Tourism

THIRD EDITION

management

NEIL LEIPER

Pearson Education Australia
Unit 4, Level 2
14 Aquatic Drive
Frenchs Forest NSW 2086

www.pearsoned.com.au

Acquisitions Editor: David Cunningham
Senior Project Editor: Kathryn Fairfax
Copy Editor: Kate Ormston-Jeffery
Proofreader: Tom Flanagan
Cover and internal design by Liz Nicholson of Design Bite
Cover illustration by Getty Images
Typeset by Midland Typesetters, Maryborough, Vic.

Printed in Malaysia, VVP

2 3 4 5 08 07 06 05

National Library of Australia
Cataloguing-in-Publication Data

Leiper, Neil.
Tourism management.

3rd ed.
Bibliography.
Includes index.
Tertiary students.
ISBN 1 86250 533 0.

1. Tourism. 2. Tourism – Management. I. Title.

338.4791

An imprint of Pearson Education Australia
(a division of Pearson Australia Group Pty Ltd)

contents

List of Figures and Tables

Figures

Tables

This third edition of *Tourism Management* has minor changes on the second (published in 2003), which was a revised version of the first (1995). Across the three editions the approach and broad structure are unchanged. The main changes in this third edition are the addition, at the end of each chapter, of discussion questions and lists of recommended readings, and the inclusion of several extra diagrams.

The book is designed for students and other readers interested in tourism and managerial work in tourism industries. Accordingly, it relates to degree-level courses with units on tourism and on business management. In these courses the book can serve as a text for the units on tourism and as a supplementary reference for the units on business management.

Most graduates of tourism courses progress to management positions, or to professional occupations where managerial issues are relevant. This book includes a substantial introduction to management theories and practices, illustrated with many examples from tourism industries. But university courses should give students much more than training to develop skill competencies.

First, such courses should be educational, aiming to develop knowledge and the kind of understanding that can underpin a range of occupations and foster inquiring, confident and self-reliant attitudes to how work relates to wider issues in the world. I've attempted to present conventional ideas about tourism and its management—followed, where appropriate, by alternative ideas on each topic. There is much scope for this in tourism. In part because it is a relatively new field, the field of tourism research and education has many contentious topics. For example, I try to demonstrate that we can never properly understand tourism if we focus too much attention on destinations, on places visited by tourists. The whole systems view, introduced in Chapter 3, presents an alternative.

Second, clear understanding and good policies are unlikely to emerge from the simplistic idea that 'tourism is an industry'. Tourism is, first of all, the behaviour of tourists and is best understood as partly industrialised behaviour, supported in part by distinctive industries. This theme is introduced at the end of Chapter 7 and is explored in Chapter 11 and subsequently.

Tourism education can be impeded by a number of expressions commonly used in writings on the subject and prone to be taken literally in key concepts such as 'tourist attraction'. Misleading metaphors of this sort often lead to distorted thinking. I've labeled them feral metaphors, following the lead of Jim Spigelman (2002), who used this term in an article exposing a source of confused thinking by administrators in the New South Wales courts, where he serves as Chief Justice. He pointed to similar confusion, from the same source, in other professional fields.

On a related matter, a lot of what is written about tourism seems to stem from one or the other of two agendas: either boosting tourism industries, or criticising them for damage caused to social and natural environments. I hope that neither agenda is seen in this book. Its overarching aim is to help readers understand tourism, along with associated themes such as environmental implications and tourism industries—not to boost or criticise.

The book is arranged in two sections. Part One, An Introduction to Tourism and its Management, has nine chapters. Understanding today's tourism requires knowing something about the past, and about how past events influenced modern patterns, so the book begins with a chapter on history. Two centrally important questions for the subject of this book—who are tourists, and what is tourism?—are discussed in Chapter 2. Then Chapter 3 sets out a systematic approach to the study of tourism, based on the concept of whole tourism systems. Chapters 4–7 provide introductions to social, psychological, geographical, economic and political dimensions.

Management is introduced in Chapter 8. Two models of managing (devised by Carroll and by Quinn) are presented, illustrated by examples from managers' roles in tourism industries in several countries. Chapter 9 sets out four case histories, illustrating management work and the nature of business activities in a travel agency, an inbound tour operator, a resort hotel, and a block of rented holiday apartments.

Part Two, Further Studies in Managing Tourism Industries, begins with Chapter 10, about environments, specifically the interactions between tourism, tourism industries and broad classifications of environments—economic, social and physical.

Chapter 11 discusses the business strategies followed by suppliers of the services and goods consumed by tourists. This leads to an approach for recognising tourism industries—combinations of organisations that are managed in ways that are strategically related to tourists' needs and other characteristics. Chapter 12 discusses four cases of organisations at the margins of tourism industries, where tourism is not necessarily the focus of managers' attention.

Attractions, an important but often ignored subject in tourism research and education, are the focus of Chapter 13. In Chapter 14, themes from several earlier chapters are combined in a case about an institution that is dependent on tourism and that has been successful as a business, a heritage museum and a tourist attraction.

Chapter 15 contains discussions on failures. Three case examples from tourism industries are presented and analysed. The purpose of exploring how and why business organisations fail in various ways is to better understand how and why organisations of similar sorts can avoid failure and, instead, survive and succeed. In other words, the purpose is pathological knowledge. This can be useful for investors, entrepreneurs and managers. While other professional fields, such as medicine and engineering, have benefited greatly from pathological research, in the business world generally and in tourism industries especially there has been little interest to date in this important theme.

Chapter 16 discusses six issues that permeate the management of tourism. Other writers have discussed aspects of three of them (seasonality, sustainable development and feedback) but the others—proliferating variety, partial industrialisation, and the question of who actually manages tourism—have not received attention elsewhere.

ACKNOWLEDGMENTS

Many individuals active in tourism research and education deserve recognition and thanks for assisting me over the years in ways that have contributed to this book. Most were acknowledged in the first and second editions, so need not be listed again here. My colleagues in Southern Cross University's Business Division, especially in the School of Tourism and Hospitality Management, deserve special mention.

I must also acknowledge students in my classes and research programs, from whom I have learnt more than some of them imagine, especially by reading their essays and supervising their postgraduate research. A dozen former students are listed among the authors in the bibliography. Having formerly studied the subject, they now become part of the subject matter.

Similarly, I gratefully acknowledge colleagues in tourism programs in many universities around the world who write for research journals and assist in the editing of these journals.

My thanks also go to many managers and other employees of a wide range of organisations, who provided me with information and ideas. In particular, I acknowledge the following persons for assistance with new material contained in this edition: Bill Wright, Managing Director of ID South Pacific, from whom I have learnt much in discussions during the past 20 years; Suteja Neka, for his generous assistance and hospitality during my research at Neka Art Museum, where he is Founding Director; and Geoff Beames, Director of Australian Wine Lodges Ltd and formerly CEO at Australian Resorts Ltd, who has drawn on his vast experience to patiently answer my questions on a wide range of tourism-related topics.

I also thank David Cunningham and his colleagues at Pearson Education Australia. David's support and guidance during the preparation of this book has been most encouraging.

John Wiley Ltd are thanked for permission to use a diagram adapted from *Becoming a Master Manager* by R.E. Quinn et al. Dr J. Jafari is thanked for permission to use his diagram 'A framework for tourism education', which first appeared in an article published in *Annals of Tourism Research*.

Neil Leiper
Southern Cross University
Lismore, Australia
nleiper@scu.edu.au

An Introduction to Tourism and its Management

part one

A History of Tourism

INTRODUCTION

Awareness of the past is necessary to understand the present, because everything in the present was determined by what has already happened. The same principle looking forward means that action now can shape the future in certain respects, an assumption that underlies all managerial decisions. A related practical reason for giving attention to history, reflecting this same principle, was observed by a philosopher who remarked that those who ignore the lessons of the past are prone to repeat its mistakes (Santayana 1962/1906). For these reasons, the theme of this book—tourism and its management in the modern world—requires historical background.

All humans observe the principle in its various applications on occasion, even if not always conscious of it. 'Learning from experience' is a term we often use. Whenever we try to avoid repeating a mistake, we are in effect attempting to learn from history. In fact, we follow the principle only to a limited extent, because attempting to know everything about the past is a waste of time and effort. The wisest attitude might be encapsulated in an old Russian proverb: 'People who stare too hard at the past are blind in one eye, but those who ignore the past completely are blind in both.' Anyone who wants to understand tourism recognises that one of the subjects to study, in outline or in detail, is tourism's history.

The quote attributed to the great industrialist Henry Ford, 'History is bunk', possibly comforts those persons who would prefer to ignore the past completely. In fact, the statement was actually 'History is more or less bunk' (Ford 1916), and the phrase 'more or less' is crucial. History can never be a totally accurate representation of the past, so everything remembered, interpreted or written by historians is an approximation. Care is needed when interpreting memories and historical writings. Besides its practical benefits, a reason for giving attention to history is one's intrinsic interest in learning about the past.

This chapter is broad in its scope. Instead of merely regurgitating the content from other publications on the subject, it presents original interpretations of events and conditions that have shaped the history of tourism. In the last section of this chapter, the theme is learning about tourism, also presented historically, showing how tourism studies have evolved over the past 100 years.

A HISTORY OF TOURISM

Long ago, people travelled in relatively large numbers as nomads, pilgrims and migrants, in smaller numbers as business traders, scholars, resort tourists, and in very small numbers as multi-destination tourists. These antecedents and early forms of tourism helped shape modern tourism in various ways, as the following discussion shows.

Nomadism

For hundreds of thousands of years all humans were nomads, people without permanent residences whose lives involved routine travelling. Writers such as Chatwin (1987, 1989,

1996) believe that nomadism, central to human existence for so long, influenced human behaviour indelibly, such that travelling is now instinctively pleasurable in favourable conditions. Although some scholars would reject this theory as unproven, it cannot easily be dismissed.

Consider the pleasure that many people now derive—a seemingly instinctive sensation—when they set off on a trip, going anywhere away from routine. Does this pleasure occur because travelling revives in our subconscious the pleasure our ancestors experienced when they travelled as nomads? This is a form of atavism, the appearance of a characteristic inherited from ancestors. Read Chatwin's (1987) *Songlines* and contemplate these ideas. The book is structured around a story of a journey in Central Australia, exploring Aboriginal culture and nomadism.

Travel for trade and business

Business travel's origins go back to when prehistoric nomads traded in goods. In Europe, archeological discoveries show that tens of thousands of years ago people were travelling long distances as traders (Delouche 2001). In the Australian context, Blainey (1982) and Chatwin (1987: 56–7) have described trading by nomadic Aborigines.

Thousands of years ago the 'Silk Road' allowed Asian and Middle-Eastern traders to traverse Asia. Seven hundred years ago the first Europeans to visit China were Italian traders. Marco Polo is the most famous, and the book he wrote about his trip has been in print ever since (Polo 1958). Later, between the 15th and the 20th centuries, colonialists from Portugal, Spain, Holland, Britain, Germany and France opened up trade routes in Asia, Africa, the Americas, Australia and Oceania. Milton's (1999) history of early voyages to the Spice Islands and Braudel's (1982, 1984) discussions of the roles of trade in the history of civilisation are noteworthy.

Business travel established many itineraries that pleasure-seeking tourists would later follow, a process summed up by the expression 'tourism follows trade'. Singapore and Hong Kong were important trading centres in the 19th century, long before becoming popular venues for holidaying tourists in the second half of the 20th century. Two factors help explain the sequence. First, business travellers returning home tell people about places they have visited, and some of these people form motivations to go there. Second, transport and accommodation provided initially for business travellers might be under-utilised, a condition which then encourages the managers of airlines and hotels to seek new users, new markets, and an obvious option—people travelling on holiday.

Pilgrimage

Visiting sacred sites has been a reason for travel in various historical eras, and in various places, for thousands of years. The origins of pilgrimage are analysed in 'Gods, graves and idols', a chapter in Jaynes' (1982) *Origins of Consciousness*, and in Sumption's (1975) book *Pilgrimage*. The custom began after humans developed the habit of burying their dead in places set aside for that purpose. Early pilgrimage involved travelling to these sites and attempting to communicate with highly revered persons buried there, in the belief that they were still alive and powerful.

The great age of pilgrimage in Western civilisation was the 500 years between 1000 and 1500 AD. Howarth (1982: 257) states that in the 11th century the five great shrines for Christian pilgrimage were St James of Compostela, St Michael of Monte Gargano, Rome, Jerusalem and Constantinople. Ten times larger than any other city, Constantinople was favoured by pilgrims because it contained two famous relics linked to Jesus Christ, the Holy Shroud (now in the Cathedral of Turin, but considered a fake) and the (reputed) Crown of Thorns, now lost.

Pilgrimage in ancient times established an attitude that can be seen among many tourists today, a concern with discriminating between authentic and inauthenic objects. An authentic relic, such as a bone believed to belong to a deceased saint, has value for pilgrims, who believe it has miraculous powers that could help them personally, by helping their prayers reach god(s) who might answer their wishes. Authenticity affects modern tourists' attitudes to souvenirs and cultural attractions, which are more valued and popular if known to be genuine rather than faked or staged. Authenticity in tourism has been explored by several researchers, such as Waller and Lea (1999).

Inclusive or prepackaged tours were first devised for pilgrims in Europe 800 years ago, when packages offered, for a single price, a pre-departure bundle of rights to use transport, accommodation and guide services. These packages became popular, and profits were made by tour operators and the church officials who cooperated in the ventures by finding fraudulent relics and advertising them as genuine, hoping that pilgrims would come to their church and spend money. Sumption (1975: 22–54) has written about saints, relics, pilgrimage and the business schemes based around them. Morris (1979: 65–6) reported that modern historians reject the line about St James of Compostela, still a very popular pilgrimage site, having any authentic links to St James. She says the site was developed by 'cunning monks who promoted its international reputation'.

Pilgrimage continues to be a major form of travel in many religions today. Every year approximately one million Muslims, followers of Islam, go on the Hajj, the mass pilgrimage to Mecca. Peters (1994) has written a history of the Hajj. It is not the largest pilgrimage event in the modern world, however. That status belongs to Kumbh Mela, staged every 12 years in India. In 2001 more than 20 million persons visited Kumbh Mela, according to newspaper reports and Internet sites. In much smaller numbers, Christian pilgrims these days visit thousands of sites, mostly in Europe, such as Santiago in Spain and Lourdes in France.

Travel by scholars and scientists

From the beginnings of civilisation, scholars and scientists have travelled to learn about the world beyond their home locality and to meet other scholars and scientists. The contribution of some of these persons to the development of tourism has been immense. Returning home and informing the public of what they had learned from their travels, they inspired many people to follow the same routes. The Dutch scholar Erasmus (1466–1536) and the English scientist Charles Darwin (1809–82) are prominent examples.

Darwin could be regarded as the first eco-tourist. The Galapagos Islands, where he discovered vital evidence for his theory of evolution, is now a highly favoured eco-tourist destination, but in fact his visits to many places have inspired generations of tourists to follow the same paths. Recommended books are *Darwin and the Beagle* (Moorehead 1982) or Darwin's *The Voyage of the Beagle* (various editions, including Internet sites).

In the modern world, tourism based around the special interest of gaining knowledge has flourished in one distinctive form, the professional conference or convention. Academic members of universities, like members of many other professions such as law, engineering and medicine, travel to conferences routinely. A distinctive industry has grown up to promote and manage this activity. It is often called the MICE industry, for it deals with *m*eetings, *i*ncentive travel, *c*onferences and *e*vents. Conference management is discussed in a book by McCabe et al. (2000) and in journal articles such as one by Oppermann and Chon (1997).

Resort tourism

Resort tourism began several thousand years ago, after humans ceased nomadic existence and settled in particular places. It involves people leaving home temporarily to visit a destination, normally not far away, for recreational purposes—for rest, relaxation and/or entertainment. This can be desirable among people whose lives are bound up in routines, whose economic circumstances allow them to get away for a while and whose imagination contains the idea that this could be pleasurable. Resort tourism has always been an exclusive activity of the relatively prosperous, which meant, for most of human history until the middle of the 20th century, a tiny minority of the population.

In ancient Greece 2500 years ago, wealthy residents of Athens and other cities periodically visited resorts. The town of Elis near Mt Olympus was a popular destination; there, every four years, people assembled for festivals based around athletics. The modern Olympic Games, since 1896, have been based on that tradition. The island of Kos was the location of the original health resort (Mumford 1961; Porter 1999), where in ancient times Greeks went to recover from illness by following theories set out by the island's leading figure, Hippocrates (460–377 BC), whose name is now best known for the Hippocratic oath, taken by all medical doctors.

In mediaeval China, a custom enjoyed by ruling families and their servants was a long holiday in a summer resort. At the time of Kublai Khan, 800 years ago, the summer palace for the annual three-month sojourn was at Shangdu (Xanadu), located 250 kilometres northwest of the main palace in Beijing. The journey took 10 days (Alexander 1994: 10).

Ancient resort tourism, like its modern forms today, sometimes involved wild and noisy entertainment. Writing 2500 years ago about pleasure cruises on the River Nile, one observer remarked (Herodotus 1987: 157):

They sail, men and women together, a great number in each boat. Some women have rattles and rattle them, others play the flute and the remainder of the women and men sing and clap hands. As they travel towards Bubastis . . . they edge the boat near the bank, and some of the women . . . scream obscenities in derision at women who live in that city, and others set to dancing, and others stand up and throw their clothes open to show their nakedness . . . and more wine is drunk than in all the rest of the year.

Resort tourism became popular, practised by wider sections of society in many countries, only in the 20th century. Going away for rest, relaxation and socialising on vacation (as Americans call it) or holidays (the British expression) is now a regular custom. One historian has described the custom's expansion as 'a middle class imitation of the aristo-cratic seasonal retreats from court and city to country estates' (Bella et al. 1985: 328). By the second half of the 20th century, better-paid members of the working classes had also adopted the custom of an annual holiday trip.

Histories of resort tourism include books by Cameron (1975) and Blume (1992) on the French Riviera, Rockel (1986) on New Zealand, and Funnell (1975) on America. Also relevant are chapters in books by Casson (1974), whose focus was the ancient world, by Davidson and Spearritt (2000) on Australia, and by Inglis (2000) on holiday travel.

Migratory travel

Humans have been migrating for hundreds of thousands of years, and in recent centuries the scale of the movement has escalated, with hundreds of millions of people moving residence. Most have emigrated from homes in the old world (in China, Europe, the Middle East, South Asia, Central Africa) to settle as immigrants in the new world (the Americas, South-East Asia, Australasia, Southern Africa).

Migration seems to reinforce the idea of long-distance travel in the popular consciousness. Surveys in Australia have shown that immigrants are more likely than Australian-born people to travel internationally (Peat, Marwick, Mitchell and Co. 1977). This can be attributed to the special purpose that immigrants have for international travel, to visit their country of birth and rekindle family links, and to the probability that the migrating experience makes people aware that travelling is feasible and interesting.

Refugee travel

Humans have travelled as refugees wherever they have felt an urgent need to escape from war, persecution, natural disaster or severe economic hardship. Recently the activities of refugees have intensified. In 2002, the United Nations High Commission on Refugees estimated that 21 million persons were in its ambit, of which 12 million were officially classified as refugees, and another one million as asylum seekers; most are in Asia, Africa or Europe (UNHCR 2002). Links between refugees and tourism are an unexplored topic, but one fact can be stated: tourists represent a fortunate and privileged category of traveller, while refugees are quite the opposite.

Commuter travel

Commuting involves travelling from home and back again on a routine basis to work or study. Between the beginning of human civilisation (when people abandoned nomadic lives and began settling in towns) and the late 19th century commuting was unknown, as almost everybody lived very close, and so could walk, to the places they visited daily.

Commuting became a mass movement in the 20th century, with the growth of suburban living and the development of transport facilities linking the new dormitory suburbs with work locations (Mumford 1961; Fitzgerald 1987, 1992). It has major effects on tourism.

Commuting is a dull routine for many commuters and, as such, contributes to boredom, triggering motivations to escape—to go on holiday trips away from the city and suburbs and away from routine existence. Commuting also leads to stress, adding to the need for escape and to seek relief from stressful conditions. Most commuters use private vehicles which, although owned primarily for commuting, become efficient and convenient means of transport for holiday trips and other types of tourism to destinations that can be reached by road vehicles.

Multi-destination tourism

Another form of travelling stems from travellers' personal interests in visiting a series of places on one trip for leisure-related experiences. This can be termed multi-destination tourism. Before 1740 such trips were very rare. A famous early tourist following this form was Ibn Battuta who, aged 20, left his home in Morocco in 1304 and visited more than 40 countries during a trip that lasted many years. He wrote about his experiences in a book that remains in print; a recommended version is edited by Dunn (1989).

Travel is torture, tourism is leisure

Although the twin terms 'travel' and 'tourism' might be used interchangably, as for many persons they mean roughly the same thing, there is an interesting difference in their early meanings. In the semi-civilised society of Europe 1000 years ago, 'travail' meant torture; criminals were subjected to travail in jail, but were not travelling anywhere. Over time, people began using 'travail' to describe their feelings while on journeys. As pilgrims, for example, they often felt travailed—felt as though they were being tortured by the discomfort of walking or riding wagons on rough roads, exposed to the weather. Over time this evolved into 'travel', meaning to go from one place to another.

Travelling often seems pleasurable because of what it represents (escape, change, excitement, the means to get somewhere) but physiologically is still, for many, unpleasant and uncomfortable. Travelling over long distances can be extremely tiring, as can be seen by observing passengers arriving at international airports after long flights. People tolerate being 'travailed' in order to get to and from destinations where they can be tourists, at leisure, seeking pleasure.

Eccentric pioneers of multi-destination tourism

Dictionaries report the origin of 'tour' as the Greek word for making a circle, which is why for many centuries 'tour' has meant a trip that returned to its starting point. 'Tour' has also meant, for at least 500 years, a circular trip for pleasure, and this extra meaning possibly evolved from the French word *tour*, meaning tower. A thousand years ago, when French was the language used by the ruling classes of England besides much of Western Europe, going on a 'tour' meant going to the tower of a castle, walking around and looking out over the scene below—leisurely sightseeing, in fact. In time, this expression would naturally have extended to trips of greater distance with the same circular itinerary, the same leisure, motivation and activities.

Certainly this sense was established in England by the 1720s, as the title and content of Daniel Defoe's book, first published in 1724, indicates: *A Tour Through the Whole Island of Great Britain*. The book is still in print (Defoe 1971). Defoe was regarded in his lifetime as an unusual person, rather eccentric, because very few persons travelled unless they were obliged to go somewhere, unless they had an objective purpose for travelling—as a pilgrim, trader or scholar. Reading the book reveals that Defoe was interested in many aspects of the places visited and so, along with Ibn Battuta 300 years earlier, can be considered a pioneer general-interest tourist.

Celia Fiennes was an upper-class woman who wandered around England on a series of trips between 1685 and 1712, on horseback and accompanied by a servant. Her diaries (Morris 1995) reveal motivations similar to those that impel many tourists today, for she recorded impressions of towns, gardens, houses, churches, local markets and people. Fiennes could be regarded as an early 'VFR' tourist, as she structured her itineraries around 'Visits to Friends and Relatives'. Between visits to their homes, she found lodging in roadside inns and the private houses of strangers.

Matsuo Basho (1644–94), on the other side of the world, was another pioneer tourist. *The Narrow Road to the Deep North* (Basho 1966) describes his tours on foot around Japan. Like Defoe, he was a literary genius. While Defoe is best known as one of the original novelists, famous for writing *Robinson Crusoe* and *Moll Flanders*, Basho is known as a master of haiku, a classic form of Japanese poetry. Travelling lightly, living frugally and carrying his simple possessions on his back in what he called 'a well-worn satchel', he was a pioneer backpacker tourist.

How society discovered the pleasure of tourism

Battuta, Basho, Fiennes and Defoe could be labelled eccentrics because their behaviour, as persons who travelled without any ulterior objective, was highly individualistic and unusual for their societies at that time. They were also pioneers, because they were forerunners of what is now common behaviour—going on trips for personal pleasure. They were unusual but not unique: historical records exist of other persons like them, at their time and earlier. How did an activity that was once rare become a popular and respectable social custom?

The process occurred first in England, among the upper classes of society, the minority of the population who had ample leisure time, could read and could afford to buy books. Many read Defoe's book about his tours. It was one of the first best-sellers, published in nine editions between 1724 and 1779, providing readers with information about places around Britain and holding up the example of an educated man who had been to these places.

Twenty years after it first appeared, another book became a best-seller in England. *Pamela*, one of the first novels, written by Samuel Richardson, 'taught the art of long distance travel', with its heroine making 'the discovery that living is not necessarily a matter of physical experiences, but that the imagination is also capable of voyages . . . of daydreams. Today, this sounds banal: in the 1740s it was as startling as discovering you could fly by flapping your arms' (Wilson 1975: 7–36). The reading public in England learned from *Pamela* what trips to distant places might be like, that the activity could be interesting and pleasurable, that tourism was not travail; and they learned from Defoe's *Tour* about features of specific places that they could visit.

Books about travel had been widely read in educated circles before the 1700s. For example, Munster's *Universal Cosmography* was published in 1544, was translated into six languages and appeared in 36 editions by 1600 (Barzun 2001: 103). But these early travel books did not inspire many readers to travel. That did not occur until the combined effects of Richardson's *Pamela* and Defoe's *Tour*.

The 'Grand Tour' of Europe

The decade in which *Pamela* was published and widely read, the 1740s, was when the Grand Tour of Europe came into fashion. Much has been written about this topic in the history of tourism. An article and book by Towner (1985, 1996) are recommended as excellent overviews. A biography of William Beckford (Mavor 1986) is a colourful account of a grand tourist who happened to be the richest—and one of the strangest—men in Europe 200 years ago. Goethe's (1970) *Italian Journey* is a famous autobiography of that writer's experiences on his tour in the 1780s.

The Grand Tour in its typical European format involved tourists from the upper classes of society. Most were young men, on long and leisurely circuits of the Continent, typically away for a year or more. Travelling independently, they were accompanied by personal servants and in many cases a tutor, appointed by their parents to provide the young man with an education while he was away. The main purpose was to provide education and training, not so much from the tutor's lessons but by first-hand experiences at classical sites and by mixing socially with members of upper-class societies in the leading cities of Europe, such as Paris, Naples, Rome and Vienna.

Most of the time was spent in cities. After weeks or months in a city, the young man would travel to the next, usually by stage coach. Grand tourism in its classical form was cultural tourism. Recreational activities were not encouraged by those who sponsored and supervised trips—the parents and tutors.

A book by Smollett (1979) is a notable autobiographical account of a Grand Tour in the 1760s. He was not altogether typical, for he was middle-aged when he travelled, was not sponsored by his parents and needed no tutor. His book, when first published in 1766, was titled *Travels Through France and Italy, Containing Observations on Character, Customs, Religion, Government, Police, Commerce, Arts and Antiquities, With a Particular Description of the Town, Territory and Climate of Nice*. It is no exaggeration, for Smollett was interested in many subjects.

In that respect, Smollett was typical in an era lasting into the 20th century, when tourists generally assumed that an international trip would probably be the only such trip in a lifetime. Tourists consequently attempted to take in many features of any place they visited, and tried to visit many places during the trip. Late in the 20th century many individuals were travelling repeatedly, and this altered the pattern of tourism.

Cultural and natural attractions

Grand tourists from the 17th to the 19th centuries focused their attention on classical art, ancient monuments, important buildings and, most notably, meeting and conversing with educated, sophisticated persons. For most of Europe's history only rare individuals took pleasure from nature. The Italian poet Petrarch (1304-74) was one of these. As a young man he climbed Mt Ventoux (near Avignon, in France) and thought the views of wilderness pleasant, an experience he found surprising. Because of that event, Petrarch was credited by Christaller (1964) as the first sightseer and thus a forerunner of modern tourism.

In fact, educated Asians were appreciating natural beauty and engaging in sightseeing many centuries before Petrarch. The evidence is in ancient writings and landscape paintings. Confucius, born 2500 years ago, wrote how 'the wise find joy on the water and the good find joy in the mountains' (1997: 147). Other writers, such as Po Chu-I in China around 800 AD, and Yoshishiga no Yasutane around 980 and Kamo no Chomei around 1200 in Japan, wrote in detail about pleasures derived from nature. This occurred mostly close to home, not on travels. Only the ruling class travelled for pleasure, moving between residences on a seasonal basis (Alexander 1994: 10; Polo 1958: 77–9).

In countries beyond Europe, however, the idea of tourism as a pleasurable and respectable activity for large numbers of people took longer to evolve. In Japan, for example, this did not happen until the 1960s, and in China the beginning of a trend was notable in the 1990s. By then, both cultural and natural attractions were established internationally as being worth attention.

Special-interest tourism

General-interest tourists like Smollett are common today, but modern tourists generally visit fewer places on each trip and in many cases become special-interest tourists. The range of special-interest tourism themes in the late 20th century is demonstrated by comparing books such as Alexander's (1994) *The Way to Xanadu*, about her trips to China, Florida, Kashmir and Ethiopia specifically to investigate the origins of a famous poem, with Lanchester's (1996) brilliant novel *The Debt to Pleasure*, set around travels in France by a character obsessively interested in food and wines. Adventure tourism is another category of special interest. Notable books include *The Life of My Choice* by Thesiger (1987) and Krakauer's (1996, 1997) *Into the Wild* and *Eiger Dreams*.

Academic overviews of special-interest tourism can be found in collections edited by Weiler and Hall (1992) and by Douglas et al. (2001). A concise review of the subject by Stear (1995) is noteworthy.

Tourism businesses before 1850

Before the middle of the 19th century the large-scale tourism industries now active did not exist, but distinctive services for tourists were provided by many kinds of businesses. Sailing ships and stage coaches provided transport, inns provided lodging and, after 1789 when the great social and political advance known as the French Revolution began in Paris, restaurants provided food and civilised places for dining. Since ancient times, tour guides have worked for hire at classical sites.

An interesting innovation was travellers' cheques—invented not, as is sometimes claimed, by Thomas Cook in the 1870s but by the Scottish banker Robert Herries in the 1770s (Booker 1994). It was an important development, as money for expenses is a vital factor in tourism. Travellers' cheques were the main solution until the 1990s, when automatic teller machines and a global network of banks combined to provide a more convenient alternative.

Before the 19th century there were few tourists. Most were rich, with servants and extensive personal contacts in the places they visited, so did not need the range of commercial services used by most tourists today. Small numbers and few demands from commercial sources for tourist-distinctive services meant there were no large-scale tourism industries.

Nature and sightseeing

Since 1800 there has been a growing interest in the natural world, in landscape and seascape. Two hundred years ago most people did not regard the natural world as interesting or beautiful. This fact can be demonstrated in several aspects of history, including the history of painting. In Europe there were few landscape paintings: art focused on portraits, religious objects and buildings. After 1800 a growing number of artists and then other people began taking an interest in nature, a trend known as Romanticism.

By late in the 20th century interest in nature was widespread, and was seen in eco-tourism and among environmental activists taking action to save endangered places and species where tourism-related developments were perceived as a threat.

In Europe, evidence of the early lack of interest in nature and the subsequent change can be seen in architecture. Before the 1800s few houses were designed to take advantage of natural scenery. Many had views over gardens or private parks but not of natural landscapes, unaltered by human design. A famous example is a house in Geneva where the English writer Edward Gibbon lived in the 1770s, a house noted in modern guidebooks because of that association. It has windows looking onto the street. It has walls with no windows on the side that could have looked out to the spectacle of Lake Leman and the Swiss Alps. A similar example is the house in an Italian village where the poet Petrarch lived in his last decades, late in the 14th century. It is well sited to enjoy a view but not built to take advantage of its situation. Petrarch's youthful experience as a pioneering sightseer on Mt Ventoux obviously did not lead to a lifelong interest in nature.

Today, all over the world, houses located with the potential for scenic views are usually designed accordingly. Hotels with scenic views from guests' rooms can charge a premium rate. Sightseeing is now a common activity among tourists, who engage in the practice and derive pleasure from it so easily that it seems to be human nature. In fact, as Adler's (1989) historical research has demonstrated, sightseeing as a leisure activity is a relatively recent innovation. Tourists in Europe several hundred years ago did no sightseeing in reference to natural phenomena. They looked at art, at buildings and monuments, but conversation was their major activity.

Great changes in human consciousness after 1800, with people perceiving beauty in landscape and the natural world and keen about sightseeing, indicate the error in thinking that it is human nature to enjoy these things. A study of history shows that while it might be human nature to seek pleasure, the sorts of experiences that are regarded as pleasurable have changed over time as a result of cultural changes in society.

Tourism in the 19th and 20th centuries

Wars and civil disturbance in Europe between 1790 and 1815 led to a reduction in travel. After 1815 in Western Europe, and later in other parts of the world, a series of industrial revolutions created conditions that led to growth in tourist numbers, to new forms of travel, and to wider itineraries. Several broad trends can be noted.

The first industrial revolution turned the English economy (and later that of other countries) away from almost total dependence on farming and towards dependence on manufacturing, via the application of steam power in rail transport and in factories. Steam trains were first used to transport materials on rails inside factories; in the 1830s the idea emerged of building railways outside factories to carry goods and people.

(Thomas Cook, the principal entrepreneur and innovator in the development of the modern tourism industry, was the first businessman to see the possibility of using railways to transport people for pleasure trips. He began business as a tour operator in 1842 with a day trip from Leicester. Several hundred workers employed in local factories, along with their families, took the tour. Cook's primary aim was not to make a profit but to provide people with a pleasant and liberating experience which, he hoped, would deter them from spending their free time and spare money on the consumption of alcohol. By the 1860s Cook was the proprietor of a large and expanding business, with customers from all classes of society taking holiday trips.)

By 1880 Thomas Cook and Son Ltd was a multinational company, with operations in countries around the globe. Along the way the anti-alcohol message was put aside, and in the 20th century most tourists using Cook's brand of packaged tours or travellers' cheques probably enjoyed a drink or two during their trips. Several histories have been written about the company and the social trends it fostered, including those by Pudney (1953) and Swinglehurst (1974).

Growing free time has been a major social trend for working people for almost 200 years. During the previous 4000 years of civilisation almost everyone worked, typically in agricultural occupations, without entitlement to paid leave for extended holidays. They did, however, enjoy many free days in the form of local festivals throughout the year. Industrial revolutions resulted in many rural workers moving to factory and office jobs in towns and cities and losing their entitlement to free days, so that by the late 1800s, in England, and in North America and Australia, most working persons were occupied at work six days a week with only a handful of public holidays in a year. As economic conditions improved, the number of public holidays grew as a result of agitation from workers' unions.

Having no entitlement to annual leave, most people before the 1930s never imagined that they might travel any longer or further than could be accomplished in a day trip. In 1936, by a convention arranged through the International Labour Organisation, the governments and major employer associations of the developed economies agreed with a trades union proposal to give everyone in paid, full-time employment at least one week of paid annual leave per year. An account of the trades unions' political campaign in Britain to achieve this goal can be found in an insightful book, *The Delicious History of the Holiday* (Inglis 2000: 106–7).

By 1960 the entitlement had extended to two weeks in many countries. By 2000, in many countries of Western Europe, the normal entitlement was five or six weeks, which is a major factor in the common pattern among Europeans to go on at least one and often two trips away from home each year. In other parts of the world, the typical entitlement to paid leave is lower, and this is reflected in a lower propensity for tourism.

Mobility options have increased greatly for tourists over the past 150 years. The trend in transport from horse-drawn modes on land and wind-powered modes at sea to steam-powered trains and ships after 1850 resulted in lower costs, greater speed, and greater capacity. This trend was amplified in the 20th century, with the introduction of diesel-powered trains and ships and, especially since the 1950s, air travel for long distance trips and private motor vehicles for most households.

Since the 1960s air travel has moved ahead of sea travel as the major mode for long-distance international travel. A major event in the history of tourism was the first commercial flight by a Boeing 747, in January 1970, from New York to London. This was the start of the era of jumbo jets and mass tourism.

As transport technology improved, the real cost of travel fell dramatically, making travel affordable for many more people. Two examples illustrate the point. Fifty years ago, an Australian on an average income buying a return ticket by air or sea to Europe had to work for 50 weeks and spend all their income on the ticket. Few people travelled to the other side of the world in those days. By the 1980s the real cost was only four weeks of work and by 2000 only three weeks. The real cost of private motor vehicles has also fallen greatly. In the 1950s, to purchase a new motor vehicle required an average Australian in full-time paid employment to use an entire year's gross income. Few people owned cars then. Now that average person earns the price of a new car in five months and that of a roadworthy used car in five weeks.

Worldwide, over the past 150 years the incomes and material living standards of most ple have improved substantially, especially in wealthier countries. Most residents of ntries with developed economies have sufficient income to afford discretionary items—non-essentials, where consumers exercise discretion as to whether to save or spend and how to spend. Holiday trips and similar forms of tourism are items for possible discretionary spending. In the business world and among professionals, rising prosperity has a similar effect. Convention and conference travel is, to a degree, discretionary expenditure.

Information about the world beyond one's immediate region is a necessary condition for persons to decide to participate in tourism. In primitive societies, for most people the world beyond home was a scary and unknown place. In the modern world, radio and TV and, to a lesser extent, attendance at schools have provided almost everyone with knowledge of places around the world that might be visited.

The factors noted above that have contributed to the huge growth in tourism over the past two centuries are not the only important contributors to this historical trend. A number of cultural factors also vital in the process and still influential are identified in Chapter 4.

THE SCALE OF TOURISM TODAY

The World Tourism Organisation's estimates of the total number of international tourist arrivals in all countries are widely used statistics for gauging the scale of international tourism. In 1950 there were 25 million arrivals; in 1970 this figure had grown to 166 million; by 1990 it was 458 million; in 2000 it was 697 million (WTO 2002). The rate of growth in tourism over these 50 years has been far greater than for most social and economic trends. For example, the rates of growth of population and of production of various items such as motor vehicles and household appliances were well below the rate of growth in tourism in recent decades.

In 2001, arrivals fell to 689 million, 8 million (1%) less than in 2000. This was the first downturn in the global statistic since 1974, caused mainly by economic recession in the USA and Japan during 2001 and, late in the year, by the sudden increase in fear of flying and of being too far from home triggered by the 11 September terrorist attacks in the USA.

Domestic tourism, involving trips within tourists' countries of residence, is a much larger phenomenon worldwide than international tourism, involving many more persons and many more trips, but no reliable statistics have been produced to show the scale of the activity. Certainly the country with the largest flow of domestic tourists is India.

In the year after 11 September 2001, while international tourism decreased slightly in some places, in many countries domestic tourism burgeoned. For example, the major Australian holiday destinations along the Pacific coast from southern Queensland to the south of Sydney saw record levels of tourism in the summers of 2001/02 and 2002/03, when many who might otherwise have travelled overseas decided instead to holiday close to home.

Tourism industries today

Tourism industries vary in scope and in size. A tourism industry might comprise many different kinds of organisations. Components in particular instances might include travel agencies, tour operators, national tourism bodies, regional and local tourism associations, airlines, cruise lines, bus and coachlines, railways, hotels, motels, backpacker hostels, caravan and camping parks, theme parks, museums and galleries, luggage and souvenir manufacturers, retail shops, casinos, travellers' cheques departments in banks, currency exchange bureaux, visitor information centres and restaurants.

Diversity is a feature of that description. Over time, many tourism industries have become more complex, as diverse organisations have emerged to specialise in particular forms of tourism, types of tourists and categories of consumer needs.

Change is another feature of tourism industries. Few business organisations in today's tourism industries existed 30 years ago. Every year, new businesses are established and a number of existing ones cease trading and disappear. There is a relatively high rate of business failure in tourism industries (McGibbon & Leiper 2001) offset by a higher incidence of new business formations. These two trends indicate favourable conditions for professional managers and innovative enterpreneurs with knowledge and understanding of tourism and its management.

The huge growth in international tourism through the second half of the 20th century noted earlier led many governments and business organisations to develop policies and strategies for tourism, mostly seeking economic gain. The growth has also created a range of environmental problems, notably in the physical, social and cultural environments of places visited by large numbers of tourists. This has led to policies and practices aimed at sustainable tourism.

There are four major interest groups in tourism industries. Tourists are typically concerned with their own personal interests associated with each trip; businesspeople and governments are often largely concerned with economic gain; environmentalists are increasingly concerned about the detrimental consequences. The eco-tourism movement (Beeton 1998; Dowling 2000a, 2000b) represents a development where the tourist's focus is on environmental issues.

Histories in specific countries and regions

While there are broad global trends, the history of tourism varies with the country and region. More has been written about the history of tourism from an English perspective than from that of all other nationalities combined. As the English have been the world's most important pioneers as tourists and as business innovators in tourism industries, anyone wanting to understand how tourism has evolved should read a selection of this literature. Recommended books and articles include those by Inglis (2000), Walton (2000), Shaw and Williams (1997), Swinglehurst (1974), Littlewood (2000) and Towner (1985, 1996).

American and British approaches to the history of tourism are reviewed by Towner and Wall (1991). Australian tourism history is explored in books by Richardson (1999) and Davidson and Spearritt (2000). Douglas (1996) has written about three Melanesian countries—Papau New Guinea, the Solomons and Vanuatu. Watkins' (1989) and Rockel's (1986) books are about New Zealand and Vickers' (1989) about Bali. Hanquin, Wong and Sik's (2001) subject is Hong Kong. Levenstein's (1998) theme is American tourists in France, Horne's (1984) museums, and Barr's (1990) the Whitsundays.

Schivelbusch's (1986) history of rail travel in Europe and the USA is especially noteworthy, for its originality and for the connections it draws between developments in railways and cultural changes. It shows how the speed of steam trains in the mid-19th century altered the way people perceived landscapes, and it analyses how rail travel led to changes in retailing and department store design in cities.

Other histories can be found in publications on motels (Baker & Funaro 1955), on hotels (Taylor 1974; Australian Hotels Association 1988; Brown & Lefever 1990; Goth 1994; Stipanuk 1996) and on hospitality (Wood 1991).

The relevance of recent history

History is not only about changes over long periods. Knowledge of events and conditions in recent months and days can be vital in understanding current issues in management. Consider the interval from 1988 to 2002 in Australia's domestic airline industry. Every year there were notable changes. Four trunk-route airlines were established and five disappeared. Ansett, one of the two major airlines since the 1950s, went out of business in 2001. In some months heavy fare discounting was prevalent. There was growth in total passenger trips over the 14 years, but in some years there were decreases, in others large increases and in some years little change.

Nobody was able to predict all these changes, but those managers with knowledge of the past were and are better able to manage current conditions. Australia's domestic airline industry is the theme in a case in Chapter 15.

Tourism in the 21st century

What will tourism be like in future—in 10, 20, 40 years from now? Knowing the future with certainty is impossible, but several propositions might be worth considering. The continuation of recent trends would result in tourism growing at a faster rate than the average change in total social and economic activity. Quite possibly, the downturn in international tourism during 2001 and 2002 will be reversed by 2003/04, just as the severe downturn in 1974 (triggered by terrorist incidents in several countries, and a 400% rise in the price of oil) was followed by recovery in 1975/6.

There will probably be continuing change in the nationality patterns of international tourists. In the 1990s there was a slowdown in the rate of growth in total trips by Americans, Europeans, Japanese and Australians, but huge growth in trips by Chinese and Indians.

Many people now have wider choices about how to use their leisure time, and widespread prosperity is allowing them to travel more often. Technologies such as private motor vehicles, working away from the office via email, mobile phones and the Internet are, in Paul Weeks' phrase, 'empowering people, giving them wider choices and more flexibility, which is changing the face of tourism' (pers. comm.).

Many people now take mobile phones and laptops with them on holiday trips, keeping in touch with work. This is blurring what was once a sharp distinction between work and leisure. Some regard this trend as detrimental, and seek to maintain the distinction; others go along with the trend, perhaps unthinkingly. The risk in the trend is that work roles intruding too far into non-work time can compromise effective leisure.

By 2000 recent developments in communication technology, such as the Internet and mobile phones, were beginning to have dramatic effects on tourism businesses. Many articles on this theme have been published in books and research journals. Sheldon's (1997) book provides an overview but is already dated, given the rapid developments in technology. Articles by Lang (2000) and Hultkrantz (2002) are interesting; the latter looks ahead to third-generation mobile broadband networks, to a unified wireless marketplace for tourism.

A number of researchers have predicted broad trends in tourism. Reviewing examples from two and three decades ago gives sufficient hindsight to assess their accuracy, and in most cases they have erred by being too optimistic. Common errors have been predictions that leisure time would continue to grow, that transport technology would continue to develop, that incomes would continue to rise, and that in combination this would produce ongoing high rates of growth in tourism. Now we can see that the underlying changes in society and technology leading to the huge expansion in worldwide tourism between 1970 and 1990 have slowed down. For example, leisure time has ceased expanding.

In Australia, entitlements for paid annual leave grew from one week in 1936 to four weeks in 1974 but have not changed in the 28 years since then. In the USA, many persons in paid employment are still entitled to only two weeks' paid annual leave. Trades unions, the institutions most instrumental in gaining workers higher pay and longer paid holiday entitlements during the middle decades of the 20th century, have become less powerful in almost all countries.

The majority of people cannot afford to be tourists, as they are too poor. This condition is most widespread in the world's impoverished countries, but it exists to some degree in countries where average incomes are high.

This short history of tourism shows that tourism has always been an exclusive activity, despite the fact that it can be described as a mass movement. This year, hundreds of millions of individuals could be counted as tourists. But they are the minority. Imagining that most people alive today are or soon will be tourists is an illusion.

RESEARCH AND EDUCATION IN TOURISM

Programs of research on tourism began 90 years ago, and developments since then have provided content for university courses that have sprung up around the world, especially since 1980. Around 1910, two economists, Picard and von Schullard, noticed that tourists visiting Austria and Switzerland, mostly from Germany and England, spent money that had interesting effects on the national economies of the former countries, and they conducted simple research on the topic (Wahab 1971, 1974). This pioneering research created a central theme for countless studies by future economists.

In Switzerland in the 1930s a group of academics formed the first team interested in studying tourism from a range of perspectives. This came about because they saw the practical use of multiple perspectives in studying tourism. The sociologists noticed how tourism affected societies, anthropologists observed effects on cultures, economists saw economic issues and so on. None studied the total picture, but in combination they might have achieved comprehensiveness, a holistic view. A multidisciplinary approach to studying tourism provides, in principle, a path to understanding the whole phenomenon.

This belief, alongside a desire to have tourism established as a legitimate subject for universities, stimulated two professors at the University of Berne to create a formal definition of tourism in 1940. When any subject or topic is studied formally, a need arises to define it, and what was needed in this instance was a definition that did not emphasise any one aspect of tourism, such as economics or sociology, but was sufficiently broad to allow all potentially relevant disciplines to contribute to a body of knowledge. Their definition is set out and discussed in Chapter 2.

American and English developments after 1960

The *Journal of Travel Research*, established at the University of Boulder, Colorado, in 1962, became the leading journal for statistically based research on its theme. In the same decade a program of education and research on tourism was launched at the University of Michigan, where Robert McIntosh wrote the first major American text in 1972, a landmark book that has developed through nine editions with various co-authors (Goeldner & Ritchie 2003). In 1973 at the University of Wisconsin-Stout, Jafar Jafari founded the *Annals of Tourism Research*. Jafari recognised that a comprehensive understanding of tourism required bringing together several academic disciplines, each with its own distinctive and potentially useful insight. *Annals* became a journal for that purpose.

In England, the University of Surrey established a pioneer degree program in tourism studies in the early 1970s, and with it two other important innovations: the publication of an influential textbook (Burkart & Medlik 1974), and the establishment of a research journal titled *Tourism Management*.

These three journals—*Journal of Travel Research, Annals of Tourism Research* and *Tourism Management*—are now deservedly regarded as the world's three leading research periodicals on tourism. They stand out among more than 40 similar journals on the subject. Among the others are *Journal of Tourism Studies, Journal of Vacation Marketing, Current Issues in Tourism, Tourism Analysis, Tourism Culture and Communication, The ASEAN Journal on Tourism and Hospitality, Pacific Tourism Review,* and *Journal of Sustainable Tourism*. A list of the English-language tourism journals in 1999 can be found in Weaver and Opperman (2000: 422).

Why research journals are important

Research journals are where most research on all sorts of subjects is first published; accordingly, these are consulted by academics, professional practitioners and students to keep abreast with developments in hundreds of specialised subjects. Tourism is one such subject. Nobody reads every article in all the journals on their subject; instead, people use journals judiciously in various ways. Those interested in learning about tourism browse through the contents of selected journals, scanning the summaries ('abstracts') of articles (many can be found via computer databases), and then reading the articles that seem interesting. Other people see articles cited in another publication and go to the journals to find them.

Publication means that a panel of referees and a journal's editors have decided that an article deserves to be made available to researchers, professionals and students interested in the subject. Then it becomes part of the (research) literature, where any article might be praised or criticised—a vital process for developing knowledge and understanding. While anyone can offer articles for publication, most are written by academic members of universities. Although writers might spend anything from 10 hours to 400 or more preparing an article, they are not paid. Conducting research, writing for journals and serving on refereeing panels are normal roles of academics on universities' staffs. Senior academics might also spend a portion of their time every week in editorial roles for the journals, again without payment from the journals.

Developments in the 1980s and 90s

During the past 20 years, for many universities and colleges around the world, tourism has developed as a theme for research and education. Many courses are promoted as vocational in purpose, preparing students for employment in tourism industries. Consequently, thousands of persons with specialist qualifications are employed in managerial and professional positions in tourism industries around the world. However, the underlying and distinctive roles of universities are research and education, without which vocational courses for professional occupations could not survive.

Research on tourism is the theme for many conferences every year. The principal event of this sort in Australia is the annual CAUTHE Conference. The Council of Australian Universities' Tourism and Hospitality Educators publishes a selection of the research articles presented at each conference. Recent annual editions have been edited by Shaw (1995), Prosser (1996), Bushell (1997), Faulkner et al. (1998), Molloy and Davies (1999), Murphy (2000), Mules (2001), Carlsen (2002) and Braithwaite (2003).

Four sources for learning about tourism

Individuals might learn about tourism from four sources: laypersons' experience, experience on the job, vocational training, and academic research and education. Characteristics of the four are described below.

Laypersons' knowledge ➤

A layperson is one who, in relation to a specified subject, has not been through a course of formal studies. Almost everybody past their early teens has a layperson's knowledge of tourism. The knowledge might have come from school studies, from reading books, from personal experience of travelling, from friends or acquaintances, from working in occupations where tourists and tourism-related businesses can be closely observed, and from the mass media (as almost everybody gains knowledge of the subject from TV, newspapers and radio).

Laypersons' knowledge generally has a number of characteristics. First, it is accidentally gained as an incidental consequence of doing something else. People generally do not go on trips in order to learn about tourism, but that might be an unintended side-effect. Second, laypersons' knowledge is individualistic—not learned as a group, as happens when students attend university. Third, most of it is shaped by the mass media.

Because of these sources, laypersons' knowledge of tourism (like many other subjects) tends to be a mixture of truths, half-truths, distortions and errors, incomplete, largely subjective, fragmented, unsystematic and uncertain. The most widely influential source, the mass media, is limited as a source of knowledge, although TV is a useful medium for gaining insight into features of tourist destinations. The commercial mass media generally are not concerned primarily with telling the truth but tend to sensationalise content to attract readers or audiences, in order to sell more of their products (those same audiences or readers, who are exploited and sold—literally, in bulk) to their customers, the advertisers. Public broadcasters such as the ABC (Australian Broadcasting Commission) and SBS (Special Broadcasting Service) are slightly different; their priority is to serve the public.

Business practice, learning on the job ➤

People working in a wide range of positions have direct involvement with tourism, and consequently acquire knowledge of tourism from learning on the job. But because most jobs touch on only a small fraction of the broad sweep of tourism this cannot be a source of broad and deep knowledge of tourism.

Evidence that working in an organisation providing services for tourists does not necessarily lead to much knowledge or understanding of tourism comes from public statements by senior managers in Qantas in 1978. The airline's main business was, and is, transporting tourists, yet when called to give information before a parliamentary committee investigating tourism, the managers freely admitted that they had never really thought much about the subject (Qantas 1978). After 1978 Qantas' managers began giving more attention to learning about tourism. An example was Qantas' involvement as sponsor in a series of research projects intended to learn more about tourism. One project, in partnership with the New South Wales government and Sydney City Council, was about Sydney as a tourist destination region (Peat, Marwick, Mitchell and Co. 1981). Another study commissioned by Qantas was the first substantial research project in Australia on Japanese tourists and their implications for Australia's tourist destinations (Leiper 1985).

Vocational training ➤

Vocational training involves courses designed to provide knowledge, skills and attitudes specific to a particular category of work. Highly useful in most occupations, it must be focused on a particular category and/or a particular organisation and its immediate operating environment, so it cannot provide extensive and in-depth knowledge of tourism.

Education about tourism in universities ➤

Academic study on any subject ideally overcomes the deficiencies inherent in other methods of acquiring knowledge. That implicit aim is never achieved completely, but any university course should go some way towards it. Ideally, knowledge acquired from a course at university is objective, presented and studied in a disinterested manner—which means, in practical terms, that the principal role of academics and students is not to promote tourism, nor to criticise it, but to learn about it. In order to learn, the main content of courses should be backed up by research. This verification gives a level of certainty and confidence to the knowledge, so it should have fewer errors and half-truths than information acquired by other means.

To achieve this, university research and education should be accompanied by a skeptical attitude. This means that good evidence and/or sound argument is required before information is accepted as knowledge. Skepticism includes the belief that knowledge is fallible, not absolutely certain, and that every theory can be challenged by new evidence or argument. If proven false or misleading, it will be replaced by a new and better theory.

Knowledge acquired from a university course on a particular subject is similar for all the students who complete that course. This helps the formation of a distinctive profession, as graduates will have similar ways of understanding their subject, use similar terminology and share similar educational experiences, so are well prepared to network and communicate with one another after graduation.

Another characteristic of the knowledge ideally gained from academic studies is its systematic quality. A method for achieving this is in reference to tourism is set out in Chapter 3.

These characteristics of knowledge gained from academic study are ideals—impossible to achieve in absolute terms but worthy aims. Nobody could find time to read more than a small fraction of the books and articles on tourism, and no lecturer or writer can be totally objective, as personal bias always intrudes to some extent. Another limiting factor is the novelty of tourism as a subject or field for academic research and education. The body of knowledge on the subject is not yet well developed.

Aims of tourism research and education

Tourism research and education has evolved through four phases in regard to its aims, according to Jafari (2002). Tourism advocacy is the name he gives to the early phase. It advocates the development of tourism. The pro-tourism aim is to demonstrate how much good comes from tourism, and in education and training the aim is to produce graduates who go out into the world and work enthusiastically and uncritically to develop tourism. Tourism advocacy of this sort is also called tourism boosterism.

In the 1970s increasing numbers of researchers, educators and commentators realised that the unlimited expansion of tourism could cause damage. This led to a change, in some places and among some persons, in the focus of research and education. A cautionary stance emerged regarding environmental issues. It recognises that (Jafari 2002: 13):

> *tourism is not all benefits and, significantly, comes with many sociocultural and even economic costs. Researchers mostly from social science fields such as anthropology occupied this position. Their resulting publications, especially characteristic of the '70s, mainly focused on the 'dark side' of the industry and cautioned host countries against its perceived and documented costs and unwanted consequences.*

In the 1980s, among some researchers and educators, the stance evolved to become an adaptancy platform. This occurred from examining different forms of tourism, and led to the argument that some are more desirable than others: 'The resulting writings favored such forms as agritourism, cultural tourism, ecotourism, rural tourism, small-scale tourism, sustainable tourism' (Jafari 2002: 15).

Jafari's fourth phase is a knowledge focus. It puts knowledge in first priority. It is based in a belief that the principal role of universities is to discover and learn, rather than push a particular view of how the world should be. This does not mean that academics and students should not engage in real-world issues, in public debate and in activism. It means that they should not allow those activities to distort the process of learning.

Progress to date in the phase in which knowledge is the principal goal is hindered by the fact that the study of tourism is a relatively recent innovation. While a substantial body of knowledge now exists, represented in dozens of specialised research journals and many books, it has not progressed to the stage of a body of knowledge that is both detailed and highly organised. In other words, there is no fully developed discipline of tourism studies.

Issues regarding a disciplinary basis for tourism studies are complex and contentious (Leiper 1981a, 2000; Tribe 1997, 2000; Echtner & Jamal 1997), but a central question is fairly straightforward. Is tourism best studied from multiple points of view, as a field for various academic disciplines such as economics, geography, management and so on? Or is it better to mix and blend disciplines into a subject that might be called tourism studies? The present book uses both approaches, as do many educational programs.

Discussion questions

1. What are three reasons for studying history, and how are these reasons relevant in studying tourism?
2. What is the basis for describing ancient nomadism as a notable historical influence on modern tourism?
3. Name five antecedents of tourism and describe how each of them influenced aspects of modern tourism.
4. What is the basis for describing Ibn Battuta, Celia Fiennes, Matsuo Basho and Daniel Defoe as 'eccentric'?
5. What evidence is there that, until fairly recently in history, humans were not generally interested in looking at sights in nature?
6. Four sources for learning about tourism can be identified, one being academic study. What are the other three, and in what ways can academic study overcome their deficiencies?

Recommended reading

Davidson, J. & Spearritt, P. 2000, *Holiday Business in Australia Since 1970*, Melbourne: Melbourne University Press

Inglis, F. 2000, *The Delicious History of the Holiday*, London: Routledge

Jafari, J. (ed.) 2000, *The Encyclopedia of Tourism*, London: Routledge

Leiper, N. 2000, Education, multidisciplinary, pp 179–82 in *The Encyclopedia of Tourism*, J. Jafari (ed.), op. cit.

Richardson, J.I. 1999, *A History of Australian Travel & Tourism*, Melbourne: Hospitality Press

Ritchie, J.R. Brent 2000, Education, pp 166–9 in *The Encyclopedia of Tourism*, J. Jafari (ed.), op. cit.

Towner, J. & Wall, G. 1991, History and tourism, *Annals of Tourism Research*, 18: 71–84

Towner, J. 1985, The Grand Tour, a key phase in the history of tourism, *Annals of Tourism Research*, 12: 297–333

Towner, J. 1996, *An Historical Geography of Recreation and Tourism in the Western World 1540–1940*, Chichester: Wiley

Towner, J. 2000, History, pp 278–80 in *The Encyclopedia of Tourism*, J. Jafari (ed.), op. cit.

Tribe, J. 1997, The indiscipline of tourism, *Annals of Tourism Research*, 24: 638–57

Tribe, J. 2000, Indisciplined and unsubstantiated, *Annals of Tourism Research*, 27: 809–13

Walton, J. 2000, The hospitality trades: a social history, pp 56–76 in *In Search of Hospitality: Theoretical Perspectives and Debates*, C. Lashley & A. Morrison (eds), Oxford: Butterworth-Heinemann

Who are Tourists and What is Tourism?

Who, among all travellers and visitors, are the tourists? And what, exactly, is tourism? Is it a form of trip, a market, an industry, a class of travel, an environmental complex linked to all this, or something else? Exploring these questions and suggesting answers are the main themes of this chapter. Almost anybody could answer these questions by drawing on insight gained informally, but these answers would be unsatisfactory compared with the quality of knowledge expected in professional and managerial work.

In many publications on tourism, a definition is noted before proceeding to discussions where the definition does not seem to fit. This has led many commentators to assume that definitions in this subject are only of academic interest. The aims in this chapter are to show that reasonably precise definitions of 'tourist' and 'tourism' can be found, and that they provide practical advantages for managers, researchers, other professionals and students. All these categories will be included as 'professionals' in the following discussion: students are on a path to a professional career of some sort.

This chapter is arranged under three main headings. It begins by discussing the absence of widely recognised definitions. Then meanings of 'tourist' are discussed and finally meanings of 'tourism'.

ABSENCE OF WIDELY RECOGNISED DEFINITIONS

Vague or imprecise meanings of words are not problematical in casual conversation. There is no lasting problem when one of my neighbours remarks that tourists are 'those foreigners you see hanging out in Byron Bay' and that she herself is 'not a tourist' when she 'flies to Sydney for a shopping spree', and when another neighbour responds with 'Yes, you are'. The only effect is a change in the topic, maintaining harmony in the neighbourly conversation. A similar difference left hanging and unexplored among professionals sharing a common interest in a tourism project could be quite problematical.

Precise definitions for 'tourist' and 'tourism' exist, but none has become generally recognised as useful in all contexts encountered by professionals interested in the subject. The fact that certain groups, such as the World Tourism Organisation (WTO) or the Bunyip District Progress and Tourist Association, use what their officials regard as 'the definition' is a formality that professionals should treat skeptically.

This is not to imply that official definitions should be ignored—merely to recommend that they not be followed slavishly. Those ignorant about technical definitions of 'tourist' used by the WTO become confused and misled when they attempt to interpret statistics from that source, but this does not mean that these definitions should be quoted and followed in every report or research project on tourism.

What about dictionaries? Despite what countless students' essays persist in assuming, ordinary dictionaries do not define words in ways suitable for academic studies or professional practice. What ordinary dictionaries (*Macquarie, Oxford English*) do is report, not define, what words normally mean in general usage. Therefore, if we were studying economics, or wanting to borrow concepts from economics for a study of tourism, *The Macquarie Dictionary* is not where we would find suitable definitions of economic concepts. 'Demand' and 'supply' are examples of words whose meanings in everyday usage and in economics are different. To discover how core terms are defined in an academic subject, professionals should turn to the specialist literature on the relevant discipline, found in libraries, journals, books, reports, and specialist dictionaries and encyclopaedias. Students of tourism can gain from following this convention. *The Encyclopedia of Tourism* (Jafari 2000) and *The Dictionary of Travel and Tourism Terms* (Harris & Howard 1996) are examples, and can serve as supplements to the discussion in this chapter.

The absence of widely recognised and universally applicable definitions is not unique to tourism, as most subjects for academic study and professional practice have the same condition. This condition is not problematical if it is understood. Take mathematics, for example, where there are at least six definitions for 'computation'. A mathematician working in more than one mathematical area can adjust to the variations appropriate to each area. Maths does not need, and mathematicians do not seek, a general and universally applicable definition of 'computation'.

A similar scheme for 'tourist' and 'tourism' will be proposed in this book. I will not suggest a single definition for 'tourist' and for 'tourism', relevant in all applications. Instead, I will identify various contexts where these terms are used and suggest appropriate types of definition for each context.

Some teachers of tourism in universities have described any attempt to define tourism as 'mindless'; they say it inhibits thinking and free-ranging inquiry. Their excuse is admirable, for if students are pedantically instructed to learn and follow *the* definition, the dull attitude of a particular lecturer or textbook writer might infect them. Education can flourish if students think about their subject's central concepts, and central to this process is thinking about how they have been or might be defined. Critical thinking of this sort goes to the core of developing understanding.

Definitions also help communication. If you and I are discussing tourists as a topic for research but have in our minds different notions of who tourists are, our discussion is unlikely to be fruitful. If you write a report about tourists without stating precisely what is meant in that report when it refers to them, each reader is likely to attach their own idea, misinterpreting your intended message. There is a famous remark by George Orwell: 'The slovenliness of our language makes it easy for us to have foolish thoughts' (1970: 157). Professionals recognising that risk and wanting to avoid foolishness try to be precise with the important terms in their subject.

The understanding of culturally loaded words such as 'tourist' and 'tourism' is helped by considering how their meanings have evolved through history. This was a topic in Chapter 1, so need not be repeated here.

The path to understanding tourism becomes clearer by concentrating first on tourists. If a person is described, classified or counted as a tourist, presumably some feature of their appearance or behaviour induces that expression. It denotes a role, when a person is some sort of traveller or visitor. The basic question is, which sort(s)?

Attempts to answer this question usually jump straight into consideration of variables such as purpose of trip or type of travel arrangement. For instance, those whose purpose is holidaying might be regarded as suitable for including in the subset 'tourist', while those whose purpose is business might be excluded. Unfortunately, that approach to answering the question can be misleading, because variables such as trip purpose are not the primary issue. The primary issue in deciding how to classify travellers or visitors into tourists and non-tourists is a question of the contexts in which the classification is being made.

Three contexts of meanings for 'tourist'

Three contexts can be identified in which the term 'tourist' is used to describe or classify travellers or visitors. These contexts have their own kinds of meanings for 'tourist'. The first context is popular notions, the second is technical definitions, the third is heuristic definitions. Once these different contexts are recognised, a lot of confusion about definitions and meanings can be resolved. Figure 2.1 provides a summary.

Popular notions about tourists ➤

In everyday communication, people use 'tourist' to identify or describe persons in a range of roles. Ordinary dictionaries report the widely recognised meanings but, as with many other words, cannot be comprehensive because many meanings and connotations attach to 'tourist'.

Different people use the expression in slightly different ways. One person might regard sightseers as tourists; another might think tourists are visitors from a foreign country who seem to be visiting for any leisure-related purpose; a third might regard people as tourists only if they are members of an organised group engaged in recreational activities; a fourth might restrict use of the expression to those staying in a resort hotel. Overlapping those possibilities is the fact that some people regard 'tourist' as a disparaging expression, implying an inferior type of traveller or an unwelcome type of visitor, while other people do not attach any negative connotations.

Because of this range of meanings and connotations, what marks out the boundaries between tourists and other travellers or visitors is impossible to define in a manner that suits everybody.

FIGURE 2.1 Three categories of meanings for 'tourist'

Category	Uses	Degrees of precision and uniformity
Popular meanings	Everyday conversation and mass media	Imprecise; wide variations in meaning; no definitions required
Technical definitions	Statistics about numbers of tourists visiting a country or region	Precision desirable; a standard definition used worldwide for 'international tourist' but different definitions used in various countries for 'domestic tourist'
Heuristic concepts and definitions	Research into tourists' activities and other aspects of their behaviour	Precision desirable in each case but no widely followed definitions; each researcher should frame a definition to suit each project

Origins of technical definitions of 'tourist' ➤

Every professional field and academic discipline has its own technical definitions as part of its distinctive jargon, the definitions pertaining to certain words or phrases used in particular settings for specific purposes. National institutions representing several countries in Europe began attempting to formulate definitions of 'international tourist' for technical purposes, especially in statistical contexts, in the 1920s. Progress on a global level in these attempts was impossible without an appropriate international institution.

Innovative leaders in matters of culture, industry, politics and public service in Europe have been pioneers of many international institutions. The first was the International Telegraph Union (now the International Telecom Union), formed in 1865 in Paris to create and manage an agreement that allowed telegraphic messages to be sent efficiently and freely across national borders. Next, in 1874, was the Universal Postal Union, which allows letters posted and stamped in any country member of the union to be delivered at no cost in any other member country to the address on the envelope. The cooperative trust at the heart of these unions became the philosophical basis for hundreds of later international institutions.

In relation to tourism, considerable progress was achieved in 1963, when an international conference on tourism was convened. Sponsored by the United Nations and by an institution known as IUOTO (International Union of Official Travel Organisations), delegates met in Rome to confer on a range of issues. Their ultimate aim was to boost tourism globally, by getting more people to travel and by encouraging visits to a wider range of countries. Their immediate goal was to find ways for countries to better coordinate certain matters involving tourism. A report contains the recommendations (IUOTO 1963).

One matter discussed, relevant to tourism management internationally, was the measurement of tourist flows. Managing international tourism is helped by knowing how many tourist arrivals occur in various countries. Knowing how many international tourist arrivals in a country are recorded month by month and year by year is useful for monitoring trends to that country, but knowing how many arrive in other countries is more useful, as it enables comparisons to be made. For instance, if country X spends $20 million advertising its features as a tourist destination and $30 million in government subsidies for tourism resource development, and a year later the flow into country Y nearby has grown by 15% while in country X there has been a 1% fall, the government and other sponsors of the $50 million campaign will need to investigate a potentially serious problem.

In order to make valid comparisons between trends in tourist flows into different countries, the statistical data about tourist flows in the different countries must be comparable. A prerequisite for achieving this comparability is that countries use the same technical definition of 'international tourist' when measuring the flow of arrivals. This has not always occurred.

In the 1970s, reports from a certain country in East Asia showed that the number of tourist arrivals was much larger than observers in nearby countries believed was realistic. Investigations revealed that every tourist coming from the USA or Western Europe was counted as two arrivals, a ploy that the minister for tourism tried to justify by claiming that as tourists from those sources tended to spend more, the arrivals data should be adjusted upwards to reflect that extra benefit. (Interested readers can find out more about this case in copies of *Asia Travel Trade* in the late 1970s.) Several cases like this, of manipulating statistics to create a positive impression, have occurred in various countries.

Another kind of distortion has also occurred in several countries. This is not the result of a manipulative ploy to deceive anyone but the result of ignorance concerning the advantages available to all countries using a standard definition. Officials in different countries have reflected on their own ideas about tourists and, from these, devised definitions for use when counting tourist arrivals. As the definitions were different, the statistics in various countries were not comparable.

These issues were discussed at the 1963 Rome conference. The conference agreed on standard technical definitions of 'international visitor', 'international excursionist' and 'international tourist'. Another outcome of the conference, helpful in ensuring that the agreement would be put into practice, was the decision to form the World Tourism Organisation (WTO), which was launched in 1974.

The WTO replaced IUOTO. Its advantage stems from the fact that its members are national governments, which gives it direct links into policy-making and law-making institutions in many parts of the world. IUOTO, on the other hand, comprised mainly private-sector organisations interested in promoting tourism but lacking direct connections with governments.

The WTO, with its headquarters in Madrid, has become an important institution in global tourism, but not so important as its own publicity pretends. Its main work is in Third World countries. The WTO has often been described, in books about tourism, as part of the United Nations. It is not. The WTO is recognised by the UN as an institution with responsibilities and information in certain matters concerning tourism. Incidentally, the World Tourism Organisation should not be confused with another institution with the same inititials, often noted as WTO in the mass media. The World Trade Organisation is a far more powerful and influential body in terms of what happens in the world's economy and the national economies of many countries.

Technical definitions of international tourist

National governments around the world send statistics about international tourists to the WTO in Madrid where the data are checked, compiled and published on the WTO's Internet site, with more detail in documented reports available for purchase. Some countries' data refer to visitors and others to tourists, with definitions applying in either case. The standard technical definitions used in statistics of international flows are as follows (WTO, *Recommendations on Tourism Statistics*, no date, p. 3):

> *For statistical purposes the term international visitor describes any person who travels to a country other than that in which they have their usual residence but outside their usual environment for a period not exceeding twelve months and whose main purpose of visit is other than the exercise of an activity remunerated from within the country visited. International visitors include:*
>> *—international tourists: those visitors who stay at last one night in a collective or private accommodation in the country visited, and*
>> *—same-day visitors, who do not spend the night in a collective or private accommodation in the country visited. This definition includes cruise ship passengers.*

Precise definitions of this sort are required before statistics can be collected about international tourists by a method that make sense internationally. An unambiguous meaning is necessary so that those responsible for collecting, processing and using the data understand what they include and exclude. Besides statistics, another context for technical definitions is legal, when governments issue tourist visas. The WTO definition is reasonably precise, although there is vagueness about the phrase 'outside their usual environment' (Smith 1999).

Technical definitions of domestic tourist

Technical definitions of domestic tourists, referring to persons on trips that do not go outside their country of residence, vary greatly among the handful of countries recording statistics on this topic. In Australia, a domestic tourist is defined for official statistical purposes (in research used by governmental tourism agencies) as a person who engages in overnight travel for virtually any purpose (Bureau of Tourism Research 2001: 61):

Overnight travel within Australia involves a stay away from home for at least one night, at a place at least 40 kilometres from home. Travel can be for a number of reasons.

This definition is used by the Bureau of Tourism Research (BTR) as the basis for collections of statistics reported quarterly and annually under the title *National Visitor Survey*. These reports are described as 'the major source of information regarding . . . domestic tourists' (BTR 2001: x) and are publicised via press releases from the ministers and commissions of tourism at Commonwealth, state and territorial levels.

The surveys, conducted regularly throughout Australia, count all purposes of trips as tourism except short-term employment paid from places visited. Under this definition, tourists include persons travelling on holidays, for work-related business, for family events such as funerals and weddings, to visit friends and relatives, for sport, for medical treatment, for study, to attend conferences and conventions, and for other purposes. In its very broad scope it is similar to the technical definition used for 'international tourist' in WTO reports.

In Britain, by contrast, official statistics on domestic tourists have counted only trips for the main purpose of holidays, and only trips of at least four nights away. Thus data about domestic tourism in Britain and Australia cannot be compared from official statistics.

Heuristic concepts and definitions of tourists ➤

Heuristic concepts are those intended to help a process of finding out or discovery, so they relate to research and learning where a researcher or student is using a concept as a basis for exploring the nature of a topic.

Accordingly, in research projects and educational courses on tourists, when the topic is their nature or behaviour a heuristic definition is needed. A definition framed for heuristic purposes has three functions. It helps professionals focus their thinking, and it removes ambiguities from the minds of the readers of reports or essays. It aids communication. Without a statement of the definition, different people involved in a project or reading its published outcomes are likely to infer different meanings or connotations because of the wide variation in popular notions about tourists.

Heuristic definitions do not have to conform to technical definitions. Because the standard technical definitions of 'tourist' are so broad, embracing travellers and visitors on trips for virtually all purposes, they are not much use in detailed research on tourists' behaviour. Individual researchers should devise their own heuristic definitions to suit the particular purpose and focus of their project. For example, a report for managers of a tour wholesaling organisation might define tourists as follows:

In this report, tourists will be defined as persons considering or making trips to international destinations and using prepackaged arrangements, on a group or individual basis.

Investigating the behaviour of tourists at environmentally sensitive sites in a national park, a heuristic definition such as this one might be appropriate:

For this research, tourists will be defined as any persons other than park employees who visit any of the special sites in the Wherearewee National Park, for any purpose.

Another example is set out below. It is intended to have wider usage as a generic definition within the heuristic context. A widely accepted definition would be useful in certain educational settings at least, because it would remove the need to restate a new definition every time the topic arose during a series of lectures and tutorials.

Generic definitions of 'tourist'

Stephen Smith made the compelling point that there is not, and probably never will be, a single definition of tourist that is accepted by the majority of researchers interested in the subject (Smith 1988, 1989). He pointed out that economists tend to perceive certain things as definitive while psychologists will perceive other things as definitive, and so on.

While Smith's point is not disputed, in this book I will seek to reveal a common thread in the views of diverse professionals interested in tourism. The belief that this is possible is supported by the fact that economists do not agree among themselves about tourists— nor do psychologists, or geographers. This does not preclude the possibility of identifying a common thread; instead, it encourages that possibility.

Three general attributes can be identified in the behaviour of tourists. These can be specified to form a widely useful heuristic definition. First, tourists are persons travelling away from their normal residences and visiting other regions in their home country or other countries.

Second, tourists' trips involve temporary periods away from their normal residences of at least one night. This excludes commuters and other day-trippers from the scope of tourists. There are logical reasons for the exclusion. If they were included, general studies of tourism would have to be biased heavily towards the distinctive circumstances and characteristics of day-trippers, because worldwide and in many cities and towns day-trippers are far more numerous than overnight-staying tourists and have different patterns of behaviour.

No maximum period need be specified in a generic definition of tourists. They can be described as being away from their normal homes temporarily for at least one night, which might be a night, a week, six months, a year or longer. No distance need be specified for the generic definition. Specifying at least one night away from home is sufficient. Many residents of cities go on overnight holiday trips that are short in distance travelled, for activities that many would regard as touristic. Suburbanites visiting the city centre and staying overnight in hotels for leisure activities such as going to the theatre or social events are one example. City dwellers going to beaches in the same metropolitan area for overnight holidays are another.

The third general attribute is that tourist behaviour is a form of leisure behaviour. It is leisure away from home. Tourists can be regarded as travellers or visitors with free time (also termed discretionary, disposable, non-obligated time). A link between tourists and leisure has been identified by writers from diverse backgrounds (Clarke 1975; Bodewes 1981; Hamilton-Smith 1987; Moore, Cushman & Simmons 1995) and can be found in many, perhaps most, academic writings on tourists' behaviour.

What is leisure? A simple description is that it comprises recreational and/or creative experiences. The former are experiences that 're-create' or restore a person—rest, relaxation and entertainment. The latter refers to creative behaviour occurring in a non-obligatory context, such as cultural and artistic activities. Leisure is a category of experiences sought and valued for intrinsic pleasure or interest. Leisure-based experiences are those that individuals regard as non-obligatory, as pleasurable or interesting, enjoyed with a sense of personal freedom. A longer discussion on 'leisure' is in *The Encyclopedia of Tourism* (Smith 2000: 354–6).

Most leisure for most individuals occurs in and near their homes, not away on overnight trips. And although tourists do not spend all their time at leisure, as they have obligations that reduce the time available for recreational and cultural experiences, their trips are a special form of leisure, a point analysed in Chapter 5.

People travelling for purposes other than holidaying (e.g. business, visiting relatives or attending conferences) in many instances spend a proportion of their time at leisure, in behaviour that observers would describe as fitting the tourist role. To that extent, travellers whose main purpose of a trip is business could be regarded as tourists.

Having analysed these three components, a definition of tourists for general heuristic application can now be set out. This should not be regarded as *the* definition; it is *a* definition:

> *Tourists can be defined as persons who travel away from their normal residential region for a temporary period of at least one night, to the extent that their behaviour involves a search for leisure experiences from interactions with features or characteristics of places they choose to visit.*

Tourists choose to visit places; their visits are not obligatory. A business traveller might be obliged to visit a city to attend business meetings, but he is not obliged to spend his free afternoon as a tourist visiting art galleries.

Nobody ever set out on a touristic trip, or set out to visit a particular place during a trip, if they perceived the experience as likely to be unpleasant and the place as lacking attractions. The same general principle could not be made about trips for business or to visit relatives. However, some tourists do choose to visit places that will cause them financial or physical discomfort (expensive places, or those lacking in amenities) because of perceiving a probability of pleasurable experiences. What about other travellers and visitors who engage for some of the time in what common sense regards as tourist behaviour? The generic definition set out above includes them, via its phrase 'to the extent that'.

This is a suitable generic definition, as it conforms to many people's idea of tourists. When a busy executive completes the main reasons for her visit to town and announces that for the rest of the day she intends to 'see the sights, go shopping and be a tourist', nobody will say that as she is in town on business, her free-time activity cannot be realistically described in that way. However, to follow the WTO concept and describe her visit to town as a tourist arrival goes against common sense.

Being a tourist has three attributes. It requires travelling, visiting, and having a leisure experience. In combination, these distinguish tourists from other travellers, other visitors and other persons having recreational or cultural experiences. In a city, tourists might be mingling with other people enjoying similar experiences, such as city residents in the museum looking at exhibits, but the combination of attributes distinguishes tourists for the purposes of general studies of tourism.

The generic definition set out above seems suitable for use in the absence of special circumstances, when a variation is preferable. It expresses what are, arguably, general features of being a tourist. It is not framed from the perspective of countries as destination, or business organisations as suppliers to tourists, or environments as recipients of impacts from tourists. It focuses instead on the distinctive behavioural characteristics that go with being a tourist.

Sorting out the three contexts

Three sets of meanings of 'tourist' serve particular purposes and fit particular contexts. Accordingly, problems stemming from contradictions or differences between meanings can be largely overcome by looking behind the semantics, to the context where the expression is being used.

The first context is everyday language, where popular notions prevail. This is a field for research if one wants to discover what people mean by 'tourist' and its derivatives such as 'touristy'. Here, researchers should avoid expressing their own opinions on the issue.

The second context is research aiming to count tourists as a distinct category among travellers or visitors. Here, a precise technical definition is appropriate and should be carefully followed when designing surveys or interpreting statistics. A similar context with the same need for precision is in legal aspects of administration, such as when governments issue visas with a specific category for tourists.

The third context is in research on tourists' behaviour. A reasonably clear and precise definition is desirable, stating clearly what researchers mean when they refer to tourists in their research project.

Failure to discriminate among the three contexts is an error in many comments and writings about tourists. Searching for a definition to put in the opening section of a report, many students, academics and paid researchers come across the WTO's technical definition and, seizing on it, graft it into their report's opening pages, implying that, as it has official status, it is *the* definition. But then the substance of the report, in many cases, includes discussion on behavioural aspects of a narrower classification of tourist than the technical definition specifies. These behavioural themes are often about holidaying or pleasure tourists, issues at variance from the definition, and so the practice leads to research that is structurally and conceptually flawed.

Why the wide scope of technical definitions?

Technical definitions of 'tourist' often include visitors and travellers that many people, probably most people, would not imagine belonged there. For example, many would not see the visitors described below as tourists. These five hypothetical visitors to a country are all counted as 'tourists', according to the technical definition recommended by the WTO:

1. A business traveller who spends virtually every waking hour during five days visiting a country on work-related matters.
2. A student visiting a country for 11 months to attend university.
3. A sick person who visits a country to have medical treatment in hospital.
4. A pilgrim who visits a country to visit a holy site, who arrives with no money and begs to sustain a frugal existence.
5. A grandmother who visits a country to be with her daughter and does not venture outside her daughter's home and the nearby shops.

If these types were discounted from official statistics, the apparent scope and value of tourism and tourism industries would be reduced by a huge amount. For example, visitors in Australia whose main purpose is business have comprised around 12% of all 'tourists' in recent years, and visitors whose main purpose is staying with relatives have comprised around 20%.

International students in Australia, officially counted as 'tourists', do not amount to a large proportion of the total, but typically they are in the country for 10 or 11 months and spend a lot on student fees and studying costs as well as living expenses. As a result, they contribute a large share to the economic impacts of tourism in reports prepared at the Bureau of Tourism Research (O'Dea 1997a, 1997b), reports whose top-line findings are widely used as official indicators of the value of tourism.

Why are technical definitions of 'tourist' so broad, and what can be inferred from the fact? From transcripts of meetings in which technical definitions were decided, notably the IUOTO (1963) conference in Rome, and from discussions with officials who participated in that and subsequent meetings on the same theme, the following explanations emerged.

First is the official explanation. The WTO's technical definition of 'tourist' was created by organisations whose primary interests are the economic consequences of tourist-visitors, including commercial benefits flowing to business enterprises and other sorts of economic benefits flowing to governments and the host community. The concerns of all those organisations relate to how much money visitors spend, what they spend it on, and trends in expenditure. All sorts of visitors in a place for at least one night typically have similar spending patterns, regardless of other differences in their behaviour. So the committee that formulated the technical definition decided to cast a very wide scope, including many kinds of visitors in the classification of 'tourists'.

The defect in this decision is that it led to a definition that every year misleads many persons. Correctly interpreting a newspaper report stating that 4 302 500 tourist arrivals were recorded in Zenda last year should not depend on readers knowing that in that context, 'tourist' means something quite different from popular notions of tourists—a far broader scope in fact. Thus, a major effect of the definition is to convey a greatly exaggerated or boosted image about the scope and apparent value of tourism.

That points directly to a second, unofficial explanation for the wide scope. Committees formulating these definitions comprised people representing organisations or institutions with 'tourist' or 'tourism' in their title. By framing the definitions very widely, more visitors could be counted as tourists, so greatly inflating official estimates of the economic value of tourism.

Who benefits? Organisations with 'tourist' or 'tourism' in their titles benefit. By artificially inflating the perceived economic value of tourism, these organisations can convince gullible administrators in government treasuries, as well as the politicians who follow their advice, that more money should be allocated from public funds to support tourism industry activities. The extra money allows tourism bureaucracies to expand, employ more staff, raise the salaries of the managers, and dispense more funds to media companies and marketing consultants.

Recipients of this largesse in Australia have included institutions such as the Australian Tourist Commission and hundreds of regional groups, such as the Bunyip District Progress and Tourist Association. The ATC has been an effective promoter of Australia as a tourist destination, but its effectiveness since the early 1980s (when its receipts of government subsidies began increasing greatly) should not be interpreted as efficiency. In absolute terms, the ATC has a larger budget than any other national tourism organisation in the world (WTO 2000b), which is odd considering Australia's current and feasible share of global tourist arrivals, quite small compared with several dozen other countries.

Many tourism industry associations in Australia and other countries have attempted to extend the ploy by casting the technical definition even wider, by including day-trippers within their association's official definition of tourists. In places visited by many day-trippers but comparatively few overnight tourists, the gains to tourism institutions can be great, but the trick succeeds only in places where distortions from common sense are not noticed.

One such place is Canberra. In the 1980s, the Department of Tourism in the Australian Capital Territory government based in Canberra adopted a technical definition of tourist which included day-trippers. Subsequently, the department's surveys of tourists' expenditures included spending by people living in surrounding towns or farms and visiting Canberra on day trips often, to shop, play sport, visit friends. This led to official reports showing that the city was earning far more from tourists than was previously assumed. The ACT government met a request from its Department of Tourism for a large boost in funds and the department was able to move into a new building, employ more staff and spend more.

From a public policy perspective, the administration of tourism would be improved if media reports about tourists' numbers and expenditures carried a note explaining clearly what sorts of visitors or travellers were included under the 'tourist' label. The suggestion is not likely to be adopted in the near future, for that would require a change in the politics of tourism. That depends on the development and spread of knowledge and understanding of tourism and related issues, a trend to which this book is aiming to make a small contribution, but a trend in a slow process.

The first meaning of tourism, when the term first appeared 200 years ago, was the practice and theory of being a tourist, a person engaged in a decadent style of travel. A more recent meaning, widely accepted since the 1960s, is that tourism is an industry. Other meanings exist. Do they all make sense? Which is most useful? The relevance of the historical evolution in the meanings of words deserves noting (Saul 2001: 223):

> *Whatever current fashion says that a word means, the same word will also carry in some invisible way the reverberations of its other, earlier senses. You may believe that you do not know what they are. You may be convinced that you are only hearing the first level of contemporary meaning. [But other levels exist] consciously for those who seek, unconsciously for others.*

Tourism as a decadent style of travel ➤

The first use of the expressions 'tourist' and 'tourism' seems to have stemmed from writings in the 1770s of Adam Smith (Wykes 1973). Smith, a Scottish scholar who went on an extended trip in Europe as a tutor, formed the opinion that the Grand Tour was a decadent custom. This led him to think of *tour-ist* and to coin the word 'tourist' to denote a decadent style of traveller. The corresponding abstract noun 'tourism' then came into use. (The reasons behind Smith's opinions are discussed in Chapter 4.)

'Tourism' denoting a decadent style of travel still has currency among many people today, who view 'travel' as the livelier, more authentic alternative. This idea is unsuitable as a generic approach for understanding and defining tourism, as it merely reflects subjective opinion.

Tourism as the theory and practice of being a tourist ➤

Around 1810, 30 years after Smith wrote about tourists, 'tourism' was becoming a recognised expression, and its disparaging sense had largely disappeared; the *Oxford English Dictionary* was later able to report its early meaning as 'the theory and practice of touring, travelling for pleasure'. Today many people use the expression in that sense, and many academic writers follow it as a definition.

Tourism as an inferior class of trips ➤

After 1840, when travel agents such as Thomas Cook began promoting tourism to the middle and lower classes of English society, 'tourism' came to mean an inferior class of trip. This meaning has also survived. It is realistic, but unsuitable for a definition used in general studies of tourism. The subject is more than class-based snobbery.

Tourism as inferior standards and lower prices ➤

Persons seeing a sign 'Tourist Hotel' would infer that it had inferior standards to those of a first-class hotel. Allied with this meaning, 'tourism' also connotes lower prices. Like the class-based ideas above, these meanings can be rejected as definitions of tourism or as foundations for general studies of tourism.

Tourism and tourists include a range of types

Taiwanese tourists on a group tour by coach in Indonesia

Delegates from various countries at a convention in Hong Kong

Adventure tourism: trekking in the Himalayas of Nepal

Tourism as a sector of regional and national economies ➤

Since 1910, economists have been studying implications of tourists' consumption and spending. For some of these economists and for a number of people impressed with their reports, tourism has come to mean a sector of regional or national economies. A person might say 'Tourism is important for Lismore' and mean, in effect, 'The consequences of tourist spending are quite important for Lismore's economy'.

This might be realistic, as tourists' activities generally do have economic consequences, but it is an inappropriate way to define tourism. Trying to define something by its consequences misses the point.

Tourism as a complex of environmental impacts ➤

As discussed in Chapter 1, Swiss academics in the 1930s formed the first multi-disciplinary group interested in studying tourism. Two professors in the group created a formal definition that regards tourism as a complex of environmental impacts (Hunziker & Krapf, cited in Burkart & Medlik 1974: 40):

> *Tourism is the sum of the phenomena and relationships arising from the travel and stay of non-residents, in so far as they do not lead to permanent residence and are not connected with any earning activity.*

This definition is widely recognised. It is endorsed by the International Association of Scientific Experts on Tourism, an academic group based in Europe, and has been quoted favourably by many writers. It has advantageous features. It is, however, unsuitable as a definition. First, its advantages will be noted.

Many academic writers favour Hunziker and Krapf's definition because it recognises the wide-ranging impacts of tourists' activities and because, from this broad scope, a large number of issues could be studied under the name of 'tourism'. It provides legitimacy for multidisciplinary research and education on the subject. By not mentioning or suggesting a discipline, it allows academics from any discipline to feel that they could be part of a university-wide program on the subject, and it prevents academics in any specific discipline from pretending that tourism is their exclusive domain. Accordingly, this definition has helped tourism studies gain acceptance and develop as a subject or field in universities.

Despite those advantages, the Hunziker and Krapf definition is hopelessly defective as a guide for research and learning. It is too broad. Applied logically, it includes a lot of human activity within the scope of tourism that common sense would exclude. Prisoners in gaol, inmates of asylums, patients in hospital, students away from home living temporarily at their university, refugees on the road and in camps, and soldiers at war are all persons who are or have been travellers, are not permanent residents of their present location, and whose presence is not based on earning money. According to the Hunziker and Krapf definition, they are all tourists.

Would many reasonable persons accept that tourism includes the 'phenomena and relationships' associated with prisoners, inmates, students, refugees on the run and soldiers at war? Probably not. This definition strays too far from common sense, and therefore does not deserve the credibilty that a large number of academic writers have accorded it by holding it up as a useful definition.

Tourism as an industry ➤

Early research on tourists focused on the economic consequences of their behaviour. The findings, in economists' minds, were reminiscent of the consequences of industries: the researchers noticed how tourists' expenditures in international destinations represented foreign exchange earnings for those countries no different from earnings derived by industries producing exported goods. Over time, an idea originally expressed as the simile 'tourism is *like* an industry' evolved into a metaphor, 'tourism *is* an industry'. According to an influential textbook: 'Tourism can be defined as the science, art and business of attracting and transporting visitors, accommodating them and graciously catering to their needs' (McIntosh & Goeldner 1977: ix).

Metaphors are seldom precise indicators to truth, because 'metaphor consists in giving the thing a name which belongs to something else' (Aristotle 1920: 71). Many other commentators, besides McIntosh & Goeldner, have given tourism a name that belongs to something else. Linking tourism to industry in a definitional sense is an example of this habit.

Certainly tourism normally has effects like those of industries. Certainly there are industries directly associated with tourism, and these can be described as tourism industries. However, these facts do not support the view that tourism should be defined as an industry. Defining tourism as an industry takes in only some of the activities of tourists and leads to irrational ideas and policies. A textbook explains this issue in the following way (King & Hyde 1989: 3):

> *The common element of all tourism is not 'the industry'. After all, a tourist may spend a night away from home at the house of a friend or relative, using a private car, and engage in no commercial transactions during the visit. The truly common element of tourism is the tourist.*

Faced with the fact that many tourists use private homes and cars to facilitate their trips and socialise with friends and relatives for entertainment, those who insist on defining tourism as an industry can become quite irrational, saying that all these things are included in 'the industry'. But these things do not function like the components of any other industry. The error in defining tourism as an industry is the error of using and believing a feral metaphor.

Tourism as a market ➤

Kaul moved from a career in airline marketing to become an academic specialising in tourism. His background carried over into his perceptions of the definitive attributes of tourism, which, he says, 'is a market rather than an industry' (Kaul 1985: 22). A similar view was proposed by two British marketers (Jefferson & Lickorish 1988). The merit of this opinion is twofold: it highlights the defects in the notion of tourism being 'an industry', and it emphasises the sensible alternative that, fundamentally, tourism is something to do with tourists themselves.

However, Kaul, Jefferson and Lickorish go too far when they define tourism as a market. Certainly, most tourists help form markets, but do they all do this? And is that a distinctive thing they do? Arguably not. Theorists in marketing (Pandya 1987; Gronhaug & Dholakia 1987) have emphasised that markets do not embrace every transaction that humans engage in. Some experiences and transactions are 'non-market'. This is notable with tourism.

Like most trips in Australian domestic tourism, a recent trip I took involved a mix of non-market and market activities. My own car was used and, as the trip was only 400 kilometres, no fuel was bought during the trip; for accommodation I stayed with relatives. Thus the transport and accommodation components of the trip had no marketing implications. We visited restaurants, and I also spent money in shops, so in those activities this instance of tourism did involve market transactions. This case exemplifies a common condition: tourism involves many activities, of which only some can be attributed to markets.

Tourism as a system ➤

Cuervo's (1967) book, Leiper's (1979) article and Mill and Morrison's (1985) book all proposed defining tourism as a system, as an interrelated set of elements such as tourists, tourism industries and destinations. Later, Mill and Leiper formed the opinion that this approach to a definition was defective. The approach had confused the activities of tourists with the sets of elements (systems) that can be useful for studying tourism.

Can tourism be all the things listed above?

Can tourism be all the things listed above? Demonstrably not. To accept that tourism can be defined in different ways is illogical, for it would require accepting that the substance of each different meaning is identical, which is clearly not the case. A market is not an industry, for example.

Certainly, all the approaches indicate things that are associated with tourism, but a definition should focus on distinctive features, not on associated items. Nobody would seriously define a university as 'sporting fields and bars where students enjoy themselves', despite the fact that sporting fields and bars are associated with universities. And while we need to understand the associated items and parts to comprehend the whole of anything, we cannot understand the whole merely by adding together the parts. That principle has been emphasised by analysts in different fields, such as Ornstein (1975) in psychology and Emery (1981) in general systems theory, and is illustrated by John Saxe's poem, 'The Blind Men and the Elephant', based on a folk story. In summary, here is its story:

Six blind men each grasped a part of an elephant and said what the whole appeared to be, from each individual's perspective. One held the trunk and believed the thing was a snake, the next held the tusk and said it must be a spear, the third held a leg and thought the thing was a tree, and so on. In truth an elephant is none of those things, and nor is it the sum of them.

Tourism could be defined as a sector of regional and national economies, but this will show only part of the picture. It could be defined as an industry, or as a market, but either of these approaches will show only part of the whole picture. Tourism could be defined as an environmental complex, but this is too vague. What remains? One early meaning stands, for it refers to the distinctive features.

A Useful Definition of 'Tourism' ➤

Tourism is the theory and practice of being a tourist: 'Tourism is, first of all, a form of human behaviour' (Przeclawski 1986: 11). A useful definition of tourism can be constructed by building on that foundation, as follows:

> *Tourism can be defined as the theories and practices for being a tourist. This involves travelling and visiting places for leisure-related purposes. Tourism comprises the ideas and opinions people hold which shape their decisions about going on trips, about where to go (and where not to go) and what to do or not do, about how to relate to other tourists, locals and service personnel. And it is all the behavioural manifestations of those ideas.*

'Ism' denotes a set of ideas or theories put into practice by persons following it. Just as idealism is the theories and distinctive practices of idealists, and socialism is the theories and distinctive practices of socialists, so can tourism be described as the theories and distinctive practices of tourists.

There is no single theory for being a tourist and no single practice that defines tourism. There are many types of tourists, so referring to 'the tourist' as a general type who follows a single set of theories is misleading (Cohen 1979). Tourism in the contemporary world includes a range of theories for being a tourist, and there is, accordingly, diversity in the practice of the role.

Alternative definitions for aspects of tourism ➤

Defining tourism as the theory and practice of being a tourist will not suit every professional and academic interested in the subject. Alternative definitions can be devised or adopted, most of which will be along the lines of the various meanings described above. Tourism can be defined as a decadent style of travel, as an inferior standard of travel, as an environmental complex, as a sector of an economy, as an industry, as a market and so on. All of these approaches for defining tourism are meaningful and useful, so long as they are applied logically. Even that can still raise problems.

A problem with most of these meanings is that, as definitions, they would limit the study of tourism to one aspect of the many that are directly linked to tourists' activities. Markets and industries, for example, are only facets of the total picture. The problem with one meaning, Hunziker and Krapf's definition, is the opposite: it is too vague.

CONCLUSION

No widely accepted definitions exist for 'tourist' or 'tourism', but comprehensive academic and professional studies of tourism should consider these concepts closely.

Three sets of meanings for 'tourist' were identified, and the contexts in which each set applies were described. A generic definition was proposed for use in general studies of tourists. It is narrower than the standard technical definitions used and is promoted by the World Tourism Organisation and other tourism-related institutions.

Several meanings of 'tourism' were identified and reviewed. Tourism is more than an issue of social class, more than what occurs in markets, more than what occurs within the domain of any industry or group of industries. One widely used definition was considered and found to be far too broad, allowing into the scope of tourism several kinds of activity that reasonable persons would exclude if they were objective about the issue.

Tourism is best defined as the theories and distinctive practices of tourists, persons travelling away from their home region and visiting other regions or countries where they seek leisure-related experiences.

Our views of the world, and perceptions of how things are or ought to be, are influenced by the stereotypes each of us hold about reality beyond our immediate or familiar surrounds. Stereotypes are inevitable and always distort the truth, but care can be taken to reduce their negative impact on our thinking.

Remarks on this process may help in reviewing this chapter. We tend to assume that we observe the real world, and then form or seek a definition of any feature that we want to study closely. Actually, these events typically happen in the reverse sequence, as Lippman (1922: 55) demonstrated:

> We do not first see, and then define, we define first and then see. In the great, blooming, buzzing confusion of the outer world we pick out what our culture has already defined for us, and we tend to perceive that which we have picked out in the form stereotyped by our culture.

Thus, virtually everyone can offer some sort of definition of tourism without having studied the subject formally, and the definitions shape what they recognise as tourism. That is how public opinion is formed. Studies for academic or professional purposes are formalised in a quite different way.

Discussion questions

1. What are the three contexts in which the expression 'tourist' carries various meanings?
2. In which two of these contexts are precise and clearly communicated definitions of 'tourist' useful and desirable?
3. Why is the WTO's technical definition of 'international tourist' not especially helpful in research on the behaviour of tourists?
4. List nine meanings of 'tourism' that have emerged successively over the past 200 years.
5. Which one of those nine meanings is most useful for understanding tourism, and why?
6. Why are attempts to define tourism as an industry misleading to those wanting to understand tourism?

Tourism Management

Recommended reading

Gilbert, D.C. 1991, Conceptual issues in the meaning of tourism, pp 4–27 in *Progress in Tourism, Recreation and Hospitality Management*, C.P. Cooper (ed.), vol. 2

Hall, Colin Michael 2003, *Introduction to Tourism: Dimensions and Issues*, Sydney: Hospitality Press

Harris, Robert & Howard, Joy 1996, *Dictionary of Travel, Tourism and Hospitality Terms*, Melbourne: Hospitality Press

Orwell, George 1970, Politics and the English Language, pp 156–69 in *The Collected Essays, Journalism and Letters of George Orwell, Vol. Four: In Front of Your Nose*, S. Orwell & I. Angus (eds), London: Penguin

Smith, Stephen L.J. 1988, Defining tourism: a supply-side view, *Annals of Tourism Research*, 15: 179–90

Studying Tourism: a Whole Systems Approach

INTRODUCTION

Chapter 2 suggested that what is really needed to study tourism is a systematic approach. This chapter explains what that involves. We often hear people say that they intend doing something 'systematically'. The intention has been taken further and formalised in academic and professional studies, within hundreds of subjects ranging from anatomy to zoology, where systems theory now has a useful role. It is, accordingly, very likely to be useful in the study of tourism.

Systems thinking has been around for thousands of years, at least since the time of the ancient Greeks. Aristotle was a systems thinker 2500 years ago. These days, countless ordinary people can think systematically to some extent. This is not to say that everyone who uses phrases like 'systematic' is in fact thinking systematically. The term has become fashionable, and is often used by those who have only an approximate idea of what it means.

If you had a list of items to buy at the shops, you might say to yourself 'I will do it systematically', and then arrange the items into categories representing different shops where they could be purchased. This is a systematic approach. It involves looking at the whole project, identifying its component sub-tasks or elements, and deciding how they best fit together.

SYSTEMS THEORY

Systems theory originated in the 1930s as an attempt to formalise and develop systems thinking. The distinctive features of systems theory are its conscious aim, which is to clarify anything that seems complicated, and its methods for achieving that purpose, which begin by identifying the system to be considered, then identifying its elements and discovering how they are arranged and interrelated. Usually a number of overlapping systems can be isolated, arranged in a hierarchy so that each system has its subsystems and superior systems.

A leading contributor to the development of systems theory was Bertalanffy, who in the 1930s realised he had to go beyond biology and integrate ideas from other disciplines in order to understand more about living organisms. To do this, he formulated theories of general systems, discovering 'a way of seeing things which were previously overlooked or by-passed' (Bertalanffy 1972a: 38).

He also introduced the concept of closed and open systems. The former is closed off from its environments, while the latter interacts with them. Tourism occurs in open systems, where environmental factors shape tourism and tourism has an impact on environments. How this occurs is discussed later.

What is a system? Jordan (1981: 24) showed that it is roughly what many people mean in everyday language when they refer to systems: 'We call a thing a system when we wish to express the fact that the thing is perceived and conceived as consisting of a set of elements, of parts, that are connected to one another by at least one distinguishing principle'. More succinctly: 'a system may be defined as a set of elements standing in interrelation among themselves and their environments' (Bertalanffy 1972a: 31).

Whole tourism systems

The easiest way to explain whole tourism systems is to begin by describing a realistic example. From the description of a trip by a tourist, we can identify a system by identifying the things that are elementary, along the lines of Jordan's and Bertalanffy's definitions.

> *Herr Schmidt, resident of Berlin, travelled to France, Spain and Italy for a holiday. Before setting out he collected information from the Berlin branch of the Italian Tourism Organisation. He drove his BMW to Paris, where he stayed three nights in his brother's home, then drove to Barcelona in Spain, where he spent two days with friends; next he drove to Italy, where he used the information collected back in Berlin to find accommodation in a hotel in Venice (the Albergo Bruno). After a week there he drove north, through Switzerland into Germany and home to Berlin.*

This hypothetical example is most appropriate, as Germans are the most numerous nationality among the world's international tourists, and France, Spain and Italy are among the most visited destination countries. How can components forming a whole tourism system be identified here? We must discover what is elementary. From the evidence, nothing certain can be inferred about Schmidt's activities in the destinations, so the elements will not be Parisian restaurants, or the sun and sea of the Spanish coast, or the gondolas and canals in Venice.

At least one tourist ➤

At least one tourist is elementary. Without tourists there can be no tourism. If Schmidt had not gone on the trip, this example of tourism would not exist. The mere existence of the Italian Tourism Office in Berlin and the hotel in Venice does not make tourism happen. These are facilities waiting for tourism, waiting for tourists to use them. Tourists are the human element in all whole tourism systems.

At least three places in each itinerary ➤

Three kinds of places, in essential and elementary roles, can be identified. First, Berlin (or Germany) is the place that generated the trip, where it began. Every instance of tourism needs such a place, so every whole tourism system has, as one elementary component, at least one traveller-generating region or country. These places generate travellers who are counted and regarded as tourists during their trips.

To reach the places he visited, and to get home again, Schmidt had to travel through places he did not choose to visit and stay a while. These places—along the autobahns from Berlin to the west, and later south along the autoroutes from Paris, then south and east to Italy—can be called transit routes. A whole tourism system is inconceivable without at least one transit route, which might be crossed by land, sea or air. Thus transit routes can be identified as another element.

He chose to visit certain cities, which then assumed the role of tourist destination regions. Every whole tourism system normally has at least one, and might have many. In theory, tourism can occur without a tourist destination region, if tourists merely wander about incessantly without choosing any place to head for or visit, but this is not usual.

At least one industry ➤

A fifth element is a tourism industry. In theory, tourism can occur without any tourism-specific industry being involved in some way, but this is not normal. Almost always, in itineraries where tourists can be observed, there will be organisations managed in ways that support or influence that activity. In this case, from the information provided, two such organisations can be identified. One is in the traveller-generating region, where Schmidt sought information at the Berlin office of the Italian Tourism Organisation. The other is in Venice, his third destination, where he was accommodated in a hotel. Thus a tourism industry, comprising those two organisations, can be identified as another element.

Nothing else is elementary ➤

Was anything else needed for the trip to happen, for this example of tourism to transpire? We could say that money and spare time were needed. These can be regarded as sub-elements, as attributes of the human element (Schmidt), as it was his money and spare time that was consumed on the trip.

We could say that good weather and peaceful conditions were needed. These can be regarded as attributes of two of the geographical elements, the transit routes and tourist destination regions. The hotel in Venice can be regarded as an attribute of the destination region as well as a component in a tourism industry.

Environments of tourism systems ➤

Around these five elements forming the whole system are all sorts of environments (social, cultural, economic, physical etc.), about which the case tells us nothing, although certain interactions may be inferred. For example, presumably the Berlin economy generated the resources—money and leisure time—required for the trip, and therefore incurred the outflow of money taken on the trip.

The economies of France, Spain and Italy gained money when Schmidt spent it. Perhaps he left a quantity of rubbish behind, after his visits to places along his itinerary. Presumably he was one of the millions of tourists who that year visited Paris, Barcelona and Venice and formed social and cultural impressions of people there. Perhaps Schmidt returned home feeling refreshed after his holiday, and in this way he and his home region derived another sort of environmental effect from this example of tourism.

FIGURE 3.1 Five elements in every whole tourism system

Element	Description
Tourists	Human element: persons on touristic trips
Traveller-generating regions	Geographical element: places where a tourist's trip begins and normally ends
Transit routes	Geographical element: places where a tourist's main travelling activity occurs
Tourist destination regions	Geographical element: places where a tourist's main visiting activity occurs
Tourism industries	Organisational element: collections of managed organisations in the business of tourism, working together to some degree in marketing tourism and providing services, goods and facilities

THE NATURE OF MODELS

Whole tourism systems, when described in words and/or diagrams, become models with great utility in studying the subject. A model is a simplified and scaled-down version of reality, representing reality in ways that are meaningful to users.

Children play with dolls and toy cars, which are models that represent, to children, real cars and real people. When designing buildings, architects make models in the form of small, scaled-down versions. Economists make a different kind of model when they study a regional or national economy, by identifying the factors that determine income and employment patterns and writing a formula to experiment with variables.

We thus use models to help our understanding of realities that are too removed, too large or too complex to work with or think about directly. There are countless models used in many subjects of academic study. The research literature on tourism contains models for all sorts of cases and topics. The models presented later in this chapter are for the big picture of tourism.

Closed and open systems

Whole tourism systems are open systems, and models should recognise that fact and its implications. A closed system is one that does not interact with environments. A series of connected pipes and bowls in a chemist's laboratory is a closed system, designed so that chemicals inside the equipment are not affected by, and do not affect, the air and other environmental factors in the laboratory.

Environments interact with elements in whole tourism systems. Social, cultural, political, economic, legal, technical and physical environments are all relevant. They shape tourism systems, and tourism in turn has effects on them. This point has not always been adequately recognised; most discussions of tourism and its environments only recognise the impact on environments, and then only in reference to places visited.

Using models of whole tourism systems

Getz (1986) was the first to use the expression 'whole tourism system', which he saw as a useful concept in planning. A number of other uses can be identified. Models of whole tourism systems provide a way of seeing the big picture, the entire scope of tourism. They remind us that tourism is not just tourists using services provided by tourism industries. Other elements, and the activities involving them, are also vitally important.

Five elements—tourists, generating regions, transit routes, destination regions, tourism industries—combine to enable tourism to occur in practice, so knowledge of all five elements and knowledge of how they interact with one another and with their environments is required to understand the dynamics of tourism. Environments depicted in the diagram of a model remind us that elements of whole tourism systems are affected by many factors in their environments, and that the process of tourism, when the elements combine, affects or influences many environments.

Models of whole tourism systems can represent particular systems, named by their geographical dimensions. Thus the Schmidt example is a Berlin–Paris–Barcelona–Venice–Berlin tourism system or, in national terms, a Germany–France–Spain–Italy–Germany tourism system. Intermediate places on transit routes, such as Switzerland on the route home, can be included for greater precision. A feature of this model is,

---

FIGURE 3.2 Geography of a whole tourism system with three destinations

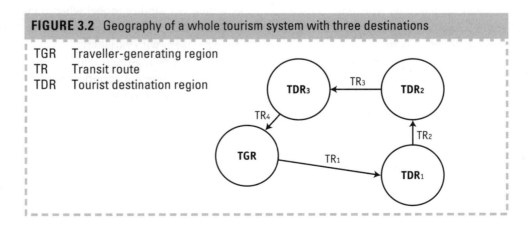

TGR   Traveller-generating region
TR   Transit route
TDR   Tourist destination region

accordingly, its geographic symbolism, as the diagram can be imagined as an overlay on a map, representing the structures of itineraries (see Figure 3.2).

The model of whole tourism systems presented in this book can also be applied to study issues and cases from different geographical perspectives. The most common application looks at tourism from the perspective of a tourist destination. An example can be seen in Henshall and Roberts' (1985) research, studying New Zealand as the focal country, as a destination for tourists from several traveller-generating countries. A similar example is Leiper's (1998) research on tourism in Cambodia.

A different perspective with the same model was used in Leiper's (1985) research on the Japan–Australia tourism system. It focused on Japan as a traveller-generating country, as a source of tourists visiting a range of destination regions in Australia. Hing and Dimmock (2000) used the same model to structure their research on the ways that political crises in Fiji have affected all elements in whole tourism systems involving Fiji. Boniface and Cooper (1994) used the model in a textbook on the geography of tourism.

In diagrams, the model can be presented in various ways to depict various ideas or perspectives. Figures 3.2 and 3.3 show it in ideographic form, as pictures resembling real-world forms.

Models of whole tourism systems can be used as a theoretical construct for studying the subject. A simple version is usually suitable here, a mono-destination case. This is shown in Figure 3.3, which is more complete than Figure 3.2. It shows all five elements and their environments. Figure 3.4 presents the model in an abstract form. This shows a simple approach for studying tourism in a holistic and systematic way.

FIGURE 3.3 A simple whole tourism system and its environments (shaded area represents locations of tourists and organisations in tourism industries)

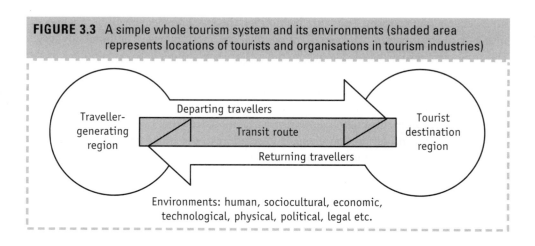

Because the model is not constructed in a way that favours any one academic discipline, it is not prone to biased or blinkered applications caused by perceiving tourism from the perspective of a single discipline. It does not describe a multidisciplinary approach to education, along the line suggested by Jafari and Ritchie's (1981) model.

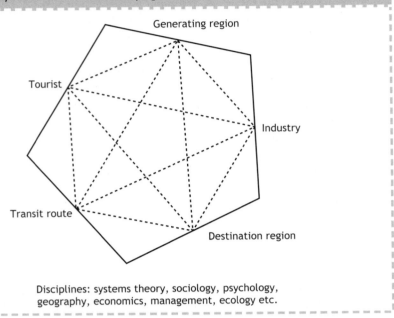

FIGURE 3.4 A systematic model for studying tourism

Generating region

Tourist

Industry

Transit route

Destination region

Disciplines: systems theory, sociology, psychology,
geography, economics, management, ecology etc.

Instead, it facilitates interdisciplinary research and study, by showing how elementary and environmental topics can be integrated and around which any traditional discipline can be applied. In other words, the whole tourism system model helps us organise our knowledge about tourism. The more we do this, the less knowledge will be fragmented into bits of information. The more we do this, the more cohesive is our knowledge. Developing cohesive knowledge, where the bits are seen to relate to one another, is the path to understanding.

Figure 3.4 suggests that any of the five elements can be used as a focal topic. Studying tourists involves considering tourists in relation to the other four elements—generating places, transit routes, destinations, tourism industries. Studying places as tourist destinations involves considering that element in relation to the other four, and so on. This method reflects a prescription for good scientific theory (Quine 1981: 90):

> A good scientific theory is under tension from two opposing forces: the drive for evidence and the drive for system ... If either were unchecked by the other, it would issue in something unworthy—in one case a mere record of observations, and in the other a myth without foundations.

Evidence about tourism comes from looking at the elements (tourists, places, organisations), at their interaction with one another and with environments, making observations using any appropriate techniques from a range of disciplines. This is balanced by the systemic structure explicit in the model, a principle that will become clearer from discussions in later chapters.

How many whole tourism systems exist?

The number of actual whole tourism systems is huge, because every itinerary route followed by one or more tourists represents, and usually recreates, another case. In some cases, millions of tourists participate every year (Germany–Italy, or England–Spain). In others, only a handful of tourists are active annually (Australia–Mauritania).

The number of subsystems is a potentially infinite quantity, as in principle every facet of a system can be dissected into its elements, which in turn can be subdivided and so on. One kind of subsystem found in every whole tourism system involves tourist attractions: Chapter 13 analyses these. Another subsystem found in all whole tourism systems is tourism industries, discussed in several chapters.

Three sorts in every large country ➤

While there might be thousands of whole tourism systems relevant to a single large country, in most countries they can be dissected into three categories, providing a simple but comprehensive way of analysing total national patterns. Taking Australia, for example, there are:

1. domestic tourism systems, where the tourists are Australian residents on trips entirely inside the country;
2. outbound tourism systems—residents going abroad—where Australia is a traveller-generating country for international tourism;
3. inbound tourism systems, where the traveller-generating countries are overseas and Australia is an international destination country or transit point.

Organisations in tourism industries often specialise in domestic, or outbound, or inbound tourism. According to King and Hyde's (1989: 3) observations on these three categories of Australian tourism, 'the industries which have developed around these three flows have evolved distinct identities and feel little in common'. Certain organisations are involved in two of the three and a minority in all three. Qantas is an example. It provides airline services for outbound and inbound international tourism, and has many domestic routes used by domestic tourists as well as the two categories of international tourists.

In very small countries there is virtually no domestic tourism, as going quite short distances takes residents over the national border and into the position of international tourists. Singapore and Brunei are examples.

One tourism industry or many?

Many commentators refer to *the* tourism industry, implying that just one industry exists to support all tourists everywhere. In practice, there are many tourism industries, each one a collection of organisations, serving tourists in particular places or particular types of tourists along particular itineraries.

Many organisations serve a number of different itineraries, so tourism industries can be thought of as networks of organisations with loosely linked activities in many itineraries. This is notable in large, multi-sector companies such as Qantas, which owns, besides international and domestic airline operations, a large tour operations company and a chain of retail travel agencies in the form of its sales offices.

In contrast, small companies, such as a 10-room motel, might derive virtually all their customers from one place and have no business dealings with widely scattered networks of organisations in other sectors, such as retail travel agencies or tour operators.

How whole tourism systems are created

All the advertising imaginable, accompanied by the most glowing word-of-mouth recommendations, does not make a country or region a tourist destination. It cannot. Beautiful scenery and perfect weather does not. Business firms or industries cannot, and nor can governments. To understand this paradox is to grasp a principle about all systems. In an article titled 'A logic of systems', Angyal provided the key to this issue when he discriminated between relationships and systems (1969: 20–2):

> *Elements forming systems do not become constituents of the system by means of their immanent qualities, but by means of their distribution or arrangement within the system. Elements are, from a holistic viewpoint, not significantly connected with one another except with reference to the whole.*

Most people practise systems thinking to some extent, but we use relationship thinking more often, because it is easier, and more useful for coping with simple issues.

Relationship thinking views the world in linear connections—step-by-step links. It notices that country X has remarkably beautiful scenery and friendly residents, two qualities that are featured in advertisements aimed at prospective tourists, some of whom go to the country, admire the scenery and socialise with the locals. Relationship thinking thus imagines that country X is inherently a tourist destination, because of its immanent qualities—beautiful scenery and friendly people.

Systems thinking discovers that the causal agents are tourists, who, preparing for a trip, create—in their minds and often on paper too—an embryonic whole tourism system, usually comprising a sequence of events along an imagined route. When they actually travel, the system becomes reality. Tourists, not destinations or tourism industries, create every whole tourism system. When they travel and visit places, a whole system comes into being, in the interactions of the elements: a tourist, at least three places in the itinerary, and a set of organisations representing tourism industries.

These organisations become productive only when tourists are present. The products of tourism industries are not, as is often imagined, things such as aircraft, hotels and service capabilities. These things are resources. They become productive when they process tourists. The products are the changes brought about in tourists as a result.

History, besides conventional relationship thinking, clouds the truth in the principle that tourism is created by a tourist and that nothing else—no spectacular sight in a destination nor efficiently promoted business—is involved inherently in that creation. This is because many places have long-established histories in their role in tourism, so it is no longer perceived as a role but as an immanent quality. In practice, tourist flows are continually being recreated, as each day and each year tourists follow the same itineraries.

TWO APPROACHES TO STUDYING TOURISM

So far in this chapter one approach for studying tourism has been described, a whole systems approach. Its foundation is a simple model. It suggests an approach used in many educational programs' core units or courses, with names such as 'Tourism Studies', or 'Introduction to Tourism'. This is an interdisciplinary approach.

Interdisciplinary approach

This involves blending into one unit or course a range of disciplines, each one an organised body of knowledge with something to contribute to the understanding of the subject. By blending them systematically, via the model, a cohesive understanding of the multifaceted nature of tourism is possible. This gives a whole-system, interdisciplinary view of tourism.

The background to this approach was the condition of tourism education and research in the 1970s. Buck (1978) remarked on two schools of thought: one focused on fostering development, business enterprise and economic benefits; the other focused on monitoring all the spillover effects, notably damage to environments. He pointed to a need for theories that would form a bridge. The weakness of two separate schools of thought is that knowledge about both is essential to understanding tourism in a comprehensive manner. However, a complicating problem when constructing bridging theories of this sort is that most academic researchers and educators lean heavily on particular disciplines, which then shape the approach of their work. Anthropology is not capable of explaining everything about tourism, nor is geography, management or any other distinctive discipline conventionally used in research and education.

Multidisciplinary approach

Usually in an educational program on tourism, units titled 'Tourism Studies' are accompanied by others with names such as 'Anthropology of Tourism' and 'Economics of Tourism'. In combination, the approach they represent is multidisciplinary, as described by Jafari and Ritchie (1981). The intended advantage of the multidisciplinary approach is that it provides in-depth knowledge on the diverse themes or issues. This is achieved by having separate units based in different disciplines. In contrast, the intended advantage of the whole systems approach is that it provide a simple method for students, teachers and researchers to follow in order to integrate the various themes or issues.

In an article that has had wide influence, Jafari and Ritchie (1981) offered a solution to this problem. They identified 16 disciplines useful in research and education on aspects of tourism. The 16 were selected as examples, not as a definitive list, as more or fewer could be used. This is a multidisciplinary subject or field, a team of teachers representing various disciplines but no bridging theories in a bridging unit or course. Thus, a course on tourism would include subjects with titles such as 'The Economics of Tourism', 'The Anthropology of Tourism', and 'Marketing in Tourism Industries'. In the discussion below, the Jafari and Ritchie model (for brevity, the JR model) will be described and evaluated.

The JR model is used for tourism courses in many colleges and universities around the world. The authors illustrated the approach with a model in the form of diagram resembling a wheel (Figure 3.5). Sixteen boxes on the rim of the wheel are 16 traditional academic disciplines. Around the rim are 16 university departments, matching the 16 disciplines, representing their academic homes. In the middle, the hub of the wheel is labelled 'centre for tourism studies'.

Labelling the hub a 'centre of tourism studies' symbolises the idea that specialists from the 16 disciplines can contribute. The JR model is especially suited to designing an

FIGURE 3.5 A model for multidisciplinary studies of tourism

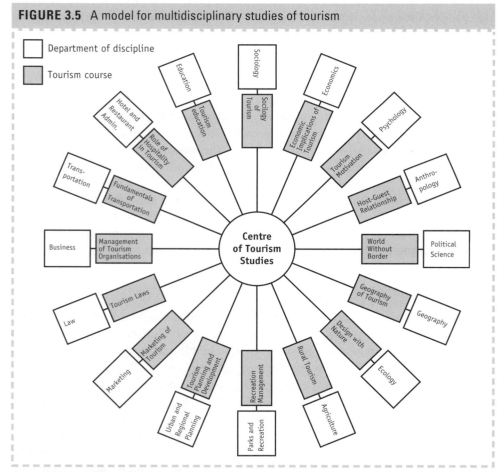

Source: Jafari and Ritchie, 'Towards a framework of tourism education: Problems and prospects' in *Annals of Tourism Research* (1981) vol 8(c) pp 13–34. Reprinted with permission from Elseivier.

educational program on tourism in a university, where persons from different academic backgrounds contribute as course designers and teachers. Certain themes can be assigned to specialists in communications, management, anthropology, economics, law, marketing etc. Each specialist is responsible for educational units that combine as a program leading to a degree or diploma. The JR model also represents an administrative approach for universities.

The JR model is useful and efficient for tourism education at university level. Thousands of students have completed such programs, and most have gone on to successful careers in tourism industries.

Multidisciplinary education can be effective if the aim is to provide students with a general education, aiming to broaden their minds and give insight into a range of subjects and diverse ways of perceiving and understanding the world. In terms of employment, this is useful for graduates leaving university without specific career aims, also for graduates planning to move on to postgraduate courses where they will receive specialised education and training, possibly for a designated profession or field of work.

Features of each approach

For many students, a course in tourism is not supposed to be a course in general education but a course on a specific theme—tourism. When that point is considered, a weakness becomes apparent in the multidisciplinary model used by many universities in tourism programs, and that is why it is often accompanied by units using a whole systems interdisciplinary model.

A multidisciplinary course comprises a series of mini-courses on economics, sociology, marketing, management and so on. A weakness in multidisciplinary courses on tourism is that students and teachers are not given a method for combining and integrating the contents of each separate discipline (e.g. geography, psychology, management, economics). The implicit assumption is that the contents of the educational program are combined and integrated into a knowledge and understanding of tourism. However, there is nothing to advise or indicate how this might be achieved. There is no bridging unit or course. Presumably the method is left to each student—left to chance and the hope that each individual student will arrive at university with competent skills in blending knowledge from diverse academic disciplines. Or perhaps it is left to each lecturer and tutor to make the connections, but the model is methodologically vacuous on this issue.

The wheel that forms the main structure of the JR model in the diagram is therefore like a doughnut. The rim might contain rich and fulfilling substance, but the middle is an empty hole. There is no method for making the centre function in a heuristic manner, a core for learning about tourism.

Unlike the JR model, the whole systems interdisciplinary model begins by assuming that the subject of tourism is best treated directly (Tourism), not merely indirectly via traditional disciplines. The latter still have important roles in an educational program but as subjects in supporting roles (e.g. Economics of Tourism, Psychology of Tourism). The advantages of this approach are that it is holistic, systematic and cohesive. The central subjects (or units) look at the whole of tourism, with an explicitly systematic method for integrating topics, issues and themes in a way that fosters cohesiveness and understanding.

Students are not left to work out for themselves how to integrate the contents of diverse subjects that have fragmented views about tourism. Thus, the empty 'centre of tourism studies' in the JR model is replaced by central units in the curriculum. 'Tourism Studies' can function methodologically, showing how this can be done. Figures 3.1 to 3.4 indicate the approach.

Despite its advantages, a weakness in the whole systems approach is that at least some important strands are unlikely to be studied in sufficient depth or detail. Another weakness is that the various strands can become blurred. A third weakness is that the method for integrating the interdisciplinary strands into a cohesive whole (Figure 3.4) is not particularly robust. As a result, while 'Tourism Studies' can be thought of as an organised body of knowledge, it is at best an emerging discipline. Tribe's (1997, 2000) rebuttal, that it is 'indisciplined', can also be noted.

Because both approaches have strengths and weaknesses, the obvious solution is to use both in an educational program leading to diploma or degree in tourism. This can be seen in the curricula of many colleges and universities, where there are two or more units with names such as 'Tourism Studies I and II' among several with names such as 'Economics of Tourism' and 'Sociology of Tourism'.

CONCLUSION

Many academic disciplines are useful in studying facets of tourism. Most of what has been learned about tourism during the past 100 years has been the result of researchers and teachers applying their specialised discipline-based knowledge and skills to aspects of tourism.

While this multidisciplinary approach has been useful, it has not been fully effective for students wanting to learn about tourism as a specialised subject for study and as background knowledge for a professional career in tourism. Nor is it fully effective for researchers engaged on multi-themed projects about tourism. The deficiency is that the contributions of various disciplines do not automatically combine, allowing students and researchers to form a systematic understanding of tourism.

To provide that cohesion in an educational course or textbook, traditional disciplines must temporarily be put to one side. Instead of beginning with questions springing from particular disciplines (How is tourism marketed?, What sort of effects does tourism have on host cultures?), a specialised course on tourism should begin with questions about tourism, especially the fundamental ones (Who are tourists, and what is tourism?). These are complex questions, and the best way to study complexities is using a systems approach.

A method based on a model of whole tourism systems provides a way to see the entire subject. In particular, it identifies five elements—tourists, traveller-generating regions, transit routes, tourist destination regions, tourism industries. The elements interact with one another when tourists go on trips. The elements also interact with various environments, as the system is open. The model suggests how the contributions of various disciplines can be combined.

The components of that model and its environmental contexts provide the structure for the chapters in this book. In Chapters 4 and 5 the central topics are tourists. In those chapters sociology and psychology are added to tourism studies, and from that blend certain management implications are derived. In Chapter 6 geography is introduced, when the focus shifts to places, the three geographical elements. Chapter 7 reviews the tourism industry from an economics perspective and shows its political significance. Chapter 10 is about environmental issues. Other chapters in this book use the model in various ways.

Many other models for studying tourism have been put forward. Notable examples include those devised by Gunn (1972), Mill and Morrison (1985) and Jafari (1987). An especially interesting model has been developed by Stear (2003). It is a much more detailed version of the whole tourism systems model discussed in this chapter. It emphasises the central role of 'attractions', showing several flows that occur when tourists make intensive and extensive use of services and goods provided by tourism industries when tourism is highly industrialised. The primary flows are industrial information; non-industrial information; money; services and goods; tourists; impacts and environmental interactions.

A comprehensive knowledge of tourism, as a subject for research and professional careers, includes familiarity with a range of models, relating to broad themes and to specific aspects of the subject. Accordingly, later chapters in this book refer to a selection of models.

Discussion questions

1. What are the five types of element in every whole tourism system?
2. What is meant by the statement 'Tourism occurs in open systems'?
3. What is the difference between tourism industries and whole tourism systems?
4. Describe three practical uses of models of whole tourism systems.
5. Give at least three examples of subsystems found in all whole tourism systems.
6. What is the reasoning behind the statement that tourists create whole tourism systems?
7. What are the three categories of whole tourism systems that directly affect most countries?
8. Name at least five academic disciplines that can be applied to understanding facets of tourism.

Tourism Management

Recommended reading

Echtner, C. & Jamal, T. 1997, The disciplinary dilemma of tourism studies, *Annals of Tourism Research* 24 : 868–83

Emery, F. (ed.) 1981, Systems Thinking, 2nd edn, London: Penguin

Getz, Don 1986, Models in tourism planning, *Tourism Management*, 7: 21–32

Gunn, C. 1972, *Vacationscape: Designing Tourist Regions*, Austin: University of Texas

Hing, Nerilee & Dimmock, Kay 2000, From Bula to bust: events, reactions and recovery strategies for tourism surrounding Fiji's 2000 coup d'etat, *International Journal of Contemporary Hospitality Management, E Journal*, 1(1): 136–48

Jafari, J. 1987, Tourism models: socio-cultural aspects, *Tourism Management*, 8: 151–9.

Leiper, Neil 1998, Tourism in Cambodia: potential, problems, and illusions, *Pacific Tourism Review*, 1: 285–97

Mill, R.C. & Morrison, A. 1985, *The Tourism System*, Englewood Cliffs, NJ: Prentice Hall

Stear, Lloyd 2003, A Model of Tourist Attraction and of Highly Industrialised (International Travel) Tourism Systems (journal article, publication pending)

Tribe, John 1997 The indiscipline of tourism, *Annals of Tourism Research* 18 : 71–84

A Sociology of Tourism

INTRODUCTION

Tourism is not so much individualistic as collective and social behaviour, because what individuals do as tourists is shaped almost entirely by what other people intend doing, are doing, or have done. Popular itineraries have been followed over the years by tens of thousands and in some cases millions of tourists. Usually they travel together, in groups of two or more. Few go solo, and those who do usually meet and mix with other tourists and with residents of the places visited. Even those who go on solo trips to remote places intending to 'do their own thing' find other tourists in the same places engaged in the same or similar activities. Thus the choice is not so much shared experiences or unique experiences but the degree of social interaction.

Sociology is the study of societies, of social groups, of roles, culture and behaviour when people are in collections of various sorts—families, neighbourhoods, teams, groups, crowds, audiences, organisations, communities, nations. There are many ways in which societies or social groups are involved in whole tourism systems, and there is thus a wide range of knowledge on the subject potentially available from sociology. This can come from specialists (sociologists), or from non-specialists drawing on the discipline in order to study aspects of tourism.

A sociology of tourism could have many themes, of which two are prominent. One set of themes studies societies in places visited, investigating how they affect and are affected by tourism. This chapter ignores that theme (it is taken up in Chapter 10). The other prominent set is tourists as social beings, which is the focus of this chapter.

Several questions will be investigated. How do sociocultural trends shape tourism? Why is 'tourist' often a negative expression, a disparaging term that suggests an inferior or unwelcome category of traveller or visitor, and what can be done about it? Is it reasonable and useful to divide tourists into types? How many are there, worldwide, and coming from and going to particular countries? What do they do?

BARZUN'S CULTURAL TRENDS

Cultural trends in societies shape the tourist flows they generate. Chapter 1 included remarks on some of these trends, and more are discussed below. These follow ideas set out by the cultural historian Jacques Barzun (2001), who has identified nine trends that have influenced many aspects of society in Western civilisation between 1500 and the present and have spread to influence societies around the world.

Tourism is not mentioned in Barzun's book, which is concerned with other issues, but all nine trends he analyses have shaped tourism, contributing to its growth, forms and present popularity. Five of the nine are discussed below—emancipation, secularism, individualism, self-consciousness and primitivism.

For the purposes of this section, tourists are persons travelling for leisure-related purposes, following the generic definition suggested in Chapter 2.

Emancipation

Emancipation, the throwing off of restrictions, is apparent to varying degrees in many aspects of societies around the world. The desire for emancipation certainly underlies the motivations of many tourists, and it can be seen in several aspects of their behaviour.

Six hundred years ago humans had no sense of emancipation, outside a religious belief that after death their souls would live on by throwing off the restraints of earthly life and moving to purgatory, then to heaven or hell. Later the sense of emancipation spread into politics, as an idea that people could throw off the restrictions imposed on their lives by kings and other absolute rulers. In this context, emancipation has been a cultural foundation in the emergence of democracy. As democracies developed, reducing the powers of kings, queens and other autocratic authorities and giving more powers to ordinary people, emancipation returned to transform religious beliefs, leading to a popular belief that people's personal and spiritual lives should not be dominated by priests, popes or other religious autocrats.

In the 19th century the cultural trend of emancipation spread to attitudes to work. Previously, people accepted that life was hard, and that arduous work with little time for recreation was unavoidable. The idea of emancipation applied to working life led increasing numbers of people to feel that they could avoid hard work, routine work and the perceived boredom associated with work. Because economic necessity and the structured nature of work made total escape impossible, this sense of emancipation led to a desire for longer intervals of rest, relaxation and entertainment.

Tourism represents for many people an ideal form of emancipation from the unpleasant aspects of work and associated characteristics of modern society. Tourism not only means time away from work but being in places away from one's own workplace and its responsibilities, stressors, managers, supervisors and colleagues. For many tourists, talking about work is tabu. The clothing worn by tourists is different from their work clothing. Resort clothes or holiday clothes are symbols of emancipation.

Secularism

Secularism is a set of beliefs that the material world is all that is real and valuable, and that life should be lived for present happiness, rather than putting off happiness until the future. A rise of secularism over recent centuries has been accompanied by a reduction in traditional religious beliefs.

In traditional Christianity, Islam, Buddhism, Hinduism and Judaism, the faithful are conditioned to focus on spiritual issues and to accept that the material world and present feelings are transient and unimportant. Under various names, heaven is held up by priests and other sources of religious authority as a future paradise. These beliefs began breaking down in the 17th century. Now, even those who retain strong religious beliefs have often become more secular in their attitudes and behaviour.

One consequence is that something called 'lifestyle' has become a valued idea in modern secular society, where various styles and ever-changing fashions are reflections of a widespread belief that people should not tolerate being unhappy or unsatisfied with their lives. Encouraged by mass media advertising sponsored by business organisations, people are conditioned to feel that the path to happiness lies in the constant consumption of goods and services. Tourism has become an important theme in the lifestyles and consumption patterns of millions of people. It is a major reflection of the cultural trend of secularism, where lifestyle involves frequent trips away for leisure experiences.

Individualism

Individualism is 'the desire that goes beyond the awareness of one's talents and demands room to improve them . . . Individualism works towards emancipation' (Barzun 2001: 60). In primitive societies there is no strong sense of self as individual apart from the community, and that reflects a fundamental truth, as it is only via relationships to others that one can develop and sustain a sense of who one is and what one represents. Individualism is a social condition that goes beyond this. It reflects a belief that one's personal wellbeing is a priority, above or at least equal to the wellbeing of others.

A central theme of individualism is the sense of individual rights, which, like many cultural trends, began as a religious idea. It began in Protestant Europe with the idea that individuals had the right to read the Bible, rather than having to listen to it being read and interpreted by authorities such as priests, which was the normal practice in Europe before 1500.

Individualism spread to politics, where it became the basis for the idea of democracy—rule by the people—where each individual has a say in government, and later spread to become a generic cultural idea. The generic idea has led to a belief that individuals can do anything they desire, so long as it is within the law. The trend to consumerism, noted earlier in relation to secularism, has benefited greatly from the parallel rise of individualism.

Tourism has not only grown because of individualism but has become more diverse in terms of the range of activities (or, in the case of those desiring to avoid activities, the range of passive pastimes) practised by tourists.

Self-consciousness

Self-consciousness is 'allied to individualism but differs from it, being not a social or political condition but a mental state' (Barzun 2001: 49). As children grow up, they begin comparing themselves with the conditions, customs and styles of others. This is an essential and useful process in development and socialisation. However, it often also leads to lack of self-esteem and need for ego enhancement.

Tourism is one medium for remedying these conditions, as it can be a form of conspicuous consumption. Going on a trip as a tourist is a means of gaining self-esteem, because it is an activity that enables each person to conform to lifestyle norms. Also, paradoxically, it engenders self-esteem because it is a privileged activity, as only a portion of the population is away at any time. Going to particular destinations and using prestigious brands is a way of gaining prestige.

In extreme but not uncommon cases, self-consciousness results in anomie, a sense of powerlessness and meaninglessness that can lead people to look for a sense of belonging elsewhere. Dann (1977, 2000) discusses anomie and ego enhancement as motivations for tourism.

Besides stimulating tourism, self-consciousness can be stimulated by tourism, as when new knowledge about foreign cultures creates the awareness that one's own customs and other cultural characteristics are not inevitable and not necessarily superior to the foreign cultures observed on trips.

Primitivism

Primitivism involves a desire for simplicity in life. As a cultural trend in Western civilisation it has existed in various forms for centuries. The idea of the 'noble savage', usually associated with the 18th century philosopher Rousseau but given that name earlier by the poet Dryden, is the idea that a high state of existence is possible in the natural world but impossible in civilised, luxurious, decadent societies.

Tourism provides many opportunities for members of civilised societies to revert, temporarily, to primitive conditions close to nature. The camping holiday, living in tents, provides the most common example. Although many campers choose that option because it is inexpensive, many choose it because it provides a brief experience of life close to nature, without the conveniences of modern housing. Adventure trips in mountains and wilderness, and trips to see primitive people in indigenous regions, are other forms of tourism that stem from the culture of primitivism.

Cultural trends in combination

The items in Barzun's list are interwoven threads in culture, combining to influence trends in society and thus in social activities in various domains, including tourism. For example, consider recent trends in spouse relationships and family formation: these include an increase in the proportion of couples living together without marriage, first marriage at a later age, higher rates of divorce, fewer children per family, and later ages for women to begin having children.

These are all manifestations of deeper cultural trends in combination: emancipation, secularism, individualism and self-consciousness. And they all influence tourism patterns. Members of a notable social group comprising couples known as DINKs (double-income, no kids) have, on average, a much higher propensity for tourism than the population at large.

'TOURIST' AS A NEGATIVE EXPRESSION

In this section no definition for 'tourist' is required, as the themes revolve around popular notions, around meanings and implications in ordinary conversations and popular thoughts.

Many people sometimes use 'tourist' as a negative or disparaging expression, in a discriminating manner, to mark out tourists as an inferior category of traveller or unwelcome category of visitor. The custom is not universal, as not everybody follows it: for many people 'tourist' is a value-free description.

However, the custom is widespread and has interesting implications, and exploring it can lead to a deeper understanding of tourism's social and cultural contexts, to which end a dozen examples are listed below.

Several examples, illustrating various aspects

Dann's (1999) article 'Writing out the tourist' shows how so-called 'travel writing' pretends that tourists are an inferior form of traveller. He cites several examples, but countless examples could be listed. Here is one by Gwen Hasler, writing in an Australian magazine (*Let's Travel*, March 1984):

> *In August, Paris is usually hot, so Parisians get out of town and leave it to the tourists, who know no better.*

Hasler's implication is that tourists as a type are ignorant. The truth, probably, is that most tourists who visit Paris in August know about the climate but have reasons for going there then. August is the main month for Europeans' holiday trips, and the climate is not a crucial factor for everyone because in Paris there is plenty to do indoors, away from the August heat, in restaurants, shops and art galleries.

In New Delhi some years ago, I was among a dozen foreigners of mixed nationalities who had met up as a result of staying in the same hotel and were discussing possible activities. Someone suggested a bus trip to Agra, a nearby city, to see the Taj Mahal. Two members of the group said that they would not go because 'The Taj Mahal is only for tourists'. Their attitude meant passing up an easy opportunity to visit a famous building. At the same time, it was understandable. In a book about alternative travellers, Neville (1970: 95) described how such types seek to maintain a sense of worth about their own experiences by deliberately avoiding the popular experiences of most travellers. In their language, 'tourists' are most travellers—ordinary people, the masses.

Besides an inferior category of traveller, the label 'tourist' can mean an unwelcome visitor. As a teenage surfer on the beaches of Sydney in the 1960s, I first became aware that 'tourist' could carry negative implications with that sense. 'Tourists go home!' was sometimes called out, more often scribbled in graffiti, by local surfers as a message to visitors—those from further away. The locals seemed to resent visitors for various reasons, especially when the surf was up and large numbers flocked in and made conditions over-crowded and unpleasant or dangerous. This negative meaning views tourists as invaders.

In the most frequently quoted book in the research literature on tourism, MacCannell (1976) gives several examples of Americans using the 'tourist' label negatively. Below are more examples, from publications in England and Australia. Several examples are needed to illustrate the many facets.

Kilvert 1870 (cited in Lambert 1950: 134):

> *Of all noxious animals, the most noxious is a tourist; and of all tourists, the most vulgar, ill-bred, offensive and loathsome is the British Tourist.*

Kilvert, like some others of superior class, did not merely castigate tourists—he tried to explain his attitude.

Review by Maloon, of an art exhibition, *Sydney Morning Herald* (17 March 1984):

Perceptive, witty, and a far cry from the tourist-clichés that our Australian painters churn out . . .

Maloon's suggestion is that tourists are never perceptive or witty and are therefore, by inference, dim and dull.

Cohen and Taylor (1978: 116):

The term tourist *has become a derisive label for someone content with the obviously inauthentic experience of staged flamenco or watered-down native food.*

These two English sociologists remark that 'tourist' is a label for naive people who can be duped by fake attractions. In many cases that is true.

Gavin Young, interviewed on ABC Radio (26 August 1985):

Traditional Samoan lifestyles are being destroyed by missionaries and tourists.

Young seemed to be implying that tourists damage traditional cultures. As a generalisation he might be correct.

Jones in the *Sydney Morning Herald* (17 June 1983):

The skies are full of package deal tourists, converging like locusts on the great cities they are rapidly destroying.

Unlike Young, Jones did not disparage all tourists, but limits the allegation that they damage places to a particular category or type of tourists, those on package deals.

In a book review in *The Weekend Australian* (13 July 1985):

Despising the American tourists she sees about her (on a visit to England) for their largeness, noisiness, and their lack of travelling manners . . .

As tourists, Americans have been more widely denigrated than any other nationality for many reasons, including—besides the characteristics noted above—blatant solipsism and questionable taste in clothing. Other nationalities denigrated as tourists in certain circumstances include English 'lager lout tourists' holidaying in Spain and Australians of similar habits behaving badly almost anywhere. More common is denigration of tourists in general, not for bad behaviour but for superficial behaviour.

Martin, cited in Lambert (1950: 212):

Tourism . . . its germ is the idea that one may learn that which is valuable, or in any way acquire virtue, by the process of being shown things. It is the passive as opposed to the active way of education. It is delusion.

Martin suggested that tourists are people seeking an education by an ineffective method. The implication is that tourists are foolish and misguided.

Trek Europa's brochure (1986):

With just fourteen people in each group, you're not a tourist. Trek Europa's maxi-waggons go incognito too, so the locals won't mark you down as a tourist. And traders won't mark up their prices for you either!

The most ironical example was kept for last. In a glossy brochure supposedly promoting a group tour company, the message conveys three reasons why 'tourist' is an undesirable state, while promoting a service that many people would say embodies distinctive features of being a tourist.

History of 'tourist' as a negative expression

The above examples cover a range of implications, all in the same broad direction—a negative view of tourists. They can serve as background for reviewing the issue historically, attempting to understand how the sensitivities around the issue have evolved.

Adam Smith, in Scotland, seems to have invented the word 'tourist' around 1770 (Wykes 1973: 13), for there is no record of it before then. At the time, many of the young men following Grand Tour itineraries had little or no interest in being educated or trained. They spent most of their time and money on entertainment. These youths, for whom Smith invented the 'tourist' label, might these days be called overprivileged and self-indulgent. The first travellers to be labelled tourists were ones whose journeys involved superficial, rushed sightseeing at designated sites. That aspect of the trips was an obligatory ritual, something that had to be done but not given much time.

Smith remarked that they usually returned home conceited and spoiled, followers of a ritual but gaining nothing useful from it. The ritual was the structured itinerary for cultural experiences at designated sites and in refined society. Smith saw the young men as 'tour-ists', following the Grand Tour ritual but not its values. This original meaning of 'tourist' has continued to the present time. In this seminal sense, 'tourist' connotes a morally inferior, decadent and deceptive *style*.

In the 1850s a different kind of inferiority evolved around a different category of travellers, people from the middle classes on Thomas Cook's tours. In resort towns of England and other countries of Europe, middle-class visitors were beginning to out-number upper-class visitors. Members of the upper classes tended to resent the arrival of the middle classes mainly because, in what had formerly been exclusive resorts, their presence was eroding the sense of superiority that the upper classes had previously enjoyed. Once ordinary people arrived, the fact and the sense of being in an exclusive venue were destroyed.

When almost all tourists were upper-class, snobbishness among tourists was not significant. After 1850, the superior classes felt their status being eroded by growing quantities of middle-class people in tourist roles seen travelling and visiting fashionable tourist destinations. The upper classes needed to deal with this sensitive and challeng-ing problem. A simple method was (and is) to denigrate the inferior classes invading what had been preserves of aristocrats and gentlefolk. The easiest form of denigration was (and is) to give them a bad name, a label with stigma, and a suitable name existed—'tourist'. What had formerly been an expression for an inferior *style* now acquired a second meaning, a traveller or visitor from an inferior *social class*.

Snobbery took deeper roots in tourism from that time. Graburn (1978: 30) remarked that 'tourism is rife with snobbery, and within each of its basic forms hierarchies of rank and prestige exist'. Snobs are people who feel insecure socially, and who suck up to those they regard as socially superior and denigrate those they regard as inferior in the hope that this will somehow bolster their own social status.

Tourists who go to particular places or stay in particular hotels because they regard these as fashionable places to be are exhibiting snobbery. There are many kinds of snobbery in tourism. In reference to Bali, ever since the 1930s tourist promotional messages have stated that tourism has almost ruined the place, while at the same time urging people to visit Bali, using its impending ruin as a reason why they should visit soon. Picard (1996: 34–8) quotes examples and points to the technique used to get around the contradiction: the previous visitors are labelled 'ordinary tourists', implying that those reading the current promotions are superior. It is a technique relying on a phony variety of snobbery.

Middle-class tourists in the 1850s began using prepackaged group tours, and by the later decades of the 1800s working-class people were also going on group tours. Thomas Cook, Henry Gaze and other entrepreneurs and their imitators made arrangements to provide not a customised or individualised service but a mass commodity, of lesser standard. Simultaneously, to serve the expanding middle- and lower-class markets, hotels were built and advertised as 'tourist-class' hotels, and railways began calling certain carriages 'tourist class', so attaching another connotation of inferiority to 'tourist'. It now also meant an *inferior standard*.

That practice continues today in some hotels, but railways and other carriers generally have abandoned it. It was used briefly by airlines. In 1954, when the world's airlines introduced a second class of service, it was called 'tourist class'. Within months, the label was amended to 'economy class', because too many airline passengers found the original term disparaging. Many people who used airlines in the 1950s, particularly those wanting to pay less than a first-class fare, regarded themselves as certainly not tourists in any sense listed in the examples above. A hundred years ago 'tourist-class' hotels were less expensive, so 'tourist' came to mean a cheap version. So a fourth factor emerged, associated with inferiority: 'tourist' as an adjective could now mean a lower than normal *price*.

For more than 100 years tourists have been regarded, sometimes accurately, as a cause of deteriorating environments in places they visit. Mass tourism tends to bring litter, vandalism, overcrowding, tawdry shops. Certain things accompanying mass tourists (commercial facilities such as hotels, service personnel, souvenir stalls, touts peddling hotels and other services) all add to connotations of 'tourists' as unwanted visitors who are *polluters* and *invaders*.

An allied fact is that many of us tend to behave with less decorum than normal when on trips. It is a natural process of leisure. Away on a trip, away from their normal environment, people normally relax their standards of decorum along with relaxing their minds and bodies. However, although many can relax without causing others concern, with many tourists relaxation becomes excessive. They dress so casually or sloppily that locals regard them as immodest, if not immoral; they are seen constantly seeking pleasure, partying late into the night, spending more money than usual, drinking too much and shamelessly displaying the symptoms. In this context the 'tourist' label denotes *moral* inferiority.

Also, many tourists are naive when they do, say or assume the wrong things in new and strange environments. They can be easy targets for slick salespersons selling over-priced or shoddy products. This creates another symbol of 'tourists', as gullible persons. Here, the label denotes *intellectual* inferiority.

Krippendorf (1987: 41–2), in an interesting and well-researched book about holiday behaviour, suggests more items that could be added to this list of ways in which 'tourist' denotes inferiority. He refers to 'the much-maligned tourist' who might be seen as 'ridiculous' (funny clothes), 'organised' (follows others, like sheep), 'ugly' (behaves as if the world owes tourists a good time, does things not acceptable at home), 'rich' (ostentatious display, conspicuous consumption), 'exploiting' (takes advantage of other people's poverty).

McGibbon's anthropological research on tourism in St Anton, a ski resort town in the Austrian Alps, contains evidence of local appreciation of the benefits gained from visitors, but also evidence that some locals curse them (McGibbon 2000: 133):

> *Although the words tourist and gast (guest) can be used interchangeably, they carry different connotations. The word tourist . . . is used when people curse tourists* ('Die Touristen!') *or stronger still* ('Die scheiss Touristen!').

To summarise, historical analysis has revealed overlapping explanations behind the expression 'tourist' connoting roles and behaviour deemed inferior or negative in some way: style, social class, knowledge, interests, wit, standards, price, attitudes, morals, intelligence. The analysis has more than academic interest. The issue has required a strategic response from tourism industries. Managers have wisely devised policies to accommodate the sensitivity of such people, as noted below.

Managing a negative expression

'Tourist' is an expression that tourism industries use cautiously or avoid in front of tourists. The airlines' change of terms in 1954 from 'tourist class' to 'economy class' is an example of avoidance. Most organisations providing services for tourists use honorific terms when referring to them: travel agencies have clients, tour operators and airlines have passengers, hotels have guests; all these and others have customers.

TOURIST TYPOLOGIES

For many years a common expression was 'the tourist', used to refer to tourists in general. It was seen in guide books, with claims such as 'Yarrawongamullee has much to offer the tourist', and in academic writings. Cohen (1979) urged an end to the prac-tice, advising anyone with a professional interest in tourism to avoid thinking in terms of 'the tourist' as a generalisation and to think instead of multiple types.

The problem identified by Cohen is that using the phrase 'the tourist' when referring to tourists in general conveys and reinforces the false theory that they are all much the same—in motivations, expectations, preferences, attitudes, consumption patterns, activities and other aspects of behaviour. The tourist goes sightseeing, is interested in particular sights, wants certain forms of accommodation, expects to be served in certain ways.

Arranging tourists into types is a useful way of avoiding that stereotype. For tourism managers, all of whom are involved to some extent with marketing, avoiding the misleading consequences is helpful. Many studies over the past 20 years have classified tourists into types. The following discussion describes several approaches for doing this. The approaches involve demographics, psychographics and behaviours.

Demographic types

Examples of 'demo' (*people*) 'graphic' (*description*) categories include age groups, genders, social classes, income levels, educational achievements, occupations, life-cycle stages, marital status, nationalities, countries of residence and regions of residence.

Demographic analysis is a traditional approach to market segmentation, used by managers in all industries providing consumers with goods and services. It has long been used in tourism industries. More than 100 years ago, Thomas Cook was providing one set of services for the upper classes of society and other sets for the middle and lower classes (Swinglehurst 1974).

When formal market research studies were first conducted on tourism in the 1970s, more attention was given to demographics because the new computer-aided research techniques enabled the measurement of demographic segments in large markets. Surveys based on interviews with carefully designed samples of several thousand persons allow reasonably accurate measurements of each demographic group.

They might reveal, for example, that persons in a certain age group have a higher propensity for certain types of trips than persons in other age groups, or that families with children under 10 have a stronger preference for certain forms of holiday resort than families where the youngest child is over 10. The main value in this sort of demographic analysis is not merely in pointing to those facts (which can be guessed with confidence) but in measuring the numbers in each segment within a regional or national market and cross-tabulating the segments. Cross-tabulation involves mixing two or more factors. It might reveal that in a national market, approximately 0.65 million persons aged between 26 and 39 with annual incomes between $40 000 and $60 000 have a strong interest in going on adventure camping tours to foreign destinations.

In recent years, countless surveys of tourists have been conducted around the world, often including demographic analysis. Examples can be found in such research journals as *Journal of Travel Research, Journal of Vacation Marketing, Journal of Tourism Studies*. There is now a growing interest among researchers from academia and from tourism industries in the topic of China as a traveller-generating country.

Ryan and Mo's (2001) research on Chinese visitors to New Zealand included demographics. They found that 69% were male, that 34% were aged 35–45 (the largest age cohort), that 63% held a college or university diploma or degree, and that 8% held a postgraduate degree. The authors concluded that, as Chinese visitors have above-average incomes and education, they are generally sophisticated persons who 'will have high expectations . . . and thus if New Zealand is to compete it will be important to ensure that those expectations are met' (2001: 17). Pan and Laws (2001) conducted research with interesting comparisons of demographics in Chinese, Japanese, Korean and Taiwanese visitors to Australia. The majority of Japanese visitors were female, while most of the Chinese were male.

A common use of the demographic perspective hinges on tourists' residences, on analysis by place of origin. For organisations interested in promoting a country or region as a destination, knowing where tourists who might well visit have their home residences is essential for placing promotional messages designed to trigger motivation for trips and visits. The relative potential of each generating region is useful in allocating promotional budgets.

For example, when managers at the Australian Tourist Commission consider which countries will be targets for advertising to boost tourism, they consider how much of the total budget will be spent in each country, and then consider how much will be spent in each region within those countries. Knowledge of total national patterns and trends has less use for marketers than knowledge about patterns and trends for regions within countries. Within Japan, promotion for foreign destinations has focused on just two regions, Kanto and Kinki, generating 80% of international trips from Japan.

Japanese tourists have been subjected to all the conventional classifications by types, in many academic and industrial studies. They have also been subjected to an unusual demographic typology, unique to the Japanese. Expressions for these types are widely used in tourism industries in Japan, USA, Australia and other countries Japanese visit in significant numbers. The types are 'silvers' (persons aged over 55, typically with grey or silver hair), 'OLs' (office ladies), 'honeymooners' (self-explanatory), and 'other males' and 'other females' (not included in the earlier types).

Is demographic analysis always relevant? Should demographic questions be included in every survey of tourists? This depends on the objectives of each survey. In a number of applied studies on tourism, demographic analysis was found to be futile, because no such variable had statistical significance. As a general rule, no survey should go to the trouble of collecting data about demographics merely for the sake of collecting.

Psychographic types

Psychographics describe differences in behaviour. The expression was coined by market researchers who in the 1980s realised that demographic methods of segmenting markets were inadequate for every condition encountered by marketers and managers. Tourist markets were one domain where this deficiency was observed.

The inadequancy of demographics was because, reflecting changes in social attitudes, more people of all ages and both genders were taking up recreational activities formerly associated with only one age group or one gender group. Grandmothers were seen bushwalking and young men could be observed at cooking classes. Particular sports and recreations formerly affordable only by the rich became more accessible to people from a wider range of incomes. In those conditions, psychographics was deemed more useful for classifying consumers in various roles, including tourist roles. It was no better as a

descriptive technique, but was regarded as having practical use as a guide t̖
management.

While they might have coined the term 'psychographic', market researc̖
merely following an approach for classifying tourists into behavioural types ι̖
already been used by anthropologists. Valene Smith (1978) was one of these. She̖ ̖ι̖
fied several types of tourist: elite, offbeat, unusual, incipient mass, mass, charter. The
anthropologist's interest is in questions of how tourists adapt to the sociocultural
environments of places they visit, and what sorts of change, if any, occur because of
tourist inflows.

Another psychographic analysis, listing 14 types, was proposed by Yiannakis and
Gibson (1992). They focused on types of 'leisure-based tourist roles'. These ranged from
'organised mass tourists', described as 'mostly interested in organised vacations, taking
pictures and buying souvenirs', to 'sun lovers, interested in relaxing and sunbathing' and
'drifters, going from place to place living a hippie-style existence'. Among their other
types are 'action seekers', 'escapists' and 'thrill seekers'.

A market research and consultancy team, the Banks Group, identified six types of
tourists in a study conducted for interests in Australia and New Zealand. Banks used
psychographic attributes and, in the fashionable mode of modern market researchers,
invented colourful labels for each type (King & Hyde 1989: 251–6)—new indulgers, big
spenders, new enthusiasts, dedicated Aussies/Kiwis, and anti-tourists.

Wanderlust and sunlust types ➤

Wanderlust and sunlust are terms describing contrasting types of tourists. Gray (1970)
seems to have been the first person to use these terms in reference to tourism. Most
tourists, on any given trip, could be described as one or the other. Individuals might mix
them during a trip, although one or the other is normally dominant. An individual might
be a wanderluster for one trip and a sunluster on the next.

Wanderlust tourism is cultural tourism in the broad sense. Wanderlust types travel to
a series of places, seeking experiences of specific sights, objects and events that can be
found in specific places. An example is a person who sets off from home in England
intending to visit Thailand and see the Royal Palace, then go to Cambodia to see Angkor
Wat, then to Bali to surf at Kuta Beach, then to Australia to see the Great Barrier Reef
and surf at Sydney's Bondi Beach.

Wanderlust trips are the usual foundation of travel writing (books noted in Chapter 1
by Basho, Defoe and Fiennes). A noteworthy example is *Empire Wilderness: Travels into
America's Future* (Kaplan 1998). Kaplan spent several months on a series of trips driving
around 15 states of his home country, the USA. Another example is *The Road to Oxiana*,
by Byron (1937), about an overland journey across Syria, Persia and Afghanistan.

The origins of wanderlust tourism are suggested by an Australian writing about a trip
to his birthplace in Hungary, where he muses about (Riemer 1993:48):

> . . . . *a great institution of the Germanic world—the walking tour, that ritualised
> enactment of the great* Wanderlust *which took generations of young Germans
> on energetic, hilarious rambles over the Fatherland in commemoration of the*

wanderings of their ancestors through the menacing forests of Gaul. There they experienced that sense of community, the absorption of the individual into the tribe, which reveals the darkest corner of the German soul—beyond individuality, pity and compassion, driven only by the instinct of the herd and the mass.

Wanderlust itineraries are usually multi-destinational. This type of tourist wants to see and feel and learn what is unique, or at least distinctive, about specific places and usually goes to a series of destinations on each trip. These tourists' behaviour tends to be motivated primarily by cultural rather than recreational needs. The Grand Tour of the 18th century exemplified wanderlust tourism. Any recreational benefits (rest, relaxation, entertainment) from these trips are often secondary and incidental.

'Sunlust' in this context does not necessarily mean a desire for being in the sun, although that is the most common form of sunlust tourism. The expression is a metaphor, derived from that common form. What is desired is a particular recreational resource, depending on the individual's motivations and tastes. It could be sun, snow, peace and quiet, noisy socialising, warm weather, cool weather, beautiful scenery, golf courses, tennis courts, good restaurants, 'people like us, our sort, our class', bungee jumps, bingo and card games, 'heavy metal music and people raging all night'. Sunlust tourism is when the tourists' main needs are for recreation. They want rest, or entertainment, or relaxation, or a mix of these three forms of recreation. Another principle distinguishing sunlusters from wanderlusters is that the things that sunlusters want are not unique to any destination. Consequently, sunlust tourism is not destination-specific. Sunlusters do not care where they go, so long as a destination suits their recreational needs and has the other necessary features, such as accommodation and adequate security.

Sunlusters tend to be mono-destination tourists, visiting one place per trip. Visits tend to be longer than with wanderlust types.

Sunlust tourism often leads to repeat visits, because when sunlusters find a place that satisfies their needs and meets their taste they feel no desire to search out alternative venues for that type of holiday. Seaside resorts, mountain resorts, and some other kinds of resort destinations function almost wholly around sunlust tourism. Sunlust tourism also occurs in metropolitan cities, although these places are popularly perceived as places where tourists go for sightseeing and other wanderlust behaviour.

The differences between wanderlust and sunlust have implications for managing tourism. The discussion in Chapter 6, where factors governing the performance of destinations are listed, indicates some of these practicalities. For example, wanderlust tourists tend not to return to the same destinations on future trips, while a sign of successful sunlust tourism is that tourists do tend to return.

Organised sightseeing facilities, by coach or any other transport mode, are likely to be less popular in a destination visited by a high percentage of sunlusters, compared to other destinations recording the same quantity of wanderlust tourist arrivals. This is partly because many sunlusters are likely to be on repeat visits and therefore no longer interested in sightseeing, and partly because sunlusters usually prefer activities with a higher recreational utility than sightseeing.

Gambling is another strategic implication of the wanderlust/sunlust dichotomy, discussed in Leiper's (1989a, 1990a) research into links between tourism and casinos. Analysing the psychology of gamblers, alongside the psychology of tourists, led to a theory that wanderlust tourists normally have less motivation than sunlusters to gamble in casinos. Evidence supporting the theory came from casinos in various locations around the world.

Wanderlust/sunlust analysis also has implications in strategies for promoting tourist destinations. Because destinations with large proportions of wanderlusters tend to have few repeat visitors, they should not be promoted in the same way as destinations favoured by sunlusters. The overarching strategy for the former should be to attract first-time tourists in substantial quantities, while a fully developed sunlust resort can use the strategy of keeping its tourist-customers satisfied rather than the more expensive challenge of chasing large quantities of new visitors every year.

Tourist types: trip purpose and visit purpose ➤

Another way of classifying tourists into psychographic types is by their purposes for trips and visits. This is not always considered a psychographic approach to classification but it qualifies as an aspect of tourists' behaviour. A lot of data are available on trip and visit purposes, in publications reporting findings from surveys. Generally these surveys follow the WTO concept of 'tourist' and include a wide range of purposes.

Caution should be used when interpreting these data to distinguish purposes of trip from purposes of visit. People might go on a trip for the purpose of business but along the way to their main destination visit another country or town for a different purpose, such as sightseeing or visiting friends. Sorting out this issue in practice is complex, as many published reports about tourists fail to distinguish between trips and visits.

One complication that is widely recognised in surveys is the existence of more than one purpose in a trip. Many travellers go on trips for multiple purposes. Usually, one purpose will be more important than the others, and surveys often identify this by asking respondents to nominate the 'main purpose' of their trip or visit.

Among total international departures by Australians, holidaying has been the leading trip purpose for several decades. Its share was 60% in the early 1980s, decreasing to 55% in the 1990s. Visiting relatives has been the second most common type, representing approximately 20% of departures in recent years. Trips for the main purpose of business rank third, with around 15%.

Among total international arrivals of visitors in Australia, holidaying has been the leading purpose of visit for two decades, and has been growing faster than other categories, accounting for 40% in 1980 and rising above 55% in the 1990s. Visiting relatives is the next ranking purpose, with a 20% share. Visits for the main purpose of business rank third, with 10%. The remaining 30% is split among purposes such as short-term employment, attending conventions, studying and in transit.

Details on purpose of visits in the two flows of tourists, to and from Australia, can be found in publications (including Internet sites) from the Bureau of Tourism Research in Canberra, the various states' Tourism Commissions, and from a regular bulletin titled *Overseas Arrivals and Departures* issued by the Australian Bureau of Statistics.

Domestic tourists in Australia show a different pattern. Holidaying is the most common purpose of trip but has a smaller share of the total, around 40% in recent years. Next ranked is visiting friends or relatives, at around 25%.

In some countries, special terms are used for describing certain purposes. In Japan, reports translated into English show the major main purpose of international trips by Japanese as 'sightseeing'. This reflects the main behaviour by Japanese on what Australians, New Zealanders and the British call holidays and what Americans call vacations. In America a 'holiday' is a public holiday, such as Christmas Day or 4th of July.

TOURISTS' BEHAVIOUR

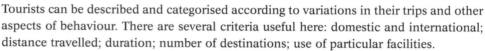

Tourists can be described and categorised according to variations in their trips and other aspects of behaviour. There are several criteria useful here: domestic and international; distance travelled; duration; number of destinations; use of particular facilities.

Worldwide, there is a trend towards briefer trips and briefer visits, according to visitor data from several countries. In Australia, for example, about half of all international visitor arrivals stay less than two weeks, and a very few stay for many months. Thirty years ago, fewer stayed less than two weeks. The trend to briefer trips and briefer visits is offset by the trend to more frequent trips and visits. For example, in recent years tens of thousands of Australians have travelled on holidays at least twice annually, a rare custom in earlier times. There are variations among nationalities: the average (mean) length of stay by American visitors to Australia has been 22 nights, for Britons 49 nights and for Japanese 13 nights.

Tourists' activities

Jafari (1987) devised a framework that can serve as a general model for what tourists do. It makes explicit the fact that tourists progress through a sequence of behavioural phases. Jafari described the model metaphorically as the activities of a diver using a springboard. Like a diver stationary on a springboard, a person begins the process of tourism in their normal, everyday routine. This first process is a phase called 'corporation'. Here is where the needs and motivations for setting out are formed. The second phase is 'emancipation', leaving the springboard, when the person travels away from their usual environment. The third phase is 'animation', up in the air above the springboard, a temporary life in the role of tourist. Next is 'repatriation', return towards home. Fifth is 'incorporation', the phase of readjusting to routine environments. Jafari's sixth process is not a phase in the experiences of tourists but it is a process always accompanying those experiences. 'Omission' refers to the ordinary current of events in tourists' home environments while they are absent.

The model makes interesting observations about the social culture of tourism. It can be applied to thinking about the commercial processes of organisations supplying tourists with services and goods, at various phases of their trips.

Moscardo (1996) surveyed tourists in North Queensland to investigate their patterns of activities. Other variables such as age, sex and transport used were also measured. The most interesting finding in her research was the identification of five types of tourist, based on clusters of activities and the indication for each type of the major age group, place of origin and size of travel party. She called the types: 'low activity beach and sightseeing'; 'high activity touring'; 'sightseeing and developed activities'; 'outdoor reef activities'; and 'nightlife entertainments'. Moscardo's research is cited here to represent hundreds of similar studies on tourists' activities that can be found in research journals.

Sources of data on activities and opinions

An annual survey of international visitors in Australia conducted by the Bureau of Tourism Research includes questions on activities, but does not need to classify tourists into types. A recent edition of the reports from these surveys (Lound & Battye 1999) found that the most widely popular activity, among all tourists (following the WTO definition), is shopping for pleasure, cited by 80% of respondents. How many of them could be described as 'shopping tourists', a distinctive type, is not known.

Insight into the questions 'What do tourists do?' and 'What are their opinions?' can be gleaned from several sorts of research. *Observing tourists* is the easiest method for discovering their activities, but it has limits. A lot of tourism happens in places that are not popular tourist spots, and not all tourists are easily recognised as such. Moreover, casual observations usually lead to biased opinions because of errors of perception. Drawing generalisations from observation is therefore risky, as the methods do not give representative views of broad patterns. Surveying tourists with *questionnaires* is a second method for gaining information about their activities and opinions, and has been the most common method used by researchers. Hundreds of articles in journals report on this method. Qualitative in-depth *interviews*, probing each individual's behaviour, can give detailed insight into activities. This is a more reliable method than a questionnaire but is more time-consuming, as the collection of information from each respondent might take half an hour or more.

Sightseeing, swimming, tea-drinking and shopping

An important point in understanding tourists' behaviour is that many recreational activities are not naturally pleasurable but are culturally determined. And because cultures change, as Barzun (2001) and others have demonstrated, particular recreational activities rise and fall in popularity. On the surface, these changes might be described as changes in fashion. Deeper analysis of how societal cultures evolve, along the lines set out early in this chapter, can reveal the deeper changes behind changes in fashion.

Sightseeing is a popular form of tourist behaviour, deserving attention in a general study of the topic. Adler (1989), writing an important study on its historical origins, showed how sightseeing has not always been a popular activity. The popular activities change over time, and the changes reflect cultural trends in society.

A similar change has occurred in peoples' attitudes to swimming as a recreational activity. Three hundred years ago almost nobody could swim, and most people regarded oceans, rivers and lakes as dangerous places that might have to be crossed while travelling, but not as places for recreational activities. On the French Riviera for several months in the 1760s, Smollett (1979) noticed only one type of person in the sea: prisoners, who were taken there periodically as a means of ridding their bodies of the lice acquired in their cells. In England at about the same time, medical doctors began recommending that patients suffering from certain ailments should swim in the sea as a cure, and this custom became fashionable. Within 100 years, by the late 1800s, what had been an activity practised as a cure for illness became a pleasurable recreation.

Tea-drinking is another custom that changed in the same way: 'Tea began as a medicine and grew into a beverage' (Kakuzo 1956: 3). In first-class resort hotels, afternoon tea is a popular recreational ritual.

Shopping for pleasure is probably the most popular activity among tourists worldwide today, although no global research is available to support that opinion. Certainly in many countries shopping is either the most or one of the most widely popular activities (Lound & Battye 1999: 53). Jansen-Verbeke (1991), Mok and Lam (1997) and Hobson (2002) are among the researchers to focus on tourist shopping. A point emerging from this research is that the forms and customs of shopping have changed.

More examples of recreational activities followed by persons in their routine lives and as tourists could be subjected to historical analysis in the manner used here for sightseeing, swimming, tea-drinking and shopping. And particular activities can be analysed to reveal how their forms have changed over the years. The sights that seemed to attract many tourists years ago are not so popular today. Douglas (1911), for example, remarked that tourists were not nearly as interested in caves and grottos as they had been 50 years earlier. Another example is the evolution of seaside recreational activities, from swimming to body-surfing to surfboard riding.

Survey research methodology

People who have access to large-scale surveys of tourists should recognise the limits of this sort of research. Designing a survey to collect information on tourists' activities or opinions poses challenges. *Where* to distribute questionnaires is a crucial issue. Distribution in various places within TDRs (tourist destination regions) in hotels and resorts, streets and shops, on beaches and at cultural sites is a common approach, but it has several deficiencies.

A sample formed by haphazardly finding respondents in hotels and other locations is unlikely to generate a representative sample of tourists in a destination region. This is because the technique is far from random in its selection of who might be surveyed within the total population of tourists present in the region at the time of the survey. A haphazard selection is not the same as a random selection, for 'random' carries special meaning in the science of survey research. It requires that all possible respondents receive an equal chance of participating.

Tourists have different velocities of circulation: some rise before dawn and spend all day on the move, while others rise at noon and do not leave their accommodation. Consequently, the technique of issuing questionnaires in accommodation places will include a disproportionately large number of tourists who spend a lot of time there and a disproportionately small portion of those who use accommodation only as places to sleep.

Leaving questionnaires for tourists to collect will elicit more replies from those with spare time to fill out surveys and fewer from those whose days and nights are already filled to capacity with activities. The result is a biased sample and misleading findings. Intercepting tourists at shops or beaches also leads to distortion, producing a non-random sample, biased towards the sorts of tourist who spend a lot of their time in those places. Perfectly random samples are impossible, but the aim of research should be optimum randomness within the constraints of the project. Cost is often the major constraint.

Another methodological deficiency, occurring when surveying haphazardly in various locations within a destination, is that tourists' answers are likely to be coloured by their immediate environment. Opinions about a TDR offered by tourists surveyed in a resort might be influenced by their opinions of that resort, which might sway their perceptions of the TDR.

A further methodological problem when surveying in a TDR is that some visitors have arrived the day of the survey, some a few days earlier and some have been there for weeks. Different stages in visits inevitably shape opinions about a TDR and distort the range of activities reported.

Besides these methodological problems, an ethical issue arises if tourists are interviewed anywhere in destinations. Filling in a survey is a kind of work task, and as such it clashes with leisure. When researchers interrupt tourists and ask them to fill in a questionnaire they are, in effect, intruding on these persons' leisure, disturbing and possibly eroding the quality of their recreational or cultural experiences. Tourists who are prone to think 'I'm on holiday, I don't want to fill in a survey' could resent this.

For all those reasons, the better time and place to survey tourists, if seeking information about activities in and opinions on a TDR, is after the visit. Interviews conducted when tourists are back at home is an obvious alternative. However, new problems then arise. Finding a suitable sample of persons who have recently visited a particular TDR within the residential population of a country can be an expensive task. Travel agents and airlines have the names of past travellers, but professional ethics do not permit the information to be divulged.

An alternative method would be to survey a large and representative sample of the population of a country, ideally in their homes, looking for persons who have recently visited the TDR or country in focus. This could give a reliable sample, but the cost would be very high. Thousands of persons might need to be approached, in a random sample of households, in order to locate 100 or 200 persons who would qualify for the survey.

Another alternative might be possible in certain TDRs if tourists can be intercepted for a survey when they are leaving—when they are departing from the airport or along a highway. All such passengers have completed their direct perceptions of and experiences in the place they are leaving, and so constitute a homogeneous set in that important respect. At airports, almost all have spare time waiting in the departure lounge or during the flight home, when questionnaires can be completed without disruption.

Photography can be used to provide researchers with useful information about tourists' activities and opinions. Several research studies reported in the *Journal of Travel Research* have involved giving tourists films (and in some cases a camera as well) and asking them to photograph activities, events and sights that they find noteworthy while visiting a TDR. The undeveloped films are mailed to the researcher, who sends copies of the photographs to the persons who took them and uses the other copies as the source of data for the research.

HOW MANY TOURISTS?

How many tourists are there? The short answer, on the worldwide scale and in many countries, is *a very large number, but not nearly as many as is often claimed*. The discussion in this section will suggest why tourist numbers are often exaggerated and will explain how the exaggeration occurs.

What causes exaggeration?

Data about tourists are often exaggerated, and a number of possible causes are apparent. In many instances the presenter might want to make the numbers seem as large as possible. Getz (1986), Hall (1991) and other disinterested researchers have referred to 'boosters' of tourism, commentators who profess expertise of some sort and who promote tourism's values and potential at every opportunity. Boosters tend to inflate the data to that end. In some cases they do this deliberately and in others naively—being confused by the statistics. Simultaneously, environmentalists who worry about damage caused by tourism and who oppose its unchecked expansion are inclined to boost the data, as this helps their argument that tourism's scale and growth are excessive. Again, like boosters, they might do this deliberately or naively.

As both groups tend to overstate the truth, the mass media tends to believe the numbers in the press releases from both kinds of interest groups. Occasional public comments from disinterested academics pointing to flaws in the data have little effect.

How the exaggeration occurs

Several factors explain how the exaggeration occurs. People tend to have subjective views for defining 'tourists', aligned with ignorance about technical definitions used for official statistics. Thus, newspapers and other mass media often present data that lead to exaggerated impressions of tourist numbers. For example, under such headings as 'Tourist Numbers Increase', they might report that 'in the past twelve months, foreign tourists visiting Australia totalled 5 101 500, which is a 5.6% increase on the previous year'. The reports often proceed to give nationality analyses of the numbers and the percentage changes from the previous year.

How do people interpret this? Research replicated over several years among novice students (to represent the general public) has revealed that the majority place the data alongside their own subjective views about tourists. They assume the data refer to visitors on holidays, or to travellers on package deals staying in hotels. In fact, as explained in Chapter 2, the data reflect technical definitions embracing virtually all visitors. People tend to assume, from published data, that there are many times more of *their* notion of 'tourist' than in fact exist.

Besides this semantic problem, statistical problems confound the issue. In particular, there is a widespread tendency to confuse quantities of tourists' activities with quantities of individual persons. As a hypothetical example, we might read that 0.8 million New Zealanders and 15 million Japanese tourists travelled overseas last year. Taking these figures at face value would lead to a false and misleading impression, because the data most probably refer to quantities of departures of residents from those two countries during one year but have been presented as a quantity of individual persons. Many people make more than one departure in a year, and this habit is growing. Multiple trippers are accounting for an increasing share of total tourist numbers year by year. Accordingly, the numbers of tourists travelling are smaller than the numbers of departures they make from their home countries. The difference in some countries can be quite substantial.

The attention given by airlines to their frequent-flyer schemes is a reflection of this fact. These schemes are designed with two aims in mind. First, they encourage members of the schemes to travel more often, the incentive being the points earned towards a 'free' trip. Second, they encourage members to remain loyal to the airlines in their particular scheme. The objective served by both aims is that the airlines carry more passengers. Of course there are no such things as 'free trips'. They are paid for indirectly in various ways.

More statistical errors occur with numbers at the other end of whole tourism systems. Reading a report stating that 'official statistics reveal that 15 million tourists visited Atlantis last year' easily leads to the inference that 15 million persons visited, but in al probability some persons visited two, three or more times during the year. The 15 million arrivals might have been recorded by only 5 million tourists. This is most probable if the country is a major destination for business travellers, some of whom travel to the same cities many times annually.

Many tourists' trips involve visits to more than one country. Several years ago, the scale of this practice was measured for international trips by Australians, New Zealanders and Japanese (Leiper 1989b). The mean average number of countries visited per trip was 2.28 for Australian residents, 2.16 for New Zealand residents, and 1.58 for Japanese. These statistics are not reliable data about wanderlust patterns because they are averages for all Australians travelling abroad, and include sunlusters.

Awareness of why tourist numbers are often exaggerated and of how the exaggeration occurs is useful for managers working with data about tourist numbers. They can take intelligent precautions when interpreting reports with statistics on the topic in order to arrive at data that are more realistic and therefore more useful in decision making.

Confusing flows for stocks

Another common error causing tourist data to be misrepresented is the tendency to interpret data about a *flow* as representing a *stock*. Like the problems noted above, this is propagated by both the boosters and the opponents of tourism growth, because exaggeration of the truth suits both arguments.

For example, environmentalists opposed to unchecked growth point to Spain, where statistics mention 50 million international tourists annually, and remark that there are as many tourists as residents, implying that the residents are being overwhelmed. Boosters use the same figures and point out that few Spaniards complain and that the national economy derives substantial gains from tourists.

The apparent 'facts' in this example are distorted, as explained earlier. Moreover, the comparison is a false one, because comparing an annual flow of 50 million arrivals with a stock of 50 million residents is irrational. To make a reasonable comparison, the flow can be converted to a stock by taking account of the average length of visit. If it was five nights, the average stock of tourists was 685 000, which is a relatively small quantity compared with 50 million residents.

CONCLUSION

This chapter's theme was tourists as social beings. The discussion began with five ideas, identified by Barzun, that underlie major, long-term sociocultural trends in society. Each of the five (emancipation, secularism, individualism, self-consciousness, primitivism) continues to have a significant influence on tourists.

The next theme was the often noted but seldom analysed question of why 'tourist' is often a descriptive expression with negative social connotations. Many examples were listed, showing the diverse aspects of this custom, which broadly fall into two categories: those depicting tourists as an inferior category of travellers, and those depicting them as an unwelcome category of visitor.

While the connotations can be explained, when the theme is considered objectively its subjective bias, often based on snobbery, is revealed. However, the analysis reveals more than that, for it points to practical issues for marketing managers and to environmental issues for policy makers and managers responsible for the impact of tourism.

Several approaches for dividing tourists into types were described. Demographic and psychographic types are the two main classifications. Within the psychographic classification, an interesting and widely useful subclassification bisects tourists into wanderlusters and sunlusters. A number of practical implications were identified arising from that analysis. Trip and visit purposes, and tourists' activities were also described.

How many tourists are there? There are a great many, but not so many as often implied in or inferred from statistical reports. Exaggeration of the truth is rife in this field. To gain a realistic appreciation of the scale of tourists activities, managers should take care interpreting statistical data. A number of pitfalls were identified. Awareness of these can assist managers in that process.

Tourists' activities can be studied using various methods. Managers draw information from several of these methods, in order to be better able to serve tourists and respond to market opportunities and challenges. Jafari's springboard metaphor is useful for gaining an overview of the entire process, beginning and ending in tourists' home environments. Several sources of information about tourists' activities were described and briefly evaluated.

Surveys using questionnaires have been the most widely used source. Several limitations of surveys and the information they discover were noted.

Sightseeing, swimming, tea-drinking and shopping, activities that millions of tourists engage in, were noted in the final section. Two points were made. One is a reminder that change is the only constant. Tourists today engage in activities that are different from those of tourists in the past. The other point is that tourists are essentially social beings, and what they do and where they go are questions that can be answered by exploring at several levels. Asking questions in a survey is one level, but the answers are usually superficial. In-depth interviews can reveal hidden issues. Analysing cultural changes in society, along the lines of Barzun's history, is a deeper level. Awareness of multiple levels is an appropriate policy for managers of tourism.

This chapter has provided a foundation for discussions in later chapters. In Chapter 5 the theme is a psychology of tourism, where the focus shifts from tourists as social beings to tourists as individuals, and where the central questions to be answered are: Why do individuals become tourists? How do they become motivated? and What causes tourism? In Chapter 10 sociology returns as a theme, where one of the topics is the interaction of tourists with residents of places visited.

Discussion questions

1. Describe any three of the cultural trends identified by Barzun as having deep effects on societies over recent centuries, and suggest how these effects are seen in tourism trends.

2. A history of 'tourist' as a negative expression for describing certain types of travellers or visitors shows that it has been linked to several aspects of tourists or tourism over the past 200 years, such as style, social class, standards, price, behaviour, morality, intellect. Describe any three of these aspects, noting approximately when they first came about.

3. What is the literal meaning of 'demographic'? What is the purpose of demographic analysis in reference to tourists?

4. What principle about tourism can be derived from considering a common pattern in the history of activities such as swimming, tea-drinking and sightseeing?

5. Name and briefly describe four possible categories in a psychographic analysis of tourists.

6. What factors seem to have led many persons and institutions to greatly exaggerate tourist numbers?

Recommended reading

Adler, Judith 1989, Origins of sightseeing, *Annals of Tourism Research*, 16: 7–29

Barzun, J. 2001, *From Dawn to Decadence: 1500 to the Present, 500 Years of Western Cultural Life*, New York: Harper Collins

Dann, G. 1999, Writing out the tourist in space and time, *Annals of Tourism Research*, 26: 159–87

Dann, G. & Cohen, E. 1991, Sociology and tourism, *Annals of Tourism Research*, 18: 154–69

Jafari, J. 1987, Tourism models: socio-cultural aspects, *Tourism Management*, 8: 151–9

MacCannell, Dean 1976, *The Tourist: A New Theory of the Leisure Class*, New York: Schoken

Moscardo, Gianna 1996, An activity based segmentation of visitors to Far North Queensland, pp 467–79 in *Tourism and Hospitality Research: Australian & International Perspectives* (proceedings of annual CAUTHE Conference, Coffs Harbour), G. Prosser (ed.), Canberra: Bureau of Tourism Research

Ryan, Chris 1991, *Recreational Tourism: A Social Science Perspective*, London: Routledge

A Psychology of Tourism

INTRODUCTION

Psychology is the study of minds and behaviour, and is particularly concerned with explanation. To some observers, explaining what happens in tourists' minds and in their behaviour is easy, requiring a simple theory—something like 'Tourism reflects a basic human motivation to get away and have a good time'. Other people, having studied tourist psychology, know that a single, simplistic theory derived from superficial observation does not explain but misleads.

In a useful overview article, Philip Pearce (2000) identifies several topics within the scope of research on tourists' psychology. Drawing on this and other sources, a number of topics can be listed.

A social psychology of tourism involves the behaviour of tourists influenced by the social groups to which they belong, a topic explored in Chapter 4. Trip/visit purpose, a simple but useful topic in psychology, reflects the broad themes of tourists' behaviour. Another topic is activities of tourists, described as 'the core of tourism experiences' (Moscardo 1996: 379). A particular purpose might encompass many different activities. Activities are all the things that tourists might do. In her research in North Queensland, Moscardo identified 56 activities. Krippendorf's (1987) research in Europe identified a similar range. Tourists' activities range from strenuous physical pursuits such as mountain climbing to idle pastimes such as resting on a beach, and range from mental concentration in a museum to empty-headedness while relaxing in a bus on a sightseeing trip.

Weber (2001) studied adventure-seeking tourism, using tourists on the 'Asia Overland Route' for examples, showing that individuals' subjective perceptions of adventure and risk and individual experiences are important in understanding tourism.

Decision making is a topic concerned with how tourists process information and images to decide among alternatives. Fodness and Murray (1997) conducted research in Florida on 585 tourists, to compare how information from different sources affects decisions. Oppermann and Chon (1997) studied decision making by tourists attending conventions.

Studies of cognition, referring to thinking and cognitive maps (the mental images of places), form a topic in tourism research. Young (1999) researched cognitive maps among tourists in the Daintree region of Queensland. Li (2000) listed three conceptual approaches to this topic. Ryan and Mo (2001) studied Chinese tourists' perceptions of New Zealand.

Sex tourism is another theme of research in the psychology of particular types of tourists. Oppermann (1998) reviewed the literature on the topic. Ryan and Martin (2001) studied how tourists respond to strip-tease acts performed as entertainment in a club. Littlewood's (2000) book suggested that more tourists' activities stem from sexual motivations that is generally believed. He might have exaggerated the issue.

Tourists' needs and satisfactions, and the associated issues of motivation, are topics in countless publications. Gnoth (1997) presented a detailed review of the research literature on tourist motivation. Hanquin and Lam (1999) investigated mainland Chinese visitors' motivations for visiting Hong Kong. Baker and Crompton (2000) studied tourists' satisfaction with destinations and the consequent activity of tourists recommending destinations.

Repeat visits were studied by Kozak (2000), in surveys of British tourists in Spain and Turkey. This topic includes the phenomenon of consumer loyalty, relevant not only to tourists' destinations but to airlines and hotels.

The above comprise only a fraction of the vast number of articles about aspects of tourists' psychology published in recent years in research journals. Notable early research on the topic includes articles by Pearce and Stringer (1991), Dann (1977, 1981), Dann and Cohen (1991), Ferrario (1979), Crompton (1979, 1992) and Mansfeld (1992).

Building on the base in Chapter 4, which was about tourists as members of social groups, this chapter aims to explain individual tourists' behaviour. Knowledge of this sort has remarkable practical potential. Managers (of anything) cannot achieve much if their knowledge is limited to description and analysis—answering the questions who? what? which? how? when? Managers that can answer the why question and explain are more competent.

This chapter does not cover all the themes or every topic of tourist psychology but focuses on aspects of understanding why people travel as tourists. The theme is explaining what causes tourism, in terms of tourists' psychology. As discussed in Chapter 3, tourists are the vital element that creates tourism, causing it to happen.

The first topic is a scientific analysis of the necessary and sufficient conditions for tourism. The second is an alternative way of answering the same question, analysing tourism as a special form of leisure. The third is another approach to the same question, focusing on two kinds of motivation, illustrated by remarks about two poems. The fourth topic approaches the theme from the opposite direction, asking why people do not travel as tourists. The fifth is the range of needs underlying tourists' motivations. The discussion draws on findings by researchers in several countries.

In this chapter tourists are defined generically, following the approach set out earlier in this book:

Tourists can be defined as persons who travel away from their normal residential region for a temporary period of at least one night, to the extent that their behaviour involves a search for leisure experiences from interactions with features or characteristics of places they choose to visit.

To discuss the psychology of other tourists beyond that definition would require a longer chapter. Persons travelling for business purposes, for example—while they might be defined as tourists in a technical context, in official statistics—have distinctive needs and motivations that are not normally present among persons travelling for leisure-related reasons.

A SCIENTIFIC THEORY EXPLAINING TOURISM

Explaining why events occur, why things happen, the causes of happenings or conditions, has always challenged philosophers. The first-known theories on causation were set out in Greece 2500 years ago. The relevance of theories on this topic to the practicalities of management can be simply stated. If managers have reliable knowledge of what causes tourism, they can be more effective with marketing and supporting resources within the scope of tourism management.

Tourism marketing is broadly intended to influence people to travel, to visit particular places and consume particular brands of services. Travelling, visiting and consuming are events. To make those events happen, their causes must be activated. Effective marketing can do this. Meanwhile, ineffective or wasted marketing includes advertising and other promotional activities that do not deal with the causes of events but with irrelevant behaviour. An ad on TV that makes every viewer smile but does not cause anyone to buy the product is an example.

Supporting and guiding marketing is tourism management. Decisions by managers put in place the resources for marketing and the resources intended for the distinctive needs and wants of tourists.

Philosophers have identified four approaches to explaining causation and one of these, efficient cause, is fundamental in modern science. The other approaches are often mistakenly imagined as the cause of something. We sometimes erroneously imagine that the consequences or outcomes of an action are what caused it. For instance, a tourist attraction might be explained by saying that a spectacular sight has 'a magnetic effect' on tourists because they move towards the sight. It does not explain what caused the process. It explains nothing. It merely uses a different phrase, usually metaphorical, to describe what has happened. This is called teleological reasoning, and is unscientific.

Efficient cause

Scientific explanations use efficient cause. This theory, applied to the issue of explaining why people go on trips as tourists, involves identifying the necessary conditions for a trip to occur, and points to the principle that when sufficient conditions exist, a trip will occur, and tourism is caused to happen.

This can be expressed as follows. Any event, from the mundane to the dramatic—me writing these words, you reading them, dog bites man, person sets off on a trip, outbreak of war—is caused when sufficient of the conditions necessary for the event exist. Just one necessary condition will not cause complex events: all the necessary conditions must be in place. This theory will become clearer from the following example.

At present I am motivated to go on a holiday trip. There is a destination in mind, and recently I collected brochures from a travel agency. My motivation is a necessary condition, but it is not sufficient to cause me to set out on a trip. I possess motivation but lack most of the means, the other necessary conditions.

These two sets of conditions, motivation and means, can be analysed to isolate their components, each of which can be regarded as a necessary condition in the process. So how does a person become *motivated* to be a tourist?

The first necessary condition is that a person must have some need, a state of felt deprivation, which might be satisfied by a trip. This could be any need (or 'motivation' as many writers call them) or any mix of needs, such as needs for rest, relaxation, entertainment, novelty, education, regression. These are described later in this chapter.

The next necessary condition is that a person must have information, forming knowledge and/or feelings about the possible satisfaction of those needs. Simply expressed, if people were totally ignorant of the world outside their home neighbourhood, they could never become motivated to travel. This is the state of babies, whose consciousness has not yet developed, and of those with serious psychological impairment.

Another necessary condition is that knowledge must lead to positive expectation that by going on a trip the needs will be satisfied. This is not always the case. Many people have knowledge of places they have never visited but have no expectation that going there would be pleasant. Expectations of satisfied needs must be greater than any other expectations relating to alternative forms of leisure, not involving tourism. A person might expect that visiting many places would be interesting and pleasant but simultaneously expect that leisure in their home region would also be interesting and pleasant. In that condition, they would not become motivated to go on a trip. The needs and expectations relating to a trip must be strong enough to motivate the person, to impel them to act. Weak motivations for any behaviour might remain latent behaviour, unfulfilled, in the mind.

Turning to the other set of necessary conditions, the *means*, three components can be identified. First, a person must have ample free time, before there are sufficient

FIGURE 5.1 Tourist's pre-trip psychological process (items 1–4) and other factors necessary for tourism

Item	Characteristics
1. Needs: state of felt deprivation	Stems from environments in TGR
2. Information, leading to knowledge and feelings about possible places to visit, things to do and see, services and facilities to use	Received in TGR, may stem from advertising and other promotional messages from tourism industries and/or from communication from acquaintances
3. Expectations about potential experiences on a touristic trip	Formed in person's mind in TGR, relating to potential satisfaction of needs
4. Motivation: a desire to take action to set off on a touristic trip	Formed in person's mind in TGR, carried into TRs and TDRs
5. Time: touristic-potential free time	One or more days free of obligations in TGR, enabling trip to one or more TDRs
6. Money and other resources	Sufficient to pay costs of trip
7. Absence of other constraints	No obligations keeping a person in their home region

conditions for a tourist trip to be caused: this might be annual leave, a weekend, or some other form of discretionary time available for leisure use. Next, the person must have ample resources, usually money, to meet the expenses of the trip he/she is contemplating. Finally, there must be no other constraints on the person going away on a trip. Such obligations are usually of a domestic nature, such as caring for sick, infirm, infants or animal members of a household, and psychological inhibitions such as agoraphobia.

The whole process is summarised in Figure 5.1.

COMPARATIVE LEISURE EXPLAINING TOURISM

As tourists have been defined as persons on trips away from home in search of leisure experiences, an interesting approach for researching why people engage in tourism would investigate differences between two locations for leisure experiences.

The link between tourists and leisure is widely acknowledged (Bodewes 1981; Jafari & Ritchie 1981; Moore et al. 1995). It can be used to explain tourism by comparing, in psychological terms, the quality of leisure in those two contexts: at and near home—the usual context, and on tourist trips—away from home for at least one night.

Many individuals' first big trip to places in their home country or internationally leads to apparent 'infection' by a 'travel bug' (Young 1973). They return home seemingly bitten, wanting to repeat the experience. What is the cause behind the travel bug? A psychological approach to the answer can be suggested that involves comparing two forms of leisure.

Leisure

To clarify the discussion, a diversion to analyse leisure will be useful. Writers with interesting ideas on leisure include Larrabee and Meyerson (1958), de Grazia (1962), Dumazedier (1967), Kaplan (1975), Kelly (1982), Dare et al. (1988), Winnifreth and Jarret (1989), and Perkins and Cushman (1993). Drawing on these and other sources, the following definition can be proposed.

Leisure is a category of human experiences found in recreational and creative behaviour pursued with a relative sense of freedom from obligations, and regarded as personally pleasurable.

Leisure is a broad category of experience, including many kinds. It might be recreational, it might be cultural, and it can be both simultaneously.

Recreational leisure recreates a person. This is any active or passive experience that restores, revives, returns a person to their former condition, which allows them to recover. For the individual, recreational leisure has three positive functions: rest, relaxation and entertainment. Rest recreates by allowing a person to recover from physical or mental fatigue. Relaxation is recovery from tension. Entertainment is recreational in its core function of restoring a person's attention and spirits when they are bored.

Usually when we have a recreational experience, two or three of these functions seem to be occurring together: we simultaneously feel at rest, relaxed and entertained, and so are inclined to sense we 'are having a good time'. Breaking recreation down into its three component functions allows a deeper explanation of the process.

Creative leisure comprises those leisure experiences that do more than recreate: they bring about something new, in somebody or something. An example is leisure spent in educational activities; afterwards the participant has new knowledge or understanding.

This definition of leisure deliberately says nothing about spare time, which features in many people's ideas of leisure. Although we tend to equate leisure with spare time (daily before and after study or work, at weekends, on holidays, in retirement), having spare time does not always produce the experiences that most people would regard as leisure. Time can be frittered away, wasted, be consumed on activities that are not thought of as pleasant—not true leisure. Everyone uses a portion of their free time on activities they regard as important but not as leisure. This might include time spent sleeping for longer than needed, doing household chores, going to the dentist.

Leisure occurs, therefore, during periods within each individual's 'spare time spectrum', a useful phrase from Elias and Dunning (1986). We might have leisure while engaged in work and other obligatory tasks, or during periods away from work. The latter is usually where most leisure transpires.

Every individual has their own preferred leisure activities, but common sentiments about ideal leisure in any activity were expressed in *The Compleat Angler* 340 years ago (Walton 1653/1930: 37):

> *It was an employment of his idle time which was then not idly spent: for angling was, after tedious study, a rest to his mind, a cheerer of his spirits, a diverter of sadness, a calmer of unquiet thoughts, a moderator of passions, a procurer of contentedness . . . peace and patience on those who professed and practised it.*

Just as successful fisherpeople are able to enjoy recreation and take home something useful (fish—a productive outcome of their leisure), so leisure in general might be recreational, or creative, or both.

Modern tourism, for most tourists, seems to be largely structured around recreational leisure. Brief interludes of creative tourism can be seen and experienced, but for the majority of tourists these seem minor. This is unlikely to change in the near future. Claims that creative tourism is large-scale and growing in popularity are widespread, often under the general term 'cultural tourism' (Brokensha & Guldberg 1992). There is insufficient evidence supporting these claims.

Comparing tourism with other leisure ➤

Tourism can be compared with 'other leisure', the category that happens in and near home and on day trips. Which of the two forms, tourism or other leisure, gives the more satisfying experiences? Obviously, no absolute answer is possible, but we can attempt a tentative answer. To discriminate requires a dependent factor, and several of these can be suggested for making general comparisons between tourism and other leisure:

withdrawal and return; duration; frequency; socialising; cost; exclusivity; discreteness. Each is discussed below.

Withdrawal and return

All leisure involves withdrawal from usual behaviour, such as work and routines, and a subsequent return to those routines. However, tourism is distinct from other leisure. It likewise involves a physical withdrawal and return, but it means going to another place, some distance away. The cliché that a good holiday means 'getting away from it all' is best understood by emphasising the last word.

Many observers have remarked that change is a dominant factor in a 'real holiday'. Mackay's research found that the change ideally has multiple dimensions: 'a change of people, a break from the same old faces, a change of scene . . . going *anywhere* makes a nice change, a change of climate and above all, a change of pace, a relief from every-day tensions' (Mackay 1977: 2). This requires going away temporarily for leisure, as a tourist. Other leisure, at or near home, cannot easily match the effectiveness stemming from these multiple dimensions.

Duration

Compared with other leisure, tourism is characterised by long duration. Tourism occurs in relatively large chunks of free time, at least one night away (according to definitions discussed in Chapter 2). Other leisure occurs in briefer respites—an hour or more after work, during breaks in a workday, at weekends. The longer duration of leisure during tourists' trips allows more productive periods of recreation and creativity. For example, a stretch of several days 'away from it all' is likely to be a productive way of getting rest and relaxation. One day of rest can be refreshing, but a weekend of rest can be much more refreshing and an entire week even more so.

Frequency

Relatively infrequent for most persons, tourism is usually practised only occasionally, once a year perhaps, while other leisure typically happens weekly, if not daily. The relative infrequency of tourism probably adds to its productive value for most individuals because of three consequences: knowing that a trip is a 'once-in-a-year experience', people tend to anticipate its pleasures keenly, then savour the experiences, and afterwards remember them clearly.

Socialising

Socialising and other sorts of interpersonal communication are more common in tourism than in other leisure. Communication is likely to occur on a frequent basis during a trip between tourists and (a) service personnel in airlines, shops, hotels and other organisations, (b) local residents of places visited, and (c) other travellers and tourists.

Stear's (1984) research concentrated on the third category, investigating social interactions among tourists. He found that the people in his survey had more frequent social interactions when they were in a coastal resort near their home city than they did with neighbours and other people at home in the city during normal weekends. Moreover, the survey respondents realised that this was a major reason why they enjoyed visiting the resort.

Other studies have shed light on this factor indirectly. For instance, in many countries international visitors are surveyed on departure, and asked 'What if anything have you enjoyed most about your visit to . . . (name of this country)?' The most frequent answer in many countries is 'meeting friendly people'. This reflects two facts. First, human beings are social creatures who enjoy company. Second, this is a vital use of leisure behaviour, perhaps the most important form of leisure (Elias & Dunning 1986).

Cost

Accommodation, transportation and other items of expense mean that tourism tends to cost more than most other options for leisure. Yet its high cost gives tourism added value in many people's minds. This is a manifestation of a general habit of many consumers, to imagine that if something costs more it is probably better value. Having decided to go on a trip and realising the high cost, many people take the attitude 'I'm paying a lot so I'll try and enjoy myself as much as possible'. A positive attitude can lead to positive outcomes.

Exclusivity

Even in its inexpensive forms, tourism is an exclusive category of leisure. This is because at any one time only a proportion of the resident population of cities or countries is absent as tourists. If an activity is generally regarded as enjoyable but only a minority of the population is engaged in it at any time, they will feel and be seen as privileged, albeit temporarily.

Compare this with other leisure: any weekend most people can be seen participating in leisure, so it is not so exclusive. The minority away on trips, feeling that they are in a sense privileged, tend to value their experience highly. Again, a positive attitude leads to positive results: people enjoy their leisure as tourists.

Discreteness

Within each individual's total leisure career, their experience as a tourist tends to stand out as special, discrete. People tend to regard holiday trips as discrete intervals in their lives, separate from and superior to other leisure.

Evidence for this can be easily demonstrated. Ask a number of persons aged over 50 to recall and describe some of the happiest and most memorable times in their lives. In many cases, holiday trips—tourism events—will be prominent examples. The explanation for this is a combination of the positive values noted above (withdrawal, socialising, frequency etc.).

Negative features of tourism as a form of leisure ➤

The positive features described above are not the entire outcome but are normally dominant. Tourism as a form of leisure has negative features compared with other leisure. These can also be explained in terms of the factors set out above.

For many people, the withdrawal and return factor in tourism has a negative side in that it involves travelling, which many people dislike, finding it stressful, scary, sickening or (a growing phenomenon among people who often travel by air) exceedingly boring. When people say they 'enjoy travel' those truths are hidden, for what they often mean is that they enjoy tourism—being somewhere different, at leisure.

Similarly, the infrequency of being a tourist has drawbacks that tend to offset the positive values to some extent. Because trips are rare events, some people try to cram in too many destinations, or too many activities at each place visited, so that instead of satisfying leisure a trip becomes laborious. Then a full complement of recreation (rest, relaxation and entertainment) is required after returning home.

But, although all the factors with positive features have their negative sides (Leiper 1990a), there seems to be a greater accumulation of positive values, which helps explain why so many people are strongly motivated to tourism.

Before leaving the comparative leisure topic, comments on the theory should be made. The argument that tourism tends to be more effective, more productive, than other leisure may seem credible. However, the entire theory has not been subjected to scientific analysis, excepting Stear's (1984) research on one point—social interaction. More research is possible on other points in the theory. Grant Cushman has pointed out this deficiency (pers. comm.), observing that the theory is not proven and that more scientific research on the theme could be insightful.

TWO POEMS BY CAVAFY

Scientific research is not the only source of insight into psychology. In two poems, the Greek poet C.P. Cavafy (1863–1933) displayed understanding of the psychology of two types of tourism. Like countless writers before and since, Cavafy used travel as a metaphor for the journey of life.

In 'The City' (titled 'The Town' by some translators), written in 1910, the poet is conversing with an anonymous person who is intending to set off on a trip, leaving the city where they have lived for many years. The person refers to a strong desire to get away from the place where nothing has worked in their favour—to escape from a city where everything is a reminder of past failures. The poet replies that this sort of attitude is futile and foolish because there is no escape if that is the motivation. Images of the city will remain in the mind of the traveller, who therefore cannot escape. The poet remarks on the futility of living in hope that things will be better somewhere else. There is a clear implication that the past cannot be avoided, and that therefore we must become reconciled with it, must learn from experiences, including failures, rather than ignoring them.

Without doubt, a proportion of tourists are like the person in Cafavy's poem. Their trips are motivated to a degree by a desire to escape, temporarily at least, from a place they find unpleasant because of their own unsatisfying and unsuccessful experiences there. Do these escapist ventures provide satisfaction? In many cases they perhaps provide only temporary relief or distraction.

In the second poem, 'Ithaka', written in 1911, a quite different message is conveyed. The poem is addressed to an anonymous person who has announced that they are setting off to travel to Ithaka. This is an island off the southwest coast of Greece, but much more than that geographical fact Ithaka is the mythical place towards which Odysseus travelled in Homer's great epic *The Odyssey*, composed around 2700 years ago. The journey from Troy to Ithaka, less than 1000 kilometres apart, took 10 years of wandering around the coastline and islands of Greece. The story in *The Odyssey* is the story of the numerous adventures along the way. In Cavafy's poem, the poet praises the person for setting off on such a journey and predicts the kinds of wonderful experiences that can be had if the traveller does not hurry.

Many modern tourists set off for a mythical Ithaka and expect to take time and enjoy every possible experience along the way, rather than hurrying with the constant image of future experiences in a distant destination. Cavafy's prescription is similar to Macartney-Snape's (1993) comments, noted in Chapter 6, about the psychological advantages of travelling at leisure and living for the moment. Accordingly, Cavafy's 'Ithaka' could be cited as a description of pure tourism.

English translations of the two poems can be found in a biography (Liddell 1976) and in collections of Cavafy's poems (1951, 1998). Homer's *Odyssey* is available in dozens of translations; a recent, widely praised version is by Fagles (1996).

WHY SOME PEOPLE DO NOT GO ON HOLIDAY TRIPS

A large-scale research project in Australia 25 years ago included, as one of its topics, a detailed investigation into why some people do not go on holiday trips, and why many are restricted from doing this as often as they would like or in the manner they would prefer (Peat, Marwick, Mitchell and Co. 1977). Unfortunately, the research has not yet been updated; while the statistics would change, the broad pattern of findings would probably be similar if the research were repeated today.

Two phases of primary research were conducted: in-depth focus groups to gain qualitative insight and then mass surveys to get quantitative data. The survey found that 92% of the adult population regarded holidays trips as desirable activities; the other 8% could be termed satisfied stay-at-homes.

The interviewers asked what problems people experienced when going on holiday trips. The major problems reported were, first, the difficulty of saving for a big holiday, cited by 46% of respondents. Next-ranked was the problem that holiday trips cost too much, cited by 30%. The third-ranked problem area comprises all the difficulties of getting away from work for a holiday—24%. Next was the set of impediments associated with household pets (cats, dogs, wombats or whatever)—18%; and fifth, problems associated with (human) babies or children in the household—14%.

Discriminating between the first and second problems might not *seem* important but it certainly was, according to the research in the focus group, which led to the separate questions in the surveys. The substantive point here is twofold. First, many people felt that what they thought of as 'a big holiday' was much more satisfying, much more desirable, than a succession of cheaper short breaks. Second, many people (about 16% of the total sample) did not regard 'big holidays' as necessarily overpriced or poor value for money, but they encountered problems trying to save the money to pay for one.

Following the publication of the research findings, the extent and nature of the problems around 'saving for a big holiday' led banks to devise and promote 'holiday savings accounts'. Most of the research report's recommendations were for governmental action at Commonwealth or state level.

Few other studies are known that have explored why people do not travel. Douglas Pearce (1987) discussed brief examples from three European countries. Haukeland (1990) reported on surveys of Norwegians. Both studies found that lifestyle has greater explanatory power than socioeconomic variables. In wealthy countries such as Norway, where virtually everyone can afford to travel, the fact that some do not is largely a matter of lifestyle choice. The major constraints in Norway were that a proportion of the population: (a) regarded a vacation trip as too strenuous, or (b) preferred shorter and briefer trips (they found day-tripping sufficient), or (c) could not easily get away from work. The proportion described as 'non-travellers' fell from 39% of the population in 1970 to 23% in 1983.

RESEARCH ON TOURISTS' MOTIVATIONS

Mackay's research: four spectra, eight motivations

Mackay's (1977) research used focus groups, comprising persons—assembled from residential communities in various localities around Australia—led into conversations about holiday trips, with the monitor leading the group towards revealing the sorts of experiences they enjoyed and why they enjoyed them. From analysing recordings of the discussions, Mackay identified a number of themes.

An important theme is that people are motivated by different needs. This reinforces the point made by Cohen (1979) that professionals interested in tourism should avoid using the expression 'the tourist' as a generic, as it implies that all tourists are much the same in terms of needs and motivations. However, a small number of general classifications of needs or motivations can be used to explain the behaviour of most tourists. This supported the observation, made in Chapter 4, that tourism is in vital ways not individualistic behaviour.

Mackay found eight broad needs or motivating factors for tourism. These are not fragmented but can be arranged in pairs, as opposites, in four spectra. Each tourist is, according to this research, located psychologically at points on each of the four spectra.

Stimulation versus relaxation ➤

Many people go on tourist trips in search of stimulation. Many go in search of relaxation. These two motivating factors do not usually occur together in the same person on one trip, because they are contrary. Being highly stimulated is not a relaxing experience.

In many, probably most, cases of tourism the tourists are somewhere between the two extremes, seeking a blend of stimulation and relaxation. In practice, what individuals want to satisfy their desires for stimulation and/or relaxation includes a highly diverse range of experiences. One person might regard a camping tour as a stimulating experience, while another might see it as relaxing.

Luxury versus 'roughing it' ➤

Some people, on some trips, want what they perceive as luxury. Others prefer to 'rough it'. The desire to rough it, to avoid all semblance of luxury, is not because of a need to save money but because of a desire to get away temporarily from the luxuries and soft living of normal routine. This helps explain why, for some of their holiday trips, a proportion of wealthy persons who could afford five-star hotels choose to sleep in tents.

Adventure versus low-key break ➤

Adventure is a personal concept. This point is discussed by Weber (2001) in her study of outdoor adventure tourism. For one person, going anywhere out of the ordinary is being adventurous, so that a three-day group tour on a bus to a nearby city in the same country for shopping and sightseeing becomes a major adventure. For another person, an adventurous holiday means taking real risks. Mountain climbing to a high peak is an example. Adventurous holidays are undertaken to satisfy, or at least dampen, various psychological needs. They can be opportunities for testing one's confidence and skills, for developing self-esteem, for status, for fun and excitement.

Low-key breaks are not adventures but the opposite, merely a time away from routine. They might be brief, just a weekend away, or might be long-duration holidays. They relate closely to the sunlust type of tourism described in Chapter 4.

Seeing versus doing ➤

Trips for sightseeing are, in many respects, passive experiences, when tourists are not engaged in doing anything else. A different type of trip is for doing things, for being physically and/or mentally active. A *doing* trip might involve going on a horseback trek, or travelling to do a cooking course, or backpacking across a country, or playing golf every day for a week.

Mackay's approach could be developed to greater sophistication by applying a detailed analysis of leisure experiences along the lines set out by Kaplan (1975). Kaplan's latent functions of leisure lend themselves to the spectra in Mackay's model.

Travel career ladders

In the 1980s the first substantial studies of tourist behaviour by Australian academic researchers were published. Notable examples include two books by Philip Pearce

(1982, 1988). Pearce's concept of the 'travel career ladder' (1988) is interesting. It refers to the sequence of trips that individuals experience and how, in consequence, they learn, progress and change as tourists.

Distinguishing needs and motivation

Several writers on psychology point out that needs and motivations should be distinguished. Needs underlie motivations. A need is a state of felt deprivation, while a motivation is like a force impelling people to act, attempting to satisfy a need. A lot of research into tourists' behaviour ignores this distinction. The distinction is more than an academic one, as it has practical relevance for managers, especially in marketing.

Crompton's research: linking psychology and geography

An insightful study into tourists' psychology was conducted by Crompton (1979), who surveyed two samples of Americans, aiming to identify the motivations affecting choice of destination. He drew attention to a contrast that has been made earlier in this chapter: the comparative ease of describing the who, when, where and how of tourism, and the difficulty of discovering the answer to the question why.

Crompton's research, over 20 years ago, remains interesting and relevant because of three features in particular. First, it identified many motivations (psychologists normally call them 'needs'), which were condensed into nine, representing a wide spectrum of tourists' behaviour. Second, it found that certain needs arise from environmental issues affecting traveller-generating regions while others arise in relation to tourist destination regions. The third feature will be noted later.

Certain needs were termed 'sociopsychological motivations', indicating that they relate to social and mental factors. These arise from conditions in traveller-generating regions and, alone or in combination, lead to people becoming motivated to leave. They are, in a sense, 'push' factors, seemingly pushing people away on trips. Included here are needs for escape from boredom, for relaxation, for prestige, for regression, for social interactions, for self-evaluation, for building and reinforcing family and friendship links.

A second category Crompton called 'cultural motivations'. These relate to conditions in tourist destination regions, as perceived by tourists pre-visit and, alone or in combination, lead to people becoming motivated to travel to particular places or particular kinds of places. They have been described as 'pull' factors, as they seem to pull or attract tourists. Included are needs for novelty and for education.

The third feature of the research was the conclusion that promotional strategies for tourist destinations are usually 'based on the assumption that tourists are attracted to a destination by the particular cultural opportunities or special attributes that it offers' (1979: 415). Crompton's research challenged that assumption, for he found that cultural factors are relatively minor in tourists' motivation. He observed that most tourism businesses, in their product and promotional strategies, ignored most of the psychological needs that motivate tourists.

He concluded that tourism industries might be following ineffective strategies by using inappropriate themes in promotional campaigns, reflecting erroneous assumptions that most tourists want to see and do things distinctive to particular destinations. So long after his research, observations in various countries seem to indicate that some interests in tourism industries are still making the same mistake.

Maslow's research on motivations

Maslow's (1982) research was about human motivation in general; it was not intended to relate to tourists, and nowhere in his writings is tourism mentioned, but, as Maslow devised one of the best-known theories on human motivation, it can be applied to tourism. He concluded that humans are motivated by many needs, which can be condensed and arranged in five levels.

At the lowest level are physiological needs—for air, water, food. Once these are satisfied to some extent, individuals become motivated to seek safety and security. Once these needs are satisfied, individuals become motivated to seek esteem, a sense of belonging, love. Once these are satisfied, individuals are motivated to seek knowledge and understanding of the world and of self. At the top level, individuals are motivated to seek aesthetic experiences.

The hierarchical arrangement helps explain the priorities of most tourists. However, any level of the hierarchy might be important in motivating a person to decide to go on a trip, and there is no automatic escalation up the hierarchical ladder. Many trips are motivated by people's desires to spend time in a healthy environment, represented in Maslow's hierarchy at the lowest level. The entire vacation might be focused around needs in that category.

TOURISTS' NEEDS AND MOTIVATIONS

Drawing on numerous research projects conducted between 1975 and 2003, a list of needs underlying the motivations of many tourists can be compiled. The sequence in the list below does not reflect order of importance, or frequency. No doubt more items could be added. Usually, a tourist's trip is motivated by a mixture of two or more needs. Discovering the mix of needs for particular tourists on particular trips is a complex research task. Asking them seldom reveals the entire mix: in tourism, as in many other forms of behaviour, a lot of what human beings do occurs as a result of subconscious motivations. Figure 5.2 is a summary of the items described below.

The need for escape from perceived mundane environments ➤

A common need in tourism is to escape temporarily from a perceived mundane or boring environment. Getting away from dull routines is possible without going on a trip but, as Mackay's research (noted earlier) emphasised, going on a trip is a method for escaping from many dimensions of normality—normal place, normal pace, normal faces and normal activities.

In modern societies, many people allow themselves to suffer from boredom. Going on a trip is an easy form of relief from boredom, for inevitably tourists experience variety. Tourism provides relief from boredom with no effort on their part. The need for entertainment is directly linked to the need for relief from boredom, as it is merely the response. Variety is entertainment. Humans need entertainment only if and when they feel bored. A person engrossed in activity is impervious to opportunities for entertainment.

The need for rest and relaxation ➤

The need to rest and relax is similar in one way to the need for relief from boredom. Satisfying these needs does not require tourism, but tourism seems an easy way to satisfy them. Rest and relaxation are the two most important functions in recreation: rest is recovery from physical or mental fatigue, and relaxation is recovery from tension and stress. Tourism is a period away from conditions that cause physical and mental fatigue—in particular, work and working conditions such as commuting. For hundreds of millions of persons every year, tourism is a major time for rest and relaxation.

The need for sunlight ➤

The need for sunlight is an important need for many tourists. Sunny places seem to have an advantage as tourist destinations. The 'sunlust' metaphor for recreational tourism is a realistic pointer to a characteristic that such places normally exhibit. The Mediterranean-type climate, characterised by long sunny seasons with a high probability of long hours of sunshine most days and a low probability of rain, is generally regarded as the ideal climate for tourism. (Incidentally, the Mediterranean climate is found in a handful of places around the world: the Mediterranean Sea and its coastline; the southern tip of Africa; near Perth and Adelaide in Australia; around Los Angeles in California; and parts of South America. Either through ignorance or duplicity, tourism promoters have claimed in advertisements that it exists in certain other countries too.)

One reason why most tourists are motivated to visit sunny destinations is because tourism generally means outdoor activities, which are more pleasant in sunlight and warmth. An additional reason for the popularity of sunny places as destinations is that the residential regions generating most tourists worldwide are places with long periods of cloudy days and cold weather (Northern Europe and the northern states of the USA). In many of these places, for months on end the daylight hours are brief. A further reason is that most people spend most of their time indoors.

There are hundreds of millions of people who see very little sunlight in their normal routines. They rise in the dark, go to work in the dark, work indoors and go home in the dark. And hundreds of millions live in places with severe air pollution, where clear, sunny days are almost unknown. The result of these factors is that many people feel a need for sunlight that is not adequately satisfied where they live, but can be found via tourism.

A deeper understanding comes from the scientific explanation of why we are motivated to seek sunlight. The following summary comes from a textbook on human anatomy and physiology (Memmler et al. 1996: 195):

FIGURE 5.2 Needs underlying motivations for tourism

Category of need	Characteristics
Temporary relief via escape from perceived mundane environment	'Boring' routines of work or home life, leading to motivation for entertainment; widespread, but not present in all tourists
Rest and relaxation	Very widespread
Sunlight	Common among residents of certain places who lack sunlight in their normal routines
Regressive behaviour	Very common among tourists, but few recognise it
Self-evaluation	Common among tourists, but few recognise it until after a trip
Self-esteem, prestige, confidence building	Common; many tourists fail to recognise it in themselves but see it in others
Social interaction	Very common
Time in company with friends and relatives	The basis of VFR tourism
Nostalgia	Occurs in many older tourists
Education, learning about the world	Very common in younger tourists
Novelty	Common but not universal
Acquisition of goods	Common but not universal

We all sense that long, dark days make us blue and sap our motivation . . . Studies show that the amount of light in the environment truly does have a physical effect on behaviour. Light exerts its effects on the pineal gland of the brain. As it strikes the retina of the eyes, light sets up impulses that decrease the amount of melatonin produced by the pineal. Because melatonin is known to depress mood, the final effect of light is to act as a mood elevator.

The need for regressive behaviour ➤

The need for regression is common and natural in all humans, and tourism provides an excellent medium for satisfying the need. Regression means reverting, normally temporarily, to an earlier state of existence and behaviour. It is most easily seen in small children, who regress often and dramatically, leading parents to remark, 'she's behaving like a baby again'. It is common among adolescents who, during intervals of rapid growth, will occasionally revert for a short while to feelings and behaviour associated with a younger stage of life. It is also occasionally seen, if one looks carefully, among adults of all ages.

Regression, within limits, is normal and healthy. It reflects the fact that life is not like a smooth curve of progressively growing up and maturing and then a smooth curve of decline. Life progresses in spurts, with occasional regression. Among adults of all ages, regressive behaviour can also be fun, and people say 'Look at them, behaving like kids, having fun'. Regressive behaviour helps children and adolescents grow up, and helps adults cope with maturity.

Tourism is an especially suitable format for regressive behaviour because away from normal contexts, behaving in ways associated with younger years is not seen as inappropriate. A tourist resort is a safe context for childish behaviour by adults. The tourist's choice of clothing is, in some cases and to some extent, an expression of regressive motivation.

The need for self-evaluation ➤

The need for exploration and evaluation of self is common among tourists. It can be, but is seldom, a conscious need in motivations to go on a trip. During leisurely vacations, away from busy activities, without pressing distractions such as work, are times when people have space to reflect and think and discover who they really are, what is really important, where they are heading in life. This does not necessarily involve time spent in deliberate self-reflection. It often occurs spontaneously.

The need for self-esteem, prestige and confidence ➤

Self-esteem, prestige and confidence are needed by all human beings. All individuals need to feel that they have worth in the eyes of others and an associated need to feel that they deserve this. Tourism provides opportunities for satisfying these needs.

Confidence building is linked to self-esteem. To set out on a trip can be a daunting experience, and completing a journey with a degree of success can lead to increased self-confidence. A big trip can develop self-reliance and the confidence that comes with it. This is especially so for young adults travelling without their parents, particularly if they go alone. The same applies to elderly persons, for whom a trip away is a demonstration, to themselves and others, that they are still capable of getting around.

Prestige issues in tourist psychology are clouded by the fact that some tourists are excessively concerned to acquire prestige and superior status, by choosing expensive destinations, first-class seats on airlines and de luxe or five-star hotels. This sort of behaviour does not necessarily reflect a need for prestige; among wealthy tourists who can afford such things, it is sometimes merely a question of choosing what is suitable. In fact, to poor people who never go anywhere, any tourist might be seen as prestigious, even the masses who visit common destinations and stay in low-rent accommodation.

The need for social interaction ➤

Social interactions are important in many tourists' motivations. All normal human beings need the companionship of other humans. We vary, as individuals, in the degree of gregarious behaviour needed, but we all need company, and show this fact by enjoying it. In modern society, many lack sufficient social interaction, or sufficient interaction of a satisfying nature, in their routine lives. Tourism provides an easy and almost certain remedy. Going on a trip almost always provides opportunities to meet and socialise with other people.

Travelling solo enhances the probability. So does travelling as a member of an organised group. Tourists usually meet and often converse with several categories of people. Other travellers or tourists, in various contexts (passengers on aircraft, guests in hotels, diners in restaurants, sightseers at popular sights) are one of those categories. Employees working in service roles are another category. When service roles in a tourism industry involve interpersonal communication, employees are usually expected, and often trained, to add a hospitality dimension to the service role. Smiles and friendly greetings are not essential when performing services for tourists, but they add hospitality, intended to make tourists feel welcome, and they often elicit a reply and lead to conversations that might be very brief but are occasionally rather longer. Trips by public carrier (e.g. an airline or railway), staying in hotels and visiting restaurants and shops can involve tourists in many social encounters of this sort every day. At leisure, and in a non-routine environment, tourists are often willing to spend time conversing at any opportunity. When service employees are not too busy, they are often willing to go beyond their obligations of providing a smile and brief greeting and will spend time in conversation. After a week or more away, tourists might have conversed, in a friendly manner, with more persons than they normally converse with in their home and work environments during a month or more.

Local residents of places visited are a third category of persons with whom tourists engage in social interaction. This can be the most valued category, providing visitors with the impression that they are meeting the real people of the country or region, not the service employees who provide hospitality as part of their duties.

In summary, from all three categories, tourism is an excellent medium for meeting people, for engaging in social intercourse, for enjoying company in a casual, non-obligated context.

Not surprisingly, when tourists are surveyed and asked what they enjoyed most about their visits, the top-ranked item is often 'meeting people'. This happens with surveys in many countries, so when this survey finding is published in newspapers and noted by local residents it should not be a source of chauvinism (absurdly extravagant pride in one's country). It should be seen as evidence that human beings enjoy meeting other humans, and that this happens in a friendly manner in countries all around the world.

The need to spend time with relatives and friends ➤

The need to maintain links with relatives and friends is linked to tourist psychology much more commonly these days than it was in the past, because many more individuals now have families and friends scattered around the country and around the world.

Geographical dispersal, along with the sense of loss it creates, motivates millions of people every year to travel for what is known in tourism industries as VFR purposes (visiting friends or relatives). As Getz (2000: 621) remarks, 'studies have revealed that this is not a homogeneous group: visiting friends can be quite different from visiting relatives'.

A related need is the building of family ties via family holidays. Many tourists' trips are motivated by desires to build bonds between members of a family, at several levels: spouses, children and parents. In families where both parents work and the children are busy with school and associated activities, in routine times there might be only brief occasions when the entire family gets together for mutual leisure experiences. A family holiday, whether it involves a couple of DINKs (double income, no kids) or a family with many siblings and a few cousins along for the trip, provides opportunities for this.

The need to indulge in nostalgia ➤

Nostalgia, 'the feeling of loss or anxiety about the passage of time, accompanied by a desire to experience again some aspect of the past . . . has emerged as a major motivation for tourism' (Graburn 2000b: 415). It leads to different forms of tourism. Visits to places known years ago and remembered fondly is one form. Graburn suggested that tourists going to 'fat farms' and health clinics might be displaying motivations of nostalgia, seeking to return to former physical states. Heritage tourism (Sofield & Li 2000) often reflects nostalgic motivations (as well as others, such as education).

The need for education, to indulge in curiosity ➤

The need for education is natural and normal in human beings. We are naturally curious, wanting to learn about the world around us. Education in this strict sense should be distinguished from schooling and training—the organised and institutionalised processes that accompanies and sometimes dominates education in schools, colleges and universities, institutions that pose under a single misleading label, 'education'. The fact that education and schooling are not the same thing is demonstrated clearly by Illich (1971) in *De-Schooling Society*.

Tourism can be an excellent medium for satisfying the need for education, for it allows individuals to personally learn something about the world by having direct experiences in places away from home. All tourists, on all trips, most probably learn something. When we are away from our home environments, in new, unusual and often strange environments, our perceptions are heightened; being more alert, we are then more likely to learn.

Many research projects on tourist psychology have found educational needs— the need to learn. However, very little research has explored the topic in depth. *The Encyclopedia of Tourism* contains 12 articles with 'education' in their titles (Jafari 2000: 166–85), but all deal with aspects of education (and training) for employees in tourism industries; none deal with issues of tourists being educated via their experiences on trips. Opportunities exist for innovative research on this topic.

The quality of education from tourism depends not only on the places visited but on the attitude and preparedness of each tourist. Tourists need open minds to receive new facts and ideas, and they need preparatory knowledge about the sorts of places and cultures they are likely to experience on trips.

The need for novelty ➤

The need for novelty is common among tourists. It means the need for new experiences, new environments, new activities, new possessions. This need is closely linked to, but is not synonymous with, the need for escape from perceived boring routines.

Needs underlying tourists' shopping ➤

Shopping is a very common activity among tourists, especially international tourists and most especially Japanese (Jansen-Verbeke 2000; Hobson & Christiansen 2002). It can be motivated by many underlying needs (Hobson 2002). Souvenir buying is a form of shopping especially associated with tourism: 'Souvenirs are material objects which serve as reminders of people, places, events or experiences' (Cohen 2000: 547).

Tourists buying gifts to take home for relatives and friends is another form, where the need might be to demonstrate that, despite going away from them temporarily, they were not forgotten. Shopping by tourists also occurs to acquire goods that are less expensive in places visited than they would be at home, and to acquire things that are not available at home. Acquiring valuable or remarkable goods can also serve tourists' needs for self-esteem and prestige.

A lot of tourists' activities in shops and shopping centres are not based on a need to buy things but on vicarious shopping: looking at goods on display, looking at other shoppers, feeling part of the crowd, feeling a sense of consuming without really acquiring anything.

Barzun's sociocultural themes

In Chapter 4, sociocultural themes from Barzun's (2001) history were analysed to show how they can help explain tourists' behaviour. They can be read alongside the discussion above on needs underlying tourists' behaviour. Each of the themes in Barzun's list can be related to one or more of the needs in the list above.

Psychological factors in sightseeing

Adler's (1989) study into the origins of sightseeing was noted in Chapter 2, but she did not explore the psychology of sightseeing in depth. Sightseeing is very often the dominant behaviour of first-time visitors to a place. In this context it is orientation behaviour, satisfying a need to develop a sense of awareness, security and familiarity with one's new surrounds. Many tourists, on their first visit to a city or region, spend their first day out and about on a sightseeing/orientation tour, to get to know the place.

Also, often sightseeing seems to be motivated by other needs, notably status, allowing a person to feel (or say) about a well-known place or sight that they have 'been there, seen that'.

A lot of sightseeing seeks to satisfy needs for authentication, as discussed by MacCannell (1976), Moscardo and Pearce (1986), Wang (1999, 2000) and others. This is linked to educational needs in many tourists, associated with the feeling of wanting to learn about the places visited. Beneath sightseeing behaviour may be several of the other needs discussed above: socialisation, novelty, education, regression, prestige. Demonstrably, a lot of sightseeing is motivated by needs for relaxation (recovery from tension and stress) and entertainment (recovery from boredom). These multiple motivations reveal the complexities of sightseeing, and managerial implications relevant to a not-so-simple form of tourism may be inferred.

MANAGERIAL IMPLICATIONS

The discussion in this chapter has attempted to explain tourists by focusing on psychological issues. Explanation of this sort is a potentially powerful tool. With credible explanations, a person can more confidently make predictions and judgments about the future, and so can plan with more certainty. Likewise, with explanations of any process a person is better able to direct resources intended to support or guide the process. Equipped to explain why things occur, we are also better prepared to control them if processes are performing poorly, or not going according to plan. These actions—planning, directing and controlling—focused to deal with any process, comprise elements of managing.

However, existing knowledge on why people travel and behave in certain ways as tourists is not sufficiently advanced to provide all the answers, and perhaps never will be. Tourists' behaviour cannot be fully explained for the same reasons that limit our understanding of other forms of human behaviour. Insufficient research has been conducted and even if more were completed, unanswered and probably unanswerable questions would remain. Despite those limits, certain lines of research, such as those discussed in this chapter, may provide indicators to a scientific understanding.

Analysing what causes tourism allows managers to take steps to promote and shape it. First, though, they should recognise that the first step in the causal chain—needs—cannot be created or shaped in the short term by tourism industries, so attempting to do so with selling or advertising is a waste of resources. This fact may be difficult to accept, for surely the first role of advertising is to make people need things?

That is merely how things seem. A more precise explanation is that a promotion campaign by any tourism organisation (Jetabout, Air New Zealand, the Coffs Harbour Tourism Association) can work on steps in the process only *after* needs exist. A campaign might be designed to inform, to give consumers knowledge and/or feelings about a tourist facility or destination. Or it might be designed to supplement existing knowledge and give consumers expectations that buying a particular branded item would be satisfying or pleasurable. Or it might assume that consumers in the target market already feel that way and be designed to heighten the expectation, pushing consumers towards the critical stage of strong motivation.

Specific findings from research projects can be useful to managers. Each one of the motivations (needs) identified above can be considered by tourism managers when assessing strategies in operations and marketing.

CONCLUSION

Describing tourists will not explain what tourists do and why. The advantage of explanatory information is that it goes below the surface and can provide plausible theories of what causes tourism. With that approach, managers are in a position to influence consumers to become tourists, to visit particular places and consume certain services. In practice, of course, an approach is not a complete kit of knowledge. It merely indicates what sorts of knowledge each manager requires, how it can be used, and how the bits fit together. Local knowledge, about particular circumstances, adds the missing ingredients.

Discussion questions

1. What are the differences between 'needs' and 'motivation' in the context of tourists' psychology?
2. List and describe the conditions that must exist before a person sets out on a touristic trip.
3. Which of the above conditions can be described as psychological?
4. Several factors common to tourism and to 'other leisure' (at and near home) can be compared to help explain why tourism is widely popular. Describe any four of these factors, and show how they can be compared in the contexts of both tourism and other leisure.
5. What have researchers discovered to be the major impediments to many people practising tourism, or at least practising it often?
6. Mackay's research identified four spectra that help explain diversity in behaviour among tourists. Describe these four spectra.
7. List and discuss at least six categories of needs underlying motivations of tourists.
8. Does tourist psychology relate to (a) one level, (b) more than one level, or (c) all levels in Maslow's hierarchy of needs? Explain your answer.
9. What are some of the useful applications of knowledge about tourists' psychology for managers in tourism industries?

Recommended reading

Cavafy, C.P. 1998, 'The City', and 'Ithaca', in *C.P. Cavafy: Collected Poems*, trans. E. Keeley & P. Sherrard, London: Chatto & Windus

Dumazedier, J. 1967, *Towards a Society of Leisure*, London: Collier-Macmillan

Gnoth, J. 1997, Tourism motivation and expectation formation, *Annals of Tourism Research*, 24: 283–304

Krippendorf, J. 1987, *The Holidaymakers: Understanding the Impacts of Leisure and Travel*, London: Heinemann

Moore, K., Cushman, G. & Simmons, D. 1995, Behavioural conceptualization of tourism and leisure, *Annals of Tourism Research*, 22: 67–85

Moscardo, Gianna 1996, An activity based segmentation of visitors to far north Queensland, pp 467–79 in *Tourism and Hospitality Research: Australian and International Perspectives* (proceedings of annual CAUTHE Conference, Coffs Harbour), G. Prosser (ed.), Canberra: Bureau of Tourism Research

Pearce, Philip L. 2000, Psychology, pp 471–3 in *The Encyclopedia of Tourism,* J. Jafari, (ed.), London: Routledge

——2003, Motivation for pleasure travel, in *Tourism: Principles, Practices, Philosophies* 9th edn, Goeldher C.R & Ritchie, J.R.B. (eds), pp 241–59, New Jersey : John Wiley

Perkins, Harvey C. & Cushman, Grant 1993, *Leisure, Recreation and Tourism*, Auckland: Longman Paul

Weber, Karen 2001, Outdoor adventure tourism: a review, *Annals of Tourism Research*, 28: 360–77

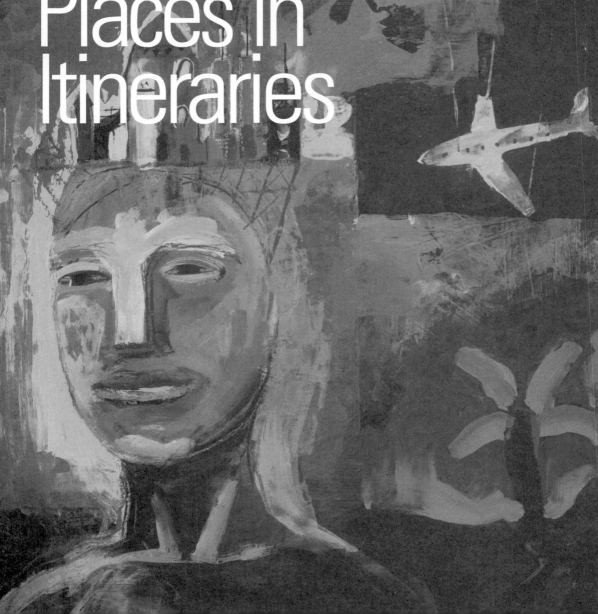

A Geography of Tourism: Places in Itineraries

INTRODUCTION

Geography is the study of the earth's surface, of places and their inhabitants, and in particular of spatial relationships. As tourism always involves places and spatial relationships, geography is useful for studying tourism. As discussed in Chapter 3, looking at tourism systematically reveals at least three possible roles for places. Every town and city is a place where the three roles can occur simultaneously; this can be observed at an airport, and involves five sets of passengers:

- One set, in the departures area, are residents of the local region—the town or city, its suburbs and hinterland—setting off on trips. A second set, in the arrivals area, are residents of the region returning from trips. These two sets mark the region as a *traveller-generating region*.
- A third set are visitors arriving and a fourth are visitors departing. These two sets mark the region as a *tourist destination region*.
- Fifth are passengers arriving in transit, flying into the airport and perhaps going to the city briefly, staying for a few hours or overnight before flying out. They have not chosen to visit the region but are passing through on their way to somewhere else. This represents the region as a node on a *transit route*, intersecting at the airport.

That analysis provides the structure for this chapter, arranged under main headings for traveller-generating regions, transit routes, and tourist destination regions, three topics elementary to tourism geography.

The approach in this chapter follows the model for studying tourism (see Figure 3.4). Studying the three geographic elements involves each one's interactive connections with all the other elements and environments.

TRAVELLER-GENERATING REGIONS

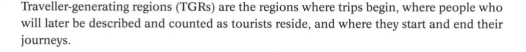

Traveller-generating regions (TGRs) are the regions where trips begin, where people who will later be described and counted as tourists reside, and where they start and end their journeys.

Absence, not dramatic presence

In contrast to the obvious signs indicating that places are destinations (the presence of tourists engaged in distinctive activities), places can be TGRs without obvious evidence. When a town, city or region generates tourists it means an absence of something—local residents (away on trips)—rather than the presence of something.

The absence is generally not problematical, as the number of persons absent at any time is usually insignificant compared with the total population. Over recent years on a typical day, the proportion of the Australian population out of the country on any sort of trip has been around 1%. In Japan and the USA it is smaller, probably below 0.5%. The proportion of the population away on overnight domestic trips (within the country of residence) is also quite small as a rule, below 5% on an average day in Australia.

The absence of anything, especially if it is benign, provokes little interest among researchers. In this instance that is one reason why few tourism researchers have focused on TGRs. In contrast, for most of these people 'tourism studies' means focusing principally, and in some cases exclusively, on places visited. With that focus, the only relevance of places where tourists reside is in research on the origins of tourists visiting particular destinations, which often extends to marketing issues.

In this book, TGRs are given more attention. They are relevant not only as the origins of visiting tourists and as the primary marketplaces for tourism industries but in other respects as well. Understanding what causes tourism, a vital ingredient in its management, requires understanding what happens in TGRs.

Multiple dimensions of traveller generation

Regions generate travellers who become tourists in several dimensions of generation. The most obvious is *spatial*, or geographical. Tourist travel is generated by a region when one or more of its residents sets out on a trip—travels spatially. Leaving a TGR means going beyond a day-trip range, going away to where an overnight stop is required. The distance from a tourist's home to a TGR's boundary varies with individual circumstances.

Second, tourist travel is generated by a region in an *economic* sense, as the resources that tourists use, consume or spend during trips have normally been generated in the economy of the TGR. People save money from income earned there and accumulate free time from activities there, such as annual leave entitlements generated from employment. Thus, in the late 1990s, the economy of Australia annually generated the resources consumed on about 50 million domestic trips and three million international trips by residents of Australia.

Culturally and *psychologically*, a place generates tourist travel when conditions there (what some writers call internal environments) shape the needs and motivations of certain residents, impelling a proportion of them to travel. These conditions have been described as the 'push factors' of tourist motivation.

At some point after setting out, tourists leave a TRG and enter a transit route (TR). Precisely when this happens varies with the circumstances of the trip and the individual. It is governed by each individual's sense and perception of home territory. In a family heading off on holidays, the small children sense they have left home territory within minutes of departing, as soon as they leave the neighbourhood and enter what to the children is unfamiliar, strange territory. Generally the change occurs when travellers using land transport such as a car leave the districts they might visit on recreational day trips, which might be several hours' travelling time. Air passengers might sense the change much sooner, on take-off, when they look down and see their home city, which becomes, consciously and dramatically, the region they are leaving.

The change from TGR to TR often gives a pleasurable sense of relaxation, and possibly excitement. This stems from the conscious or subconscious process of escaping from, if only temporarily, familiar places and routines, and escaping to somewhere else.

None of the dimensions (spatial, economic, cultural, psychological) provides in itself a way of fully understanding why places generate touristic travel. In combination they can provide a more complete approach to that understanding.

Gross and net travel propensities

Concepts for measuring the size and trends in activity in a TGR include gross and net travel propensities. These are measurements that provide a more detailed and precise understanding than the commonly used concept of simply measuring the number of departures (Schmidhauser 1975).

Assume that a region has a resident population of two million, and in one year 610 000 residents set out on 1 405 000 touristic trips; in the next year, the population grew to 2 040 000, and the flow grew to 622 000 individuals making 1 505 000 trips. The gross travel propensity is the total trips generated divided by the population. The net propensity is the total number of persons making those trips divided by the population. Gross travel propensity grew from 70% to 74%, while net travel propensity remained virtually constant at 30%.

Analysing the activity in this way indicates that most of the trips generated by this hypothetical region are made by a minority of its population, who make, on average, more than two trips per year. Trend data, more precisely, reveal that the increase in the second year did not come about from more people travelling but from a small increase in the average number of trips by those who did travel.

In practice, these twin measurements are difficult to calculate in reference to most regions. Leiper (1984, 1990a: 118–40) calculated the measurements over several years in reference to international travel by Australians. The research was conducted for academic interest, but was useful in the late 1980s when Qantas management saw its relevance for applied research underway for the design of a new promotional device, frequent-flyer schemes.

While gross and net travel propensity may have certain uses, they do not explain what determines the size and characteristics of a traveller flows from a TGR. If reasonably precise explanations were known, a statistical model could be devised and used with benefits for organisations managing tourism. A first step is to identify and describe the factors shaping patterns of traveller generation.

Factors shaping patterns of traveller generation

Although relevant factors can be suggested, as listed below, precise methods for measuring several of them have not progressed far to date. The goal, ideally, would be a formula that could explain with some precision, and therefore predict, the size of flows.

Size of population ➤

The larger the population of a place, the more travellers are generated from it, as a general rule. This principle applies to towns, cities, regions, countries. It is one reason why India generates more tourists than any other country. Most of them are domestic, travelling within India. It is the main reason why Sydney is Australia's and Auckland is New Zealand's major TGR.

Gross economic prosperity ➤

Germany, the USA, France, the UK and Japan were the world's leading generators of international tourists in recent years (WTO 1999). These countries are all relatively prosperous. Russia's population is larger than any of them but is not so prosperous, and this is a major reason why fewer Russians travel internationally.

China's major cities, such as Beijing and Shanghai, emerged as important and rapidly growing TGRs in recent years. In 2001, national tourism promotion offices representing several countries around the world began giving much more attention to tourist markets in China. The underlying reason for the growth is China's rapidly developing economy.

India too, has experienced rapid economic growth in recent years. Because both countries have very large populations, and because prosperity is spreading to large and expanding middle classes, these two countries seem to be on a path to becoming major generators of international tourism.

Distribution of income and wealth ➤

Brunei is a small country known as one of the richest countries in the world, specifically because statistics show its per-capita GNP (average per person gross national product) near the top of the world's rankings. However, an enormous share of the income and wealth is in the hands of one family, and most of Brunei's residents are not nearly so fortunate.

The USA is another country where some persons are extremely wealthy with enormous incomes while many are relatively poor, so the high average wealth and income in the USA are not indicative of its population's propensity for tourism. Countries in Western Europe have a more even spread of wealth and income, and this is reflected in a higher net travel propensity among their populations.

Many people say that through the 1990s there was a broad trend for the rich to get richer, the poor poorer and more numerous, and the middle class to shrink as many slipped into the poorer category. Other commentators have produced statistics to dispute the accuracy of these allegations. If the trend is real, it will affect trends and patterns of tourism, as the middle classes of the world have provided the great majority of tourists in recent decades, especially for international tourism.

Hong Kong exemplifies a distinction between wealth and income. In the years 1997–2002 the average price of shares on the HK stock market fell notably, reducing the wealth of tens of thousands of Hong Kong residents who owned shares. The number of tourist trips by Hong Kong residents decreased, and analysts believe this can be attributed more to the reduction in wealth than to any reduction in income. The explanation is that while their share portfolios were worth a lot, wealthy HK residents felt

Tropical sunset in a Fijian island resort

comfortable about going on frequent trips; when they saw the value of their shares falling, they felt financially insecure and cut back on travel.

Spare time in large chunks ➤

Relatively large chunks of spare time are required for tourism. This is axiomatic, as trips briefer than one night away from home fall outside the scope of most definitions of tourism. Annual leave and weekends are the principal contributors to largish chunks of what can be termed tourism-potential free time.

Accordingly, countries where everyone in paid employment is legally entitled to several weeks of annual leave on full pay each year and two days off work every week are generally countries generating large tourist flows. This helps explain why populations of continental countries in Western and Northern Europe have a high propensity for tourism. In France, Germany, the Netherlands, Norway, Sweden and several other European countries, persons in full-time paid employment are legally entitled to at least five weeks' paid leave per annum. Tourism generation is rather lower in countries such as Australia (where the minimum annual leave entitlement is four weeks), less again in New Zealand (where it is three weeks) and less again in the USA (two weeks).

When minimum leave entitlement in a country rises, a sudden rise in tourism generation could be anticipated, a substantial rise in the number of holidays and similar types of trips. This last occurred in Australia in the years after 1974, a year when the Australian Council of Trades Unions (ACTU) conducted a successful court case to boost minimum annual leave entitlements from three weeks to four.

Demographics ➤

In June 2002, findings from the 2001 Australian census were released to the public by the Australian Bureau of Statistics. Among the demographic trends discovered, by comparing the statistics with those collected five years earlier, were rises in the average age of the population, increases in single-parent families and divorce, and a tendency to have fewer children.

Demographic trends give clues to changing trends in tourist travel generation. The tendency to have fewer children and an allied tendency by women to postpone the time they commence having babies—two trends that have been notable in Australia and in similar countries for several decades—have contributed to the high propensity in the population generally to go on holiday trips. Several young children in a household, and especially the presence of a baby, inhibit many families from going on trips.

The age pattern of a population also affects its propensity for travel. Young adults have a higher propensity, on average, than those in advanced middle age. An ageing population tends to generate more tourism for a while; then, when a relatively large proportion of persons are elderly, it tends to generate less.

Tastes and preferences ➤

People have different tastes and preferences, and these can vary from one region to another, shaping the number of persons in the population who travel as tourists and influencing the sorts of trips and the patterns of itineraries.

Different national cultures tend to have different preferences or tastes for many leisure activities, including tourism. The needs are the same for all humanity: leisure activities are motivated by needs for recreation (rest, relaxation, entertainment) and for creative pursuits, but different cultures tend to seek satisfaction of all those needs in culturally determined ways. Accordingly, different nationalities would be expected to have different levels of interest in tourism.

Other constraints on travel ➤

Lack of money and perceived lack of free time are common constraints on travel: these factors were itemised under an earlier heading. However, in every country there are people who are constrained from travelling by personal or family circumstances. Illness, infirmity, serious disability, agoraphobia (extreme fear of open spaces) and a need to take care of aged or disabled relatives are examples.

In some countries, political constraints restrict the population's freedom to travel, domestically or abroad. Totalitarian governments, such as those in North Korea at present and the USSR from the 1920s to the 90s, impose restrictions principally to keep the mass of the population out of contact with the world.

In other instances, a temporary restraint has been applied for economic reasons. In 1997 the government in South Korea requested the people to abandon plans for international trips other than on business, because the nation's economy was in a precarious state. Most obeyed willingly, and during the next three years few Koreans went abroad. In Indonesia, where the economy has been precarious for years, the same result is achieved by a pricing strategy. The government imposes a tax levy, called a fiscal, on any citizen going out of the country. Only well-off persons or those on subsidised trips are travelling abroad.

Transport facilities for trips away ➤

A region requires transport facilities for locals wanting to go to other places, and the nature of those facilities affects the region's capacity as a travel generator. For example, when a provincial city has its airport upgraded to international status, the city and its surrounding region usually produces a surge in outbound international travel. This consequence tends to be obscured. Instead, when provincial communities make plans for international airports they publicly support the proposal with descriptions of more visitors coming in to develop the city and its hinterland as a tourist destination.

Fares and other prices ➤

Demand for travel and tourist services, like that for many other goods and services, is price-elastic. If fares alter substantially, demand for tourism is affected. A fare with high price elasticity is one where a change in the level of the fare leads to a proportionately large change in the demand for tickets. There is evidence that air fares are highly price-elastic in certain markets.

In Australia in the 1990s, when Virgin Blue and other discount airlines began operating, low fares led to a huge rise in the number of passengers. (The fact that the lowest fares were unsustainable, because the airlines were losing money, is a separate issue.)

Exchange rates ➤

In June 2003, the Australian dollar was worth $US0.65. Australian residents visiting the USA found most prices rather high compared with home. During the previous two years, however, the $A had risen 30% against the $US, which meant that between early 2001 and mid-2003, the USA became a less expensive destination for Australians. Other things equal, this could have led to a rise in the number of Australians visiting the USA and fewer residents of the USA visiting Australia.

Foreign currency exchange rates are published in daily newspapers and on Internet sites. They have great impact on the scale and directions of international tourism, because most tourists are constrained by budgets; when exchange rates vary, the costs of alternative itineraries fluctuate. Comparing countries over long periods gives clear signs of the effects. Thirty years ago relatively few Singaporeans visited Australia, largely because of an unfavourable exchange rate: $S1 was worth $A0.30. Since 1970, Singapore's economy has grown remarkably and the rate has changed; now the two currencies are almost equal in value. Thirty years ago $A1 was worth $US1.20, and Australian tourists in the USA and in most countries around the world were in an economically fortunate position.

Promotion ➤

The amount and effectiveness of advertising and other promotion can affect the volume of travel generated by a region. Where large outbound markets exist, promotional campaigns can be vigorous and highly competitive. Consider how many tourism-related advertisements are seen and heard in large cities. People who watch commercial TV and read popular magazines and newspapers are inundated with images and messages about countries and regions to visit, about airlines for getting there, resorts and hotels, car rental and packaged holidays. Seemingly continuous promotions are reminders of tourism as a generic activity and also of specific places and services. Continuously receiving informative and persuasive messages, consumers are induced to keep moving towards decisions to go on trips.

Tourism promotion is only one theme in a vast array of promotion for all sorts of goods, services, experiences and ideas. In combination the message is 'Consume, spend money and be satisfied, for if you cease consuming you will be unhappy'. The message is untrue, of course, but many of us are deceived at least some of the time.

Tourism industries in TGRs

A fully developed industry for tourism has linked operations—usually by nominally separate organisations—spread across the geography of whole tourism systems, in TGRs, TRs and TDRs.

In TGRs, business organisations in tourism industries are those serving the distinctive needs of tourists pre-trip, and are therefore located in places where trips are caused and where they begin. They include retail travel agencies, the promotional branches of national (and large-scale regional) tourism organisations, the marketing arms of tour operators and wholesalers, and luggage retailers. In one sense the most important of all are public carriers such as airlines and buslines, whose role in reference to TGRs is to transport people away on trips and bring them home again.

Managers of marketing organisations in TGRs monitor trends by looking for changes in the factors that shape demand—the 11 factors listed above.

The cause of tourism and the relevance of TGRs

Chapter 5 contained a discussion on what causes tourism. The explanation relates to the geography of tourism in one important respect. The process of a person becoming motivated for tourism occurs in his/her home locality, which becomes the centre of a TGR if and when the person travels.

Tourism is caused by certain events in TGRs. Therefore, any activity by managers of tourism to stimulate more tourism in a primary sense must involve doing things in TGRs. A theory useful for understanding what causes tourism is summarised as follows (Stear 1984: 16):

> *The explanation is based on the deterministic axiom that events are caused by present or past phenomena or relationships of phenomena, whose identification is logically possible. It assumes that an event (in this case a touristic departure) is caused by the interaction of sufficient conditions within a region, in this case a perceived traveller generation region.*

Determinism is a philosophy permeating modern science. It is based on a belief that what happens cannot be influenced by anything in the future or by anything unknowable, so fate or god(s) or willpower or luck are not reasons why things happen.

Necessary conditions and sufficient conditions are things we can know about, if we observe and think carefully, so they are concepts used for discovering what causes any action or event to occur. Why does an apple fall from a tree? A person with a little knowledge of science might say 'Because of gravity'. That is a *necessary condition*, as in space, where the effect of the earth's gravity is absent, objects do not fall (as seen in videos from spacecraft); but gravity is not a *sufficient condition*, as in a gravitational field (on earth) not all apples fall to the ground. Therefore, we should not say 'Gravity caused the apple to fall'. There must be at least one more necessary condition—*the absence of constraints*. Fallen apples are the ones whose stems linking them to trees have broken free. These two necessary conditions occurring in combination become sufficient conditions; and so, if the tree is in a gravitational field (a reasonable assumption) and if a stem holding an apple to a tree breaks, the apple is *caused* to fall. The event *will* occur, and a precise cause has been identified. The event is logically determined.

This theory explains the causes of all sorts of actions and events, including the event of a tourist setting out on a trip. In Chapter 5, this theory of causation was introduced as a theme in tourist psychology. It is brought in here again to demonstrate how the processes in the causes of tourism occur in traveller-generating regions.

> *Rebecca, setting off from her home in Takapuna for a holiday in Surfers Paradise, might personally attribute the event to free will and personal effort (she really wanted to go on a holiday, and saved the money), or to fate (her new best friend suggested that they go together to Surfers), or to a prayer answered (her boss gave her permission to take leave during a busy time in the office). In reality, none of these things caused the trip, although some of them might have been contributing factors.*

Understanding causation is useful in any managerial and professional work. It is useful in tourism because, if a manager or marketer decides to take actions to stimulate tourism in the primary sense, the actions must be directed at people before they leave home, when they are in TGRs. Planning the actions must consider or research all necessary conditions, and then should implement actions on any conditions found to be lacking or deficient.

As the discussion in Chapter 5 showed, those actions can include building consumers' (a) knowledge of places they might visit and services they might use in trips, (b) positive feelings about the places and/or services, and (c) expectations that by going on a trip, or by visiting particular places and using certain kinds of services, their touristic needs will be satisfied. In a travel agency, a consultant might assume that clients already have the necessary knowledge, feelings and expectations, and so can focus on (d) inducing motivation so that they make a decision and set out on a trip. In some cases, the consultant notices clients wavering because of some perceived problem, and in these instances might have to work on (e) removing a constraint, before they decide and act, paying for the tickets and setting off.

Rebecca's trip to Surfers Paradise can be attributed to causes in the form of neces-
sary conditions occurring in her home town, Takapuna. There she developed her
knowledge *of Surfers Paradise, then formed* positive feelings *about the place as a*
possible venue for a holiday, and this led to an expectation *that it would be a pleas-*
ant place to visit and then the motivation *to act in ways that would result in her*
going on the trip.

Rebecca's knowledge *of Surfers might have come from diverse sources: seeing TV*
ads, reading magazine articles, hearing the hairdresser raving about her own expe-
riences. Her positive feelings *and* expectations *probably began and developed dur-*
ing those processes. Her motivation *to do something might have emerged while lis-*
tening to her new best friend suggest that they go to Surfers. She began saving
money and visited the Takapuna Travel Agency, which added to her knowledge,
shaped her feelings, raised her expectations and strengthened her motivation to
save the money and go.

When all was ready, Rebecca became extremely insecure, sensing an acute fear
of flying. She urged her best friend to forget Surfers and go on a bus tour instead.
Her friend phoned the travel consultant, Rebecca was called in for a chat, and the
consultant used her professional skills in helping her get over her irrational fear.
Once this constraint *was absent, all the necessary conditions were in place and the*
two friends set off.

Tourism is caused by events and conditions in TGRs. The discussion above, in its
hypothetical illustration and theory, describes and explains how and why certain pre-trip
events and conditions in TGRs are vital in the process of tourism. Tourism is caused by
events and conditions in TGRs. Some have been placed there as promotional devices,
by interests from TDRs (tourist destination regions) and from organisations in tourism
industries, such as airlines and tour operators. Other events and conditions shaping
the pre-trip process stem not from any person or organisation interested as a matter of
routine in promoting tourism but from the social and cultural environments of TGRs.

TRANSIT ROUTES

Many places are visited by very large numbers of people on tourist trips but record little
if any economic impact and have virtually no tourism industry. The city of Calais records
more than 15 million visitors annually. It contains features that might be remarkable
attractions: the city centre was destroyed by bombs in the 1939–45 war and was rebuilt
as a replica of old Casablanca. Yet most of the tourists who visit Calais do not go to the
city centre and most are probably quite unaware of its replicated association; the only
significant economic activities serving the huge numbers are in transport and duty-free
shopping on the city's fringe (Rivais 1993). Calais' major role in tourism is as a point on
popular transit routes.

Geographically, part of every whole tourism system is where a traveller has left home but has not yet reached a place he/she regards as a tourist destination for that trip. This is an intermediate zone where the principal *travel* activity of tourism occurs, as distinct from *visit* activity in destinations. The discussion under this heading deals with four topics: (a) alternative roles of transit routes (TRs); (b) efficiency of TRs; (c) management strategies of businesses on TRs; and (d) certain problems for places with significant dual roles, as points on TRs and as tourist destinations.

A special role for transit routes: pure tourism?

For many tourists, probably the majority, TRs have a supporting role, for they are the paths that must be traversed to get from home to a tourist destination, to additional destinations in many cases, and then home again. For certain tourists, however, TRs are the principal places in itineraries. Weber's (2001) article on outdoor adventure tourism described this theme. She discussed it in reference to the Asian Overland Route, a 'classic trip of modern times' (2001: 365). For certain tourists on this kind of trip there is no destination in mind. They travel and stay with any place or event that takes their interest. They live in the present. A particular mental attitude is required to sustain this behaviour, for there are frequent intrusions that tempt us, in everyday life and when we are tourists, to focus not on experiencing the present but on hopes and expectations of a future where we will have really interesting and pleasant experiences.

An Australian adventure tourist expressed these ideas well, after his third climb to the top of Mt Everest. For his first two ascents, he flew to Nepal and then flew to the base of the mountain before climbing it. For his third trip he took an extra month and walked from sea level, for the fun of it. Incidentally, that made him the first person to truly climb Mt Everest. The book of the trip is titled *Everest from Sea to Summit* (Macartney-Snape 1993: 130):

> *Much of the expedition experience is lost by flying in. Modern modes of travel all suffer the same flaws: the sense of journey, so fundamental to life, is diminished and the quality of that portion of life is all the poorer. By making the object of the journey the destination rather than the journey itself, we rob ourselves of an important element in living. I truly believe that to really live is to be engrossed in the moment. Waiting for the future kills experience, wastes life—as if our purpose is merely waiting to die.*

In what could be termed pure tourism there are no tourist destinations, there are only traveller-generating regions and tourist routes. It might be seen as an ideal, a worthy one, but it is one that most business persons in tourism industries would be loath to promote. Tourism as an industrialised commodity depends on creating hope and expectations of a pleasant future, and this requires creating images in consumers' minds of tourist destinations.

A strategy suggesting that people are better off living in the present would be contrary to the major interests of tourism industries as currently structured. In fact, it would be contrary to the interests of capitalism in general, which depends on sustaining a widespread mood of dissatisfaction with current conditions alongside hope and expectations for future happiness—not in heaven but on earth, and not too far into the future.

Transit route efficiency

'Accessibility' is an expression often used to describe the relative ease or difficulty in reaching tourist destinations. Factors determining accessibility can be bisected into those found in destinations and others, usually the more important, found in TRs leading to destinations. An efficient TR is a path giving easy access for large numbers of travellers. This is always a comparative issue, depending on which whole tourism system and which travellers are being discussed.

Describing the Maldives or Maroochydore as a tourist destination that is 'easily accessible' without asking or implying 'From where?' is meaningless. Once that is known, distance and transport costs immediately come to mind as relevant factors. They are, but several additional factors may also be important.

Distance often seems a critical factor affecting tourism. In Australia, the phrase 'the tyranny of distance' has become well known since a famous history book with that title was published almost 30 years ago. The title refers to the perception that the very large distances between scattered parts of the continent and between Australia and the developed and culturally similar countries of Europe and North America have been a 'tyrant', imposing difficulties on Australians in terms of national economic development, trade, business and tourism.

Travel time ➤

In fact, distance is not a critical factor. It merely seems that way to people with an unfulfilled desire to easily reach somewhere far away, and that is certainly a common perception. In the latest edition of *The Tyranny of Distance*, Blainey (2002) added a comment that distance is not always the real issue. It is travel time.

Modern technologies in transport by air, sea and land have speeded up popular forms of long-distance travel so that travel times on many TRs have been reduced greatly, improving the efficiency. Giant steps in this process were the development of steam-powered railways and ships after 1840, motor cars and motor coaches after about 1910, commercial jet aircraft after 1950 and, especially, wide-bodied jets since 1970.

There have been no major advances since 1970, and new technology is unlikely to speed up mass tourist travel in the next decade or so. It is available, is currently feasible technically, but is probably not feasible on marketing and economic criteria. Despite this, every year tourism boosters in Australia publicly forecast that new, faster aircraft models are about to be introduced, cutting travel times and resulting in many more tourists coming from abroad. Hindsight has shown that these forecasts were little more than daydreams, probably induced by spending time in the company of marketing representatives from Boeing. Two examples among many culled from old documents will be noted here. In 1964 a politician informed the Commonwealth parliament that 'by 1971, Sydney would be only five hours from Tokyo and San Franscisco' (Gibson 1967, in Hansard HR 41: 415). The chairman of the Australian Tourist Commission said in

1967 that Australia 'would be served by supersonic jet aircraft by 1972 and rocket vehicles by the 1980s' (Bates 1967: 11).

In recent years such authoritative predictions, at least from some sources, have become more cautious and less exciting. A senior official from Tourism New South Wales predicted in a speech that 'by 2005 faster jets will take two hours off trips between the USA and Australia' (G. Buckley 2002).

Fares and other travel costs ➤

The lower the fares, the more efficient the TR, as fare levels are critical influences on most people's decisions to go on trips and decisions about where to go. The period 1950–1974 saw real costs of long-haul travel fall greatly, via developments in aircraft technology and rises in real incomes, and the huge increase in TRs' efficiencies resulting from those trends was a major contributor to growth of worldwide tourism in that era.

Since 1974, trends in the real costs of travel have stopped falling and are now beginning to rise, while energy prices go up and while technologies and real incomes stagnate. This is making many TRs less efficient and will, if the trend continues, lead to changes in tourism patterns worldwide. Broadly, the effect will be lower demand for distant destinations and higher potential demand for tourist destinations closer to home.

This is already being seen around several large cities. In recent decades, destinations have developed in the hinterland fringes of Auckland, Sydney and Melbourne, for example, drawing primarily on markets in the nearby city.

Availability of a carrier and other transport facilities ➤

Factors so far noted may be the most obvious influences on a TR's efficiency, but a basic one is the availability of a public carrier, a transport service for public use, such as an airline, railway or coach service. Where this is not available, tourists have to provide their own means of transport or not use that TR. Where roads are also lacking, the options (and thus the TR efficiency) are reduced further.

Capacity ➤

The capacity of any TR limits the quantities of tourists visiting the destinations it services. Overcrowded roads near large cities in peak holiday seasons demonstrate this condition. Faced with long delays, some people postpone trips and some travellers turn and go home, abandoning their trips.

Frequency of services on public carriers ➤

Imagine that, instead of dozens of flights daily between Melbourne and Sydney, leaving at different times, just one huge aircraft capable of holding 6000 passengers made one return trip. For many travellers the service would lose convenience, and in some cases this would mean not making the trip. Frequent services are a factor in a TR's efficiency because they allow travellers to integrate their movements along the TR with other activities at each end.

Changes in transit ➤

Changing trains or aircraft in transit makes a TR less efficient. More tourists use a TR where direct links are possible. This is why organisations attempting to develop a place as a tourist destination try to persuade carriers to provide direct services linking the place to its major traveller-generating regions.

Cambodia's best-known tourist attraction is Angkor Wat. Until 1998, international tourists would fly into Cambodia at the capital, Phnom Penh, and change to another airline for a flight to Siem Reap. Now Siem Reap's airport handles international flights, so many tourists fly straight there. The result is more tourists, but for briefer visits.

Discomfort ➤

Travel over long distances tends to be uncomfortable, physically and mentally. Airlines especially, and all public carriers, are strategically managed to disguise the reasons for the discomfort and to compensate for its occurrence. Disguise and compensation is achieved, to some extent, via certain themes in promotional messages and by the provision of certain facilities, services and films on board. These work to some extent, but a TR can be regarded as inefficient to the extent to which it is regarded by travellers as uncomfortable.

Perceived safety ➤

Perceptions of safety and its opposite, risk, are critical issues. This applies especially to air travel, although 150 years ago many people were fearful of rail travel, for what now seem like naive reasons (Schivelbusch 1986).

Poros, in the Greek islands, has three geographical roles in tourism: generating region, transit point and destination region

Horrendous attacks on the World Trade Center in New York and the Pentagon in Washington on 11 September 2001 led to a sudden and substantial rise in the number of people around the world perceiving air travel as risky and a large rise in the level of perceived risk. These conditions triggered a sudden and substantial fall in the number of people travelling by air for tourism and most other purposes. Managers of airlines around the world reduced the number of scheduled services and laid off many employees. Statistics collated in early 2002 by the World Tourism Organisation showed that global international tourism, measured in terms of arrivals of international tourists, had decreased by several percentage points on an annual basis. It was the first sustained fall since 1974. In mid-2002, reports from several places around the world were showing signs of recovery.

The truth is that air travel has never been safer than since 12 September 2001, when managers of airports and airlines began raising the standards of safety. For many years, services by major airlines have been the safest mode of travel, in terms of injuries and deaths compared with the number of passengers and distance travelled. Perceptions and emotional feeling, not truth and reasoning, is what governs a lot of human behaviour, especially in risky circumstances, and many people will take time readjusting to the fact that air travel is comparatively safe.

Reliability ➤

How reliable is the X Coachline in terms of its performance in departing on time as per its published schedule? How reliable is the Y Rail in terms of arriving on time? How reliable is the Z Airline in terms of not often having flights delayed because of what airlines always call 'technical problems'? The record of carriers in this respect shapes the efficiency of TRs.

Attractions along the way ➤

Some TRs have scenery or other features that passengers find interesting, enjoyable or mildly entertaining diversions from tedium, and these can all add to the efficiency. Marriott's model of tourism systems' geography, described by Douglas Pearce (1987), recognised that some TRs are noteworthy in this respect.

Marriott identified two categories of TR, termed *access route* and *recreational route*. The former is the quick way, the latter more pleasant but probably slower. Marriott's concept can be seen in a practical design feature of the Michelin road maps, widely used in Europe. They show direct routes in red and what they call 'tourist routes' in green, the latter having special scenery or other features. This allows motoring tourists to plan itineraries according to their priority: getting somewhere quickly or meandering to enjoy the country. Airlines are not easily able to use this factor in TR efficiency.

Schivelbusch's (1986) study of rail travel contains a brilliant discussion on how, 100 years ago, people developed new abilities to interpret and enjoy landscapes seen from trains. The analysis has relevance for wider issues of managing tourism. It shows how and why enjoying landscapes seen from fast-moving transport is not a natural ability. It is, rather, something modern cultures have learned.

Stopover points ➤

Stopover points are where journeys are broken for any reason, such as for picking up and putting down passengers, refuelling, for passengers to rest and eat, to use a lavatory, or because there is a distinctive feature worth experiencing. The suitability of facilities and services at these points affects the efficiency of the TRs on which they are located.

One category of attraction businesses on transit routes uses a skimming strategy. A distinctive feature is displayed where it can be seen by passing motorists. It could be a truly big banana, a very large sheep, a giant concrete bull, or a huge plastic prawn. Those cultural markers of provincial Australia can be seen, each with one or more shops offering goods and services, at Coffs Harbour, Goulburn, Wauchope and Ballina. Seeing the 'Big Thing' as they approach it, motorists on the road for some hours know that here is a place suitable for a brief rest, where there are restrooms and a shop. The manager's business strategy is to entice as many visitors as possible and to derive a small profit per sale on a large volume of turnover.

Places in dual roles: TRs and TDRs

Many places have substantial numbers of visitors for whom these places are TDRs, and large numbers passing through for whom the places are points on TRs. Although anyone familiar with tourist-related businesses can recognise the existence of the dual roles, in most places nobody knows with any precision their relative sizes. Moreover, according to governmental tourism organisations in Australia and New Zealand, the dual roles do not exist. Officials in these organisations have tended to see tourism in overly simplistic ways, clouding their own and others' perceptions of what really happens. Places visited by tourists are all assumed to be destinations: 'transit route' or similar expressions are not in their jargon.

A result is that the scale of these dual roles cannot be measured from official tourism statistics. Official statistics such as those reported by the Australian National Visitor Surveys and International Visitor Surveys assume that all places visited by tourists are 'destinations'. In practice, this overestimates the size and performance of most destinations, while disguising the fact that many places are also functioning as transit points.

Managers of businesses dealing with tourists are normally aware of these potential pitfalls. Usually they tend to specialise in either of the two roles, some organisations dealing mainly with transit travellers and others dealing mainly with visiting tourists. Strategic mistakes can occur if the two are confused. The Big Banana case study later in this book illustrates that mistake.

TOURIST DESTINATIONS

More has been written about destinations than any other element in tourism systems. This can lead to the inference that the study of tourism is the study of destinations and that everything else is peripheral. Certainly the most dramatic aspects of tourism occur in destinations—crowds of tourists doing the things and using the facilities that represent popular notions of tourism.

The discussion below focuses on only a few of the myriad topics relevant to tourist destination regions. Examples in the academic literature on the theme are books by Laws (1995) on destination management, Page (1995) on cities as destinations, and King (1997) on island resort destinations.

What are tourist destinations?

Tourist destinations are a category of traveller destination, in the literal sense that they are places that travellers head towards, including destinations to visit and the final destination, home. Tourist destinations can be defined as places where travellers choose to stay awhile for leisure experiences, related to one or more features or characteristics of the place—a perceived attraction of some sort. In that process, travellers cease being travellers and become tourists. The choice might be made pre-trip, or after setting out from home.

Size of TDRs

How large are tourist destinations? In one sense they are as small or as large as anyone wants to regard them. However, a standard concept of size is useful for thinking about, researching and discussing the geography of tourism. This is helpful for distinguishing tourist destination regions (TDRs) from tourist destination countries.

The boundary of a TDR can be regarded as the feasible day-tripping range around a tourist's accommodation, encompassing the area that tourists might typically visit on day trips. Going further requires shifting to new accommodation, when tourists move to what is, in effect, another TDR. In theory, each hotel or other accommodation base where a tourist stays for a night is the centre of a TDR, but to simplify discussion the popular centres (e.g. the middle of a city and the nucleus of a popular attraction) can be regarded as the centres of many TDRs.

Singapore and other very small countries comprise just one TDR. Tourists staying anywhere in the country can reach any other part on day trips. There is no need to move accommodation in order to see all of Singapore. Large countries comprise thousands of TDRs. This variety has interesting practical implications for tourism management, discussed in Chapter 16.

In practice, TDRs vary in size, but the concept of a standard size for the purpose of research has useful implications for describing and analysing, planning and managing large areas such as an entire country. It can resolve the apparent confusion expressed by one tourism minister when he added an unscripted comment during a speech: 'There is a need for more research and planning of Australia as a tourist destination . . . or maybe that should be a collection of destinations. Is there one or many? We don't seem to have thought about that question' (Brown 1986).

Shapes of TDRs

TDRs vary in shape. A circle is useful for abstract models, as shown in the diagrams in Chapter 3. In reality, some are roughly circular, as happens with TDRs formed around the centre of a city, while others might be long and narrow, as occurs with resort strips such as the French Riviera and Australia's Gold Coast. Tourists on these resort strips typically move along the coast on day trips but seldom venture far inland. Some island TDRs are shaped like a hoop. In Tahiti, for example, many tourists go on day trips around the island's coastline but few go inland.

How tourists perceive TDRs

Different tourists tend to perceive the same TDR in different ways. Variables shaping perceptions include tourists' social and cultural backgrounds, education levels, taste or preferences, previous visits, form of travel arrangements, past travel experiences and, a very influential variable, the time available for spending in each place. Another interesting variable is the direction from which they came to a place.

Laurie Lee, an English teenager backpacking around Spain in 1939, visited Gibraltar and recorded in his notebook how 'to travellers from England, Gibraltar is an oriental bazaar, but coming from Spain I found it more like Torquay' (Lee 1985: 141). Torquay is a town in England. In 1939 Gibraltar had many English residents.

Sight is the most important sense in most modern tourists' perceptions of places they visit (Adler 1989). Smells, sounds, taste and tactile senses are also influential, to varying degrees. All kinds of senses tend to be sharper than usual in tourists arriving in new places, and this is arguably one of the underlying explanations for the pleasure in tourism. As tourists, away from our normal environment, our senses become more alert, certainly in the early days of a visit to a place we have not visited previously.

Environmental issues in TDRs

TDRs are the places in whole tourism systems where various kinds of environmental effects of tourism are especially notable. Some of the effects or influences are viewed as benefits of tourism, such as the revenue for businesses stemming from visitors' expenditures and all the secondary effects of that spending, such as employment and, at a national level, earnings of foreign exchange. Other kinds of effects can be damaging. These issues are discussed in Chapter 10.

Do TDRs compete with one another?

Countries, along with many regions, cities, towns and villages, have promotion offices that issue advertising and other marketing activities intended to persuade tourists to visit that region, city, town or village rather than others, and these activities are signs of competition. A range of writings can be found on competitive marketing issues relating to tourist destinations (Pearce 1997; Crockett & Wood 1999; Day et al. 2002).

Destinations also differ in terms of planning and design, and this can have similar effects. Planning and design issues for tourist destinations have been discussed extensively in the literature (Gunn 1972, 1993; Getz 1992; Dredge 1999).

However, to imagine that competition is a dominant force in relationships among TDRs is misleading. Competition and cooperation occur simultaneously, and either might be more important. In wanderlust tourism tourists visit a series of TDRs, and in this sense the places are in cooperative relationships. This is widely recognised, leading to cooperative marketing programs by a number of countries or regions. Hundreds of examples could be cited.

Henderson (2000) describes alliances for cooperative destination marketing in the Greater Mekong, involving several countries through which the Mekong River flows. Prideaux and Cooper (2002) and Leiper (2002) have discussed cooperative marketing by tourism interests in the 10 countries of ASEAN (Association of South-East Asian Nations). In the 1950s the main purpose of the Pacific Asia Travel Association (PATA) was to foster cooperative promotion by countries around the Pacific Ocean. In Europe, cooperative marketing among tourist destinations is highly developed, arranged via the EU (European Union) and other institutions.

Genesis: how places become TDRs

A widely accepted theory is that tourist destinations normally originate when small numbers of tourists of the adventurer type visit (Plog 1974; Pearce 1989). This theory can be expressed more precisely by saying that many TDRs began their roles in tourism as points on TRs. Typically they were visited by highly independent wanderlust tourists with ample leisure. Here are examples, each slightly different.

Capri is described in modern Michelin guidebooks to Italy as 'one of the highlights of world tourism'. In Douglas' (1911) essays on Capri, he noted that the Blue Grotto, the island's most celebrated feature, has always been an irrelevance for locals but became famous internationally in the 1830s. Two visitors from northern Europe were responsible for the publicity. In 1827 Hans Christian Anderson and a friend were travelling around Italy and stopped off on Capri, where they became fascinated with the Blue Grotto. They wrote about it and it became famous throughout Europe. Tourists went to Capri specifically to see it. An island on a TR evolved to become a TDR.

Hawaii's first role in tourism was as a port of call for passengers on trans-Pacific ships, on pleasure cruises and on line voyages between California and Asia and Australia (Farrell 1982). This role emerged in the early 1900s. Passengers told acquaintances about Hawaii and over time, when a trickle and later a flow of tourists set out with intentions of spending time in Hawaii, the islands evolved as a tourist destination.

Surfers Paradise is another example. In the 1930s it was a point on a TR, not the centre of a TDR. This history comes from interviews in the 1970s with two elderly men. In the 1930s 'Surfers Paradise' was the name of Jim Caville's pub on the main road, situated on what is now the corner of Cavill Avenue; it was not the name of a town or district. The pub enticed passing surfers with cold beer—paradise for surfers returning after a hot day at the beach. The beach that now bears the name was not a surfer's paradise. Surfers deemed it not worth visiting. The surfers, mainly residents of Brisbane, drove past on their way to the better surfing beaches to the south, especially Coolangatta, but they stopped off on their way home.

Koh Samui and a number of other tiny islands of Thailand in the Gulf of Siam are mass tourist destinations. This is a fairly recent development. In the 1960s the only travellers' accommodation on Koh Samui was a couple of primitive huts rented by a shopkeeper to backpackers coming and going by tramp steamers that moored in the lagoon. Usually the huts were empty, for nobody seemed to stay long. After a stopover for a day or more, enjoying tropical fruit and other pleasures of a peaceful tropical island, the backpackers continued their journeys, on the small ships going north to Bangkok or south to Songkhla. Koh Samui was a tourist destination for these travellers, but not one that they all knew about before travelling in Thailand. It emerged while they were travelling along a TR.

Like most theories, this one has exceptions that test the rule. Monaco was not a TR before it became a TDR. Smollett's (1979/1766) observations on the Riviera and Cameron's (1975) history indicate that when Nice was becoming the centre of a fashionable TDR, in the late 1700s, Monaco—15 kilometres east—was a rocky hill where no tourists ventured. Monaco was established as a TDR in the 1870s when Louis Blanc developed the legendary Monte Carlo casino and other features. Incidentally, Blanc invented the name 'Monte Carlo' for the precinct where the casino was built because he believed it would have more promotional impact than 'Monaco'.

Theories of destination evolution and development

Two books by Douglas Pearce (1987, 1989) present several theories on how places emerge and evolve as tourist destinations. Gunn's (1988) *Vacationscape: Designing Tourist Regions* also describes and illustrates a number of theories on the topic. Under the next two headings, two widely known theories are discussed.

Plog's theory of destination change ➤

Plog's (1974) article 'Why destinations rise and fall in popularity' was based on research conducted among air passengers. Plog identified two personality types. *Allocentric types*, few in number, are individuals who prefer unfamiliar places and enjoy risks. They are the ones who first visit new destinations. Over time, these places become known to more numerous *psychocentrics*, the masses who prefer destinations that are becoming popular, that have been endorsed as pleasant and safe. When a destination becomes well known among psychocentrics, it becomes a mass destination. Eventually the psychocentrics start to move on, after learning about other destinations, and the formerly popular place sees a decline in visitor numbers.

S.L.J. Smith (1990a, 1990b) argued persuasively that Plog's theory is unproven and defective because the research techniques used were the wrong ones for this sort of research, and could not logically have given the results Plog claimed.

McDonnell (1994) tested Plog's theory empirically, using the same techniques as Plog. McDonnell used Plog's questionnaire and survey design method to interview two samples of Australian tourists, one lot going to Bali and the other to Fiji. McDonnell had knowledge of these destinations, having worked as Qantas' station manager in both places, and believed that Australian tourists in Fiji would show a leaning towards a psychocentric personality, while those in Bali would be more inclined to the allocentric. His research found no significant difference, and he concluded that Plog's theory was flawed.

Another criticism of Plog's theory, not raised by Smith or McDonnell, stems from a philosophical review of what it says. This leads to a conclusion that the theory is merely a tautology, not an explanation. It merely describes, using jargon about types, how some places grow in popularity as tourist destinations. Typological analysis is useful as description but not for explanation or prediction. Plog's theory does not explain why destinations rise and fall in popularity.

Destination life cycle theory ➤

The most widely discussed theory in tourism studies is the destination life cycle, first proposed by Butler (1980). Hundreds of articles and many books have discussed it. Articles by Prosser (1995), Luntorp and Wanhill (2001), Agarwal (2002) and Hovinen (2002) are noteworthy.

The theory regards destinations as living things and as therefore moving through the same sort of life cycle as animals and plants. They are born, grow rapidly through childhood and adolescence, then their growth rate slows until, in maturity, vitality stagnates and life eventually goes into decline towards old age and death. Destinations supposedly display this cycle in their visitor numbers, according to the theory. Numbers go up, remain up for a while, stagnate, then go down; ultimately, the place ceases to exist as a notable destination for tourists. One benefit of the theory is that it has stimulated an enormous quantity of research. While much of it is mundane and trivial, many discussions are interesting and informative.

Why is this theory popular among researchers, consultants and teachers interested in tourism? Three reasons can be suggested.

First, the theory is based on a description of trends that are virtually universal among TDRs. All TDRs have fluctuations in visitor arrivals. Numbers go up, stay up for a while, then fall by varying amounts, then in many cases rise again. Anything that moves or fluctuates seems to be alive, so 'life cycle' seems to be a realistic way of describing the fluctuations.

Second, the theory suggests opportunities for managerial intervention. By appropriate actions at the right time, a TDR's apparently mature phase can be prolonged and its decline in late maturity can be halted or possibly reversed. Possibilities for this action include advertising, to induce more tourists, and renovation of the TDRs facilities, to improve satisfaction levels (Agarwal 2002). Managerial intervention to prolong the upper-level performance of a tourist destination is an especially pleasing prospect for business entrepreneurs and local governments with investments in tourist facilities in any destination that seems to be heading for late middle age. Because of this point, the life cycle theory is widely popular among consultants, who charge fees for giving advice on the precise kinds of strategies required to stimulate and revive a particular destination where visitor numbers are stagnant or decreasing. A theory supported by articles in research journals can help create a prestigious image around consultants' proposals and reports. Moreover, the term 'life cycle' is a subtle selling point for consultancy projects. Life cycle implies ultimate death, but consultants with a prescription for eternal life offer hope to owners of fading tourist facilities.

Third, the theory is popular because it is simple. Most humans take an immediate liking to any theory that offers a simple explanation for a complicated issue. The basic ideas of destination life cycle theory can be quickly grasped and conveyed to students by any lecturer capable of getting chalk on his coat. This might be one reason why the theory is prominent in the syllabus of so many courses, and why it is in so many research articles.

Despite its popularity, the theory is seriously flawed. In many, possibly most instances where it has been applied, the theory has been either useless or misleading. Destination life cycle theory does not explain fluctuations in visitor numbers and is useless for predicting them.

Hovinen's (2002) research provides adequate evidence to support those opinions. He was the first person to test the theory, in the early 1980s. Twenty years later he tested it again in the same TDR, a district of Pennsylvania. He found signs of growth, stagnation, decline and rejuvenation—all occurring at one time. These contrary trends were in different forms of tourism occurring in the TDR. He concluded that the theory of destination life cycle is fundamentally flawed. Lundtorp and Wanhill (2001) tested the theory using long-run time series and found it made no sense. They dismissed it as intrinsically flawed, describing it as 'no more than a statistical caricature of the real world' (2001: 947). Both articles, by Lundtorp and Wanhill and by Hovinen, give reasons why they rejected the theory. There are additional reasons for doing so, which add to the strength of the rejection.

A central defect in the theory is one that occurs in many areas of tourism research. The theory is based on a feral metaphor. Tourist destinations are not living things, and interpreting them via a life cycle metaphor is potentially misleading, possibly leading to confusion and error. The life cycle concept has been taken out of its normal context and put, metaphorically, into a theory about tourist destinations where it is likely to behave like any feral—wildly, out of control, and not reliably as people hoped it would.

Tourist destinations might seem to be living things because they are alive with tourists. But TDRs cannot live independently, any more than a human leg could live if it were amputated. The lively quality of destinations as destinations is entirely the result of tourists coming in from somewhere else. There is no life in tourism industries located in TDRs if there are no tourists to serve. There are few things on earth so lifeless as a hotel with no guests or a theme park with no visitors. The life in tourism occurs at the level of whole systems. Life comes to TDRs from TGRs. Instead of trying to fit life cycle theory into explanations of tourism by focusing on destinations, more might be gained by applying the theory to whole tourism systems interacting with environments.

Another defect in destination life cycle theory is evident in the way some commentators and researchers interpret all rises in tourist arrivals as signs of a growing destination that is progressing towards maturity and all falls as signs of advancing age.

A simple theory labelled 'life cycle' invites that interpretation and has been repeated in countless articles and reports.

In fact, a fall in visitor numbers over a few years might be a short-term dip on a long-term upward trend line; and vice versa, a rise might be a short-term rise in a long-term downward decline. The result is that even the most precise statistical data cannot be taken as signs of where a destination is currently located on its so-called 'life cycle'. An analogy might clarify this point. If a child became ill, and remained ill for several months, no medical doctor would interpret the decline in vitality as a sign that the child's life cycle was in decline, even if its condition was life-threatening. Illness and death in childhood are never attributed to geriatric issues, to stages in life cycle.

A third defect is equally serious. Carefully examined, most of the fluctuations in visitor numbers at tourist destinations have nothing to do with conditions in the destination. Most are caused by events in external environments.

The same analogy used earlier can clarify the point. Consider the changing vitality of a human being or any other animal over a normal life span. Rapid growth and much vitality are evident early on, in childhood and adolescence, then slower growth and less vitality, then a trend in middle age towards less vitality and eventual decline towards stagnation and death. However, the trend line of vitality is seldom smooth, for there are normally disruptions, sudden downturns caused not by the stage in life cycle but by illnesses or injuries, events caused by factors in external environments. Recovery leads to an upturn, an increase in vitality that cannot be attributed to life cycle but regression to the trend line. The fact that old folk often recover from injuries and illness and return to their former level of vitality reinforces the point.

Remembering that analogy, consider tourist trends in a sample of destinations where fluctuations over several years have been interpreted as representing the life cycle of tourist destinations. In fact, many of the increasing and decreasing trends were caused by events and conditions in external environments.

Increasing prosperity in traveller-generating countries often leads to increased tourism into tourist destinations, and decreasing prosperity triggers the opposite trend. An outbreak of war, or sustained terrorist attacks, can lead to a severe downturn in tourism. After a war, or after a terrorist campaign, the return of peaceful conditions can be quickly followed by growth in tourism. A severe typhoon or hurricane can devastate the resorts on a tropical island, leading to a year or more of falling tourist numbers; later, when repairs are completed, the numbers begin rising again. A change in a country's government policy can lead to more or less money being spent on promoting the country as a tourist destination, with corresponding shifts in visitor numbers. All these and other changes are changes in the environments that affect tourist numbers in a given destination and have nothing to do with the internal characteristics that could reasonably be attributed to the stage in its life cycle.

The proper aim of criticising a theory is to provide better theory. As Karl Popper (1959) showed, scientific knowledge advances not by finding support for a theory but by demonstrating why it is false. This leads to a search for a better theory, one that more realistically explains the things that the discredited theory had purported to explain. Destination life cycle theory, assumed by many researchers over the past two decades to be valid, should now be assigned to the archives of history—as a former theory, now discredited, shown to be false.

To understand why destinations rise and fall in popularity requires considering whole systems, not merely what happens in a destination. It also requires distinguishing between the internal functioning of the systems and factors in their external environments.

What makes TDRs popular?

What are the factors shaping TDRs' evolution, making a place popular or inhibiting that process? Several can be easily identified. Attractions, accessibility, amenities and affordability make up one simple, but not sufficiently detailed, formula.

In one interesting project, Braithwaite et al. (1998) sought to identify the success factors for tourism in 13 regions of eastern Australia. In order of importance, the factors were local attractions, infrastructure, marketing and promotion, government support and local champions (i.e. persons willing and able to lead and manage). The following list has all of those factors and a number of others.

Attractions ➤

Without features or characteristics that seem attractive to potential tourists, a place will not become a tourist destination: that is, there must be something perceived as probably pleasurable to experience in person. If nothing is perceived as likely to satisfy their individual preferences for leisure experiences, tourists will not go to the place, or will not linger if passing through.

Usually TDRs that attract many tourists and sustain popularity for long periods are places with multiple attractions of the sort that evolve without planning for tourism in mind. This can be observed in the world's most popular TDRs, which are cities such as Paris, New York, Rome, Venice, Cairo, London, Sydney, Los Angeles. Large and cosmopolitan cities are especially popular. They are popular among wanderluster and also sunluster types. This has been reported by hotel employees in Sydney, for instance, who have noticed an interesting trend. Twenty years ago many American and European tourists coming to Australia were on packaged trips for wanderlust-type itineraries, visiting several regions including Sydney. Now, increasing numbers are flying to Sydney, staying there for a vacation, then going straight home. These sunlust types tend to be independent of any package arrangements, and largely independent of pre-trip travel agency booking services for accommodation. Instead, they book their hotel personally, via the Internet or telephone.

Accessibility ➤

Before large numbers of people will choose to visit a place as a tourist destination, the place must be relatively accessible. This depends on the transit routes leading there being efficient, as discussed earlier. It also requires that the place has open gateways, without excessively restrictive policies for visiting tourists. Where foreign tourists are required to first obtain visas, for example, this deters some potential visitors.

Tolerance ➤

Residents of a region must tolerate the presence of visitors for the place to function as a tourist destination and grow in popularity. They do not have to be friendly for this to happen, merely tolerant. In the 1960s and 70s Teheran was a popular destination for international tourists. Then came the rise of anti-Western sentiments, fanned by a new government in Iran led by Islamic fundamentalists who wanted to rid the country of corrupting Western influences. Tourists were made to feel unwelcome in public, and soon the only Westerners to visit the city were travellers on business and diplomatic missions, who did not need to move about in public places, and a small number of backpackers. The latter had to take special precautions (Dalrymple 1989). Conditions began to change in the 1990s with a new government and more moderate policy. Western tourists began trickling into the city again.

Tolerance is not synonymous with friendliness. There is no evidence that places where locals do not display friendliness to tourists are places that tourists avoid.

Security ➤

The list of things that make people feel insecure about trips and about visiting particular places is long. The more distant and different the proposed destination, the longer the list, as sensations of insecurity seem linked to how exotic the place appears. This issue is critical, because tourism is practised to bring pleasure to the practitioners and any significant threat to security immediately diminishes those prospects.

Life-support and comfort systems ➤

Tourists require some standard of life-support and comfort systems in the places where they choose to stay. Accommodation is the major item here. Different types of tourists have different preferences and standards. In terms of security and life support and comforts, tourists generally seek a mix of familiar and exotic environments.

Some want more familiarity and less of the exotic, so they choose TDRs not too different from their home region. In particular, they choose TDRs where there are hotels or other forms of tourist accommodation that cater specifically to tourists of their type, and these places provide what could be called a 'bubble' or 'cocoon' of life support and familiar comforts in the foreign, exotic destination. Examples are those American tourists who would not think of staying anywhere except the Hilton or Holiday Inn if they were visiting Istanbul, where for years the Hilton advertised 'genuine US hamburgers' in case anyone needed reminding of why the Hilton was in Istanbul. The same principle operates in Sydney, where in the 1990s most Koreans on packaged tours stayed in Korean-owned hotels.

Adventurous types choose TDRs that seem more exotic and less familiar. They might enjoy staying in what to them is exotic accommodation, eating strange food, and, in few cases among Western tourists, doing without Western-style lavatories for days or weeks on end. Even in these cases, familiar comforts are usually present. AusVenture, an upmarket adventure trek operator in the Himalayas, provides chairs for its trekkers, carried through the mountains on porters' backs; at night, Scotch whisky and sherry are served.

Cost and benefit advantage ➤

Costs of getting to and visiting a place have a direct effect on its popularity as a tourist destination. Inevitably, cost comparisons are made by persons on a budget contemplating trips with alternative destinations in mind.

Another comparison is made regarding each place's potential for satisfying experiences, an assessment reflecting each tourist's needs and preferences for particular kinds of experiences. One person's decision may be heavily weighted by cost, another's by security, a third by attractions.

Information diffusion ➤

For a place to develop as a TDR, there must be information diffused to inform potential visitors about features and conditions that might influence them to become motivated to visit. Those features and conditions include the items on the above list.

Tourism industries in TDRs

Of the three geographical elements, TDRs are where the largest and most diverse collections of organisations in tourism industries are found. TDRs in the early stages of evolution might have few, if any, organisations in the business of tourism: tourist visitors use the same facilities as local residents—finding accommodation in private houses, and finding their own amusements.

A tourism industry develops when and if tourists visit in greater numbers, especially the type who need particular kinds of accommodation, need help to find and interpret natural attractions, or need artificial attractions such as theme parks and staged entertainment. These tourists add demand to local markets, as do pioneer tourists (buying the same goods and services as residents), but they also create distinctive tourist markets. These include markets for accommodation in different forms and standards, attractions of different sorts, local tours, tourist-specific banking services, information, and (most diverse of all) consumer goods ranging from cheap souvenirs to expensive items in boutiques.

Understanding how places function and evolve as tourist destinations is useful in any management role involved with tourism. To develop that understanding, theories of the kind set out above need to be reviewed against a number of actual places. This is best done in the field. Studies of particular places as tourist destinations are useful.

CONCLUSION

A simple whole tourism system has one TGR, one TR and one TDR. A lot of tourism has this geographical structure, but many tourists visit a series of destination regions in what can be termed multi-destination tourism.

A detailed analysis of multi-destination patterns among international tourists visiting Australia was conducted in research by Tideswell (2001). She identified nine noteworthy itineraries and gave each type of tourist a label. These included 'round Australia tourers', who typically spend 26 nights in the country and visit five regions; 'three state tourers', 13 nights in four regions of Victoria, New South Wales and Queensland; and 'Sydney to Queensland coasters', 26 nights, four regions.

This geography of tourism has been about places represented in various permutations in tourists' itineraries, so that from all possible itineraries a general principle can be recognised. At least three distinct places, in three different roles, are active in every tourist's trip. To understand the geography of tourism, all three roles must be observed. Overly simplistic ideas about tourism tend to focus on just one of those roles—tourist destinations—because that is where tourism is most apparent, most dramatic, and where beneficial and detrimental impacts on environments are most easily noticed.

Managing tourism involves activities in places in all three roles. Marketing by certain organisations is most effective when it involves promotions distributed in generating regions. Moreover, because tourism cannot be accomplished in one place alone, and because few managers are highly skilled in the art of ubiquity, the effective management of tourism requires some degree of coordination and cooperation among managers situated in different places. This is not unique to tourism, for most industrialised processes are geographically scattered. In most industries, management strategies work to reduce geographic fragmentation, by clustering the processing of resources in a few places in order to gain economies of scale and scope. This clustering strategy has little potential in modern tourism, which means alternative and often less productive means of gaining efficiencies must be used. It has less potential because the main resource of tourism industries are tourists, who are relatively free to go where they choose. As Krippendorf observed, 'the timber industry processes timber, the tourism industry processes tourists' (1987: 40).

The analysis in this chapter suggested a number of factors that shape the performance of places in tourism systems. Managers of all sorts of organisations in the business of tourism are more competent if they understand how places are performing.

Another theme was diversity. While certain factors can be identified as likely to be shaping the performance of places in all three of their potential roles, unique factors affect each place. This is why detailed local knowledge is needed for effective tourism management, which cannot easily be transferred from one location to another. However, as tourism depends on connecting places in an itinerary, the management of tourism is likely to be more effective and efficient when it involves cooperation between individual managers located at different places.

Because tourism involves so many places, virtually every region on earth, and because each place is unique in some respects, effective managers must not only have good knowledge of the region where they are personally based but should be outward-looking—knowledgeable about places away from their own patch that are linked to it in itineraries. This applies in all directions: from managers with bases in generating regions looking out to other places as transit routes and destinations, to managers whose work arises from their base as a destination and who then look outside to transit routes and generating regions.

Discussion questions

1. What is the basis for describing one of the three geographical elements in whole tourism systems as having 'an absence' of persons?

2. What are three reasons explaining why many researchers, writers and consultants involved with tourism have accepted Butler's theory of tourist destination life cycle?

3. While many researchers, writers and consultants have accepted Butler's theory of tourist destination life cycle, others have criticised it as being defective and misleading. Describe the grounds of these criticisms and give your views.

4. Why can Plog's theory, about why destinations rise and fall in popularity, be rejected as an explanation for such fluctuations?

5. List and describe factors in TGRs that lead to tourism. Present your answer in terms of a particular person, real or imaginary, in some real place in its role as TGR.

6. List and describe factors that can contribute to a place becoming a popular TDR. Present your answer in terms of a particular place—a town, city, region or country.

7. What is meant by so-called 'pure tourism'? Which element normally found in whole tourism systems is absent in this condition? Why would certain business interests in tourism industries be opposed to the concept?

Recommended reading

Blainey, Geoffrey 2002, *The Tyranny of Distance* (2nd edn), Melbourne: Text

Braithwaite, Dick, Greiner, R. & Walker, P. 1998, Success factors for tourism in regions of eastern Australia, pp 69–96, in Hall & O'Hanlon (eds), *Rural Tourism Management: Sustainable Options* (conference proceedings), Ayr: SAS

Dredge, Dianne 1999, Destination, place, planning and design, *Annals of Tourism Research*, 26: 772–91

Hall, C.M. 1996, *Tourism in the Pacific,* London: Thomson International Business Press

Hall, C.M. & Page, S.J. 2001, *Geography of Tourism and Recreation: Environment, Place and Space* (2nd edn), London: Routledge

Laws, E. 1995, *Tourist Destination Management: Issues, Analysis and Policies,* London: Routledge

Leiper, Neil 2000, Are destinations 'the heart of tourism'?: the advantages of an alternative description, *Current Issues in Tourism*, 3(4): 364–8

Macartney-Snape, Tim 1993, *Everest from Sea to Summit,* Sydney: Australian Geographical Society

Page, S.J. 1995, *Urban Tourism,* London: Routledge

140   Pearce, Douglas 1987, *Tourism Today: A Geographical Analysis*, London: Longman

——1989, *Tourist Development* (2nd edn), London: Longman

——1997, Competitive Destination Analysis in Southeast Asia, *Journal of Travel Research*, 35(4): 16–24

——1999, Tourism in Paris: studies at the microscale, *Annals of Tourism Research*, 26: 77–97

Smith, S.L.J. 1990a, A test of Plog's allocentric/psychocentric model: evidence from seven nations, *Journal of Travel Research*, 28(Spring): 40–3

——1990b, Another look at the carpenter's tools: a reply to Plog, *Journal of Travel Research*, 28(Fall): 50–1

The Tourism Industry: Economics and Politics

INTRODUCTION

Businesses supplying services, goods and facilities used by tourists have been referred to collectively as 'the tourism industry' or 'tourism industries' only since the 1960s. Before then, no reference to an industry linked to tourism or travel has been found. Despite the new expression, nothing new of substance was created, as tourists had been using the same sorts of items for ages. In other words, the expression 'tourism industry' was a new way of describing things that had existed for a long time but had not been regarded as components of an industry.

This raises interesting questions. How and why did the idea emerge of describing organisations associated with tourists as 'an industry'? Why did this happen in the 1960s and not earlier, in the 1920s for instance?

A second theme explored in this chapter is how the recognition of the tourism industry occurred and how it is often described and defined. A third theme is the idea's utility. What practical use is served? As will be shown, the adoption of the expression 'industry' signified a strategy with economic and political implications, enabling certain interests to gain substantial advantages. This is one reason why the issue is not merely academic. A fourth theme focuses on a contentious issue. While many people recognise the tourism industry as a realistic entity, others disagree. An aim in this chapter is to clarify this issue but not resolve it. Resolution requires a more detailed discussion, set out in later chapters.

The sides in the dispute do not argue over the fact that tourism has value, for anyone with common sense knows broadly what is meant when they read statements like 'the tourism industry does a lot for the economy'. The dispute is about the real nature and scope of this industry. The clarification in this chapter suggests a scheme that recognises two concepts of tourism industry. Each is realistic and appropriate in a particular context, but one is highly misleading when used in the wrong context, which often happens.

HOW THE IDEA OF A TOURISM INDUSTRY EMERGED

We live in a highly industrialised world, where material wellbeing and entertainments are largely supported by industries, as most of the goods and services we consume come from organisations, large and small, that are components of industries. Three hundred years ago the world was not like this. Industries as we now know them did not exist. Instead, goods and services were produced by labourers on farms, tradesmen in workshops and domestic workers at home.

The change to an industrialised world involved a number of complicated developments, sometimes called industrial revolutions. The industrialisation of tourism is part of that change and in this case is a process that is not and probably never will be complete. Tourism, like many other forms of human behaviour, is partly industrialised.

The development of modern industries

Around 1700 the beginnings of modern industries occurred in the West Indies, in the production and distribution base of sugar (Mintz 1985). Around 1750, in ways that led to huge economic development in England, later in other parts of Europe and later again in other places around the world, the production and distribution of many other kinds of goods become industrialised, notably via the development of factories for manufacturing.

The precise basis of industrialisation is disputed, although researchers agree that several factors contribute to the process. Mintz (1985) and Buckminster-Fuller (1972/1946) make a strong case for believing the central factor is a radical change from an economy based on independent producers to one based on combinations, on industrial chains and networks, on cooperative and collaborative links between and among producers and distributors.

Other changes accompany that central factor. These include specialisation and division of labour, large-scale organisations, new sources of energy, technical developments, innovations in capital flows and in legal arrangements for doing business, the movement of populations from rural settings to cities, provision of general education, greater roles for managers, geographical expansion of markets and wider scope for trade. Together, these factors contribute to gains in productivity, so that more goods are produced, at lower costs; and, with national economies becoming more productive, workers are able—usually via political action and trades unions' efforts—to gain higher wages. A result is higher material standards of living, with people consuming a wide range of goods and services.

Industries permeate many aspects of individual lives and of societies, economies, politics and cultures. An organisation is described as being a unit in a particular industry if its activities contribute, in an industrious manner, to the production or marketing of a distinct category of goods, service or experience. An industrious manner is purposeful, persistent, routine. The garden in my house contributes to the production of vegetables but it is not in a vegetable industry, as this activity is not the purpose of the garden: the garden is mainly trees, shrubs and weeds. Besides, the activity is not assiduous: growing vegetables there is an occasional activity, not a constant routine.

Industries can overlap, so that one organisation can be in more than one, especially if it is sufficiently large. Publishers such as Pearson Education are in the book-publishing industry and also the education industry. Being in two at one time might require allocating resources to both. Publishers of academic books, for example, have certain employees working as editors and others who visit universities to promote sales.

Before the 1960s, references to collections of organisations providing services for tourists used expressions such as 'the tourist trades'. Now, the expression 'tourism industry' is widely used in everyday communication, the mass media, academic and professional dialogue, and governmental reports. Three separate factors came together to allow this idea to form and become accepted. The first was a natural evolution in language, when a simile of 'industry' became a metaphor. The second was a new concept in economics. The third was a political and economic need that led certain people to use

FIGURE 7.1 Three factors that came together and led to the widespread perception of tourism as 'an industry'

Factor	How the factor contributed to the perception
A simile evolved into a metaphor	The view that tourism is 'like an industry', because of its economic impacts, evolved via casual communication to 'is an industry'
Fisher's valid concept of 'tertiary industries', where managed services are the main activity, gained wide acceptance in the 1950s and 60s	A wide range of business organisations provide services used by tourists (information, transportation, accommodation, security, hospitality, entertainment etc.)
Desire among certain business organisations, notably hotels, to gain recognition by governments and the benefits flowing from this	By notionally combining all organisations supplying items to tourists, the combined effect was promoted as 'an industry' in public relations campaigns

the first two factors to rethink what tourism involves and apply the new idea in public relations. The three factors are summarised in Figure 7.1 and explained below.

Similes and metaphors of 'industry'

Researchers began studying the effects of tourists' spending on national economies in Europe about 100 years ago. The effects reminded them of the effects of industries. Like industries, international tourism resulted in more income for businesses, more foreign currency for national economies, and more employment. The similarity was noted by a growing number of economists during the 20th century. Over time, the simile 'tourism is like an industry' evolved via casual word usage, as often happens with similes, to become the metaphor 'tourism is an industry'.

The difference is irrelevant to economists interested in tourism, whose main concerns are measuring and analysing the effects of tourism on economies, not defining the scope of an industry.

During the 20th century the metaphor came to be accepted as realistic by many persons. This came about via a process that has shaped opinions in many areas of business and politics, a process noted in a famous remark from one of the 20th century's most famous books (Keynes 1973/1936: v):

Practical men, who believe themselves to be quite exempt from any intellectual influences, are usually the slaves of some defunct economist. Madmen in authority, who hear voices in the air, are distilling their frenzy from some academic scribbler of a few years back.

Most people interested in tourism who, since the 1960s, have become slaves to a defunct economist's concept of industry, would probably describe themselves as 'practical'. There is no problem in the way they acquired the concept, as similes evolving into metaphors and shaping language are not normally problematical, and is a natural process of language development (Jaynes 1982). The risk is that certain metaphors go feral and lead to mixed-up thinking, a process that excessively practical people might not notice.

Recognising service industries

An intellectual development in the 1930s provided the link that allowed the metaphoric tourism industry to be easily accepted as a realistic idea. This was a scheme devised by a young researcher employed in the Sydney head office of the Bank of New South Wales, now the Westpac Banking Corporation.

Fisher (1935) devised a conceptual scheme for arranging industries into three sorts: primary, secondary, and tertiary. He is not widely known for the invention, which is now a theme in economics courses describing modern economies and is widely known among educated persons. Primary industries such as farming, fishing and mining industries are those which extract commodities from the land or sea; secondary industries manufacture goods; in tertiary industries the central process is servicing.

Before Fisher, nobody seems to have regarded collections of service organisations as industries. Nobody had seen that the same principles of industrialisation that had been applied to manufacture and distribute goods since the earliest industrial revolutions were now being applied to the preparation, marketing and performance of services. Fisher's observation, that many services were becoming industrialised and should be recognised as such, gradually came to be acknowledged, first among economists and later in wider society. By the 1960s references to banking industries, insurance industries and other tertiary industries were becoming common in the mass media. These references laid foundations in modern culture for somebody to recognise tourism industries.

Since the 1960s, tertiary industries have become widely recognised for four reasons, just as Fisher predicted: (a) they are where most people are employed and (b) where most economic growth occurs; (c) they are a major source of rising living standards, because once people have ample goods they typically spend increasing proportions of their incomes on services. Flowing from these reasons is (d) that governments now recognise selected tertiary industries as appropriate targets for interventionist policies, intended to boost national and regional economies. For example, in several countries today, governments provide money and supportive facilities for tourism development in ecoomically depressed provincial regions away from major cities.

That is what Fisher was advocating in 1935. Ironically, the country in which he wrote his book was one of the last in the developed world to adopt the idea. In the 1960s, Australian governments' policies for economic development were still harnessed to old ideas about farms and factories, although the beginnings of change were apparent.

When other collections of organisations providing services gained recognition as industries, providers of services to tourists—especially owners and managers of large hotels—realised that advantages could be gained if their organisations obtained the same collective recognition. The main advantage would be greater profits, potentially available if governments recognised an industry deemed worthy of support via large subsidies and reduced taxation.

Simultaneously, people involved with community associations in various regions were becoming more aware of the potential economic benefits for wide interests in a community if more tourists visited their region and spent money. They too came to see that if tourism were recognised as an industry, governments would be more likely to provide support in various forms to develop and promote regions as tourist destinations.

Consequently, in the 1960s businesspeople involved with tourism began using terms such as 'tourism industry' or 'travel industry' in newsletters, press releases, speeches and other publications. This process began in the USA and Britain and became an international custom. Simultaneously, community leaders in many regions began using the same expressions. Thus the initial use of the expression 'tourism industry' involved a politically useful alliance of business leaders serving their individual commercial interests and civic leaders serving communitarian economic interests. Some individuals straddled both sides of the alliance, which in some cases gave them more influence and status.

An influential report containing ideas for developing tourism in Australia, prepared by a team of researchers from the USA (Harris, Kerr, Forster & Co. and Stanton, Robbins & Co. 1965), made extensive references to an industry. The report led to the government's decision to establish the Australian Tourist Commission in 1967.

The formation of the World Tourism Organisation in 1974 and its public relations messages during its formative years spread the idea of tourism as an industry, as did the first academic texts on the subject in the same decade. The formation of the World Travel and Tourism Council (WTTC) amplified the message further. The WTTC comprises approximately 100 individuals, all chief executive officers of major private-sector companies: airlines, hotels and resorts, tour operations and travel agencies. Besides direct communications with governments, messages on behalf of their collective interests are directed at opinion leaders among journalists, academics and politicians. The WTTC's slogan, *'Tourism, the world's largest industry and creator of jobs'*, is repeated in all its public relations messages, alongside a message to governments: the industry will grow further and deliver more economic largesse if governments support it more, in ways that the WTTC will suggest.

In universities, many academics engaged in research on aspects of tourism have helped propagate the message that tourism is an industry and that it is a very large and valuable one. Articles in journals such as *Annals of Tourism Research* often open with remarks along the lines of 'Tourism is widely acknowledged as one of the largest industries in the world'. What does this sort of message seek to achieve? It has never been merely recognition. What the WTTC, WTO and countless other associations affiliated with tourism in various countries wanted (and continue to want) are the real advantages that can follow recognition of an industry: support from banks and investors; and, most valuable of all, assistance from governments.

Banking issues ➤

In the 1960s, business leaders with interests in tourism could see how their activities, compared with interests in manufacturing, mining and farming, were disadvantaged in terms of banking issues. This occurred to some extent in several countries.

In Australia before the 1980s the banks were reluctant to make large loans or arrange capital finance for tourism-related ventures. This was largely because bankers did not fully understand how tourism-related businesses operated, being more attuned to farms and factories. It was also because tourism-related businesses were seen as bad risks, being typically small-scale enterprises with a high incidence of failure. If all the providers of services and goods used by tourists could be recognised as forming 'the tourism industry', however, collectively they could be presented to bankers, and to the business community in general, as a large and notable force in the economy. Bank policies might change as a result.

Seeking subsidies for promoting destinations ➤

Since the 1960s, business interests in many countries have used the idea of the tourism industry in campaigns to ask governments to subsidise the costs of promoting tourist destinations. In some countries, such as Britain, New Zealand and Australia, governments had been providing small subsidies for this purpose for decades. The campaigns begun in the 1960s sought much larger sums from governments' treasuries and, to a remarkable degree, have succeeded since the 1980s.

Globally, the numbers of tourists grew steadily through the 1950s and 60s, but each year more countries and regions were spending more money on advertising and related promotion. A reasonable belief developed that without sufficient efforts of this sort, countries and regions would record falling shares of tourist markets. This belief, that destinations were becoming increasingly competitive, created the perceived need for increasingly large expenditures on advertising and other promotional activities.

A widely used strategy among modern business entrepreneurs who proclaim beliefs in self-reliance and competitive economies is to find ways of using 'OPM' (other peoples' money) to pay for as many things as possible to help their businesses and their personal accounts prosper. A large source of OPM is governments' treasuries, and one of the functions of modern public servants and politicians is finding politically credible ways of dispensing it to appropriate sectional interests. To convince governments of the wisdom of allocating large sums of taxpayers' funds to subsidies for tourism interests, representatives of tourism-related businesses had to devise a strategy based on plausible arguments. Four tactics have been used in the strategy.

First, measuring by surveys how much is spent by tourists in a country over a year produces statistics that can be held up as representing the direct value of the tourism industry to the country's economy. Expenditures by an identifiable category of consumers (tourists) were held up to suggest the worth of an identifiable industry (tourism).

The second tactic has been to emphasise that tourism is indeed an industry. Horne (1976) and Drake and Nieuwenhuysen (1988) noted how governments especially favoured interests that they recognised as defined industries. Those writers did not fully explain why this is so, but another provided an answer. In political and governmental dialogue in modern Western countries, structure is a revered attribute (Saul 1992), and the simplest way to see structures in a regional or national economy over and above specific persons' interests (e.g. specific companies) is to recognise industries. A government subsidy to a private-sector company is politically risky, but giving the same sum to 'an industry' can be politically advantageous if public relations are in place. An industry association, representing the collection of companies, is normally essential for this tactic to succeed without controversy.

The third tactic has been to stress the line that more money is needed for promoting tourism because of the increasing competitiveness among destinations, and that when more visitors arrive their spending will lead to benefits across the economy. Economic gains attributable to the tourism industry have been calculated in numerous research and consultancy reports. In Australia, the report by Harris, Kerr, Forster & Co. and Stanton, Robbins & Co. (1965) was an early landmark. Recent examples include two from the Bureau of Tourism Research (O'Dea 1997a, 1997b).

Finally, and most significantly, there has been an argument that the tourism industry is unable to generate the necessary sums of money required for promoting destinations and that the public purse, via the government's treasury, is the only alternative. From time to time free-market ideologues in the treasury have opposed this argument, by pointing to an anomaly. If the tourism industry is really one of the largest in the country, why does it need so much government support? Moreover, if it is growing so rapidly, why does it need more every year?

The answer, according to its lobbyists, is a twofold one. Tourism is a huge but seriously handicapped industry, handicapped by its fragmented nature and its free-rider problem. (These twin issues are teased out later in this chapter.) Only government support in the form of large subsidies and other assistance, so the argument goes, can remedy these handicaps. As will be shown later, the economic issues are real and substantial. The political issues are another matter, for the question can be asked whether the tourism industry truly represents all tourism.

Recognition of the tourism industry in Australia ➤

Leaders of tourism associations decided on a broad strategy in the late 1960s. Aiming to change perceptions in the minds of key publics, they had to create the impression and build it into a belief that tourism was an industry—was valuable economically and deserved governmental support.

Public relations campaigns throughout the 1970s achieved the goal by the decade's end. The first real steps, simple recognition, occurred in 1972–75 when Whitlam's Australian Labor Party government was in office in Canberra. It established a Ministry of Tourism. In 1976 the newly elected Liberal Coalition government scrapped the Ministry and abandoned any semblance of tourism policy.

Three years later, responding to lobbying by tourism industry interests, the government changed tack. The policy change followed the receipt of report from a parliamentary inquiry (Select Committee on Tourism 1978). The government re-established the Ministry and announced that tourism was now recognised as an industry deserving substantial support and, backing up its words with money, raised the Australian Tourist Commission's budget by 300% in one year. In the years since 1979, the Commonwealth government has put increasing amounts of public money into tourism promotion and development, mainly as subsidies for the ATC.

After 1979 new campaigns were launched, notably in the USA and Japan, promoting Australia as a destination. The Australian government spent $20 million in 1980 supporting the tourism industry. Through the 1980s and 90s lobbyists sought increasing levels of assistance, and successive governments agreed to meet the requests. By 2000 the support reached $100 million. Probably it was a good investment, as the number of visitors had increased greatly, and substantial economic gains had flowed to many business interests and to wider communities in the form of more employment opportunities.

Describing and defining the tourism industry ➤

By 1980, recognition of the tourism industry was well established in public opinion and in government policies in many countries. There have been many attempts, in various countries, to describe and define it. The following description by a Canadian researcher is typical of descriptions internationally (S.L.J. Smith 1989: 10):

> *Consider your last vacation. You may have purchased a travel book from a local bookseller and read about a new resort that appealed to you. You booked a reservation at the resort through a travel agent and reserved an airline seat at the same time. While waiting for your departure date, you bought new luggage and resort clothing. When the departure date arrived, you called a local taxi company to get a ride to the airport and then rented a car at the other end. While on the trip you ate in local restaurants, danced in local clubs, bought local crafts, and visited some attractions. You purchased gasoline for your rental car and picked up a few sundries at a drugstore. You may even have visited a clinic for treatment of sunburn. Part way through the trip you called home to tell everyone how wonderful the vacation was ... You made tourism-related purchases from a bookstore, a travel agent, three different commercial transportation companies, an accommodation establishment, several food service operations, different retail shops, a medical clinic, and a telecommunications business ... In addition to these direct providers of tourism commodities, one can identify other types of organisations and firms that help support the tourism industry.*

While descriptions are relatively easy to formulate, the same cannot be said about definitions on this topic. A report from the Australian Department of Tourism claimed 'the diversity of the industry makes it difficult to define', but stated that it 'consists of many different types of businesses' (Department of Tourism 1992: 5). It listed 'the core of tourism business' as (1992: 5):

Accommodation: hotels/resorts, motels, hostels, caravans, camping; Transportation: airlines, cruise ships, rail, car rental, bus/coaches; Attractions: man-made, natural; Food & beverage: restaurants, fast food, wine merchants; Travel agencies; Tour Companies; Souvenirs; Luggage; Hotel and restaurant suppliers; Taxi services; Cameras and film; Maps, travel books; Shopping malls; Service stations; Sporting events; Banking services; Reservation systems; Auto clubs; Entertainment & arts venues; Museums/historic sites; Construction/real estate; Distillers/ brewers/bottlers; Motor vehicles; Airplane manufacturers; Motor fuel producers; Clothing manufacturers; Communications networks; Education and training institutions; Recreation/sporting equipment; Food producers; Advertising media; Cartographers/printers.

The Department of the Treasury expressed the same idea more precisely than the long descriptive form used by Smith (1989) and the Department of Tourism (1992). The Treasury's report (1977: 1212) stated:

The tourism industry is defined, not in terms of the production of particular types of goods or services, but in terms of the circumstances in which goods and services are consumed. Thus the sale of a particular good or service to a tourist is counted as 'tourist expenditure' while the sale of the same good or service to a local resident is not. As a result of this difference in concept, the tourist industry overlaps the usual classification of industries defined according to the goods and services they produce.

Another way of expressing this definition is that when tourists spend money, on anything, the money is deemed to be revenue of the tourism industry, which comprises the direct recipients of the money.

The utility of this concept of the tourism industry

Several practical uses stem from this concept of the tourism industry, as described and defined above. These uses are identified in the following sections.

Identification of sectors in tourism industries ➤

As a result of the broad scope arising from the descriptions and definition noted above, a custom has developed of classifying the components of a tourism industry by sector. Each sector comprises suppliers of similar items, such as transport and accommodation. The sectoral arrangement gives a sense of structure to a tourism industry. It enables employees in different lines of business to see how they fit into the larger and complex whole. It helps people better understand tourism industries.

Discussing 'the tourism industry' as a generic term, when activities in specific places is not the topic, the number of sectors varies. Depending on detail required, anything from three to 10 or more could be identified. A seven-sector analysis is shown below. It cannot be precise; in the real world there are fuzzy boundaries between sectors. This example can be described as a highly developed tourism industry:

1. A *marketing specialist sector* of a tourism industry comprises retail travel agents, tour wholesalers, and promotional agencies of national and regional tourism organisations. The sector's main locations are in traveller-generating regions, places where people make decisions about trips before setting off, the best places for selling and other promotional activities.

2. A *carrier sector* includes public transport specialists such as motor coach, airline, railway and shipping lines. The main activities are along transit routes, but this sector's activities reach into generating and destination regions.

3. An *accommodation sector* includes organisations providing lodging and related services such as food and drink to tourists. Its main location is in tourist destinations, and it also functions at points in transit routes. Examples are resorts, hotels, motels, traveller hostels, condominiums, holiday apartments, camping grounds, caravan parks and guest houses.

4. An *attractions sector* is made up of organisations aiming to provide tourists with leisure experiences of any kind. Its locations are mainly in destinations, and also along transit routes. Theme parks, roadside attractions, museums, art galleries, entertainment and sporting venues are included.

5. A *tour operator sector* contains organisations that assemble or conduct prepackaged arrangements for tourists. Ingredients packaged might be transport, accommodation and attractions, using services drawn from organisations in those sectors. This sector is located in all three geographical elements of whole systems. In traveller-generating regions there are outbound tour operator-wholesalers; in transit routes and destination regions, inbound tour operators and local operators of various kinds.

6. A *coordinating sector* includes units within government tourism departments that attempt to coordinate operations or developments of any other sectors. It also includes similar units within global, regional and industrial tourism organisations.

7. A *miscellaneous sector* is the convenient category for left-overs. It takes in souvenir, duty-free, luggage and all other retail shops where tourists spend money, banks providing travellers' cheques and other banking services, currency exchange bureaux, car rental businesses and travel insurance companies. It includes suppliers of all goods and services not included in the other six sectors, used by tourists, where the suppliers have appropriate policies and strategies for tourism.

Many small-scale organisations are active in just one sector, but larger ones might be active in several. Qantas Airways has activities in three: the marketing specialist, the carrier and the tour operator sectors.

In practice, in specific cases—in particular whole systems—a tourism industry might not have all seven sectors listed above. A basic tourism industry might contain:

▮ *attractions*, as described in the list above;

▮ *accommodation*, as described above;

▮ *amenities*, such as restaurants and other sources of food and drinks, as well as retail shops providing a range of goods and services.

This sort of basic tourism industry can be found in many places functioning as destinations or stopover points in transit routes, where tourists do not use travel agents or tour operators for pre-trip packages or other pre-trip arrangements and do not use public carriers (e.g. airlines) to reach the destination. Instead, the tourists make their own arrangements and use their own vehicles for transport.

Increased investment ➤

Recognition of the tourism industry by governments in many countries in the 1980s was followed by greater levels of investment in the promotion of destinations and the development of resources used by tourists. Increased investment in training and education programs helped improve the knowledge and skills of new recruits and existing employees. In the 1990s there was a notable increase in the number of research projects on tourism. Australia's Co-operative Research Centre in Sustainable Tourism, a joint venture involving several universities and companies, used government subsidies to sponsor dozens of new projects every year.

Banks become more willing to invest ➤

With the growing recognition of the tourism industry, banks and other financial institutions dealing with businesses have been more willing to deal with tourism interests than they were before. This allows investors more scope for raising capital.

A focus for government policy ➤

Reflecting their need for structures (Saul 1992), governments—more precisely, politicians and public servants—require focal points before industrial policies are formulated; in the case of tourism, this became clear during the 1970s. Institutions representing the tourism industry in general, in its various sectors and in its activities in specific regions, have become media for communication with governments.

In Australia the generic institutions now include the Australian Tourist Commission (a national promotional agency officially reporting to the Commonwealth parliament), the National Office of Tourism (a unit within a public service department), the Australian Tourism Export Council (a private-sector association of inbound tour operators and affiliated organisations interested in promoting international tourism to Australia), and the Tourism Task Force (a lobby group representing several dozen large hotels and affiliated businesses).

Tax concessions ➤

For many years, tourism businesses were denied the same tax benefits allowed to businesses in industries enjoying government recognition. An advantage flowing from the recognition that has developed since the 1960s has been a more extensive range of tax benefits. In Australia before 1979, for example, depreciation costs for buildings were not allowed as tax deductions by companies operating hotels and other forms of tourist accommodation, while deprecation costs on factory and farm buildings were allowed as tax deductions. The difference meant that tourism accommodation enterprises paid proportionately more income tax, making their cash flows relatively smaller and their investments much less appealing to capitalists and bankers.

This restricted tourism entrepreneurs' access to investment capital, increased their costs of capital and lowered their after-tax profits. When the owners of tourist-use buildings were granted the right to claim depreciation as a tax deduction, those disadvantages were removed.

Government subsidies for promoting destinations ➤

Australian governments had been giving token levels of support for tourism promotion since 1928, when ANTA (Australian National Travel Association) was formed as a private-sector club for conducting advertising and publicity about Australian tourist destinations in a small number of international generating countries, such as the UK and USA. Every year ANTA received a small subsidy, a token gesture of approval, from the Commonwealth government. Meanwhile, Australian state governments had been supporting their railways with promotional agencies called tourist bureaux, which by the 1970s had evolved into departments of tourism.

In 1967, the Australian government established a national promotional agency to promote Australia as a destination. The Australian Tourist Commission (ATC) replaced ANTA in this role, and, as a governmental commission, had potential access to larger subsidies. Ten years later, however, its expenditure on international promotion was tiny, compared with amounts spent by many other countries. The ATC's annual budget in the late 1970s was only $3 million, and it could not afford to spend nearly as much as most countries.

The contrast was dramatically revealed in an analysis of expenditures on tourism advertising in the USA, by all countries, presented in a paper prepared for a parliamentary inquiry (Leiper & Stear 1978). It showed that Australia ranked 43rd in spending by all countries being promoted as tourist destinations, spending about the same amount as Bulgaria and Tunisia. The paper received prominent attention in newspapers, where it was held up as evidence of neglected opportunities for developing inbound tourism to Australia. This was at a time when the Australian economy needed more foreign exchange, due to a deteriorating balance of payments. Inbound tourism seemed an obvious remedy, if a way could be found to make it grow. More money spent on advertising and other promotions, aiming to induce more international tourists to visit, seemed an obvious remedy.

The parliamentary inquiry on tourism (Select Committee 1978) received advice from dozens of interest groups and a handful of disinterested academics. Much of the advice recommended that the parliament should instruct the government to properly recognise tourism as an industry and increase spending on its development. In 1979 the Minister for Tourism put in place a number of policies to that end (described elsewhere in this chapter).

Pride and professionalism among employees ➤

Being 'in the tourism industry' gives thousands of employees a sense of pride and professionalism, leading to widespread advantages for them, for their employers, for their customers, and for the economy. Pride in one's work is a desirable condition for everyone directly involved—in this case workers, tourists and employers. The feeling encourages workers' motivation, which can lead to higher and more consistent standards of service.

Growing recognition of the tourism industry as a large and thriving entity has led to its becoming regarded as a field for professional careers, not just a place to work for a while, and not just as a source of income. In 1960s Australia, as in many other countries, most employees working in hotels, restaurants and tour operations regarded their jobs as temporary occupations, merely a source of income. Without intentions of remaining for long, they had little interest in education for a career, and their employers had no interest in trying to train them beyond the immediate requirements of routine tasks.

Years ago, service work in hotels, restaurants and similar places was regarded as work that most people would avoid if possible. It was a low-status occupation, revealed as such in many historical records, including George Orwell's famous autobiographical *Down and Out in Paris and London* (1933).

There is no doubt that since the 1970s the new image of tourism as a large industry generally appreciated by the community has helped alter attitudes towards service work in some parts of the world. It is not a universal trend, of course. In many places service workers are underpaid and exploited, and service work is still regarded in these places as something only desperately poor persons would seek. Ehrenreich's (2000) book *Nickel and Dimed: On (Not) Getting By in America*, based on her investigative journalism in Florida's hotels and restaurants, is notable in this context.

Nationalistic themes have been undertones of propaganda used by tourism industry institutions in Australia, New Zealand and some other countries to encourage service workers to feel proud about their work. This is achieved by invoking the image of tourism as one of the country's largest and most valuable industries and linking this image to the workers, encouraged to feel patriotic for their large contribution to the nation's economy.

A convenient focus for environmental concerns ➤

'The tourism industry' has been a convenient focus for environmental activists concerned with two types of environmental damage associated with tourism. In Australia, activist groups such as The Wilderness Society and the Australian Conservation Foundation conduct campaigns to protect land with valuable natural features. This can give rise to both types. First, they might call on the tourism association in the region where the land is located to add its voice to their campaign, by pointing out that the natural feature needs preserving because it is a valuable resource for tourism. Many cases where this happens occur every year. In another type of protest, the tourism industry is cast in the role of villain. This occurs when property exploiters plan to build tourist resorts in places that will destroy the natural habitat of endangered species or damage the recreational amenity of members of the local human species.

Environmental activists protest. Property exploiters hire public relations companies, some of whom will promote anything if a fee is on offer and are usually able to get support from at least some members of a local tourism industry association. The media then begins publishing stories about the thousands of jobs that will be created if the resort is built and about the need for 'balance' between those desirable outcomes ('progress') and the 'regrettable damage' to environments. Environmental activists step up the protests.

The phoney issue of 'balance' is seldom discussed in the public relations battles that follow. (The issue is analysed in Chapter 10.)

Many cases of both types of environmental issue linked to the tourism industry have occurred in Australia since the 1960s. Newpapers carry accounts of these cases.

THE CONTENTIOUS TOURISM INDUSTRY

The idea of a tourism industry as described and defined above, as the supplier of all things to all tourists, is contentious. Critics in countries including the USA, Australia and New Zealand have argued that the idea is conceptually flawed, and that it leads to faulty decisions in practice. This dispute is explored below.

Critics and what is said in response

There is no dispute with Fisher's view that many services used by tourists can be industrialised to some degree, nor with the view that various tourism-specific industries can be identified among the organisations involved with tourists. What the critics dispute is the claim that lumping all such organisations together makes the collection a single entity, the tourism industry. They say that this is an imaginary industry, not a real one, because the entire collection does not function in the ways that industries function.

In response to these critics, the message from lobby groups has been blunt, emphatically repeating that 'tourism is an industry'. In Australia that emphatic message was especially notable in the late 1970s. A speech in 1979 by the then Minister for Tourism in the Australian government, Phillip Lynch, repeated at least six times that 'tourism is an industry'. The reiteration could be inferred as a sign that Lynch and his advisers were concerned that the message was not winning enough hearts and minds.

In the USA in the 1980s the controversy led a professor to poke fun at the people behind the campaign to gain recognition for the tourism industry by describing them as 'a bunch of businessmen in search of an industry' (R.C. Mill, pers. comm.), a description of considerable precision.

In Australia in the 1990s the controversy was observed by a woman who had retired after 10 years as a financial trader in the city and who launched an adventure tour business in a seaside resort town. After a year immersed in her new business and the local tourism association, she remarked on the difference between her former field of work and her new field. 'People working in finance', she said, 'do not sit around discussing the existence and scope of the finance industry and worrying because outsiders can't see it'. Many more examples of this sort could be listed.

A huge fragmented industry with a free-rider problem?

The tourism industry is often described as fragmented, and this characteristic, along with the associated free-rider problem, was one of the justifications in requests that governments pay large subsidies for promoting tourist destinations. Its alleged fragment-ation is also the basis for the critics' argument that tourism is not really industrialised in the way its boosters claim. Before explaining the argument, I will describe the alleged characteristic of fragmentation.

Fragmentation in this case refers to a condition where the industry's component business organisations can be bisected into the following categories.

The first category comprises organisations such as travel agents, tour operators, tour wholesalers, airlines, cruise-ship lines, hotels, and other forms of commercial accommo-dation used by tourists, theme parks, duty-free shops, and souvenir shops. These organisations share certain characteristics. They all provide some kind of service related to the distinctive needs of tourists. Reflecting the first characteristic, many and in some cases all of their customers are tourists or travellers. Also, they club together, recognising their common interests in fostering travel and tourism. One important aspect of the clubbing tendency is a willingness to participate in tourism industry associations and to contribute money and effort to cooperative programs for promoting tourist flows into the places where they are operating.

The second category comprises an enormous range of business organisations, provid-ing all sorts of goods and services used by consumers generally. General retailers are included here: supermarkets, department stores, pharmacies, newsagents, food shops, hairdressers, clothing and shoe shops, bookshops, shops selling electrical appliances, household durables and motor vehicles. They share four characteristics relevant to the issue under discussion.

They all have tourists among their customers, but usually the proportion of tourists to total customers is relatively small. Because they supply such a wide range of goods and services purchased by tourists, they are the direct recipients in many regions of a sizable share of total spending by tourists. For various reasons they generally do not join and participate in tourism industry associations and, furthermore, they typically reject invitations to contribute to cooperative programs for promoting tourist flows into the places where they are operating. Moreover, managers of most of these businesses have no conscious awareness of their alleged industrial affiliation. Asked if they are in the tourism industry, most will say 'no'. Because of these chacteristics, this second category of organisations are the reason why many observers have described the tourism industry as 'fragmented'.

Among academic writers, Burkart (1981a, 1981b) and S.L.J. Smith (1988, 1989, 1991) have been forceful advocates of the legitimacy of the view that the tourism industry includes both categories of organisations: those that specialise in tourism, and those who supply most of the range of goods and services and give the industry its fragmented quality. The same view appears to be shared by most academics writing about tourism, by public-sector agencies responsible for tourism and by groups such as the World Tourism Organisation and the World Travel and Tourism Council.

A consequence of fragmentation is that tourism associations in towns around Australia and similar countries have employees who spend time soliciting for members. This involves trying to persuade retailers of all sorts of goods and services that because they have tourists among their customers they are part of the tourism industry and should be actively helping with promotion and development campaigns. A common slogan used in public relations to encourage this involvement is 'Tourism—Everybody's Business'.

Generally these campaigns have failed, for most businesses have not taken steps to make tourism their business, despite the fact that they earn income from tourists. The failures have not deterred the sponsors, mainly public-sector agencies such as Tourism New South Wales, from continuing the campaigns year after year.

Free riders on tourism promotion

Businesses that earn a portion of their income from tourists without doing anything to promote tourism, not contributing to community and regional promotion, are, in a sense, 'free riders' on the promotional campaigns that are funded by others. Understanding the free-rider problem is helped by knowledge of the economic theory of public goods. While these are called 'goods', they are more often services that are used freely by members of the public and are provided normally by governments, because markets do not provide them.

An example is street lighting. Everyone in a street at night uses it, without paying, because asking for payment is not feasible. No private-sector company wants to set up a business to light public streets because it is a service that cannot be feasibly marketised. Governments pay for street lights by using tax revenue, collected from all taxpayers. Street lights are a communitarian service—a public good, not a marketised service.

Promoting a region or country as a tourist destination can be seen as a kind of public good. Markets do not generate sufficient money to pay the costs of these promotions. Why should hoteliers or tour operators spend money independently, or contribute money to a pooled fund for marketing Australia as a tourist destination country, or for their local region, when they might get nothing in return but might see other hotels, tour operators, supermarkets, restaurants and other businesses getting more income from the tourists who have been induced to visit because of the promotion? These 'others' are the free riders: like fare evaders on a bus, they ride for free on promotion campaigns that they have not paid for.

The free-rider problem is much larger than the 'fragmented industry' issue, because all sorts of businesses supplying goods or services to tourists are affected by it. Market theory advises against private expenditure on marketing tourist destinations. According to marketing theory, such expenditures are akin to purely charitable donations, given without any thought of personal benefit, and businesses generally are not sufficiently charitable to support other businesses in that way.

A solution to the problem is the same solution used for hundreds of years in relation to public goods: convince governments that tourists visiting a region or country provide a public good, that free-rider problems prevent the tourism industry from paying for the promotional campaigns that persuade them to visit, and that therefore, governments should pay most, if not all, of the cost.

In order to convince governments to do this, lobbyists and public relations experts hired by the tourism industry have spent a lot of time and money issuing messages to persuade politicians and the opinion leaders who shape government policies of a number of points. These are that (a) tourism is an industry; (b) the economic benefits it brings to destinations are substantial; (c) these benefits are spread all over the economy, because 'tourism is everyone's business'; and (d) the fragmented nature of the tourism industry and its free-rider problem means that promotion should be treated as a public good.

Referring to the political status of the tourism industry in Britain, a commentator remarked that 'it is because tourism is perceived as a growth industry, as a wealth and jobs creator, that it is so powerful' (Hewison 1988: 239–40). The same can be said in many other countries. 'Perceived' is the key word. The political power of the tourism industry in Australia is seen in the fact that its leaders and lobbyists have been able to raise the level of subsidies provided by the Commonwealth government from $3 million in the late 1970s to well in excess of $100 million by 2000.

Why 'tourism industry' as economic impact seems dubious

Critical thinkers have suggested that in fact there is not one industry but many tourism industries. This view has been advanced from many sources, ranging from American business consultants Kaiser and Helber (1978) to a minister for tourism in the Australian government (Hockey 2002).

Stronger critics go further. They agree that there are many tourism industries, but point to the fact that most of the organisations supplying tourists with services and goods, the so-called 'fragmented' units, are not really in the business of tourism and therefore not in any tourism industries. They point out that for an organisation to have a business relationship to a specific type of consumer requires recognising the distinctive characteristics of those consumers and acting in ways that meet their distinctive needs. These qualities can be seen in hotels, travel agencies, tour operators etc. They also claim that for an organisation to be part of an industry requires, axiomatically, that it has industrious activities—purposeful, persistent, routine.

These two conditions are certainly found among organisations that provide services for the distinctive needs of tourists, such as hotels, travel agents and tour operators. These organisations relate to tourists in a businesslike and industrious manner. These qualities are usually absent in the commercial dealings between most suppliers of goods and services and consumers that just happen to be tourists. For example, supermarkets do not normally treat consumers who happen to be tourists in any distinctive way. The fact that tourists are often among the customers and have economic impact is incidental, not a fact with any relevance to the supermarket's business strategies or its policies regarding industrial associations. Supermarkets and countless other kinds of suppliers of goods and services used by tourists are normally not in the business of tourism.

In popular tourist destinations, a supermarket's manager might decide that there is good sense in treating tourists in a distinctive way—targeting the tourists with special promotions, for example. In such cases, a supermarket could be described as being in the business of tourism. But cases like these are the exception, not the general rule.

Butchers, bakers and candlestick makers

To imagine that a tourism industry is created by tourists wandering around and spending money, converting resources into an industry by their presence and activity, is just that—imagination. The same imagination alongside simplistic ideas about what actually constitutes an industry could see left-handed persons in the butcher's, baker's and candlestick-maker's shops and decide that these shops must be in the left-handed industry. If anyone proposed that this idea had practical implications for those shops they would be regarded, quite properly, as being seriously out of touch with reality.

The error in principle beneath these imaginative leaps is the mistake of 'using a single construal for paradigm development' (Oliva & Reidenbach 1987: 136). Tourists and left-handed persons are single construals. Their presence might be construed as an indicator for the existence of an industry, but one cannot use one indicator to infer that. Moreover, using an indicator on the demand side of tourism economics is wrong-sided for identifying an industry. Industries are the sources of supply in tourism economics.

To identify industrial activity in tourism systems requires a supply-side view, by examining how businesses are managed. It cannot be guessed by looking for tourists, which is what S.L.J. Smith (1988) implied when he referred to a 'supply-side view', although Smith's perspective has been described as 'a so-called supply-side view' (Gilbert 1991: 18).

SUMMARY: TWO CONCEPTS OF TOURISM INDUSTRY

Since the 1960s, two concepts of 'tourism industry' have developed. Distinguishing between them, in order to use each one in an appropriate manner, is important. A summary is presented in Figure 7.2.

The tourism industry according to tourists' expenditure

The commonly recognised idea of the tourism industry, based on measuring tourists' expenditures, is useful and appropriate for describing the economic effects of tourists' spending and the consequences of their use of resources. It is useful for seeing where the money goes and monitoring trends. Those are the only truthful applications of the idea. Beyond those applications, the idea has limits that should be observed but are often ignored. It is quite inappropriate for making comparisons with other industries. Claims that the tourism industry is larger than other industries are irrational when they rest, as they always do, on this idea.

An error of principle is the assumption that one industry can be defined by unique criteria. All industries must be defined by similar concepts and measured by the same criteria if people are to speak meaningfully about one industry compared in any way to others.

FIGURE 7.2 Two concepts of 'industry' associated with tourism

Concept	Basis and scope	Uses and limitations
The tourism industry is everything linked with tourism	All activities of all tourists are inferred to reflect 'the industry'	Useful as a measure of tourism's economic impact, but misleading as a guide for management, policy, planning and sustainable tourism
Tourism industries as collections of organisations in the business of tourism, working cooperatively to some degree and possibly competing	Any such industry includes only organisations with business strategies focused on tourists and with linkages via managed cooperative networks	Useful as a guide for management, policy, planning and sustainable tourism. It reduces the size and importance of tourism industries (but not of tourism). It is difficult to identify and measure such industries, as every supplier must be assessed

The concept of the tourism industry based on tourists' expenditures has no relevance to business management. To suggest, as many tourism boosters have, that every organisation supplying goods or services to tourists is in the business of tourism is to be out of touch with reality. For more than a decade, governmental agencies such as Tourism New South Wales have issued countless posters asserting that 'Tourism is Everybody's Business'. The campaign might comfort its believers, but it confuses the gullible and wastes public money.

In summary, several beliefs about 'the tourism industry' have depended more on faith than on rational understanding, and accordingly have not really helped tourism interests to gain full acceptance in the wider business and political communities. Recently, the CEO of a large company in the business of tourism expressed dismay that 'after all these years, many public servants as well as managers in the wider economy still do not accept that tourism is a large and valuable industry'.

Tourism industries according to business management

Tourism industries exist. They vary in size and in composition. All comprise a number of organisations in the business of tourism. All of these business organisations (travel agencies, tour operators, hotels, motels, airlines, cruise lines, theme parks and others) are managed with tourists in mind. Some of these tourism industries operate worldwide, others are localised.

In terms of the seven-sector analysis set out earlier in this chapter, many tourism industries contain business organisations from all seven sectors, and some have a less diverse sectoral spread. In combination, tourism industries supply only a portion of the goods and services consumed by tourists. That is the basis for describing tourism as partly industrialised, a concept that is explored in more detail in a number of later chapters.

CONCLUSION

This chapter began by identifying the origins of the idea of the tourism industry. It then described how the idea was spread and how it came to be widely recognised. Certain practical uses were identified: these are in the domains of public relations, inside and outside organisations involved with tourism. Another practical use is in economics, referring to the economic impacts of tourism.

Those practical uses are based not on any substantive observations of a real industry in a functioning sense, akin to other industries, but on a notional one, imagined from observing huge numbers of tourists doing all sorts of things and making guesses about 'the industry' presumably behind all these activities. Subjected to scrutiny, and thought about in a precise way, the image of a huge industry supplying everything to tourists can be seen to be erroneous and misleading (Tolstoy 1997/1910: 233):

> *Many statements which are accepted as truth because they have been passed down to us look like truth only because we have never tested them, never thought about them in a precise way.*

The tone in sections of this chapter has been skeptical, appropriate when one of the emerging messages is that an economic image has been devised and used for a variety of political purposes, some admirable and others questionable or erroneous. In Chapter 11 the discussion will identify a number of ways in which tourism industries are formed and managed. More detail relating to the industrialisation process will be explored. Argument and evidence will reinforce the view that tourism industries are real but the process of industrialisation is limited, unlike many other sectors of modern economies. This limits the scope of tourism management.

Discussion questions

1. What are the three categories of industry identified first by Fisher in the 1930s? In which category do tourism industries fit best, and why?

2. The expression 'tourism industry' first emerged comparatively recently, after 1960. What were three factors that came together when the idea of a tourism industry emerged?

3. In what ways has the idea of 'the tourism industry' associated with the economic effects of tourism been useful in relation to pride and professionalism among employees?

4. The title for Chapter 7 refers to 'economics and politics': in what ways is the commonly recognised idea of the tourism industry linked to economics and politics?

5. What are 'free riders' in the context of tourism industries? Why are they seen as problematical?

6. How is the free-rider problem normally solved?

7. Two concepts exist for the 'tourism industry', one based on the receipt of tourists' expenditures and one based on business management practices. Which of the two is larger, and why?

8. Why are two concepts of 'tourism industry' useful for understanding the topic?

9. List the sectors in a highly developed tourism industry; give each sector a name and give examples of business organisations in each sector.

Recommended reading

Buckminster-Fuller, Richard 1972, Designing a new industry, pp 153–220 in *The Buckminster Fuller Reader,* James Mellor (ed.), London: Penguin

Hall, Colin Michael 1994, *Tourism and Politics: Policy, Power and Place,* Chichester: Wiley

Pretes, Michael 2003, Tourism and nationalism, *Annals of Tourism Research* 30: 125–42

Schivelbusch, W. 1986, *The Railway Journey: The Industrialization of Time and Space in the 19th Century,* New York: Berg

Smith, S.L.J. 1991, The supply-side definition of tourism, *Annals of Tourism Research,* 18: 312–18

Management
and its Roles
in Tourism
Industries

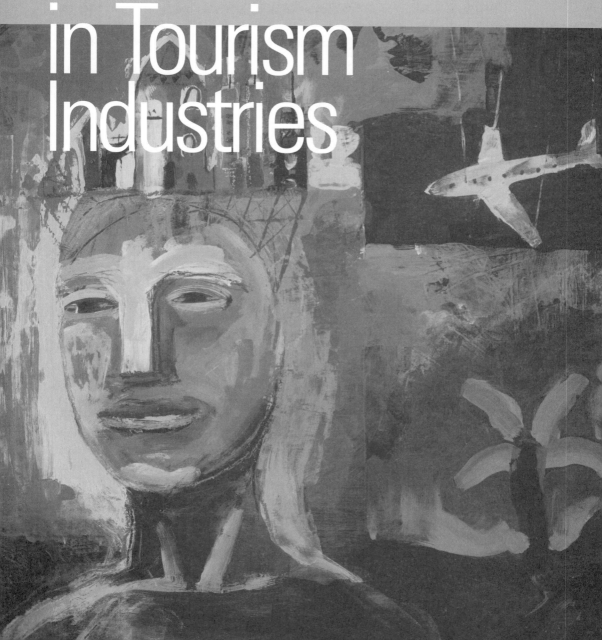

INTRODUCTION

Management issues have emerged sporadically in earlier chapters, where the main theme was tourism systems. In this chapter the relationship is reversed. Theories of management are the main theme, illustrated with descriptions of managers' practical work in examples drawn from tourism industries.

More people are studying management now than ever before. Jobs requiring managerial competence are plentiful, growing in number, well-paid and with prospects for progression to highly rewarded positions in a range of occupations across many industries. For many people managerial work is interesting because of its challenges, and also its variety, in two senses—work roles and work locations. Managers are seldom stuck in one place all day. As a profession, it suits those who want to participate in managing organisations, in the private and public sectors, that serve society in beneficial ways.

'Management' is an expression with overlapping meanings. It refers to people who manage, knowledge about managing, and functional activities or roles of managers. As these meanings are not contradictory, the variations are not problematical.

The discussion below begins with remarks about standards. The next theme is the distinction between managerial work and the work of the organisations being managed. A key question, 'Why do organisations have managers?', is explored in a section about schools of thought in management. This leads to a description of the work of managers. Three brief sections round off the chapter, based on the following questions. Which, among all their roles, is central—managers' most important role? What do successful managers need to know? Who actually manages tourism?

STANDARDS OF MANAGEMENT PRACTICES

High and low standards of management practice can be found in many industries. Seeking to improve the average, an industry Taskforce on Leadership and Management Skills conducted 20 studies over the period 1991–94 (Karpin 1994b). Led by practising managers, the taskforce was financed by the Australian government and supported by a number of major corporations, while academics from universities provided the research.

Its report contains recommendations about management education. One reason for low standards of managerial performance might be that few Australian managers have formal education at tertiary level: only 20% of senior managers have degrees, compared with 85% in both Japan and the USA (Ashenden & Milligan 1994: 41). The condition might be worse than indicated, because degrees held by managers seldom have much management content. A little knowledge on a subject can be a dangerous thing, and can lead to misplaced confidence.

While most managers have high ethical standards and a sense of social responsibility, some are obviously deficient in these areas (Saul 1992, 1995, 2001). In 2002, top managers in several giant American corporations, most notably Enron and WorldCom, were revealed as corrupt, using fraudulent techniques to take many millions for themselves while damaging the corporations they were supposed to be managing, causing major problems in the wider society. Tens of thousands of employees lost their jobs, and economic problems rippled across the economy (Krugman 2002; Overington 2002; Chancellor 2002; Gottliebsen 2002). Similar cases have been revealed in Australia, described in hundreds of reports in newspapers. In this book, I do not discuss ethics, but readers can go to books by Solomon (1992) and Singer (1993). Issues of civic values in management, related to ethics, are raised at various stages in this book.

RESOURCES, ORGANISATIONS AND MANAGING

Resources

Managing always relates to resources. A person cannot be a manager without having power over resources, that is, they have an organisation of some kind to manage. In the context of management, an organisation is a collection of resources that a manager can influence, in all its broad components, by decisions and actions.

For example, in my study today the resources I am managing include books, materials and equipment on the desk, organised to make my work efficient and effective, which makes it easier. My diary has a plan for the working hours. Looking at the clock periodically provides a control device around that plan, allowing time management.

Any collection of any items can be regarded as an organisation (Feibleman & Friend 1945), and understanding the links between managers and organisations can be helped by considering the differences between unmanaged and managed organisations. The former can be seen in the natural and human worlds—piles of rocks caused by landslips, swarms of bees, crowds of sightseeing tourists. These unmanaged organisations might seem chaotic, but surrealist philosophers such as André Breton believe that there is no such thing as chaos. Chaos, they say, is an illusion. What other people might perceive as chaos is, in the surrealist vision, unrecognised and as yet uncategorised order.

While few managers know much about surrealism, all practising managers implicitly display agreement with it, for managing depends on recognising the potential for order in organisations and involves fostering some kind of order. Stone masons manage piles of rocks by sorting them into categories for different purposes, bee-keepers manage swarms by applying smoke, and swarms of tourists can be managed too, by various methods.

Organisations

Organisations are commonly referred to by labels designating their legal or structural status, such as company, corporation, firm, enterprise, business, partnership, association, commission, group, department, division, party, team. 'Organisation' is a convenient expression embracing them all. Organisations have different sizes, purposes, aims, strategies, structures and cultures, leading to different approaches and methods by managers. Consider two extremes, small and large.

Small organisations are often established with three primary purposes benefiting the proprietors: giving them something to do, giving them an income, and allowing them relative independence—as their own boss. Thus, a small motel can use simple strategies and basic business methods for a single line of business, supplying transit accommodation; and it needs only a simple organisational structure, one or two employees sharing all managerial and operational tasks.

Giant corporations and large public service departments often have complex purposes with multiple aims, and require large organisations with complex methods and elaborate structures combining bureaucratic, entrepreneurial and political characteristics.

Management generally relates to organisations with one or more human beings as members and with goals or reasons for existence, goals consciously set by humans; they are 'purposeful' organisations (Ackoff & Emery 1972). When conditions *seem* relatively chaotic, people remark that the organisation has a management problem. This indicates a fuller statement of a principle noted earlier.

Managing is about imposing and maintaining order of some kind in purposeful human organisations, appropriate to their aims. Worth emphasising is the phrase 'of some kind'. There are different kinds of order, reflected in different values in different schools of management thought. Relevant to all of these schools is variety. Managing involves dealing with variety: sometimes enhancing it, sometimes reducing it. Waelchli's (1989) article on the theme is recommended for readers interested in exploring management theory. Waelchli's ideas are discussed later in this book, in relation to an issue of tourism management.

The relationship of managers to the organisation they manage can be regarded systematically and depicted in a diagram with three elements: (a) managers, (b) an organisation being managed, and (c) managerial work (Figure 8.1).

The element to the left in Figure 8.1 are managers, one or more persons who make decisions and take action that influences an organisation from within. They might or might not have 'manager' in their job title: that is merely a question of official status, not relevant to the question of who actually manages. The large element to the right depicts an organisation. Its components, not shown in the diagram, are called its resources. The middle element is managerial work. Managers and managerial work are shown as separate elements in the diagram to emphasise an important point. When somebody is appointed as a manager, this in itself does not indicate that managerial work is also present. Managerial work requires doing things, behaving in ways that actually manage. Arrows leaving the managerial work element in the diagram include two sorts: some go into the organisation, symbolising the internal work of managers, within the organisation; others go out, symbolising managers' work on links between the organisation and its environments.

Managing inside and outside organisations ➤

Managerial and organisational elements overlap, which is also symbolic. Managers are members of any organisation they manage, active inside it, but they also detach and go outside, in two senses.

FIGURE 8.1 A managed organisation system

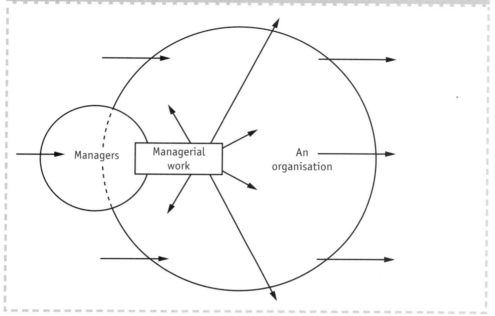

For example, hotel managers go out to visit other hotels, to see what is happening there and to meet other managers. They go out to meet important competitors and customers. They visit suppliers of resources, so food and beverage managers learn about new kitchen equipment by visiting trade shows where new designs are displayed, and finance managers visit banks to learn about alternative ways of raising new capital. They also go out in a mental sense, seeking objectivity in their thinking, trying to look at their own organisation as an outsider might.

Managerial work and organisational work ➤

The distinctive work of managing an organisation is not the same as the work of the organisation managed. Managers' work ideally makes an organisation effective and efficient, while a working organisation creates and delivers goods and/or services.

Managers become involved in both sorts of work. They normally spend a portion of their time in hands-on work, providing services to consumers or making things. While all good managers do this, it is not managing but something done to help out, or to keep in touch. Managing comprises such activities as leading, decision making and coordinating.

The products of managers are managed organisations. These are organisations that are effective and efficient. An effective organisation does the right things—fulfils its purposes. An efficient organisation fulfils its purposes without wasting its resources and without damaging the environments it shares with other interest groups, unless it pays the full costs.

Strategic management and operations management ➤

There are two kinds of managing, often overlapping, referred to as *strategic management* and *operations management*. Senior managers are more heavily involved in strategic issues, while middle and lower levels of management are more involved in operational issues. In many modern organisations there is a trend to blur these hierarchical divisions, via policies of empowerment, involving all employees in strategy formulation and implementation, via the use of teamwork (Wall & Wall 1995).

Top managers, middle and lower management ➤

Top managers have been described as 'the strategic apex' of organisations (Mintzberg 1991b), in the sense that they are the ones who normally make the most important strategic decisions. The CEO (chief executive officer) is at the peak. Middle-level managers are those below the top levels. Where does middle begin? A useful indicator is that top managers include the CEO and those who report direct to the CEO.

Where is the line between middle and lower? Few people describe their own jobs as 'lower management'. Those managing below the top level feel better if their position can be described, by themselves and others, as 'middle', to avoid the opprobrium of 'lower'. The same false consciousness applies in social class divisions, where these days everyone outside a handful at either end of the spectrum wants to be perceived as middle class.

How important are CEOs? ➤

There is a widespread public opinion that CEOs and other top managers are not as valuable as their large salaries and emoluments would imply. There is no doubt that since the 1980s many top managers have been overpaid, especially via the corrupting practice of share options (Kohler 2002).

An opposing opinion is implied in a book by Finklestein and Hambrick (1996). Their research found that CEOs can make vitally important contributions to the performance of organisations. Market prices for managers, expressed in salary levels, support this conclusion. Many managers in the middle levels are paid two or three times the average of other persons in full-time work, and in top management the remuneration can be much higher again.

Inputs, processes, products and other outputs

Drawn into organisations from their environment are resources, which include employees (usually the most important resource), finance, equipment, technologies, raw materials, information and knowledge (an increasingly important resource). Managing these inputs is vital to an organisation's work.

Processes are all the activities occurring while resources are being applied in the work of an organisation. In a hotel, for example, the processes include receiving requests for a room, arranging for rooms to be booked for each guest, preparing rooms for use, receiving guests on arrival, escorting guests to their rooms and explaining the facilities, assisting guests with their requests for information or special needs, and cleaning.

These things might seem to 'just happen', but if they are not managed in some effective way the processes are prone to fail in some degree. Managing does not always require a supervisory role. Mintzberg's (1991b) analysis of 'organisational configurations' shows how, in certain cases, best practice is achieved if workers are allowed to work independently, with managers not interfering or overseeing.

Leaving the organisation are its outputs, including products, byproducts, waste and other environmental emissions. What are the products of tourism businesses and tourism industries? Many writers have tackled this question and almost always state that the products are the things provided for tourists to use and enjoy, ranging from facilities and services in a hotel to the coaches and guides provided by a tour operator. Managers might say that a particular airline 'has a great product', referring to its in-flight service and food, its aircraft, its performance in terms of keeping to timetables and so on.

Here is a different view. Facilities and service capabilities are not products of hotels, as the purpose of having these things is to be productive—to produce something. A hotel's facilities and service capabilities are its resources, not its products. The products are guests who have been accommodated, just as a tour operator's products are customers who have been on the tours and an airline's products are passengers who have been delivered (ideally, along with their luggage) to their intended destination.

This view points to interesting concepts for services management. Thinking about whether a business has products or services leads to terminal confusion. Managing services involves managing (a) the resources being applied as inputs for capability; (b) the processing or servicing, which involve roles or performances; and (c) the product, the changes that occur as a consequence of the servicing. The products of tourist industries are persons who are changed as a result of their experiences as tourists, including the experience of receiving services.

Normative and descriptive theories of management

Discussions about management usually involve two kinds of theories. Distinguishing between them, and understanding what each kind does, is essential to understanding general discussions on management. One kind is prescriptive theory, sometimes called normative theory; the other is descriptive theory.

Prescriptive theory ➤

Many practitioners and researchers look for better methods of solving managerial challenges, and the solutions they come up with are known as normative theory, also called prescriptive theory. Examples are set out in books with titles such as *In Search of Excellence: Lessons from America's Best Run Companies* (Peters & Waterman 1991) or *The Deming Management Method* (Walton 1986).

Descriptive theory ➤

Other researchers seek to discover what managerial work involves. This is not always apparent from superficial observations. Descriptive theories do not judge managers' performance, nor do they recommend or invent new or better methods. They aim to reveal and explain underlying realities. Most of this chapter presents descriptive theories, with occasional dashes of prescriptive comment.

The best-known descriptive theorist on management is Mintzberg (1991a). Case studies in the USA led him to identify the broad characteristics of managers' work, under three headings: interpersonal roles, informational roles, and decisional roles. Dunford (1992) set out a useful summary of Mintzberg's descriptive theory. The discussion later in this chapter will draw on research by Carroll and by Quinn, whose descriptive analyses of managers' roles are similar to those set out by Mintzberg.

Why do organisations need managers?

Organisations in which nobody is managing in a formal sense might go at least partway to fulfilling their purposes, by muddling along. In this way some organisations survive, a few succeed, some collapse. Tourism-related organisations in this category are found among community-based, non-profit associations set up by volunteers for the purpose of promoting a town or region. Those operating without formal managers or with inadequate managers (because of lack of funds) might struggle to survive and achieve little. This indicates a reason why managers are needed: to give organisations a better chance of surviving and fulfilling a purpose.

Investors' first priority is almost always the protection of their capital, with the second priority being income or capital gains. Most investors lack the competency, motivation, time and/or energy to personally manage the organisations in which their funds are invested. Simultaneously, they are cautious about who might be trusted with that capital. Accordingly, few shareholders place investments at high risk by allowing workers to muddle along as self-selecting, informal managers. Instead, shareholders select directors to govern, and these, as agents of the owners, select managers.

Managers can then be regarded as agents of the owners of organisations. Agency theory has thus been a useful source of theories about management, but it does not explain the whole picture.

SIX SCHOOLS OF THOUGHT

During the past 100 years, several schools of thought about management have been devised. Each comprises a set of values, theories and methods. Old schools do not always disappear and so, in most modern organisations, traces of overlapping schools can be found. Six are discussed in this chapter. In a sense, each represents prescriptive theories, for each contains advice on how to manage. The advice reflects certain values in the organisation being managed or, more precisely, values of the owners. In this chapter, however, the aim is merely to describe and explain them, not to present them as prescriptions.

The rational goals school

The rational goals school of management refers to the methods and reasons for managing the sort of organisation that developed in new industries around 100 years ago, notably in the manufacturing of steel, explosives and automobiles. It is sometimes called Taylorism, after an activist known as the founder of scientific management (Taylor 1972/1911).

Managers who follow Taylor's prescriptions emphasise clear goals based on rational thinking. They aim to maximise production and revenue while minimising costs. Sharp distinctions are maintained between managers and workers. Employees below managerial status are not expected to think, just to do as directed. Furthermore, work should be divided up among different departments, with the aim of producing as much as possible, and workers should be given very simple tasks requiring minimum training. Workers should be closely supervised. Workers should work while managers manage.

Merkle (1980) and Morgan (1986) have written about the leading theorist of the rational goal school, F.W. Taylor. The man's personality was strange, but he contributed greatly to the world's industrial development.

Before Taylor's work became well known, around 1912, common sense suggested that the only way to produce more was to work harder, or to work longer hours. An English professor, Jevons (1888), had shown that this was a flawed idea, from his experimental research on different designs for shovels, but the discovery was not widely adopted by industrialists at the time and it did not change common sense. Nor did Jevons see any managerial implications: his focus was on technical developments and how they can create added value. By using improved technology (e.g. a better shovel) a worker can become much more productive, more than by working harder or longer.

Taylor noted Jevons' research, and publicised his own, which became widely known in academe and industry. His intellectual contribution, suitable for his time, was to teach that productivity in the new industries around 1900 should not be the responsibility of workers but should be totally the responsibility of managers. Taylor designed and promoted detailed methods for managers to implement his theory. Common sense slowly changed as a result. In the 20th century managers came to accept that working smarter, by managing resources intelligently, was the best path to higher productivity.

While that broad theory is now widely accepted, some of Taylor's other theories have come into disrepute, especially those that encouraged managers to treat workers as inferior human beings, with no potential beyond unskilled labour.

Remembering that Taylor's theory emerged around 1900 will help explain its characteristics. At that time many workers were barely able to read and write, so could not do complex work requiring those skills. Many people were looking for any sort of unskilled work in the cities, where new technologies of mechanisation were being applied to rapidly expanding new manufacturing industries. Crude ideas derived from biased interpretations of the Bible and of Darwin's (1964/1859) *Origin of Species* encouraged industrialists to feel justified in exploiting workers. The principle of survival of the fittest was used by managers to justify this policy to themselves and others. It encouraged managerial attitudes that disparaged the intrinsic worth of workers, who were treated badly, paid a pittance, made to work long hours, often in dangerous conditions where many were killed or injured.

Certain ideas in the rational goal theory remain in use today, in certain organisations. Some managers believe that workers should be exploited—although these days they would not say so publicly. The belief that managers should be responsible for all decision making remains current in some circles. That began to change in the 1980s, when a trend to empowerment was noted, but in many organisations the trend has not progressed. Empowerment involves managers giving up certain decision-making powers, handing them over to workers. An empowerment scheme in a resort hotel is a theme in a case later in this book.

A hundred years ago, Taylor's prescriptions also suited the political needs of company shareholders and directors, who felt threatened by trades unions and working-class political movements. Taylor provided a theory justifying the conservatives' desire to keep ordinary people in subservient and ignorant positions on the job, which carried over into social environments off the job. Again, there are traces of this attitude current today.

The internal process school

Fayol (1987/1916) was another early theorist whose ideas are reiterated in many modern texts. Fayol saw managing as a process with five linked functions: planning, organising, commanding, coordinating, controlling. His 14 principles of management are designed to assist that process (Quinn, Faerman, Thompson & McGrath 1990: 6).

Chandler's (1977) historical review of management in the Du Pont company is also relevant to the internal process school. It emerged in business organisations that had grown to become well-established early this century. The overarching goal of managers is to keep their organisations in a stable state, growing steadily and avoiding problems.

Procedures manuals are a sign of the internal process school of thought in application, for their purpose is to ensure stability in the way processes are performed. Clearly expressed hierarchies, showing each level of employee from the lowest-paid operative to the chief executive officer, are also important. The ultimate value is a smooth and efficient flow of work, so the managers' main roles are coordinator and monitor. By monitoring closely, managers can take steps to correct things if an organisation strays from its path of steady growth. The internal process school is widely followed in modern industries, and is found in many larger hotels, airlines and tour operators.

The human relations school

Values associated with employees as individual humans emerged in management theory and practice in the 1920s and developed over the following decades. Trades unions and progressive intellectuals were expressing the view that workers deserved to be treated like humans. World War II (1939–45) accelerated that development. Millions of ordinary workers came to realise that they, the working classes, had borne the major burden of the war and deserved a better life in the peace that followed. The Declaration of Universal Human Rights (by the United Nations in 1948) reinforced the attitude.

The creation of more than 100 independent nation-states between 1946 and the 1960s, from what had been colonial empires, further contributed to a belief that all humans were capable of participating in running their own affairs—were capable of managing.

Increasing numbers of managers came to realise that the old ways of treating workers, as inhuman resources to be exploited, were ineffective in newly emerging forms of industry.

An Australian researcher, Elton Mayo, conducted experiments in American factories in the 1930s and proved what other intellectuals had been suggesting, that the social treatment of workers at work affects their productivity. The experiments demonstrated that when workers received attention by managers, productivity went up (Mayo 1945, 1987). A striking fact about Mayo's famous experiments is that workers became more productive not as a result of improvements in physical aspects of their working conditions, such as better lighting, but merely as a result of managers paying attention to them in an apparently sympathetic manner.

When Mayo's findings spread, prescriptive theories began to change. Managers learned that they might be able to build commitment and morale among workers by paying attention to them. The application of Mayo's theory in the rise of the human relations school of management is widely interpreted as a sign of progress in civilisation, but a cynical alternative interpretation is worth noting.

Merely paying attention to people does nothing for them personally other than to give them a feeling that they are worthy of attention. It is the cheapest form of manipulation. Managers learned an easy and inexpensive method for raising or sustaining productivity, at least in the short term. Smarmy types, who keep close contact with employees and always behave in a friendly manner but always have an excuse for postponing the promised pay rise or improved working conditions, exemplify this practice.

Another aspect of the human relations theory has much more merit, for it recognises differences between people. Under the rational goal theory espoused by Taylor, workers are treated the same, based on an 'average man' notion. This leaves human capacities underutilised. Individuals have different capabilities and personalities, so they can be more productive collectively, as an organisation, if they are treated as individuals.

The human relations theory has been widely followed to some degree in many modern organisations. It has never totally replaced, in any known business organisation, the earlier theories of rational goals and internal processes, but has a moderating effect on their excesses.

When human values contradict the values of the rational goal theory, sometimes the older theory dominates, and this might be detrimental for all parties. For example, management by objectives (MBO), a popular technique praised by widely admired authorities such as Drucker (1955), clearly represents the rational goal model. But, according to Deming (Aguayo 1990), MBO is counterproductive.

The open systems school

Open systems models of management are conceptually like the open systems models of tourism described in Chapter 3. The year 1954 is a symbolic date for their emergence.

This is when the Society for General Systems Research was founded by Ludwig von Bertalanffy, Kenneth Boulding and others. The Society's early work had no interest in management, although Norbert Wiener suggested the idea of applying systems theory to management.

Wiener (1950) is famous as the founder of cybernetics, the science of automatic communication which helped the development of computer technology. He seems to have been the first to recognise that business organisations can be regarded as systems interacting with their environments, meaning that the performance of an organisation (its survival, success, productivity or failure) is not just a matter of internal process. It also depends on how an organisation reacts to threats from environments and on how it responds to opportunities offered there. Awareness of these ideas encourages managers to look outside their organisations, trying to understand environments.

Knowledge of open systems theories is not required by managers; they do require a frame of mind that thinks in terms of open systems. Not all managers have that attitude. Some are constrained by, or personally suited to, the internal process model of management, looking inwards.

Porter's (1980, 1985) theories about managing competitive strategies, widely followed in modern industries, are based implicitly on an open systems model. He described how successful managers think of their organisations as firms in an industry with features of an open system. The strategy then is to position the firm, using its strengths and overcoming its weaknesses (internal process factors) while taking advantage of any opportunities and avoiding any threats in the firm's environments (open systems factors).

The cooperate and compete school

While there was a growing school of thought in the 1990s that advocated cooperative networks among business organisations (Holmes 1995), comparatively few researchers are exploring the interrelationships of cooperation and competition.

The theory's origins can be found in early writings on sociology (Veblen 1904) and economics (MacGregor 1931/1911). Not until Penrose (1959) was the idea of simultaneously competing and cooperating made explicit in management writing. Penrose saw that business firms are often successful when they compete with other firms, and she also saw that cooperative activities are very important. Penrose seemed unsure which was more important and did not explain the functions of the two factors. She showed no signs of having read much prior research on the topic, and called competition 'God and the Devil'.

Best (1990) developed Penrose's ideas, drew on more research, showed where the cooperate and compete theory was working particularly well (Japan and Italy), and showed how the theory's denial was causing economic and managerial problems in other places, notably the USA. He saw cooperation as more important, but emphasised that competition is needed too.

In certain countries, notably the USA, competition is held out by many economists and their acolytes as a supremely desirable condition for the economy at large and for industrial prosperity. In Australia, recent governments have sought ways to encourage ever more competitiveness, while cooperative processes are implied to be anti-competitive, a cause of economic problems. Hilmer's writings (1985, 1993) were influential in conveying this ideology in Australia, despite the fact that the evidence and arguments they contain are flimsy as generalities. (This is usually the case with ideological writing, as anyone who has read a range of books by political or religious zealots will know.)

The competing values school

A sixth school of thought in management was described by Quinn (1988). From studying hundreds of practising managers, Quinn, like other descriptive theorists who have looked at the topic, identified a number of work roles. He discovered something more, and this is the most distinctive feature of his findings.

The values followed in a manager's roles are not consistent, but are in a sense competing with one another. For instance, at 9 am a manager might take decisive action that reflects the rational goal school of thought and at 9.30 make a decision reflecting the values of the internal process school of thought. Later that morning the same manager does something reflecting the values of human relations; suddenly, thinking and decision making swings to open systems, then switches back to internal process. The switching is not necessarily haphazard, random or sequential. Nor should it be viewed as foolish. It probably reflects the particular challenge or task being faced at a particular time in a busy day.

What professional practitioners and the academic literature lacked before Quinn developed his model and published his book (1988) was a theory that explained this diverse, inconsistent and seemingly contradictory approach. The later book by Quinn, Faerman, Thompson and McGrath (1990) has a fuller discussion of this theory.

After students of management have read about the diverse schools of thought but before they study Quinn, they might assume that the schools of thought are mutually exclusive, and that a manager should be consistent, following one or other of the schools. Quinn demonstrated that this is an unrealistic assumption. His theory is remarkably realistic. Before describing it, I will present another researcher's findings.

CARROLL'S CLUSTERS OF MANAGERS' ROLES

Having identified several theories reflecting the values in managerial work, the theme now shifts to the work itself. What do managers do? After surveying hundreds of managers, Carroll (1988) identified eight 'job activity clusters', described below. Original interpretations, not in Carroll's research, are also presented. The order in the list below does not signify order of importance or chronological sequence.

Managers are planners

World Expeditions Pty Ltd, a Sydney-based adventure tour operator, plans certain things in similar ways to other well-managed operators of packaged tours. Tour parties' departure dates and itineraries are planned more than a year in advance. Hotels and airlines have to be selected and bookings made to arrange transport and accommodation for the estimated numbers of tourists and guides in each party. In a typical year, about 200 groups go to Nepal, India, Pakistan, Tibet or Bhutan, 500 to remote regions of New Zealand and Australia, and dozens to other countries.

Planning these trips requires careful attention to detail. Many adventure tour operators have failed as businesses, or struggled as unprofitable hobbies, because their managers' only strong skills were in operating adventure tours, not in planning and other roles of management.

All managers plan. Planning is always concerned with the future. Almost anything about an organisation's future might be planned: operations, human resources, cash flow, materials, technologies, marketing, implementation of strategies, as well as capital decisions.

Planning means thinking through the important issues in how a desired future might and can be shaped. It involves making orderly preparations for probable and possible future conditions. It involves thinking about what is feasible. It means making judgments as to what will probably happen, what might happen, and what should be done soon before these future times arrive. It involves deciding on a series of steps to reach a desired goal. Without a planning component, managing might be reduced to its least effective approach—no preparation, but a willingness to cope with circumstances as they occur. In managerial jargon, when conditions become hectic, this coping approach is called 'fighting fires', and is prone to causing errors.

Not all success in business stems from planning as a preliminary step. A multi-billion-dollar business in car rental developed without any initial planning for anything beyond a small-scale enterprise conducted at home (Fucini & Fucini 1987).

Managers are representatives

All managers represent the organisation that employs them. When Geoffrey Beames addresses university audiences as a guest lecturer he represents Australian Wine Lodges Ltd, where he is the founding director and CEO. When he addresses employees of Australian Wine Lodges, he also represents that organisation. Representation can thus be external or internal to the organisation being managed.

Managers cannot determine *how* they will represent their organisations, because this is ultimately decided by the images formed by observers. However, they can try to create an appropriate image. This is why meeting people personally is important, why conversational skills are useful, and why style is important. Styles of clothing, grooming, speech, body language are all symbolic issues, giving off messages and so creating images in people's minds about managers and therefore about the organisations they represent.

After the first minute in a representative role, the substance of what managers do or say is more important than style. Few defects are more serious in the representative role than style without substance.

Managers are investigators

Managers investigate. In other words, they research. This stems from a need to know about what is happening, or what has happened, and a recognition that existing knowledge is deficient. No manager can know, or need to know, everything relevant to their job and so must decide what they most need to learn.

Not all investigations require sophisticated research methods, but they do require intelligent concentration. The managing director of Ausfurs, Rob Hayter, regularly investigates certain topics using a simple method. Ausfurs has a chain of shops in Sydney selling Australian products, mainly to tourists. Hayter occasionally walks around shopping centres, observing activities in shops patronised by tourists.

Certain investigations use more formal methods to collect and analyse data. Management information systems (MISs) are the most formal. Specialist books explain how various MISs can be designed and used (O'Brien 1990; Ahituv & Neumann 1990). The MIS is where managers integrate information from diverse sources, such as operations supervisors, accountants, market researchers, marketers, sales personnel and engineers. Certain types of investigations should use the formal approach of scientific research (Emory & Cooper 1991; Sakaran 1992).

Managers are negotiators

All managers had the opportunity to practise negotiation when they were offered appointment, with their work conditions and, most negotiable of all, salary and benefits. Negotiating is a process whereby two or more persons communicate over some transaction that may benefit one more than the others. Managers negotiate a lot, on a range of issues.

Managing an inclusive tour business requires contracts with suppliers of each component in the various packages. This requires negotiations with managers in airlines, coachlines, hotels and so on. Topics negotiated include how many units are needed, at what price, when, the standard required, and the methods of payment. In mass-market packaged tour operations, skilfully negotiating contracts may be the most significant factor in the profitability of the venture, as margins can be slim (Koloff, Moore & Richardson 1989).

A subtle approach in negotiating is to compete within a cooperative policy, seeking an 'I win and you win too' outcome. Axelrod's (1990) *Evolution of Cooperation* is a good introduction to strategies for simultaneously competing and cooperating. See too Singer's (1993) *How Are We to Behave? Ethics in an Age of Self Interest*, and Covey's (1989) *Seven Habits of Highly Effective People*.

Managers are coordinators

Managing requires coordination. Almost anybody can coordinate resources in a small organisation, which is reflected in the observation that most people are capable of managing their own households. Coordination becomes more difficult in large and complex organisations.

Coordinating involves arranging resources so that organisational processes transpire smoothly, so that each step occurs in its proper sequence, minimising the conflicts that arise among flows of resources, among workers and working departments. This ensures that the right persons and resources are doing the right things at the right times.

For example, Sea World, a theme park near Surfers Paradise, described in a case study by King and Hyde (1989), presented a coordination issue. The organisation was originally structured in four departments. A new manager changed this to 10. The extra departments might have helped the organisation's work, but 10 as compared to four would require more resources in the coordinator role. Also, frequent-flyer programs, a promotional device used by airlines since the 1980s, were first devised to operate as a separate scheme within each airline. When the concept was extended to include several airlines in each scheme, the marketing gains from each scheme were amplified but more coordination was required.

There are many useful coordinating techniques but no generally applicable best method. Mintzberg (1991b) suggested guidelines for coordination methods suitable for particular types ('configurations') of organisations.

Managers are evaluators

Managers evaluate, which is similar to what many textbooks call controlling. Consider the work of a maintenance manager in a large resort. Maintenance is vital in resorts, because if it is neglected there will be breakdowns and excessive wear-and-tear in rooms and equipment, leading to operational problems and dissatisfied guests. Managing maintenance involves many managerial roles; here, one item in the evaluator role is noted.

Every month, the maintenance manager (in some hotels and resorts the title is 'chief engineer') evaluates information in reports listing all the maintenance items conducted during the past month, and the costs for each one. Some are 'jobs' (renovating a room, or repairing an air-conditioner) and some are routine 'processes' (lawn-mowing, cleaning the grounds). The reports are assessed in comparison to the budgeted maintenance items for that period, and their costs. The differences, or variances, are investigated if they are too large.

The craft of managing includes knowing what should be evaluated, and how often. The science of management provides technical skills, which show how to evaluate. These skills are in accounting, research methods, marketing, operational management and computer technologies. Few individuals are highly skilled across that range, but most managers develop basic skills in all areas.

Managers are staffers and change agents

Managers are responsible for staffing organisations. Initial activities are planning human resources, then recruiting, which means finding a pool of potential employees and then selecting, finding from the pool the persons best suited to the job. After employees are appointed, managers are responsible for training them, helping them become productive employees. An ongoing activity is staff development, which means encouraging and assisting individuals to fulfil their potential by education, training and career progression.

The increasing importance of staff development results from two contrary trends. First, organisations are changing in many ways, adapting to new conditions and exploiting new opportunities in technology, finance, marketing and so on. This means existing ways of operating must also change, so the behaviour of people in organisations must adapt. However, most individuals' natural tendency is to resist changing if there is no pressing need to do so, if they feel comfortable. The responsibility of managers in staff development is to be a stimulus for change, to make development systemic, an element in the organisation's vitality.

Broadly, staff can be developed in three respects: in their knowledge, their skills, and their attitudes. Research by Daruwalla and Weiler (1995) found that training programs in Australian hospitality industries have often focused on knowledge and skills development, neglecting attitudinal issues. They cited a study by Craig-Smith and French (1990), which indicated a need for change towards 'a clear Australian imprint'.

In larger organisations staff development responsibilities are usually assigned to specialist personnel, but this arrangement is not universal. Townsend's (1970) book about his remarkable career as CEO at Avis Car Rentals made the point that staffing roles are best performed by line managers at top, middle and lower levels. Townsend closed down Avis' personnel department.

Managers are supervisors

Supervising means taking responsibility for and exercising direct authority over the work of other persons. It can be done in various ways. At the Russell Hotel, a boutique hotel in Sydney with 10 employees, the manager says her work includes relatively little supervision because the staff work effectively without anyone watching over them. Regular staff meetings are held, so the team can communicate on a range of matters.

A different kind of supervising is a constant role in Paula Layton's work as a shift manager in a large restaurant. She describes supervision as her main role. She spends most of the shift watching over the operational personnel—chefs, cooks, kitchen assistants, waiters, cashiers and cleaners.

The complete manager: a perfect princess?

Carroll's list of activity clusters can be remembered by the acronym formed by listing, in sequence: *p*lanning, *r*epresenting, *i*nvestigating, *n*egotiating, *c*oordinating, *e*valuating, *s*taffing, *s*upervising. An all-round manager, competent in all eight roles, is a *princess*.

This indicates the main reason why managing is a difficult job to do well alone: an all-round manager is multiskilled. Many individuals are highly competent in certain job clusters, average in others, deficient in others. This is how career managers can point to a need for ongoing education and training, to build up their weaker roles, besides developing their strengths. It is also why a managerial team can be useful, if it contains individuals with a blend of competencies and if their personalities are such that they can coordinate their individual strengths and weaknesses.

Quinn's model can be explained using a diagram (see Figure 8.2). A circle is divided into quadrants, each representing one of the four major schools of thought in management, each with its dominant value. The four are placed in a specific arrangement, so that opposing values are shown as opposites, which suggests that they are competing. It is described as a competing values framework model of management.

Each quadrant has two distinctive roles, making eight roles in all. Quinn et al. (1990) identified, for each of the eight roles, three skill competencies, so in total his model has 24 skill competencies. The eight roles are described below.

Managers are directors

Director roles occur when managers make decisions and issue directives to other persons that define problems, select alternatives for action, generate rules and policies, make strategies, or give instructions.

Three skills in this role are taking initiative, setting goals, and delegating. They relate to the rational goal model of management, aimed at getting more productivity. Geoffrey Beames exemplifies the 'taking initiative' skill. For some years various people had tinkered around with resorts in Australian wine regions, catering to tourists with a special interest in wines and vineyards. Beames, after working in top management positions in airlines and island resorts, took the initiative to further develop and properly implement the concept when he founded Australian Wine Lodges Ltd.

FIGURE 8.2 Management work: eight roles and four competing values

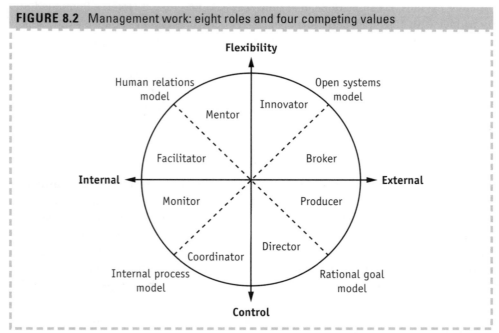

Source: R.E. Quinn et al., *Becoming a Master Manager: A Competency Framework* (1990) New York, Wiley. This material is used by permission of John Wiley & Sons Inc.

Managers are producers

'Making resources productive is the specific job of managers, as distinct from (their) other jobs' (Drucker 1980: 18); this role complements directing, as both roles are aimed at raising productivity. The role is aligned with the values of the rational goals school.

The three skill competencies are creating conditions where others can become motivated, personal motivation and productivity, and time and stress management. Managers highly skilled in this role are not difficult to find in any sizable industry, for every successful organisation has at least one individual who is known for his/her ability to get things done.

Mohan Oberoi is a wonderful example of excellence here. From an impoverished childhood in India and a first job in the 1920s in a lowly position earning $3 a month, he rose to become CEO of Oberoi Hotels, a company he founded. By 2002 it had grown to a chain of 35 de luxe and first-class properties in seven countries. Asked the reason for his success in an interview by Seth (1992), Oberoi, then aged over 90, revealed in his answer three classic signs of a productive manager. He said, 'I never postpone till tomorrow what I can do today and I live simply and have very few personal needs'.

A related issue: greed and lack of civic value ➤

A sharp contrast exists between Oberoi and those CEOs and other top-level managers who desire enormous wealth, high status and luxurious living. The mediocre performance or failure of many organisations during recent years has been blamed on CEOs and other top managers using their positions to build personal wealth from excessive remuneration packages and neglecting their responsibilities to others (Kohler 2002; Balzar 2002). Haigh's (2003) article is recommended reading for anyone studying the topic. There is no doubt that certain highly paid CEOs are worth their pay, as research by Finkelstein and Hambrick (1996) has indicated. The problem is that those who occupy upper-level managerial positions might then assume that they are entitled to be paid many times more than the employees they oversee, merely because they are in a top management position.

The underlying issue is greed and its correlate, a lack of civic values. A comment made by Adam Smith 200 years ago is worth quoting: 'He is not a good citizen who does not wish to promote, by every means in his power, the welfare of the whole society of his fellow citizens' (Smith 1790, cited in Saul 2001: 99). Adam Smith is regarded by many entrepreneurial managers as a great thinker about business and free markets, and his remarks on those themes are often quoted; his remarks about social responsibilities do not receive nearly so much attention.

Some managers assume they have a right to use their positions in any way they choose, within legal limits. What is widely ignored is the principle underlying the contract between owners of a company and the society in which it operates. It adds a legal dimension to the point made by Smith.

The legal right to form and operate a company began as a contract, in which society, in the name of the government, gave that right and its various advantages. In return, owners of companies and their managerial agents were supposed to use the rights and advantages 'for the public good' (Bella et al. 1985: 290). The idea that companies have a right to be exploited for private gain by shareholders and managers and that this can be done regardless of public interest, regardless of social welfare, is a corruption of the civic values and responsibilities that were central to the history of company law.

Managers are coordinators

The coordinator role relates closely to the internal process model. It is required where stability and smooth operations are needed. This applies to many organisations, to some extent. Three key skill competencies are planning, organising, and controlling.

Organisations that grow and become more complex will depend more and more on coordination. The tourism organisation with the greatest dependence on this role might be Accor, the world's largest tourist-related company. In 1994 it employed 145 000 persons in 132 countries, and its activities included 2200 hotels, 700 public restaurants, 1100 travel agencies and 5000 car rental agencies (Steinmeyer 1994).

Managers are monitors

Like the coordinator role it sits alongside in the diagram, monitoring relates closely to the internal process theory. Three key competencies are reducing information overload, analysing information with critical thinking, and presenting information by writing effectively.

Skills in critical thinking help managers make good decisions, and knowing which issues require decisions allow them to concentrate on decisions that will make a difference. Drucker (1980) says that in modern, turbulent environments, managers should concentrate on three key issues: liquidity, productivity, and the costs of the future.

A productivity issue in many hotels relates to overbooking. In busy times, hotels sensibly accept more bookings than there are rooms available for any night, because a percentage of bookings normally remain unfilled because of 'no-shows'. Critical factors for managers are deciding, during very busy periods, how far to go with overbooking. Too little means lost income, while too much creates problematical guests who cannot be accommodated. Schirmer (1994) investigated how overbooking was managed in a sample of hotels on Queensland's Gold Coast. Her study revealed that managers in different hotels had different approaches.

Managers are mentors

Being a mentor involves developing an understanding of yourself and others, being skilled at interpersonal communication, and spending time to develop subordinates. Organisations where staff development is a high priority need a sprinkling of managers who are skilled mentors—persons with experience who are able and willing to nurture the younger or less experienced.

Nguyen Thi Ngoc Lien, a senior manager in Vietnam's National Tourism Office, is active in all three mentor roles. In 1991 Vietnam recorded 300 000 arrivals of international tourists and aimed to double the number quickly. Key strategies for reaching the goal were training young staff, the managers of the future. No doubt Lien is keenly aware of her own youth when she spends time with trainees: during the war in Vietnam that ended in 1975 her own youthful experiences were sacrificed, as she was severely injured in battles as a platoon leader in the army (Hwu 1992).

Managers are facilitators

To be a good facilitator requires skills in team building, participative decision making and conflict management. The facilitator role is located opposite the producer role, which points to the fact that when a manager is engaged in facilitator roles, the organisation is not being productive.

Meetings of staff enable managers to be facilitators: building team spirit, allowing all staff to feel that they are participating in decisions, and reducing conflict. Some managers call too many meetings, other too few. Katie Lahey discovered the latter defect when she moved from being general manager of the Victorian Tourism Commission to the corresponding position in the Sydney City Council: 'One of the things I found early on in the SCC was that most of the staff were completely in the dark as to what was going on. For example, they'd never had a general staff meeting' (Lahey, quoted in Larkin 1994: 41).

Managers are innovators

Being innovative means doing new things, or old things in new ways, in order to do better and in order to adjust to change. Skill competencies are living with change, creative thinking, and managing change.

Soon after Robyn Thurston took over as manager at the Russell Hotel, she innovated with marketing management. Formerly, like other small hotels, the Russell had been promoted independently, not participating in tourism industry marketing schemes. This was because managers of boutique hotels traditionally distance their hotels from images of mass tourism connoted by industrial marketing. The innovation was based on an opinion that appropriate kinds of industrial marketing could be used without necessarily forming that image. Thurston purchased mailing lists of American travel agents and contacted several, also forming links with inbound tour operators in Sydney. The outcome, two years later, was a doubling in the number of American guests. Many became regulars.

Three benefits flowed from this. The ambience in the hotel is sociable and personal, which regular guests anticipate and first-time guests readily feel. Staff find working there pleasant, and tourists find visits to Sydney enjoyable. The hotel as a business gained higher occupancies and income, while the manager was able to reduce the costs of promotion. The higher the proportion of repeat guests among total guests, the less a hotel need spend on promotion.

Innovating is the opposite of coordinating. The solution is not to seek a balance, for that expression implies an equal share. It is to seek the appropriate mix. Sometimes innovating should cease for a while, in order to consolidate. Sometimes coordination should be ignored temporarily, while innovating.

Managers are brokers

Three key skills in the broker role of managers are building and maintaining a power base, negotiating agreements and commitments, and presenting ideas—orally, in writing and in other ways.

Brokers are opposite monitors in the diagram. This suggests that some personalities might be better adapted to one role and lacking in the other. Ralph Reed, CEO at American Express 50 years ago, seems to exemplify that condition. He opposed and resisted proposals, over several years, for American Express to introduce a credit card (Grossman 1987). Other persons were convinced, by analysing market trends and critically thinking through the implications, that American Express would be highly successful as a credit card operator. An Amex card ('Don't Leave Home Without It') would complement the other travel and tourism services marketed by the company. Reed assumed that it would take business away from Amex travellers' cheques. Eventually Reed was obliged to agree that his analysis was flawed, and that an Amex card could be established. Offsetting any inability as an analyst and critical thinker, Reed was apparently skilled as a broker—able to build and maintain a power base within the company, which gave it stability in an era of growth.

What is the central role of managers?

The keystone role is coordination. It occurs at two levels. In combination the two levels of this role are vital for managing, and they permeate other managerial activities. Managers typically coordinate the deployment of many kinds of resources in organisations: employees, data, knowledge, raw materials, equipment, cash, investments, technology and so on. This vital coordination role has been summarised as follows. Every organised human activity—from the making of pottery to the placing of a man on the moon—gives rise to two fundamental and opposing requirements: the division of labour into various tasks to be performed and the coordination of those tasks to accomplish the activity (Mintzberg 1991b: 332).

Besides coordinating organisational systems, managers coordinate another sphere of behaviour, another system. Managers coordinate managerial work when a person coordinates her or his own work as manager, or coordinates other managers' work. For simplicity, the diagram in figure 8.3 shows the roles in Carroll's model. The process can be described as follows. From observation, or judgment, or information or some other stimulus, a manager determines that managerial activity is needed. Is it planning, representing, investigating, negotiating or something else, or some combination? The manager decides. Whichever role is activated, it might directly affect the organisation or may lead to another elementary role in the management system. All the roles are

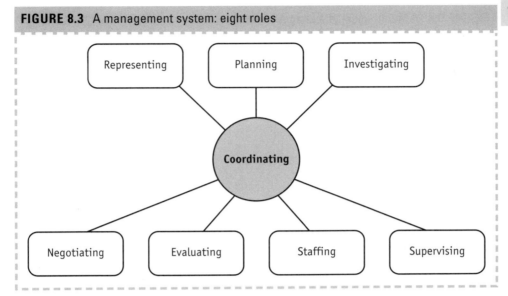

FIGURE 8.3 A management system: eight roles

interrelated, via the coordinator element, and all are interrelated with the environment within which managing occurs—an organisation.

In this model of a management system, originally presented in Leiper's (1989c) study of control systems, the coordinator element is as a kind of central clearing house for managerial work, linking all managerial roles (Figure 8.3).

Linear models and systemic models

Management textbooks often depict Fayol's model of five functions, shown as a sequence in a diagram: planning comes first, followed by organising, next is directing (originally called commanding), then coordinating, and finally controlling. The results of controlling become feedback to another round of planning, and so the cycle is reiterated, as shown in Figure 8.4.

Figure 8.4 may look systematic, might seem good theory, and is often described in textbooks as 'systematic'. However, it is linear, not systematic, and is a misleading description of processes in managerial practice. Figure 8.3 is more realistic. It is systematic, not linear, as it shows activities as a collection of interrelated elements, not a series in a line. There is no standard cycle in Figure 8.3, which represents managing as a flexible collection of roles. Figure 8.4 does not admit flexibility: it has planning first, in a reiterated cycle ending in controlling. An example will demonstrate the practical difference in the two theories.

Every month, managers typically receive reports from accountants that the managers use as evaluation and control devices. Assume that a report has shown sales were 15% above budget but direct costs were 30% above, so that, instead of a sizable profit flowing from the jump in sales, the company has incurred a loss. What does the manager do

FIGURE 8.4 A linear model of managerial roles

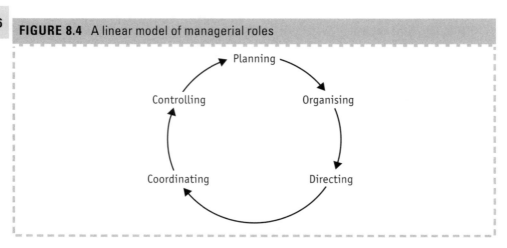

next? This depends on which theory is followed—Figure 8.3 or Figure 8.4. Which is a more accurate description? Which is better for understanding what managers actually do? It is Figure 8.3.

According to the linear model in Figure 8.4, controlling is always followed by planning. This theory suggests that the manager should note the incongruent movements in sales and costs, possibly do something about it as part of the control function, and consider them in planning adjustments to next month's budget. Controlling is implied to be related to other roles only via the cycle, via planning.

A more realistic way of describing the normal sequence is this. After seeing last month's unexpected results, the manager would shift straight from evaluator role to monitor role and analyse the data, applying critical thinking to discover broad causes as to why sales and costs trends have gone awry. (Perhaps they would go into director mode and delegate this analytical task to another manager.) Once the broad causes were identified, the manager would shift to the investigator role to discover the background reasons. In this role, they could draw on the MIS (management information system), perhaps using a simple research approach (asking blunt and direct questions) or scientific research method, or a blend of the two. The monitor role's activities—analysing data, critical thinking, presenting complex information in clear writing—might come into play again.

Once the reasons were known, the manager would decide what to do to correct the problematic trends of costs rising at a greater rate than sales. This decision-making process occurs in the coordinator role, according to Figure 8.3, from where a number of options are open. Perhaps the manager will decide that if the main cause of the problem is found to be understaffed departments, the solution will be in the staffing role: recruit more staff. If the reason is found to be certain employees not following proper policies, the solution will be in the director role—those persons given strong instructions to correct their behaviour.

Perhaps other actions would follow. These need not be discussed, as the example has served its purpose, showing that the system of managerial roles shown in Figure 8.3 is a more realistic description of what actually happens than the linear series of roles in Figure 8.4.

What do managers need to know, to support their diverse activities? Eight items or themes of knowledge are as follows:

1. Managers need knowledge of the organisation(s) in which they are employed, which they are managing. This means getting to know the people, the history, the processes and so on. This takes time to acquire, which is why managers who remain with the same organisation for a number of years can be highly competent and highly valued.

2. Managers need knowledge of the industry or industries in which their organisation participates. This requires knowledge of the component organisations that form these industries, and of the ways the collection cooperates and competes. It also suggests a need for studying past trends and the possible directions for future industrial change. This takes time to acquire, which is a reason why many managers stick to one industry for years, even if they switch employment among organisations within it.

3. Managers need knowledge of the markets in which their organisation participates. These include consumer markets—which, in tourism systems, comprise persons willing and able to go on trips. They also include supplier markets, which comprise other organisations, suppliers providing items such as oil and other energy sources, equipment, food, beverages, kitchen utensils, computer hardware and software.

4. Managers should have a well-developed knowledge of management, acquired from wide reading and from completing the increasingly available formal studies.

5. Most managers have knowledge of at least one specialisation besides management. Again, this does not necessarily require formal qualifications but might come from intensive reading, perhaps some formal studies, and from on-the-job learning. Many managers have knowledge of science, or accounting, or marketing, or research, or engineering, or tourism, or some other subject.

6. All managers deal with people. Thus, knowledge of behaviour (psychology) or human cultures (anthropology) or behaviour in groups of people (sociology) are useful parts of any manager's knowledge.

7. Managers need self-knowledge. Those who know their own character, and their strengths and weaknesses, are more capable of succeeding as a manager.

8. Managers need general knowledge, about wide-ranging topics. Experienced managers find all sorts of knowledge useful in some aspects of their work. Two applications are in representative and negotiator roles, where conversational skills on topics with no relationship to work are often critical factors in success.

Who manages tourism?

Implicit throughout this chapter is an assumption that management is about organisations of the sort used in the illustrative examples: travel agents, tour operators, airlines, hotels, and governmental tourism agencies. In fact, managers and other employees of these organisations are not the only people managing tourism. They normally share the role with other categories of people who are handicapped as managers, a fact that means the whole process of tourism management cannot be as effective as one might imagine. These other categories include, in particular, tourists. (The issue is explored in Chapter 16.)

CONCLUSION

The themes in this chapter were theories of management and their application in managerial work. The diversity of skills, knowledge and values shaping managers' roles was emphasised. Awareness of this diversity can give us wider and deeper understanding of what being a manager really involves.

Awareness of the particular skills and knowledge behind each role can guide an individual's career development, for it indicates that the education and training required to develop as a manager does not focus on merely one or two roles. In a team of managers working together, the relative strengths and weaknesses of members in the team can be complementary, giving the team overall strength, but in practice this requires careful attention to teamwork and team management.

Several schools of thought, or philosophies of management, were identified and described. Using Quinn's model of competing values, the four major schools of thought can be seen to be associated with particular roles. In most purposeful organisations there is a need for each of these roles. Competent managers recognise that principle—rather than adopting the naive attitude of assuming that a manager can and should be consistently 'the director type' or consistently 'the mentor type'. The art of managing includes the sense to know when each type is appropriate.

Discussion questions

1. What are three reasons for the fact that more persons are studying management now than ever before?
2. Describe the basic links between managers, managerial work, organisations and organisation work.
3. What is meant by the observation that managers' work occurs inside and outside the organisations in which each manager is employed?
4. What are the products of business organisations in tourism industries? Give examples relating to airlines, resort hotels, and any other kind of organisation in this category.
5. Why would managers in tourism industries be interested in the products of these industries?
6. List and briefly describe six schools of thought in management.
7. In a typical business organisation involved with tourism, do managers follow just one school of thought about management, or does their work typically reflect more than one school?

➤ 8. Quinn's model of management is described as 'competing values'. Does this mean it is applicable in competitive markets, or something else?

➤ 9. Carroll's model of managerial roles can be described as a 'princess model'. What is the basis for that label?

➤ 10. Among the various roles of managers, which one is arguably the central role?

➤ 11. Answering the question 'What do managers need to know?' leads to the realisation that successful managers have developed personal competence in eight categories of knowledge. What are they, and why is each category useful?

Recommended reading

Chandler, Alfred D. Jr 1977, *The Visible Hands: The Managerial Revolution in American Business*, Cambridge, MA: Harvard University Press

Finkelstein, S. & Hambrick, D. 1996, *Strategic Leadership: Top Executives and Their Effects on Organisations*, St Paul, MN: West Publishing

Haigh, Gideon 2003, *Bad Company: The Cult of the CEO*, Quarterly Essay, issue no. 10, Melbourne: Schwartz Publishing

Quinn, Robert E., Faerman, S., Thompson, M. & McGrath, Michael R. 2003, *Becoming a Master Manager: A Competency Framework* (3rd edn), New York: Wiley

Waelchli, Fred 1989, The VSM & Ashby's law as illuminants of historical management thought, pp 51–76 in *The Viable System Model: Interpretations and Applications of Stafford Beer's VSM*, Raul Espejo & Roger Harnden (eds), Chichester: Wiley

Walton, Mary 1986, *The Deming Management Method,* New York: Putman

Business Organisations in Tourism Industries

This chapter is about four organisations, all active in the business of tourism and participating in tourism industries. They were selected to describe what this twin set of involvements can involve, in a range of examples including large, medium and small organisations. In one case, the main activities occur in a traveller-generating region; in the other three, in tourist destinations.

The theme is descriptive, not prescriptive, so the discussions do not include making judgments about the standards of management or making suggestions for improvements. In fact, all four cases are well-managed, relatively successful businesses.

The Karpin Taskforce on Management Education conducted research across all sectors of the Australian economy, in a project sponsored by the government and assisted by business leaders attempting to find ways of improving management standards via educational initiatives. It found that (Karpin (1994b) 4, parenthesis added):

A breakdown of management performance into its components indicates a reasonable performance in functional areas (e.g. office administration, financial, human resources and sales management, information systems) but poor performance in the strategic and cross functional area—entrepreneurship and management development.

Both broad areas are discussed in this chapter, with a leaning to the latter, which is for many students and practitioners the more interesting.

All four cases are about businesses based in Australia, but they are not unlike similar businesses in other countries. World and Country Travel is a small, independently owned travel agency in a busy shopping mall; it is managed by the owner. ID Tours South Pacific was included to represent inbound tour operators, important 'behind-the-scenes' components of tourism industries whose activities are relatively unknown to the general public. Novotel Opal Cove is a four-star resort hotel managed by Accor, one of the largest organisations in world tourism; the case describes organisational structures and management systems. Sandcastles is an apartment block designed for holiday rentals; what seems on the surface to be a relatively simple managerial arrangement is shaped by three sets of agreements and a licence.

WORLD AND COUNTRY TRAVEL

World and Country Travel was chosen to represent retail travel agencies, the front-line sales arm of tourism industries. The term 'travel agent' takes in several types. Retail travel agents are those dealing direct with consumers—people going on trips. They are the ones typically seen in shopping centres.

Other types include wholesale travel agents. 'Wholesale' implies an intermediate marketer, in the business of supplying retail travel agents with items to sell that the wholesaler has obtained from a third party. Prepackaged tours are distributed to retailers by tour wholesalers, sometimes known as wholesale travel agents. In some cases the wholesaler and retailer are from the same company. Other sub-categories include general sales agents (GSAs) and consolidators. *The Australian Travel Agency* (Harris & Howard 1994) defines these terms.

The business of retail travel agents can be analysed systematically to see that managing an agency involves managing five sets of responsibilities and roles: (a) consumers or clients; (b) principals; (c) the travel agency as a business, and its owners; (d) employees; and (e) external environments. The five are described below.

> *World and Country Travel is a small-scale, single-outlet agency in a regional city in Australia. It is owned by Camilla Fedrant, who is also the manager. Two employees, June and Henry, work for her on a permanent part-time basis, and occasionally a casual is engaged.*

Travel agents' five sets of responsibilities

Retail travel agents have responsibilities to their clients, their principals, their owners, their employees and to wider interests. Retail travel agents can provide a range of services for their *clients*. The term 'client' is favoured by travel agents for referring to their customers, probably because it connotes a professional image. 'Client' comes from the Latin 'cluere' meaning to listen, which indicates that a person whose work involves clients listens to each individual, in order to deal with their needs on a personal basis.

Travel agents also have responsibilities and perform associated roles for their *principals*. All agents, in many fields of business (e.g. real estate and travel), have principals behind them. The principals are the persons or organisations represented by the agents. Principals behind real estate agents are the sellers of properties; principals behind travel agents include airlines, hotels, tour operator-wholesalers, car rental firms, travel insurance firms and others. Roles performed by travel agents for their principals require managerial input or support.

Travel agencies as business entities have relationships to the *owners* of the business, and this affects the first and second relationships. Travel agencies are owned by shareholders, partners or a sole trader, who expect that the business will earn sufficient profit to pay them dividends, beyond any wages they might draw personally. Travel agencies also have *employees*, such as travel consultants, who depend on the agency's survival and prosperity for their work and income. Finally, travel agencies have responsibilities that give rise to roles related to *wider interests*.

Below, these five sets of relationships are analysed, several roles are identified, and certain issues are noted.

Relationships with clients ➤

Travel agencies' clients include the general public, where individuals arrange and pay for private trips; and commercial clients, where an organisation arranges and pays for trips made by its employees, on trips for business or work-related purposes.

World and Country Travel depends almost entirely on the general public. Twenty years ago it was a more diverse business, with dozens of commercial accounts besides the general public, but most of the former have drifted away. In the 1980s major airlines and two large-scale travel agencies set up specialist teams in the city to compete for commercial accounts, and World and Country Travel could not offer the same discounts and services (e.g. credit) that were being offered by these specialists. As a result, it is not as profitable as it once was, and the manager, Camilla, says that her staff have had to work diligently and strategically to service its customers and win new ones.

The business of travel agents depends on what each client needs. Seven roles performed by agents for clients can be identified, and these constitute the relationship: motivating, informing, booking, purchasing, planning, organising, supporting.

Motivating sales prospects

This role is not required for most clients. However, some individuals visit travel agencies with unspecified needs, just feeling that a trip of some sort might be a good idea. Effective selling skills by travel agents can arouse motivation in these individuals, who then decide to go on a trip. Camilla's managerial responsibilities include ensuring that her agency's front-line employees ('consultants') have the competencies necessary to sell. Sales skills relevant to this role, and several others listed below, are vital in travel consultants.

Informing consumers

Many people seek information, about many aspects of proposed trips, from travel agents. The topic might be prices (What's the cheapest air fare to Hobart?) or holiday plans within a price budget (What sort of holiday could I afford if I spent $2000 for two weeks for an overseas trip?) or sources of information (Where can I get information about farm-stay accommodation in Ireland?). Sometimes the questions are about space availability (Is it necessary to book many weeks in advance if I want to fly to Germany for Christmas?) and often the questions require travel agents to make comparisons (Which cities in China besides Beijing do you recommend that I visit during my tour? or Which brand of package, Jetset or Jetabout, gives the best value for a holiday to Thailand?).

Information offered clients is not always a reply to a question but given to add to the client's knowledge of some aspect of the trip, to make them less uncertain, more motivated, more satisfied. Camilla Fedrant says that, while a lot of information can be found via the on-line computer systems in the agency, good travel consultants need a better than average general knowledge of the world's countries, regions and cities. They also need to know the sources of information among airlines, hotels, tour operators, national and regional tourism bodies.

Making and confirming reservations

Many clients need reservations made before they finalise plans for a trip. Travel agents can book (reserve) the use of a range of services—a seat on a plane or coach, a room in a hotel or motel, a place in a group tour and so on. Increasingly since the mid-1990s this is being done via websites, on-line computer systems. Years ago, letters or telephones

Visitor Information Centre, Kempsey

were used, and often a delay occurred before the client's booking was confirmed. A benefit of on-line computer systems is instant notification that the booking has been accepted.

Selling

On behalf of their clients, travel agents purchase services from principals and issue a voucher to the clients. The voucher (a ticket in the case of airline travel) gives the client a legal right to the service. The money paid in various forms (cash, cheque or credit card) becomes the legal consideration that establishes that right.

Most travel agents do not sell their own service. Like real estate agents they sell something belonging to their principals, and earn all their income on commissions from those sales. The service of the agent (the provision of information, making reservations, confirming, planning etc.) is normally provided to clients at no cost to the client.

In this way travel agents are not like professionals such as lawyers, medical practitioners and architects, who work on a fee-for-service basis and do not need to sell anything for commissions. Nor are they like those in another type of established professions (university academics and medical officers in public hospitals), who provide each service free and do not need to sell anything for commissions, as their income is derived from a government subsidy to their employer institution—deemed a public good—topped up by a fee from consumers for a wide range of non-specific services.

Planning clients' trips

Some clients need help planning their trips. A planning role exists most clearly if an agent draws up a specialised itinerary, but it exists also if the agent provides advice, about a proposed itinerary or about the brands to use (which airlines, which hotels etc.).

'Itinerary' usually means, to travel agents, a document. It sets out details on many features of each client's itinerary (route); direction (a given route often has at least two possible directions); schedule (the time spent at each place); duration (total elapsed time); dates and times for key events (flights and check-ins and check-outs); facilities to be used (names, locations, and phone numbers of hotels and inbound tour operators to be used).

Organising clients' trips

Most travel agents help their clients organise their trips. Providing a checklist of 'things to do before leaving home', giving tips for packing, for clothes to take or how much money to take, and in what forms, are examples of this role.

Camilla's policy is that the consultants provide a pre-departure checklist for every client, even those who are frequent travellers. She says that setting off on big trips, busy people who travel often usually have so many things on their mind that they might overlook simple things that can cause problems, so a professionally prepared checklist is helpful. For all the others, infrequent travellers, there are organisational issues that they might not be aware of, or might not understand.

Supporting the management of clients' trips

Underlying all the roles noted so far is a supportive role. In this sense, agents are available to assist their clients in any way that might be expected (within reason) on travel-related matters. After travellers have returned home, their travel agent might contact them to chat about the trip, to learn whether the holiday was pleasurable and to see whether all the services were as expected. A combination of the roles noted above (planning, organising, supporting) goes some way towards managing the client's trip.

Relationships with principals ➤

Five roles, described below, constitute the main threads of the relationships that retail travel agents have to their principals. These are: representing, selling and promoting, collecting information on bookings, providing financial services, and gathering market data.

Representing principals

Travel agents represent their principals in the specific markets in which each agent is based. The relationship of travel agents to their principals is based on a representative role. It occurs because hotels, airlines and the like cannot afford to maintain a presence in all geographical locations where markets exist for their services. Meanwhile, maximising sales of those services depends on widespread promotion and, more importantly, widespread opportunities for travellers to make bookings and buy tickets and vouchers. The problem is solved by the appointment of agents, widely spread geographically.

Qantas, for example, has only a few sales offices in certain cities. Were they the only places where that airline could be marketed, Qantas would not sell many tickets. In practice, most are sold in agencies. Every retail travel agency represents Qantas, merely by displaying symbols of travel and tourism.

'Accredited travel agents' are those who legally are entitled to hold themselves out as representing a certain principal or set of principals. Many agents are described as 'IATA accredited', which means they represent all members of the International Air Transport Association, a group comprising most of the world's major airlines. The consequence of this accreditation is that the agent is supplied with a stock of blank tickets and the technology for issuing tickets. A non-accredited agent can sell as a sub-agent, which requires going to an accredited agent for the tickets. The latter are sometimes known as consolidators, as they consolidate the sales in several agencies; they could also be described as ticket factories.

Selling and other promotional roles for principals

Travel agents promote their principals' services. They do this in two broad ways: one is by displaying posters, brochures and decals, and by selling that principal's services; the less obvious way is simply by promoting travel and tourism in a generic sense.

Consumers see a travel agency and two things are likely to happen. They are reminded of the possibility of going on a trip, and they assume that any sort of trip-related service can be arranged there.

Camilla Fedrant remarks that new travel consultants might naively imagine that working in a retail agency will not require sales skills. She says that unless those skills are developed, the employee does not last long.

Collecting information on bookings

Travel retailers collect information on bookings for airlines, hotels and other principals, sending it via computer or other media. This information is vital for efficient operations in each airline, hotel, tour operator and so on. The Manhattan Hotel case, presented in Chapter 12, explains one important aspect of this role.

Providing financial services

When a client pays money to a travel agency, the money does not belong to the travel agency. Instead, the agent collects it on behalf of the principals whose services have been purchased by the client. Because this money does not belong to the agent, it cannot be used in any way by the agency, for paying wages or rent for instance. It must be lodged in a trust account and remitted periodically to the principals.

Gathering market data

Every retail travel agency is a potential source of data about market trends in its district. Principals tap into this source. Managers in airlines, tour operators and wholesalers, car renters, travel insurance companies, regional and national tourism organisations, and in other trip-related principals tap into this source. Principals employ sales representatives who call on travel agents, perhaps seeing six or more per day, and one of their functions is to collect information.

Relationships with the owner ➤

As noted already, World and Country Travel's owner, Camilla Fedrant, also works as the manager. Managing in a small-scale business like this one is a part-time role, as Camilla spends most of her days working as one of the travel consultants. Putting that fact aside,

Tourist-related businesses span a wide range of sizes

Right: Made's bicycle rental business in Ubud, Bali

Below: The Golden Bay, a resort hotel on Larnaca Bay on the Mediterranean near Nicosia

she regards one duty of Camilla the manager as looking after the interests of Camilla the owner. In agencies where the managers and owners are separate persons, that distinction is clearer.

The manager's first role for the owner can be termed a steward, looking after the owner's interests. As manager, Camilla has an obligation to herself as an owner looking ahead to retirement and selling the business 10 years from now. A manager has a duty to protect and conserve the value of the shareholders' investments. An allied managerial responsibility to the owner is to use the resources efficiently and effectively in ways that earn a profit, some of which can be returned to the owner. The business should be returning a profit on top of what Camilla earns as manager.

Relationships with employees ➤

Managers are responsible for providing a safe working environment. The legal basis of this is expanded by Camilla's personal view that working environments should be more than safe: they should be pleasantly comfortable and stylish. Managers are increasingly taking some of the responsibility for helping employees to develop a career. Education and training courses of various sorts are part of the approach here. In a wider context, on the job, the mentoring and facilitating roles of managers (described in Chapter 8) are important here.

Relationships with other interests ➤

Camilla Fedrant is active in the city's Chamber of Commerce, a role she sees as helping her business community and her own work-based responsibilities, as by supporting commerce in the local district she is helping her own business. She is also active in the Australian Federation of Travel Agents, and is a volunteer worker in a local charitable association.

CONCLUSION

World and Country Travel is like many small-scale, independently owned travel agencies. It is probably feeling the effects of more travellers using the Internet as a means for obtaining information about principals' services and prices and for making bookings, bypassing travel agents (Lang 2000). Camilla has also negotiated a franchise arrangement with one of the national chains of travel agencies, a path that most independent agencies have been down before now.

ID TOURS SOUTH PACIFIC

ID Tours South Pacific Pty Ltd represents an important category of business organisation in tourism industries but a category that is relatively unknown among the general public. Inbound tour operators (ITOs) do no advertising in the mass media, and have brochures that are not displayed in travel agencies and seldom seen by any tourists. As 'inbound' implies, these organisations are involved with tourists coming into a region or country. More precisely, they are involved only with particular forms of inbound tourism.

ITOs participate extensively and intensively in tourism industries, by cooperating closely with other organisations in the same line of business, yet their clients or customers are not tourists, nor any other kinds of travellers or visitors. That paradox, once explained, is helpful in understanding the business strategies and routine activities of ITOs.

More than 100 businesses are listed under the heading 'Inbound Tour Operators' in a recent edition of *Travel Trade Directory* (Reed Business Publishing), which attempts to list all components in the Australian travel and tourism industries. In 1994 there were four large ITOs, each with notable shares of the market for ITOs in Australia. Thomas Cook, one of these, opened the first inbound office in the southern hemisphere, in Melbourne in 1872. By 2002 the pattern had changed, as noted below.

ID Tours began 101 years after Thomas Cook set up its first Australian branch. In its first year, 1973, ID Tours employed just four persons in one office, in Sydney, and handled 24 tours for 501 tourists visiting Australia. During the next 20 years it grew to become one of the leading ITOs in Australia.

Now, in a typical year, ID Tours handles more than 9000 tours (ranging in size from small parties to large groups) and in excess of 25 000 tourists. It is Australian-owned and is closely affiliated with a New Zealand company, which uses the same name in order to present a single presence in markets in the northern hemisphere. This is a useful policy, as many tourism organisations in the northern hemisphere involved in arranging trips to the Asia–Pacific region perceive Australia and New Zealand as a single destination area.

Besides being prominent in market share, ID Tours is a leader in qualitative ways, winning awards from travel and tourism industry associations and from the wider business community.

Its founder and managing director, Bill Wright, is widely recognised for his achievements and, among other leadership roles outside ID Tours, has served as a member of the New South Wales and Australian Tourist Commissions. For several years he has been a director of the Sydney Aquarium Ltd, at Darling Harbour, and in 2001 was appointed chairman of the board.

Having set out the background, the theme now shifts to the main focus of the case, a discussion of ID Tours' business activities.

Two broad kinds of business

ID Tours' business activities can be classified into two distinct types. One is focused on leisure travel, mainly involving Japanese tourists coming to Australia, and represents ID Tours as a traditional ITO. The other is focused on corporate travel, and mainly involves American and British visitors in Australia on company-sponsored trips of some kind.

This activity represents ID Tours in what is described by Bill Wright and other executives in this field as a destination management company. The two types of business are discussed below.

Inbound tour operations

Koloff et al. (1989) described ITOs' functions thus: they 'assemble, quote, book and organise the land content of a tour product, in the country in which they operate. This land content amalgamates a number of services, (1989: 272). The services might include coach transport, hotel accommodation, entertainment, meals in featured restaurants, tour guiding, and air transport between regions in the destination country.

ITOs have several kinds of clients or customers: all of them are other organisations in the business of tourism. The main ones are tour wholesalers (sometimes known as outbound tour operators) based in another place, usually another country. ITOs in Australia deal with tour wholesalers based in Japan, the USA, Singapore, the UK, Germany, Korea, China and other countries. ITOs thus provide an industrial link, part of a distribution channel, between tour wholesalers located in traveller-generating regions and suppliers of accommodation and other services located in tourist destination regions where the ITO is located.

Another kind of client is retail travel agents serving FITs (fully independent travellers/tourists) and one-off groups. The relationship with them is essentially similar to that with tour wholesalers. The difference is that FITs and one-off groups via retail travel agents usually require more personal attention—and pay for it. More precisely, what an ITO does depends on what a particular client requires, and this reflects the needs of the tourists.

ITOs provide six functions ➤

In serving clients, ITOs carry out up to six functions: itinerary planning, quotation costing, documentation, liaison and coordination, quality control, and final accounting. Some of these are described below.

Itinerary planning is not an everyday function of ITOs, because most tour wholesalers and travel agents have good knowledge of the geography and services available in places their clients visit. However, itinerary planning can be an important ITO function for clients serving special-interest tourists and VIPs ('very important persons'), in fact all the types who want (and can afford) special treatment. For example, the Japanese Prime Minister's wife made a private trip to Australia, and a travel agency in Tokyo associated with the government asked ID Tours in Sydney to arrange her itinerary.

Quotation costing is a routine function, occupying many staff at ID Tours for part of the time every week. Precise mathematical skills are essential for this work. It is triggered by tour wholesalers arranging a packaged trip or series of trips; they normally ask several competing ITOs to indicate whether they would be interested in participating by quoting, which means stating the costs of each service to be included in the package in specified destination regions. To do this, staff of the ITO contact hotels, coachlines, airlines, restaurants, theme parks etc., and get quotes from them relating to the numbers of tourists and the kind of service required, as indicated by the tour wholesaler. The ITO then adds a mark-up to cover its own direct costs and overheads, and a profit margin, and the total amounts go into a quoted costing provided to the tour wholesaler.

Winning a contract ➤

The tour wholesaler's decision as to which ITO will get the contract depends on several factors, one being the cost. A lower cost is a possible reason for a tour wholesaler selecting one ITO over others, especially in mass-market tourism, because this gives the wholesaler two possible benefits. It can decide to market the tour at a lower price, to gain more sales, and/or it can retain a higher profit margin. However, the reputation of an ITO, developed from its reliable service in the past, can also be very important.

Large-volume packaged tours typically have small margins. Net profits of tour wholesalers in large-volume markets are often below $10 per package sold, which is a fraction of 1% of the price paid by consumers; this is a smaller profit margin than in most consumer goods and services (*The Economist*, 28 October 1989: 63–4). Reasons for this condition are discussed by King and Hyde (1989) and King (1991).

Specialist niches in the FIT trade can give ITOs larger profit margins but on smaller volumes. While FIT is an acronym for fully independent tourists—those with individually customised services, specially planned and hosted for one or two persons or a small party, they are not really 'fully independent' if they come within the scope of a tour operator, but the term is used to distinguish them from tourists in group tours.

Liaison and coordination are functions of looking after tourists, on behalf of the tour wholesalers or travel agents who dispatched them. This involves a hosting role, which usually commences with what is known as a 'meet-n-greet' service at airports.

Behind the scenes ➤

Behind the scenes, the coordination function requires the ITO's staff to contact hotels, coachlines and other service suppliers to ensure that everything is ready and according to specifications. This is a vital point emphasised by senior managers at ID Tours, expressed in its stated goal: error-free tours.

Quality control involves staff in the ITO checking, by personal inspection, of standards and styles of services and facilities in hotels, motels, farm-stay houses, coachlines, restaurants, theme parks and other places used, or potentially used, by tourists under the supervision of that ITO. This might occur at the request of a manager wanting a restaurant to become an optional inclusion in packaged tourism, or it might occur during spot checks in hotels. Managers and supervisors from ID Tours say they are sometimes able to offer advice to managers and suggest improvements to the places they have checked over, especially smaller establishments.

Reasons for ITOs' existence ➤

ITOs exist because tour wholesalers, and to a lesser degree retail travel agents, need them. They need ITOs in order to support prepackaged tourism. If there were no prepackaged tourism, ITOs would not exist in their present form. There are several reasons why tour wholesalers (and travel agents selling FIT packages) use ITOs. These reasons underlie the functions described above, and are further explained below.

Managers and operational staff in ITOs have (and continuously develop) expert knowledge of the country where they live, in terms of its roles as a tourist destination. This knowledge spans all the items discussed in reference to destinations in Chapter 6, but is more precise and updated often. Based in Australia and New Zealand, ID Tours' managers and operational staff travel intensively rather than extensively in those countries, building networks of contacts and amassing knowledge of key features and facilities. This knowledge, and the personal contacts forming a component of it, are valuable resources in the design, construction and operations of prepackaged tourism. Tour wholesalers draw on this specialist knowledge and contacts by using ITOs.

A second reason why tour wholesalers need ITOs is that without them, tour wholesalers sending tourists abroad would have to establish offices and employ staff in destinations. The costs could be prohibitive relative to the amount of work to be done. A preferable arrangement, in many cases, is for tour wholesalers to use an ITO as an agent. An ITO can gain economies of scale, achieved by the consolidation of many small orders, if the ITO looks after the destination-specific needs of several tour wholesalers. ID Tours is an example. In 1994 ID Tours in Australia was serving 40 different tour wholesalers, from several countries, with a large proportion of the total volume coming from just three of those tour wholesalers. By 2002 the pattern had changed, not because of the increase in tourist numbers coming into Australia during those eight years but because of a strategic decision. (An explanation is set out later.)

A third reason why tour wholesalers need ITOs is that most tourists who use prepackaged tours require some degree of personal attention to be available in the countries they visit. Even tourists not being personally escorted might feel insecure about being in a foreign country without somebody close at hand who is responsible for helping them with any problems that might emerge. Because it has offices and resident staff in several cities of Australia and New Zealand, ID Tours is able to provide a wide-ranging service to meet this need. Phone lines are open 24 hours a day to provide immediate response.

Synergy ➤

By consolidating many small orders flowing from a number of tour wholesalers, an ITO can create a synergistic process—the basis of productivity in modern industries (explained in Chapter 11). Synergy is achieved by an ITO consolidating several tour wholesalers' orders.

When ID makes a contract with a restaurant or hotel, it can plan to send tourists there from different tour wholesalers. The consolidated volume may allow ID to negotiate a lower cost, reflecting economy of scale. The consolidation per se, different orders amalgamated, creates additional productivity through economies of scope.

Another source of ID's synergistic productivity is the computer technology within the organisation and linking ID to other organisations. One of the directors, Michael Mannington, was responsible for guiding the design, installation and performance of successive generations of computer technologies used for day-to-day activities, such as maintaining files on each tour, and for managerial activities. Recently, ID adopted 'Tour Plan', a brand of software specially designed for use by ITOs.

ITO business strategies

As noted earlier, although ITOs are very much in the business of tourism, tourists are not their clients or customers. One of the managers at ID summed up the issue by remarking that 'our only real clients are tour wholesalers'. This is because the deals and contracts that form the basis of business for an ITO are mainly with tour wholesalers. ID, like most ITOs, has no contractual relationships with tourists. It looks after tourists while they are visiting Australia, on behalf of the tour wholesalers (and retail travel agents) in other countries who have dispatched those tourists. Deals and contracts made between ID and hotels, coachlines, restaurants etc. are vital but secondary; they occur because of deals made with tour wholesalers and, to a lesser degree, retail travel agents.

Therefore, ID's critical business strategies have involved forming and maintaining relationships with tour wholesalers. In 1994 there were about 40 such relationships, of which three were on a large scale: Japan Creative Tours (JCT), a wholesaling subsidiary of Japan Airlines; Nippon Travel Agency (NTA); and Qantas International Holidays (QIH). All three relationships are based on Japan–Australia/New Zealand tourism. In 2002 a different pattern existed, triggered by dramatic changes in the mid-1990s, when JCT and NTA expanded their direct activities in Australia and ceased using Australian ITOs. This reduced ID's income by almost half. It demonstrates the risk of one company becoming highly dependent on one or two sources of business.

ID responded to the challenge by actively seeking new business from several medium- and small-scale tour wholesalers, especially those involved with Japan–Australia programs. By late 2002 it had virtually recovered to its mid-1990s position in terms of volume of activities and is now in a more secure condition, as its business risks are spread: it is no longer highly dependent on three large-volume clients.

In 1994 the major competitors of ID were four other inbound tour operators in Australia. They were Thomas Cook's inbound tours division, Silver Fern, JCT and NTA. Eight years later, in 2002, a different pattern existed. Thomas Cook and Silver Fern were no longer active as ITOs in Australia, and the major competitors of ID were Southern World Vacations (Japan), which is a New Zealand-owned ITO, JTA (Japan Travel Agency), which is owned in Hong Kong, and Japanese-owned ITOs, such as Jalpak (formerly JCT), NTA and Japan Travel Bureau.

Different types of tourists

ID handles different types of tourists, and these require slightly different handling, and slightly different strategies: groups, FITs, shore excursions, conferences and incentives.

Tour groups can be divided into three sub-categories. The largest comprises tourists on general-interest holidays using a prepackaged tour from a tour wholesaler's series. A series might run for months, with tourists arriving from abroad every few days. Some are escorted group tours, where a party of typically 20 or 40 tourists move about together, with an escort or tour manager provided by the tour operator. Others are independent tours, where all the tourists arrive on the same flights and might stay in the same hotels but follow their own itinerary and arrange their own day-to-day activities. An alternative to a series is known as an ad hoc tour, a one-off. Another type of group is for tourists on special-interest trips and technical-interest trips.

For most types of tourists, routine procedures for an ITO are similar. Passengers are met at airports when they arrive in Australia or New Zealand. Documents are handed over, notably vouchers for each prepaid service (usually prebooked), such as accommodation, meals in restaurants, trips on airlines or coachlines, use of rental cars, and admission to theme parks and to cultural performances.

Suppliers

Suppliers used by ID in 1994 included virtually all the major hotel chains in Australia and New Zealand, selected farm properties, coachlines such as AAT Kings, Clipper, Murrays and Hegarty, restaurants such as The Waterfront, JoJo and Sydney Tower. In 2002 a different mix was in place, with Murrays the most important coachline and a much wider range of restaurants being used. ID contracts with a dozen shipping lines to conduct shore excursions for cruise passengers, at ports in eastern Australia, New Zealand and a number of Pacific islands.

At the end of each month, each hotel, coachline and restaurant in ID's programs sends vouchers collected from tourists to ID's office in Sydney, as a claim for payment. The vouchers are matched with records on file and the payment processed. The sign of a well-managed ITO is prompt payment to suppliers. If payments are delayed, suppliers can be seriously disadvantaged and the industrial system of tourism eroded. This is where some ITOs can cause problems. Lacking sufficient finance for their own activities, or being badly managed, they pay their suppliers well after the due dates.

ID as a destination management company

The expression 'destination management company' (DMC) emerged in the 1990s, signifying a type of business that a number of ITOs had been performing previously but which was then growing in scale and becoming a distinctive field.

DMC roles are similar to ITO roles in two respects: both look after international visitors in a tourist destination country, on behalf of clients in traveller-generating countries where the visitors come from.

DMC roles are different from ITO roles in several respects. The visitors in the DMC roles are not tourists on holidays who normally pay for and arrange their own trips, but are visitors on some sort of business-related trip, for a conference, convention or on an incentive tour, and in all cases have their expenses paid for by a sponsor. Also, a DMC deals not with tour wholesalers and travel agents in traveller-generating countries but direct with the companies arranging the trips. Thus, in its DMC role, ID's clients are conference organisers and incentive travel companies, based in most instances in the USA or UK.

The many acronyms used widely in the business of travel and tourism might seem confusing to new students. However, a characteristic of employees in tourism industries all over the world is familiarity with this sort of jargon. There are dozens of commonly used examples. Lists explaining what they mean can be found in books such as Harris and Howard's (1996) *Dictionary of Travel, Tourism and Hospitality Terms.*

Conferences ➤

Conferences are a type of business whereby a DMC is able to adapt the resources used in group tourism (in an ITO role) to the similar needs of conference delegates. In this instance ID's clients might be associations hosting conferences with international delegates, or might be a specialist conference organiser. Sydney and Melbourne have become popular conference venues recently, and this type of business is expanding in Australia.

Incentive travel schemes ➤

Australia's largest market for inbound incentive programs is in the USA. The clients of DMCs in this instance are incentive and motivation tour specialists. Incentive tourism involves schemes to reward winners, among certain groups of workers, for achieving more than they would without incentive.

Schemes are set up, for example among 5000 commission salespersons in the USA who sell a particular brand of life insurance, or among 20 000 persons all selling a particular make of automobile. The winners might be the 200 persons (or 500 or 1000) who achieve the largest sales increase in a year. The prize, for them and their partners, is a fully paid trip to a destination chosen by the incentive tour operator. Incentive tourism from its major source, the USA, has tended to favour destinations such as Hawaii, Britain, Continental Europe and, recently gaining popularity, Australia and New Zealand.

Incentives are used because clever salespersons who are paid on a commission basis tend to stop working for more sales as soon as they reach a certain level of personal income each month, but will often keep working throughout the month, gaining more sales, if there is an impressive prize such as a fully paid trip to be won. Before incentive schemes with non-cash rewards such as international trips were introduced, many salespersons were only working only two weeks a month; now they typically work longer, and sell more.

The amount of business and profits for DMCs winning contracts to handle large-scale incentive groups can be considerable. Imagine a group with 1000 persons in Australia for 10 days on a first-class, all-expenses-paid visit. Estimate the amount of money spent on hotel accommodation, coach travel and incidentals, and calculate how much a DMC might earn if it were to charge a fee that represented a few percentage points of the total sum.

In most cases, DMCs do not earn a percentage-based margin, as applies with retail travel agents and normal ITO activity. Instead, they negotiate with their principals to provide specified services for a set fee.

Organisation structure

ID in Australia employed 45 persons as full-time staff in the Sydney head office in 2002, plus several dozen more in October to March, the busy season. There were also 10 staff in the Gold Coast, Cairns and Melbourne offices. The New Zealand company is smaller. In other parts of the world, ID has three offices in Japan (in Tokyo, Osaka and Fukuoka), two in the USA (California and Chicago) and one in London. In terms of persons employed, ID is a relatively large organisation compared to most ITOs.

ID's offices in Japan, the USA and the UK are marketing branches, not locations for inbound operations. In those locations, ID sells to and services tour wholesalers of various sorts who are sending tourists to Australia and New Zealand. Each office explores new business opportunities.

The offices in Japan have also been responsible for preparing quotations for Australian itineraries for passing on to the Japanese tour wholesalers. In what CEO Bill Wright described as 'a major change', in 2002 he was preparing to shift the Japanese quotation work from Japan to Australia. This will reduce staffing in Japan and enlarge it in Australia. The reason for the change is the very high costs of maintaining office employees in Japanese cities; the costs of staff and their overheads are lower in Australia.

ID and the Sydney 2000 Olympics

The Sydney Olympics in 2000 was a major event for ID. A total of 200 extra staff were engaged, mostly for a period of weeks before and during the Games. A special 'ID Olympics Division' was established so that this big event would not cause undue disruption to normal operations and the other staff.

Two senior managers were engaged for the Division on three-year contracts, starting in 1998. Only two other personnel from ID, including CEO Bill Wright, were involved with its Olympics Division. The three-year contracts reflected the importance of planning and other preparatory activities during the lead-up to the Olympics. A vital part of these activities was winning competitive contracts, and ID was able to win a contract with a number of sponsoring organisations, in particular Coca-Cola, the largest sponsor. As a result, ID looked after 12 000 sponsored visitors to the Olympics.

Sponsors of events such as the Olympics are organisations that give money to help with expenses for the Games in return for publicity at the event. Promotional banners and other signs displaying the brand names and logos of Coca-Cola and other sponsors were widely displayed at the 2000 Olympics, intended to induce more people to buy the sponsors' products. The sponsors also used the event to invite sponsored visitors to attend the Olympics as fully paid guests at the sponsors' expense. These visitors included important business clients and political associates of the sponsor companies.

Past and future trends

ID grew at a remarkable rate in its first 30 years. One might imagine that any ITO formed in Australia in the 1970s would have done so well, given the huge increase in inbound tourism since then, but in fact no ITO in Australia has grown as much as ID over these 30 years. Several other ITOs that were small-scale, newly formed businesses in the 1970s had disappeared by the 1990s. ID's survival and success might be partly due to luck, but are mainly due to entrepreneurial initiatives and good management.

What sort of organisation will ID be in the future? Over the long term, opportunities will be shaped by entrepreneurial initiatives and management, but several external factors might also be important. One is the trend in packaged tourism into Australia and New Zealand. If more inbound tourists became highly independent, like most trips in domestic tourism, the market for ITOs in these countries will diminish even if tourist numbers rise. Perhaps the growth in tourism from China will sustain and further develop the large flow of prepackaged business. Possibly conference and incentive travel relating to the DMC role will continue to grow strongly.

History reveals that no business organisations remain static for long. They change by adapting, or die. Long-surviving organisations in the world's tourism industries are not many, but they have changed in order to survive, as historians of business have shown: Pudney (1953) and Swinglehurst (1974) writing about Thomas Cook; Grossman (1987) about American Express. They have changed their strategies, devised new kinds of services, found or developed new markets. ID is changing in substantial and subtle ways. The range of tourists it now handles suggest that new kinds of services and new markets are part of its long-term strategy.

NOVOTEL OPAL COVE RESORT

'Novotel' is one of Accor's brands, designating a particular standard and style of hotel. Accor uses five brand names to distinguish grades of the hundreds of properties in its worldwide operations, a practice used by increasing numbers of hotel chains (Littlejohn & Roper 1991). Accor's five-star brand is Sofitel and Novotel is the four-star brand; Mercure is the brand for three-star, Ibis is two-star, and Formule 1 is the brand for Accor's one-star motels.

Opened in 1989, Novotel Opal Cove Resort is a medium-sized (151-unit) tourist accommodation property. It is owned by an investment company with the management rights assigned to Accor Asia Pacific Ltd, a Sydney-based subsidiary of Accor, a French company. In this case, topics discussed are facilities for guests, the nature of the organisation and its markets, managerial policies and practices. An ongoing economic problem, stemming from a decision in 1985 that with hindsight can be described as a mistake, will be described.

Physical setting and facilities

Opal Cove is six kilometres north of Coffs Harbour, between the Pacific Highway and the beach. The resort occupies 38 hectares, most of which are open lawns and a golf course, and adjoins public reserves along a beach. The beach has no road access, so the resort has a spacious, away-from-it-all atmosphere despite its location only five minutes from a busy provincial city.

Accommodation at Opal Cove comprises 151 units, of which 131 are rooms and 20 are villas. Support facilities include two restaurants, a bar and a cocktail lounge, two swimming pools, spa pools, tennis courts, gymnasium, sauna, and a golf pro shop.

There is a very large lobby, comparable to those sometimes found in hotels with 400 rooms. This reflects two facts in the original architectural plan. First, Opal Cove was designed to cater for large conferences: when several hundred conference delegates are present, a spacious lobby is useful in a number of ways. Second, the original plan, conceived in the overly optimistic 1980s, was to build 262 rooms in two stages. The second stage has not been constructed.

Besides the big lobby, the resort's conference facilities include six fully equipped function rooms suitable for meetings, ranging from a board of directors to an association with 550 persons in attendance. The two restaurants and bars also reflect the needs of a resort catering to conference delegates besides other guests.

Organisation structure at Opal Cove

Six persons report directly to the general manager. This statistic (in this case six) is referred to as span of control, 'the number of employees reporting to one manager' (Dubrin & Ireland 1993: 174). Opal Cove's general manager says that six or seven is appropriate, given the nature and size of the organisation and its business. Many textbooks on management discuss the factors affecting the span, observing that while conventional theories say that seven is a desirable maximum, there is a trend in some sorts of organisation towards wider spans. As the number of subordinates always increases arithmetically while the complexity in the superior manager's work always increases exponentially (Pearce & Robinson 1989: 328), that trend cannot be taken far.

The positions of the six managers reporting to the general manager were, not necessarily in order of importance: (a) financial controller, (b) resort sales representative, (c) food and beverage manager, (d) grounds maintenance manager, (e) chief engineer, and (f) duty manager, rooms. Those six positions and many others are depicted in Figure 9.1. It shows a hierarchical organisation arranged in up to six levels. Later, an additional senior manager position was created, reporting direct to the general manager—the human resource manager. Previously the HRM functions were carried out by the GM and other senior managers. The investment in a specialist person for this role reflects a growing emphasis in the resort industry on the importance of staffing. Opal Cove seems to be at the marginal size, where the creation of a specialist HRM was always desirable but not considered economical in the early 1990s.

Opal Cove's organisational structure reflects the usual principle of division of labour. Individuals specialise in particular tasks. One basis of this policy is that it puts individuals in positions where they are currently best suited, recognising that everyone has relative strengths, a particular set of skills, knowledge, experience and personality that

FIGURE 9.1 Opal Cove's organisational chart

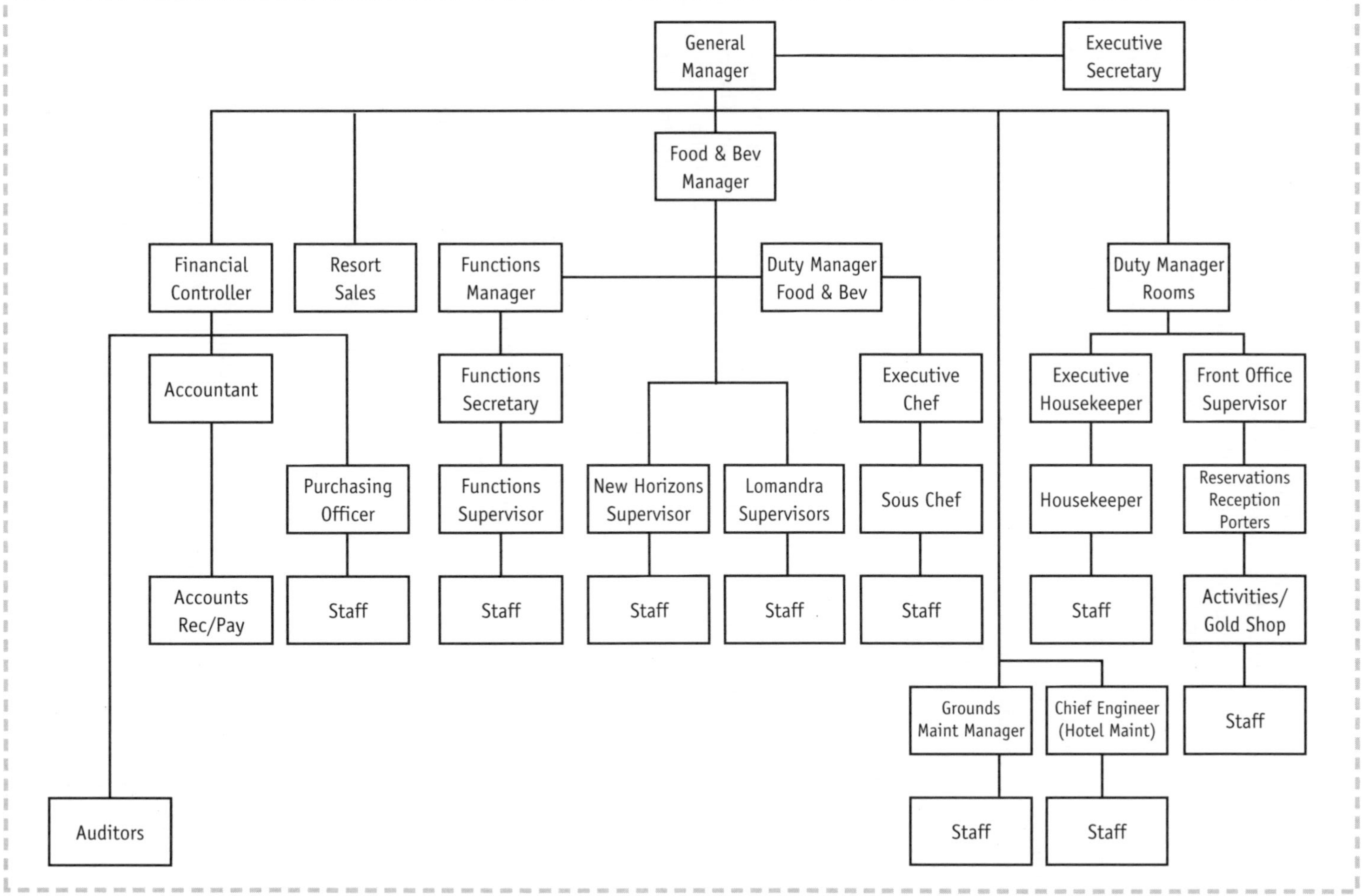

Source: Opal Cove, General Manager's office

matches the requirements for a particular position. Thus, the organisational structure reflects a staffing strategy.

Another principle in the design of many organisational structures is a controlling strategy. Opal Cove's night auditors illustrate this. Like most hotels with several functional managers, Opal Cove has employees in this designation (see the position shown in the lower left corner of Figure 9.1). These staff compile and check reports of each day's activities, to have ready for the general manager to review first thing in the morning. Their work involves compiling reports on operations that come under the responsibility of the duty manager, rooms, and the food and beverage manager. However, the night auditors do not report to either of those managers but to the financial controller. In this respect the financial controller's department functions, as its name implies, as a managerial control on the work of the operational departments in rooms, food and beverage.

There are other examples in Opal Cove's organisational chart of this controlling strategy. The chart for Opal Cove ends with the general manager, but that person is not an independent entity. He (the last two people in the position were men) reports to the Accor area manager for New South Wales and ACT, based in Sydney. Opal Cove is one of eight properties in that area manager's domain.

Markets and marketing ➤

Guests at Opal Cove can be analysed in many ways. By purpose of visit, approximately 60% are at leisure, 30% are conference delegates and 10% in other categories. This is a different mix from that in other resorts in the region, as Opal Cove has a higher proportion of conference delegates. By geographical origin, almost 90% of guests are from New South Wales, of whom 85% are from Sydney. Only 2% are from outside Australia, and these are mostly on holidays from New Zealand.

Opal Cove's general manager has on hand precise information (daily, monthly, yearly) on the mix of guests by various analyses, such as those broadly indicated above.

Almost all bookings are made by guests contacting the hotel direct, rather than via travel agents or other intermediaries. This is unlike many other resort hotels of comparable size, although similar to other resorts in Coffs Harbour. Certain effects of this feature are noteworthy. One is that the marketing of Opal Cove is done almost entirely by Opal Cove staff, rather than via links into the marketing sector of travel and tourism industries. A second effect is that for typical bookings Opal Cove does not have to split the price paid by guests with outside interests that have helped get that booking. Accordingly, the average room rate is higher than it would be if all bookings came via the travel trade.

Despite this high level of self-reliance, as part of their marketing some of Opal Cove's managers periodically attend trade breakfasts with travel agents in Sydney. At these meetings, hotels and other industry principals (airlines, tour wholesalers) can promote their products to agents in an informal setting. The reason why managers from resorts such as Opal Cove attend is that a few extra percentage points in room occupancy gained from travel agents can be the critical margin in meeting performance targets.

Opal Cove's important marketing activities are direct mailings to targeted prospects. In the leisure segment, these are mostly individuals or families who have previously stayed at the resort. For the conference segment, the prospects are key individuals in selected organisations, mainly in Sydney and Melbourne.

In school holidays periods, especially from Christmas to the end of January, Opal Cove is typically fully booked by guests who are either repeat visitors or persons coming on recommendations. In many other months of the year, while there are always guests on holidays, Opal Cove's business is highly dependent on winning contracts to host conerences. In Australia, the conference markets (for all sizes of venue) are highly competitive. Opal Cove has one staff member based in Sydney working as a promotional representative, targeting conference organisers, and working closely with the general manager (at Coffs Harbour) to win contracts.

If a conference organiser wants a quote for accommodation and services, the policy is to have a quote prepared and delivered within 24 hours. Opal Cove then tracks the prospect by contacting them every few days until the decision is made as to which hotel will host the conference. When Opal Cove wins a contract, the conference team at the resort begin action. If some other hotel wins the conference, Opal Cove's general manager investigates why, by contacting the lost prospect to complete a 'regretted business' form, which is filed for later review. In this way, over a period, a pattern of information is compiled, identifying what sorts of conferences are and are not being hosted at Opal Cove, along with the pattern of reasons.

The local resort industry

Opal Cove's neighbours include five resorts within one kilometre. Two of them, Nautilus-on-the-Beach and Pelican Resort, are similar in size to Opal Cove; another two, Aanuka Resort and Pacific Palms, are significantly smaller; and one, Pacific Bay, is larger. Pacific Bay, as the largest and newest of the resorts close to Opal Cove, is in some ways the market leader.

Managers of the properties keep in touch, and monitor what each is doing. These resorts compete with one another in several ways, but they also cooperate to some extent. The most overt evidence of competition among these resorts are roadside signs with the names, symbols and lists of facilities displayed. Sometimes, these resorts also use temporary roadside signs to promote special prices.

Managerial work at Opal Cove

One of the best-known studies of what managerial work actually involves is 'The Manager's Job: Folklore and Fact' (Mintzberg 1991a). Managerial work at Opal Cove reflects several of the points that emerged in that research. The managers tend to work long hours. Managers in Novotel resorts typically work 60 hours a week, six days a week in busy periods, and only a little less in quieter periods.

Another finding from Mintzberg's research was that managers' jobs are not dominated by routines. This is one reason why managerial careers are widely desired. However, managers' jobs do have routines. For example in a Novotel, the general manager's first activity after arriving in the office is to review the previous day's events. The data are waiting on a standard form, 'Daily Trading Report', prepared by the night auditor. The second routine activity is to decide whether anything needs to be done as a result of the information in that report, and the next activity is to implement that decision in an effective way. A second priority, another daily routine, is to inspect the daily 'Incoming Arrivals Report' prepared by computer at the front desk. This lists names, addresses and other information about all guests who checked in during the previous 24 hours. It also lists advance bookings, up to one month ahead.

Asked which aspects of his job give him the most personal satisfaction, one of the Novotel's managers said 'seeing satisfied guests, and exceeding my profit target'. He also said that every day he feels a sense of personal pride when he walks around the building.

How Accor manages standards

Accor sets precise standards for facilities and services in each of its properties. These standards are specified in manuals for each of the brands, so managers at Opal Cove follow a manual titled *Accor Asia Pacific: Novotel Resorts Standards of Operations and Facilities*. Each item is described in unambiguous terms, so that at every Novotel property the managers know exactly what is expected. From Accor's perspective, and more importantly from the guests' perspectives, the benefit of this standardisation is that it allows people away from the property to assume that all Novotels will maintain certain minimum standards across a number of items.

Periodically, one of Accor's managers visits Opal Cove and checks each itemised facility and service against the specifications in the manual, to determine whether or not the standards are being achieved. This can be termed a managerial approach for achieving planned standards.

An alternative is a market approach, which uses guests' behaviour as the indicator. For example, if significant numbers of guests complain about defective facilities or services, the hotel's administrators might decide to make improvements. In fact, Accor hotels use both approaches, but the principal one is managerial. The reason is that data in the form of guests' opinions are less reliable, less comprehensive and less representative as indicators of standards than data collected from a managerial approach.

Opal Cove's MIS

All Accor hotels follow a standardised MIS (management information system). A detailed MIS manual is provided by Accor to guide managers in the procedures. Its main output is a monthly performance report for each property, a report containing more than 200 pages. The contents are detailed and comprehensive, covering 'virtually everything', in the words of one manager. Within 15 days of the end of each month, copies are sent to head office (Accor in Sydney) and to the owners of Opal Cove. The resort's managers also use the report. To indicate the contents, Table 9.1 shows a representative extract, one day's trading report in 1994, relating to food and beverage

TABLE 9.1 Extract from the daily trading report, Novotel Opal Cove

Covers	Lomandra, breakfast	52
	Lomandra, lunch	9
	Lomandra, dinner	46
	Horizons	5
	Room service, breakfasts	6
	Room service, lunch	2
	Room service, dinner	13
	Pool bar	15
	Banquets	202
	Total covers	350
Average check $	Lomandra, breakfast	$11.76
	Lomandra, lunch	$6.83
	Lomandra, dinner	$25.55
	Horizons	$46.90
	Room service, breakfasts	$12.75
	Room service, lunch	$10.75
	Room service, dinner	$13.88
	Pool bar	$4.18
	Banquets	$32.50
	Total covers	$25.76
Beverage revenue $	Lomandra, breakfast	$0.00
	Lomandra, lunch	$48.30
	Lomandra, dinner	$424.75
	Horizons	$209.00
	Room service, breakfasts	$0.00
	Pool bar	$103.25
	Banquets	$5,971.25
	Cocktail bar	$557.25
	Mini-bars	$123.00

sales. For each outlet (each restaurant—Lomandra and Horizons, room service etc.) the total number of covers are reported, the number of meals served, and the revenue bisected into food and beverage.

In the monthly report these data are shown as actual performance, budget performance and variance—the difference between actual and budget. In that way, the managers (and owners) can analyse the performance and determine precisely where aspects of operations varied from budget. Variances give pointers to managers, indicating which items need their attention.

Opal Cove's general manager supplies a monthly report to head office in Sydney, which includes: (a) trading figures for the month and the year to date and other performance items, following the MIS guidelines; and (b) information on major non-routine events, such as equipment breakdowns, or termination of employment for salaried personnel.

Managerial meetings

The routine procedures and standardised methods described above might imply that all managerial work at Opal Cove and within Accor is highly regimented. In fact, the managers have considerable independence. For most of the time they are left alone, to get on with their own work in their own way.

There are a number of scheduled meetings, but these are not so frequent that they dominate day-to-day activities. The top seven managers at Opal Cove meet as an executive committee every two weeks. Because this is not a large group, and reflecting the personal style of the organisation, the meeting is not excessively formal. One of its main purposes is to allocate new jobs (tasks) and dates for completion to individual managers, and to review progress on current work.

Every three months all the general managers of Accor properties in Australia meet for one day. Scheduled meetings are not their main form of communication, but they are a vital form. Between scheduled meetings, informal communication face-to-face and by telephone or fax are the more usual means for managers within Opal Cove and within the Accor group to pass on information.

Problem areas

Asked to name 'the problem areas for managers of a resort like Opal Cove', one of the Novotel's managers identified two principal ones: 'having a consistent product', and 'meeting budgets for revenues and costs'. He then identified three staff-related areas: staff training, staff awards, and staff morale. Besides those day-to-day problem areas, which are common in many hotels and resorts, at Opal Cove there is another set of underlying problems.

In 1985 Opal Cove's main building was planned to contain 260 rooms, to be built in two stages. However, only stage one, with 131 rooms, was constructed. This seems to have been a wise decision, as there was a high probability that the larger capacity would have incurred ongoing losses. The downside is that Opal Cove's income-earning resources are limited to 131 rooms and 20 villas but some of its cost-incurring fixed resources are on a much larger scale.

One of those fixed resources is the large lobby. Another are the lifts, which have capacity for moving guests, staff and supplies to and from 260 rooms, and which therefore are underutilised and expensive to operate (in terms of energy consumption and maintenance) on a per-room basis when only half that number of rooms are earning revenue. A third item is the air-conditioning plant, also designed for twice as many rooms as now exist. Then there are the swimming pools, which are larger (and so more expensive to maintain) than needed for a resort of Opal Cove's scale. Likewise, the golf course is expensive in relation to the scale of the resort.

A simple solution might seem to be a decision to build the second stage, adding another 130 rooms. Then the variable revenue base and the shared facilities would be balanced. Managers at Opal Cove cannot change their property's economic handicap, but it does have ongoing managerial relevance, because performance ratios of fixed costs to variable revenues and costs will be unfavourable in comparison to other properties of similar scale.

The next case is also about a tourist accommodation business, but a rather different type. Instead of a large resort owned by a large corporation and managed as a unit in an international, branded chain, this one is owned and managed by four persons in partnership.

SANDCASTLES HOLIDAY APARTMENTS

This case is about rented accommodation, where owners of units (apartments in a strata plan) have assigned management rights to a team of professional managers. Sandcastles is a block of 36 two-bedroom apartments on Ocean Parade, Coffs Harbour. Ocean Parade's northern end is a tourist precinct, as several dozen sites in the Parade and nearby streets contain houses and apartments rented as holiday accommodation, along with several motels.

In a tourist precinct

The precinct's development has been influenced by official zoning by the city's strategic planners, but more influential over the years has been the evolution of markets and entrepreneurial initiatives as demand has developed for tourist accommodation in the neighbourhood. Next to an ocean beach, the location of a large bowling club, and in a quiet part of the city, the precinct has contained rental holiday houses and flats for at least 30 years. Now these premises vary in many ways, in age, size, architectural styles, rental tariffs, management and marketing methods.

Most tourists in the precinct, and by far the majority staying at Sandcastles, are couples and families with children, on holidays to enjoy the warm weather, beach and range of outdoor activities in the region. Lawn bowlers constitute a small but notable segment of visitors staying in this precinct. Unlike Victoria's, Coffs Harbour's bowling greens do not close for winter. Not so far from Melbourne as clubs in the far north of the state or over the border in Queensland, the Coffs Harbour clubs are visited by two kinds of lawn bowlers from the south. Many come for tournaments, for several days. Others visit for weeks on end, a winter sojourn.

Built in 1982, the three-storey Sandcastles block was converted to strata title in 1989 and the 36 apartments (known as 'units' under strata title) were subsequently sold; in 1994 there were 20 owners of the 36 units, all offered for rent to tourists. Owners seek a number of benefits from investing in units such as these: security of capital, income from rentals, capital gains and, in some instances, personal use for holidays. The units occasionally change ownership.

Managerial agreements and licence

Sandcastles is managed by a team comprising four persons in partnership: Linn and John Keelan, and Carol and Max Burt. This team bought the management rights in 1991 from a previous management team. There are three sets of agreements in place, and a licence, which influence how Sandcastles is managed.

First, the four managers have an agreement among themselves as to how they will share the work and benefits. A feature of this agreement relates to time schedules and living arrangements. Managing this property does not require all four managers being present simultaneously. Instead, the two couples can share the work. For periods of approximately 10 days, one couple lives on the premises, in the apartment adjoining the office, taking responsibility for day-to-day duties. Time on duty can be tiring, as described later, but, with this kind of managerial roster, each person can have much more leisure time than many other kinds of managers. The roster also allows one couple to be on site while the other couple travels away on promotional trips.

Second, there is an agreement in the form of a legal contract collectively signed by the Keelans and Burts as managers and by the secretary of the body corporate, representing the owners. This contract requires some of the managerial team to reside at Sandcastles at all times, and to maintain the body corporate's common property, which comprises gardens, driveways, office, swimming pool, spa pools, barbecue, sauna, corridors and stairways. For this work, the body corporate pays a fixed fee to the managers.

Third, there is a set of contracts between the managerial team and each of the owners, contracts which govern the marketing and administration of the rentals. For this work, the managers receive a commission, a percentage of the rental income, so there is a financial incentive for the managers to work towards maximising the income from rentals.

From the analysis above, two legally distinct but interwoven roles can be discerned in the managers' total work. They are stewards of the property, with authority and responsibility for care and maintenance of the building and grounds; they are also the business managers of the 36 units, with authority and responsibility for marketing, operational and administrative activities needed to attract and serve tenants.

Since 1993, managers of this sort of property in New South Wales must hold a licence. This governs certain managerial procedures, discussed later.

Markets and sources of business

Virtually all tenants at Sandcastles can be described as tourists, in an official technical sense and also following widely used heuristic concepts. Moreover, the property is designed, managed and marketed in ways that focus on distinctive charactersitics of certain categories of tourists. Sandcastles certainly can be described as being in the business of tourism.

Among the other apartment blocks in the precinct, a number are exclusively in the business of tourism, while others, such as the high-rise Pacific Towers, accommodate a mix of permanent residents and tourists and are marketed and managed accordingly, simultaneously in two lines of business. This makes managers' efforts complicated and, in some respects, divided. At Sandcastles, by concentrating on short-term rentals for tourists, managing the business is less complex.

The largest source of business at Sandcastles in 1994 was repeat trade, customers in the literal sense. This source was not as great as it might be, for potentially it would be almost 100%, and then very little marketing expenditure would be required. At present it is below 40% in most months, but the trend is upwards in the long term. Other significant sources in 1994 were guests' recommendations to acquaintances—termed 'word of mouth'—retail travel agencies, and a tour wholesaler. Ansett Holidays uses Sandcastles (along with other properties) when bundling air transport to and from Coffs Harbour with accommodation, then selling the packages in places such as Melbourne or Sydney.

Marketing Sandcastles

Marketing rented holiday apartments could be done with a minimalist policy, involving a promotional sign visible from the road, occasional small advertisements in the 'Holiday Resorts' classification in newspapers such as the *Sydney Morning Herald* or Melbourne's *The Age*, and a person sitting in a reception office waiting for prospective guests to call in, write or telephone. At the other extreme, it could involve the managers investing a lot of time, expense, creativity and energy, including trips to selected market-places—the key traveller-generating regions.

Sandcastles' managers lean towards the latter policy, within reason. They market the property assiduously. Most new business comes from their own efforts, with a minor share coming from travel agents and Ansett.

The managers believe that a carefully designed brochure is essential for this kind of business. Prospective guests might decide whether or not to seek a booking on the basis of images formed from a brochure's pictures and words. If they are deciding among alternatives, brochures might be determining factors.

When the Keelans and Burts acquired the management rights in 1991, Sandcastles' existing brochure seemed deficient. However, as 19 000 copies were in stock, the supplies were used while a new one was designed. In 1993, after a lot of planning and preparation, it was ready and 20 000 copies were printed. The out-of-pocket costs (not including managers' time) for design, photography and printing were $11 000. It is a single sheet, on glossy paper with colour photos, presented folded in half.

The front has a photo from the air above the ocean looking towards Coffs Harbour, a heading, 'Sandcastles Holiday Apartments', and a tag below 'In the heart of Coffs Harbour'. Inside the brochure and on the back are six photos showing facets of Sandcastles: the swimming pool and building, two happy young guests in a spa pool, older guests at tables near barbecues, and two shots showing the inside of units; there are also four photos of sites in or near Coffs Harbour: a sightseeing cruise, whitewater rafting, porpoise pool, and a surfing beach; the other illustration is a map showing where

Sandcastles is situated. Features of Sandcastles' accommodation and recreational facilities are briefly described. The brochure is sent to people asking for copies, given out at travel shows, issued to retail travel agents in selected cities and towns, placed in tourist information offices in Coffs Harbour and elsewhere, and handed to guests for passing on to acquaintances.

Including features of Coffs Harbour in the brochure was a planned strategy. It reflects a belief that many holiday-makers need specific images and information on what to do and see in a region, and that this helps sell the accommodation.

Promotional trips by the managers are an important part of Sandcastles' marketing. One kind of trip involves attending travel trade shows. Sandcastles' managers attend five or six of these every year, in places such as Brisbane, Sydney, Melbourne, Canberra and Hobart. Another kind involves visiting travel agencies in those cities and selected country towns. A third kind of promotional trip was participation in a delegation from Coffs Harbour tourism interests on a promotional tour in New Zealand in 1993. Market research in Queensland had revealed that each year more than 7000 New Zealanders have holidays in rented apartments similar to Sandcastles on the Gold Coast. This is regarded as a market segment in which Coffs Harbour's tourism interests should be more competitive. One year after the 1993 trip, only negligible effects had been noticed, which suggests that either a different strategy is required or that the segment is not feasible.

Star ratings influence the number and type of guests using particular tourist apartments. In New South Wales, a widely followed rating system is administered by the National Roads and Motorists Association. (Unlike most European countries, Australia has no governmental agency that issues ratings of tourist accommodation.) Sandcastles is rated four-star. Periodically, an inspector from the NRMA visits to review the rating against current standards. If it were reduced to three-star, the impact on the business would be significant. To keep Sandcastles' four-star rating, the owners (on the managers' recommendation following a report by the NRMA) recently spent $60 000 on improving certain facilities in the 36 units.

Tariffs at Sandcastles are on a weekly basis, except at Christmas. The rate includes linen, weekly service, undercover security parking, and use of the recreational facilities listed earlier. Pricing policy can be critical in successful marketing. If tariffs are too low, the business is not maximising its income, even though demand for accommodation might be high; and if tariffs are set too high, demand will be reduced. Finding an appropriate level requires that the managers carefully monitor market patterns and trends.

Communicating with the owners

Owners of rental units under delegated managers typically want to be kept informed, and managers who can keep owners satisfied in this respect are being professionally responsible. Sandcastles' managers use a number of media for this role. There is a formal meeting once a year when the unit rental business is discussed, along with issues relevant to the body corporate.

The *Sandcastles Newsletter* is sent to the units' owners four or five times each year. There are routine monthly reports to each owner, showing the income and expenses of their unit and enclosing a cheque. The amount is a monthly dividend, representing the net income from their unit(s) less an advertising levy, body corporate charge and the managers' commission.

Staffing and organisation at Sandcastles

Sandcastles' organisational structure comprises four managers, five cleaners who service the units, and a part-time gardener. Units are serviced weekly, and also after each tenant departs. The managers do much of the operational work, such as answering the telephone, reception, office work, responding to guests' requests and pool cleaning. Cleaning standards are vital to the success of good-quality holiday accommodation units offered for rent. Any deficiency, however small, will be noticed by guests, and can dissuade them from returning and from recommending the place to other persons.

Because each apartment at Sandcastles has a fully equipped kitchen and laundry, there is more scope for cleaning defects than in a hotel room. Linn Keelan says that 'good cleaners make the building a success'. Sandcastles' managers have carefully selected and nurtured a team of five persons who fulfil this key role competently, and there is little staff turnover. Some apartments in the neighbourhood have given less attention to this factor.

While the individual managers have free time when they are off roster, their working schedule can be arduous. The managers' working day begins at 6 am with pool cleaning and other tasks, and seldom ends before 11 pm, seven days a week.

Hirum Reports

In its first few years of operations, Sandcastles' monthly performance reports and profit and loss statements for the 36 units was a time-consuming task, occupying one of the managers for one week in every four. This was reduced to a half-day per month after Sandcastles acquired a computer program, 'Hirum (unit management trust reservation system) Reports—Holidays and Permanent', designed by Hicaliber Software at Southport. The program was designed specifically for managers of rented apartment buildings under strata title, where detailed reports must be prepared every month for each owner. The system is approved by government bodies involved with strata title management and produces, besides reports for managers, reports for accountants and auditors, necessary for the managers' quarterly audit.

Data inputs are fed in daily as events happen: a guest arrives or departs, a bill is paid, a cost item is charged. At month's end, the computer amalgamates all the data and produces print-outs showing reports and accounts for each unit, including the amount to be paid as dividend to the owners.

Licensed managers

In 1993 the New South Wales parliament passed a bill that requires managers of rented, strata title apartment blocks to hold a licence as an *On-Site Residential Property Manager*, issued by the Real Estate Services Council. The bill was modelled on a Queensland Act, where licensing has been mandatory for several years. John Keelan was one of the initiators of the legislation. He said that previously a number of incompetent and/or unscrupulous persons had been able to gain employment as managers and had caused problems, especially for owners. One of the features of the Act is that a licensed manager must keep properly designed trust accounts for the income earned by each owner's units. These are audited in the normal way for other kinds of trust accounts.

The initial effect is greater security for owners. In the long term, licensing the managers probably benefits all interested parties: owners, managers, employees, commercial suppliers and guests. It can also be seen as a sign of greater professionalism in this category of managerial work, and as an indicator of a higher level of industrialisation in this category of tourism.

CONCLUSION

The four cases presented in this chapter—about a retail travel agency, an inbound tour operator, a resort hotel, and a block of holiday rental apartments—represent just some of the many kinds of business organisations in tourism industries.

In each case, the organisation is in the business of tourism, purposefully supplying services useful for tourists and, in the inbound case, for tour wholesalers and retail travel agencies. In each case, the organisation is cooperating with others in the business of tourism, forming linkages that are the very basis of tourism industries,

The four cases illustrate certain principles set out earlier, in Chapter 8 on the subject of management. As depicted in Figure 8.1, in each case there is an organisation with resources under the authority of managers. The work of these managers—inside and outside their organisation—is directed at making their organisation efficient and effective. Various schools of thought about managing can be discerned, as guiding principles shaping the managers' work. Various managerial roles can also be identified, from the Carroll model and the Quinn model.

The distinguishing features in these four cases that enable them to function in tourism industries are not that tourists spend money and have economic impact, but in the ways the four organisations are managed. Thus the cases help clarify the point made in Chapter 7, that economic impact is not the best way to understand the nature of tourism industries. The better alternative is the theme to be explored in Chapter 11. It involves the management of business strategies and cooperative linkages.

Discussion questions

1. Retail travel agents have five sets of responsibilities, to five categories of what might be described as stakeholders: what are they?
2. In their relationships with their clients, retail travel agents perform up to seven roles: what are they?
3. Give examples of the various kinds of principals with whom retail travel agencies have dealings.
4. In their relationships with each of their principals, retail travel agents perform up to five roles: what are these roles?
5. If inbound tour operators' customers are not tourists, who are they?
6. What is the basis of incentive travel schemes?
7. What are the roles of inbound tour operators in incentive travel?
8. Accor is a multinational corporation operating hotels under several brand names, each representing a particular grade of hotel: what are the names of Accor's brands?
9. Describe the methods used in Accor Asia Pacific Hotels for managing standards.
10. At Sandcastles Holiday Apartments, as in many other similar businesses, three sets of agreements are in place that govern the way the business is managed. Who are the parties to each of these three sets of agreements?

Recommended reading

Harris, Robert & Howard, Joy 1994, *The Australian Travel Agency*, Melbourne: Hospitality Press

Laws, Eric & Cooper, Chris 1998, Inclusive tours and commodification: the marketing constraints for mass-market resorts, *Journal of Vacation Marketing*, 4(4): 337–52

Richards, Greg 2001, Marketing China overseas: the role of theme parks and tourist attractions, *Journal of Vacation Marketing*, 8(1): 28–38

Accor Asia Pacific http://www.accorresorts.com.au/

ID South Pacific http://www.idtours.com/

Australian Federation of Travel Agents http://www.afta.com.au/

Sandcastles http://www.totaltravel.com/travelsites/sandcastle/

Further Studies in Managing Tourism Industries

part two

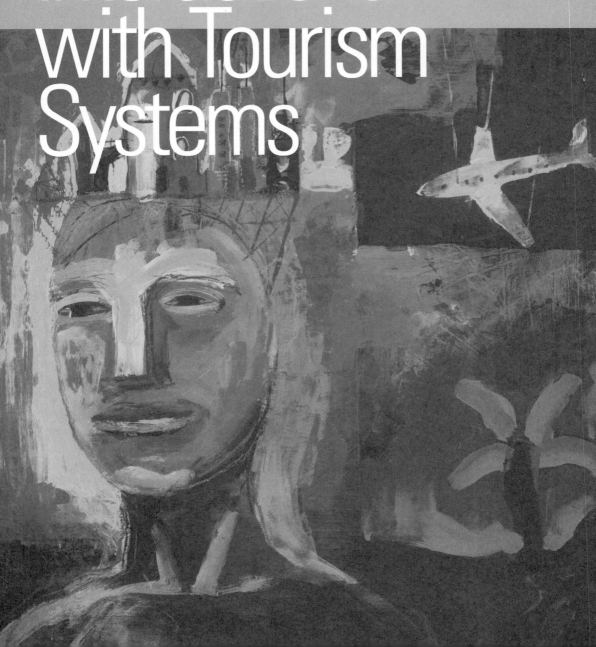

Environmental Interactions with Tourism Systems

INTRODUCTION

The environments of anything are the surrounding contexts that might affect it in any way and that might be affected by it. That is an extremely broad description. Thinking about environments begins with some kind of description and proceeds to an artificial idea, a model, in order to select particular facets or themes. Everybody does this, because (Lippman 1922: 11):

> . . . the real environment is altogether too big, too complex and too fleeting for direct acquaintance. We are not equipped to deal with it . . . We have to act in the environment so we have to reconstruct it on a simpler model before we can manage with it.

No matter how much time we spend, we cannot possibly perceive—let alone know or study or manage—all aspects of our environments. 'Environment' is also a multifaceted concept and is seen subjectively, shaped by the sensory perceptors and cultural backgrounds of each observer. The following paragraph describes some of my perceptions of my present environment. If others were here, they might not perceive the environment in the same way I do.

The room is furnished with a desk, two chairs, a bookcase. There are two travel posters and four photographs, which remind me of certain people and events. The air is cool but comfortable. Through the window are trees, two houses and blue sky. The only sounds are from birds in the trees and children in the park. On the desk are several items: computer, electricity bill, a magazine, press clippings, a diary, paper, pencils. On the floor is a waste bin half-full from yesterday's activities.

The description could be said to include physical, cultural, technological and economic environments. Different processes are evident, for the environment has effects on me and I have impacts on the environment. A better description than 'impacts' is that environments and systems interact. Certain interactions could be termed positive if they seem beneficial, according to a particular perspective and value, while others could be regarded as negative and others as benign.

In a book still often quoted, Mathieson and Wall (1982) presented a literature review of research on impacts of tourism; they remarked that three environmental categories (economic, social and physical) are useful for focusing discussions but represent an arbitrary approach, as 'the distinction is artificial for, in reality, the boundaries between the categories are indistinct and their contents merge' (1982: 3). This reflects the principle Lippman (1922) noted: that arbitrary models are necessary for thinking about and discussing environments. Besides the three categories used by Mathieson and Wall, others could be used (e.g. technical, political, legal).

Commentators and researchers usually see the links between tourism and its environments as impacts of tourism on environmental aspects of destinations. That is where the most important and controversial effects are noticed. This chapter begins by identifying simple ways of perceiving environments and showing why simplification is necessary. Environmental issues relating to destinations are discussed. The second half of the chapter proposes an alternative approach, not found in the existing literature on tourism. It looks at links between environments and all elements of tourism systems, not merely destinations. This does not contradict the first half of the chapter but adds to it. An ecology of whole tourism systems is suggested and its managerial implications are noted.

USUAL PERSPECTIVE: IMPACTS IN PLACES VISITED

Research on tourism–environment interactions can be found in hundreds of books and dozens of journals, one of which, *The Journal of Sustainable Tourism*, specialises in a subject relevant to these interactions. Almost entirely, this large body of research has traditionally focused on one broad theme, the impacts of tourists and tourism industries on the environments of places visited.

Within that broad theme, most individual commentators and researchers focus on just one category, usually economic or sociocultural or physical. Relatively few have tried to deal with many categories. Among those few, Mathieson and Wall's (1982) book and Ritchie's (1992) prize-winning essay, on environmental trends likely to shape tourism in the 21st century, are examples.

Which category of environmental impact is most important? This is a matter for judgment, and depends on the background, perspective, values and training of the person making the observations. This can be seen from a review of 23 studies on environments of places visited, where the reviewer found 'varying emphasis . . . given to economic, cultural and environmental issues, depending on the background of the writer' (Pearce 1989: 5). Douglas Pearce's word 'environmental' refers to physical environments.

Below are facts and ideas relating to three kinds of impacts of tourists and tourism industries on places visited.

Economic impacts in places visited

Tourists are usually temporary consumers in the places they visit. They stay for a while and typically consume a range of goods and services, spending money, then they leave. As tourists, most people spend more money per day than they do in their normal routines, for a number of reasons that need not be listed here.

A large flow of tourist-visitors tend to spend money on a wide range of goods and services, and also tend to use free facilities, with the result that their presence has an impact, direct and indirect, on virtually every part of the place's economic environment. Several types of economic effects on places visited are described below. Figure 10.1 is a summary.

Foreign exchange earnings ➤

International inbound tourists brings foreign currencies into a national economy by cash, credit cards, travellers' cheques and, increasingly popular, bank transfers via automatic teller machines. (The distinctive advantages of ATMs compared with other methods for foreign tourists are convenience, security and familiarity.)

When international tourists prepay before departure for the use of certain facilities, as happens with packaged tours that include accommodation or other items, the cost of the accommodation is sent to the hotel in the destination country by the travel agent or outbound tour operator.

FIGURE 10.1 Nine economic effects of tourism

Items	Comments
Foreign exchange earnings	An important effect of inbound international tourism
'Tourism gap' in national balance of payments	A misleading illusion that can cause concern among any tourism booster ignorant of economics
Business incomes	Huge in some cases, notable in many more; present to some degree in almost all organisations
Jobs supported by tourism	Many, but not nearly as many as claimed by tourism boosters
Personal incomes	Effects flow to more persons that those with jobs in tourism industries
Government income	Very large sums, especially via various taxes
Economic multipliers	Real, but not unique to tourism and a widely misunderstood effect; very difficult to measure accurately
Regional economies	Large metropolitan regions gain most; a few small regions gain a lot
Recreational and cultural facilities shared by local residents and visitors	Most notable in large cities

For most countries tourism is a minor contributor to foreign exchange earnings; in a small number of countries, including New Zealand and Australia, it is an important item; in a very few countries, it is the largest item. Foreign exchange earnings are essential to the economic vitality of national economies, and this helps explain why national governments around the world have tried to foster inbound tourism. International inbound tourism is a form of export, and, to acknowledge that fact and exploit the political advantages accruing to any institution involved in exports, the Inbound Tour Operators Association in Australia recently changed its name to ATEC, the Australian Tourism Export Council.

Inbound tourism is often described as an 'invisible export'. This is because the foreign exchange it earns is credited in the national accounts to an item known as 'invisible earnings', which includes insurance premiums, shipping fees and tourism. This accounting system was designed 60 years ago, when international tourism was a very small-scale activity, and is clearly out-of-date. International tourism in fact was never 'invisible', and these days is more visible than ever. Tourists in large numbers can be easily seen, as can the facilities and operations of tourism industries.

There remains another anomaly in the way tourism is measured as an export. Traditionally, tourism has been measured in terms of arrivals—as an inbound flow— because, for more than 100 years, all travellers arriving in each country have been screened into categories by immigration authorities to determine who should be allowed in and under what sort of legal status or visa. This created the tradition of describing foreign tourism as 'inbound' tourism. The term belies the fact they they are, from an economist's perspective, a kind of export.

From the perspective of national economic management, international tourists should be counted when they leave each destination country, as exports—not when they arrive. We could then say that Australia, for instance, received an unstated number of international visitors last year, processed them in tourism industries, and then 'exported X million tourists and gained as a consequence \$Y billion in export earnings'. This arrangement would enable international tourism to fit more neatly into discussions of its effects on national economies.

Tourism 'gaps' in balance of payments ➤

Positive foreign exchange earnings and a consequent positive balance of payments allow national economies to import a range of goods and services to sustain material well-being without having to sell capital resources to foreigners, or to go into debt.

Estimates of earnings from inbound tourists are recorded as credits in accounts of each country's national balance of payments, following the standard method of national accounting used globally. Meanwhile, estimated expenditure abroad by residents of the same country are recorded as debits. The net figure, the difference between the amount a country earns as an international tourist destination and the amount it spends as an international traveller generator, is called the 'travel gap' or 'tourism gap'.

Collier correctly remarks that 'it should not be assumed that a deficit on the tourism balance of payments is always a bad thing' (1989: 268). Like many other commentators, he understates the point. The gap is an abstraction, and its measurement and consideration in national policy is irrelevant. There is no real problem if a country has a large negative tourism gap, any more than if a country has a large gap in its balance of payments related to imports versus exports of oil, or computers, or any other item. Problems occur only when the total balance of payments (all items combined) is negative to a large degree, and remains that way.

Business incomes ➤

Tourists' expenditures in places they visit are reflected as incomes of the suppliers of the goods and services purchased. Because a large number of tourists usually purchase a wide range of items, a wide array of business organisations earn revenue from tourists, either directly or indirectly. This economic gain stems from both sorts of tourists, international and domestic.

Personal incomes ➤

Residents in places visited by tourists might earn all or part of their income from tourists, if they work as employees in a business deriving revenue from tourists. People earn income from the same source if they are shareholders in companies earning profits from tourists. Because tourists' expenditure is spread into all sectors of national economies, all employees and shareholders can be said to earn a portion of their incomes from tourism, directly or indirectly, to varying degrees.

Governments' income ➤

Governments derive income from tourists in several ways, and the large amounts help explain why governments have shown increasing interest in promoting international inbound tourism especially. A lot of governmental income derived from tourists is indirect, via taxation. This comes from taxes on incomes—business and personal—that are derived from tourists. Another source, usually minor in comparison, is the revenue of government-owned businesses earning income from tourists.

Governments in many countries gain revenue from tourists' spending if there is some sort of transactions tax. In several countries, a service tax is imposed on hotels and restaurants. In a number of Asian countries a service tax is also imposed on restaurants serving foreign tourists; the rate is usually 10% on the bill. In many countries there is a transaction tax on all marketised items; this is called VAT (value-added tax) or GST (goods and services tax). In New Zealand, GST began in 1986 at 10% on everything sold, and was raised to 12.5% in 1989. The bulk of the revenue collected from VAT or GST comes from residents, but the amounts collected from foreign tourists can be substantial. For instance, if foreign tourists spend $5 billion in a year, the government may collect $50 million on a 10% GST, an amount sufficient to pay for a lot of facilities and services, useful for residents as well as visitors.

Taxing tourists can be seen as equitable, as they use many public facilities and services without paying; if they are taxed, via GST, they contribute to the costs. In Australia, a 10% GST applies to certain items only, but the sums raised by governments from tourists in this way are huge.

Employment: many jobs, but not as many as is often claimed ➤

Many jobs are supported by tourism. Jobs are wholly supported by tourism if all the consumers of goods or services provided by an employing organisation are tourists. This would normally be the case in a resort hotel, or with a tour operator.

Much more common are jobs supported partly by tourists and partly by non-tourists, such as local residents. This is because tourists' spending is spread across all types of goods and services, to a varying degree. Virtually all tourists spend money on food; some spend on hotel accommodation; at the other extreme, only a few tourists spend money purchasing cars, houses or furniture.

Misleading propaganda messages, spread in the mass media by tourism boosters, greatly exaggerate the number of jobs in tourism industries. The World Tourism Organisation and the World Travel and Tourism Council have been the great global fudgers. Tourism Training Australia, the Australian Tourist Commission and the National Office of Tourism have issued similarly fudged figures in this country.

There are not 120 million persons employed by tourism worldwide and there are not one million in Australia. An analysis of tourism employment, explaining how the errors occur, can be found in a research journal (Leiper 1999a). The true numbers are closer to 40 million and 300 000. The errors occur because those doing the calculations assume that all the money spent by tourists goes into supporting real jobs, held by individual persons. In practice, that is not so. In every country, only some of the money spent supports real jobs held by individual persons; most of the expenditure is spread thinly over the entire national economy and helps support every job in the country.

What the technicians in the WTTC, WTO and Australia's Bureau of Tourism Research actually estimate is the number of equivalent full-time jobs supported by tourism. These comprise a number of real jobs (positions in hotels, tour operators, theme parks, travel agencies, airlines etc.) and a much larger number of notional 'jobs', representing the combination of tiny fractions of every job in the country. Unfortunately, when the estimates fall into the hands of public relations agents working for the WTO, WTTC and other boosterist institutions representing tourism industries, they typically write press releases that portray the numbers of equivalent full-time jobs as real jobs. This can make 'the tourism industry' seem very large, and help create the political advantages described in Chapter 7.

Figure 10.2 presents a matrix describing an analytical approach that could give a more truthful picture. The matrix cannot show statistics for its four categories, because no detailed research studies are known that have attempted to divide the employment sustained by tourism, in any country or region, into the four categories.

Economic multipliers ➤

Economic multipliers apply to all aspects of regional and national economies. They describe how one item of economic activity, such as a person spending money, has

---

FIGURE 10.2 Four categories of employment supported by tourism

	Directly involved with tourism	Indirectly involved with tourism	Total employment effects
Real jobs supported (full- and part-time)	a	b	a + b
Other EFTJ (equivalent full-time jobs)	c	d	c + d
Total employment effects	a + c	b + d	a + b + c + d

ripple-like effects when the recipient spends it and so on through successive rounds of economic activity. Multipliers are calculated as ratios. Thus, if $1 spent eventually creates $2.50 in spending in the same region or country, the expenditure multiplier is 2.5.

Because most tourists spend money, and because governments and other institutions are interested in how much this spending affects economies, in recent decades economists have been calculating the size of tourism multipliers in many places. Among many articles on the topic is one in *The Encyclopedia of Tourism* (Fletcher 2000). Unfortunately, while most of the research literature on tourism multipliers gives details on how they are calculated, most of the literature, including that article, fails to mention their practical utility. Before addressing that theme, the theory of tourism multipliers will be outlined.

When tourists spend money it becomes revenue for the recipients—the suppliers of goods or services, such as shopkeepers or hoteliers. Later, the shopkeepers and hoteliers will spend some or all of that revenue, for paying wages to employees and purchasing new goods to sell. Afterwards, from that spending, a third round of spending is triggered, when the secondary recipients spend a proportion of what they received. Then a fourth round, and so on. From the original expenditure, in each successive round of spending, over time, the sum of money circulating in a particular economy (a town, region or country) becomes smaller. This is because recipients seldom spend all they receive within the economy in question. They might save a portion, or send a portion out of the economy, as happens when a business buys something from another place, or when a person sends money to a relative living elsewhere, or when a company sends profits to a distant shareholder. Therefore, eventually the rounds of spending triggered by the original spending by a tourist will cease.

The *expenditure multiplier* is the sum of spending in all rounds divided by the original spending. If tourists in a region spend $120 million annually which, over several rounds of spending, generates total expenditure in a given economy amounting to $204 million, then the tourist expenditure multiplier is 1.7 (204 divided by 120).

Several kinds of multipliers could be calculated. One is the *expenditure multiplier* described above. The *employment multiplier* is an indicator of how many jobs are sustained in an economy as a consequence of an original sum of expenditure; the *income multiplier* indicates how much income is created. The three kinds of multipliers will normally have different values.

Methods for calculating multipliers with any degree of accuracy are highly complex, and only specialist econometricians need the competence. Managers involved with tourism do not need those skills, but because multipliers are mentioned widely in discussions about government tourism policies, a theme with implications for managers, there are advantages in understanding what the multipliers represent, what they do not represent, and their practical uses. Learning that the tourism expenditure multiplier in the Bunyip Region is 1.34 might be satisfying for some people, might give them a warm inner feeling supporting their belief that Tourism Is A Good Thing, but the knowledge in itself has no practical use.

Economic multipliers are not unique to tourism. They can be calculated for any kind of economic transaction. This indicates their practical use, which is allowing comparisons between sectors of an economy as a guide to good government policy. Statistics from a few years ago in Fiji illustrate the point.

Inbound tourism was contributing 12% to Fiji's gross domestic product, and more growth was possible. To increase tourism would require expenditure on promotion. As private-sector businesses were unwilling to finance the extra promotions, the government would have to make a policy decision, to determine whether more public resources should be allocated to tourism. The decision was shaped by the values of two multipliers. Economists estimated the tourism income multiplier in Fiji to be 0.94 and the sugar income multiplier to be 1.47. In those circumstances, if the government's priority was to boost incomes in Fiji, the best policy would be to allocate more resources to developing sugar and not so much to tourism. A balanced outcome, giving an equal amount of assistance to sugar and tourism, would have been wrong (Central Planning Office 1985).

In those circumstances, owners and managers in Fiji's tourism industry would be wasting their energy if they accused the government of making a bad decision. The fact that boosting tourism would create more income for Fiji might be true, and no doubt would have received a lot of attention in the messages from public relations consultants hired by tourism interests. That is irrelevant. What is relevant is that every extra $1 in sugar income would create a greater rise in total incomes in Fiji than an extra $1 in tourism income.

Another practical use involves calculating a multiplier in a particular economy for several years, to monitor any significant trends and to interpret what they indicate.

Regional and national economies ➤

When tourists visit any place and spend money, the local economy gains to some extent. Popular regions can gain hugely. If the tourists are entirely domestic—people who live in another region in the same country—the nation's economy gains nothing, because all that has happened is a transfer of money from one region to another. Domestic tourism does not do much for a nation's economy in terms of incomes and employment. International inbound does.

Leisure facilities for locals ➤

Consider theatres, cinemas, opera houses, art galleries, museums and concert halls in cities such as Melbourne, Sydney, Paris, London and New York. There are almost always tourists in the audience. Without them, the cities would have fewer of these facilities and the cost of seats for locals would be higher. Visitors and residents in many places, especially large cities, share many kinds of leisure facilities. Tourists in large numbers can make a difference to a facility's economic feasibility, so more locals are able to use it because tourists help support it.

This example demonstrates how different facets of the environment are linked. Tourists using theatres means direct economic impact in the form of extra income for the theatres, which simultaneously means indirect economic impact in the form of more theatres available for locals, at lower prices, which simultaneously affect social and cultural environments. Also, the structural presence of theatres can be regarded as one of tourism's effects on physical environments.

Street market in The Rocks, Sydney

The example also suggests why environmental benefits of tourism are not intrinsic but depend on particular conditions. Leisure facilities might be shared by tourists and locals if the two groups have common tastes and comparable incomes, as happens with theatres in large and cosmopolitan cities. It does not happen in every tourist destination.

Economic effects in destinations are generally beneficial ➤

The items listed above, especially in combination, are generally beneficial to the economic environments of destinations. Alongside these, there may be negative economic impacts or costs. Less is known about economic costs, such as the higher inflation and land values caused by tourism. The available evidence indicates that when places are visited by tourists, economic gains are the general rule. However, as the next section will show, economic benefits tend to be offset by social and cultural costs.

Social and cultural impacts in places visited

How does tourism change societies and cultures in places visited? What are the characteristics of guest–host interactions? In what ways are the changes beneficial or detrimental? 'Guests' and 'hosts' are labels for tourists and the residents of places they visit. Often the ideal connoted by the labels is not realised, so the visitor does not behave or feel like a true guest and the local does not feel or behave like a true host.

Five characteristics can be identified in interactions between tourist-guests and local-hosts. These are not universal characteristics, but generalisations.

First the interactions tend to be transitory, not permanent or long-lasting, and so there is seldom any commitment, by guest or host, to giving their relationship qualities found in long-lasting relationships between people.

Second, the relationships are typically quite brief and expected to be so. This means that each local (host) typically has only a short encounter with each tourist (guest), and neither party believes it will be an encounter developing into a substantial relationship of the sort that develops among neighbours and friends. Of course there are a few exceptions, as with all general theories: examples could be cited of individuals who have become close friends (and more) as a consequence of meeting as tourist and local resident.

Third, in mass destinations each host typically encounters a continuous flow of guests, and has transitory and brief communications with many of them. If many of the tourists are from the same generating country, and from a similar social class, and if they behave in similar ways regarding their attitude towards the locals and the activities they engage in as tourists, then inevitably over time the locals will form a blurred image of any individual differences among them. Examples of this pattern can be observed among Parisians' opinions of tourists from the USA and among the Balinese opinions of tourists from Japan and from Australia.

Fourth, the relationships are unbalanced in a number of respects. Hosts are in familiar territory and going about routines, while guests, as a rule, are in unfamiliar territory and engaged in non-routine behaviour. Hosts are often at work, while guests are at leisure. Most contacts between hosts and guests occur when hosts are in serving roles and guests are expecting to be served, and often the hosts are trying to sell things to the guests, which are two factors inhibiting the sort of balanced relationship that is best for social interaction.

Finally, most contacts between hosts and guests are not spontaneous. They occur as a result of the structural and functional features of mass tourism. Tourists are welcomed on arrival in hotels and restaurants by employees whose job requires that their manner be warm and smiling. Tourists arriving at these places expect to be looked after because they have paid for that right, and many also expect a warm, friendly and smiling manner. After a paid 'host' has welcomed several thousand tourists in this way, the friendly manner can become difficult to maintain. A remarkable English film, *O Lucky Man*, dramatically portrayed how its hero, a naturally warm and smiling young man, began working as a travelling salesman and changed after several years of hardening experiences into a depressive who could not smile even when he tried. A book titled *The Managed Heart: Commercialisation of Human Feeling* (Hochschild 1983) discusses broad aspects of this theme, describing what it calls 'emotional labour'.

These five characteristics explain why relationships between tourists and locals are often shaped and damaged by the stereotyped images that each party holds and has reinforced about the other. Stereotyped relationships inevitably create a sense that the other party is inferior in certain ways (Goffman 1964). This can happen even if the other party is superficially treated as an equal, or as a superior. Because of this, tourism in many forms is not conducive to mutual understanding between people who meet or are in close proximity as 'hosts' and 'guests'.

Tourist-guests are often valued by local-hosts for the economic benefits they bring, and might be treated as superior because of that value. This becomes part of a stereotyped notion of tourists that handicaps the social interaction of guests and hosts. Locals perceive tourists as lacking individual personalities because their behaviour and/or appearance conforms to a mass stereotype, and tourists simultaneously require certain sorts of homage because they are big-spending consumers. Overlaying those broad images are stereotypes about particular categories of tourists. On Queensland's Gold Coast, for example, casual conversations with locals will reveal that many have stereotyped images of Japanese tourists and also of 'Mexicans', the term they give to tourists or recent immigrants from Australia's southern states.

In places such as Papua New Guinea and Fiji, where international tourists come into contact with hosts whose recent ancestors lived a primitive lifestyle, the conditions are likely to be extreme: '(R)elations between tourists and recent ex-primitives are framed in a somewhat forced, stereotyped, commercial exploitation model characterised by bad faith and petty suspicion on both sides' (MacCannell 1992: 270).

Six factors in negative social impacts ➤

From the perspectives of residents in tourist destination regions, there are many factors behind the negative feelings they often form about tourists. Six are described below.

Tourists exceeding social carrying capacity

In mass tourist destinations, being hospitable becomes increasingly difficult for locals if their neighbourhood or town seems to have been taken over by tourists, who then appear as invaders. Doxey (1975) found that over time, when numbers approach and pass a region's social carrying capacity, the attitudes of hosts towards guests go through a sequence of stages.

The first is euphoria, when tourists are welcomed wholeheartedly. Next is apathy. Then comes irritation, the beginning of strain, then antagonism, when a definite anti-tourist feeling becomes apparent. Finally there is xenophobia, intense dislike of any outsiders, foreigners especially. Social carrying capacity is different from physical carrying capacity; the latter is simply the accommodation spaces available for visitors.

Problems of strained hospitality are real, but have been exaggerated by many commentators, especially when referring to whole countries. Turner and Ash (1975) made an error in this regard that many subsequent commentators have repeated, perhaps because they do not understand a simple principle about tourism. Turner and Ash remarked that Spain was hosting 35 million international tourists annually, but, as the resident population was only 34 million, social problems were inevitable. The clear implications were that there were more tourists than locals and that the locals must feel threatened in some way. The remark and implications are misleading.

The 35 million tourists were not all in Spain at the same time; the 35-million statistic refers to a flow over a year, and on an average day in the mid-1970s there were only 800 000 international tourists in Spain, which represents one tourist for every 40 Spaniards. Also, the geographic distributions of the two populations were different. The 800 000 tourists were mostly clustered in a small district (Torremolinos, Palma etc.). Most Spaniards live in cities and towns where tourists are relatively few in number and where they cluster in a few precincts. Few tourists visit residential suburbs or industrial districts.

Problems of social strain from tourism can be severe at the level of a neighbourhood or precinct, but as a rule are less severe, and might be insignificant, in whole towns, cities and countries. In cities such as Paris, New York, Hong Kong, Singapore, Bangkok, London, Sydney and Los Angeles, which can be described as mass tourist destination regions, large numbers of tourists can be observed in only a few precincts, while most parts of these cities and their suburbs see relatively few tourists. Overall in these cities, the stocks of tourists are only a small fraction of the resident populations.

In many small towns the reverse is true. In the resort town of St Anton in Austria, in the 1990s the resident population of 2500 was usually outnumbered by overnight visitors, comprising approximately 180 000 tourists per annum towards the end of the decade, besides several thousand seasonal workers (McGibbon 2000: 118–19). Total tourist-nights in the town were approximately 970 000, which represents 2650 on an average night. In the ski season the average was approximately 4400, or two visitors for every resident. Byron Bay, one of Australia's best-known resort towns, has an even more pronounced imbalance during peak times, when 25 000 overnight visitors are in town along with fewer than 9000 locals: three visitors for every resident. Moreover, in Byron Bay, day-trippers can greatly outnumber overnight visitors.

A principle is that problems of tourism exceeding social carrying capacity can be most accurately analysed as a local issue at the level of town or precinct, not as a metropolitan or national issue.

Debasement of local culture by commoditisation

Greenwood's widely quoted study described how Fuenterrabia, a small Spanish town, saw its local traditions destroyed as a living culture when, over several years, its festivals became popular tourist attractions, promoted by commercial interests in and beyond the town. 'The commoditization of culture does not require the consent of the partici-pants . . . Once set in motion the process seems irreversible and its very subtlety prevents people from taking any clear cut action to stop it' (Greenwood 1978: 137).

Increases in tourist numbers visiting festivals in some towns have been so great that the locals' roles have become submerged and their cultures debased or destroyed. Near the end of his life Hemingway was reminiscing in Pamplona, and remarked on the increased tourism there. He had visited several times previously during Fiesta de San Fermin, a festival in July each year famous for one of its events, the fighting bulls running through the streets. He remarked, in 1959, how 'there were not twenty tourists when I first came here nearly four decades ago. Now, on some days there are close to a hundred thousand in the town' (Hemingway 1985: 97).

Solo, a city in central Java, has an annual pageant when the *kraton*, the palace of the Sultan, is the setting for traditional music and colourful parades of people dressed in traditional ceremonial costumes. Among thousands of locals, the total quantity of foreign tourists at the festival recently has been fewer than 100. Unlike Pamplona and hundreds of other places, Solo's pageants have not yet been swamped by tourists.

Even where there are very large numbers of tourists, not all local cultural traditions are destroyed. In some ways they can be supported. Manning (1979) discussing Bermuda, Noronha (1979b) and Vickers (1989) on Bali, and Andronicus (1979) on

Cyprus all pointed to local factors that can conserve local cultures, while exposing aspects of them as mass tourist attractions. Noronha (1979b: 201) remarked:

> *Most careful observers of Bali have maintained that tourism has not destroyed Balinese culture. Why is this so? One possible reason is that customary ties with the bandjars are so strong . . . A second is that tourist routes are well defined, and tourism only touches the fringes of Balinese life . . . A third and probably most important reason in that tourism offers Balinese opportunities to profit from what they have always done: dancing, painting and carving.*

Not all societies are so culturally resilient as Bali, Bermuda and Cyprus, and therefore Greenwood's pessimistic view may be more typical of what is happening worldwide. Evidence for pessimism is found in many sources, such as Butterworth and Smith's (1987) photo-essay on the commoditisation of Maori cultures in New Zealand, and reports on Koori cultures being commoditised by tourism interests in Australia (Hawke 1992). Recent research in Bali is not so optimistic as Noronha was, years ago (Picard 1996; Leser 1997).

Damage by demonstration effects

Foreign tourists, behaving naturally and doing the sorts of things tourism usually involves, demonstrate foreign cultures. They demonstrate behaviours, attitudes, and what is often termed 'lifestyles', in front of local residents. In particular, they demonstrate a lifestyle of sustained and indolent leisure. Younger and easily impressed people in host societies see this demonstration without realising that for 12 months or more the tourists have probably been working, saving to pay for a holiday. Not fully recognising that fact, hosts might assume that a life of leisure, in all its demonstrated forms—idleness, playing, self-indulgent spending—is normal and central in modern societies.

Tourists also demonstrate a materially rich lifestyle, by spending more each day than most locals, especially in Third World destinations, earn in a year, and by spending on what Veblen (1970/1899) termed conspicuous consumption. Many services and goods consumed by tourists are highly conspicuous, non-essential and status-claiming. Locals see or hear all this, and see how tourists are served in airports, restaurants, shops, bars, theme parks and hotels. Tourists are seen to be attended by servants in one form or another. Servants clean their rooms, bring drinks and food to their room or in restaurants and bars, drive them to sights and shops, and hoteliers wishing to impress guests have the service personnel do things with a grand show of service. Veblen demonstrated how conspicuous consumption (unnecessary, excessive, but obvious) is valued by status-conscious consumers.

Obviously not all tourists who participate in these things are excessively concerned with status, but that is irrelevant here. The point is that locals perceive the excessive consumption, and attribute significance to it, which reinforces in their minds a stereotyped image of tourism.

Tourists also demonstrate a highly mobile lifestyle. Locals who might never have travelled beyond the next town are impressed by tourists' freedom to range from country to country.

Many tourists behave in ways that transgress local customs. Often the transgressions are minor and unintentional, so merely build stereotyped images. An Australian in England, for example, may talk in familiar, friendly ways to unknown locals, to persons who might be from a different social class and who cannot possibly discern from the accent whether this tourist is a common yobbo or a member of the upper class—and, worst of all, has begun talking in a familar way without being introduced. Thus, for the past 150 years, the English have formed stereotyped images of the Rude Australian. The process requires a clash of both customs and ideologies. Many Australian tourists in England are incapable of easily adapting to local customs, while many English (in England) are incapable of socialising with strangers who cannot be slotted into a certain social class (above, below, or equal to their own—it does not really matter), which is often necessary for smooth social relationships between strangers in England. The result is stereotyped image-forming on both sides.

Adapting to the culture of a new country is a very difficult role. It cannot be learned in a few weeks, even with study. Nothomb's (1999) factually based novel shows that even with fluent skills in the language and months of residing and working in a foreign country, the outsider is still prone to making cultural mistakes that can lead to offence or embarrassment. No doubt this is partly why many tourists behave very cautiously, and why many avoid the issue by keeping inside an escorted group.

Other examples of clashing customs that lead to stereotyping include Western tourists in Asia not showing reverence to older persons, appearing semi-naked on beaches, refusing to haggle over prices in markets, kissing one another in public, behaving in inappropriate ways in temples, and displaying emotions in public. Conversely, on Australian beaches, certain types of foreign tourists can be observed staring ('perving' in local jargon) at naked or semi-naked bodies, when the local custom dictates that, as Robert Drewe's book *The Bodysurfers* puts it, 'ogling is out of the question'.

So much for the demonstrations. The demonstration *effects* are the effects of these demonstrations on local societies and cultures. The primary effect is the creation and maintenance of stereotypes, about tourists in general, about foreigners, and about particular nationalities. Secondary demonstration effects flow from these, and tend to be detrimental when the destination is a materially poor country and the tourists are from a rich country.

Children, teenagers and easily impressed adults in the host society are inclined to envy the lifestyle demonstrated by tourists—its material riches, its leisure and mobility and its self-indulgent freedom from traditional customs. If envy becomes strong desire, problems emerge in the host society. Teenagers wanting material riches in a country where jobs are scarce are tempted to gain money by crime or prostitution, or by emigrating, all detrimental to the local society. If their ambition cannot be achieved in any way, the teenagers can become excessively frustrated, then apathetic or anomic.

Older and conservative members of host societies often develop a different sort of secondary effect to the demonstrations. They come to regard tourists as decadent influences on the local society and its cultures. Thus, they may accept inbound tourism for its economic benefits, but form anti-tourist attitudes in other respects. Thus, the demonstration effects can widen the generation gaps in host societies.

Low-status jobs

In mass tourist destinations, the majority of jobs involving direct contact with tourists are low-paid: preparing rooms and meals, serving in simple tasks, cleaning up afterwards, waiting at tables, bars, hotel front desks or telephones. These jobs have relatively low status. They are often available on a casual basis, rather than on permanent arrangement. They usually mean working shifts. For each and all of those reasons they are avoided by most workers if other jobs are available.

In Florida, Ehrenreich's research (2000) showed dramatically how and why only desperately poor persons would work in some of the hotels and restaurants, not so much because they are low-status jobs but because they are very badly paid, exceedingly tiring, and are under managers who often treat workers very badly.

Neocolonialism

Since 1945, more than 150 countries have become nominally independent nations. Formerly these were colonies of British, French, German, American and other empires. In newly independent nations there are concerns about neocolonialism, about slipping back to colonial status while nominally free and independent of a former imperial power.

Certain activities of multinational companies in tourism industries have been described as neocolonialist, a term meaning that a foreign organisation is treating the host country as a colony, a place to be exploited with only token regard for the aspirations of locals and their sense of national sovereignty.

Manifestations include the following. In foreign-owned hotels, the best jobs are often kept for persons from the foreign country in which the owners of the hotel live. Profits are repatriated to shareholders abroad. Company directors in a distant country influence government decisions in the host country. Thus, while the relationship between one country and another might have changed *nominally* when a colony gained independence, the real economic and political relationships can remain the same—imperial and colonial.

Rodenburg (1980) distinguished three kinds of tourist accommodation in Bali: (a) 'large industrial', his term for five-star hotels, owned by interests outside Bali; (b) 'small industrial', which are economy-class, smaller hotels, some of which are owned by Balinese; and (c) 'craft' (i.e. non-industrial), the home-stay guesthouses, all owned by Balinese. Rodenburg found that the Balinese economy gets most economic benefit per dollar spent by tourists using category (c), because virtually all the money spent remains in Bali. Tourists using other categories tend to spend more per day, but much goes out of Bali. His estimates of leakage were 40%, 20% and zero for categories (a), (b) and (c) respectively.

Tourism and immoral conduct

Behaviour that many persons regard as immoral occurs where large numbers of people live or gather. Drug use and prostitution are examples. These and other activities deemed immoral by some persons will occur in mass tourist destinations, with a proportion of tourists involved.

Hall (1991) cited prostitution and crime as examples of immoral conduct fostered when places become popular tourist destinations. Chesney-Lind and Lind (1986) discussed the issue in relation to Hawaii, while Walmsley et al. (1983) looked at crime–tourism links in Australia, and Hong (1985) presented press reports on tourism–crime–prostitution links in Asia. Opperman (1998) and Ryan and Martin (2001) have presented further research on sex tourism.

Tourists can be relatively easy (and profitable) targets for thieves, for they carry money and other valuables and spend a lot of time in public places. Meanwhile, tourists' hotel rooms are good targets for robbers. Robberies on a tourist's last night of a stay in a hotel are more common, because this gives robbers an advantage: the chances are the victims will not postpone their departure if this causes great inconvenience, so the victims do not report and follow up the crime with local police. Knowledge of when individuals are planning to check out is not difficult to obtain in a hotel where records are not treated in confidence or not kept securely.

Three parties gain when tourists are victims of theft or robbery: the criminals, and two parties located far away, in traveller-generating regions. These are insurance industries, which make profits on travel policies, and travel agents, who take large commissions (often 25% or more) for selling the policies. If there were very little crime against tourists, fewer policies would be sold.

Two parties lose. Tourists lose as individual victims, and lose collectively by paying high premiums on travel insurance. Business interests in tourist destinations lose if crimes against tourists are perceived to be common, because this will deter potential tourists. No doubt countries with the worst reputations for theft and robberies against tourists would be visited by more tourists if the crime incidence were lower.

1000 year old Church in Cyprus, a World Heritage site

Tourists as invaders: instinctive hospitality? ➤

Tourists arriving in a place are invaders of territory that local residents regard as theirs, because the arrival of any stranger challenges what Ardrey (1967) calls the territorial imperative. One stranger is sufficient for a local to feel this challenge; mass arrivals merely amplify the feeling. Ardrey does not mention tourism, but his findings can be applied to this context.

Threats of invasion felt by locals must be eliminated or reduced. The question is, how can locals retain their sense of territorial imperative while tolerating tourists? Three ways, not mutually exclusive, will be suggested.

One way is by perceiving these invaders as merely temporary visitors, not come to stay permanently and not likely to cause harm as individuals. This can be achieved by recognising the invader as a tourist. The label applied to an individual signifies a false threat to territorial imperative. The problem remains that while each individual tourist may be a false threat to territorial imperative, mass tourism is not.

A second way is by showing hospitality. A display of hospitality towards strangers approaching or entering one's territory is behaviour that is instinctive and/or learned for coping with threats of invasion. Ardrey believed it was instinctive and—here is the key principle—he showed that threats of enmity by invaders produce displays of hospitality by residents. In other words, his research suggested that hospitality is instinctive.

If an invader responds positively or neutrally to the display of hospitality, the resident perceives that the threat is over, that the visitor has accepted the welcome and will not pose a real threat. The disruption is temporary, the visitor is not a real invader. Ardrey found this process occurring among animals and birds. Regardless of whether it is instinctive or learned behaviour, it has implications for human beings, and has particular relevance for the encounters of local residents and tourists in places they visit.

For example, it reveals an unintended benefit in campaigns by tourism booster groups encouraging locals to show hospitality towards tourists. Examples of these campaigns include the Kiwi-Host training programs sponsored by the New Zealand government since 1990, and its copycat Aussie-Host program in Australia and all the less formalised campaigns in many towns and countries that encourage people to be nice to tourists. Superficially, these are intended to make tourists feel welcome. In fact, they are probably doing something else besides. They are training residents in a natural method of coping with false threats to territorial imperative.

There are limits to the strategy. Large quantities of visitors become an invasion. A different kind of limit stems from attitudes of insecure residents. MacCannell (1992: 188) reported that in districts of California 'popular bumper stickers say *Welcome to California . . . Now Go Home!*'. This represents another way by which locals, at least in some places, cope with threats to territorial imperative. They display a symbol of hospitality but hold up a blatant reminder, to themselves and others, that hospitality has a very brief shelf life. There is in such behaviour a contradiction and a false consciousness covering it, a guilt-based process which, according to MacCannell, 'manifests itself at every level of thought, behaviour and organization' (1992: 80) in postmodern communities. He saw Orange County, home of Disneyland and other symbols of the present age, as the archetypal postmodern community.

New Zealand has not yet acquired the same degree of postmodernist culture found in California, but New Zealand's official tourism policies on this issue display another sort of contradiction and false consciousness. The government conducts annual surveys to measure what Doxey (1975) originally called a 'tourism irritation index'. In New Zealand this index has been inverted and termed a 'tourism acceptance index'. Thus the survey findings, widely publicised in the mass media, consistently show favourable results. Inverting Doxey's technique is a contradiction, and represents false consciousness and denial, because it pretends that the normal tendency is for a host society to accept increasing numbers of tourist-visitors.

All sorts of communities might be able to adjust to some quantity of tourist-visitors. Damage to local societies and their cultures might be severe if the rate of growth in tourist numbers is high. What this reflects is a flexible social carrying capacity. A local population might now be comfortable with x number of tourists per day, and in a few years might be comfortable with x plus y. Ultimately, continual increases in mass tourism must pass the limits of hospitality, when the locals lose any real sense of territory.

MacCannell (1992) drew attention to another issue, overlooked in discussions of tourism's impacts. Tourism is one form of mass movement, and another is mass migration of mainly poor persons from Asia, Latin America, Africa and Eastern Europe into the cities of North America, Western Europe and Australia. The sense of threats to territory felt by established locals in places such as Orange County relates to tourists and also to new immigrants, especially those coming as refugees of some sort.

Impacts on physical environments of places visited

Physical environments comprise the natural and what used to be called the manmade, now called the built, environment. Cohen (1978) provides an explanation of the relationships between tourism and the physical environments of places they visit. Among many other useful and comprehensive discussions on the topic are those by Douglas Pearce (1989) and Nepal (2000). Budowski (1976, cited in Mathieson & Wall 1982) identifies three possible kinds of relationship between tourism and physical environments: (a) independence—no impacts; (b) conflict—tourism damaging environments; and (c) symbiosis—mutual benefits for tourism and physical environments. The first possibility is very rare, so is not discussed here. The second and third are taken up below.

Conflict ➤

Damage to physical environments has been attributed to tourism and facilities of tourism industries. Quality of water and air, the state of vegetation, wildlife, fragile ecosystems and the aesthetic qualities of built environments are all relevant. A huge literature, constantly growing, exists on the subject. A common observation has been that mass tourism damages the very features of physical environments that make places attractive to tourists. Hotels, shops, roads, theme parks, signposts and other facilities can detract from, and might even ruin, the beauty of landscape or the peaceful state of wild places, and those qualities are what many tourists desire.

Damage caused to coral reefs by tourists exempify Cohen's (1978) principle that the worst damage occurs when tourists enter the most fragile, least resilient ecosystems. Coral reefs have been killed in this way, so that where living coral and coloured fish teemed, admired by tourists, today there are dead, colourless coral and no reef fish. Individuals might imagine their personal activities to be harmless. The damage caused by a single act might be minimal, but thousands of tourists all acting the same way can collectively cause serious damage. Thus, coral reef damage is caused by combined effects, over a period, of many thousands of individuals walking on the same reef at low tide and collecting coral for souvenirs. The same principle of mass effects can be seen with picking wildflowers, disposing of small pieces of rubbish in the bush, taking wood from trees for a fire, or disturbing wildlife while seeking close-up photographs.

Worldwide, more people are becoming responsive to the problems of the natural environment. In Australia today, probably most organisations in the tourism industries are managed with some degree of consideration for environmental matters. A number of organisations take special care to protect and, where possible, enhance certain environmental values. Case studies collected by Harris and Leiper (1995) and the National Office of Tourism (1996) describe examples of how this can be achieved. (These are discussed in Chapter 16.)

Five kinds of damage to built environments have been linked to badly designed or inadequately managed resort developments. Architectural pollution—ugly buildings or buildings quite inappropriate to their setting—is the most glaring kind. An example is the first large hotel built in Bali, a high-rise built at Sanur by Americans in the 1960s. The Balinese later attempted to introduce a policy that allowed no future building to go higher than palm trees. Regrettably, the Balinese lost control of property regulations for buildings on their island when the corrupt Indonesian President Soeharto and his cronies decided in the 1970s to invest in large-scale resort developments in Bali (Aditjondro 1995). By 1999, when large-scale protests by students and workers in Jakarta forced Soeharto to resign, a lot of damage had been done.

In Australia a regrettable mistake was allowed on Hamilton Island in the Whitsundays where a resort with high-rise buildings was constructed in the 1980s. This was despite expert advice that the plans were inappropriate for island environments—not matching the physical features and clashing with most tourists' expectations of tropical island holiday experiences. The main beneficiaries of high-rise in such places are investors such as Keith Williams, who exploited Hamilton Island in building the resort according to his own ideas of how the world should be.

Ribbon development, where buildings sprawl along a road or coast, is another damaging impact. The ribbon development along Australia's Gold Coast is an example. Toward the ends of the ribbon, buildings tend to increasing bad taste. Another problem occurs from overloading infrastructure, by putting more accommodation capacity in a place than the water supply, power, roads or sewerage can handle.

Damage can occur when planning of physical facilities segregates locals from tourists. The physical division can affect other facets of the environment, as revealed with Sydney's Darling Harbour precinct. Hailed by its sponsors and creators in the 1980s as having huge potential for tourists and Sydney residents, it appears to be failing to achieve its aims. One design problem is that resident communities immediately to the west are cut off from Darling Harbour physically by busy roads and blank back walls of large structures, two signals to them that the precinct is a separate place, beyond easy reach. They are also detached socially, because facilities in the precinct do not match their preferences or budgets. The result is that those visiting are either tourists or day-trippers from distant suburbs. Darling Harbour has few customers in the true sense. Lacking customers—individuals who make a custom of being there, who belong there—the precinct is not so successful. The only regulars in Darling Harbour are its workers.

A trend damaging environments in many national parks is the use of helicopters for non-essential purposes. Helicopters are popular with some rich tourists because they save time getting to distant spots, allow unsurpassed sightseeing and a quick turnaround for long ski runs. Helicopters are also popular with some park rangers because they are fun, give a sense of power and high status, and save time and effort getting around. Helicopters are accepted by many tourists and recreationalists because they can be used in emergencies to save lives if someone is injured or lost.

But for the majority of visitors to national parks and beaches, helicopters are intruders that destroy peaceful and quiet environments. More than this, helicopters destroy a deeper value in national parks, especially in wilderness zones. These places are valuable because people need to escape temporarily *from* technology and other features of industrial societies, and escape *to* wholly natural environments where those features are absent. A true wilderness experience cannot be compromised. When helicopters roar overhead, usually quite low, the experience is destroyed for those below, on the ground. Moreover, helicopters intruding on these experiences cause a shock, precisely the kind (but not so prolonged) caused by other industrial technologies in factories, mines, mills and heavy traffic. Schivelbusch (1986) has described and analysed these industrial shocks, and shown how they have shaped the experiences of tourists.

The utility of national parks for the majority of users is diminished by the increasing use of helicopters, which have real benefits for only a small minority. A true wilderness experience is damaged even by the knowledge that four-wheel drives and helicopters will come in to search for missing persons. Those sorts of insurance facilities are needed in the ordinary recreational zones of national parks, but by keeping them absent from wilderness zones two sets of park users, each wanting a slightly different sort of experience, can be better served. This sort of management policy is an example of matching different kinds of resources to different market segments.

Symbiosis: tourism in harmony with its physical environments ➤

Not all relationships between tourism or tourism industries and physical environments is damaging and involves conflict. In many instances it is symbiotic. A symbiotic relationship is a mutually beneficial one, advantageous to both sides.

Four types can be identified in the links between tourism and physical environments: (a) tourism issues have stimulated the restoration or rehabilitation of precincts, sites, buildings and objects; (b) tourism issues have led to the transformation of usage of precincts, sites, buildings and objects; (c) tourism issues have led to the conservation of natural features—parks and wildlife; and (d) tourism issues have led to management schemes being adopted to conserve physical environments.

Borobodur, the giant Buddhist temple in Central Java, was falling into decay until UNESCO spent tens of millions of dollars in the 1980s to restore it. The temple was deemed to have world heritage value, and simultaneously valuable for developing the tourist destination region centred on Jogjakarta. By the 1990s its value as the nucleus of a tourist attraction had grown to attract hundreds of thousands of visitors annually.

The Marais district in Paris, containing buildings and streets older than the city's well-known districts, has been restored since the 1960s for its value to national heritage and for its potential as a tourist precinct. Forty years ago the Marais was not marked on popular guides; now it is included and, while not so popular as Champs Elysees or Montmartre, is visited by many tourists interested in the city's culture and history.

The Rocks district in Sydney is comparable to the Marais. In the 1960s The Rocks was a neglected and run-down zone between the central business district and the harbour, where few outsiders ventured. Following the Parisian model and possibly inspired by André Maurois' writings about the Marais, in 1970 the New South Wales government established The Rocks Redevelopment Authority, and within 10 years The Rocks had become one of Australia's most popular attractions for tourists. It contains the oldest buildings in Australia, many built in convict times, and among its dozen pubs are at least three advertised as the oldest in the country. It could be described as Australia's archetypal cultural heritage area. Many old structures and sites have been transformed into new forms useful to tourists, so conserving features of the physical (and cultural) environment. The Argyle Arts Centre and the Old Sydney Hotel (both in The Rocks) were once warehouses. The Powerhouse Museum in Sydney was once a generator of electricity, then for many years an empty building. In its new form, it has become a museum visited annually by millions of locals and tourists.

The Victorian Alpine Commission exemplifies management schemes. The VAC has managerial authority over all matters in the alpine region of Victoria. Before the VAC's formation, a number of fragmented authorities were responsible for different aspects of the alpine region. As a consequence, environmental damage was occurring because of issues that fell between the specific responsibilities of the various groups.

AN ECOLOGY OF WHOLE TOURISM SYSTEMS

As described above, traditional perspectives for studying tourism's impacts have looked only at impacts in places visited by tourists. That vision takes in only a fraction of tourism's total impacts, a large fraction admittedly. A wider view, to take in all impacts, is achievable by thinking in terms of whole tourism systems and by looking at the environments interacting with all elements in those systems.

The model presented in Chapter 3 suggests that impacts of tourism occur on environments interacting with five elements. There are impacts in the three kinds of places in every tourist's itinerary: traveller-generators, transit routes, and tourist destinations. The first of those is overlooked in most discussions. A holistic perspective also points to impacts on tourists, and on organisations, especially those in tourism industries. These multiple perspectives are described below. By bringing the impacts together in reference to whole tourism systems, an ecological system can be suggested.

Tourists

Tourists incur personal costs, mainly the time and money spent on trips. They also incur opportunity costs, which are the activities, experiences, money or things that they could have had instead of a trip. Having incurred various costs, the question arises: what do tourists receive in return?

Any trip inevitably *changes* participants in some way, even if the changes in some cases are neither profound nor long-lasting. The changes might be beneficial, or damaging, or a mixture.

The changes are often beneficial. After holiday trips, many people are rested, relaxed, refreshed, and/or entertained. Any of those changes can be regarded as evidence that one impact of tourism is that the central participants—tourists—are recreated by recreational experiences. Besides recreation, many persons learn or otherwise develop as persons as a consequence of experiences during trips, so there are educational or other creative impacts.

Other impacts on tourists might be detrimental. During and after trips, tourists may become ill. Clark, Clift and Page (1993) researched tourists' illnesses, ailments and treatments. Some return home physically and mentally fatigued from excessive activity while away. A number probably return home more ignorant than when they set out, as a consequence of misinformation acquired during the trip.

Discussed and analysed in Chapter 5, the 'travel bug' refers to a practice of many individuals who make a habit of tourism. They go on frequent trips. Common sense indicates that this is because the gains for tourists from tourism are pleasant and satisfying.

Tourist destination regions

As described earlier in this chapter, tourist destinations generally gain economically but can incur damage and unrecouped costs in other aspects of their environments, such as their natural and built environment and their sociocultural characteristics.

In places that are at least moderately successful as destinations, local residents and visitors are likely to be committed to protecting any environmental qualities that seem worthy of protection and prone to damage, but this is not easy to accomplish. (The issue is taken up in Chapter 16.)

Transit routes

Research and professional commentary should distinguish between two elementary roles of places visited by tourists—transit routes and destinations. Places along transit routes are usually visited briefly, by travellers who do not expect these visits to provide the quality of experience desired in tourist destinations. For the same reasons, places on transit routes that are not also large-scale destinations do not usually gain much economically from tourism. However, a large number of passing tourists, and their transport facilities, can cause considerable damage to environments.

A major form of environmental damage caused by certain forms of tourism has been generally ignored in discussions about tourism and environments: it is the damage to the biosphere caused by aircraft vapour trails. For several years a small number of environmental activists and scientists have been claiming that aircraft are causing serious damage. However, their arguments have been circumstantial and lacking strong scientific evidence.

In September 2001 a scientific study was possible because of an unplanned experiment, and was conducted by David Travis and a team of climatologists from the University of Wisconsin. Their study is reported in *Nature* (Travis 2002). For three days after 11 September, all air traffic in the USA was grounded as a security measure, as the government feared another terrorist attack. For those three days, Travis and his team collected data from 4000 weather stations in the 48 mainland states, and compared the maximum and minimum day and night temperatures for the three days with data going back to 1971. Because thousands of commercial flights were cancelled for those three dates in 2001, the thin blanket of cirrus clouds that forms from water vapour leaving jet engines was absent, allowing daytime temperatures at ground level to rise and night-time temperatures to fall. The loss of this cloud cover led to a 1.98-degree increase in the difference between high and low temperatures over the USA. This is the first irrefutable proof of the effect of aircraft contrails on climate.

Traveller-generating regions

What are the impacts on a place when its residents go away as tourists? More significantly, what are the impacts when they return? There are potential benefits and costs. A place functioning as a traveller-generator temporarily loses population and there are economic costs, such as the money transferred to other economies to pay for the trips. There are also opportunity costs of the temporarily absent population.

There are potential benefits that the place's society and economy receives in return for costs incurred. These are gained after the tourists return home. These benefits are not automatic but contingent; they depend on the characteristics of individual tourists and their trip experiences. Broad generalisations can be suggested, as follows.

When people go on trips as tourists they are seeking recreational and/or creative experiences. If successful, they return home changed in beneficial ways. The question for the present topic is this: do any of these individual benefits flow into the home environments of returned tourists? The question does not seem to have been investigated by empirical research focused specifically on tourism, but it corresponds with a similar question about leisure. The concept of leisure as a social instrument (Kaplan 1975) is relevant here.

Persons returning home after successful leisure-based trips to other regions or

Nepalese porter and international tourist on expedition in the Himalayas

countries can make contributions, and often do, to their home societies. Going away tired and tense, they should return fresh and relaxed. These benefits will, inevitably, flow on to their home society and its economy. The simplest form of benefit is seen in the higher productivity of organisations where workers have become invigorated as a result of trips away. Kaplan emphasised that leisure is more than a social instrument, and should be seen as more. Accordingly, the main beneficial impacts of tourism in generating regions can and should be seen as in terms of advantages gained by individuals. That philosophy does not mean that leisure does not also function as a social instrument.

The simple beneficial impact of a reinvigorated workforce might be less important, and is certainly less durable, than other complex benefits. Societies in most countries are richer to some degree, in non-economic terms, because a proportion of their populations go away as tourists and, returning home, contribute to society in educational, artistic, or other ways.

Broinowski (1992) called this a transfusion of ideas. She described artistic, philosophical and other changes in Australian cultures that have come about partly through transfusions of ideas by persons returning from trips to Asia. (No doubt the same sort of transfusions could be revealed from trips to other parts of the world; Broinowski's research focused on Asia.) Her examples, her transformers, are artists, writers, musicians and others from Australia who have spent periods of leisure—recreation and creativity— in China, India, Japan, Indonesia and other Asian countries: 'As more Australians visited Asian countries . . . an efflorescence in what might be called the living arts took place, enlivening Australian tastes in food, clothes, sport and entertainment' (Broinowski 1992: 167).

Are changes like these beneficial? Broinowski clearly believes they are. There is no doubt that Australian culture in 2002 is very different from 1962, for example, when few Australians travelled internationally. Many factors have contributed to the changes—immigration, mass media, technology, economic development, international tourists visiting, Australians going on international trips and returning.

The sort of changes noted by Broinowski were analysed by Toynbee (1935) in reference to a wider theme. His analysis supports her opinion, and gives it a wider context. Studying the history of civilisations, Toynbee devised a phrase, 'withdrawal and return', for a crucial process in his theory explaining how civilisations develop. He described famous persons from the past 3000 years who made major contributions to the development of their civilisation after spending periods of time away from home at leisure, visiting other countries, in different cultures, engaged in what can be termed recreative and creative leisure. Their behaviour, in effect, can be termed tourism, even if the individuals do not match the popular stereotypes of tourists.

Mumford (1961) drew on Toynbee's ideas in his study of the history of cities. He described how the ancient Greeks travelled away from their city residences to visit what were in fact tourist resorts, where they experienced recreational and creative leisure. Returning home, they enlivened their home civilisations. Mumford referred to the major resorts as three centres in the following passage (Mumford 1961: 135–6):

> From these three centres flowed currents of vital energy . . . which brought to every Greek city a whole stream of unifying and self-transcending ideas and norms of life . . . [The Greeks] experienced that process of withdrawal and return which both Patrick Geddes and Arnold Toynbee have demonstrated historically is an essential mode of human growth.

The 'three centres' were the archetypal resorts of Greek tourism 2500 years ago. What is remarkable is that the specialised products of the three can be aligned with specialised functions of leisure noted in Chapter 5: rest, relaxation, entertainment (all comprising recreational leisure), and creative leisure.

The archetypal resorts were on the Aegean island of Kos, and at two places on the mainland, Olympia and Delphi. Kos, the world's first health resort, specialised in rest and relaxation: tourists go to these sorts of resorts to recover from mental and physical fatigue, to relax, and to recover from stress. Olympia, site of the games, was principally a resort for entertainment, and recovery from boredom. Delphi's specialised resort product was creative more than recreational: the Greeks visited Delphi to consult the oracle, to gain advice about important decisions thay had to make back home in business, civic and personal matters.

The argument that tourism contributes to the health and civilisation of societies in traveller-generating regions has interesting implications for tourism management and government tourism policies. These issues are taken up in later chapters. For now, the argument can be accepted as plausible and as going a step beyond the opinion held by scholars of leisure such as Bell (1928), Huizinga (1950) and Larrabee and Meyerson (1958). These writers see the quality of a civilisation as being ultimately represented in the qualities of the leisure experienced by members of a civilising society.

Toynbee, Mumford, Meyerson and Broinowski go a step further by observing that leisure spent creatively in distant places, temporarily away from home, can enhance a civilised society after the individuals return. This does not mean that all tourists can or should confer these benefits on their home society, but it does indicate an effect that a proportion of tourists convey.

Organisations in tourism industries

Prospering organisations in tourism industries are evidence of the positive impacts of tourism. The impacts include revenue sufficient to pay expenses, and, in entrepreneurial enterprises, interest on capital and a return for risk. As in other industries, certain organisations survive and others fail and disappear.

An ecological system

Having identified environmental impacts relevant to each element in whole tourism systems, we can suggest an ecology of tourism, with interesting conclusions. What follows is only indicative, because ecological theories are fraught with the problems of any new discipline (Saarinen 1982). Ecology, the study of ecosystems, is an application of general systems theory, and so it differs from conventional sciences (Flanagan 1988: 167):

> *Where sciences such as physics, and even much of biology, seek to reduce the world to its simple elements, ecology seeks to understand how the simplest constituents interact to give rise to the living world we actually perceive with our senses.*

An ecological view involves whole tourism systems (see Figure 10.3). This is based on certain assumptions but designed to reveal interactions that are recognised only with a broad perspective. The assumptions are: (a) tourists spend money during trips; (b) most expenditure remains in places visited and there is no substantial leakage to generating

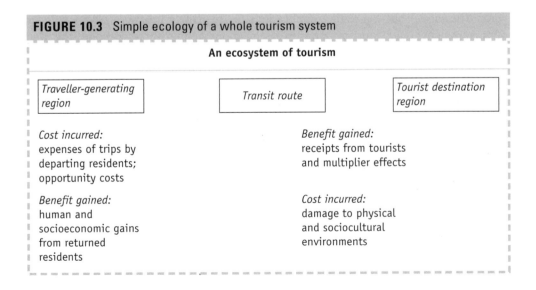

FIGURE 10.3 Simple ecology of a whole tourism system

An ecosystem of tourism

Traveller-generating region	Transit route	Tourist destination region

Cost incurred:
expenses of trips by
departing residents;
opportunity costs

Benefit gained:
receipts from tourists
and multiplier effects

Benefit gained:
human and
socioeconomic gains
from returned
residents

Cost incurred:
damage to physical
and sociocultural
environments

regions or elsewhere; (c) tourists derive satisfaction and value from their experiences; and (d) environmental damage and cost impacts in places visited are balanced by economic benefits accruing there.

The fourth assumption is the most speculative. In practice, it can be regarded as a prescription for good management at a regional level, through governments working closely with tourism interests. All costs and benefits accruing to places visited by significant numbers of tourists should be measured by host communities, ideally working via their own governmental agencies. If damage to environments is found to exceed economic gains, the excess should be recouped from tourist-visitors either directly or indirectly via charges on certain facilities and services. This is a clear example of the 'user-pays' principle, however difficult it might be to apply. Tourists use free environments and free public goods of the places they visit and often cause damage to certain environments. They should not be allowed to use these things without paying the costs of that use. Likewise, business organisations established specifically to make money from tourists use environments and public goods, and the same principle should apply there.

Given the assumptions above, a traveller-generating region incurs a cost, the price of trips, balanced by the benefits reflected in (and conveyed by) its residents returned home changed in positive ways by their experiences. Meanwhile, transit routes and tourist destination regions benefit economically from tourists' expenditures, but incur costs on their sociocultural and physical environments. Under normal conditions, the benefits and costs *in each region* are in balance.

This model suggests, first of all, that looking for some kind of environmental balance across the system is futile if the only places considered are places visited by tourists. This is because another place, a traveller-generating region, is elementary in the ecology of tourism. The big picture also indicates the futility of imagining that each category of environmental impact can be managed to show positive impacts in each region. Rather, places visited by tourists are likely to be damaged in social, cultural and physical ways. The model has interesting implications for managing tourism and for policies of governments and tourism industry associations, implications beyond the one noted above.

Good policy should acknowledge the ecology of tourism, but should establish organisations and management systems to carry out measures, including: (a) minimising the damage caused by tourism and its spillover effects, and (b) collecting some of the economic gains from tourism and its spillover effects, via special taxes or some other means, to pay for monitoring organisations.

The model also points to the view that good tourism policy at the regional and national levels should not merely concern incoming tourists. A comprehensive policy also encourages local residents to travel as tourists to other regions and countries.

Ecological vision is a way of bringing together all the components of a system, in order to describe and understand processes in the living world. The living world of tourism has often been seen myopically, not ecologically, when its environmental impacts were imagined to be only in places tourists visit. A broader vision leads to a different level of understanding.

Industrialised and non-industrialised tourism ➤

Complications to the model sketched above are many. In practice, economic benefits are seldom confined to places visited, for at least two reasons. Leakage means that a proportion of tourist-visitors' expenditures leave the region or country. Pre-trip expenditure, especially for prepaid services to be used in places visited, means that traveller-generating regions can gain significantly in economic terms, perhaps more than tourist destinations.

Say a tourist prepays to a travel agent, before leaving home, $1000 for accommodation and other facilities and services to be consumed in other places during a trip, and that the arrangements are based on a package assembled by a tour operator in the tourist's home country. Possibly the hotel is also owned in the country where the trip begins. In this case, most of the $1000 could remain in the traveller-generating country, with only a small sum of money going to the colonial destination country to pay the direct costs incurred by the hotel.

The example indicates that analysing impacts across the geographical spread of a whole tourism system can be done in more detail by considering the degree of industrialisation, a concept described in Chapter 11. When tourism is relatively independent (non-industrialised), there are few, if any, cooperative linkages between organisations in generating regions and destination regions, and thus most expenditure occurs after leaving home. At the other extreme, as tourism becomes more highly industrialised, there is more involvement by pre-trip businesses such as travel agents and outbound tour operators.

Also, the degree of industrialisation correlates with the extent of managerial responsibility for the environmental impacts of tourism. To date, no scientific empirical research has been conducted to test this question scientifically. Certainly many organisations that are in the business and industry of tourism have managers that are more likely to recognise environmental impacts in their district (Harris & Leiper 1995). Possibly, in many other organisations providing goods or services to tourists without being in the business of tourism, managers will be less aware of, or involved with, environmental issues associated with tourism.

Activists who accuse the tourism industry of neglecting the problems caused by environmental damage associated with tourism might be accusing the wrong institution, or hitting only part of their proper target. As shown in Chapter 11, ideas about 'the tourism industry' as a monolith, supplying everything used by all tourists, are illusory. Some environmental impacts of tourism have no links with tourism industries.

The questionable issue of 'balance' ➤

In many controversies relating to conflicts between the interests of tourists or tourism industries on one hand and an environmental interest on the other, the concept of 'balance' is invoked. The implied suggestion is that both sides of the controversy deserve a balanced share of the outcome. 'Balanced' implies, and is often inferred to mean, approximately equal shares.

This is often a phony idea, a strategic ploy, when invoked in controversies. It is a public relations tactic intended to sway an argument. If an EIA (environmental impact assessment) on a proposed resort development finds that the construction will cause serious harm to a fragile environment, and if the value of that environment is assessed as greater than the value of the resort, the proposal should not proceed. 'Balance' belongs in bicycle riding, dancing and politics; when it is brought into policy-making processes for managing environmental issues, care is needed to avoid distorting the issue and the outcome.

Environmentally sustainable tourism ➤

Many writers have discussed the concept of sustainable tourism and its close relative, ecotourism. Examples include books by Tisdell (1990), Hall (1991), Harris and Leiper (1995), Middleton (1998), Mowforth and Munt (1998), Beeton (1998), Swarbrooke (1999), Honey (1999) and the World Tourism Organisation (2000a). Buckley's (2001) review is also noteworthy. The focus of discussion has usually been restricted, like most other research into tourism and its environments, to sustainability in places visited by tourists. The key question has been this: under what conditions is a destination sustainable, gaining economic benefits and incurring minimal damage to social, cultural or physical environments?

Before environmental problems were recognised, tourism development was based on two assumptions. Destination regions were assumed to deteriorate. Other places were assumed to be always available as 'new and unspoilt' destinations. In the 1970s, the possibility was recognised that degraded destinations could be restored and recycled. The prospect emerged that tourism might occur in ways that caused minimal damage to environments in destinations. This condition is said to be sustainable tourism. How to achieve and maintain it is, in theory and practice, quite complex (Tisdell 1990; Buckley 2001).

Without disputing that opinion, a different view of sustainability is provided by ecological approaches of the sort described earlier in this chapter. The key question is this: under what conditions is a whole tourism system sustainable?

The best possible management applied to sustain the qualities of a region or country as a tourist destination will not be sufficient to ensure that tourism development is sustainable. This is because for any place to be an effective destination, other places must function effectively as transit routes and traveller-generating regions, so sustainable tourism depends on environmental conditions in at least three locations. Those conditions need not all be positive. In fact, deteriorating physical and social environments support tourism development—if the deterioration occurs in traveller-generating regions. There, poor-quality physical and social environments for residents will motivate escapist tourism. This trend has been active for years.

Environmental damage of various sorts is increasing in many cities, and includes: overcrowding, ambient noise, air and water pollution, excessive traffic and risk of crime. Simultaneously, while cities around the world are places where many residents are poor they are also places of economic prosperity for a minority of their populations, a minority who make up, worldwide, hundreds of millions of people. These prosperous residents are able to afford temporary escapes from unpleasant cities, spending holidays in places that are perceived to have comparatively attractive environments. The fastest-growing traveller-generating regions in global tourism patterns during the 1990s were cities in East Asia, where increasingly prosperous middle-class societies reside amid deteriorating environments—Soeul, Tokyo, Osaka, Manila, Taipei, Bangkok and Jakarta.

So what sorts of environmental qualities sustain tourism? Economic prosperity in traveller-generating regions is necessary. Political stability along transit routes is necessary. And environmental qualities in potential tourist destination regions must be perceived, from traveller-generating regions, to be attractive for leisure experiences.

A destination may be environmentally degraded from an objective assessment, but if tourists subjectively imagine it to be sufficiently attractive in key features they will often be willing to tolerate the degraded environment. The tolerance is possible because tourists are on temporary visits, not staying permanently, and because tourists use comfortable and secure accommodation that protects them from unpleasant environmental conditions. (A longer discussion on sustainable tourism is in Chapter 16.)

Discussion questions

1. One category of environment with which tourism systems interact is the physical environment: name and describe at least three other categories.
2. Why is the description of inbound tourism as an 'invisible export' now out of date?
3. List and describe four types of effects on the economic environment of national economies that arise from inbound international tourism.
4. List and describe three types of economic multiplier.
5. What is the practical use of calculations for economic multipliers?
6. List and describe four types of negative effects on sociocultural environments of places visited by tourists.
7. The links between tourism and the physical environments of places they visit have been put into three categories: what are they?
8. Referring to the five elements in whole tourism systems, outline what is meant by an 'ecology of whole tourism systems'.

Recommended reading

Beeton, Sue 1998, *Ecotourism: A Practical Guide for Rural Communities*, Melbourne: Landlink Press

Bossevain, J. 1996, *Coping with Tourism: European Reactions to Mass Tourism*, Oxford: Berjhann

Buckley, Ralf 2001, Sustainable tourism management, *Annals of Tourism Research*, 28: 523–5

Ding, P. & Pigram, J. 1995, Environmental audits: an emerging concept in sustainable tourism development, *Journal of Tourism Studies*, 6(2): 2–10

Fredline, Elizabeth & Faulkner, Bill 2000, Host community reactions: a cluster analysis, *Annals of Tourism Research*, 27: 763–84

Hunter, C. & Green, H. 1995, *Tourism and the Environment: A Sustainable Relationship?*, London: Routledge

Tourism Management

McGibbon, Jacqueline 2000, *The Business of Alpine Tourism in a Globalising World*, Rosenheim: Vetterling Druck

Mowforth, M. & Munt, I. 1998, *Tourism and Sustainability: New Tourism in the Third World*, London: Routledge

Nepal, Sanjay 2000, Tourism in protected areas: the Nepalese Himalaya, *Annals of Tourism Research*, 27: 661–81

Pigram, J. 2000, Environment, pp 193–5 in *The Encyclopedia of Tourism*, J. Jafari (ed.), London: Routledge

Wall, Geoffrey 2000, Impacts, pp 296–8 in *The Encyclopedia of Tourism*, J. Jafari (ed.), London: Routledge

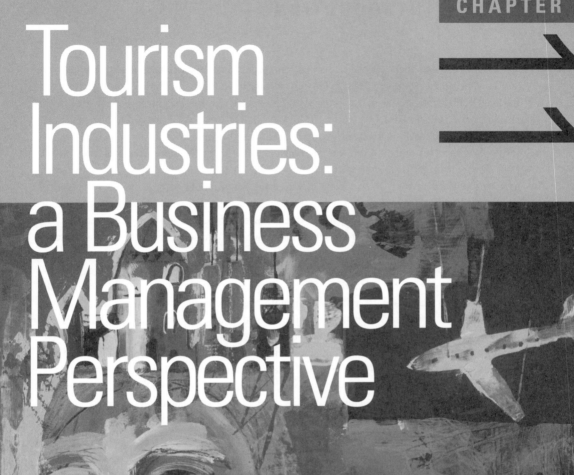

Tourism Industries: a Business Management Perspective

INTRODUCTION

This chapter explores theories of business and managerial issues in organisations supplying services and goods direct to tourists. The theories are mostly descriptive, explaining practical issues in the real world. From this base and from analysis, prescriptive theories emerge—suggestions for managers and policy makers.

A range of strategies is involved when organisations specialise in tourism. A similar range is involved when other organisations, not specialists, decide to target tourists as a segment within their broader markets. The discussion shows how both these types of organisations normally participate in tourism industries. It also explains why many organisations supply tourists with services or goods without being in the tourism business and without participating in tourism industries. In other words, it shows how and why tourism—the behaviour of tourists—is partly industrialised. The condition is problematical in certain respects but is inevitable to some degree and has advantages for various types of tourists.

Extending a theme raised near the end of Chapter 10, this chapter teases out two threads: being in a line of business related to tourism, and being in a tourism industry, twin conditions normally intertwined in practice. Understanding them requires separate analyses, so I first discuss business strategies aimed at tourists, then show how tourism industries function, explaining how this also involves managerial decisions and the strategic use of resources. Combining core ideas from the two sections in a diagram (Figure 11.1) graphically illustrates key concepts of partial industrialisation.

Later sections show how the degree of industrialisation is shaped by factors other than business strategies, and how it can vary among different types of tourism, in different places and over time. The partial industrialisation syndrome has implications for all stakeholders in tourism. Explaining the syndrome also raises interesting but generally ignored differences between economics, markets, business strategies and industrial structures.

BUSINESS STRATEGIES AIMED AT TOURISTS

An organisation is active in a line of business related to tourists when its managers recognise distinctive characteristics of tourists and deploy the organisation's resources to deal with them. In this condition, an organisation does not passively accept the tourists' presence but has deliberate strategies for dealing with them. A strategy may be aimed at tourists in general or a particular type or category.

For many organisations tourists, along with other travellers or visitors displaying broadly similar characteristics, comprise all or almost all of the consumers. Examples include travel agencies, tour operators, hotels, backpacker hostels, motels, holiday apartments, airlines, coachlines, cruise ships, duty-free shops, souvenir shops and others. As they specialise in tourism, these organisations' strategies and operations are managed with tourists in mind.

Business strategies are more complicated in a second category of organisation, those that do not specialise in tourism, where consumers comprise a mix of tourists and non-tourists, the latter being mainly residents of the local region. These organisations might or might not be managed in ways that recognise tourists as a market segment and, accordingly, might or might not treat tourists in a distinctive way with a focused business strategy. In this second category there is no universal rule for guiding managers to the best decision. The presence of tourists among customers of a shop, restaurant or bar is not sufficient justification to put it in the tourism business. Tourists' expenditure might be highly valued by organisations in this second category, but that is not sufficient reason for managers to decide that tourists represent a market segment requiring a business strategy. Merely because tourists' spending affects the economics of virtually every business organisation supplying goods and services for consumers does not mean that every organisation should be managed in ways that recognise tourists.

Of course, in many cases in this second category tourists do represent a feasible market segment. In these cases an organisation can profitably go into the business of tourism. It should be decided on a case-by-case basis, by managers assessing the conditions relevant to each situation and reassessing conditions periodically.

Why certain organisations have business strategies for tourism

Organisations that specialise exclusively or largely in tourism need business strategies centred around tourists, in order to achieve the organisation's purpose, which is the provision of services or goods suiting one or more of the distinctive needs of tourists. These distinctive needs include transport, accommodation, packaging, guiding and souvenirs. Successfully achieving the purpose should also enable well-managed organisations to achieve their objectives, which, in the private sector, means earning sufficient profits to maintain the business and to satisfy shareholders and other stakeholders.

In public service tourism agencies and similar not-for-profit communitarian organisations, the main objectives might be to use tourism as a means of bringing economic benefits to a town, region or country. In a slightly different category, organisations with the overarching goal of heritage conservation might use tourism as a means of making money to support that goal; the Neka Art Museum, the subject of Chapter 14, is an example.

Organisations not specialising in tourism but deriving a portion of income from this source must decide for or against having business strategies focused on tourism, as a market segment. Extra income from this source can in certain cases add a useful contribution to total revenue, greater than the costs and efforts of the targeted strategy. Examples include Goodings' Supermarket, described later, and several cases studied by Firth (2002).

Roles of business strategies

Many strategies discussed in books and journals are prescriptive theories intended as guides for business organisations to be more competitive (Porter 1985; Mintzberg

& Quinn 1996; Johnson & Scholes 1999). Although some writers view strategy almost entirely in terms of competition, for many organisations the need to be competitive is not always a pressing issue, and it is not the fundamental issue for business strategy. Being competitive is the fundamental issue in a different application of strategies, in military battles during wars. That is an important difference but it is ignored by many writers on business strategy, who refer to writings about warfare and become preoccupied by ideas about competition, implying that it is ubiquitous and always dominant in strategic management for business.

There is widespread agreement that strategy is about deploying resources to achieve goals. This is true for armies in battles and for organisations in business. In order for a business organisation to achieve its goals, it must fulfil its purpose. Primarily, therefore, business organisations' strategies are about achieving the purpose of each organisation, which is not beating the competitors but satisfying the customers. This is often confused with a search for profits and competitive advantage.

To clarify the confusion, the widely respected business management authority Peter Drucker (1968, 1974) has emphasised in writings over many years that the purpose of business is to create customers, by providing goods or services in ways that satisfy consumers' needs.

Business strategies represented in a marketing mix

Strategies that enable an organisation to achieve its purpose in reference to tourists are represented in its marketing mix, formed and applied with tourists (or some category of tourists) in focus. A marketing mix combines products—based in goods and/or services, promotional activities, prices, and distribution activities. Several writers have suggested a more sophisticated mix, including more components, but the four-item mix is sufficient for now. Putting a marketing mix into practice necessitates general managers (with authority over marketing managers) deciding to allocate the necessary resources for its proper implementation.

Goods and services can be designed and managed to meet particular, distinctive needs or characteristics of tourists. This can be seen, for example, in the activities and facilities of travel agencies, tour operators, resort hotels, souvenir shops and luggage shops.

Promotional activities (advertising, publicity, selling, sales promotion, public relations) can be designed and managed to meet particular, distinctive needs or characteristics of tourists. This can be seen clearly in advertisements for packaged tours, for cities, regions and countries as destinations, for airlines and cruise lines.

Prices can be designed and managed to meet particular, distinctive needs or characteristics of tourists. This can be seen clearly with air fares at discount levels, with conditions suiting tourists, such as advance purchase, minimum time away, and with prices for packaged holidays, where several components (e.g. transport and accommodation) are included at a total price below what might be available if the components were purchased separately.

Distribution can be designed and managed with the same intention. The distribution function in tourism industries involves managers' decisions as to where to place facilities, services and promotional messages: which countries, which regions, which sites and, in the case of promotional messages and purchasing opportunities, which media. The increasing use of the Internet for promoting and selling tourism-related items is dramatically altering this area of strategy (Sheldon 1997; Law & Leung 2000; Lang 2000; Hultkrantz 2002).

Competitive strategies

Competitive strategies are used when managers take action to gain an advantage over competitors or to protect their own organisation's interests from predators. Often the contest is in a market, where competitive strategies aim to capture market share from other suppliers or to protect market share from predatory competitors.

Merely being active in a market does not represent genuinely competitive behaviour, just as the mere presence of a sporting team in a match does not necessarily mean it is always competing. Every sports fan has seen teams cease being competitive before a match is over when players on one side realise they have no hope of winning but keep playing, keep the game going without really competing, until the final whistle.

Competitive business strategies can be classified into several kinds. Theories have been put forward by many writers, including Ansoff in the 1960s and Porter in the 1980s and 90s, to describe and explain the range (Mintzberg 1991c: 70–1). Focusing on characteristics of tourists (or a category of tourists) is basic, underpinning any competitive strategy in this area. Then, to compete with other organisations present in the same market or field, an organisation's managers must decide among several possible choices of differentiation strategies: in design—offering something truly different; in quality; in image; in price; in support facilities or supplementary services. The general approach is to create differences between an organisation's marketing mix and that of its competitors.

The differences might be real or imaginary. In tourism industries' promotional strategies, as in many other areas of consumer goods and services, image can be a powerful force, so the tactical aim is perceptions of differentiation in consumers' minds. For this to be effective, consumers have to believe the differentiated image, when in many instances it is faked: 'Marketing is often used to feign differentiation where it does not otherwise exist—an image created for a product or service' (Mintzberg 1991c: 75). There is a large body of research on destination image in tourism: an article by Gallarza, Saura and Garcia (2002), especially its bibliography, is a guide into the literature.

The vertical axis in Figure 11.1

From the discussion so far, a spectrum of possible strategic positions can be identified, represented in Figure 11.1 by the vertical axis, with its range of positions.

Positioned at and near the top of the axis are organisations competing strongly for tourists' custom via intensive business strategies. At the bottom are organisations that passively accept the presence of tourists among other customers but have no business strategy aimed at tourists. Other organisations are between these extremes. To date,

FIGURE 11.1 Partial industrialisation: four positions of organisations directly supplying goods and services to tourists, in terms of business strategies and industrial cooperation

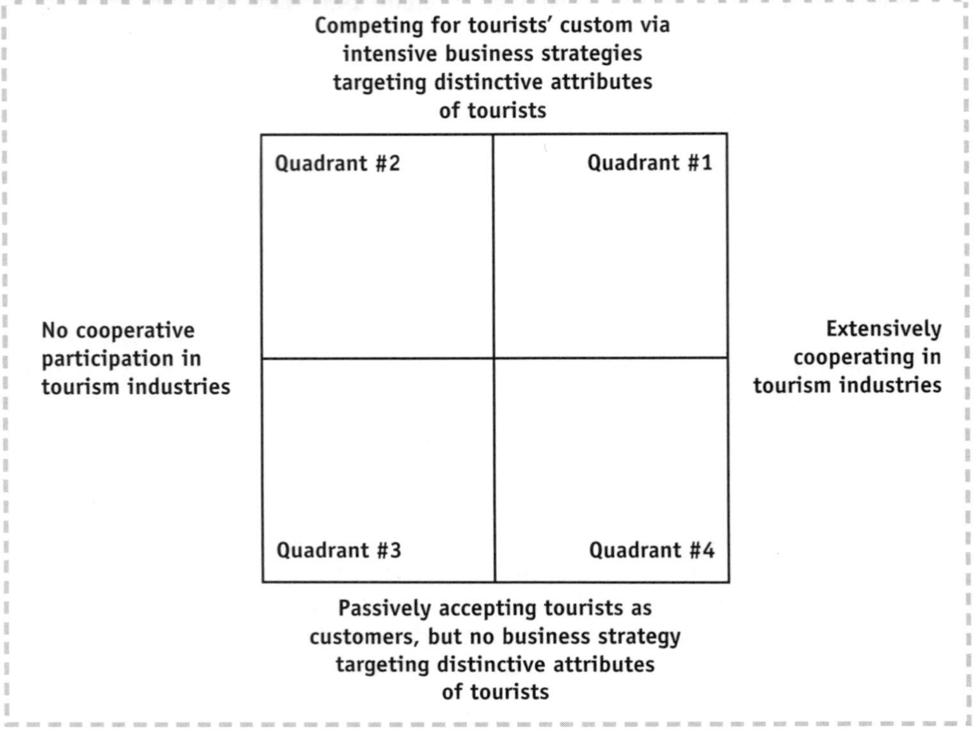

Competing for tourists' custom via
intensive business strategies
targeting distinctive attributes
of tourists

Quadrant #2	Quadrant #1

No cooperative   Extensively
participation in   cooperating in
tourism industries   tourism industries

Quadrant #3	Quadrant #4

Passively accepting tourists as
customers, but no business strategy
targeting distinctive attributes
of tourists

no research method has been developed to measure each organisation's position, but estimates can be made.

For example, at or near the top are most travel agencies, tour operators, resort hotels, promotional agencies, visitor information centres, souvenir shops and other types of businesses specialising in tourism. Also at or near the top are organisations where managers have implemented business strategies that target tourists, treating tourists as a market segment. Examples might be certain supermarkets, restaurants, pubs, food shops, clothing shops, department stores, or virtually any category of organisations providing any sort of goods or services used by consumers.

At or near the bottom of the vertical axis are many retailers of general goods and services; these include most supermarkets, restaurants, pubs, food shops, clothing shops, department stores, or virtually any other category of organisations providing any sort of goods or services used by consumers. All these might be positioned anywhere on the vertical axis. Decisions for or against having a business strategy for tourism, and regarding its type, intensity and duration, rest with the managers of each organisation and depend on their assessment of the circumstances, available resources and opportunity costs in each case.

Market segmentation decisions

What is involved in managers' decisions in these cases? How do they decide whether their organisation should be in the business of tourism or supplying tourists incidentally? A pioneer thinker on business strategy drew attention to a difficulty that can cloud the issue (Drucker 1968: 66):

Nothing may seem simpler or more obvious than to answer what a company's business is . . . Indeed the question looks so simple it is seldom raised, the answer so obvious it is seldom given. Actually 'what is our business?' *is almost always a difficult question which can only be answered after hard thinking and studying. And the right answer is usually anything but obvious.*

If tourists are among the customers of a business organisation, they might be a market segment. To be more than a hypothetical segment, action is necessary, which means tourists, or some of them, become targets for marketing activities. That strategy, identifying and targeting a market segment, has been recommended often to wider business communities by leaders of many regional and national tourism associations and by a number of governmental tourism agencies. A slogan used to encourage the trend is 'Tourism Is Everybody's Business'. Alongside publicity about an allegedly large and growing industry ('The World's Largest Industry'), the catchphrase tempts entrepreneurs by pointing a path to profits. For more than a decade it has appeared in countless promotions by tourism booster groups in several countries. In Australia it has appeared on posters and other items in campaigns arranged by public-sector agencies such as Tourism New South Wales.

However, only a minor proportion of entrepreneurs and business managers from the business world at large have been seduced by the silly phrase, which might be testimony to the majority's common sense. As advice, the phrase is potentially misleading. The path to understanding why it is misleading is not very complicated, but requires clear thinking. The discussion so far in this chapter has provided analysis and reasoning on the issue. More analysis follows, supported by evidence from case research.

Restaurants A and B might be neighbours and both find that tourists account for 20% of revenue, but in A's case tourists are a market segment while in the case of B they are not, because segmentation strategies are not feasible for B. Successful strategic decisions about segmentation are not linked to the percentage of tourists in the market, nor to how dependent a restaurant is on tourists as against non-tourists. The tiered hierarchy of organisations in tourism industries proposed by S.L.J. Smith (1988), reflecting degrees of economic dependency on tourists, might be interesting to economists but has limited relevance for business managers or marketers.

Marketing specialists have generally agreed on a theory for determining whether or not a collection of consumers in a market represents a feasible segment for targeting. The theory is set out in many texts (e.g. see Kotler et al. 1994: 132–3). The theory says that several conditions are necessary. As a preliminary the segment must have some distinctive characteristic to which at least one item in the marketing mix of the organisation contemplating the market can relate. Then, the segment must be (a) identifiable and measurable, so that it can be valued and compared with the costs of targeting. It must be

(b) accessible, so it can be reached and served effectively. It must also be (c) substantial, sufficiently valuable to warrant the costs of targeting, and (d) actionable by the organisation considering it, a condition depending on the resources and opportunity costs of the organisation.

An example of non-actionable segments occurred with a small airline company whose marketing staff identified seven potential segments but realised the airline was too small to develop separate strategies for each one (Kotler et al. 1994: 133).

These necessary conditions are common in markets served by organisations serving a mix of tourists and non-tourists, but sufficient conditions—all the conditions applying in one organisation—are rare. This explains why most organisations selling goods or services to tourists as well as non-tourists are best managed by ignoring tourists in their business strategies. The theory of market segments exposes the flaws in the boosters' warcry, 'Tourism Is Everybody's Business'. Anyone who insists on believing it would also believe, if they were consistent, all sorts of bizarre assertions along the same line. Would any rational person believe that as 10% of consumers in a shopping mall are left-handed, the mall is in 'the left-handed industry', or that the presence of a group of students studying their books in a public park means that the park is in the education industry?

Cases in Chapter 12 illustrate segmentation issues in more detail. Superficial observations are an unreliable means of knowing whether certain types of organisations are, or should be, in the business of tourism. Close inspections, to discover each organisation's business strategies, operating environments and resources, are required. Firth's (2002) research is also noteworthy for this topic.

Business strategies of 'marginal tourism firms' in Sydney

In and near Sydney's CBD (central business district), Tracey Firth surveyed managers of organisations 'that were not obvious tourism providers and that supplied goods and services to the population at large including a mix of tourists and non-tourists' (2002: 84). She used the term 'marginal tourism firms' to describe them, indicating that they were not like firms specialising in tourism. Sydney was 'chosen as the sampling area because it has Australia's largest concentration of tourists and tourist-related consumption . . . The tourist precincts where the survey was conducted were Darling Harbour, The Rocks, Circular Quay, China Town, the CBD' (2002). Respondents included 80 managers of 30 restaurants, 30 retail shops, 15 entertainment or attraction businesses and five shopping centres.

Of the 80, in 24 cases the managers said they were 'unsure' of tourist numbers and in another 55 cases the managers said there were 'significant numbers of tourists' among their customers. In the one other case, the manager said there were 'very few'. Most of the 55 firms with significant numbers of tourists among their customers had no strategy to target them. Only 24 cases were following a business strategy of targeting tourists. Firth concluded that 'tourist numbers and associated expenditures were not found to be an accurate measure of a firm's involvement in tourist markets and industries' (2002: 105).

After completing the survey using a questionnaire and quantitative research, Firth conducted detailed case studies based on in-depth interviews with managers in a sample of 11 organisations in the same geographical area and known, in each case, to have significant numbers of both tourists and non-tourists among the customers. She set out detailed information analysing each case (2002: 107–71). Seven of the 11 were targeting tourists, to varying degrees and for diverse reasons; they included four retail shops, a bar/restaurant and two attractions. Four were not targeting tourists, for various reasons; they included two bar/restaurants, a retail shop and a department store.

Firth's findings support the points set out earlier in this chapter. In seven cases where tourists were targeted, and in the four where tourists were not targeted, the managers had reasoned it was a worthwhile policy, and gave practical justifications supporting their decisions.

Goodings Supermarket was another case discussed by Firth, using secondary sources. There is probably truth in the assertion that usually supermarkets and most other types of retail shops are not in the business of tourism, even though they often have tourists among their customers. 'Usually' is a key word here, for there are exceptions: the common practice should not be interpreted as a universal rule (Firth 2002: 77–8):

> Unlike many supermarkets that target the general population, Goodings implemented several [additional] initiatives aimed at attracting tourists. These included the provision of additional products that were known to be popular with tourists in the area . . . Prices at Goodings were also higher than other supermarkets, [an advantage they could exploit because] there was no other supermarkets within a two mile radius. Bilingual employees were recruited to more effectively communicate with the numerous international tourists . . . The supermarket offered less variety in grocery items than normal supermarkets and instead added gift items such as a large array of Disney merchandise, luggage, underwear and first aid items. Whilst locals also shop at Goodings, the decision [by Goodings' management] to focus on tourists came about because numerous hotels and motels, some of which have self-contained units with kitchens . . . surround the supermarket. Therefore it was assumed that visitors staying in this accommodation would most likely cater for themselves rather than dining out in restaurants every night.

Goodings' approach would not suit most supermarkets, even in places where there are many tourists, but there is no doubt that it would be appropriate in certain cases. Each manager should assess conditions for each case.

Seasonal business strategy

In places where tourism is highly seasonal, certain types of organisations supplying goods or services to the public at large have business strategies targeting tourists only during times of the year when large numbers of tourists are present. For example, a milk run might not deliver to camping grounds when few tourists are present but might make daily deliveries during the busy weeks, when the consumers of milk in a camping ground become a feasible market segment.

Having discussed business strategies, the theme now shifts to industrial participation. The horizontal line in Figure 11.1 represents a range of possible positions of organisations in relation to tourism industries. At or near the right end of the line are organisations participating extensively in one or more of these industries; those at the left end are not participating, even though they might be supplying goods or services direct to tourists.

Explaining these possibilities is the theme of this section. The first step required for the analysis is forming a reasonably clear concept of 'industry'. Tourism industries must share certain industrial characteristics with other industries if the expression is to have any sense. The first aim of this section is to identify these characteristics.

What is an industry?

'Industry' is often mentioned but seldom defined by economists, because they typically regard industries not as focal topics for study but as vaguely sketched backgrounds while studying related topics, such as market conditions under varying degrees of competition or the performance of firms (Porter 1980, 1985; Baumol & Blinder 1988; Best 1990). Porter described certain types of industries (emerging, fragmented etc.) but did not define industry.

Although modern economists have typically neglected to focus on industries, economists in the early decades of the 20th century and more recently researchers in certain other disciplines, along with practising managers, have focused on the nature of industries (Marshall 1895/1920; MacGregor 1911/1931; Robinson 1931; Buckminster-Fuller 1946/1972). For comments on the widespread ignorance about what industries are, along with a message dispelling and clarifying the confusion, Richardson's (1972) article is recommended.

Early research on industries by Marshall was developed in the 1920s by MacGregor, Robinson and others. In the 1930s the process stopped because, as Robinson remarked many years later in a forward to Best's (1990) book, all the economists at Cambridge University (where the early research on industries had been conducted) dropped their interest in industries and switched to new issues introduced by Keynes, concerned with ways for governments to deal with economic depressions.

Research by Penrose (1959), Richardson (1972) and Best (1990) represents a revived interest in industries among economists. In the meantime, independent thinkers in the USA, Britain and Japan also discovered the key theory through their own genius applied to close studies of working industries, not needing to read academic studies on the subject. Buckminster-Fuller studied ship-building and house construction and discovered what made all industries function, between inventing geodesic domes and other useful things. Deming, a famous statistician and management theorist, also seems to have developed an understanding of industries without studying earlier scholars on the subject. Richardson, an academic economist, seems to have worked out the theory

after realising that contemporary, conventional ideas about industries were unable to **267**
explain much about them.

Cooperation: the basis of industries and sports ➤

So what is the obscure theory about industries, described by relatively few researchers
but implicitly understood, as a result of practical experience, by many managers? It
involves cooperation. Certain kinds of cooperation, sometimes termed combination or
collaboration, among a collection of business organisations is what makes the collection an industry. This is what the early economists knew, what later economists
including Penrose, Richardson and Best rediscovered, along with Buckminster-Fuller
and Deming.

Competition certainly exists within many industries, but its role is secondary as it
'works within the grip of a certain amount of combination' (MacGregor 1911/1931:
204). By 'combination', MacGregor was referring to the effects of cooperation. Competition and cooperation are not mutually exclusive. Both can occur simultaneously in
industries and in many other institutions. The principle that competition is secondary
and normally subservient to cooperation is not widely recognised, yet it is fundamental
to a range of activities, including industries and sports, in civilised societies.

In the popular consciousness, encouraged and to some extent shaped by the mass
media, business and sport are constantly presented as activities in which competition is
the central issue and the antithesis of cooperative behaviour. Because most people spend
more time watching sporting events (especially via TV) than looking closely at business
activities, and because the mass media emphasise the competitive aspects of sport, many
'lessons' about the competitive nature of business management use metaphors and other
allusions drawn from sports.

Careful analysis can reveal that not only are many of these allusions misleading, but
their basis in sport is generally the result of mistaken perception. A brief discussion
on sporting myths will add support to the argument about the relative importance of
cooperation and competition in all aspects of civilisation, including modern industries.

How sporting myths obscure reality in business ➤

Persons who favour more competition for every industry typically assert that the 'level
playing fields' of sporting matches are useful models for business policy. The implications
are that intensive competition among businesses is more likely when 'the playing fields'
of business (i.e. markets) are 'level', not giving any competitor an advantage, and that
intensive competition is a desirable condition. (The reasons why many influential
persons strongly advocate more competition in the business world are outside the scope
of this discussion. Worth noting is the fact that most of these advocates are themselves
in powerful positions, associated with large and well-entrenched companies.)

Superficially, allusions linking sport and business might make sense, giving more
credence to the ideas that competition is the core of sport and business and that intense
competition is always desirable. In fact, the allusion is misleading, for there is no such
thing as a perfectly level playing field in field sports, such as football, hockey and polo;
even if it is physically level, the wind or sunshine gives one end an advantage. If playing

fields were perfectly level, teams would not follow the convention of changing ends at half-time. The purpose of the convention is to prevent one team from having a competitive advantage, derived from an uneven playing field, or wind or sunshine, throughout the entire match.

In the business world, markets are usually much more 'uneven' than most playing fields. Thus, if the sporting analogy were honestly applied, a rule for business would be introduced to 'change ends' halfway through each financial year. Every half-year all companies could be required to swap their business premises and equipment with their competitors. These prospects are ludicrous, but they expose the absurdity of the level-playing-field metaphor as applied to markets in the world of business.

An underlying analogy from sport to business is even more pervasive and misleading. This is the widely assumed idea that sports are primarily competitive contests and the opposite of cooperative behaviour. In fact, sporting matches in the modern world are based primarily on cooperation. Competition occurs within the bounds of a cooperative framework, as players in both teams cooperate when they agree implicitly to follow the conventions and rules of the game they are playing. When a referee or umpire issues a penalty, it means a team has gone beyond the cooperative basis of the game. Players who repeatedly break the rules are sent for a spell in a sin-bin, or sent off for the rest of the game in response to a more serious transgression. In sport, cooperation is therefore superior to competition, although it is the competition that spectators focus on and appreciate, and that players also typically enjoy.

The cooperative foundations of sports are a feature of modern, civilised societies. In primitive societies sporting contests can be fiercely competitive, almost wars. Football's origins in England, centuries ago, were brawls between mobs from opposing villages competing to capture and run off with a ball, without rules or referee. In modern times a primitive sport of that kind is the national sport in Afghanistan, buzkashi. Hundreds of horsemen fiercely compete in a wild melée to pick up and carry off a dead goat. Polo, originating across Afghanistan's southern border in Pakistan, is a highly refined form of buzkashi, still competitive but only so far as its conventions and rules allow. The addition of conventions and rules converted the wild buzkashi into civil sport.

A gradual incorporation of cooperative behaviour into sports as they evolved, and therefore a gradual restriction on the limits of competitive behaviour, can be viewed as a sign of an evolving, more civilised society. Similar processes explain the evolution of civilised business activities in industrialising economies. Just as outsiders might regard polo as a wild melée of horse-riders obeying no rules, spectators who lack the in-depth knowledge that comes from practical experience in business management, such as many economists and social commentators, notice competitive activities on the surface and overlook the underlying cooperation that sustains industries and makes them productive.

Cooperation and competition in business ➤

In the business world, relationships between organisations are a complex mix of competition, cooperation and coexistence. Competition can be useful for stimulating innovations and efficiencies, but cooperation is normally more important as it involves participants combining in various ways to get the productivity that makes industrial activities effective and efficient. Perrow, in his book *Complex Organisations*, commented on the relative roles of competition and cooperation: (Perrow 1986: 174)

> *Standard Oil and Shell may compete at the intersection of two highways but they do not compete in the numerous other areas where their interests are critical such as foreign policy, tax laws, import quotas, government funding of research and development, highway expansion, internal combustion engines, pollution restrictions and so on.*

Perrow's comments imply that to the senior managers in the global oil industry, cooperation is more important than competition. The same conclusion emerged in Sampson's (1975) detailed analysis of that industry.

Studying managerial trends in several major industries in the USA, Chandler (1977) explained how the old idea of so-called 'market forces' with their 'invisible hands' arranging processes via competition is a defective vision of how modern industries operate. During the 20th century the way organisations and industries operated came increasingly under the influence of managers' visible hands—visible if one looked for them—and managers normally seek cooperative solutions rather than the more costly competitive alternatives.

Geographic clustering as one sign of industry ➤

An important aspect of the cooperation at the core of industries is seen in the way component organisations cluster together. Silicon Valley in California is a major location of the world's computer industry: thousands of nominally independent enterprises are located there. In older, traditional industries the same principle of clustering can be seen in ancient cities of the Middle East, Asia and Africa. Baghdad's Sheik Omah Street contains hundreds of tiny workshops forming the city's car-repair industry. Within it are smaller specialist industries, each geographically clustered, for the workshops are grouped according to their specialty—engine blocks, radiators, windscreens, panels and air-conditioners. In manufacturing zones behind traditional marketplaces of ancient cities (Cairo, Istanbul, Teheran) the same sort of industrial clustering by specialty products can be seen, one location specialising in making pots, another in jewellery, a third in clothing.

In none of these cases was the clustering the result of planning and administrative decrees from a government or an industrial association. It emerged over time as a natural process of industrial structure, the result of countless small decisions by nominally 'independent' entrepreneurs. Why does this clustering occur?

A superficial explanation is that the location is a marketplace, where buyers and sellers meet, and there are economies of scope and of scale if industries can be located close to markets. This is not the complete reason. Clustering also reflects a need for cooperative behaviour, for it enables easy communication, in person, among managers and workers in the component business organisations, all with common interests in many issues relating to work roles and whatever is being produced—computer software, windscreens or whatever.

Geographic patterns following the same principle can be seen in most tourist destinations. Hotels of similar standard are often located in close proximity to one another. At the northern end of Australia's Gold Coast along a strip of highway are several large theme parks (Movieworld, Dreamworld, Wet 'n' Wild) and a number of smaller-scale facilities; collectively they form the Gold Coast's theme park industry.

Why do organisations cooperate? ➤

Why do organisations cooperate and form industries? Organisations are governed by people, so the issue can be approached by asking more questions: why do people cooperate, under what conditions does this occur, and, in particular, what are the links between cooperative and competitive behaviour? Axelrod's (1990) book is a classic on these questions. It shows how cooperation and competition can occur simultaneously; why cooperation often leads to better outcomes for all stakeholders, in certain circumstances; and it sets out four principles for encouraging cooperative behaviour.

The benefit of industrialisation, compared to other methods of production and marketing, is that it enables large-scale production, greater productivity (more outputs per resource input), and greater managerial control over quality and other matters. The first and second advantages mean lower costs and hence lower prices which, combined with greater outputs, lead to higher material standards of living for consumers and greater profits for industrialists. Of course, industrialisation is not appropriate for all kinds of products and services. Only certain forms of tourism are suited to a high degree of industrialisation.

Four early industries ➤

Common features of cooperative behaviour can be seen among otherwise independent organisations that formed pioneering industries in sugar, pottery, travellers' cheques and packaged tourism. The purpose of the cooperation is clearly implied in these examples.

Mintz (1985) showed how a sugar industry formed in the Caribbean in the early 18th century when managers coordinated two stages of production—plantations and mills. Neither could be very productive operating separately but together, in cooperative combination, they became a sugar industry. Other forms of cooperation in this seminal industry included management-imposed coordination of the labour force, such as time coordination, with managers specifying set times for work—unknown in pre-industrial systems. In earlier times, before these 18th century innovations, sugar production and distribution was the work of uncoordinated farmers and merchants, and sugar was very expensive, sold at prices beyond the budgets of most people.

Josiah Wedgewood industrialised pottery manufacture and marketing in the mid-18th century (McKendrick 1959). He introduced coordinated steps and cooperative processes. His other innovations included: in production, standardised designs, clocking-in of workers (i.e. time-consciousness) and training schemes; and, in marketing, grading of products, partnerships with merchants, and public relations campaigns to create customers by fostering a belief that certain styles of pottery were fashionable. Before Wedgewood, pottery was manufactured as an uncoordinated, casual, cottage-based activity, and its marketing was left to chance.

Robert Herries invented travellers' cheques in the late 18th century, a service requiring cooperation between multiple banks and merchants (Booker 1994). His persistent efforts to make the invention work largely focused on getting banks and merchants in several countries of Western Europe to participate in a cooperative manner.

Thomas Cook began arranging tours in the mid-19th century and was the pioneer of the modern form of packaged tourism (Pudney 1953; Swinglehurst 1974). In order for packaged tours to function, he formed and managed cooperative links between nominally separate organisations in retailing, wholesaling, transport, accommodation and attractions.

A definition of industry ➤

Building on ideas set out above, and on Buckminster-Fuller's (1972: 161) insight, a definition of industries can be proposed:

> *An industry comprises a collection of three or more productive units that are managed to be assiduously active in similar or related lines of business, using compatible technologies and coordinating the activities via a cooperative approach to achieve synergistic outputs and constantly improving performance. The activities transform resources, via processes involving division of labour, into products with some degree of homogeneity.*

One elementary unit in industry has the role of coordinating the work of the others: it is management. As explained towards the end of Chapter 8, the main function of managers is coordinating the work of others. Working independently, or relying on imperfect markets to coordinate activities, separate units seldom achieve the same productivity.

Synergy is an outcome when cooperation is properly implemented; it is the ability of two or more components in a functioning system to achieve more in combination than they could independently. Sometimes called the $1 + 1 = 3$ principle, it occurs in productive teamwork, where the output of a team is greater than the sum of the outputs of its independent members.

The concept and the word come from biology: the power of an animal's limb is greater than the sum of the power of the limb's muscles working independently. Anyone who has played in a smoothly functioning sporting team develops a sense of what synergy is about. Anyone with practical experience in a functioning industry, especially if the work involves links between different business enterprises, knows the same sense.

A business enterprise is not restricted to one industry and, in practice, industries overlap. However, participating in an industry requires maintaining cooperative links, and because this requires effort and expense, small-scale enterprises tend to specialise because they cannot afford to maintain simultaneous links into several industries; their managers decide on the best option. Wyndham Estate Winery, discussed in Chapter 12, followed this policy for many years. The winery catered for tourists' visits but was not a participant in tourism industries.

How tourism industries function

Certain types of tourist-related businesses, notably tour wholesalers and travel agents, are intrinsically components of tourism industries, as their core activities depend on cooperating with others in the same or related lines of business. Organisations in any other type of business, involved with any kind of goods or services used by consumers, might also be components, if their managers actively cooperate with organisations in tourism industries.

Cooperation occurs when a person is simultaneously aware both of the need of another person and of an ability and obligation to help that person (Kagan 1998: 162). Kagan remarked that honey bees are not cooperating with flowers when they carry pollen. The behaviour might seem cooperative to human observers, because it is mutually beneficial, but it lacks the essential motivations of cooperative behaviour. More than a dozen examples can be listed of cooperative links between organisations in the business of tourism (see below). Each involves work and resources applied by managers of the participating organisations, conscious of the mutual benefits to participants.

Researchers interested in tourism management have discussed certain items from the examples below; strategic alliances, for instance, have been discussed by many writers since Lane's (1986) early article on the topic, 'Marriages of necessity: airline–hotel liaisons'. Since the mid-1990s a flood of articles has appeared on strategic alliances in the mainstream literature of business strategy (see especially Reuer 2000; Koza & Lewin 2000; Stuart 2000), and these provide useful theories that could be applied in research and practice relating to tourism. Strategic alliances are a generic form of cooperation, and several of the items below come within this ambit. What has been lacking in earlier writings on tourism industries, with few exceptions (Leiper 1990b, Crotts et al. 2000), is an overview of the multiple forms of cooperation.

Principal–agent links ➤

Principal–agent links, always requiring cooperation by the participants, are important in most tourism industries. Retail travel agents are commercially linked to their principals, the organisations each agent represents in its local market. They include airlines, hotels, motels, tour operator-wholesalers, travel insurers, and car renters. As described in the case about World and Country Travel in Chapter 9, the link is established when principals accredit agents, allowing them to sell the principal's products and paying commissions for sales achieved.

Forming and maintaining these cooperative arrangements requires time, costs and enterprise. Who gains? Ideally the principals gain by getting more sales, the agents gain by earning commissions, and consumers gain from the convenience of booking and buying travel arrangements without having to contact the distant principals who will ultimately provide the service. Broadly and synergistically, industries and markets gain.

Packaged tour arrangements ➤

Packaged tours, also known as inclusive holidays, were originally for organised groups but these days are mostly for 'independent' tourists—independent of groups. Created by travel agents or tour operators, packages require the cooperation of at least three parties, typically carrier and accommodation units brought together by a managing unit.

Reservation systems ➤

Reservation systems are widely used for transport, accommodation, packaged tours and other items. As with packaged tours, their functions for tourists include providing security and saving time. Reservation systems involve common technology shared cooperatively by organisations such as travel agents, airlines, hotels and tour operators.

Cooperative R&D ➤

Powers (1992) noted that worldwide more than $US3 billion was spent in the late 1980s on developing new technologies for computerised CRSs (central reservation systems) for airlines, hotels and related sectors in tourism industries. The very high cost led large companies to form partnerships, to share the costs, the work and the benefits of this research and development. Powers observed three megasystems emerging: Sabre, where the major investor is American Airlines, stands alone; the second is a collaboration between Apollo (a joint USA–Europe effort), Galileo (European) and Gemini (Canadian); the third, another collaboration, between Worldspan, Systems One, Abacus and Amadeus, representing European, US and Asian sources.

Other examples of cooperative research could be noted, although the practice is not so widespread as it might be. Market research studies are sometimes sponsored by consortia, where the partners cooperate.

Standardised products ➤

Coordinated product design among superficially competitive organisations is common in tourism industries. Most airlines on similar routes, for instance, use similar aircraft and similar in-flight facilities. Many airlines' meals are produced in the same kitchen. Dozens of airlines using Sydney airport share just two kitchens. Hotels in each class have relatively similar rooms. In many regions, most operators of sightseeing tours follow similar itineraries. All this is done consciously by managers, normally for a range of reasons, and cooperation is present in most of them. Economies of scope and of scale are two of the reasons.

Graded products ➤

Standardising products can lead to a higher order of cooperation, a higher order of industrialisation—graded products. In airlines, grades are described as first class, business class and economy class. In the different international airlines, such as Qantas Airways, Singapore Airlines and Thai Airways, the first-class facilities (seats and food) and services (in-flight entertainment) are much the same, as they are in business or economy class.

In many countries, certain types of tourist accommodation are graded. In some places the labels are 'de luxe', 'first class' and 'tourist class'; more common, in other places, are stars, from five down to none. In Australia, motorists' associations such as the NRMA (National Roads and Motorists Association) were pioneers in this work (Leiper 1980c).

Standardised and graded goods, facilities and services are signs of an industry. In tourism industries these enable retail travel agents to offer their clients hotel bookings, for example, with confidence that the quality will suit the client, even though the agent has not personally seen the hotel. This added knowledge in distant markets and distribution channels helps an industry function more effectively and more efficiently.

Generic products? ➤

Generic products are standardised—perhaps graded, but unbranded, so outputs from different sources are not easily distinguished. The term is used in supermarket retailing for low-price soap powders etc. Generics represent a higher degree of industrialisation, an extension of standardised and graded products. There are no generic products in tourism industries yet: a hypothetical example would be packaged tour brochures on display in a travel agency (or on an Internet site) without showing the names of the tour operators, airlines or hotels in the package.

Cooperative pricing policies ➤

In most markets aimed at tourists, suppliers cooperate in subtle ways on pricing. The most obvious evidence is in air travel, where price competition is not the usual condition. Instead, a new fare from one airline is usually copied quickly by other airlines on the same route, in the same industry. Research by AGB McNair (1986) and others has found that Australian airlines seldom engage in price competition over long periods.

Why? Uniform and stable prices are advantageous for suppliers at large. There are also benefits for consumers in relatively stable prices, even though prices may be higher than would result in perfectly competitive markets. This is because wildly fluctuating prices can make consumers feel uncertain about value.

Agreements between employers and employees ➤

A sign of a developed industry is standardisation in agreements, between employees and employers, in various organisations in the same field of work about pay and working conditions. There are no labour awards spanning all sectors of tourism industries, and there probably never will be, but in Australia awards were first negotiated in the 1980s that specifically deal with certain jobs in those industries (Palmer & McGraw 1990).

A shift away from industrial awards towards 'enterprise bargaining', where each worker bargains with the employer for wages and conditions, was evident in Australia in the 1990s. To date (2003) the trend has not progressed far in tourism industries.

Industrial training schemes ➤

Training schemes to prepare people for work in a particular industry exemplify cooperative management at the industrial level. These schemes depend on managers from organisational components of the industry meeting and agreeing on what the training should be designed to achieve, so they can advise the trainers on the required outcomes.

These schemes also depend on employers from different organisations recognising the qualifications in their recruitment and staffing practices. These arrangements for training schemes serving tourism industries began in Australia and New Zealand in the 1970s and have proliferated since then.

Intra-industry careers and networks ➤

A sign of an industry is employees regarding a collection of organisations as their career field, with individuals moving among jobs within 'the industry'. There is scattered evidence that this happens widely among employees in tourism industries. Careerists move from job to job among and between travel agencies, tour operators, airlines, hotels, national tourism offices and the like. This is possible because there is a body of common knowledge across the field, as research by Airey and Nightingale (1981) revealed. Knowledge gleaned in one job can be usefully taken on to another.

Similarly, people employed in tourism industries in any city or region tend to form personal networks, keeping in touch. This happens informally, via telephone or over lunch, also at meetings of industry associations and, in fact, while people are maintaining all the examples of cooperation in this list.

Exchange of useful information ➤

A widespread and important manifestation of an industry is that people working in different component organisations exchange mutually useful information. This happens widely in tourism industries. Managers of hotels in many cities and regions inform one another about each hotel's room occupancies, average room revenues and other items.

The practice seems more common in large-scale hotels in large cities and major resort towns; it is uncommon among small-scale hotels and motels. The reason for the difference seems to be that proprietors and managers of smaller-scale enterprises are more bound up in competitive ideologies, believing that knowledge about business must be kept 'commercial in confidence' because disclosing it to competitors would give away a competitive advantage. By this indicator, larger hotels tend to be more industrialised than small-scale hotels and motels which, in contrast, are in many cases not so much part of an industry but a collection of fragmented enterprises.

A lot of information is exchanged widely among all sectors of tourism industries. A prominent example is data on movements in whole tourism systems (traveller departures and tourist arrivals, country by country and region by region) published by the World Tourism Organisation on the global scene and by the Bureau of Tourism Research on Australia. The data, often more detailed that any published for all to see on Internet sites of those institutions, are used by managers in travel agents, carriers, accommodation, attractions, tour operators and tourism coordination bodies, among others.

BSP (Bank Settlement Plan) is another example of the cooperative basis of tourism industries. Its participants include accredited travel agents, most airlines, and many hotels and tour operators. While it is primarily a scheme for coordinating payments from travel agents to airlines and other principals owed revenues collected from consumers, an important byproduct is information that gives a precise insight into market trends on a fortnightly basis.

In Australia, the data were for many years kept confidential by the principals. In the late 1980s the biweekly reports began being leaked to trade newspapers, which published them. A number of managers from larger principals and larger travel agency chains expressed strong opposition to this practice—more evidence of a competitive ideology working against the common interest. The opposition withered and the publications continued.

John Haddad, managing director of Federal Pacific Casinos, 'stresses the co-operative aspect between potential competitors' (King & Hyde 1989: 168). Haddad mentioned regular meetings of managers from different casinos, superficially in competition, for the exchange of information on matters of mutual interest, such as security procedures. Countless more examples of managers cooperating like this could be found.

Industry associations ➤

Associations of business organisations are a major medium of cooperation at the centre of many industries, and there are perhaps more in tourism than in other kinds of industries. *Traveltrade Yearbook*, published in Sydney and Auckland, lists many examples.

Some associations try to span all sectors of travel and tourism industries in a region, a country, or multinationally, as with WTTC (World Travel and Tourism Council) or PATA (Pacific Asia Travel Association). Many deal with interests of a particular sector but usually include members from affiliated fields. IATA (International Air Transport Association) is a cooperative grouping of more than 100 airlines, and is used as a medium for airline industry discussions and for representing airlines in dealing with governments, hotels' associations and travel agents' associations. AFTA (Australian Federation of Travel Agencies) and TAANZ (Travel Agents Association of New Zealand) mainly look after the interests of travel agents, but the members includes airlines, car rental firms and tour operators. Members of Australian Tourism Export Council (ATEC) are inbound tour operators and allied businesses from several sectors of Australia's inbound international tourism industries. Tourism Task Force (TTF) is an Australian association comprising large city-based hotels and affiliated businesses.

Industrial associations have several functions, all relevant to the theme of cooperation in industries. The exchange of useful information on mutual concerns is a common one. Some associations conduct jointly funded promotional campaigns, to boost a particular destination or class of product, requiring a cooperative effort. Co-managed research projects are another possibility. Many of these associations are quite active in promoting the interests of members via public relations aimed at governments and the mass media. Internet sites of each association are useful for learning about their membership and activities.

Advertising and publicity messages ➤

Advertising and publicity are not commonly viewed as cooperative activities because their obvious role is promoting particular brands of hotel or airlines, or particular places as tourist destinations. They seem to be competitive actions, however (Berger 1972: 131):

. . . in advertising and other forms of publicity, one brand competes with another, but it is also true that every publicity image confirms and enhances every other. Publicity is not merely an assembly of competing messages: it is a language in itself which is always being used to make the same general proposal. Within publicity, choices are offered between this cream and that cream, between this car and that car, but publicity as a system makes a single proposal.

The publicity system of tourism industries makes the single proposal that people should go on trips. One TV ad proposes flying United Airlines while another proposes British Airways; one publicity story in a newspaper proposes staying in a Novotel hotel while another describes Parkroyal; one brochure is all about inclusive packages under the Venture Holidays brand while the next brochure on the travel agency's rack is from Trafalgar Tours; this week's promotional feature in the travel section of the weekend *Sydney Morning Herald* is about New Zealand while last week's feature was Malaysia.

Thus each promotional item, from in some cases competing sponsors, is simultaneously serving overlapping, common interests—each particular item, and tourism industries in general. The overlap might not be easily recognised by persons mentally bound up in the dogma of competitiveness.

Thomas Cook seems to have recognised it 140 years ago. Pudney's (1953: 151–2) history of Cook's business described how its promotional publications, *The Tourist* and *The Excursionist*, carried advertisements for other tour operators with whom Cook was competing, such as Henry Gaze. Pudney attributed this to Cook's sense of 'friendly competition', which totally misses the point. Berger's theory, that promotional systems normally have generic benefits besides benefits for brands, explains how it can be attributed not to friendly competition but to Cook's understanding, as an insightful business practitioner, of the ways in which cooperative activities can develop markets and industries.

Summary: cooperation in industry

Structures and productivity of modern industrialised economies cannot be attributed solely to competition in markets. A more important factor is cooperation, in various forms, among component units of industries. Cooperation sometimes evolves spontaneously, sometimes emerges as a consequence of actions by organisations seeking a self-interested goal, and sometimes happens because far-sighted individuals in key organisations recognise the synergistic potential of cooperative processes. Regardless of how it occurs, once it is recognised, cooperation in most forms can be fostered and managed.

If component units of industries did not work in unison to some degree there would be no functioning industries; there could only be industries in a notional, imaginary sense. This points to a defect in excuses about an allegedly huge and ubiquitous thing called 'the tourism industry' being 'fragmented' or, as some commentators have called it, 'a disorganised industry'. To the extent that there is fragmentation or disorganisation, there is no functioning industry.

None of the forms of cooperation listed above is, in itself, an essential criterion for the industrialisation of tourism. Tourism industries evolve when a number of forms of cooperation are in place. Thus there is no single step that shifts an organisation from being totally outside to totally inside a particular industry. There is, rather, a series of steps in a number of possible forms of cooperative behaviour.

This list of cooperative forms is not exhaustive. No doubt others exist that could be identified. As industries develop, change and disappear, the forms and degrees of cooperation change. Part of the challenge for managers is to decide which forms are most important at particular times. Another challenge is to invent and apply new forms.

Overt and covert signs of an industry

Observing the diverse forms of cooperation reveals how industries are internally structured, behind the superficial components of industrial structure expressed in terms of sectors. The sectors of tourism industries (marketing specialists, tour operators, carriers, accommodation etc.) are overt signs of their structures, just as a building's walls and roof are overt signs of its structure. Inside a building's walls and roof are the unseen components that hold it together, and hidden inside an industry are structural links that outsiders do not see, or do not recognise as structural and functional. Knowledge of both kinds of structure leads to a deeper understanding of how an industry functions, and how it can best be developed and managed.

The horizontal axis on Figure 11.1

Any organisation with any kind of link to tourism could be assessed for its cooperative behaviour with other organisations of this sort and placed in a position along the horizontal axis in Figure 11.1. Those with extensive and intensive cooperative activities would be placed on the extreme right, and those with no such activities on the left. Many are between the extremes. To date, no methodology has been developed for gauging and measuring the precise position of organisations in this model, but this is certainly feasible. In the meantime, approximate estimates are possible.

Quadrants in Figure 11.1 ➤

The vertical and horizontal axes divide Figure 11.1 into quadrants, and the analysis to date enables a hypothetical arrangement of all organisations supplying goods or services direct to tourists to be placed in the four locations, depending on each organisation's business strategies (vertical axis) and industrial participation (horizontal axis).

Quadrant #1 is the normal location of organisations specialising in tourism, such as travel agencies, tour operators, regional and national tourism organisations, international institutions, airlines, coachlines, cruise lines, certain railways, motels, hotels, holiday apartments for rent, camping grounds and caravan parks, hostels, theme parks, souvenir and luggage shops, and any other organisations that specialise in tourism.

Quadrant #3 is the normal location of organisations supplying goods or services direct to tourists in a passive, incidental manner, without business strategies for tourists and without cooperative participation in any tourism industries. In many towns, cities and regions, a very large number of organisations are in this category.

Quadrant #2 is the location of organisations supplying goods or services direct to tourists and using a business strategy in that work, but not participating in any tourism industry. Relatively few organisations are in quadrant #2, because a business strategy for tourism is normally more efficient if accompanied by a number of the cooperative links in the list above.

Quadrant #4 is also a relatively uncommon location. An example of an organisation here is a shop selling clothes or food that has no business strategies for tourism but is a member of the region's tourism association. The proprietor's motivation for membership might be a sense of civic duty, aligned with a belief that inbound tourism is good for the local community.

Different and shifting positions within each quadrant ➤

The positions of particular organisations in any quadrant depend on their positions along the vertical and horizontal axes. Thus, a tour operator with intensely directed business strategies for a particular type of tourist and with an extensive range of cooperative links to tourism industries would be located in the top right-hand corner of quadrant #1, while a motel with relatively weak business strategies and maintaining only token membership of one or two industrial associations would be towards the botton left-hand corner of the same quadrant (#1). If the motel later began liaising with tour operators, providing accommodation as a component in packaged tours, its position would shift in a diagonal direction, up and to the right.

Shifting between the quadrants ➤

A newly established business, such as a motel or block of holiday apartments, might begin in quadrant #2 and later shift to quadrant #1 by joining the regional tourism association. Various other shifts between quadrants can occur.

Practical uses of Figure 11.1 ➤

The diagram represents a model of four broad strategic positions that various organisations might occupy in relation to tourism. As such, it demonstrates how and why tourism is partly industrialised in terms of the activities of individual business organisations.

By measuring and plotting the positions of a sample of organisations in towns, cities and regions, an assessment could be made of the level of industrialisation of all the organisational resources in those places. Different places would be different in this respect, and variations would occur over time. The relevance of these assessments is that they indicate the degree to which tourism is being supported by organisations with strategic and industrial relationships to tourism. As a general principle, the higher that degree, the less the need for governmental support and involvement.

Partial industrialisation syndrome ➤

Partial industrialisation is not a single theory. It is better described as the partial industrialisation syndrome, a collection of theories that describe, explain and stem from a condition found in reference to tourism and a number of other categories of human activity, such as education and entertainment. In modern tourism there are several consequences of the syndrome. These are described in Chapter 16. Policies and strategies for dealing with these consequences can be much better informed if there is recognition and understanding of the syndrome, and that is helped by Figure 11.1 and the accompanying discussion in this chapter.

A WIDER VIEW OF PARTIAL INDUSTRIALISATION

Organisations are not the only resources supporting tourism. Accordingly, the analysis to date, focused on organisations, does not give a complete picture of partial industrialisation. The following analysis attempts this, building on earlier theoretical research on the theme by Leiper (1990a, 1990b) and drawing on complementary research by Stear (2002).

Three perspectives on resources used in tourism

Perspectives of three kinds of stakeholders are relevant to understanding resources used in tourism.

First, there is the perspective of individual tourists. Each makes choices, on each trip, about the degree of tourism industry usage he/she requires. One tourist makes her own arrangements to travel to a nearby seaside town, where she stays in a friend's apartment; another books arrangements via a travel agent for a trip to several cities using airlines, hotels, coach tour operators and guides. The first example is non-industrialised tourism, the second is highly industrialised tourism.

Next is the perspective of organisations supplying goods or services, where managers make decisions about the degree and type of tourism industry involvement the organisation will have. This perspective was explored earlier in this chapter.

Third is the perspective of resident populations in places visited by tourists. These people make decisions or, very often, see decisions that affect them made by others about the degree of tourism industry development that occurs in their town or region.

Categories of resources used by tourists

Four phenomena associated with tourism can be distinguished (see Figure 11.2): economic resources, markets, businesses, and industries. They differ in size. Close observation will reveal how tourism—the activity of tourists—is always greater than the economic resources used in tourism, which in turn is larger than tourist markets, which in turn tend to be larger than activities of organisations in the business of tourism, which in turn are usually broader than the scope of tourism industries. An explanation for this descending scale is set out below.

FIGURE 11.2 Tourism and economic resources, markets, businesses and industries

How tourism leads to other phenomena

Tourism = activity of tourists,
so places become traveller-generators,
transit routes and tourist destinations

Scarce resources used by tourists (basis of tourism economics)	Unlimited resources used by tourists (e.g. scenery—no economic relevance)
Tourist markets, or tourist segments in larger markets	Non-marketised tourism: no transactions, or no rights in transaction (e.g. use of personal house, car)
Tourist-oriented business strategies (e.g. resort hotel)	Business strategies not oriented to tourists (e.g. store with occasional tourists among shoppers)
Tourism industries (tourist-oriented businesses working in cooperation)	Non-industrial tourism resources

Economic and non-economic resources ➤

Tourism includes many sorts of behaviour—mental, physical, social and economic. The economic dimension is restricted to that part of tourism depending on limited resources, such as money, facilities and services, where allocations have to be made. Non-economic tourism (not the same as 'uneconomic') includes all the rest. Sunshine, for example, cannot be allocated among tourists. Whether there are two persons or 10 000 enjoying the sun has no economic implications. As only part of tourism has an economic basis, the economics of tourism is smaller in scope than tourism. The top section in Figure 11.2 describes this analysis.

Marketised and non-marketised resources ➤

Markets and marketing are expressions sometimes used precisely, and very often loosely. The loose expressions are metaphors and similes, describing all sorts of transactions and promotions that are *similar* to markets and marketing. Genuine markets and marketing involve transactions between parties where there is also an exchange of property rights, a principle stressed by marketing theorists (Bain & Howells 1988). Property rights are either rights to ownership, where goods are exchanged, or rights to temporary use, where rights to services or facilities are provided.

Much tourism is marketised—when tourists obtain legal ownership of goods (e.g. food, souvenirs) and legal rights to use services and facilities (e.g. airlines, hotels, tour groups). Tickets and other vouchers are normally the evidence of rights being exchanged in transactions.

Much tourism is not marketised. Some cannot be. All tourists display what is described by marketing theorists as 'non-market behaviour' (Gronhaug & Dholakia 1987). As any market depends on limited resources, the non-economic part of tourism is outside the scope of marketised tourism. This is depicted in Figure 11.2. No market exists when tourists look at scenery or mingle with the crowd in a public place, even if commentators remark (using a feral metaphor) that the tourists are 'in the market for experiences'.

Non-marketised tourism also involves economic resources that are not marketised. Many tourists use personal possessions, their own or their friends' and family's vehicles, houses, recreational equipment. No exchange of rights occurs when this happens. Tourists also use non-marketised personal services such as help and advice or recommendations from family, friends and strangers offering casual, informal assistance in different ways.

Non-marketised tourism also includes tourists using public goods: 'The market cannot solve the problem of supplying public goods' (Sugden 1986: 3). Public roads, street lighting, parks, toilets, signposts, and services such as police, garbage, public hospitals and libraries, information bureaux can be used by anyone, and no rights are exchanged when they are used. Usually there is no price. The fact that administrators of public goods use expressions such as 'markets' and 'marketing' is not evidence that markets exist. It merely signifies that the administrators have borrowed the jargon from marketers.

So, for a number of reasons, tourism is part-marketised, and while that proportion will vary in different circumstances it will always be smaller than the proportion using economic resources, as Figure 11.2 depicts.

Business strategies and passive acceptance of tourists ➤

The scope of tourism potentially available for business organisations is limited to the scope that can be marketised. Within that scope, only a portion is normally feasible for business strategies, because of the limits of market segmentation and other factors discussed earlier in this chapter. Thus, in Figure 11.2 the box representing tourism-oriented businesses is smaller than the one above it representing tourist markets and market segments.

Tourism industries and non-industrial resources ➤

As discussed earlier, in many places there are organisations with business strategies aimed at serving tourists but not participating in any tourism industry; they are represented by quadrant #2 in Figure 11.1. The condition means that the scope of tourism industries tends to be smaller than the scope of all business organisations with strategies for tourism. The lowest section of Figure 11.2 depicts this point.

Summary analysis: seven types of resources used in tourism

Stear (2002) summarised the analysis of resources used in tourism by identifying seven types. Each has been described in various sections of the discussion earlier in this chapter:

■ free goods and services, natural and built, such as beaches, scenery and interesting buildings;

■ social goods and services forming 'public goods', such as roads, street lights and sanitation;

■ organisations that only incidentally serve tourists: many (but not all) cafes, book-shops, supermarkets etc.;

■ tourists in each party providing, for themselves and their travelling companions, trip management, transport, accommodation etc.;

■ tourists' friends and relatives who provide accommodation, transport, company and food;

■ resources from other tourists, including information and companionship;

■ organisations in tourism industries providing, usually on a commercial basis, transport, accommodation, entertainment, food etc.

The purpose of this analysis was summed up by remarking that tourism industries 'can only ever supply, perform or be responsible for *some* of the goods and *some* of the services and *some* of the experienced phenomena that make up the total trip experience of every tourist on every touristic trip' (Stear 2002). This explains, succinctly, why and how tourism is partly industrialised.

Index of industrialisation ➤

Figure 11.2 has a sloping line representing divisions of all the factors leading to part-industrialisation. The line's slope and position vary with circumstances, and in different types of tourism. For example, outbound tourism from Japan in recent years has been highly industrialised. Most tourists have depended on services from tourism industries. In the 1980s about 90% of outbound Japanese were buying transport and accommo-dation packages before departure (Leiper 1985); in contrast, domestic tourism in Australia in recent decades has had low degrees of industrialisation (see Figure 11.3).

Reports from the Bureau of Tourism Research reveal that more than 80% of domestic tourist trips were self-sufficient for transport, using personal vehicles; and that 60% were self-sufficient for accommodation, using private holiday houses or the homes of friends and relatives. Most needs of Australian domestic tourists in recent years have been served by organisations or persons with no business or industrial links to tourism. Describing those two extremes, Figures 11.3 depicts approximate levels of industrialis-ation for two sets of tourism in Australia: visitors from Japan and Australian domestic.

The ratio of expenditure on goods and services supplied by organisations in tourism industries (the seventh category in the list above) to total expenditure (in all categories) can be termed the *index of industrialisation*. It ranges theoretically from 100% to zero. For example, if a tourist (or collection of tourists) is supplied with services worth $1000, of which $600 comes from organisations in tourism industries and the other $400 comes from organisations beyond that industry, the index will be 60%.

FIGURE 11.3 Industrialisation compared: Japanese and Australian tourists

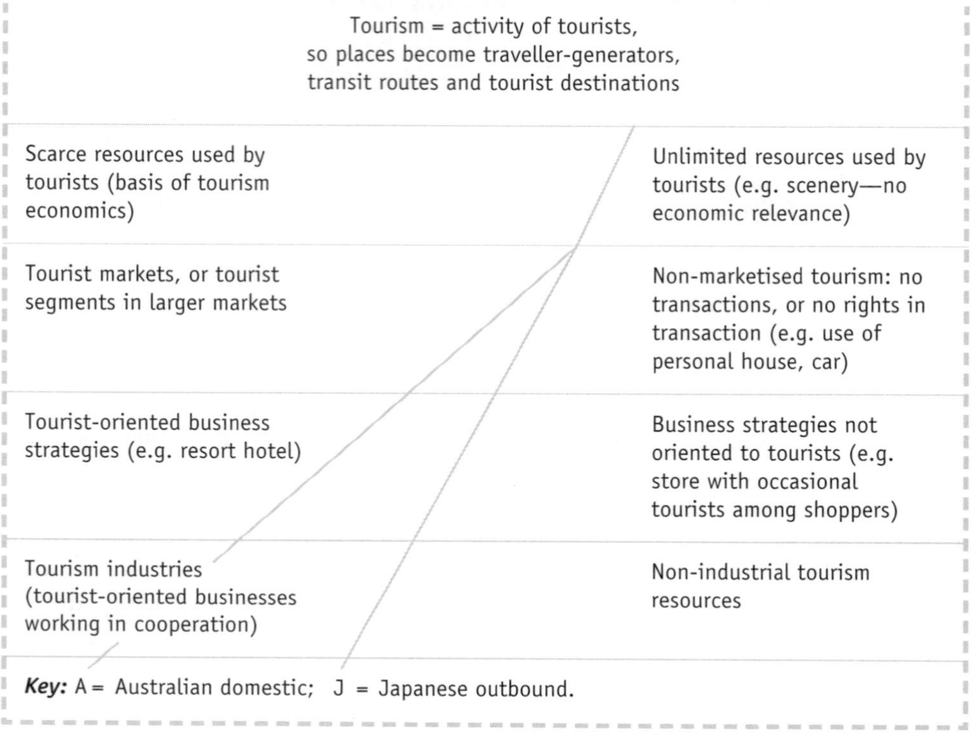

Tourism = activity of tourists,
so places become traveller-generators,
transit routes and tourist destinations

Scarce resources used by tourists (basis of tourism economics)	Unlimited resources used by tourists (e.g. scenery—no economic relevance)
Tourist markets, or tourist segments in larger markets	Non-marketised tourism: no transactions, or no rights in transaction (e.g. use of personal house, car)
Tourist-oriented business strategies (e.g. resort hotel)	Business strategies not oriented to tourists (e.g. store with occasional tourists among shoppers)
Tourism industries (tourist-oriented businesses working in cooperation)	Non-industrial tourism resources

Key: A = Australian domestic; J = Japanese outbound.

CONCLUSIONS

Tourism is part-industrialised, to varying degrees. It is supported and shaped by many factors, some of which are organisations of various types. Some of these organisations are in the business of tourism and some are in other lines of business. Some in the business of tourism are also functional components of tourism industries, others are not.

Industrialisation involves nominally independent resources, in functionally or geographically separate organisations, becoming strategically active in a tourist-related line of business and cooperating in some significant way. The cooperation creates synergy, in the form of productivity gains.

Several examples of cooperative processes at the core of tourism industries were identified. Some occur without conscious effort by managers, examples of what Mintzberg terms 'emergent strategies, where patterns developed in the absence of intentions' (1991d: 14). All of them may occur sequentially with the deliberate intent of managers, examples of what Mintzberg terms 'deliberate strategies', which might be planned or arise from another deliberate action. Thus tourism industries are created, sustained and developed by various business organisations when their managers and operating personnel establish and sustain usefully cooperative links with one another.

The realisation that tourism is part-industrialised poses a major challenge to the conventional assumption that tourism is wholly industrialised. For example, attributing all the credit for economic benefits associated with tourism to 'the industry' becomes an unrealistic assumption and an untenable policy. Likewise, 'the industry' cannot be blamed for all the damaging impacts of tourism on physical, social and cultural environments. Implications of part-industrialisation are relevant for decisions in many aspects of whole tourism systems, such as marketing, management, environmental impacts and development policies. In Chapter 12, a number of case histories are presented; themes explored there include partial industrialisation at the level of single organisations. In Chapter 16, broader implications of tourism's partial industrialisation, affecting regions, tourists, whole systems and environments, are identified and discussed.

Discussion questions

1. Describe how business strategies targeting tourists can be seen in the marketing mix used by organisations in the business of tourism. Use in your answer one or more examples of organisations that supply tourists with services or goods.

2. Is the slogan promoted by many booster organisations, 'Tourism Is Everybody's Business', a realistic reflection of the real world of business?

3. Why is it that not all organisations that are direct suppliers of services or goods to tourists have business strategies targeting tourists? Is it merely that they do not appreciate the economic value of tourists, or is there some other explanation?

4. Explain the following principle: the presence of substantial numbers of tourists in the market served by an organisation does not in itself mean that tourists are a feasible market segment.

5. Explain why, in sports and in business activities of civilised societies, competition normally occurs within frameworks of cooperation, with cooperation more important than competition.

6. Describe briefly how the innovations of Robert Herries in reference to travellers' cheques and Thomas Cook in reference to packaged tourism depended on cooperation.

7. List and describe, with brief examples to illustrate, at least six kinds of cooperative activities, practised by nominally independent business organisations, that have the effect of creating tourism industries.

8. List seven types of resources used in tourism that enabled Stear's analysis and conclusion that 'tourism industries can only ever supply, perform or be responsible for some of the goods and some of the services and some of the experienced phenomena that make up the total trip experience of every tourist on every touristic trip'.

9. Describe what is meant by the observation that normally, tourism is partially industrialised.

10. If you were a minister in the government of a country, discussing with other ministers and advisers how much financial subsidy should be given to promote tourism, how would the theory of partial industrialisation shape your thinking?

Recommended reading

Axelrod, R. 1990, *The Evolution of Cooperation*, London: Penguin

Best, Michael 1990, *The New Competition: Institutions of Industrial Restructuring*, Cambridge: Polity Press

Buckminster-Fuller, Richard 1972, Designing a new industry, pp 153–220 in *The Buckminster Fuller Reader*, James Mellor (ed.), London: Penguin

Penrose, Edith 1959, *The Theory of the Growth of the Firm*, Oxford: Basil Blackwell

Richardson, G.B. 1972, The organisation of industry, *Economic Journal*, 82: 883–96

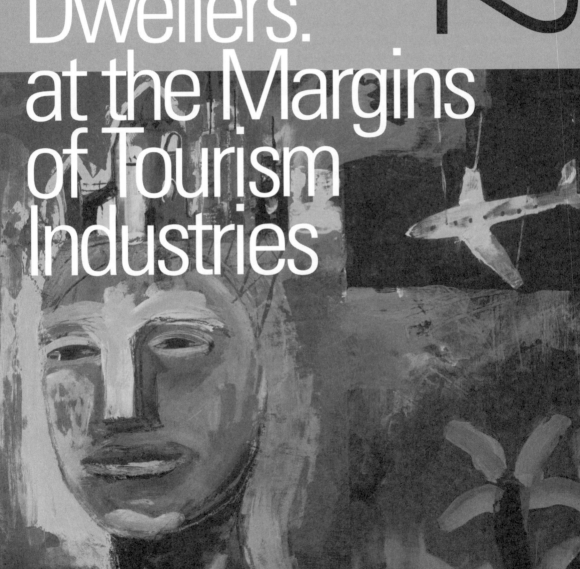

Fringe Dwellers: at the Margins of Tourism Industries

INTRODUCTION

Chapter 9 described cases representing a range of organisations directly supplying goods or services to tourists, in the business of tourism, and participating in a strategic sense in tourism industries. The examples were a retail travel agency, a tour operator, a hotel and holiday apartments. Chapter 11, in contrast, discussed why many organisations that also directly supply goods and services to tourists are not in the business of tourism and do not participate in tourism industries. Instead, they passively accept tourists as consumers, without treating them as a market segment, without doing anything substantially to target them in any aspect of a marketing mix. The discussion was largely theoretical, but accompanied by brief examples.

The discussion concluded that no general principle exists for guiding managers to the better alternative between targeting tourists and not targeting them, between participating and not participating in tourism industries. We cannot say that every restaurant should be managed to be in the business and industry of tourism or that all supermarkets should not. The best decision can be made only after assessing the conditions relevant in each case.

This chapter provides detailed discussions on cases in marginal conditions. These are fringe dwellers, organisations at the margins of tourism industries and, in certain instances, shifting their strategic position.

Research in fringe conditions has been very useful in other fields of knowledge, because it highlights what occurs at the margins, and in some cases reveals transitional shifts. Darwinian theories of evolution, for instance, were largely formed and scientifically supported from research on islands (Quammen 1996: 17–34). On islands and, on continents, coastlines—the fringe of land and sea—are where many major discoveries are made in biology, zoology and other fields. Thus focusing on fringe dwellers in research into business strategies and industrial structures relating to tourism is following an established and fruitful tradition in research methodology.

The cases presented below are about the Manhattan Hotel, the Summit Restaurant, Wyndham Estate Winery (all in Australia) and, as a combined case, six farm-stay properties in New Zealand. Certain managerial issues are explored: why did managers follow particular policies and strategies, and what were the outcomes?

What emerges is more evidence for the argument that tourism is part-industrialised behaviour, not a wholly industrialised phenomenon. As noted in Chapter 11, the cases are far from unusual, being typical of many organisations supplying goods and services to tourists in an incidental way, without deliberate strategies promoting tourism and without participating in cooperative programs for promoting tourism at the regional level.

This policy has been criticised by persons in many tourism industry associations, who have castigated managers of enterprises that earn income from tourists but do not actively support these associations, calling those managers fools (for not taking full advantage of opportunities in 'the world's largest industry') and parasites (for taking advantage of promotion schemes that they have not helped finance). Before judgment can be made as to whether or not either of these criticisms is justified, there is a need to investigate how and why organisations follow particular strategies, and what outcomes result. The appropriate method for this investigation is detailed case research.

THE MANHATTAN HOTEL

The Manhattan Hotel was in Potts Point, near Kings Cross, Sydney, for several decades until the building was converted to apartments in 2001. This case study was conducted over several years during the 1980s when, with 160 guest rooms, the Manhattan was a three-star hotel serving the middle to lower end of the market. Its guests could be described as tourists of various types: virtually all were visitors to Sydney, and many were on holiday. The hotel's small bar and restaurant were mainly for guests, not promoted to the public at large.

New manager, big problem, new strategy

In 1982 the Manhattan changed ownership and Gary Connell was appointed as manager, his first work in hotels, coming from a club management background. The hotel was unprofitable. Room occupancy (RO) was low, fluctuating around 40%. Connell's main objective, to reach profit, was to improve RO. To do this, he announced a strategic intent 'to get the hotel plugged into the tourism industry'.

Superficially, his statement might seem strange to anyone using the concept of *the tourism industry* based around economic impacts (described in Chapter 7) because in that simple sense the hotel was already in that industry, as it provided accommodation for tourists, earning its income from tourism. However, Connell's ideas reflected realistic thinking by a practical manager, not abstract ideas about the economics of tourism. He realised the Manhattan was in the business of tourism but sensed it was not really participating in any tourism industry. He regarded 'being in the industry' as operational and strategic possibilities, not as economic impacts. His term 'plugged into' reflected a desire to participate in networks of travel agents, airlines, tour wholesalers. His implicit theory of industries matches the one set out in Chapter 11.

At the time, in 1982, virtually all the guests staying at the Manhattan came in off the street or made their own reservations; only a tiny proportion came from bookings through retail travel agents. None were on packaged arrangements, as the Manhattan was not in any tour operator's program. Connell saw potential for many bookings from travel agents and tour operators. He regarded 'being in the tourism industry' as a managed option, requiring conscious effort, and not as a state of affairs determined by the touristic status of the guests and related economic impacts. In 1982 the Manhattan was in the business of tourism, but on the fringes of, not participating in, tourism industries.

Three strategic objectives ➤

The primary objective was to use industrial participation as a means of bringing in more guests. Travel agents and tour operators can provide links between a hotel and potential guests that make a great difference to the hotel's RO and income.

A second objective was to boost RO during low periods. Activity at the Manhattan fluctuated hugely. Some nights RO was below 20% and on others above 70%. Extreme seasonal fluctuations were also notable, with holiday periods the peaks. Connell reckoned that by getting bookings from travel agents and tour operators, extra demand could be generated in low periods.

A third objective was to get advance information. Operating independently, management at the Manhattan could not predict how many rooms would be occupied in the coming hours and days. Sometimes at 5 pm RO was 30% and remained at that level all night; on other days many guests arrived unexpectedly during the evening and night.

The managerial problem caused by unpredicted fluctuations involves resource allocation. If a hotel manager knows that RO will remain around 40% for the night, staffing levels can be set accordingly. But if RO unpredictably jumps to 70% during the evening, extra staff are needed; if these are unobtainable for the next morning, standards of service go down. Alternatively, if staff are scheduled for work but not needed because RO remains low, operating costs are too high in relation to income. The greater the percentage of guests booking via travel agents and tour operators, the better a hotel manager is able to predict RO.

The Manhattan's strategic shift ➤

In 1982 the Manhattan was in the tourist hotel business but had minimal participation in any tourism industry. It was in quadrant #2 in Figure 12.1. By 1983 the position had shifted to quadrant #1. It had moved into tourism industries.

Connell had established links with travel agencies (using the Australian Federation of Travel Agents to make the contacts), with inbound tour operators (via the Inbound Tour Operators Association, now the Australian Tourism Export Council), with selected airlines (Qantas and Air New Zealand) and with the New South Wales Department of Tourism (now Tourism New South Wales). As a result, average RO increased and a growing percentage of guests came from trade bookings. Some were fully independent travellers and others were using inclusive tours, which combined transport (typically flights from New Zealand) with accommodation. Tour wholesalers became involved in arranging these packages and distributing them to retail travel agents in New Zealand.

In brochures, the Manhattan was listed among dozens of other accommodation houses in Sydney, with a photograph of the building and itemised details. Fluctuations in RO became less extreme, and management had advance information on the arrival of many guests.

In 1989 the strategic position was still in quadrant #1. The hotel had again changed ownership. New managers described the current business as being approximately evenly split between Australia and New Zealand. Most of the latter was coming in the form of packaged trips.

FIGURE 12.1 Partial industrialisation: positions of certain organisations directly supplying goods and services to tourists, in terms of business strategies and industrial cooperation

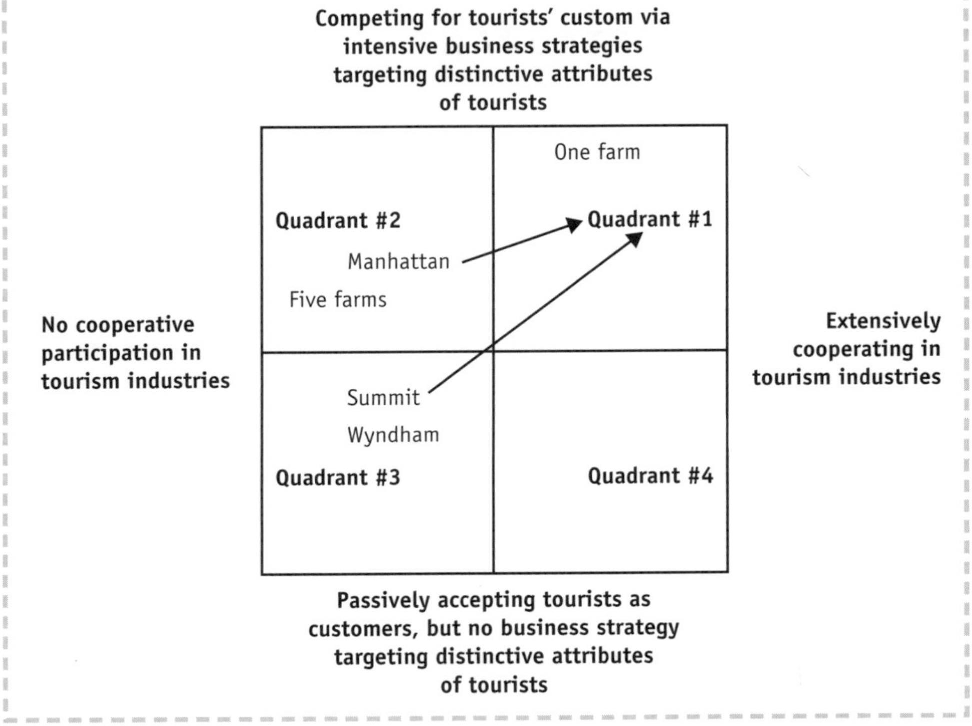

Competing for tourists' custom via
intensive business strategies
targeting distinctive attributes
of tourists

One farm

Quadrant #2 ➤Quadrant #1

Manhattan

Five farms

No cooperative
participation in
tourism industries

Extensively
cooperating in
tourism industries

Summit

Wyndham

Quadrant #3 Quadrant #4

Passively accepting tourists as
customers, but no business strategy
targeting distinctive attributes
of tourists

Was the strategic change successful? ➤

Achieving the three strategic objectives are apparent improvements, but they do not *prove* that the strategic shift was a success. What remains unknown are precise trends in RO, revenue, costs and profitability. To determine this, inspection of the hotel's accounting records would be necessary. The research did not extend to this.

What can be noted is that participating in an industry incurs costs. In this case, the main cost was that the Manhattan's net average room revenue was almost certainly lower in 1983 than in 1982, because of two factors. Travel agents earn a commission, normally 10% of the room rate charged. In addition, tour wholesalers are supplied rooms at below the rack rate by at least 10% and, depending on market conditions of supply and demand, possibly as high as 40% below rack rates. Therefore, the three gains (higher RO, less extreme fluctuation in demand, and advance information on demand) were offset to some degree by lower average room revenue, and might possibly have been totally negated.

Those gains and costs are what should be assessed in a manager's decisions before a strategic shift is made from the margins of an industry to participation (or vice versa).

Managers of hotels who participate in tourism industries do so in the belief that the gains will exceed the costs.

THE SUMMIT RESTAURANT

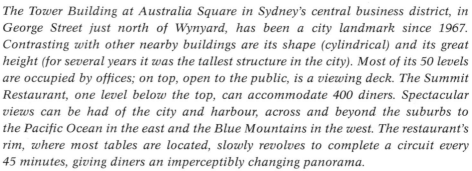

The Tower Building at Australia Square in Sydney's central business district, in George Street just north of Wynyard, has been a city landmark since 1967. Contrasting with other nearby buildings are its shape (cylindrical) and its great height (for several years it was the tallest structure in the city). Most of its 50 levels are occupied by offices; on top, open to the public, is a viewing deck. The Summit Restaurant, one level below the top, can accommodate 400 diners. Spectacular views can be had of the city and harbour, across and beyond the suburbs to the Pacific Ocean in the east and the Blue Mountains in the west. The restaurant's rim, where most tables are located, slowly revolves to complete a circuit every 45 minutes, giving diners an imperceptibly changing panorama.

The Summit lost its status as Sydney's highest restaurant in 1982 when Centrepoint Tower opened, with two levels of restaurants near the top. However, the views from the former are superior in important respects. Located a kilometre north of Centrepoint, The Summit provides closer views of Sydney's Harbour and Opera House.

From its beginning, The Summit was popular among diners in the market for first-class restaurants in Sydney and, especially because of its views, was also popular among tourists who prefer first-class restaurants, especially those on their first visit to Sydney. However, from 1967 to 1987 the manager followed a strategy of keeping on the fringes of the tourism business. The position during those 20 years was quadrant #3 in Figure 12.1. It was not in the business of tourism, and not participating in tourism industries.

Speaking at a conference to discuss commercial development in Sydney, the managing director of Summit Restaurants Ltd remarked that his restaurant was not in the tourism industry. Oliver Shaul's remark provoked a minor controversy among certain persons in the audience, notably representatives from the New South Wales Department of Tourism. According to them, this restaurant was very much in the tourism industry. Shaul's notion challenged their belief, but did not provide a detailed explanation. This was sought later, by me, as an exercise in academic research.

The information set out below comes from interviews with Shaul and his staff and from closely observing the restaurant's operations and marketing over the period 1982–90. (Before this period of research, since 1973 I had come to know the restaurant as a frequent customer for business lunches.)

Many tourists, but no market segment

Shaul knew that his restaurant was economically dependent to a notable degree on tourists. He said that surveys over the years showed that approximately 20% of diners were tourists, in a broad sense—visitors to Sydney from around Australia and abroad. Nominally, tourists were a market segment. However, a nominal market segment is not always a real one, as collections of similar consumers do not always form market segments. For instance, no restaurant is known that treats diners with blue eyes as a market segment. A market segment becomes real and effective only when a collection of consumers is targeted by business strategies. This is not always feasible.

From 1967 until 1987 The Summit did not target tourists. The restaurant's products and services were were not designed specifically for tourists, nor were the prices, distribution or promotion aimed at tourists. The strategies were targeted at those persons in the Sydney population *at large* who were willing and able to dine in first-class restaurants, not discriminating between local residents and tourists.

This shows why Jafari's (1987) ROP/TOP theory, favoured by some students of tourism, can be misleading as a principle of target marketing. Jafari's theory divides products into resident-oriented products (ROPs) and tourist-oriented products (TOPs). The theory is too academic, too removed from reality; it misses the precise nature of practical business strategies. Relatively few businesses target residents; instead their marketing is aimed at the public at large, not discriminating between residents and tourists.

Three reasons were behind Shaul's decision not to target tourists. All three supported his decision that to target tourists would be uneconomical, and not in the best interests of the restaurant. The first reason was linked to the fact that the majority of diners at The Summit were residents of Sydney, mostly there for work-related lunches or dinners with clients and work colleagues. Shaul believed that most of these diners would not favour a restaurant that was seen by them to be a tourists' restaurant. Too many of the wrong type of tourists in the restaurant, or promotions that advertised the place as a venue for tourists, could create that undesirable image. Similarly, he believed that the type of tourists who do visit first-class restaurants 'like to go to restaurants that are frequented by locals, and this is very important as far as the public face of the restaurant is concerned' (pers. comm.).

A third reason is that in Sydney from the 1960s to the 90s the tourist population was highly heterogeneous. Most tourists were independent. Relatively few were on packaged arrangements and, of those, most followed individual and unscheduled activities while in Sydney, not group tour itineraries. A minority used hotels. Instead, private homes of friends and relatives in Sydney were the common form of accommodation. These characteristics meant that the tourist population in Sydney was not easy to identify and reach with advertising and other promotional activities.

To be useful, a nominal market segment must meet four necessary criteria: measurability, accessibility, substantiability and actionability (Kotler et al. 1994: 132–3). All must exist. In the case of The Summit from 1967 to 1987 these were not all present, so there was no feasible tourist market segment for the restaurant to target.

The Summit's strategic change ➤

In 1988 The Summit Restaurant changed its business strategies. Japanese tourists became a market segment. Estimates by staff during the period 1989–90 were that on a typical day anywhere between 50 and 200 Japanese tourists dined there. This had not developed accidentally. Oliver Shaul had strategically moved the restaurant into the business of tourism and into a tourism industry.

Two factors led to his decision to make the change. A new taxation regulation introduced by the Australian government in 1986 removed restaurant expenses from the list of allowable tax deductions. Thus the government ceased to subsidise restaurant bills of businesspeople, meaning a 50% increase in the cost of dining out for those persons, which caused a noticeable downturn in the number of Australian taxpayers dining in restaurants, especially in expensive restaurants such as The Summit. Accordingly the restaurant market became turbulent. Restaurant managers tried competitive strategies to win greater shares in a shrinking market. Some turned to a new market, to tourists. Shaul was in this category, and he was well prepared to succeed.

In the late 1980s a huge increase was apparent in the numbers of Japanese visitors in Sydney. In 1986/87 arrivals of Japanese visitors in New South Wales were estimated at 151 900; in the following year there were 270 400—a 78% increase (Bureau of Tourism Research 1989: 109). Virtually all of them visited Sydney, more than 80% were on prearranged packaged tours, and most of these tours were arranged by a handful of tour operators in Japan (Leiper 1985). These conditions offered scope for market segmentation. Any item that the major Japanese tour operators included in the list of options in popular tour packages would be in a strong position to succeed. Shaul made contracts in Tokyo with several outbound tour operators, who then included The Summit as an item in various brands of packaged tours marketed in Japan for trips to Australia. The tourists received a voucher for dining at the restaurant.

Thousands of Australian entrepreneurs were trying to gain a toehold or competitive advantage in Japanese tourist markets in the late 1980s and early 90s. Most were unsuccessful. Why did Shaul succeed in this respect? The following section points to the answer.

Industrial preparedness ➤

Oliver Shaul's restaurant career began in 1939, and from 1949 he was also active personally in tourism industry associations, even if his restaurants were not. In 1949 he joined the Australian National Travel Association (the original name of a group that claimed to represent all components of Australia's tourism industries; its later names have included Australian Tourism Industry Federation and Tourism Council Australia). Shaul was a founding member of the Pacific Area Travel Association (later the Pacific Asia Travel Association) in 1951 and the Australian Tourist Commission in 1967.

Those time-consuming activities might be regarded as wasteful if his policy was for his restaurant business to remain beyond the fringe of tourist industries. However, the activities had strategic purpose, providing Shaul with an industrial network, built over several years, which he used to gain a competitive advantage in the late 1980s.

From the 1960s Shaul travelled abroad frequently, he or one of his executives visiting Japan every year. They got to know the executives of Japan's major tour operators on a personal basis, and came to understand Japanese tour operations. These facts indicate that Shaul regarded tourism as potentially relevant to his restaurant's long-term interests, years before the potential was realised in practice. His involvement with tourism associations can be regarded as a defensive corporate strategy, which defended Shaul's investments in restaurants. It gave him knowledge and personal contacts that could be used, if needed, should the restaurant's traditional market fall away. What was being defended was capital investment. His largest restaurant, The Summit, required considerable capital. For example, he said that he spent more than $1 million on refurbishments in 1989.

Unlike many entrepreneurs and managers who have tried unsuccessfully to capture profitable shares of Japanese tourist markets, Shaul had been preparing for this in a number of ways over the years. His success, set alongside the failure of many other restaurateurs to attract Japanese tourists in any quantity, exemplifies a remark in Farrell's study of tourism in Hawaii: Japanese tourists 'patronise a number of retailers attuned to their tastes and patterns of buying, and would-be competitors attest that it is an extremely difficult market to crack. Selling to the Japanese is an art mastered only by a few' (Farrell 1982: 336).

Gains offset by costs? ➤

Was The Summit's move into the business and industry of tourism a worthwhile one for the restaurant? Given the decreased demand from the restaurant's traditional customer base, the strategic move was probably the best option. It led to the opening up of a sizable and growing market comprising a regular flow of diners.

Offsetting those gains were costs. One cost item was trips to Japan. Another is that the average expenditure by tourists paying by voucher is lower than that by The Summit's traditional customers. Moreover, three businesses share expenditure by tourists on packages: besides the restaurant, tour operators and retail travel agents in Japan take a cut.

This means that the move into tourism probably lowered the average revenue per cover at The Summit. It changed the economic conditions of the firm. Also, the strategic change almost certainly lowered the image Shaul originally sought to protect; one indication is that among the best-selling 'fun' books in Sydney in 1994 is one titled *Life's Little Instruction Book*, whose prescriptions include 'steer clear of restaurants that rotate'.

The strategic shift after 1987 can be depicted as a move to quadrant #1 in Figure 12.1. It almost certainly contributed to the fact that The Summit survived as a profitable venture when some other restaurants in the city were incurring losses and several went out of existence. In 1994 this survival allowed Oliver Shaul, then planning retirement, to sell The Summit to Accor Ltd in a multi-million-dollar deal.

WYNDHAM ESTATE WINERY

Information in this discussion comes mainly from observations at the site on several occasions between 1983 and 1997 and from discussions with staff, including detailed discussions with the managing director in the late 1980s.

The winery and its vineyards are old, established in the 1800s. They were purchased by the McGuigan family in 1970, as a base for a new company, Wyndham Estate Wine Ltd. In order to raise capital for expansion, in 1977 most of the shares were sold to Quadrax Pty Ltd, an investment company owned by Stan Hamley, who became chairman of Wyndham.

The managing director was Brian McGuigan. He was responsible for management and marketing, besides wine-making. Wyndham became known for good-value, above-average quality wines. McGuigan used his considerable skills in public relations alongside his knowledgeable enthusiasm for wines to promote his brand and wine generally.

The winery was open to the public. Visitors came in to look, talk about wines, taste and buy wines, and eat at the bistro. Most of these visitors could reasonably be described as tourists. Casual observers would infer that the winery was in the business of tourism and a component of the region's tourism industry. (Those inferences reflect ideas about 'the tourism industry' described in Chapter 7.)

Closer inspection of managerial practice and discussions with the managing director about Wyndham Estate's strategies led to a different conclusion. Through the 1980s, Wyndham was not participating to any notable extent in tourism industries, and McGuigan did not regard Wyndham as being in the tourism business.

Wyndham Estate as a tourist attraction

Wyndham Estate is located in the Hunter Valley, near Branxton, where there are expansive vineyards and about 60 wineries. The district has become an increasingly popular tourist destination, because of the wineries, since the 1960s. Most tourists come from Sydney, by private car or on coach tours. Increasing numbers stay overnight in motels, pubs, resorts and other accommodation houses.

Compared with others in the district, Wyndham's winery and cellars are in old, substantial and distinctive buildings. These function as nuclear elements of tourist attractions, in terms of the theory in Chapter 13. A parking area in front of the winery has the capacity for dozens of vehicles. Staff serve in a tasting and sales room, and in a bistro.

McGuigan estimated in 1983 that Wyndham ranked in the top three wineries in the district in terms of visitor numbers. He kept no records for the estimates, but guessed that daily numbers at Wyndham varied from 50 to 500.

Wyndham and the local tourism association ➤

Relationships between Wyndham and the Hunter Valley Tourism Association are pertinent to the case. Like other regional tourism groups, the HVTA's members have a shared goal of promoting tourism into their region. Dependent on members for a large proportion of their funds and voluntary work, associations of this type need as many members as possible and need active types generous with time and money.

Based in Newcastle, the HVTA covers a large region in which vineyard districts represent a small but distinctive portion. Several wineries, including Wyndham, were HVTA members in the 1980s, but most were not active members. Their managers did not attend many meetings and they seldom donated time or funds to special projects for tourist promotions.

Noticing McGuigan's exceptional skills in promoting wine, the HVTA wanted him to become more active in promoting tourism. However, McGuigan regarded Wyndham as being in the wine, not tourism industry, and did not give as much support as some persons presumed was desirable for his own interests and those of the HVTA.

McGuigan's strategies for Wyndham Estate ‰

McGuigan recognised the value of tourism, and its potential for growth, in relation to the economy of the Hunter Valley and his own company, Wyndham Estate. However, his assertion that Wyndham was not in the business of tourism was justification for not becoming more involved in the HVTA. He followed the principle that entrepreneurs should determine precisely which line of business to follow and, having made the decision, focus on it (Drucker 1955). 'Stick to your knitting' is how this prescription was described by Peters and Waterman (1991).

The reasoning is that each organisation's managers can only fully master the knowledge, skills and interpersonal networks relevant to one field, or closely related fields. If an organisation tries to be active in different fields of business, it is likely to fail in at least one. This theory is most relevant for smallish organisations (such as Wyndham), which do not have sufficient resources, especially managerial time, to develop several SBUs (strategic business units). Interviewed on this issue, McGuigan illustrated the practical side of the theory. Active in the wine industry, he attended frequent meetings of associations linked to wine in the Hunter Valley, in Sydney, and beyond. Time given up from normal work and leisure for these meetings was considerable, leaving him no time for meetings on other topics such as tourism.

With hundreds of tourists coming to the winery most weeks of the year, and with income earned from selling them wine and food, Wyndham displayed superficial evidence of being very much in the business of tourism. But McGuigan decided that tourists would not be a primary market and not a targeted market. Wyndham's primary markets were in cities such as Sydney, Melbourne and London, where many wine drinkers live, and this is where Wyndham's major promotion was directed. In this context, *any* time and money spent promoting tourism to the winery could be seen to have an opportunity cost, representing so much less available for promoting wine sales in the primary markets.

Pricing strategies at cellars in vineyards ➤

Pricing strategies are salient. Many tourists expect prices to be lower at the cellars in vineyards than in city shops. They realise that city prices include costs of transport and profit margins for distributors. Looking at prices in wineries in several wine-producing regions of Australia and New Zealand, two categories can be discerned. Only one type of winery offers discounts at the cellars.

Most numerous are the 'cellar-door bargain sellers', generally small-scale producers where prices are lower than one might expect to pay for a comparable bottle in a city shop. The second category, including Wyndham, could be called the 'fixed-price channellers'. Prices at these wineries are virtually the same as prices for the same bottles in cities. This difference is a clue to discovering whether a winery is being managed to be in the tourist business or the wine business. The cellar-door bargain sellers are usually in the tourist business, while fixed-price channellers are in the wine business. An explanation follows.

If a winery has an urgent need for income, and in particular cash flow, a useful strategy will be to sell wine cheaply to visitors, impressing tourists with the idea that they are buying from the cellar at something close to the cost of production. Low price is an incentive for tourists to visit that winery and, more significantly, provides an image of economic gain for tourists. After spending many dollars on transport and accommodation on a trip to vineyards, many visitors are likely to imagine—and tell acquaintances—that they scored a bargain by saving a few dollars buying wine. Wine-makers using this strategy are often those unable, for various reasons, to sell most of their output in cities.

Meanwhile, other wine-makers, including Wyndham, are able to sell virtually all their production in cities, so do not need to discount prices to get income and cash at the winery. More importantly, if wine-makers like Wyndham discounted prices at their wineries, they would be inducing consumers to travel and buy large stocks there, sufficient for many months' consumption, instead of buying a comparable quantity over a series of trips to their neighbourhood retailer in the city where they live. The effect would be disastrous for the winery, because city retailers would lose sales and would then refuse to stock and sell those brands. Not all consumers would bother making trips to the wineries to stock up, so many would switch to other brands that were conveniently available.

Wine-makers like Wyndham, using well-established relationships with wholesalers in distribution channels of wine industries and depending on those channels for most of their sales, must protect the channels by maintaining good relationships with wine wholesalers and retailers. Undercutting the retailers' prices is a certain way of ruining the relationships.

Wyndham's policy regarding tourists ➤

Tourists visiting Wyndham's neighbourhood were regarded by McGuigan as an opportunity to publicise wine (particularly the Wyndham Estate brand) more than an opportunity to sell it. If they came in they could buy wine, but not at a notable discount. Tourists' visits were promoted by signposts, but not by contacting tour operators or placing advertisements in traveller-generating regions.

By welcoming those who visit the winery, McGuigan believed that they could learn about the wines and would, afterwards, look for the Wyndham brand and other Hunter Valley brands in wine stores. Thus the passing flow of tourists represented an opportunity to create *future* customers. That was the main utility of tourism to Wyndham: an opportunity for public relations to help its primary field of business.

Hungerford Hill in contrast with Wyndham Estate ➤

Hungerford Hill Winery, located nearby, had strategies very different from those of Wyndham. In the 1980s Hungerford developed a wine theme park and retail shopping centre, with rural style and wine as features. Formerly the site had contained only a winery and cellar. In 1983 it had several dozen shops (leased to retail entrepreneurs), three restaurants, children's playgrounds, a winery and cellar. More tourists and day-trippers visited Hungerford than all other wineries in the district combined. A major source of income for Hungerford was, apparently, expenditures and leasehold incomes generated by tourist-visitors in the shops, restaurants and cellar. Hungerford had managers focusing on the theme park, rather than on wine-related activities.

The success of the whole venture was linked directly to the numbers of visitors and how much they spent, so the key strategies were aimed at getting more visitors, which meant promoting tourism and day-tripping, and ensuring that visitors enjoyed themselves. Hungerford employed managers involved in the business of consumer retailing, entertainment and tourism. These are linked areas with common knowledge, like shopping centres in mass tourist destinations. Hungerford Winery can be placed in quadrant #1 in Figure 12.1.

Wyndham's strategic position ➤

Throughout the period under discussion, Wyndham's strategic position was in quadrant #3 in Figure 12.1. It was on the fringe of the business of tourism, not putting resources into developing its tourist trade, and on the fringe of the region's tourism industry. McGuigan had carefully considered these positions and saw no reason to change.

The performance test ➤

Central to the HVTA's argument against McGuigan's policy is that by not promoting tourism he was ignoring a wonderful opportunity to make money. If he were to give more attention to tourism, according to some commentators (e.g. the HVTA), many more visitors would go to the winery and Wyndham Estate would prosper.

How valid is that argument? It might seem reasonable on its own, out of context. An objective test would be to consider Wyndham's performance in terms of normal criteria for private-sector companies. If the performance were poor or mediocre, there would be grounds for concluding that McGuigan had made a bad decision by focusing his strategies and resources on wine and neglecting tourism.

Records show that Wyndham Estate Wine Ltd was an outstanding success as a company and as a participant in the Australian wine industry. Reports in the *Australian Financial Review* give consistent data to back up that claim. For example, over the four years to 1988, Wyndham's revenues grew at an average annual rate of 35% (*AFR*, 2 September 1988), many times faster than the economy at large. In the year to June 1989 revenue was up by 50% on the previous year, to $51 million, and profit was up 46%, to reach $10 million (*AFR*, 17 September 1989).

In the two years after the 1987 share crash, few companies in any industry in Australia grew so rapidly and with such high profitability. This is best revealed in a table headed 'The hero stocks of the last two years' (*AFR*, 21 December 1989), which showed the top 25 from the 1100 listings on the Australian stock exchange. Wyndham Estate ranked

17th. Moreover, much of Wyndham's growth came from exports. Begun in 1982, to Canada alone, by 1986 exports were going to 17 countries (Forde 1986). By 1989 more than 50% was exported, as Wyndham's market share grew (Knight 1989). Wyndham became one of the major contributors to the Australian wine industry's growth as an earner of foreign exchange. Had McGuigan spent resources developing links with tourism, the probability of his achieving success on the scale he has achieved by concentrating on wine would be remote. There is ample evidence that his strategies were the optimal ones for the interests of his company, its industry and the Australian economy.

To argue that Wyndham Estate would have been more successful as a company had it given more attention to tourism ('the largest industry in the world') is like arguing that Cathy Freeman and Ian Thorpe would be more successful as sportspersons if they gave more attention to Rugby ('the game they play in heaven'). Arguments along these lines are myopic and out of touch with reality.

Postscript

In 1989, Wyndham's major shareholder, Quadrax, incurred huge losses when another company in which it had a majority shareholding, Budget Rent-a-Car Australia, went broke. To make up his loss, Quadrax's owner sold his large holding of Wyndham shares. Brian McGuigan tried to buy them, but was outbid by the South Australian winemaker J.C. Gramp Ltd, so he left Wyndham to set up an independent company and was soon marketing under a new brand, McGuigan Brothers. The Wyndham brand joined that of its new owner to become Orlando-Wyndham.

In the 1990s wine tourism markets in the Hunter Valley burgeoned and McGuigan Brothers adopted a rather different, multipronged strategy from that followed in the previous decade by Wyndham. As managing director of a rather different company in quite different conditions, McGuigan decided that the best policy was to promote wine and tourism.

FARM TOURISM IN THE MANAWATU

Here we discuss six organisations in the same line of tourist-related business, farm-stay tourism, all located in close proximity. Farm tourism is well-established in Europe, and in the 1980s began a period of growth in New Zealand and Australia when many farming families, facing falling incomes, ventured into tourism. Frater (1983), Haines and Davis (1987) and Philip Pearce (1990) have researched the topic.

The cases below were investigated by me and by Cheyne-Buchanan (1992). Aspects of the first survey, not reported in Cheyne-Buchanan's article, investigated whether and how each farm was participating in tourism industries. All six were certainly in the business of tourism, but only one of the six was active in any strategic sense in tourism industries. The difference in performance is interesting.

The Manawatu region

The Manawatu region of New Zealand is suited to farm tourism. It has pleasant rural scenery, and is convenient for domestic tourists from anywhere on the North Island and for international visitors travelling through the main north–south route. The regional city is Palmerston North, with a population of 70 000.

A report for the city council, Manawatu Regional Tourism Marketing Plan: Inventory *(1989), listed 20 farm tourism properties. Three others in the region are listed in the* New Zealand Bed and Breakfast Book *(1989). Of the 23 total properties, in 1990 only six were open for business, and each was contacted as part of the study. The proprietors were Morris, Fryer, Charlton-Jones, Barnett, Fraser and Collecut. All six cases were couples, with both partners active in some way in the venture.*

Five places had two bedrooms allocated to paying guests and one had three. Thus the regional stock of farm tourism supply was not large: just 13 rooms. Prices in 1990 ranged from $60 per night for a single room and no meals, up to $118 per night for two persons and three meals. Asked to nominate 'one main reason' for offering accommodation to paying guests, four of the six couples gave a social factor, 'meeting people'; and the other two gave economic factors, 'a business venture' and 'utilising assets on the farm'. However, as the accommodation and meals were being sold at prices designed to cover costs and make a profit, there is little doubt that all six proprietors regarded economic returns as pertinent.

In all six farms, the sources of guests were diverse. Five were getting some guests from travel agency bookings, which was the major source across the six in total at 55%, according to estimates by the proprietors. Relying on estimates and guesses, the proprietors seemingly lacked records that analysed these patterns and trends. A further 13% came via bookings made at the tourist information office operated by the city council in Palmerston North. For referrals, a 10% commission is paid to the agents or the information office.

Guests came to the farm off the road after seeing a sign (11%) or making an independent booking (31%). Some of the latter may have resulted from recommendations; most were from guidebooks. Three of the six properties were listed in farm-stay brochures (*New Zealand Farm Holidays* and *New Zealand Directory of Farm and Home Hosts*) distributed freely in certain markets by travel agents and tour wholesalers. Five of the six were listed in one or the other of two directories, *New Zealand Bed and Breakfast Book* or *Jason's Budget Accommodation*.

Which business, which industry?

The six properties were all in the tourism business, more precisely in farm tourism. On average, the six were only marginal participants in tourism industries, represented by their links with travel agents, the city's information office, and tour brochures and guidebooks. Thus, as a set, the six could be represented in quadrant #2 in Figure 12.1.

One of the six was rather different. It can be placed in quadrant #1. It was the only case where 'business venture' was the main reason for taking in guests. It was one of the cases deriving custom from travel agents and listed in brochures and guidebooks. It was the only one whose proprietor was a member of the NZ Association of Farm and Home Hosts and claimed to be an active member, attending meetings regularly.

Four of the other five proprietors were ignorant as to the Association's existence, and none of the others was a member of any tourism-related association. The unusual farm-stay proprietor was the only one of the six reporting contacts with other farm-stay proprietors. This occurred via the Association, with farms outside the Manawatu.

Compared to the other five, the unusual farm was participating in tourism industries to a greater degree. It could also be described as the most successful farm-stay property of the six surveyed, for it had more guests and its proprietors seemed most satisfied with their farm-stay activities. This indicates that participating in tourism industries, as a managerial strategy, may be very useful for organisations in the business of farm tourism.

CONCLUSIONS

Several interesting points are revealed in the cases discussed in this chapter. The cases are not unique, as Firth's (2002) research in the later 1990s revealed. Thousands of organisations can be found that provide services or goods to tourists, depend on that income to some extent, but are not in the business or industry of tourism. In some instances the policy is beneficial for the interests of the organisation, and in other instances it will be a handicap. These cases demonstrate that involvement with or dependence on tourists are not relevant factors determining that an organisation has (or should have) strategies targeting tourist business or participating in the operations of tourism industries.

Outcomes of different strategies followed by managers in these cases do not point to general principles relevant to all kinds of services and products used by tourists. There is evidence that the restaurant, the hotel and the winery were all following strategies most suited to their own best interests at particular times and under particular circumstances. Yet the three cases followed different courses.

The cases suggest, therefore, that to advise managers of all enterprises around the fringes of tourist markets that they should or should not target tourists and should or should not participate in tourism industries is deficient advice, based on bad theory. Generalisation represents bad theory in these circumstances.

Discussion questions

1. What were the three objectives sought by the manager at the Manhattan Hotel behind his aim of getting the hotel 'plugged into the tourism industry'?
2. What was the strategy used to achieve that aim?
3. At the Summit Restaurant for 20 years there were always many tourists among the diners but, according to the manager, The Summit was not in the tourism industry. What did he mean by this remark?
4. What were the environmental changes that led the manager at The Summit to make strategic changes to take the restaurant into the business of tourism and into participation in a tourism industry?
5. How does the concept of opportunity costs help explain Wyndham Estate Winery's strategy, during the 1970s and 80s, of not investing managerial time and other resources in tourism?
6. With hindsight, looking at the performance of Wyndham Estate Winery, was its management wise to ignore the advice from the local tourism association that Wyndham really was in the tourism industry and should have been promoted strongly as a tourist venue?
7. What does the evidence in the three major cases in this chapter (Manhattan, Summit, Wyndham) tell us about the slogan promoted by many tourism boosters that 'Tourism Is Everyone's Business'?

Recommended reading

Firth, Tracey 2002, *Business strategies and tourism: an investigation to identify factors which influence marginal firms to move into or remain on the fringes of tourism industries*, unpublished PhD thesis, Southern Cross University

Tourist Attractions: a Scientific Analysis

Nobody would set off on a tourist trip without the probability of experiencing attractions of some sort, no tourist would choose to visit a place for longer than a transit stop if it lacked them, and tourist guidebooks generally dedicate more space to attractions than other topics. These three points indicate that attractions are the principal focus of tourists' behaviour.

Accordingly, attractions should be a major topic in any general study of tourism. Paradoxically, most general text books on tourism say little about attractions. Are the writers deceived? In a valuable article on the topic, Philip Pearce (1991: 47) remarked that 'it is, perhaps, deceptively self-evident that tourist attractions are important'.

What are tourist attractions? How do they function? What theories about attractions might be useful for managers in tourism industries? These are the broad themes of this chapter. Everybody can list tourist attractions, some famous internationally and others known within one country or region: Angkor Wat, Disneyland, the Eiffel Tower, Kuta Beach, Kakadu National Park, Sydney Opera House, the Big Banana, whales at Byron Bay, Bledisloe Cup matches. What is not widely understood is what apparently causes tourists to be attracted to these sights, places, objects and events. That question is a central theme of this chapter.

RESEARCH ON TOURIST ATTRACTIONS

Useful early studies of attractions include those by Ritchie and Zinns (1978) and Ferrario (1979), presenting classifications of attributes of places such as natural beauty, climate, named sites, and culture.

Classifications are useful for describing different features of attractions, but they do not explain much. Additional methods are needed because 'tourism researchers and theorists have yet to fully come to terms with the nature of attractions as phenomena both in the environment and in the mind' (Lew 1987: 554). Moreover, discussions on the topic are often unscientific, according to another commentator (Stear 1981: 91):

> Most of the literature on tourist attractions is descriptive, case-specific, and not explanatory in the general or specific case. A preponderance of teleological interpretations posing as scientific explanations plagues this issue.

As will be shown below, Stear's criticisms apply to a lot of what has been written on the topic. Many writers obscure the way attractions function by using feral metaphors in their definitions and descriptions. Terms like 'attraction', 'draw', 'magnetism', 'pull factor', 'gravitational influence' imply that the thing itself has power to influence tourists' behaviour, that an attracting force stems from an immanent attraction.

It is a false implication. Places, buildings, objects and events that are commonly known as popular tourist attractions (Bondi Beach, Disneyland, Gracelands, the Empire

State Building, whales, pandas) have no power to influence tourists' behaviour in any way. So-called 'tourist attractions' do not function in the literal way the term suggests.

Examples of misleading general statements on the topic include 'tourist attractions are by definition anything that attracts tourists' (Lundberg 1985: 33); 'attractions might be site attractions or event attractions . . . both of which exert gravitational influence upon non-residents' (Burkart & Medlik 1974: 44); 'by definition an attraction is magnetic. If it does not have the power of drawing people . . . it fails to be an attraction' (Gunn 1972: 37), 'sometimes natural and historic features have intrinsic attracting power' (Gunn 1979: 71) and, most blatantly, 'I believe that tourist spots do have some inherent, unique quality which attracts tourists' (Schmidt 1989: 447). Taken literally, such statements are nonsense, yet these authors invite readers to take them literally by using words such as 'intrinsic' and 'inherent'. Expressions such as these imply and reinforce stereotypes of tourists as mechanical things whose behaviour cannot be explained in the same way as humans.

How can researchers and professional analysts get around the problem? One solution is to place risky expressions inside quotation marks ('attraction', 'magnetism') the first time they are used in a report, to indicate that a literal meaning is not intended. An alternative warning is a note when a report discusses attractions, such as 'It is important to recognise that magnetism is not somehow an inherent quality' (Pigram 1983: 193). Here Pigram was emphasising that in tourism, as in other human contexts, certain expressions are used as metaphors that should not be taken literally, because 'metaphor consists of giving a thing a name that belongs to something else' (Aristotle, *Poetics*, 1920).

Expressions like attraction, gravity, pulling power, magnetism have literal meanings in the physical world. The earth literally attracts falling objects, by gravitational force, and magnets really do attract iron, by magnetic force. The process involves an inherent

Tourists at scenic lookout above Coffs Harbour, Australia

quality in the attracting thing which reaches out to physically change a'
things within its field. Using these expressions metaphorically, in rel
behaviour, is a natural process of language. 'Tourist attractions' are like
of the physical world, *like* the earth with its gravity, *like* real magnets. Beiu.
17th century, the metaphor was irrelevant because scholars believed all movements
(of planets, objects, animals, people) were caused by similar processes. In the 17th
century new knowledge about causes of movement emerged, and 'Newton's laws of
motion make it all the more clear that physical behaviour is a quite distinct thing from
animal behaviour' (Jaynes 1973: 178). Many persons writing about tourist attractions
seem to have missed that distinction because the way they define them, alongside
tenuous explanations of how they function, might easily lead to inferences of a pre-
Newtonian or metaphysical kind.

What is required for an alternative approach to understanding tourist attractions
is a model that avoids these problems. MacCannell (1976) proposed a model that is
radically different from earlier ones, and which can be adapted to this purpose.

TOURIST ATTRACTION SYSTEMS

A discussion on attractions begins with a definition that is strikingly different from those
quoted above (MacCannell 1976: 41):

> *I have defined a tourist attraction as an empirical relationship between a tourist,
> a sight and a marker—a piece of information about a sight.*

MacCannell avoids any suggestion that a sight has inherent power to cause tourists to
direct their itineraries or attention towards it, and introduces information as an elementary component of every attraction. His definition is the foundation for understanding
what attractions are and how they really work.

The definition requires a slight amendment before it is useful as a general model, as it
refers to sightseeing, which is common but not universal. Many unsighted persons enjoy
tourism and many places are visited by sighted tourists who do no significant sightseeing
there (for a number of reasons) but who engage with other forms of attractions.

Gunn (1972) recognised that attractions involve more than sights, and so avoided
'sight' as a concept in the general model he developed. Instead, he used 'nucleus' to
denote the central component. By substituting 'nucleus' for 'sight' in MacCannell's
model and making a number of additions, a general model of tourist attractions can be
proposed that fits into the systems approach for tourism studies:

> *A tourist attraction system comprises three elements: a tourist or human element,
> a nucleus or central element, and a marker or informative element. A tourist
> attraction comes into existence when the three elements are connected. Tourist
> attraction systems are open systems, interacting with environments. They are sub-
> systems in every whole tourism system.*

In the discussion to follow, the three elements are treated in turn—tourists, nuclei, and markers. The topic can be integrated with the systems approach discussed in Chapter 3. A principle of systems theory is the hierarchy: every system has its subsystems and superiors. Because tourism without attractions is inconceivable, a key principle emerges. Every whole tourism system must have at least one attraction subsystem. Every tourist trip requires at least one attraction comprising a tourist, a nucleus, and information received by the tourist about the nucleus.

Tourists

Tourists are persons seeking satisfying leisure experiences on trips away from home. This means a search for nuclear elements of attractions that individuals can experience in person. Two broad categories of theories about psychology can be combined to explain how tourist attractions work. The two categories, discussed in Chapter 5, are content theories that reveal the contents in motivation (a range of needs), and process theories that explain the sequence of steps between the emergence of a need and the motivated action to satisfy it.

Content theories of tourists' psychology reveal that they are motivated by a wide range of needs. These might include the need for rest, relaxation, novelty, education, sunshine, regression, self-esteem, or prestige. Each of these classifications of needs is manifest in motivations or desires for particular kinds of experiences or activities. Few if any tourists are motivated throughout a trip by just one need; instead, normally a range of overlapping needs shapes their behavior and, in particular, their interest in specific attractions.

Process theory of tourists' psychology reveals how the connections occur between a tourist with a need and a place where that need might be satisfied. Markers, information about nuclear elements, have an essential role in the process, linking tourists into attraction systems. This process is not automatically productive, because tourists' needs are not always satisfied. In other words, attraction systems may be functional or dysfunctional, to varying degrees.

This summary of tourists' roles in tourist attractions will become clearer during the course of this chapter, as the other elements are described in detail and a number of examples are added for illustration.

Nuclei

A nucleus, the central element in all tourist attractions, might be *any* feature or characteristic of any place that a person visits or contemplates visiting. Some nuclei are highly popular, experienced by tens of thousands of tourists annually: St Petersburg's Hermitage Museum, Australia's Great Barrier Reef, New Zealand's Abel Tasman National Park, historic sites in Greece such as those at Delphi and Epidaurus, the Borobodur monument in Java, the Coral Coast in Fiji, the Salzburg festival in Austria.

Popularity is not necessary for a tourist attraction to be recognised by professionals interested in tourism, for if we restrict our thinking to superficial ideas, our understanding is handicapped and professionalism is impossible. A tourist attraction might be a nucleus plus marker and just one single tourist. A unique nucleus, the focus of attention by perhaps one lone tourist, is the friend or relative visited during a trip.

Methods for classifying nuclei ➤

Classifying nuclear elements may be done in several ways. One method, akin to Lew's (1987) cognitive perspective, is to classify nuclei according to tourists' experiences. All potential nuclei in a place could be classified according to the needs with which they correspond.

For instance, a place with a Mediterranean-type climate has, for many tourists, a nucleus satisfying their touristic needs for outdoor recreation in many forms. A place characteristically quiet and peaceful matches a need for rest. A place where people are very friendly and hospitable towards visitors has a nucleus matching tourists' needs for socialising. Examples representing those three kinds of places can be easily imagined.

Despite its apparent value, that method of classifying nuclei by tourists' needs has limited use on its own, as needs are insufficiently specific. What is relevant is not the need but the specific desire that it stimulates when a person becomes motivated to satisfy the need. For example, three persons all needing relaxation might decide to go on trips but want quite different experiences: the first wants any seaside resort with a good book to read, the second decides to hike 100 kilometres across Tasmania's Cradle Mountain-Lake St Clair National Park, the third joins a group tour to Machu Picchu and Lake Titicaca.

This distinction between *needs* and *wants* helps explain why practical research into links between tourist markets and tourist attractions has tended to be descriptive and case-specific, two attributes noted by Stear (1981: 4). A *need* common to many individuals might be expressed by different wants or demands, exemplified in the three cases noted above. Conversely, a *want* might reflect a number of different needs. You and I might both want to go on a sea cruise around the Pacific visiting New Caledonia, Vanuatu and Fiji. Beneath that shared want, you might need a restful holiday while I need entertainment. This diversity is relevant to tourist behaviour (Mill & Morrison 1985: 4), as it is to leisure behaviour in general (Kelly 1982: 1–2).

Another method of classifying nuclei is in environmental categories. The natural environment includes topography, flora and fauna. Topography refers to the detailed features of a particular region or place, and unusual or distinctive features of landscape are usually nuclei in tourist attractions. Examples are Mount Kosciuszko, the highest peak in the Snowy Mountains; the geysers at Rotorua; Lake Como in northern Italy; Niagara Falls; The Nut at Stanley in Tasmania; Mount Kinabalu, highest peak in South-East Asia; the Grose Valley in the Blue Mountains National Park.

Flora refers to plants, trees and flowers. Places with distinctive collections of flora can be especially popular with tourists. Good-quality parks and botanical gardens inevitably add to a city's popularity. The world's great urban parks and gardens, such as Central Park in New York, the Retiro in Madrid, Hyde Park and Kensington Gardens in London, and the Botanical Gardens in Bogor, Melbourne and other cities are all examples.

A garden can become popular through having a rare or famous specimen. In 1994, a giant tree that had been thought extinct for thousands of years was found growing in

Pub in The Rocks, Sydney. The sign showing the date of the first hotel on the site was added when the precinct began to develop as a popular place for tourists

small quantities in one limited area of the Wollemi National Park. From the seeds, a new tree named the Wollemi Pine was added to the Botanical Gardens in Sydney (inside an iron cage until it grew, to prevent theft) and its presence led to even larger numbers of visitors.

The built environment encompasses cityscape, particular buildings, monuments, archaeological sites. The sociocultural environment includes ordinary people and famous individuals, language and dialect, regional food and drinks, arts and crafts, social customs, historical objects.

Technological environments include applications of science, in functional industries or in staged displays. Technological museums are highly popular, the greatest being the Deutsches Museum in Munich and the Smithsonian Institution in Washington, DC. Working factories are also in this category. Tours of breweries are especially popular, for reasons that the research literature on tourism has not yet explained.

Making lists of nuclear elements in attractions is useful in analysing the potential of any place, as a step in the preparation of marketing or development plans by national, regional and local tourism authorities. Instead of a single classification method, multiple methods applied to the nuclei of a region are likely to provide a deeper appreciation of their role and potential.

Spatial distribution of nuclei

Nuclear elements of attractions are located in all parts of whole tourism systems but function in different ways. Their major locations and major functions are in tourist destinations. Along many transit routes, attractions also function, with the nuclei located here and operating in much the same way as in destinations.

A subtle difference applies in traveller-generating regions, where trips begin and end.

As individuals, we all observe features of our own home locality that are foci for tourists, the nuclei in attractions, but we cannot *be* tourists in our home locality. We can play a tourist-like role there, by having recreational activities based in sights and other things that might be tourist attractions.

Within tourist destinations or transit routes, different types of nuclei have different spatial patterns. Certain types can be described as general to the region, meaning that they can be found throughout the designated place. Throughout Italy one would expect to find manifestations of Italian culture, such as the language and examples of the national cuisine and wines. Throughout Tuscany, a region with large numbers of tourists, one would expect Tuscan cuisine and the regional wines such as Chianti.

Other types of nuclei have narrower spatial distribution, limited to a particular district, city, town, precinct, village, site, building, room. Each distribution has implications for understanding tourists' behaviour, linked to the structures of their individual and collective itineraries. Gunn (1972) provided useful theories about the design and management of areas surrounding a nucleus. He introduced the terms inviolate belt and contiguous zone.

Environments of nuclei: inviolate belts

Inviolate belts are the immediate surrounds of a nucleus. They have a number of functions. Tourists normally approach and enter a nucleus through its inviolate belt, where they experience 'physio-psychological conditioning and reflecting' because their 'mental set or anticipation of the attraction has much to do with their reception and approval when the feature is reached' (Gunn 1972: 40–1). Examples of this function of inviolate belts can be seen at cathedrals, churches and art galleries. The entrance path and entrance lobby act as an inviolate belt, conditioning the visitor for a religious or artistic experience. Visitors might be talking loudly in the street, but as they walk along the entrance path and into the lobby their voices drop and often conversation ceases.

Another function of inviolate belts is protective. A fragile and valuable nucleus, such as a unique artwork, can be protected from damage by a managed space. Famous and valuable artworks displayed in a gallery often have special protection of some sort. In Amsterdam, one of Rembrandt's most famous paintings, 'The Night Watch', has its own special room with special security devices. In the Louvre in Paris, Da Vinci's famous portrait of the Mona Lisa is in a long gallery with other paintings and art objects but has a glass screen positioned between this most famous painting and the public. These devices serve as a second inviolate belt, so that special paintings are inside at least three: the forecourt of the gallery, the gallery building, and the special room or screen for the special painting. The effect reminds the viewer that these are special objects.

Within the Kosciuszko National Park, the Snowy Mountains Wilderness Area is designated by signposts and information plaques on the side of the road just above Charlotte's Pass, the highest village. These inform visitors that the Wilderness Area higher up, encompassing the highest mountain ranges, is a very special part of a special area of land (the national park) and is especially protected in various ways. Visitors learn what they are not permitted to do there. The result is that visitors sense that the Wilderness Area is a very special experience.

Zone of closure (Gunn 1972), or contiguous zone, refers to the area immediately outside an inviolate belt. This zone is where facilities and services should be located. If they were allowed to intrude on the inviolate belt, the quality of the tourists' experiences would deteriorate. In countless locations around the world, this issue indicates a conflict between the interests of tourism (the behaviour of tourists) and the perceived interests of tourism industries.

Commercial operators selling souvenirs, food, drink and parking space are more profitable, in the short run at least, when these facilities are located as close as possible to the nucleus of an attraction. A shop selling souvenirs of visits to Notre Dame Cathedral will sell many more if is located across the road than if it is located a kilometre away.

Gunn argued that the zone of closure with its facilities and services is an essential part of a tourist attraction, but that it must not intrude on the inviolate belt. Countless thousands of businesspersons around the world have tried to fudge this issue in their desire to make more money. Left to market forces (i.e. the desires and tactics of businesspersons), the nuclei of tourist attractions are damaged in various ways by commercial interests, and the quality of experiences is diminished. Shops, stalls and advertisements encroaching as close as possible to special places represent commercial decadence, the tragedy of the commons (Hardin 1974/1969).

The solution, followed in certain locations in countries around the world, is for governmental intervention, representing the common interests of tourists and the local industry, to take precedence over the interests of individual commercial enterprises. After appropriate research, a plan and an administrative regime can decide where an inviolate belt and a zone of closure are to be located and how they are to operate.

Borobodur is a huge Buddhist monument in Central Java, constructed 1000 years ago. In the 1970s there were several hundred stalls selling souvenirs, food and drink clustered at the base of the temple. At one side of these commercial ventures were a parking area and public toilets. The whole site was a dirty, crowded, mess. UNESCO planned and implemented a total rehabilitation of Borobodur, a project needed mainly to prevent the temple's collapse from water eroding its interior over the past thousand years. The rehabilitation included the removal of all the services and facilities. When the project was completed, all the services and facilities were located 400 metres away from the monument. Visitors now pass though a gate and walk across an empty, peaceful space, an effective inviolate zone. Simultaneously, the zone of closure provides a well-designed range of facilities and services.

The first-known case of a special place being rearranged in this way is described in the Bible (Mark 11). Jesus Christ believed that a temple was a place for religious practices, not for commercial transactions; so, without any official authority to do so, he threw out the money-changers, who presumably set up their businesses in new locations outside, in the street.

In some sites, the problem is not the intrusion of commerce but the lack of appropriate services. Philip Pearce (1991) cited research at one of the world's most popular attractions, Niagara Falls. Despite recording 11 million visits annually, and being described as 'the world's greatest five minute experience', Niagara Falls could not, at that time, be regarded as a wholly successful attraction, because of deficiencies in its zone of closure. Survey research in 1987 found that a third of visitors were quick to criticise the lack of adequate on-site information, signage, traffic and parking. Pearce also mentions research at Stonehenge in 1985 which revealed similar problems with the attraction—deficiencies in its zone of closure.

Attraction mix and hierarchy ➤

A tourist might set off from home with a single experience in mind. Much more common is when each tourist on each trip is involved with multiple nuclei. *Attraction mix* is a useful expression for this combination. Within a mix, different nuclei are more significant than others. This can be expressed by classifying nuclei in a hierarchy of *primary/secondary/tertiary attractions* relevant to an individual tourist or to a given population of tourists in a flow (arrivals in a country over a period) or stock (the temporary population visiting a place at any particular time).

A primary attraction influences a tourist's decision to visit the place where the nucleus is located. This requires information in some form received by a tourist, information which, interacting with the person's needs, stimulates motivation and a decision to go to the place or, if already there, to stay a while. A secondary attraction is a feature or characteristic that is known about before a person visits a place but which is not influential in shaping their itinerary. A tertiary attraction is something unknown pre-visit but discovered by a visitor.

Analysing the attractions in any place (site, precinct, city, town, region, country) by primary/secondary/tertiary classifications can help describe and explain behaviour patterns of individual tourists and, by extension, collections of tourists. This in turn is useful in a range of marketing, planning, and other managerial issues.

Uluru National Park in Central Australia provides examples of the distinctions. The primary nucleus for most tourists involves the central feature of the park—Uluru, also called Ayers Rock. The Rock is something to look at, ponder, climb, photograph. Secondary nuclei might include Aboriginal customs on display, something most tourists would expect to experience in the park. A tertiary nucleus would be anything unexpected by a tourist before visiting the park that the tourist found interesting or pleasurable.

Markers

Markers are items of information (oral, written words, pictures) received by a tourist about anything that could be the nucleus of an attraction. MacCannell's (1976) seminal use of the term emphasised that markers are not the media conveying the information; they are not the signposts but the signs they convey, not the guidebook but the information it contains. Markers comprise information received by tourists about nuclei.

MacCannell discussed two kinds of markers, which he labelled 'off-sight' (located away from the object of sightseeing) and 'on-sight'. A more detailed analysis, involving several forms of marker and several locations and functions, can be developed. It is set out below, and offers the possibility of a fuller explanation.

Media and locations of markers ➤

Where do tourists receive markers? And in what media are markers conveyed? First and mainly, everyone, at home and in everyday routines, learns about potential attractions in places away from their home region.

We acquire bits of information from diverse media: from TV, from radio and the press, from books, from conversations. If we are at the phase of planning a trip, we might visit a travel agency and acquire more information of places we might visit. Other markers are received while travelling, and more during visits to tourist destinations. Some are received before visiting the site of an attraction (as happens with posters and brochures promoting local attractions displayed in a hotel) and some received at the site.

Labels for these different categories are useful in discussing their roles. 'Detached marker' refers to information received away from the nucleus. This category can be divided into 'generating marker', received pre-trip in traveller-generating regions; and 'transit marker', received after departure. A 'contiguous marker' is information located with the nucleus.

Examples of contiguous markers include the information passed on by a guide in the Bogor Botanical Garden that it was founded 200 years ago by Raffles, whose name is now more widely known from the famous hotel named after him, or the information read from a plaque beneath a painting viewed in the National Art Gallery of Australia that it is titled 'Mount Kosciuszko' and was painted in 1864 by von Guerrard.

Functions of markers ➤

Every attraction system includes at least one functioning marker. Markers are linking elements—between tourist and nucleus, between tourists and sights, objects, precincts, regions, countries, events. Many attraction systems contain multiple markers with

Contiguous markers, Dorrigo National Park, Australia

overlapping functions. An attraction might be defective because it has too many markers, or because the markers are conflicting or deficient in some way.

These principles become clearer after reviewing a list of separate functions that marker elements can perform in attraction systems.

Certain markers trigger motivation

People must have information about what might be experienced before they can form positive expectations about travelling as tourists. The principle arising from this is that at least one *generating marker* is necessary, referring to something that can form a *primary nucleus*, before an individual can become motivated to set off on a touristic trip.

Certain markers help tourists decide where to go

At least one detached marker, referring to a place-specific nucleus, is normally required for a tourist to decide which destination(s) to head towards. The marker might occur either pre-trip or in transit. In 'pure tourism', discussed in Chapter 6, markers are not needed for this function.

Certain markers are used in planning itineraries

A series of detached markers is necessary for planning itineraries of multi-destination tours. Guidebooks, national or regional tourism offices, and travel agents help tourists with this function. Independent tourists might use markers only from sources outside tourism industries, although these days most tourists are influenced to some extent by information from industrial sources.

Certain markers help tourists decide what to do each day

Markers often influence tourists' decisions about day-to-day activities. On vacation, a person might hear or see an advertisement for a golf course, or for scuba diving, and become motivated to participate. Many resorts publish daily weather bulletins for guests, information that often helps them decide on activities for the day. Variations on this are ski resorts' daily bulletins about snow conditions, and beach resorts' bulletins about sea and surf conditions.

On escorted group tours, the medium is often the tour leader or escort, who describes the coming attractions of the trip, for the day, the night, or for the next day or two. Often these descriptions involve a choice, with each member of the party deciding which option he/she will take. There are usually benefits when a tour escort describes coming attractions. These might add to expectations and motivations, leading to greater enjoyment.

Certain markers help tourists locate an attraction's nucleus

Certain information from media, such as maps, roadside signposts and local people from whom tourists ask directions, have the function of helping tourists reach the place they are seeking.

Certain markers tell tourists that they've arrived

Signposts at the entrance to a theme park, hotel or town are typical media for this function of contiguous markers. Most markers name the nucleus to which they refer ('Welcome to Dull Center, Wyoming'), information enabling the nucleus to be identified and distinguished from other similar ones.

Certain markers enable tourists to form images

Certain names of nuclei have positive connotations affecting tourists' attitudes and the images they form about certain places. This may contribute to motivation and add to satisfaction, which is why organisations promoting places or events often coin names that seem to have promotional appeal in target markets.

An early example was Monte Carlo, a name invented in the 1860s in a tourist promotion campaign (Cameron 1975). The promoter, Louis Blanc, believed that the official name, Monaco, had little value in tourist promotion, so he invented a new name for a section of the principality.

Costa del Sol ('Coast of the Sun') is one of many names for parts of the Mediterranean coast that were devised to promote the coast to tourists and to real estate buyers. A name like this produces warm thoughts in Northern Europe during winter.

Surfers Paradise is a name (of a suburb and its beach) that has been a factor in the growth of Australia's Gold Coast as a popular tourist destination. Both words, 'surfers' and 'paradise', create positive connotations and produce synergy.

Certain markers help tourists remember past experiences

Certain markers help people remember touristic experiences. Photographs are the most popular medium for this function. A major advance in photographic technology was invented by a tourist for this very purpose. Wanting a method other than water-colour painting for recording the scenery at Lake Como, Fox Talbot devised the technology in 1839 (Sontag 1979).

Postcards are another popular medium. 'souvenir' acquired its English meaning in the 19th century when large numbers of English began visiting Paris. They encountered street vendors, selling postcards and other items, who solicited for customers by approaching tourists and offering items *pour souvenir Paris* ('for remembering Paris').

Certain markers provide meaning in tourism

Information is essential to give meaning to any touristic experience. Douglas Pearce (1999) analysed three types of tourist attraction in Paris, with special attention to the meanings conveyed by markers. MacCannell (1976) discussed this in detail with reference to sightseeing, using examples from several countries. He showed that markers give meaning for tourists, relating to the sights they experience.

A theoretical problem he solved was the common case of a tourist encountering a sight (or site, or event) for which they had no information. For example, imagine you are in a foreign city, Samarkand possibly, and you see a distinctive building. It has no signs, is not listed in your guidebook, and there are no locals about to ask. You have no idea what it is. Can it be regarded as a tourist attraction if one of the elements, a marker, is missing?

What happens in this case is a switch in function. The distinctive and unknown building for which you have no information fails as a nucleus. But obviously, if a tourist has become fascinated with it—even for a few seconds—there must be some kind of 'tourist attraction'. What happens is this. The strange building becomes information, because it tells you (the visitor) something about Samarkand. The failed nucleus becomes a marker, and something else—the city or the region—emerges as a nucleus. This is a common experience of tourists.

Certain things interest tourists only because of the meanings conveyed by markers, not because of anything remarkable or distinctive in the sight itself. MacCannell gives examples from Europe and the USA. An Australian example, related to me by Lloyd Stear after a trip to Central Australia, concerns a small waterhole on the Todd River. Many tourists go there, look at it, photograph it, although it is much the same as thousands of other waterholes. What makes this one the nucleus in a tourist attraction is information, on a plaque, that tells visitors it is the original Alice Springs, near the town that now bears that name.

An Egyptian example comes from E.M. Forster's introduction to a guidebook for a famous city (1922/1982: xx):

> *The 'sights' of Alexandria are in themselves not interesting, but they fascinate when we approach them from the past, and this is what I have tried to do by the double arrangement of history and guide.*

The principle that at least one marker is essential to give meaning to an attraction applies to all types of attractions, not just sightseeing. Only during the past 100 years has swimming been widely regarded as a pleasant activity and a popular one among tourists. Why has that trend occurred? It cannot be because swimming is naturally a pleasant recreation for humans. Were that so, Europeans would not have waited until the 19th century to indulge in it, and Balinese would have taken to the sea for recreation before the 1970s.

Swimming, like other forms of recreation, is an activity that cultures have learned to enjoy, a slow process requiring information that developed the attitude that this could be pleasant. Information is necessary to that process. The process is what sociologists call acculturation, and might evolve over decades. Without markers, many recreational activities are meaningless.

MODELS OF ATTRACTION SYSTEMS

The diagram (Figure 13.1) shows a model of a typical attraction, revealing the main components and their linkages. The process begins pre-trip or pre-visit when a person receives information (a detached marker), which reacts with certain needs and stimulates motivation leading to a decision to travel (the same information is now a generating marker), putting the person into a certain role (a tourist).

The tourists are pushed by their own motivation towards the phenomenon indicated by the marker. Arriving at the phenomenon (nucleus), tourists have experiences of

FIGURE 13.1 A tourist attraction system

A tourist attraction is a systemic arrangement of three elements: a **person** with touristic needs, a **nucleus** (any feature or characteristic of a place they might visit), and at least one **marker** (information about the nucleus).

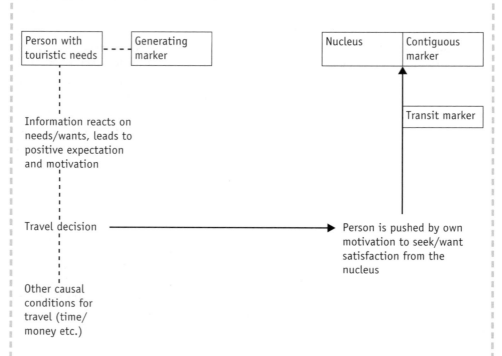

The **generating marker** is information received before setting out for the place where the nucleus is located; the **transit marker** is information received on route; the **contiguous marker** is at the nucleus. The diagram depicts how 'attractions' really operate: tourists are never literally 'attracted', 'pulled' or 'magnetised', but are motivated to experience a nucleus and its markers when a marker reacts positively with needs and wants.

some kind that might be satisfying or unsatisfactory, to varying degrees. The quality of the experience is shaped by their direct perceptions of the nucleus, and its immediate surrounds (inviolate belt), by their personal interests and knowledge, and by a range of markers received about this nucleus. The visitor might use facilities and buy goods from the shops in the zone of closure. These can also affect the quality of the experience.

Figure 13.1 shows how the linkages occur, how a tourist attraction is structured and how it functions. There is no teleology. Tourists are not depicted as attracted in any literal sense; there is no 'gravitational influence', no 'magnetism, no 'pull factors'. Instead, past and present events have determined the behaviour. Tourists are *pushed* (an appropriate metaphor, as the literal meaning does not contradict reality) by their own motivation, triggered by at least one marker towards a nucleus.

MacCannell (1976) suggested that attractions develop in identifiable phases. He illustrated the process by referring to religious sites, suggesting that other sightseeing objects, of a secular kind, follow the same phases. Several researchers have applied this theory to a variety of particular cases, providing a deeper understanding that can be interesting academically as well as useful for planners and managers. A notable example is Seaton's (1999) study of the battlefield of Waterloo, the site of a popular tourist attraction since 1815.

The naming phase ➤

The first phase is naming. Soon after any number of tourists begin paying attention to anything it is given a name. In the pre-history of tourism this process began among pilgrims, who first travelled to communicate with the revered dead (Jaynes 1982). To protect the saintly relics these were entombed, and buildings were constructed over them. The place and the building were given a name, that of the interred saint, which is the first phase of sight sacralisation—naming (MacCannell 1976: 44). Thousands of cathedrals and churches today are known by the names of the saints buried there. St Peter's in Rome is perhaps the most famous example.

In due course, names would be chosen without any substantial link between site and saint. So far as is known, there is no Mary buried in St Mary's Cathedral in Sydney. This artificial contrivance, intended to give sacred aura to a site and a building, has been used by tens of thousands of churches and by even more commercial sites, such as hotels and guest houses with inauthentic names made up for image-building purposes.

Benson's (1929) amusing account of English guest houses begins with remarks on their phony names—Wentworth, Blenheim and Balmoral. Each connotes aristocratic associations, when in fact the houses with these names in his book are frequented by persons from the lower middle class.

Visiting the Kosciuszko National Park, many tourists on their first visit ask which of the peaks is Mt Kosciuszko, the highest place on the Australian mainland. After it is pointed out, few tourists ask about the others. The name is the key to this common occurrence.

If a site, sight, object or event lacks a name, it has not begun its evolution as the nucleus of a tourist attraction. It is just a site or whatever that tourists might notice. To climb any of the dozens of named mountains in the Himalayas (such as Everest, Dhaulagiri, Annapurna) earns status, while climbing any of the dozens of not-quite-so-high and unnamed peaks can be a challenging and intrinsically rewarding experience but one that earns no status, because of the lack of a name. A conversation that demonstrates this point occurred at a party in Sydney a few years ago: 'I climbed a mountain in the Himalaya', he said. 'Which one?' she asked. 'It doesn't have a name', he replied. She knew then that his mountain-climbing exploits were not so remarkable and he, noticing her expression, wished he had not mentioned the topic.

When certain places become popular, names are inevitable. In Darlinghurst, Sydney, 30 years ago, a restaurant opened for business with no name. It became known as 'the no names restaurant'. Any taxi driver, told that name, could find it. By the 1990s there were several restaurants in Sydney using the same device but with blatant emphasis, so that in Norton Street, Leichhardt, there is now a large sign 'No Name Restaurant'. Once this occurs, the place is probably no longer relying on regular patrons from the neighbourhood but has become a place for tourists, as well as excursionists from other parts of Sydney.

In certain cases tourist attractions have names that are technically the wrong names, or at least accidental. This issue is interesting academically and can provide extra information (markers) passed on to tourists who might be interested in such things. A site in Belgium known as Waterloo is a famous attraction visited by large numbers of tourists every year since the site acquired its fame in 1815, as the place where Napoleon's army was finally defeated. However, the battle occurred at Mont St Jean, 'which is the name the French came to call the battle and one which would have gained general acceptance had Napoleon won' (Seaton 1999: 140–1). Waterloo was the name of an inn, several kilometres from the battlefield, where the general in charge of the victorious English army had slept the night before the battle. It is a striking example of the principle that history is written by the victors.

Framing and elevation phase ➤

This is the second phase, normally occurring after naming. Framing something, whether it is a painting, a national park or festival, has two consequences. It puts a boundary of some sort around the thing being framed which not only implies that it is worthy but encourages viewers (tourists) to focus their attention on what is inside the frame. Elevating something in some way, actually putting it into a higher position or virtually doing so by describing it as special, adds reasons for people to give it their attention.

As with many other aspects of modern tourism, the framing and elevation of attractions has its origins in early religious practices. At ancient religious sites, as the numbers of pilgrims grew the tombs were displayed more prominently, framed and placed on pedestals. This allowed more viewers to see it but also implied that it was important, worthy of attention. There is also a hint with dead saints that the highest placed ones are nearer to heaven, the most important. (The same symbolism is seen in organisational charts presented in hierarchical format, showing the CEO at the top and the ordinary workers at the bottom.)

The same phase, framing and elevation, occurs with secular attractions, such as artworks. Every painting on display in the Louvre has been framed, signifying it is worthy of hanging. Framing any painting is a certain method for giving it more status. In most cases, however, the major dispenser of status is the painter, who has arranged for his/her own paintings to be framed.

The enshrinement phase ➤

Enshrinement is the third phase. In MacCannell's analysis of religious sites as evolving attractions, in cases where pilgrim numbers have grown the building itself has acquired a sacred reputation, allied with but distinct from the sacred status of the relic interred inside. Thus the church known as St Cassian's is regarded as sacred because it is a

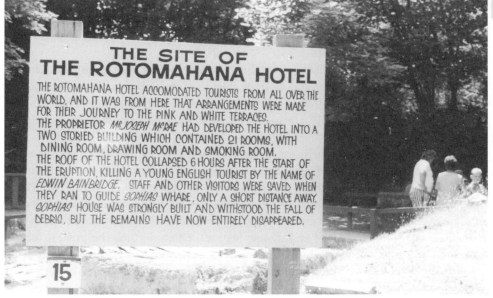

A sign that becomes the nuclear element of an attraction system, since the building it describes no longer exists

church, not because it is the burial place of Cassian (a patron saint of teachers, he was killed by ungrateful students).

Gracelands, visited by hundreds of thousands of tourists annually, is often described as a shrine, which it is. A shrine is a place or construction that is revered not for its intrinsic qualities but because of its close association with a person, an object or an ideology that is highly revered.

The great art galleries are shrines. Every day, thousands of tourists flow into the world's most famous galleries, such as the Prado in Madrid, the Louvre in Paris, the Hermitage in St Petersburg, the Uffizi in Florence without knowing much, in some cases, about any of the artworks inside but with a feeling of reverence for the gallery, based on the knowledge that it contains culturally important works of art. Enshrinement is another way of explaining an aspect of the theory of inviolate belts.

The duplication phase ➤

A final phase is duplication, when copies (or replica models, or pictures) of the nucleus are made. In practice, as observations around popular attractions will reveal, replicas and postcards of both the inner nucleus (saint) and outer (church building) are used in this manner. In Rome, in the tourist precinct near St Peter's and the Vatican, tourists buy postcards depicting those two buildings and the succession of popes who have lived and worked there.

At other places, in secular forms of tourism, tourists can buy postcards of Mickey Mouse and of his retirement home, Disneyland, of Mona Lisa and the Louvre, of

Elizabeth II and Buckingham Palace. In effect, these replications represent the evolution of two related, overlapping attraction systems, sharing a common theme (Disney, popular culture; art, high culture; royalty, icons of celebrity—persons who are famous for who they are, not for what they do).

The third phase of evolution (enshrinement) is, in effect, the emergence of new nucleus from the inviolate belt and zone of closure of an earlier nucleus, so there are now two attraction systems, or what can be called a molecular structure of nuclei.

Subsequently the new nucleus acquires its own inviolate belt. We can see this in many 23

well-known cases. Forecourts, landscaped grounds, and embellished entrances of famous buildings are examples. Souvenir stalls and fast-food shops are not allowed in the open space leading to Buckingham Palace, St Peter's Cathedral, or the Louvre. These open spaces function as inviolate belts. Sometimes this can be achieved with regulations, in some cases the land must be purchased by the proprietor of the attraction to keep that immediate environment free of undesirable features. Often, in time the process recurs, and another attraction evolves as a new nucleus forms out of an inviolate belt. This process, molecular compositions mutating, represents an explanation for the formation of one kind of tourist precinct.

Disneyland entered the third phase immediately after opening as a theme park in 1954, when the park itself came to be seen as an attraction, a site with significant meaning for millions of people, a sacred status allied with but distinct from the sacred status of Mickey, Donald, Minnie and others who were, in a sense, entombed inside.

Dysfunctional evolution of attractions ➤

Artificially pushing the evolution of a tourist attraction might seem advantageous for commercial interests, but can be problematical. For example, there are unlikely to be

Tour guide describing mosaics for tour group at 'The House of Dionyos', remnants of a 1700 year old Roman villa near Paphos, Cyprus

many sales of duplicates and postcards depicting an attraction that is still relatively new, not well known, not yet really worthy of enshrinement let alone duplication. This is where slavishly following simple ideas about advertising and marketing, without due attention to cultural undertones or unforeseen events, can lead to business problems.

Atmosphere as an attraction system

The analytical method outlined earlier helps explain the apparent atmospheric appeal of many places and events. Merely saying that a place has a certain atmosphere (New Delhi is exotic, Rome is romantic, Hill End is historical) might be useful in advertising and other promotions, but does not explain *why* or *how* that atmosphere is formed and thus how it might be managed, developed, promoted, or sustained with appropriate policies.

To explain this, the approach is to identify specific nuclei, specific markers and specific kinds of tourists. In combination, several nuclei and several markers are usually necessary, plus at least one tourist, for atmosphere to be created as a tourist attraction.

For example, Hill End is often perceived as historic by tourists with an interest in Australian colonial history. Visitors can observe the remnants of the old town, now reduced to one hotel and one store where there once were 50 hotels and stores. Visitors are informed, by markers of various sorts, about the town's history. The combinations (multiple nuclei, many markers) create the perception of historic atmosphere in a tourist's mind.

Tourist precincts and festivals

Certain nuclei are so special for particular tourists (one or many) that they can stand alone, spatially or in time. Highly popular sights (Taj Mahal, Grand Canyon) or events (Olympic Games, Melbourne Cup) are examples.

For most tourism, however, clustered nuclei are more important than any unique feature. Clustering is based on more than symbiosis, things working together. It involves synergism (the 1 + 1 = 3 principle), where a combination is more than the sum of the parts. This can occur in several spatial categories: a room, building, site, precinct, town or city, region, country, continent. An example of a room functioning in this way is in Madrid, where 20 portraits by El Greco of 17th century Spaniards are in one room of the Prado. The clustering makes the room a focus for many tourists. No particular portrait is important in that process.

'Tourist precinct' is a useful concept for designating a small zone in a town or city where tourists congregate because of clustered, synergistic attractions. The term was adapted from the term 'precinct' used in urban planning and adapted for use in tourism research in a study relating to towns in Australia (Leiper 1981b). Examples of tourist precincts can be seen in almost any city, especially metropolitan cities visited by large numbers of tourists. Sydney, for example, has several: Circular Quay and the Opera House forecourt is the most popular; others include Dixon Street (the centre of the Chinese quarter), the Queen Victoria Building, and a number of precincts within The Rocks—the oldest part of the city. These places have no single dominating nucleus,

Contiguous marker on sign post
at hot springs near Rotorua,
New Zealand

even if they seem to have an architectural centrepiece.

Piazza Navona in Rome is one of that city's tourist precincts. Many tourists on this piazza seem to pay little or no attention to Bernini's Fountain of the Four Rivers, the grand embellishment in the middle of the square. Similarly, Kathmandu's Durbar Square is that city's most popular tourist precinct, and while many people, at least on their first visit, look up for a glimpse of the legendary Living Goddess, the square functions as a tourist precinct because of other factors.

Tourists are attracted to these places, and enjoy leisure time there, because of multiple features, which synergistically give the place character or atmosphere, contributing to an interesting or pleasant experience. These features include other tourists and locals using the place for leisure. Each particular feature might not in itself be sufficient to influence tourists' itineraries, but in combination a synergistic effect operates, and the place is deemed sufficiently attractive to spend leisure time there. Shopping malls, art galleries, zoos and theme parks all function as tourist precincts.

Disneyland, the archetypal theme park, is a recreational and tourist precinct. Michael Real (1977) studied the place and its visitors. Disneyland comprises a number of sites that could be described as mini-theme parks. The popularity of Disneyland is partly because of synergy, the combination of themed experiences form a cluster. Tomorrowland, Adventureland, Fantasyland and others are located in one precinct, large but sufficiently compact for visits to several sites in one day.

While all nuclei have spatial dimensions, some are also located in time, when an event is the focus. Here, too, in many instances synergistic clustering of little events is the focus and real basis of the attraction system. A typical festival comprises many events, major and minor, scheduled into a short period, clustered. Each little event may have no motivating influence on tourists, but in combination, with a unifying theme, they form the nucleus for an attraction.

The Olympic Games provides an interesting example. Few people would visit merely to see a 20-second foot race and fewer still would attend to see synchronised swimming, but when hundreds of little events are packed into two weeks, the resulting big event is deemed worthy of attention by many persons.

Cultural festivals in thousands of towns and cities function as tourist attractions in the same synergistic way. A famous example is the Fiesta in Pamplona every July, best known for the running of the bulls through the streets, seen on global TV every year, but in fact a combination of many different events. Its popularity as an event for foreign tourists owes a lot to Hemingway's writings, first in a popular novel (1926) and later in a book of memoirs of a summer travelling around Spain. His description of the Fiesta begins 'Pamplona, overcrowded with tourists and characters . . . for a week we averaged three hours' sleep a night' (Hemingway 1985: 97).

CONCLUSIONS

This chapter set out a discussion about attractions. Blending selected aspects of theories from two writers, Gunn and MacCannell, provided a basis for developing a more comprehensive set of theories about tourist attractions.

Tourists are elementary parts of attractions, and are not merely consumers or users of some discrete sight, event or experience. If no tourist ever visited the Tower of London, or the Great Wall of China, these things would not be tourist attractions. Markers too are elementary, not merely promotional or logistic tools supporting the attraction.

Tourist attractions do not operate in a literal sense. The expression is metaphorical, a risky one if taken literally in research, yet that is what a number of scholars seem to have done when they invite readers to believe that, in tourism, 'attraction' can be inherent or intrinsic. Instead of this non-scientific approach, a three-element model allows a determinist explanation of what attractions are and how they function.

A topic not discussed in this chapter is authenticity. Are attractions that portray inauthentic experiences, such as fake history and distorted culture, always problematical? Does tourism typically represent inauthentic experiences, as the pejorative sense of 'tourist' or 'touristy' often suggests? The theme has received attention from a number of researchers, including MacCannell (1976), Cohen (1979), Philip Pearce (1991), Wang (2000) and Halewood and Hannam (2001).

Another topic not explored in this chapter is the role of organisations whose business is tourist attractions. Two cases in Chapters 11 and 14 are on this topic. The attractions sector of tourism industries has developed in recent years, with new forms and a trend to larger-scale enterprises. An industry association directly involved with attractions is the Tourist Attractions Association of New South Wales: 'Initially conceived as a simple forum for contact and discussion between attraction operators, the Association has broadened its charter to become a voice for the attractions sector of the tourism industry' (TAANSW 1993).

At the beginning of this chapter an observation was made that attractions are a relatively neglected topic in the scholarly literature on tourism. Why is this so? To some extent the explanation is that most elements in most attractions do not constitute components of tourism industries. Most attractions are in the non-industrialised part of tourism, on the fringes of but outside tourism industries. Nuclei such as scenery, beaches, incidental displays of local culture and customs are all examples. Likewise, most markers stem from sources outside the tourism industries. These include the non-advertisement content of television and the mass media generally and, most common of all, messages about attractions received casually from personal acquaintances in everyday conversation.

Meanwhile, most of the scholarly literature on the operations of tourism relates to organisations in tourism industries—to hotels, airlines, tour operators, national and regional tourism authorities, theme parks, casinos. Certain distinctive attractions are in that list (theme parks, casinos), but these represent a minor portion of the spectrum of attractions. Theories discussed in this chapter have potential applications for a wide range of problems and opportunities faced by managers, planners and policy makers responsible for many tourism-related issues.

Discussion questions

1. Why is the expression 'tourist attraction' misleading if taken literally?
2. What are the three elements (that must exist) in every instance of tourist attractions?
3. What are the roles of inviolate belts, according to Gunn's theories for tourist attractions?
4. Describe a tourist attraction with an effective inviolate belt.

5. Describe a tourist attraction where the inviolate belt is ineffective.
6. What is the zone of closure, according to Gunn's theories for tourist attractions?
7. What is meant by primary, secondary and tertiary attractions?
8. How might the theory of primary, secondary and tertiary attractions be used by a manager overseeing the design of a marketing campaign for a large tourist destination, such as a city, region or country?
9. Where, in the geography of whole tourism systems, are the marker elements of attractions located?
10. List and describe at least six functions of marker elements in tourist attractions. Use examples to illustrate your answer.
11. How does the theory of attractions comprising tourist/marker/nucleus operate in the case of a tourist in a strange city seeing a quite remarkable building for which he/she has no information?
12. What are the phases in the evolution of tourist attractions, according to MacCannell's theory?
13. What practical uses exist for the theory of attraction evolution?
14. What is a tourist precinct? Explain this in terms of a theory of tourist attractions.

Recommended reading

Gunn, C. 1988, *Vacationscape: Designing Tourist Regions* (2nd edn), New York: Van Nostrand Reinhold

Henderson, J. 1997, Singapore's wartime tourist attractions, *Journal of Tourism Studies*, 8(2): 39–49

Lew, A. 1987, A framework of tourist attraction research, *Annals of Tourism Research*, 14: 533–75

Lew, A. 2000, Attractions, *The Encyclopedia of Tourism*, J. Jafari, (ed.), London: Routledge

MacCannell, Dean 1976, *The Tourist: A New Theory of the Leisure Class*, New York: Schoken

Pearce, Douglas 1999, Tourism in Paris: studies at the microscale, *Annals of Tourism Research*, 26: 77–97

Pearce, Phillip 1991, Analysing tourist attractions, *Journal of Tourism Studies*, 2(1): 46–55

Seaton, A. 1999, War and thanatourism: Waterloo 1815–1914, *Annals of Tourism Research*, 26: 130–58

CHAPTER

14

Managing a Successful Tourist Attraction: the Neka Art Museum

After visiting the Neka Art Museum, many tourists would probably agree that it is quite successful in several respects. Displaying remarkable originals in various styles of painting, it provides cultural experiences that are interesting and educational. Many visitors would agree that it deserves its reputation as the best and most popular art museum in Bali and would also endorse the recommendation in a guidebook: the Neka 'should not be missed'.

Given those points, the Neka is a suitable case for this chapter, where the aim is to illustrate a number of theories set out in earlier chapters, relating to management (Chapter 8), the partial industrialisation of tourism (Chapter 11) and tourist attractions (Chapter 13). In particular, the aim is to show how those theories come together as themes in a real example. The case also explores the reasons for the Neka's success and simultaneously attempts to identify any weaknesses in its performance and management. Not explored, and beyond the scope of this study, is the artistic merit of the paintings.

The research was made possible by the willing cooperation of Suteja Neka, the founder and director of the Neka Art Museum, and Made Parnatha, manager of operations, especially during three weeks in January 2002 when several interviews were conducted. The project was also informed by observations on the site and conversations about museums with tourists there and elsewhere in Bali. Memories of four previous visits to the Neka, between 1981 and 1999, provided extra background.

An overview is the first topic below, leading into a discussion of links between museums and tourism. The third topic is an analysis of the Neka Art Museum as a tourist attraction. The fourth is visitor trends and patterns, the fifth is organisation and management, and the sixth identifies reasons for the Neka's popularity among tourists compared to other museums in Bali. A final topic raises a question about the long-term viability of the current approach to strategic management at the Neka.

An interesting issue emerged from analysing visitor numbers over 60 consecutive months from 1997 to 2002. During this period, three disastrous events triggered sharp downturns in the numbers of tourists visiting Bali. Data from the Neka provide indications of the shape and durations of these downturns, and to what extent they affect long-term trends. After the October 2002 bombing of the Sari Club in Kuta, with its tragic loss of life, the immediate effect was, once again, a sharp decrease in tourist numbers going to Bali. Can the historical trends from 1997 to 2002 give clues for predicting the longer-term effects?

THE NEKA ART MUSEUM

In 1966 a young schoolteacher, son of Bali's most famous wood-carver, began selling paintings as an after-hours sideline. In the same year the Bali Beach Hotel, the island's first large resort, opened and in 1969, an international airport (Kam 2001a: 115):

[Seeing] foreign tourists taking home Balinese paintings, Suteja Neka realized the need to preserve Balinese art . . . and began collecting high quality art to encourage the market and give opportunities for artists. His choices were based on whether pieces had special qualities and portrayed characteristics of Bali . . . He avoided works that copied those of other artists.

In 1975 Suteja Neka toured museums in Europe and realised that Bali also needed museums in which high-quality works representing its artistic heritage could be preserved and displayed in their original environment. In 1976 he established a museum, 2 kilometres northwest of the centre of Ubud. When it opened there were 45 paintings in the collection. Over the years, the collection has grown via acquisitions and donations and the museum has expanded with the construction of more buildings on the site. By 2002 there were 312 paintings exhibited and another 48 in storage because the available wall space could not properly display the entire collection. The site occupied by the museum is almost 1 hectare (9150 square metres), and there are 2580 square metres of floor space in seven buildings designed after traditional Balinese architecture. The open land within the site comprises gardens, lawns, paths, access road and parking area.

Eight categories of paintings are exhibited, including five by Balinese painters. They are: classical puppet style; Ubud style; Batuan style; Young Artists style; and Contemporary Balinese Painting, embracing several artistic styles. One category is titled 'Contemporary Indonesian Art', these are paintings by artists from Indonesia's other islands; another, 'Artists from Abroad', has works by foreigners in Bali. Included are paintings by Dutch, Swiss, Malaysian, Japanese, Australian and American artists. The Arie Smit Pavilion has paintings by that Dutch-Indonesian, resident in Bali for many decades. Another has several distinctive drawings by I Gusti Nyoman Lempad, perhaps Bali's most famous artist, who died in 1978 aged 116.

MUSEUMS AND TOURISM

Museums have been defined as 'institutions for the collection, preservation, exhibition and explanation of cultural and natural phenomena' (Graburn 2000a: 400). Accordingly, their mission is to serve humanity, and especially the society of the country or region in which they are located. For a number of reasons, many museums are also popular with several types of tourists.

Research on museums in a tourism context includes studies by Jansen-Verbeke and Rekom (1996), Harrison (1997), Tufts and Milne (1999), Swarbrooke (1999), Munsters (2001) and Richards (2001), Museums are discussed or noted briefly in many broad studies of tourism with geographical or historical themes.

In the 18th century, participants on the Grand Tour of Europe viewed art in grand private homes and in cathedrals, but in that era museums for the general public did not exist. Since the 19th century, and especially since the middle of the 20th century, many public galleries and museums have opened, but the geographic pattern is not uniform.

Entrance to the Neka Art Museum

'All over Europe there has been a veritable museum explosion' (Richards 2001: 62), but in Asia no explosion has occurred and museums are not common. Most major cities in Asia, especially national capitals, have a few museums, but they do not seem especially prominent in tourism. Museums are not mentioned in *Tourism in South East Asia* (Hitchcock et al. 1993), and in its 200 pages Picard's (1996) book on cultural tourism in Bali gives only three lines to museums.

In fact, Bali is an exception to the Asian pattern, for there are 20 museums on the island, besides hundreds of art galleries. In Bali, 'art gallery' means a place where art is for sale, while 'art museum' signifies a collection for cultural heritage. This custom differs from the convention in Europe, where 'gallery' is a generic term.

Why do tourists visit museums?

Richards (2001) points to opportunities for cultural experiences via tourism, and describes museums as 'experience factories'. An alternative, but not contradictory, way of answering the question can be suggested. In museums, tourists can conveniently acquire authoritative impressions or knowledge of the cultural or natural phenomena of a country or region. Museums are efficient sources for satisfying, to some degree, two common needs beneath touristic motivation: the need to learn something about places visited, especially their cultures; and the need for authentic experiences (MacCannell 1976; Wang 2000). The reputation of a museum is closely linked to its role as an arbitrator of authenticity.

Wang (2000) begins his discussion of authenticity issues in tourism by remarking that the issue began in museums and art galleries. That is untrue. As discussed elsewhere in this book, pilgrim-tourists were concerned about the authenticity of religious relics many centuries before anyone was interested in viewing art. However, Wang is correct in noting the authoritative role of museums and its relevance for tourism. Art deemed worthy of a place in a museum is normally considered authentic in several respects: originality of style, quality within its school, and painted by the designated artist.

Museums suit a range of tourists. At one end of a spectrum are tourists of the type that are content with superficial impressions. At the Neka, many of this type can be seen. They move around the exhibits, seldom pausing for more than a few seconds in any spot and seldom spending more than five minutes in any room. Some tourists of this type look closely and briefly at every item, but some look at only a small selection of paintings in each room, giving the others an overall glance. At the opposite end of the spectrum are those who spend time studying the paintings, often consulting a guidebook, discussing the works with a companion or tour guide, or retracking their steps to revisit a particular painting. At the Neka, as in other art museums around the world, tourists representing both extremes of the spectrum and positions in between can be observed.

Controversies exist around the way certain museums select and present particular aspects of culture in order to shape public perceptions. For instance, there is much controversy regarding the National Museum of Australia: see 'How not to run a museum' (Windshuttle 2001), a response by Morgan (2002), and subsequent rejoinders. This theme is outside the scope of the present research and, in any event, so far as is known there have never been any controversies regarding the Neka.

The Neka's mission

The Neka's mission, or 'superordinate goal' (Waterman et al. 1980), is to preserve Bali's artistic heritage in its original environment, for the benefit of humanity and in particular

Suteja Neka with his wife Ni Gusti Made Srimin

for Balinese. However, in its superficial role and as its business activity, the Neka Art Museum is a tourist attraction. That is how it earns money to carry out its mission.

Tourists at the Neka ➤

Arriving in the lobby, visitors are welcomed, directed to enter names and nationalities in a register, and asked to pay an entrance fee, currently (in 2002) 10 000 Rupiah (approximately $US1). The fee is not obligatory, so those who do not want to pay are courteously treated and allowed to enter. Very few tourists do not pay, and some contribute more than the nominal amount. A leaflet is available, describing the art in the various pavilions. A guide service is available for a fee.

Tourists typically spend between one and two hours on site. Before departing, most browse in the lobby, where books, art posters and postcards are displayed for sale, and then enter the cafe, at least for the views from the terrace overlooking a spectacular valley.

THE NEKA'S ROLES IN TOURIST ATTRACTION SYSTEMS ON THE MARGIN OF TOURISM INDUSTRIES

As shown in Chapter 13, a tourist attraction system comprises a nucleus, a tourist, and a marker. In many instances there are multiple, overlapping markers, along with multiple, overlapping nuclei, forming the basis for experiences by tourists whose needs and other characteristics are also diverse. Any art museum popular with tourists is an especially notable example of this overlapping diversity, as the following discussion will demonstrate.

Chapter 11 tells us that tourism is not an industry, is not wholly industrialised behaviour, but is best understood as the behaviour of tourists, which is partly industrialised. Broadly, tourists use a range of resources, some supplied by tourism industries (forming the industrialised part of their behaviour) and some from other sources (the non-industrialised part). The Neka Art Museum is a suitable case for illustrating practical aspects of this theory. It is in the business of tourism but does not operate as a component business organisation within any tourism industry. It does not practise strategic or operational cooperation with other organisations in the business of tourism, which is the necessary condition for an industry. The Neka's policy on this point is based on the fact that, to date, it has not needed to work closely with tour operators, hotels or other similar organisations for its success.

These two themes—tourist attraction systems and partial industrialisation—are illustrated throughout the discussion below.

Nuclear elements of attractions at the Neka

Attraction systems involving art museums have multiple nuclear elements. These include: museums as a conceptual possibility for tourists' experiences; a specific museum as a possible site to visit; and the physical embodiments of each museum—the site, buildings, interiors, type of items on display and staff who assist tourists.

The entire collection of paintings on display represents a nuclear element for most tourists who set out to visit an art museum. The Neka's collection, arranged in eight categories (described earlier) is well designed to suit these tourists, who, after a visit, probably feel that they have had a comprehensive overview of Balinese paintings.

Because the Neka collection comprises originals of high quality, because of the range of styles, and because of the manner of display, tourists probably appreciate the distinctive difference of the paintings there compared to those on sale in the dozens of commercial galleries and thousands of shops in other locations in Bali. The fact that paintings in a museum are not for sale adds to the perception that they have special value, are beyond price and outside the world of commerce. In sharp contrast, many of the paintings displayed for sale in Bali are obviously fourth-rate and amateurish, even to a non-expert's assessment and, as many tourists discover, can be bought for sums far below their advertised price.

Various categories of paintings are distinct nuclei for some persons—those who visit or revisit principally to view one specific category, such as the Ubud-style collection at the Neka. Another level of nuclei comprises works by particular artists, such as the Lempad drawings, exhibited in their own room. Another level comprises specific items, such as 'Mutual Attraction' by Aziz, the painting at the Neka that possibly gets closer attention from tourists than any other on display.

All these nuclei are, in a real sense, manifestations of the Neka as an organisation in the business of tourism, as they have been put on display to serve tourist markets. If the collection had been assembled to preserve cultural heritage without regard for tourism, a different and less expensive method could have been used.

In tourist attraction systems based in art museums there are also nuclei not put in place by the museum or any organisation in the business of tourism. These comprise tourists, who quite often become the focus for other tourists' attention. This happens in two ways. Tourists can often be seen looking at other tourists and obviously taking an interest in their appearance or behaviour. This presumably occurs when viewers become a little bored looking at paintings, and find other visitors an interesting distraction. The other way is when conversations are struck up between strangers visiting a museum, often beginning with an exchange of opinions on a particular painting or painter. In museums as in many other kinds of places, other tourists form the basis for tourists' experiences, becoming the central element of a type of attraction.

Tourist elements in attractions at the Neka

A second set of elements in attractions are tourists seeking experiences. At the Neka they are diverse: different in nationalities, levels of interest, tastes, knowledge of art and amount of time to spend there.

Some are visiting because the Neka is on an itinerary prepared by a tour operator. These tourists represent highy industrialised tourism. They include those on group tours and others, quite numerous, who visit alone or in family parties with personal tour guides. Many tourists in Bali hire their own tour guides, either for a series of trips over several days or for a single day.

Others represent relatively non-industrialised tourism, and are substantially independent of tourism industries. This type can be identified by the absence of a tour guide inside the museum or a tour escort waiting with a coach or car in the parking area. Independent tourists at the Neka use a range of transport modes. They walk from Ubud, or use bicycles, motorbikes, rented cars or the public mini-buses.

Marker elements in attractions at the Neka

Tourists might learn about the Neka from its own publicity. Suteja Neka has a flair for getting publicity stories about his museum into newspapers, magazines and TV. Probably more common are tourists who learn about it from guidebooks. In Bali, as in many other places, tourists with an interest in cultural attractions buy guidebooks to gain information.

In *Travelpack Bali*, the Neka is described as a place that 'should not be missed' (Sheehan 2000: 51), and *Lonely Planet Indonesia* says it is 'the best place to learn about Balinese painting' (Turner 2000: 438). Similar endorsements are in other guidebooks. These bits of information can function as generating markers, stimulating and triggering decisions to visit.

To a casual observer, this information in guidebooks might be seen as evidence that the Neka is promoted via links between its director (or managers) and the writers and publishers of guidebooks, and that this represents participation in a tourism industry. In fact, Suteja Neka and his managers have no role in the publicity given to their museum in guidebooks. The writers normally seek independence, in order to be able to present their own opinions and to give guidebooks credibility among readers. During my visits, Suteja Neka was keen to discover whether and how his museum had been described in a guidebook I carried.

Oral information ('word of mouth') shared among tourists is a common form of marker in tourist attraction systems, typically coming from non-industrial sources. For example, I learned about the Neka from a woman in Kuta in 1981, as one tourist conversing with another. The information from that woman became a generating marker, as the way she described the place triggered a decision to go there. The next day in Ubud, I sought directions from a group of men in the street. A man pointed to a mini-bus and said the trip would take five minutes. As I was already on my way there, this information served as a transit marker. Presumably neither the woman in Kuta nor the man in the street had any interest in boosting tourism to the Neka but were merely passing on information—being civil, not behaving strategically in an industrial context, not working at a job. An industrial context would require that they passed on such information in a routine, assiduous, purposeful and rewarded role.

The many bits of information acquired by tourists during their visits in a museum are contiguous markers, occurring while tourists are at the nuclei, the central elements in attraction systems. Contiguous markers at the Neka include information from sources such as the signs at the entrance and on buildings, the leaflets, the staff who answer questions and, the most often used contiguous markers, the bits of information written on plaques under each painting. At the Neka, plaques alongside each painting are in English and Japanese. All these contiguous markers reflect the Neka's strategy: it is in the business of tourism. Another common type of contiguous marker in a museum is comment about paintings offered by other visitors; this type is outside the scope of the museum's business strategy: it is not designed, planned or managed by the museum.

Several functions of markers were identified in Chapter 13. Some markers trigger the motivation to visit a place. Other functions include helping tourists to plan itineraries, to know that they have arrived, to form a sense of place, and so on. The most important function is that certain markers enable tourists to gain a sense of meaning from the experiential leisure at the core of tourism.

Discussions with several tourists (Japanese, American, Australian and Norwegian) about their experiences and opinions of the Neka were not in sufficient detail to be certain as to precisely what sense of meaning was derived from their visit, or which markers were most important in the process. Certainly most said they were pleased to have had the experience. Most carried guidebooks, and those interviewed inside the museum had been observed paying close attention to these books and to the plaques alongside paintings. This analysis, indicating overlapping nuclear and marker elements, helps explain why for many tourists visiting a museum like the Neka is a rich cultural experience. There are many cultural themes and objects and many sources of information. Some markers and nuclei are within the scope of the museum's management and reflect its strategic focus on tourism, and some are outside that scope.

VISITOR TRENDS AND PATTERNS

All visitors are requested to enter their names and nationalities in a register in the entry lobby at the Neka Art Museum, so these registers are a source of reasonably accurate data on numbers. Table 14.1 shows large fluctuations annually. Table 14.2 shows Japanese as by far the most numerous nationality among visitors to the Neka. That might reflect their strong interest in staged culture, and probably also stems from the fact that Japanese tourism in Bali is highly industrialised. The increase in Taiwanese visitors is notable. Indonesians made up between 3% and 4% of visitors in the four years.

Most Japanese are on programs designed and managed by tour organisers, who would regard an escorted trip to a museum as a suitable inclusion in itineraries. The Neka is approximately two hours by car or coach from Nusa Dua, the resort hotel zone where most Japanese stay. For many of these tourists, the Neka serves as one of the points on a full-day tour.

The sharp falls in visitor numbers at the Neka in 1998 and 2001 probably match falls in total tourist numbers in Bali. There are no suggestions of a decrease in the propensity of tourists to visit museums, or of a trend away from the Neka to other museums. The total numbers of tourists visiting Bali is not known, because many fly in direct and many fly via Jakarta. Therefore, an accurate estimate of the proportion

TABLE 14.1 Annual numbers of visitors, 1997–2001, Neka Art Museum

Year	Number	Change
1997	80 248	
1998	63 989	−16 259 (−20%)
1999	81 234	+17 245 (+27%)
2000	99 974	+18 740 (+23%)
2001	85 917	−14 057 (−14%)

Source: entries in visitors' book at entrance desk.

TABLE 14.2 Nationality of visitors to the Neka Art Museum, 1997–2000

Nationality	1997	1998	1999	2000
Japan	64%	59%	56%	71%
Germany	6%	7%	9%	4%
USA	6%	7%	7%	6%
Australia	4%	5%	5%	3%
Taiwan	1%	3%	4%	10%
Others	19%	19%	19%	6%
Totals	100%	100%	100%	100%

Source: analysis of entries in visitors' book.

visiting the Neka cannot be made. Falls in total tourist numbers in Bali in 1998 and 2001 can be attributed to events that caused many potential visitors to avoid Indonesia.

Figure 14.1 shows peaks (each August) and months of sharp downturns, notably May–June 1998 and October–November 2001. From 1997, Indonesian tourism suffered from the effects of the Asian currency crisis and other problems (Leiper & Hing 1998). In May 1998 Indonesia's image as a safe destination was severely damaged by riots in Jakarta, with hundreds killed, events leading to the end of Soeharto's dictatorial regime.

In September and October 1999, the insecure image was reinforced by media reports of mass demonstrations in Jakarta, where tens of thousands of citizens protested outside the parliament, opposing a security bill that if passed into law would again have given the army sweeping powers over the people. Also in those months, Indonesia's rule over East Timor ended, with violence by groups wanting to remain Indonesian inflicted on those wanting independence. The violence intensified perceptions internationally that Indonesia was not a safe tourist destination.

A negative image was further reinforced in September 2001, when the attacks that month in New York and Washington were found to be the work of Islamic terrorists. As home of the world's largest Islamic population, Indonesia was viewed by many people around the world as a quite dangerous place to visit. Widespread perceptions after 11 September of higher risks in flying also led to a sudden fall in tourism. Interestingly,

FIGURE 14.1 Monthly trends in visitor numbers at the Neka Art Museum

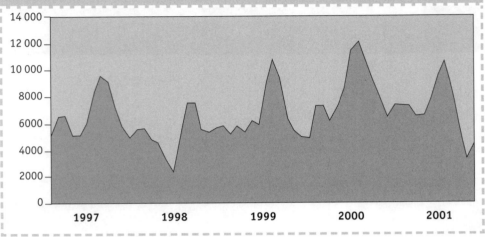

Source: entries in visitors' book at entrance desk.

after each sharp fall, the line soon reverts (figure 14.1) to the normal trend, with visitor numbers recovering. From the lowest point, for example (June 1998), visitor numbers climbed to peak again in August. The low point in late 2001 (after 11 September) was not as low as that in 1998 after the Jakarta riots. Table 14.2 indicates that growth from Japan has been a major factor in the recoveries and the long-term growth, and that Taiwan is also important in these respects.

Figure 14.1 certainly shows that tourism to Bali in the past has been resilient, with numbers recovering to the long-term trend line after previous tragedies. The effects of the October 2002 bombs at the Sari Club on future tourist numbers in Bali might be far more severe than any of the events noted above. Many more persons were killed in the May 1998 riots, but that tragedy occurred on a neighbouring island, Java, in the city of Jakarta, and the riots did not involve many attacks on foreigners but on local shops and certain residents.

ORGANISATION AND MANAGEMENT

Two overlapping organisations are directly involved. In 1982 Suteja Neka formed Yayasan Dharma Seni (Art Devotion Foundation), an advisory body for the museum. The YDS has characteristics of Mintzberg's (1991b) professional and missionary configurations, its members comprising Suteja Neka and a group of comparable art experts committed to Bali's cultural heritage. The YDS's roles relate to the museum's 'superordinate goals, the fundamental ideas around which a business is built . . . its main values' (Waterman et al. 1980: 25). It provides advice about the collection and broad heritage policy.

Employing 25 persons, the principal organisation that manages and operates the museum reflects Mintzberg's entrepreneurial configuration. There are three middle managers and relatively few technical and administrative personnel. The structure's key part is its strategic apex, in the person of Suteja Neka; the prime coordination mechanism is direct supervision by him.

An organisational chart is displayed in a large, open office in the main building, where the director and three assistants have desks. It shows a conventional hierarchy: at the apex is the director, and on the line below are the three reporting direct to him. These managerial positions are labelled 'assistant, curator', 'assistant, operational' and 'assistant, finance'. Lower levels comprise 21 positions—administrative and security personnel, gardeners, cleaners. There is no marketing manager. Promotional activities revolve around Suteja Neka, who seems to have connections for getting publicity in the mass media.

An assessment of the way the Neka is managed, based on observations during visits and on interviews with Suteja and various employees, leads to the opinion that it is reasonably strong in all seven areas of the 7S framework (Waterman et al. 1991): these are structure, strategy, staff, style, skills, systems, and superordinate goals.

A BUSINESS STRATEGY FOR TOURISM...

The Neka's business strategy does not stem from plans but occurs as patterns and perspectives (Mintzberg 1991d). In their relationship to tourism, the strategies illustrate another dimension of partial industrialisation, as the following explanation will show.

Tourists in the Neka Art Museum

The Neka is in the business of tourism. The museum is designed for exhibiting art to visitors who are almost all tourists of some sort, and aspects of its design and operations are concerned with meeting distinctive needs of tourists visiting a museum.

. . . But no substantial links into tourism industries

However, the Neka is not substantially participating in any tourism industry. It has no cooperative arrangements—strategic, operational or commercial—with other enterprises involved with tourism, which is an essential condition for industrial participation (discussed in Chapter 11). Tour operators who take tourists there make no arrangements with the museum. Instead, visitors on organised tours arrive without notice, and pay the entry fee like other visitors. Tour operators wanting to take tourists to the Neka are welcome there, but they are not encouraged to do so by any commercial arrangements, largely because to date there has been no need for such arrangements.

The Neka's location is not a 'museum industry zone', as it is located 1 kilometre from the nearest museum and does not have the cooperative benefits that stem from industrial zoning. Many museums in various major cities (e.g. Paris, London and Jakarta) are geographically clustered.

Moreover, before the current research, visitor records had not been closely analysed in terms of nationalities for several years. Everyone asked said that Japanese formed the majority, but nobody knew the exact percentage. As the total trend has been growth, there has been no need to invest time and expense in forming and sustaining relationships with tour operators, and no need to have staff analysing the visitor registers to collect information useful in such relationships. Thus, being in the business of tourism but not participating substantially in any tourism industry seems to have been an appropriate policy. Absence of threats from other museums to its position of market leader among museums in Bali underlines the appropriateness of the Neka's policy of not forming strategic links with tour operators and other sectors of tourism industries. It does not need to compete via strategic business management, because it has other advantages.

Explaining the Neka's popularity

From observations and interviews at the Neka Art Museum and from similar research (in less depth) at other museums in Bali, several reasons were identified to explain the popularity of the Neka. Why has it been successful as a tourist attraction? Its art collection, assessed in its entirety, is probably the best in Bali, and this is a very important factor. The collection gives the Neka an edge over other places where tourists see art—especially the countless commercial galleries and shops. The collection is large, has diverse styles, is high-quality and is presented in an aesthetically pleasant, informative, non-commercial setting.

Age is another factor. Established in 1976, the Neka has had ample time to become widely known as a place worth visiting.

Its location is a neighbourhood northwest of Ubud where several upmarket resorts,

Organisation Chart on the wall of the administrative office, Neka Art Museum

restaurants, boutiques and galleries have opened in recent years. This location, on the fashionable side of Ubud, has been fortunate, or was perhaps the result of intelligent foresight. The large parking area inside the grounds, adjacent to the entrance, provides space for dozens of vehicles. This is especially useful for tour operators with coaches, particularly if they are transporting tourists who do not want to walk far in the open air.

The prominence given the Neka in guidebooks on Bali has certainly contributed to its popularity. There is no doubt that many tourists in Bali use guidebooks as reliable sources of information for decisions about where to go.

The large number of Japanese tourists in Bali in recent years has been a major underlying factor in sustaining visitor numbers. This is because most Japanese in Bali are consumers in highly industrialised tourism. Their activities, especially their visits to places such as art museums, are determined for them by tour operators and other manifestations of the Japan–Bali tourism industry. It is also because, apparently, a large proportion of Japanese tourists in Bali have a strong interest in cultural displays.

On all these criteria, the Neka has advantages over Bali's other museums and, as noted above, it has not had to compete in any substantial strategic or tactical sense.

The Puri Lukisan is an older museum, opened 20 years before the Neka in 1956, but it lacks parking facilities, so vehicles must find parking spaces in Ubud's busy main street and visitors must walk along a path through a steep gully, a condition that deters potential visitors and tour operators. Museum Agung Rai and Rudana Art Museum were founded only recently, in the mid-1990s, and are not yet widely known. Moreover, their location in Peliatan and Teges, 2 kilometres south of Ubud, is a disadvantage, away from fashionable precincts and cultural sites. Both these museums have a number of splendid paintings, but neither has a collection comparable to that in the Neka. A fourth large institution, the long-established Museum Bali, is in Denpasar, where there is little to interest tourists and where traffic is now so congested that few tourists go there.

A POSSIBLE WEAKNESS?

The Neka is very dependent on Japanese tourists for its commercial viability. (As shown in Table 14.2, these represent more than half of all visitors and seem to be growing in relative importance.) Two signs of possible weakness in its business strategies can be inferred. One is the risk that if, for any reason, the Japan–Bali tourism system were to go into decline, decreasing numbers of Japanese tourists in Bali could lead to substantial decreases in the number of visitors at the Neka and serious problems for its economic viability. The other sign of possible weakness is that for unknown reasons, relatively few non-Japanese tourists in Bali visit the Neka. For example, in recent years the number of Australian tourists visiting Bali has been about the same as the number of Japanese, and the former are typically there for longer visits, and yet Japanese outnumber Australians at the Neka by 12 to 1. Relatively few Australians in Bali visit the Neka, and the same is true of Americans and several other nationalities.

Why is this so? Management at the Neka has not conducted any research that might give an answer and point to a strategy for strengthening the customer base.

CONCLUSION: BROADLY COMPETENT MANAGEMENT

A number of reasons have been identified for the Neka's popularity as a tourist attraction. There is another set of factors, without which the museum would not be successful as a museum, as a tourist attraction, or as a business enterprise. These are the managers and staff, including, most especially, the director and founder Suteja Neka.

At the head of an organisation of competent staff with almost no labour turnover, Suteja Neka's personal contributions in several ways have been vital in the success.

Severe setbacks occurred in some years, and in these slow periods when the museum's income did not cover its costs, the operations were subsidised from Suteja Neka's other business activities, such as the Neka Art Gallery, a commercial venture in Ubud. Thus, like the great museums of Europe and America, this one in Bali has been sustained with philanthropic help. More substantially, Suteja Neka's personal commitment, enthusiasm and leadership are all apparent. In their research, Finkelstein and Hambrick (1996) showed how and why success in certain organisations depends to a notable degree on the top manager. The Neka Art Museum appears to exemplify that principle.

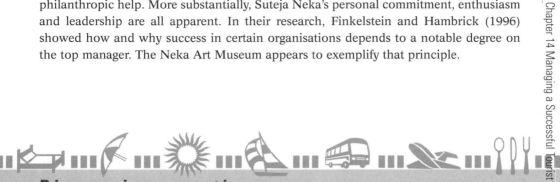

Discussion questions

1. What are some of the reasons why tourists visit museums?
2. What are the various types of nuclear elements in tourist attractions that exist in an institution such as the Neka Art Museum?
3. What are the various types of marker elements in tourist attractions that might be observed in relation to an institution such as the Neka?
4. What is meant by the remark that the Neka Art Museum is in the business of tourism but does not need to participate substantially in tourism industries?
5. What factors seem to explain the fact that more tourists visit the Neka than other art museums in Bali?
6. An analysis of tourism at the Neka Art Museum revealed a possible weakness in its tourist business. What is it, and what could be done to remedy it?

Recommended reading

Neka, S. & Kam, G. 2000, *The Development of Painting in Bali: Selections from the Neka Art Museum* (2nd edn), Ubud: Yayasan Dharma Seni

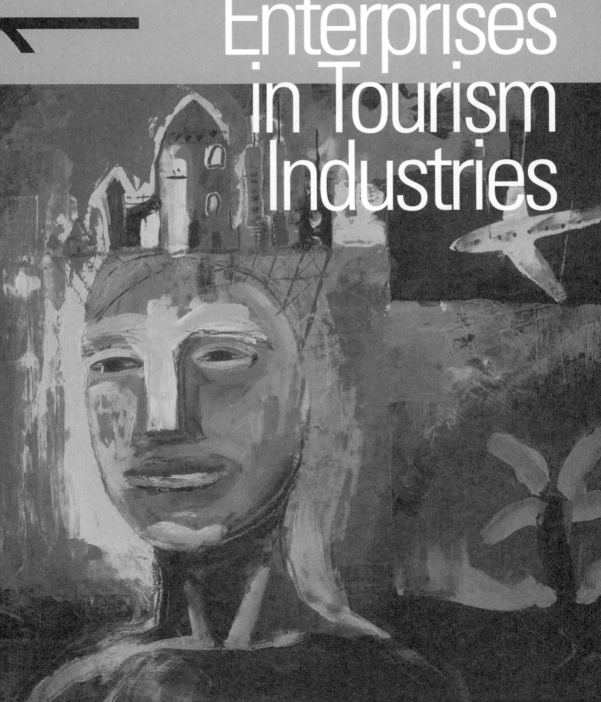

Failing Enterprises in Tourism Industries

Successful businesses are all alike; every failed business is a failure in its own way. This allusion to a characteristic of failures has been adapted from the opening line of Tolstoy's *Anna Karenina*, where it is applied to failure in a quite different area of human activity. The adaptation suits one of the findings from the case histories in this chapter.

The purpose of discussing failed tourism enterprises is to illustrate some of the aspects of failures and to identify and discuss their causes. The aim is to demonstrate that by studying failures, by attempting to understand how and why business organisations fail, managers are better able to avoid failure with their own organisations and are better positioned to be successful.

During the years immediately preceding 2000, the British government spent $A2000 million on the design, construction and development of what was supposed to be one of the world's most popular attractions in the millennium year, the Millennium Dome in London (Comptroller & Auditor General 2000). Instead of the forecast 12 million visitors in that year, an average of 33 000 per day, the project was a flop—a failure of huge proportions. While many thousands of visitors were recorded on some days, the totals were way below the forecast: on some days there were fewer than 200 visitors (Walter 2000). The Dome failed in multiple respects—as a visitor attraction, tourism icon, public investment and business enterprise. Some people found it a most interesting experience; many others found it tediously dull and irrelevant, and from its second day of operation it lacked that highly desirable guarantee of success in any kind of mass entertainment and culture—word-of-mouth endorsement from previous visitors. The Dome was, quite possibly, the greatest failure in the history of tourism. It has been discussed in many newspaper articles, and no doubt a number of detailed research studies will appear on the topic. Exactly why it failed would require careful analysis.

The three cases discussed in this chapter also led to widespread media attention in their own constituencies; none is exactly like the Dome, although one, about a theme park, is similar. It too was built with capital investment, supported by a feasibility study prepared by a firm of well-known business consultants who professed expertise in tourism—but a feasibility study that was seriously faulty. Planning is no guarantee of success.

In the business world, and in professional and academic writings on business, failures do not gain widespread interest. In fact, the topic is generally avoided. There are very few articles in the research literature on tourism about failures, despite widespread acknowledgment of the fact that tourism industries have a relatively high incidence of failure among their component businesses (McGibbon & Leiper 2001). Before presenting the three cases, an explanation is suggested for the lack of interest in learning about failures in business and in tourism.

MANY PEOPLE AVOID THINKING ABOUT FAILURES

The sight, mention or thought of failure in any kind of activity seems to make many people uncomfortable. Possibly this is because they are subconsciously afraid that failure is infectious, and that if they look too closely they might become infected themselves.

Another possible explanation is that the sight, mention or thought of failure can remind us of our own deficiencies, and the fact that none of us is perfect and all of us fail in some of the things we attempt. Because of these reminders, our human inclination is to avoid focusing attention on failures. When we do, they are usually being presented as objects of fun—something to laugh at. Clowns in a circus get most of their laughs by falling over, by tripping over buckets and ladders, by failing spectacularly at simple routines.

The best-known case of enterprise failure in tourism and hospitality was probably depicted in the TV comedy series *Fawlty Towers*, where the central characters are the earnest and sincere but hopelessly incompetent Basil, the proprietor, and Manuel, the earnest, sincere but equally incompetent waiter. Each is a failure in his own way. Fawlty Towers, the hotel depicted in the series, along with Basil and Manuel, have become comic symbols for everything a resort hotel and its staff should not be. The series was based on the experiences of its writers, John Cleese and Connie Booth, at the Gleneagles Hotel in Torquay in England in the 1970s. Its proprietor, Donald Sinclair, was extremely displeased at being the model for the character of Basil, but presumably deserved it.

In sharp contrast to their general lack of interest in taking failure seriously, many people respond enthusiastically to success stories occurring in virtually any field of activity. Individuals who are notably successful in any sport, entertainment, recreational or cultural activity, politics or business very often become well known because of that success. If they are very successful beyond their local region, they may eventually become celebrities, persons who are famous merely for being famous, for being who they are, for their name, regardless of the original reason.

Explaining the popularity of successful role models involves the opposite reasons noted above for explaining the unpopularity of failures. Looking at or reading about a success story makes many people feel good, partly because there is a mystical sense that the success might 'rub off'. It is also because any success can remind even the least accomplished people that they too have potential for some sort of success. In many instances this is comforting and distracting, so a couch potato watching a TV screen where athletes are racing for a world championship might feel good because the images create the notion that he too might—just might—one day get off the couch, give up the pizzas and be a success in the local sports club.

Why professionals study failures

In many fields of academic research and professional practice, the attitude to success and failure is the opposite of that in popular, everyday existence. Many researchers in academia and the professions take great interest in failures. They study failures carefully, and are not so interested in success. A number of examples help explain why this is so.

Consider a field of human activity in which academic research and professional practice are very closely linked: medicine. Medical researchers and practitioners seldom show much interest in healthy humans but take great interest in sick, diseased and malformed humans. When a person dies after a long and generally healthy life, the cause of the death is not a topic of concern: they died of old age, of inevitable degeneration.

But when somebody dies before old age, or becomes very ill, they become a case for autopsy (a postmortem examination to discover the cause of death) or for pathology (the study of disease, an examination of a sample from their body to discover what disease is causing the illness). Case research based on pathology and autopsy has been a major contributor to the huge increase in knowledge of medical matters that has occurred over recent centuries—especially the 20th century, when methodologies and techniques for pathology developed rapidly (Porter 1999).

Why do medical researchers study death and disease? In order to discover the causes, so that practitioners can take steps to prevent or reduce their incidence in future. Much of what is now known about medical practice for curing people of illness and disease, aimed at keeping them healthy and prolonging life, has come from studying failures.

Consider civil engineering. In the past 100 years few bridges have fallen down; in the 19th century, however, when railways were being built, many bridges collapsed, in many instances with large numbers of fatalities. A number of engineers began studying the causes. Their research led to changes in the way bridges and other large buildings were designed and contructed. Petroski (1992a, 1992b, 1994) is the principal historian of research by engineers into failure. In university courses in which civil engineers are educated and trained, the failure of structures is an important theme.

Consider warfare, battles and related military issues. In the study of warfare, a central theme has been investigating why wars and battles were lost (Adkin 1996; David 1997; Durschmied 1999). David's research, focusing on 30 battles during the past 2500 years, identified five broad causes of failure. In military academies, where officers are educated and trained, this theme is always prominent.

Consider space exploration. In 1986 the American 'Challenger' space shuttle exploded soon after take-off, killing the seven astronauts. An official inquiry found the cause only because one researcher was fiercely independent, capable of thinking objectively and prepared to reveal the real cause, which other committee members wanted to hide (Feynman 1999).

Consider land exploration. Glen McLaren's (1996) history of the early European explorers of Australia showed that in the first 50 years of European settlement, 1788–1838, most explorers not only made many mistakes, leading to failed expeditions, but failed to learn from their own experiences and the experiences of others who had failed in attempts to explore the Australian continent. In the 1840s, Ludwig Leichhardt brought a different attitude to the field. Leichhardt studied the failed expeditions of the past and learned what to do differently, in effect what to avoid in terms of equipment, supplies, organisation and strategy. He then made a number of successful expeditions (and finally, just one failure: he became lost, died somewhere, and his body was never found). More importantly (for us at least), his successful methods, derived from studying failures, became a model for the next generation of explorers, who succeeded in opening up the Australian continent to new settlers.

Other examples from various fields of human endeavour could be cited, but the point has been made. In professional work, an understanding of the causes of failure is highly useful, and in professional-level education and training pathological approaches to the subjects, whether these are human bodies or railway bridges, is an integral theme.

The point of focusing on failures is to learn how to survive and succeed, but this idea does not have many followers among academics involved with business, management and tourism. Only a handful of studies can be found in the literature (e.g. Argenti 1976; Peacock 1984; Boer 1992; English et al. 1996). In contrast, there is an almost over-whelming focus on success stories.

Fred Hilmer, former dean of the Graduate School of Management at the University of New South Wales, is now CEO at Fairfax, one of Australia's large media companies. In one of his books on business and management, Hilmer writes 'I have concentrated on success stories because I am sure we can learn more from successes than from failures' (Hilmer 1985: xi). One wonders how he could be so sure of an opinion that contradicts a principle well recognised in many fields of learning. He offers no supporting argument or evidence for his opinion, but goes on to remark that 'a mindset shapes the way a person feels, interprets communications and acts' (1985: 2).

Hilmer's belief in studying success is not uncommon in the circles in which he moves. It is seen as a common theme of stories in the business pages of newspapers and in text-books on management. The usual patterns are to attribute failures to bad management (without really explaining how bad management led the failure) or, in textbooks, to show how good management was able to overcome a challenging situation that threatened to lead to failure.

Why do these common patterns occur? Perhaps they reflect some sort of ideology (a set of beliefs that obscure the truth) in managerial circles. A 'mindset' is often ideo-logically based, as the term implies. A set mind is not a mind open to ideas. Regardless, there is little doubt that there is something odd about the shortfall. Many fields of professional knowledge have depended heavily on studying failures, but in business, management and tourism the theme is uncommon.

All books written for academic readers—students, researchers, teachers—should attempt to present some uncommon ideas for their field, ideas drawn from other fields, and this chapter is one such attempt.

THREE CASES: OVERVIEW

Three cases were selected for inclusion here, on several grounds. Each is about a busi-ness organisation involved directly with tourists, but each represents a different sector of tourism industries and a different kind of failure. One case is about a failed management scheme in a large resort hotel. Another is about an airline that failed as a business and was liquidated. The third is about a theme park that failed as an investment and was sold at a fraction of its capital cost.

Le Lagon Pan Pacific Resort is a case involving a scheme devised by the Japanese general manager of a large resort in Vanuatu in 1994, intended nominally to improve and sustain service standards. It failed spectacularly. Ansett Airlines is a case involving the failure and collapse, in 2001, of one of Australia's largest airlines, leading to enormous losses of national significance. The Big Banana was a successful roadside attraction that was developed into a theme park in 1989 and failed within six months, leading to losses of $30 million. The causes of the failures in the first case were obvious to many observers. In the second and third cases the causes were quite complex, not apparent from quick and superficial observations. Moreover, in the Ansett case, the main cause identified in the discussion to follow will probably clash with the preconceived opinions of some readers.

LE LAGON RESORT

▬▬➤

For 30 years Le Lagon, located near Port Vila in Vanuatu, has been one of the best-known resorts in the islands of the southwest Pacific. Originally French, it was owned and managed by Japanese during the period of this case study, 1993–95. The case involves an unusual staffing strategy devised by the general manager, Takahiro Iio, who introduced a scheme that changed the way Le Lagon operated by dramatically altering the roles of its employees.

Superficially a resort hotel with 108 accommodation units, Le Lagon was changed to operate as eight small hotels, arranged in clusters around shared resort facilities used for all eight, such as front desk, swimming pool and restaurants. The eight clusters were operated by independent teams of workers, without supervision from the general manager's office or line managers.

What was introduced might be described as 'managing without managers'. The scheme applied a combination of three prescriptive theories: (a) that breaking up big organisations into small teams will improve productivity and quality; (b) that empowering workers, giving them the right to make decisions on matters that might otherwise require managerial authority, will also improve productivity and quality; (c) that improving service quality requires innovation, especially in the way service employees are managed. On the evidence available, the scheme failed—badly.

Le Lagon's business, markets and industries

Although Le Lagon's public areas, such as the resort's grounds, pool and golf course, were comparable to five-star standard, at the time of this study most of the accommodation units could be graded three-star. The physical setting is beautiful: tropical gardens with palms, bougainvillaea and other species, and idyllic water views. The resort had two restaurants, three bars, a large swimming pool, a private beach, and a shopping arcade (see Figure 15.1).

Guests' activities include all those found in most large resorts in the tropics. There are free watersports facilities, such as catamarans and what the brochures describe as 'surf skis' (but there is no surf), a golf course, tennis courts, and bicycles. Typical guests seem

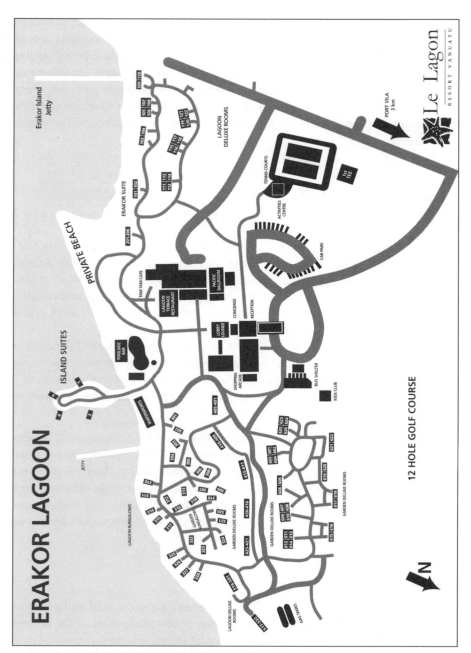

Source: Reproduced with the kind permission of Le Lagon Resort, Vanuatu.

to spend most of their time in passive relaxation—lying around the pool, in their rooms or on the beach, or sightseeing in Port Vila, often rated the most pleasant town in the Pacific islands.

As with all sunlust resorts, where the process is recreational tourism and the products

are tourists who, by the end of their visit, are rested, relaxed and entertained (i.e. recre- **351**
ated), Le Lagon's main markets are not far away on the other side of the world but close
at hand, in the large traveller-generating regions of Brisbane, Sydney, Auckland and
Melbourne. Few tourists from Europe or the USA visit Le Lagon. Australians and
New Zealanders on holidays represented more than 70% of Le Lagon's trade. Japanese,
New Caledonians and residents of other nearby countries also visited on holiday,
accounting for another 15% or so. The remaining 15% were holidaying tourists from
distant countries, business travellers from around the world on brief recreational
stopovers, and conference delegates. At the time of this study, most conferences at
Le Lagon were meetings of Vanuatu governmental and public service personnel.

More than 90% of guest nights were on packages (inclusive tours), so Le Lagon was
highly dependent on outbound tour operator-wholesalers in Australia in particular.
Major suppliers were Connection Holidays and Swingaway in Australia, Aspac and
Passport in Auckland and JAL and Kintetsu in Tokyo. In all, there were 12 tour
operator-wholesalers supplying Le Lagon from Australia, four in New Zealand and
12 in Japan.

Packages that typical guests purchased pre-trip for holidays at Le Lagon included air
transport, seven nights' accommodation, and transfers between Port Vila airport and the
resort. Prices per person in 1994 on a popular brand, Swingaway, using a twin-share
room, were $A1028 ex-Brisbane, $1118 ex-Sydney, and $1239 ex-Melbourne.

Organisational structures before 1994

From the 1960s to the early 90s, Le Lagon's organisational structure was typical for resort
hotels of comparable size. Total employees numbered 170, of whom 25 were managers.
The managers' positions were structured in a hierarchy, with a general manager and an
assistant at the apex. Other senior managers included a food and beverage manager,
rooms manager, front office manager, chief accountant, chief engineer, guests services
manager, and executive housekeeper. The remaining 18 managers occupied supervisory
levels. The 145 non-managerial workers were arranged in functional groups such as
housemaids, cleaners, gardeners, grounds staff, pool attendants, chefs, cooks, kitchen
hands, waiters, bar attendants, receptionists and clerks. This structure could be described
graphically with a conventional organisational chart. An example is in the Novotel Opal
Cove case in Chapter 9.

Staff training for the new scheme began in November 1993. Implementation began in
early 1994. The scheme was called PHAD, an acronym for 'Perfect Hospitality from
Arrival to Departure'. By October, 60% of employees were participating, and the aim
was to quickly achieve 100%.

PHAD and the 7S framework

PHAD was a multidimensional change in the human organisation at Le Lagon.
Although not based consciously on this particular theory, the issues in PHAD can be
described against the backdrop of a theory set out by Waterman et al. (1980, 1991),

known as the 7S framework. PHAD affected Le Lagon's strategies, structures, staffing, style, skills, systems, and superordinate goals. The 7S framework is a theoretical system that proposes that effective organisational change requires changes in those seven elements of organisations. Attending to only some elements might prove ineffective.

Believing that high standards of personalised service can give a hotel a strategic advantage over other hotels, Mr Iio saw PHAD's primary objective as the acronym indicated, 'perfect hospitality from arrival to departure'. The competitors of Le Lagon were (and are) in Vanuatu, Bali, Fiji, New Caledonia, Hawaii and, most prevalent, along Australia's east coast. To raise service standards, PHAD was a scheme wherein the 145 operational employees at Le Lagon were given the responsibility, the authority, the freedom, the incentive and the team support to manage their own work.

Takahiro Iio said, in an interview in October 1994, 'I am empowering all staff to make decisions on any matter about service to guests. That is the key. They do not have to check with me or anyone else' (pers. comm.). Under the new policy, if a guest experienced less than desirable service, the staff member directly involved could decide that the appropriate action was a refund of money. Often they could fix the problem in other ways.

Structural changes could be seen in four ways. Le Lagon's 108 accommodation units were divided into eight clusters, each comprising about 13 neighbouring units. Each section was allocated a team of 12 workers. Workers were given badges to wear, showing that they were PHAD members, and displaying their section (team) colour.

Supervisory and most middle-manager positions at Le Lagon were gradually abolished. In 1993 there were 25 managers; by late 1994 only 10.

Team members in the eight clusters were expected to spend some of their time working in their own accommodation section, and other time working in common facilities such as the front desk, restaurants, bars, water sports and so on. Each team was given authority to arrange how this was done.

Staffing under PHAD meant that each team member was involved in all services provided to guests at Le Lagon. Mr Iio intended that when the system was fully implemented, within two years, there would be no division of labour. Workers would no longer be designated housemaids, cleaners, pool attendants, waiters, room service attendants or front office clerks. Workers would be PHAD team members, active in all those duties.

Style is manageable, according to Waterman et al. (1991: 312). In a resort hotel, guests perceive the style of the place partly in terms of how the employees behave and appear. In conventional resorts, employees are seen in specialised functions: housemaids, porters, managers. Le Lagon aimed for another distinct style. All workers were to perform generic functions, rather than specialist roles. Skills in the PHAD scheme required each employee to be multiskilled, competent and willing to do many different sorts of work. To achieve this, education and training would be vital processes, and would require more time and care than with conventional, narrowly focused skills training.

Systems in the 7S framework are the procedures, formal and informal, that make the whole operation function, minute by minute and month by month. Takahiro Iio's policy was to make systems as simple as possible. He said he detested formal MISs (management information systems) with their reports, memos, detailed statistics and routine meetings. He described this as 'management nightmare'. He said the alternative was to allow workers to get on with their work, unimpeded. They were to create their own procedures. If a team needed to hold a meeting, they did. If they decided to change methods, they could.

When guests arrived, immediately after being welcomed, PHAD principles were outlined to them. Members of the team present at the time introduced themselves and stated that the team would look after all the guest's services. Within two days, a guest would meet all 12 team members.

Superordinate goals are 'the fundamental ideas around which a (particular) business is built' (Waterman et al. 1991: 313). Listening to Takahiro Iio describe PHAD, there was little doubt that it was the superordinate goal at Le Lagon. Of course, the resort's owner in Tokyo may have had a different goal, and Pan Pacific Hotels might have had a different goal again, but these were corporate and marketing issues, separate from the management of the resort.

The origins of PHAD ➤

Learning about Mr Iio's innovation, anyone might attribute PHAD to his Japanese background and/or his study of management. PHAD represents the application of three ideas in combination: small teams, empowerment, service quality. These ideas have been widely discussed in academic and professional writings (Reich 1987; Berry et al. 1990, 1992; Carr 1992; Lovelock & Wright 1999; Lockwood 2000).

Each idea has been applied in many organisations with varying success, in many kinds of industry. Hyatt Hotels and Resorts had an empowerment program a decade ago (Brymer 1991). In Australia, Ballantyne (1994) found that many large-scale hotels and resorts were using worker empowerment to some degree. Service quality is a prominent issue for managers in hospitality and tourism industries (McCabe & Weeks 1999).

Mr Iio said he did not find the ideas for PHAD in the literature and did not copy anything in Japan. He found the idea in the USA. Travelling there and staying in family-operated bed-and-breakfasts (B&Bs), he noticed the warm hospitality and high standards of service, and noticed how each person was competent and willing when performing any task. Appointed general manager to Le Lagon, he saw the opportunity to adapt certain principles of small-scale B&Bs to a large resort. He said he was able to introduce such a scheme because he is not merely general manager at the resort but a director of the company that owns it.

The Honda effect ➤

Japanese management in general has a reputation for clever strategies, a talent supposedly stemming from Japanese cultural traditions. One of the famous success stories that gave rise to this reputation was Honda's rapid capture of large shares in motorcycle markets internationally, a move that led to the closure of several European and American manufacturers of motorcycles.

The Boston Consulting Group reported, in a study commissioned by a British government worried that more industries might collapse from Japanese competition, that Honda's success was another example of strategic planning based on Japanese culture (BCC 1975, cited in Pascal 1984/1991). Research at Harvard University came to the same conclusion (Purkayastha 1981). Pascal had doubts. He interviewed the six Japanese executives who, a decade earlier, had managed Honda's entry into the USA. He found that they had no strategic plan, no structured approach to managing, and had made many mistakes as they tried to learn from Americans about the motorcycle market. Success came after several failures, hard work, innovative thinking, experimentation and a little luck.

PHAD is an example of what Pascal termed a 'Honda effect'. It is the illusory effect in outside observers' minds that clever innovations by Japanese managers reflect Japanese culture and are mysteries not easily understood by foreigners. Several managers of European ethnicity based in Vanuatu described the PHAD scheme as an example of Japanese-style management, never guessing that it had been copied from America.

Evidence of PHAD's success? ➤

Mr Iio said that the scheme was very successful. He produced, as support for his opinion, a monthly survey of guests, summarised in a report headed 'PHAD Ratings'. These were, he said, higher than in any other hotel in the Pacific-Asia region. With the ratings were verbal comment, written by guests, published on one page of a newsletter (*Tok Tok Journal*) for guests and staff. The page contained quoted comments from approximately 40 guests. Typical comments (names omitted) were:

People are very friendly and helpful. I didn't want to go home . . . Nelson, NZ

Have visited many countries and found Vanuatu to be the best. We were thoroughly impressed and very satisfied . . . Koshiga City, Japan

What a happy, happy, ambience. Just stay as good as you are . . . Waverley, NSW, Australia

Nothing is too much trouble. Stayed at many hotels, the staff here are simply the best . . . Elanora Heights, NSW, Australia

In late 1994 contrary evidence existed, which indicated that PHAD was not as successful as the general manager claimed and might, instead, be a failure. Two middle-level managers in two other resorts in Vanuatu scathingly dismissed PHAD as 'a gimmick'. Both used the same expression. (Neither used the obvious pun, 'a fad'.) Both said it was causing serious problems among staff at Le Lagon and was leading to deteriorating standards of service.

In the research literature, suspicions of the true worth and intent in schemes to empower workers were widespread in the early 1990s. Editors of the journal *Training and Development* felt the need to conduct a survey (1992, Vol. 47: 1) headed 'Is empowerment a sham?' to seek readers' opinions.

However, every new method that changes working arrangements is controversial. Opposition broadly comes from two sources. First, workers tend to be uncomfortable if asked to change the way they work, especially when the type, scale and permanence of impacts on them personally are not known with any certainty. Second, supervisors and other managers tend to become uncomfortable if asked to try a new theory of management, for the same reasons. Research into Taylor's famous innovations in management theory and practice 100 years ago (see Chapter 8) shows this clearly (Merkle 1980: 27, 32):

> *Neither workers nor management were pleased with the Taylor system . . . At every stage of the system's development, Taylor met bitter opposition . . . Although Taylor characterised management resisters as narrow-minded old capitalists, the truth was that Taylorism took control from old-style management just as surely it had from labor.*

A second set of evidence questioning the worth of PHAD came from casual conversations on a flight from Port Vila to Brisbane in October 1994. Ten tourists who had stayed at Le Lagon were asked their opinions. Eight were critical. None criticised the attitude displayed by staff—described as friendly, hospitable and service-oriented. However, all eight critics made similar remarks on other matters. These concerned aspects of the performance of staff—such as rooms not properly cleaned, the run-down nature of the place, unsatisfactory laundering of sheets and towels.

How can those negative comments be true, contrasting against high ratings in the official survey? One possibility is that the critical tourists were a quirky sample, representing some of the 1% who had offered negative comments in the official survey. This is highly improbable. A second possibility is that guests tend to hold back negative comments while in a resort, when filling in questionnaires, but are more likely to express true feelings in conversations with other tourists after leaving the place, on their way home, which is when the 10 casual conversations occurred. A third possibility is that the research method behind Mr Iio's survey was flawed as the data came from an unrepresentative sample of guests, so did not accurately portray opinions of the total population of guests at Le Lagon. Surveys using questionnaires filled in by self-selecting respondents are unlikely to give representative results (Emory & Cooper 1991: 243).

Implications of the change to PHAD

PHAD was risky. It departed from widely held prescriptive theory for empowerment programs. Brymer's (1991) discussion of empowerment in American hotels emphasises that middle managers have important functions under empowerment schemes, even though their work changes. Indeed, Brymer described middle managers in empowerment programs as 'the key to success' (1991: p 60). Carr (1992) also emphasised important new roles for middle managers. Under empowerment programs their roles as supervisors of workers diminish, but they adopt the roles of leader, teacher, coach and mentor. The risk at Le Lagon is that middle managers were not used in those ways; they were encouraged to resign and were not replaced.

Of the middle managers at Le Lagon in 1993, more than half, 15 out of 25, had left by late 1994 and had not been replaced. Indications were that more would be going. All of the middle managers were expatriates from Britain, Australia and New Zealand, who saw themselves as separate from the indigenous workers in all respects.

Mr Iio said he had decided to break down these barriers. One example was his decision to remove the perquisite, formerly enjoyed by all the managers, of dining freely in Le Lagon's restaurants. His decree was that the restaurants were for guests, not staff, and that managers might eat freely in the employees' canteen. He said that this helped build teamwork. Mr Iio said that he personally ate regularly in the employees' canteen. He said that this new policy had particularly upset middle-level managers, who had then resigned.

The success or otherwise of a scheme like PHAD cannot be assessed accurately until it has been operating for a long time, as 'it takes months and even years to produce successful self-managing teams' (Carr 1992: 46). Objective research, on several aspects of the scheme, would be required to test its true viability. Gossip from managers in nearby resorts and opinions collected from ad hoc interviews with 10 tourists do not amount to reliable data.

Happy Christmas in Vanuatu, but not at Le Lagon

Before Christmas 1994 there were rumours that the Japanese were negotiating to sell Le Lagon. Increasing numbers of staff began staying away from work. Over Christmas, a peak season, guests found that nobody was in the kitchens or restaurants to prepare and serve meals, and few workers were in the rooms or grounds. A deputation of angry guests marched on the resort's administration centre.

In January 1995 an announcement was made to the Port Vila media that the resort was being sold and the Japanese were pulling out. The buyers included a consortium of Ni-Vanuatu business leaders and a local community trust. Southern Pacific Hotel Corporation was taking over the management, and proposed upgrading the resort to meet the standards of its Park Royal brand.

A rumour circulated in Port Vila in early 1995 that the PHAD scheme had been a ploy to impress the Vanuatu government. The rumoured aim related to taxation. The alleged ploy was that because Le Lagon had made special efforts to give its Ni-Vanuatu workers special advantages, the Japanese owners of Le Lagon deserved special treatment from the government. The aim, according to the rumour, was to have a tax levy, normally imposed on the seller of a business, rescinded in this case. Perhaps the rumour is true, but false rumours abound in competitive business circles, and foreign companies are often targets.

CONCLUSION

Irrespective of that rumour, PHAD was a flop. It failed because it was poorly designed and badly managed. Empowerment schemes using teams to improve and sustain high standards of service work can succeed, but are likely to fail if they use the approach and methods devised at Le Lagon. The major error was in removing middle management, leaving 145 employees to fend for themselves.

The case also serves as a lesson in skepticism regarding reports prepared for an organisation regarding its activities. The PHAD ratings, with their positive statistics, might have given warm inner feelings to the general manager and his associates, but they were obviously based on a biased survey. Anyone with training in research methods should have questioned their validity.

In early 1995, a member of the group of managers at Southern Pacific Hotel Corporation in Sydney was asked whether they, the new managers of Le Lagon, intended keeping the PHAD scheme. The reply was succinct. The scheme was finished. The new owners had no thoughts of reviving it. Middle-management positions would be reinstated, following the normal practice in large resorts.

ANSETT AIRLINES: AVOIDABLE FAILURE

After 66 years, one of Australia's two largest domestic airlines ceased operations in September 2001. What happened, why it happened, and what could be done to prevent a similar collapse of a major Australian airline in the future, are the themes of this case history.

The airline ceased operating, passengers with tickets lost their rights to be carried, members of the frequent-flyer program lost the accumulated value in their points, employees lost their jobs, the company was liquidated and wound up, the assets were sold to pay creditors (who will lose most of their debts owing from Ansett), and the owner lost most of the investment. Secondary effects of the collapse—affecting many people, businesses and tourist regions—were even greater.

Hundreds of reports in the mass media have laid the blame for Ansett's failure with management. There is no doubt that bad management and bad corporate governance by the directors were factors, but the underlying cause of the failure was something else. It was the excessively competitive market, a condition brought about as a deliberate policy of the Australian government. Operating in that condition, a team of world-class managers would not have saved one or the other of the two major airlines from serious problems.

Ansett's collapse and the immediate reaction

Rumours of problems in Ansett Airlines circulated around Australia's business communities in late 2000 and into 2001. In the first week of September serious financial problems were revealed (Gilchrist & Niesche 2001). On 12 September Ansett was placed in the control of an independent administrator to deal with debts of $A3 billion and operating losses of $A8 million per week, and on the following day all operations ceased (Creedy et al. 2001). The same week, on 11 September, attacks with hijacked aircraft destroyed New York's World Trade Center and a section of Washington's

Pentagon. Ansett's problems were not associated with those events.

Throughout history, terrifying or highly disturbing events with no definitely known cause usually trigger a search for a culprit or, if none is known with certainty, a scapegoat to quickly hold up to blame. That was the reaction to the events in the USA, and in the following weeks signs emerged to support the first suspicions. After Ansett's failure, suspects of a different sort were immediately identified by the media, by protesters at airport rallies attended by thousands of unemployed Ansett workers, and by members of the Australian government. The fault was placed with the directors and top managers in Air New Zealand, Ansett's parent company since 1999. As with many company collapses, the problem emerged as a financial crisis, but this was only the superficial sign of other, non-financial problems.

A short history of Ansett Airlines

Under a governmental regime known as the two-airline policy, from the 1950s to the 90s, Ansett Airlines shared a regulated duopoly on domestic trunk routes around the country with TAA, a publicly owned airline established in 1948 by the federal government. Ansett and TAA also operated on many provincial routes to outlying cities and towns. Ansett and TAA each maintained, under the policy, approximately 50% of the national market for domestic air travel.

Gordon Mills, a professor of economics at the University of Sydney, summarised what happened in Australia as a result (see also Table 15.1), in a quasi free market (Mills 2001: 5):

> The airlines (Ansett and TAA) were left to regulate the market using their own market power. They easily saw off Compass I and II (a new airline that lasted only months in its two entries to the market). And for a decade consumers have paid some of the highest airfares of any moderately competitive advanced country . . . The two airlines gained a false sense of security from their ability to engage in predatory pricing—on the rare occasions when an entrant raised its head. So they had insufficient incentive to reduce staffing levels and other inflated costs. For Ansett, the outcome has been disastrous.

In the USA in 1978 the domestic airline industry was partly deregulated, leading to intense competition with price discounting and new entrants. In Australia, as often happens, an old US model, built in 1978, was seen by some persons as worth adopting. This happened in the 1980s after Ansett changed hands, becoming a 50/50 share partnership of Rupert Murdoch's News Corporation and TNT, another wealthy Australian-based multinational, chaired by Peter Abeles, with its origins and main activities in freight trucks.

Abeles successfully pushed his friend Bob Hawke, the Australian Prime Minister, to deregulate the domestic airline industry, claiming that more competition would benefit everybody but probably believing that Ansett would benefit most. The Prime Minister could not do this merely on the basis of his friend's advice, so a committee of inquiry was appointed, the Independent Review of Economic Regulation of Domestic Aviation

TABLE 15.1 Domestic airlines in Australia: a 14-year history

Year	Pass trips (m)	Change	Conditions, events
1988	17	+8%	Ansett and Qantas active: market growth
1989	13	−25%	Early growth, then pilots' strike
1990	15	+20%	Strike ends, Compass enters industry
1991	20	+26%	Growth, Compass fails
1992	21	+5%	Slower growth, Compass II enters, fails
1993	22	+7%	Growth
1994	25	+12%	Growth
1995	27	+7%	Growth
1996	28	+5%	Growth
1997	28	+1%	Small growth; extensive discounting
1998	28	—	Stagnant
1999	29	+3%	Marginal growth
2000	31	+7%	More growth, Virgin and Impulse enter
2001	32	+1%	Impulse fails, market slows, Ansett fails; market turbulence after 11 September

(IRERDA). A large research project was commissioned to provide background information, involving 20 000 interviews with passengers at 52 airports and dozens of interviews with airline and travel industry executives.

The project produced a detailed report for IRERDA (AGB McNair/Leiper 1986), which stated, among other things, that the airlines were widely viewed as providing satisfactory services, but lower fares would lead to increased demand for air travel. IRERDA decided that the best strategy was to add more airlines, in the belief that this would result in greater competitiveness and lower fares. The government took the same view. The report for IRERDA has not suggested this strategy.

Ansett had approximately half the market, with Qantas now holding the other half since taking over TAA. In 1996 Ansett's ownership changed again. TNT sold its 50% share to Air NZ for $A325 million. In 2000 News Corporation sold its 50% to the same buyer for $A580 million, so Ansett was now a subsidiary of Air NZ which, having invested an additional $A150 million, had a capital investment in Ansett of $A1055 million (Westfield 2001).

Under the government's policy of promoting more competition by encouraging new airlines, Impulse Airlines and Virgin Blue Airlines began operating on Australia's busiest routes, centred on Sydney. Impulse lasted only months before voluntarily closing, after consuming too much capital and failing to become profitable.

Ansett's subsidiaries in 2001 included several small-scale airlines active on rural and provincial routes around Australia. These included Hazelton, Kendell, AeroPelican and Skywest. Another subsidiary was Traveland, a chain of 104 travel agencies with 750 employees (Petty & Towers 2001). The Ansett group had 147 aircraft, mostly small models used on rural and provincial routes but including more than 30 large aircraft, such as 20 Airbuses (A320-200) and 11 Boeings (747s, 767s and 737s), on the inter-city trunk routes and internationally (Goodsir & Doherty 2001).

Almost all the larger aircraft were leased, adding to the periodical costs of operations but adding nothing to the value of Ansett's assets. Ansett also owned terminals in airports, notably a large terminal at Sydney opened in 2000, representing a capital investment of $A160 million.

Consequences of Ansett's collapse

Airport records show the number of aircraft taking off and landing; by comparing the four days before and after 12 September, a substantial downturn becomes apparent. The decreases were 32% at Sydney, 35% at Melbourne and 30% at Brisbane (Mega-logenis 2001). On that and following days 50 000 persons with Ansett tickets were carried free by Qantas, using aircraft rushed in from abroad to help with the national emergency caused by Ansett's collapse. The downturn in global aviation following the 11 September tragedy in the USA meant that aircraft normally used on international routes were sitting idle.

Employees of Ansett and its subsidiaries, approximately 16 000 persons, were out of work. Because the failure of Ansett had not been expected and because they faced losing not merely jobs and incomes but legal entitlements to holiday and long-service payments (for many individuals, tens of thousands of dollars), these people were hurt and angry. Protest rallies were held throughout September at Sydney, Melbourne, Brisbane and Adelaide airports.

The drama of unemployed Ansett workers was prolonged, helping the story to remain a media news item, by uncertainty about a possible revival of Ansett's operations. The official administrator (initially PricewaterhouseCoopers, replaced a week later by Andersons) negotiated with other airlines and outside investors on possible deals to lease the Airbus fleet for use on the now underserviced routes, especially Sydney–Melbourne and Sydney–Brisbane.

Negotiations were unsuccessful, but on September 29 a small number of Ansett flights recommenced on the Sydney–Melbourne route as a venture by the administrator. Approximately 1000 employees were rehired, but there seemed little likelihood of the revival becoming more than a skeleton operation (Boyle & Field 2001). Within months, the revival failed and Ansett Airlines ceased altogether.

Because the Ansett group had carried almost half of all air travellers within Australia and because it was the sole airline servicing several towns, the direct effect on the country was severe and widespread. Provincial cities far away from metropolitan capitals were left with no air service, as Ansett had monopolies on certain routes (Megalogenis 2001).

Ansett had been a sponsor of many sporting teams, which helped sustain nationwide competitions in various codes of football as well as basketball, netball, swimming and cricket. Without Ansett, and with Qantas' flights heavily booked, the viability of several sporting competitions involving teams that lack large incomes from TV networks was looking dubious. Similar problems meant that a number of performing drama, dance and arts companies were obliged to cancel tours.

Tourism in Australia has always been impeded to some extent by the high costs in time and money of reaching scattered parts of a large country. While the major tourist destination regions are Sydney and Melbourne, several distant places normally reached by domestic air are important in the country's tourism systems.

Moreover, many towns scattered around the country are not important to the national tourism economy but are themselves highly dependent on tourism for their own economic vitality. Ansett's demise was a serious problem for tourism in Australia, especially when international long-haul tourism was heading for a large downturn because of the effects on mass psychology of the 11 September tragedy. In late September, businesses in Australian tourism industries were reporting that between 20% and 30% of bookings placed by overseas agents for the coming season had been cancelled (Sandilands 2001c).

Star Alliance was a factor compounding the problems, because it has been integral to a crucial strategy for Ansett's important role in inbound tourism. The Alliance is a cooperative network of 14 airlines, the largest such network in global aviation. (Qantas is a member of a smaller cooperative network, One World.) Passengers gain discounts and can 'earn and burn' their frequent-flyer points by keeping to either Alliance airlines or One World airlines, and many international visitors have been induced to come to Australia, and travel by air within Australia, as a result. About 32% of international visitors, or 1.5 million annually, flew into Australia with a Star Alliance airline in 2000, and a proportion of them used Ansett while in Australia (Sandilands 2001c). Without Ansett flying to provincial destinations away from the capital cities, a proportion of that inflow was lost to Australian tourism.

Another effect of Ansett's failure was on retailers in airport terminals. This disaster was greatest at Sydney, where dozens of retailers were locked out, unable to enter their business premises, when the terminal was closed and the doors locked (Harley 2001).

Blame somebody . . . blame management

Another consequence of Ansett's collapse was a search for somebody to blame. Most reports in the media, along with ministers in the Australian government, blamed management at Air New Zealand (Bartholomeusz 2001; Koutsoukis 2001a; Koutsoukis et al. 2001; Lecky 2001; McCrann 2001a; Sexton & Crichton 2001; Westfield 2001). Ample evidence supports the opinion that Ansett had been badly managed in some respects at various times over the years, certainly during the latter part of Reg Ansett's chairmanship in the 1970s, certainly when Peter Abeles was in charge in the 1980s, and certainly in some respects since 2000 under Air NZ.

As a predominantly domestic airline, Ansett should have been relatively easy to manage, as it largely avoided the complexities that bedevil managers of international aviation (Doganis 1987). However, sheltered to some extent from either competition or strong government regulation, Ansett's managers and directors had been lax and deficient on many occasions since the 1960s.

Reg Ansett's greatest fault as chairman in the 1960s and 70s was probably his failure to plan for the fact that most of his top executives were around the same age and would retire together. Nothing was done to properly train a cohort of young managers to succeed them. This led to an interval of weak management, followed inevitably by an interval of poor corporate performance, which enabled the TNT–News Corporation partnership, formed for the purpose, to buy the airline (and its governmental subsidies) at a bargain price.

The subsidies were a real prize. The government guaranteed Ansett's borrowings, enabling low-interest loans. There are rumours that the TNT–News Corporation partnership's main interest in buying Ansett was to get this privilege and use the cheap capital for its broader business ventures.

During September 2001 many commentators in the media (examples noted above) referred to aspects of bad management at Ansett since the 1980s. Bad decisions regarding capital expenditure were made by Peter Abeles, who foolishly assembled a fleet of aircraft comprising different models and brands. The effects were high maintenance costs and inflexible fleet deployment, becoming worse over time as the aircraft aged.

Ansett Airlines employed far too many people in relation to its activities, thus incurring diseconomies of scale and imposing excessive problems of proliferating variety on managers. There was also a widely acknowledged fact that since the early 1990s Ansett had been undercapitalised, needing huge amounts of new investment capital to upgrade its ageing fleet of aircraft.

Under Air NZ, the management of Ansett has been portrayed as especially deficient; see the headings of the articles by Koutsoukis et al. (2001) and Lecky (2001). Air NZ's first and major mistake with Ansett was made when its board of directors paid far too much when it purchased Ansett. Instead of paying what the company was worth, it offered News Corporation a premium, presumably because of a strong and irrational desire to acquire the second 50% of the company. Once this was done, Air NZ directors were inclined to regard Ansett as owing Air NZ as much as could possibly be recouped on the investment. Air NZ controlled Ansett's finances and other assets, with cash management and similar functions centralised in the NZ head office (Long 2001). This encouraged Air NZ managers to regard Ansett in Australia as merely a branch operation, to support head office if problems developed at home. That is what happened.

Air NZ itself was in deep and worsening trouble, with its shares twice suspended from trading on the stock exchange after falling drastically in value. Predictions in September 2001 were that Air NZ would be taken over by the NZ government to enable it to continue operations (Griggs 2001; Todd & Crichton 2001).

While the criticisms about deficient management have substance, certain facts seem to have been ignored by those who cite this as the principal cause of Ansett's failure. Ansett had been badly managed at various times throughout its history, which leads to the question, why did it go bust in 2001? Was the standard of management so much worse under Air NZ, or did accumulated effects of bad management over many years finally become unsustainable?

At other times, Ansett seems to have benefited from strong and effective management, according to various sets of information in annual reports, although results were mixed.

Ansett's CEO under Air NZ in 2001 was Gary Toomey, who formerly had been for three years a successful joint managing director at Qantas. Were his managerial methods and performance different in the two airlines? Also notable is the fact that in the late 1990s the CEO at Ansett was Rod Eddington, who seems to have been a successful manager, now CEO at British Airways and also a director of Qantas.

There is evidence that the Australian government could be blamed for not dealing with the problems faced by Ansett and Air NZ, problems that Prime Minister John Howard and his ministers knew about (Koutsoukis 2001b). Throwing the blame on Air NZ might have been a ploy by Howard to deflect public attention from his role in this episode of Ansett's story.

Singapore Airlines, which owned 25% of Air NZ, was willing to invest new capital to fix the problems at Ansett and Air NZ, but the idea was delayed and eventually thwarted by the Australian Prime Minister, despite the fact that his senior ministers advised him to go along with it.

Thus a reasonable conclusion is that management deficiencies, as well as dithering during 2001 by the Howard government, were the triggers of Ansett's collapse. The necessary condition for it to occur, however, was a deeper issue.

Calling for revived competition

While putting the blame on management, Prime Minister John Howard and many other commentators were also saying that Australia must resurrect 'a competitive airline industry'. Certain reporters in newspapers were in this category, supporting their opinion with quotes from politicians and business leaders (Koutsoukis 2001a; Kohler 2001; Sandilands 2001c). Emphatic calls for revived competition seemed to imply that the return of competition was more important than the return of the lost airline services, via references to 'the fundamental issue of restoring domestic airline competition' (quoted in Sandilands 2001c).

Fundamentalism of this sort seems misleading and detrimental, and the emphasis on competition for airlines is a clue to a deeper problem. Excessive competition is the underlying explanation of Ansett's demise, as the following analysis will explain.

Myth and reality about competition

If the talk about competition being the ultimate virtue for every industry was a true reflection of their values, members of the Australian government and the technocrats in the Australian Consumer and Competition Commission (ACCC) should have publicly celebrated Qantas' victory and Ansett's demise. This did not happen.

Of course, what should be valued most by everyone with proper common sense is not competitive markets but an effective industry, capable of providing adequate and appropriate services.

What is hidden behind the calls for competitiveness? And why is it always persons in powerful positions who favour competition everywhere? It might have something to do with the fact that the powerful, those in entrenched places in markets, those on the high sides of playing fields alongside their well-positioned associates in parliament, have a competitive advantage, and are pleased if competition continues while they continue to score points.

In Australia, it might also reflect a desire among dull careerists in many occupations (politics, academia, the media etc.) to imitate anything that is popular in the USA. Copycat behaviour is a way to avoid real thinking and, in this case, blurs the fact that American markets for many things, including airline services, are quite different from those in Australia. The USA's larger population, wider geographic dispersal of the population, and scattered locations of large cities with busy airports, in combination create conditions that suit a very different airline industry.

In any event, by the 1990s any objective observer could see that the deregulation policy in the USA had not worked in the long term. After its introduction in 1978, many new airlines were formed and fares dropped. By the late 1980s most of the newcomers had disappeared and fares were back to pre-deregulation levels on many routes.

In Australia, calls for revived competition in domestic airline services after Ansett's collapse often invoked the 'level playing field' model. As seen in Chapter 11 this is a misleading ideology, a belief system that is not based on reality but obscures it for a political purpose. A discussion in Chapter 11 shows that cooperative behaviour, not excessive competition, is what enables an industry to function.

Excessive competition is especially inappropriate for Australia's domestic airline industry because, as the Ansett case demonstrates, the demise of a major company leads to widespread national problems. Simple economics teaches us that without competitive markets, prices (air fares) will rise. Management can point to the obvious alternative: fares can be managed and kept low by an external regulator.

Ansett's collapse was caused by the competitive market in which Ansett operated in Australia, made hazardous for the two major airlines (Ansett and Qantas) by the recent addition of new airlines such as Impulse and Virgin, invited in by the government. The small-scale discount airlines were allowed to scavenge on trunk routes, eroding the income of the two majors so that one was unlikely to survive. In that context, Ansett's management and luck needed to be only marginally worse than Qantas' for it to be the one that failed.

Even if both airlines had been favoured by management practices of world-class standard, one would eventually have failed in those conditions. This is because marginal revenues for the two major airlines were being eaten away by the discounters on what should have been highly profitable trunk routes for the two majors, such as the Sydney–Melbourne, Sydney–Brisbane links. Large profits normally earned on those routes can be used to cross-subsidise less profitable or unprofitable routes.

The opinion that excessive competition was a major factor in Ansett's demise is not unique to this book: for Sykes (2001) and Mills (2001) advanced much the same argument. So did the CEO at Qantas, at least implicitly. Geoff Dixon, interviewed about the issue on TV news, said 'I do not believe there is room for two full-service airlines' (Channel 7, 29 September).

Warnings of Ansett's demise

The federal government was warned that Ansett was in trouble and that huge problems would follow if it collapsed. People in the airline industry knew that Ansett was struggling to remain viable. Reliable sources in Qantas have told me that James Strong, the former managing director of Qantas, conveyed warnings to the government on several occasions. Prime Minister John Howard has been quoted stating that his government was getting the opposite message. Rejecting suggestions that the government should assist Ansett to recover from seemingly fatal financial wounds that became public knowledge in September, John Howard was reported as saying (Howard, quoted in Koutsoukis 2001a: 13):

> *The corporate sector can't have it both ways. It can't assert rugged individual freedom and the right to do as it chooses to the greater glory of the market, but when things get into difficulty turn around and expect governments to bail them out.*

Qantas warned the government of the problem, saying that a free market was not in the best interests of the airline industry and was leading to a disaster, so the Prime Minister's statement is disingenuous. He may well have heard company chiefs from other industries calling for free markets, but not every chief was sending that message to Canberra and, as Howard has never suggested that such calls have come from airline chiefs, his statement reported by Koutsoukis seems like duplicity given its context—a statement about airlines.

John Howard's attempts to spin the issue can also be inferred as evidence that he was caught in an ideological bind. His policy was to advocate competition, and this is simpler to do if applied universally, to all industries. Discriminating, deciding that in some industries government policy should foster competitiveness while in others the policy should go in another direction for the common good, requires complex and difficult dealings with a wide range of business interests. Instead of the difficult political work required in that strategy, a politician can relax in comfort by hiding behind a simple idea, repeating as mantra that competition is good for everyone.

Foreign ownership of airlines

A complicating factor was that the Australian government had allowed Ansett to be sold off to a foreign company, Air NZ. This meant that detailed information about trends in Ansett's business performance was not being kept in Australia but in New Zealand, where Australian observers could not be closely aware of what was happening with Ansett in the short term. It also meant that decisions about Ansett by top managers and company directors were being made in New Zealand by persons whose first duty was to the parent company, Air NZ. When the going got tough for both airlines in 2001, the directors apparently looked after the parent company's interests to the disadvantage of the subsidiary company in Australia.

Similar problems have occurred in other countries in which a major airline was owned and controlled by foreign investors. For example, in Cambodia in 1994 the national airline, Royal Air Cambodge (RAC), was sold to Malaysian Airline Systems (MAS), and serious problems developed because the major airline was under foreign control (Leiper 1998).

CONCLUSION

Ansett's failure was triggered by bad management in Air NZ and by delays in the Australian government's handling of problems with aviation policy in 2001. The underlying cause of the failure was the excessively competitive condition faced by Ansett after 1999.

The consequences of Ansett's collapse demonstrate that in Australia, airline services between distant cities and other scattered locations should be regarded as a vital public utility. These services are too important for the community, for business, for national sports, for touring performing art groups and for national and regional tourism interests to leave at risk in the 'invisible hands' of 'market forces'. They should be managed in a visible manner, by managers with visible hands, under a regulatory regime sponsored by the government. Moreover, they are too important to be placed at risk under foreign ownership. Just as Qantas must, by law, be majority-owned in Australia, so any airline that acquires a significant share of the domestic market should be subject to the same law.

One year after Ansett's collapse, in September 2002, approximately 16 000 former employees were still owed $400 million in entitlements, an average of $25 000, and 3000 remained unemployed, according to a newspaper report (Creedy 2002). The size and timing of their payout will depend on the sale of the company's assets. Gary Toomey, the former CEO, was also unemployed but had received a $3.5 million 'golden handshake' in 2001 when he resigned (Creedy & Bryden-Brown 2002).

BIG BANANA: A BIG FAILURE IN 1989

Thirty years ago 'Big Things' began appearing along Australian highways. The first, at Nambour in Queensland, was a pineapple. Big Things along provincial roads represent provincial themes: Big Pineapple, Big Trout, Big Ram, Big Cow, Big Oyster, Big Prawn, Big Bull. This discussion focuses on the fluctuating fortunes and changing business strategies at the Big Banana between the 1960s and the 90s.

Origins of the Big Banana

In 1963 a scientist, John Landi, began a study of bananas in Coffs Harbour, centre of Australia's premier banana-growing region. At his plantation he set up a road-

side stall to earn money. Inspired by Hawaii's Big Pineapple, Landi proposed to the Coffs Harbour Banana Growers' Federation that they pay half the cost of constructing a larger-than-life banana as a generic promotional symbol next to his stall. The idea sparked the first of many stories on this topic in The Advocate, *a local newspaper. The Big Banana was built in 1965, at a cost of £1200. It was controversial. Many persons in Coffs Harbour did not like it and, worse, regarded it as shameful and detrimental to the district's interests.*

The district was being proudly advertised to prospective tourists, prospective immigrants (and others not so fortunate), as the 'Pacific Beautizone'. According to the sensibility of the Coffs Harbour civic leaders supporting that campaign, a giant artificial banana is not a thing of beauty. It was the sort of thing they imagined might be seen on a road in places like Queensland; besides, it had unmentionable connotations, which in 1965 made respectable people feel uncomfortable.

In 1972 the controversy was largely resolved. A respectable chain of department stores in Sydney decided to use bananas as a theme for their summer promotional displays, a decision that caused a rethink in Coffs Harbour. If Grace Brothers imagined that bananas might promote retail sales in Sydney, then Coffs Harbour could believe that an oversized model of the fruit was the ideal symbol for boosting tourism in Coffs Harbour. Promotional campaigns named Banana Coast and Banana Republic were soon devised, and the Big Banana acquired the status of regional shrine.

The Big Banana as a popular 'pit stop'

The Big Banana in the 1970s and early 80s can be analysed as a successful business system comprising several elements. The 15-metre fake banana lying on its side was its central element. Travellers stopped to see it close up, touch it, walk through it

and take photographs of one another posing around it. From the shop alongside they bought drinks, souvenirs, packaged snacks, postcards, honey and bananas. A parking bay accommodated cars and tour coaches.

A large sign told everybody that this was indeed the Big Banana. An important adjunct was the spacious public toilet, a welcome relief for travellers, who had been on the road for hours in many cases. Economically, the business depended on sales in the shop. Everything else was free.

The Big Banana was more than just another roadside attraction. It was a highly profitable business. Tourists and other travellers journeying along the highway found that, however incidental in their total trip experiences, a brief stop at the Big Banana satisfied a range of needs. The bundled psychological satisfactions represented, in fact, the heart of the successful business strategy. Transiting tourists still stop because it is a convenient place to rest, buy petrol, use a toilet, buy a snack. It is one of the better-known 'pit stops' on the Pacific Highway.

Developments in 1989: Big Banana theme park

In 1988 the Big Banana was sold to a large horticultural company, which had a highly successful business based on growing and marketing vegetables and fruit. The new owner's idea was to establish a theme park around horticultural displays, with supplementary rides, food and shopping. One of the directors, Bob Johnson, took the lead in furthering the proposal. A subsidiary company, Horticultural World Pty Ltd, was established for the theme park. A manager was employed, which allowed Johnson and the other directors of the parent company to continue with their other business interests. With approval of the parent company, the manager hired two consultants. Total Project Control Pty Ltd was engaged to plan the redevelopment, while a firm of management consultants with extensive experience in tourism, Horwath and Horwath Services Pty Ltd, was engaged to conduct feasibility studies for the new business, to ensure that the large investment was likely to return a profit.

Two levels of strategies can be identified in the development proposed in 1988, as follows. The top level is a corporate strategy, of the sort described by Andrews (1980/1991), Ansoff (1965) and others. The directors envisioned potential, at the banana site, for strategically expanding the horticultural company. This strategy is one of the four kinds of diversification identified by Galbraith (1983/1991). Making money by growing and selling fruit and vegetables, and opening up vast markets in Asia, could be complemented by using horticulture as a theme in tourism. The second level of strategy is a business strategy, involving a certain kind of marketing mix aimed at particular types of consumers. Rumelt (1980/1991) and others have discussed theories for this level of strategy. If thousands of tourists every month were visiting an attraction and spending, on average, $5 in the shop, why not create added attractions and services up the hill behind the banana, additions that surely would induce the average visitor to spend much more and would also attract greater numbers than were stopping off to use the lavatories and buy a Coke?

The Big Banana could be developed as a distinctive theme park, a small version of

Disneyland and Brisbane Expo but with environmentally appropriate style, endemically suiting Coffs Harbour.

Optimism was encouraged by signs that Australian tourism was in boom phase, with large increases being recorded in numbers of visitors, especially from the USA, Japan and New Zealand. Brisbane Expo had recorded, in 1988, millions of visits. Its marketing manager was signed up for the position of marketing manager at Big Banana. Other encouraging signs were Japanese investors inspecting properties in Coffs Harbour while their Australian agents willingly described to locals the fortunate prospects in the near future when many Japanese tourists would be visiting.

The feasibility report for the theme park

The report on the feasibility study by Horwath and Horwath was presented to the directors in July 1988. The report came to optimistic conclusions. It estimated that the theme park would capture, over each year for five years into the future, high penetration rates of several target markets: transient tourists passing along the Highway; domestic (i.e. Australian) tourists staying in Coffs Harbour; day-trippers from surrounding districts; international visitors in Coffs Harbour; and residents of Coffs Harbour and district (Table 15.2).

The highest projection was for international visitors: the report projected that 60% would visit the theme park. The lowest was for residents of Coffs Harbour: 15% penetration rate in the first year, falling to 10% in future years.

Those penetration rates were applied to optimistic predictions about future growth in tourist arrivals in Coffs Harbour, for example 120 700 international tourists and 439 600 domestic tourists in 1990/91. The report forecast that total visitors to the Big Banana in 1993/94 would number 1 108 600. This came from adding the units in segmentation analysis. The report projected a cash flow from operations, before debt costs and income tax, of $5 872 000 in 1989/90, rising to $7 375 000 in 1993/94 (Horwath & Horwath 1988: VIII-6). The main revenue source in the report was admission fees, projected to earn $6 655 000 in 1989/90, when 924 300 visitor arrivals were expected, paying

TABLE 15.2 Market segmentation forecasts for Big Banana

Segment	Number of visits ('000)	% of total
Coffs residents	9	1
Area residents	10	1
Domestic tourists	499	45
International tourists	94	8
Transient tourists	496	45
Total	1 108	100

$7.20 (mean average) per head. Smaller sums of revenue were projected to come from lease payments from food and beverage outlets, retail outlets and a farmers' market, and 'a minimum figure of $275 000 per annum' from corporate sponsorship (1988: VIII-3).

After reviewing the feasibility study, the finance industry provided the additional funds required and the theme park was built, stretching up the hill behind the banana. The precise cost is unknown: reliable sources say about $22 million was invested, of which more than half came from the parent company and almost half from three Australian banks. The largest bank investment (about $5 million) came from AGC, a subsidiary of Westpac.

A concrete rail with a train was the most expensive capital item. It was for transporting visitors on a meandering route up the hill and back, through a plantation, alongside lakes where a monster lurked underwater, rearing up its grotesque iron head and spraying water as the train passed, and on to a number of stations.

At these, tourists could alight and rejoin later services. At one station a hydroponics vegetable farm was built. At another, inside a large tin shed, tourists could see displays of ecological notions and futuristic technology. The next was another shed where verandas gave spectacular views over the sea. Inside were tables for 100 diners, a bar, a dozen open kitchens and signs for European and Asian cuisines.

Up and down at Big Banana

A large yellow-and-black sign announced 'The Big Banana Theme Park'. The first months of trading were a great success, with thousands of visitors. Suddenly the growth in numbers faltered, then fell rapidly and continued falling. Within months of opening, by late 1989, the business was technically insolvent. The directors of the parent company realised that the managers of the subsidiary company might have made some blunders, so Bob Johnson stepped into a CEO role.

He quickly implemented strategies for dealing with crises, of the sort described by Starbuck et al. (1991), and strategies for trying to turn around failing ventures (Hofer 1991). He found, for example, that the manager of the subsidiary company had employed four times as many staff as were needed to operate the business at full capacity. Johnson reduced costs by slashing overheads, and boosted sales using new, low-cost promotional tactics. Within two months, in early 1990, the business was earning more income, at lower costs, sufficient to cover operating expenses but not nearly enough to pay the interest bill to the bankers.

Unable to raise alternative capital at cheap rates in Australia, Johnson went to Tokyo and obtained finance from a major bank, sufficient to pay out the Australian bankers and save the impending collapse of the theme park. He said that AGC refused to accept the Japanese money, preferring to force Horticultural World into liquidation, which would give AGC a small part of its capital back. The cheque was returned to Japan. Johnson suspected that AGC's managers were frightened to take the Japanese money, which would have saved AGC from any loss, because this would have exposed certain details of their role in the whole deal to scrutiny from their superiors in Westpac.

In 1990, a year after opening, the theme park was placed in receivership. The bankers used the law to have an official receiver placed in charge. While trading in receivership it was offered for sale, and in 1992 was sold to the highest bidder in order to repay the creditors at least something of their losses.

Reverting to the original strategy

A successful bid by Kevin Rubie was a fraction of the $22 million that had been invested there three years earlier. He paid less than $2 million for the assets and business name and said it was the best deal of his career. Under his direction as on-site manager, after 1992 the operation was scaled down and the strategy changed in several ways.

There was now no entry fee. The restaurants on the hill were closed and the train runs only on busy days. Two small buses, cheaper to operate than the train, convey tourists (for a small fare) up the hill to the views, plantation, hydroponics farm and display of ecotechnology. Alternatively, they can walk up for free.

A principal focus of business strategy, in terms of earning money, now seems to be sales in the roadside shop, as it had been prior to 1989. Income from tours to the top of the hill is secondary. With a relatively small amount of capital invested, $1 million as against $22 million, the Big Banana after 1992 needed far fewer visitors to break even. It could be economically sustainable on a smaller scale.

Reviewing the 1989 investment

The feasibility of developments like the one at the Big Banana in 1989 depends on five major issues: strategic management, capital investment, market potential, market penetration rates and cash flows. If any is seriously deficient or, more importantly, if they do not match up, the proposal is highly risky. Certain managerial and marketing issues such as staffing and promotional strategies are secondary, not crucial; usually they can be fixed if found to be defective.

Development proposals for the Big Banana in 1988 were deficient in most of those five issues. An aggravating factor was the fact that the feasibility study prepared by Horwath and Horwath was accepted as valid by all the investors, possibly blinded by its professional tone, detailed data and optimistic conclusions—three common characteristics of expensive reports from consultants.

Business strategies for the theme park, outlined above, might have seemed reasonable to those transfixed by casual (or detailed) stories of a tourist boom. However, the markets for the new business strategies were too small in relation to the amount of capital required (as will be shown below). Moreover, the new strategies largely killed off custom from the established markets, passing trade (another point explained below). This meant that the probability of sustaining a positive cash flow was about zero. The theme park should have been seen as doomed from the outset. That it went ahead suggests that senior officials in certain Australian banks might lack competence in judging the feasibility of business proposals. The sums involved in this case meant that the decisions were not made at local branch level but in head offices of AGC, the

Commonwealth Development Bank and the State Bank of NSW. That the proposal went ahead also indicates that entrepreneurs can launch grandiose visions if they are skilful in selling the visions—and themselves—to bankers and tourism boosters. None of this is news or unusual, as Sykes' (1994) case histories have shown.

An unusual feature of the collapse of the Big Banana was its immediacy and speed. The theme park opened, enjoyed a few busy weeks (mainly because many locals came for a look) and then crashed. This is a strong indication that something was seriously flawed in the original design and in the feasibility study. The development would not have proceeded without Horwath and Horwath Services' (1988) report. After the collapse, Bob Johnson reviewed the report and decided to commence a legal claim against Horwath and Horwath.

Finance, cash flow and visitor flows

The financial feasibility behind the $22 million theme park can be analysed. The following data have been prepared without specific information from anybody associated with the Big Banana, or any documentary sources. It shows broad-based estimates.

To service capital of $22 million in the late 1980s, the business needed a net return of at least $3 million annually, assuming that the cost of capital was around 12%. (It was probably more.) This is $8219 on an average day. There was also a need to cover operating costs and earn a profit.

How much money would an average visitor spend in this sort of theme park? Assume, generously, an average of $30, a mean in a range of, say, $10–$50 for individuals. Expenditure items include entrance fee, rides, goods such as food and drink consumed, food and drink taken out, film and souvenirs. For the purpose of analysis, the restaurant's kitchens and bar are assumed to be part of the company operating the theme park; in practice, they were leased.

For this average $30 revenue, the businesses would incur direct costs of, say, $15 to pay for supplies. This would leave $15 to contribute to overhead expenses such as wages, rates, office costs, advertising etc. and to service the $22 million investment—also, ideally, to return a profit to the entrepreneurs.

Assume that the overhead expenses were $3000 per day. (They were probably more.) Combining the estimates, the first 200 visitors every day of the year would, in effect, cover the overheads (200 × $15). If another 548 arrived, the daily cost of the $22 million of capital investment would also be covered (548 × $15 = $8219). Thus, the business needed 748 visitors (200 + 548) per day, on average all year, to break even. If an average of 749 or more was achieved, the business would become profitable. The probability of averaging anywhere near 749 was quite remote. This is explained in the following analysis of markets.

The crucial questions in analysing markets for roadside attractions and theme parks is not the size of the total market—all the persons who might visit—but the size and likely penetration rates in key segments. Segmenting a market can be done in many ways. Traditional methods, by demographic variables such as age, gender, place of residence and occupation, are not relevant to this issue and can be misleading if managers always focus on them.

Analysis of key segments

An approach suiting this case begins by identifying three categories of persons: (a) permanent residents of the region; (b) tourists travelling along the highway, past the Big Banana; and (c) tourists staying for leisurely visits in the region. These are discussed below. The segments have different psychographics in relation to possible visits.

Permanent residents in the region of a theme park often provide a significant percentage of the park's customers. The brief boom at the Big Banana when it reopened as a theme park in 1989 was caused not by tourists but permanent residents of the region. Curious about a new and unusual park, a high percentage of locals came to see. Most never returned for repeat visits. Repeat visits by locals sustains Disneyland (Real 1977), and is important at Dreamworld and other theme parks.

Why few locals revisited the Big Banana is not salient to this analysis, because even if many had, the population is too small to generate much demand. Theme parks on Queensland's Gold Coast draw on a local resident market numbering two million in the day-tripping range. Disneyland has 30 million. The Big Banana has fewer than 100 000. Thus the Big Banana was relatively dependent on tourists, compared to the norm for theme parks.

The second segment comprises tourists passing by, in transit, passing through Coffs Harbour by private vehicle, line coach or tour coach, perhaps stopping overnight but not visiting for longer than two nights. These people are on trips for holidays or to visit friends and relatives, but regard this region as a point in transit, not a tourist destination; this is reflected in their behaviour, affecting the sites they visit in the region. This market segment, which can be termed 'transiting tourists', is huge in this case.

Baker's (1994) research identified Coffs Harbour as the second-largest stopover point for transiting tourists in New South Wales after Sydney, but did not estimate quantities. Estimates can be drawn from other sources, such as data collected in domestic tourism monitors and international visitor surveys for the period 1986–89, reported in *Tourism Trends in New South Wales* (Bureau of Tourism Research c. 1990). Another source is four surveys of visitors in 1992 and 1993 reported in the *Coffs Harbour Tourism Association Newsletter* in November 1993. The four surveys found that between 52% and 61% of visitors staying at least one night regarded the region as a transit point.

From those sources the number of journeys past the Big Banana by transiting tourists (including overnighters) can be estimated at between 1 500 000 and 2 000 000 per year, or about 300 per hour in daylight hours, in the late 1980s. This estimate counts movements in both directions, north and south, and assumes that most travel by day. Because of Brisbane Expo and other bicentennial events, 1988 was a boom year, up 20% or so. Volumes decreased in 1989, back to normal. A small proportion of persons in this transit segment visited the Big Banana in its original form, before 1989. But the segment is huge, so a small proportion is a very large number. For example, a market penetration rate of 5% represents 87 500 visitors per annum.

Whatever the quantities of transiting tourists who visited the Big Banana when it was a roadside attraction before 1989, far fewer visited the theme park thoughout the period 1989–91. There are sound reasons for the decrease. Transiting tourists tend to avoid sites that occupy an hour or two, which is what a theme park requires. They prefer short stops, as their typical priority is getting to destinations. Money is another factor. The theme park's entrance fee obviously deterred motorists who would have stopped before 1989.

The third segment of the market was identified as tourists staying for leisurely visits in the region. Many of these people, on holidays of various sorts in Coffs Harbour and nearby districts, have the necessary conditions to become visitors to a theme park: free time, motivation, and money to spend on pleasant (or time-consuming) experiences. This tourist visitor segment is small compared with the transit tourist segment. Its size in the late 1980s is estimated at about 300 000 tourists per annum. But the penetration rate achieved by a theme park could be much higher among tourist visitors than among transit tourists. A 10% penetration rate might be feasible. It is unlikely to be greater than 10% in a theme park such as this one.

In terms of the theory of attractions set out in Chapter 13, the Big Banana was the nucleus in a secondary attraction, not a primary attraction, for many tourists. Very few persons would travel to Coffs Harbour from distant homes for the specific purpose of visiting the Big Banana.

The main market had to be visitors already in the region. Surveys by the local tourism association, noted above, found in several months that between 10% and 16% of visitors said they 'might be attracted' to the Big Banana. Assume that 10% did go there. This gives a total of 30 000 per annum, or 82 visitors per day on average.

Estimates for the three market segments can now be assembled. Table 15.3 compares estimates of market size, penetration rates, visitor numbers, income and break-even data for the two kinds of business: roadside attraction versus theme park.

The profitability and low risk of the Big Banana as a roadside attraction is evident. Total visitors are 119 300, which is 9% above break-even, a comfortable margin. In contrast, the theme park is revealed as a very bad idea. Revenue per visitor is higher from entrance fees and other charges, but visitor numbers are way below those under the roadside attraction option. The lost market share is in the huge transit segment.

At 52 000 visitors per annum, the theme park option is operating at only 19% of its break-even point. To achieve break-even it would have to boost penetration rates sixfold across the market. That is impossible. In the tourist visitor segment, at 10% the penetration is already near peak potential. The alternative would be penetrating the transit segment to 14%—absolutely impossible.

CONCLUSION

In the emergent strategy from 1965 to 1988 and revisited after 1992, the Big Banana's main market is passing travellers, tourists in transit. The successful strategy positions the Big Banana on a transit route in whole tourism systems. Huge numbers pass by, so a low

TABLE 15.3 Big Banana Theme Park: feasibility analysis

Estimated item	Roadside attraction	Theme park
Local residents	90 000	90 000
Pentratation rate	2%	5%
Market potential	1800	4500
Transit tourists	1 750 000	1 750 000
Pentration rate	5%	1%
Market potential	87 500	17 500
Tourist visitors	300 000	300 000
Penetration rate	10%	10%
Market potential	30 000	30 000
Total visitors	119 300	52 000
Break-even visitors	110 000	273 000
Capital invested	$1 million	$22 million
Total as % of B/E visitors	109%	19%
Profitability forecast	Profits probable	Huge losses certain

market penetration rate is sufficient to attract large numbers spending small amounts of money. It requires a market-skimming strategy, in a very large market. The probability of failing to gain sufficient consumers is low.

From 1989 to 1991, when the Big Banana was a theme park, the principal markets were tourists visiting the region for longer periods than a transit stop. This strategy positioned the Big Banana in a tourist destination region. It is a much smaller market, so a higher penetration rate was required, which would be difficult to achieve. It required a market-dipping strategy in a small market. The probability of failing to attract sufficient consumers was higher than before. Also, the amount of capital being risked was much higher.

Losses of $22 million were directly shared by Johnson and other investors and by the three banks that loaned finance. Public opinion in Coffs Harbour is that local businesses and workers also lost money, perhaps $8 million, when the theme park went broke. Thus the total loss might have been $30 million.

Losses such as these are paid for, indirectly, by everyone with any sort of interest in the Australian economy—wage earners, consumers, businesses, investors, taxpayers, borrowers. That is why large business losses should be matters of public interest and why decisions behind failed investments should be studied. Economies cannot avoid losses on some investments. However, by studying past failures, by pathological research, the incidence or severity of future ones might be reduced.

MORE RESEARCH NEEDED

The three cases discussed in this chapter are not intended as a statistically representative sample of all failures in tourism industries. Each case had its own distinctive problems:

each failed in its own way. However, many other cases could be found that failed in the same ways. The PHAD scheme at Le Lagon has its parallels in countless hare-brained schemes dreamed up by innovative CEOs. It was based in a good idea (empowerment) but was badly designed. The failure of Big Banana was largely due to excessive enthusiasm, blinded by boosterist attitudes to tourism and by a seriously flawed feasibility report prepared by consultants advertising expertise in tourism—conditions that might have been mutually reinforcing and that have occurred in many other cases. Ansett's demise could be attributed to bad decisions by top management and to the excessively competitive context imposed on the domestic airline industry by Australian governments in recent years.

The three cases only touch on the wide range of issues and causes associated with failures in tourism industries. More research in needed on the theme, using a variety of approaches and research methods, looking at diverse types of organisations and enterprises. Despite the lack of interest in this theme in the past, not merely in regard to tourism but in relation to businesses in general, there are signs of an emerging awareness that it is an important, useful and interesting theme to research. Countless opportunities are available for projects by students and academics who take up the challenge.

Discussion questions

1. Why do many people avoid thinking about failures and prefer instead to focus on success stories?

2. What are the advantages, in business management and in many other professional activities, in studying failures?

3. What were the defects at Le Lagon Resort in the general manager's PHAD scheme, supposedly intended to improve service standards?

4. What were the causes of the collapse, in 2001, of Australia's second-largest airline, Ansett Airlines?

5. A detailed feasibility study and plan were prepared, by a well-known firm of business consultants specialising in tourism, for the new theme park at Big Banana, yet the venture was a financial failure. Does this mean that feasibility studies and business plans are a waste of time and money?

6. What were the major errors in the feasibility study prepared for the new theme park at Big Banana?

Recommended reading

Easdowne, Geoff & Wilson, Peter 2002, *Ansett: The Collapse*, Melbourne: Lothian

Petroski, Henry 1992a, History and failure, *American Scientist*, Nov–Dec, pp 523–6

Petroski, Henry 1992b, *The Evolution of Useful Things*, New York: Alfred Knopf

Issues in Tourism Management

INTRODUCTION

This chapter contains discussions on a selection of issues relevant to tourism management. Seasonal fluctuations occur in virtually all tourist flows and in many places are regarded as problematical. Sustainable tourism is recognised as an increasingly important issue. Feedback is a widely noted aspect of information flows affecting tourism and its management. Proliferating variety is a common issue in many managed systems, but has not been discussed by other researchers on tourism. Another issue overlooked is a simple question: who actually manages tourism? Five sections of this chapter analyse these issues in the context of two core concepts in this book, namely whole tourism systems and partial industrialisation.

Several writers, including a number cited in Chapter 3, have followed a whole systems model in research on tourism. Chapter 3 indicated that such an approach is useful when thinking about many issues. This chapter will demonstrate the point further. The whole systems approach encourages visions of tourism and its management that other kinds of approach do not easily see.

Partial industrialisation was described and analysed earlier in this book, namely in Chapters 11, 12 and 13. Broadly, the concept expresses the fact that only a portion of resources used directly in tourism stems from tourism industries, from the collections of cooperating organisations in the tourism business, while the other portion comes from other sources. Partial industrialisation is an issue for tourism managers because it provides insight into the limitations of strategies and operations of tourism industries. In this chapter the issue is shown to be relevant to many other issues affecting the management of tourism.

SEASONAL FLUCTUATIONS

Tourism fluctuates with the seasons, in terms of the numbers of trips, tourists, and associated variables such as expenditures, rooms occupied, workers in employment and business profits. Busy times of the year in destinations are known as high or peak seasons, quiet times are low or trough seasons, and the intermediate periods are shoulder seasons. These expressions come from observing the shape of a typical graph depicting the pattern over a year.

In fact, seasonal patterns are only one category of fluctuations that follow patterns over time; others include daily patterns (certain days of the week usually have more tourist movements than other days) and hourly patterns (certain times of the day see more activity). This discussion focuses on seasonal issues.

Hall (1991: 131) noted that the seasonal nature of tourism is 'one of the most significant drawbacks to tourism development'. Butler (2000: 521) agreed, stating that 'seasonality is one of the most distinctive features of tourism in many parts of the world and is generally viewed as a major problem'. Peat Marwick (1977) provided extensive alleviating its problems.

Extreme seasonal fluctuations cause economic problems. In high seasons, the numbers of tourists wanting transport, accommodation and recreational facilities might be so great that they cannot all be satisfied. In low seasons, the numbers might be so few that resources are idle or underutilised. This represents idle capital investment in tourism industries, incurring fixed costs but not earning income.

Many workers are affected by seasonality. In high seasons some are excessively busy, and in low seasons, if they are employed on a casual basis, are laid off. This suits many but is disliked by others. Mill and Morrison (1985: 231) stated that seasonal fluctuations underlie criticisms of tourism industries that hire in busy months and retrench in quiet months. Where a tourism industry is excessively dependent on casual employees, the standard of service can be inadequate.

Seasonal fluctuations can also be problematical for tourists. Many are disadvantaged by going on trips in peak seasons when top prices are charged and popular sites are overcrowded. In low seasons, tourists might spend less money but feel dissatisfied if few other tourists are on hand to provide company and an atmosphere of conviviality.

Seasonal fluctuations in whole tourism systems

What causes seasonal fluctuations? Seasonal characteristics of destinations, such as climate, are often a major factor. Summertime in seaside resorts is the peak, because that is when most tourists want to be there, while winter is best in ski resorts. Peak times depend, to some degree, on the way particular tourists use each destination.

In the Himalayas, winter is the high season for tourist treks because the weather is dry and clear, ideal for trekking. It is not the best time for mountaineering, for scaling the high peaks. One of tourism's greatest seasonal concentrations is in Mecca, where, during one week in the Muslim month of *Dhu al-Hij-jah*, the major annual pilgrimage rites (*hajj*) occur in the city because of long-established custom.

Occasionally a high season shifts. For more than 100 years the high season for tourism on the French Riviera was winter; in the 1920s, it shifted to summer. Turner and Ash (1975) explained why and how this occurred—a change caused by cultural and social changes among tourists. The change led to fashion changes in recreational behaviour in many countries and led to suntans becoming fashionable after 1929.

Theories attributing seasonal fluctuations only to what happens in destinations ignore another element in tourism systems. A holistic view reveals that seasonal variations might be caused in traveller-generating regions, where social traditions develop for large numbers of persons to go on holiday trips at certain times of the year. In the Australian population, the most popular time for holiday trips is between 26 December and 31 January. Many people go then to destinations where it is the ideal time for holiday visits, but many go to places where this is not the case. For example, through the 1980s and 90s Bali was the most popular overseas holiday destination for Australians and the peak month for their visits was January, the worst month for holidays in Bali because it is the season when clouds and rain are common.

Seasonal fluctuations and variations in industrialisation

Seasonal fluctuations tend to be less extreme when tourism is highly industrialised and greater where tourists are independent of tourism industries. Domestic tourism in Australia and in New Zealand is relatively independent of tourism industries and has large extremes in seasonal patterns. In contrast, international tourism into and out of those two countries is highly industrialised—mainly because, as both countries are islands, tourists are dependent on airlines and associated organisations such as travel agents in tourism industries. Statistical data are published on monthly patterns; these can be assessed to confirm the point. The explanation follows.

Under conditions of independent tourism, the major interest group or stakeholders are tourists. Using mainly non-commercial facilities for transport (personal motor vehicles) and for accommodation (private homes of friends and relatives), they are normally not concerned if these facilities are not used for tourism during most of the year.

Under conditions of highly industrialised tourism, the major stakeholders are investors with ownership interests in hotels, airlines and theme parks. The managers of these organisations, as agents of the owners, are responsible for the productive use of the resources, which generally means avoiding losses and earning profits. Accordingly, managers take actions to prevent, if feasible, the resources remaining idle or at low levels of productivity. The more capital investment is tied up in a resource (e.g. in large hotels or airlines), the more responsibility falls on its managers to seek an economical return on the investment. The manager will assign sales and marketing staff the task of boosting room occupancies and revenue.

Managing seasonality

The most common managerial policy regarding the seasonality issue is to accept that its problems cannot be totally overcome but that extreme fluctuations can be moderated. Using casual labour, engaged for busy periods and laid off in quiet times, can lower costs on the supply side. Meanwhile, demand management is achieved by synchromarketing, an expression used by Kotler et al. (1994) referring to coordinated strategies designed to improve the short-term matching of demand and supply. The aim is to induce a transfer of demand from the peak season into the shoulder and low seasons.

Airlines and hotels often aim promotional campaigns at consumers, travel agents and tour operators. The inducement for consumers is usually lower prices—cheaper fares. Travel agents might be induced to sell more in low seasons by offering them higher rates of commission ('seasonal overrides') or giving prizes to the travel consultants who sell the most. Tour operators are induced to push off season packages.

Seasonality under totally industrialised tourism ➤

Under hypothetical conditions of total industrialisation, how might seasonal fluctuations be managed? Synchromarketing would be used, but more powerful strategies would be added. One possibility would be to regulate the weather. This strategy conjures up images of resorts inside huge domes where the sunshine and temperature could be planned and controlled, creating ideal conditions every day. In that condition, the weather ceases to be an (unmanageable) environmental factor affecting tourism; instead it becomes an element in the management system of the destination. In ski resorts, artificial snow-making is used to extend the season.

Strategies would also be directed at traveller-generating regions to eliminate or counteract additional causes of seasonal fluctuations. For example, more than 50% of all annual holiday leave taken by Australian employees occurs in just 17% of the calendar, in December and January. In principle, this pattern could be regulated and altered to smooth out the fluctuations. There are a number of ways this could be managed.

One is a roster, used by industrial organisations that need to maintain constant labour input all year because seasonal shut-downs are technologically or economically impractical (oil refineries) or are socially undesirable (police, hospitals). In these sorts of organisations, employees are rostered to take annual leave at designated times, so that at all times a constant percentage of employees is on leave.

Imagine a totally industrialised economy, where all workers were members of organisations that were managed in a coordinated manner to achieve totalitarian goals, such as maximum productivity. A condition that allowed half the workforce to go on leave simultaneously would conflict with that goal, so a universal roster scheme, across the entire economy, would be introduced. Labour input to productive activity would be maximised, while there would be no seasonal fluctuations affecting tourism systems.

Perhaps there are those obsessed with productivity who see that policy as desirable and feasible. In practice it would be very strongly opposed by large numbers of people, for a number of reasons. The totalitarian argument that the scheme would benefit everyone because it helped 'the whole system' would carry little weight with individuals who saw disadvantages for themselves personally. The main reason for opposing a scheme like this is that it intrudes on and erodes what people regard as a basic right—how and when each individual uses the time that is 'mine' and 'free'.

Cognisant of that constraint, lobbyists wanting to attack the problems of seasonality by changing patterns of leave-taking do not ask governments to regulate the leave of all employees. Instead, they suggest modifications around the fringes, by staggering school leave in different parts of the country. This strategy was introduced, on a limited scale, in several parts of Australia during the 1980s.

FEEDBACK: AN ISSUE IN THE MANAGEMENT OF TOURISM

'Give me some feedback on what's been happening' is a request everyone understands. The term began as jargon among systems theorists 60 years ago. In popular usage it means information given to one person from another who has been closer to the source. That closely reflects its original meaning in the 1940s (Bertalanffy 1972b; August Smith 1982), referring to the portion of any system's outputs that become one of its inputs in a later period. The first person to discuss feedback in human organisations was Norbert

Wiener (1950), the inventor of cybernetics. The issue explored below revolves around differences between two categories of feedback, natural and managed.

Natural feedback and managed feedback

Analysing applications of systems theory in management, Stafford Beer (1975: 10) distinguished between feedback that occurs spontaneously or automatically in a given system (e.g. a thermostat) and another kind of information, often *called* 'feedback', which depends on a request. Managers often make requests such as 'Give me feedback on the sales promotion'. Beer pointed out that information requested is not natural or pure feedback, because it does not occur as a automatic process in a system. If it did, the manager would not have to make the request. Therefore, he suggested, our under-standing about all kinds of systems is helped if we distinguish between natural feedback (referring to spontaneous, automatic or natural cases) and managed feedback.

Feedback has been discussed by many writers on marketing (e.g. Kotler & Anderson 1987) and on marketing in tourism-related businesses (Morrison 1989; Reid 1989). These writers seem unaware of Beer's distinction. What they refer to is managed feed-back, as exemplified in this quote: 'good feedback means getting regular information from and about sales representatives to evaluate their performance' (Kotler & Anderson 1987: 612). Natural feedback occurs spontaneously and costs nothing; managed feedback must be created and therefore has a cost. That is the practical reason for the distinction.

Both kinds of feedback in tourism systems ➤

Both kinds of feedback occur to varying degrees, in many forms, in all tourism systems. By far the most common kind is natural feedback, when tourists pass on information about their own experiences to other tourists met while travelling or later, back home, to friends and acquaintances. Natural feedback includes information circulating among tourists within a destination region, among tourists at various stages of their itineraries, and, after their trips, between tourists and residents of their home regions.

Word-of-mouth recommendation (for or against) is natural feedback, and is an important influence on tourism trends. Nolan's (1976) prize-winning research was the first of many studies showing how credible word-of-mouth information can be in tourism.

Managed feedback also occurs in various forms. Within a traveller-generating region, managers of businesses such as travel agencies, airlines and tourism promotion offices request and collect information about market trends in that region. They are interested in learning about trends in the numbers of residents setting off on trips, in terms of numbers, itineraries and pre-trip services purchased. Within a tourist destination region, managers of businesses such as hotels, theme parks and tour operators request and collect information about visitors' activities within the region.

At a macro level, managers of various businesses in tourism industries request and collect information from sources across the geographical spectrum of whole tourism systems. Hotel managers obtain information from travel agents and outbound tour operators located in distant places that serve as traveller-generating regions for the destination region where the hotels are located. Also, national tourism organisations such as the Australian Tourist Commission or the Thai Tourism Authority collect information, by means of various kinds of surveys, to test and measure the interest among resident populations of various countries in visiting Australia or Thailand.

Feedback and partial industrialisation

Natural feedback occurs regardless of the degree of industrialisation. It is a natural process of tourism. However, when tourism is highly industrialised, the collection of natural feedback by managers in tourism industries is relatively simple and economical. At the other extreme, under conditions of highly independent tourism, managers in tourism industries do not have this advantage. Why this is so, and what it implies, is explained below. The explanation will be demonstrated by contrasting two kinds of tourism. Referring to tourism as partly industrialised implies varying degrees.

Highly industrialised tourism occurs when tourists make intensive and extensive use of services offered by tourism industries. Pre-trip they use travel agencies and outbound tour operators; they travel on airlines or other public carriers in the business of tourism; they use hotels or similar commercial accommodation; they visit theme parks and go on organised sightseeing tours.

Independent tourism, in contrast, occurs when tourists make little or no use of services offered by tourism industries. They plan and arrange their own trips, use their own vehicles for transport or use public transport of the sort not distinctly related to tourism, use private homes for accommodation and avoid theme parks, guided tours and similar institutions.

Under highly industrialised tourism, managers in tourism industries can easily collect opinions and other information from tourists, because of two facts. First, under this condition tourists are, by definition, consumers or customers so can be approached and asked for information by the supplier organisation as a routine phase of the consumption process. Second, in many instances tourist-consumers provide suppliers with their names, home addresses and additional items of demographic information. After trips, back home, tourist-consumers can be contacted by those business organisations with names and addresses on file. This allows the conduct of inexpensive surveys to collect facts and opinions.

Even if that routine is not followed, travel agents often collect post-trip opinions informally, when former clients call into the agency for a chat or to book another trip. Information collected is routinely passed on by travel agents to their principals (airlines, tour wholesalers, hotels and national tourism offices). The information is passed on in a number of ways, the most common being when principals' sales representatives contact travel agencies. Thus managers in tourism industries are able to tap into natural feedback of whole tourism systems. The cost is small, as there is no direct expense incurred in surveying or collecting the data that the sales representatives amass during their normal duties.

In totally industrialised tourism—a hypothetical condition—samples of *all* returned tourists could be routinely surveyed, and the data collected could be circulated widely among organisations involved in supplying services at various points in itineraries.

In contrast, with independent tourism there is no easy and economical way for managers in tourism industries to tap into feedback in order to collect tourists' opinions. Missing are consumer–supplier links and principal–agency links.

What is the alternative for managers of businesses and governmental tourism bodies interested in these tourists' opinions? They can tap into natural feedback, but to do so must establish special data-collection systems, requiring special effort and considerable expense if done properly. To collect valid and reliable information, scientifically designed market research studies are required. These involve random samples of the residents in each market area, discovering persons who have recently been away on trips and asking them for information about the places visited, the purpose of the trips, and facilities used.

The costs of conducting surveys of this sort, in ways that generate useful findings, are too high for the budgets of most organisations in the business of tourism. Funded on a cooperative basis via a governmental agency, on a regional or national scale, this sort of research can be economical. In Australia this is the basis of the National Visitor Survey, a government-funded continuous survey to collect data about recent trip patterns.

CONCLUSION

The feedback issue illustrates one aspect of how highly industrialised systems are able to work productively in the interests of their component organisations. International tourism systems to and from different continents, or to and from island countries such as Australia or New Zealand, are examples where this can be achieved. The practice of domestic tourism in those two countries offers a contrast, as most domestic tourists in both Australia and New Zealand are independent; accordingly, the role of tourism industries is quite minor in relation to the huge numbers of tourists.

This is one of the more important, though less obvious reasons for justifying publicly funded research into the behaviour of tourists, arranged via governmental agencies such as Australia's Bureau of Tourism Research.

PROLIFERATING VARIETY AND TOURISM MANAGEMENT

All management theories and practices can be understood as responses to one underlying problem—how to deal with variety (Beer 1959; Waelchli 1989). Reading Beer or Waelchli might not be necessary for understanding why this is so; an outline can be set out here.

Every managed organisation—ranging from a small business with one proprietor doing all the work to a multinational corporation with thousands of employees in many countries—operates in conditions of constant change, caused by eternally changing environments. The result is constant change in the factors dealt with by managers. In other words, a manager's work is never complete, as changing environments will constantly throw up new opportunities and problems requiring attention. Variety proliferates and so managerial initiatives and reactions proliferate.

The scientific explanation involves the 'Law of Requisite Variety' (or 'Ashby's Law', as it is sometimes called), originating in cybernetics with application in management (Beer 1959, 1975, 1979; Schoderbeck et al. 1988; Leiper 1989c; Waelchli 1989). Beer illustrated the issue by noting the fact that inexperienced managers often express a desire for simple control systems, which later prove ineffective as they lack the complexity to deal with real-world variety (1959: 44):

> *One often hears (from managers) the optimistic demand, 'Give me a simple control system, one that can't go wrong!' The trouble with simple controls is that they have insufficient variety to cope with variety in the environment. Far from not going wrong, they can't go right.*

To be effective, there must be as much variety in a management system as there is in the system being managed. Countless examples of this principle could be found in tourism industries. Here just one facet will be described. It relates to the geography of tourism.

Proliferating geographical elements in world tourism

An accurate description of modern tourism is that it involves proliferating geographical elements around the world. Over time, more and more places are becoming generating regions, transit routes and tourist destinations. Compared to any time in the past, there are now more places around the world actively involved in tourism. Every city and town generates travellers who become tourists during their trips. Every city and town hosts some quantity of tourists every year; relatively few villages are not visited by at least one tourist occasionally.

Millions of tourists travelling from and to all these places means that a lot of other places have become points along transit routes. In summary, modern tourism is a phenomenon likely to be manifested virtually anywhere on earth. Why is this so?

Proliferating variety in tourists' itineraries primarily stems from three facts: (a) modern tourists are relatively free to go almost anywhere they choose; (b) small but significant numbers choose to go to places off the beaten track; and (c) this means visiting places that formerly were seldom, if ever, visited by tourists.

Independent tourists who, for any reason, tend to avoid using facilities intended for tourists are more numerous now than at any time in history. By using self-sufficient means of travel such as walking or cycling, or using ordinary public transport in each locality, there are few limits to their itineraries.

Less variety in highly industrialised tourism

If a primary cause of proliferating variety in tourists' itineraries is independent tourism, what would happen under the opposite condition, namely highly industrialised tourism?

If all tourism came entirely within the scope of tourism industries, there would be far less variety. There would be fewer tourist destinations and transit routes. The range of destination choices available to people contemplating trips would be much smaller than it is now. Policy makers would decide which places were destinations, and no tourists would be allowed to visit places not in that range. By administrative, marketing and legislative means, that strategy could be implemented under conditions of totally industrialised tourism. This strategy would be in the tourism industry's interests, for two broad reasons.

The first reason is economic. If a given quantity of tourists is dispersed to a large and growing number of destinations, the economic interests of tourism industries suffer. On the other hand, if the same quantity were restricted to a few destinations those interests would gain, by economies of scale, economies of scope, lower unit costs and larger profits.

The other reason is managerial. Fewer regions being visited means less variety to be managed, which means the fundamental tasks of managing are less complicated, are simpler, which in turn means that managers are more likely to achieve their organisations' goals, whatever these might be.

Reducing the number of available destinations, by restricting tourists to a smaller range of optional places to visit, is a strategy that would produce whole tourism systems that could be managed more effectively and more efficiently than the real-world condition of an unrestricted range of options. No other strategies, alone or in combination, could produce the same effects. Strategies such as (a) improving communications, (b) devoting more attention to human resources management, (c) slicker marketing, (d) improved planning or (e) better coordination might seem like solutions to problems of proliferating variety. In practice, they do nothing to reduce variety, and are little more than bandaids on its symptoms.

Bringing about greater concentration is hypothetically a superior strategy. It is, however, deficient, in two ways. The overarching fact is that contemporary tourism is nowhere near totally industrialised. Simultaneously, in the culture of modern society, freedom of choice about where to go is an entrenched value, a right.

The first case below is not about tourism but iron manufacturing, and illustrates two extreme circumstances. Its purpose is to explain, by analogy, what happens with variety and its managerial consequences under contrasting conditions: low and high levels of industrialisation. The second and third cases concern countries where problems arising from proliferating tourist destinations, problems common in Australia and many other countries, are not a significant issue. The purpose of these cases is to illustrate a major aspect of proliferating variety as a managerial issue, rather than point to Asian examples of how it might be solved. In fact, the Hong Kong and Singapore cases below have avoided the issue in one major respect by good fortune, not by good management.

Two methods of manufacturing iron ➤

A scientific method for investigating high and low degrees of industrial involvement in tourism would, ideally, require observing a given case under both conditions. Performances and environmental impacts under each condition could be compared.

No empirical examples are known in tourism where that method can be applied, and a laboratory experiment is impossible. However, there is a real-world experiment that was closely studied in another sphere of human activity, one with economic, social and managerial implications.

Between 1958 and 1965, two quite different methods were used in China for manufacturing iron. At first, manufacturing had very low levels of industrialisation. Later it was manipulated in the opposite direction. What happened under the two methods has lessons for other socioeconomic systems (e.g. tourism) in which levels of industrialisation can vary. Here is what happened.

In 1958 China's economy was very poor, ruined by hundreds of years of colonial exploitation and 30 years of war. As a central part of his 'Great Leap Forward' for China, Mao Zedong decided to boost production of iron by a method quite different from the iron industries of other counties. During 1958 some 60 million peasants were forced into a campaign called 'backyard blast furnaces', which involved the building of very small factories and mines in rural and urban districts.

Chairman Mao believed that small-scale backyard production, involving part-time iron workers who spent the rest of their time as farmers, was economically and culturally the best method for a revolutionary communist society. He (and many others) claimed that by this strategy China would quickly become a major producer of iron and steel, which would help other sectors of the economy develop in spectacular manner.

Backyard blast furnaces were a dramatic failure. The quantity of iron produced was a tiny fraction of the amount predicted and all sorts of damage was incurred to the wider environment, which hurt the already parlous economy. In particular, 60 million peasants were physically tired by the labour in the mines and blast furnaces and were distracted from their normal work, so food production decreased, causing severe hardship around the country. The failures contributed to what became known as 'Chairman Mao's Great Leap Backwards'.

After 1960, the tiny mines and blast furnaces were closed and a quite different method for manufacturing iron was adopted. The Chinese government built a small number of large-scale mines and large blast furnaces, with the other characteristics of modern iron industries such as technical expertise and professional managers on site. This was the conventional method used in other countries since the 19th century. Wheelwright and McFarlane (1970), Breth (1977) and other researchers have reviewed the topic, focusing on its economic and political issues. Economists' and political scientists' reviews of the case ignored a managerial dimension in the problems of the backyard blast furnace campaign.

One reason the campaign failed was that it was unmanageable, because it had too much variety: too many mines, too many blast furnaces, too many workers. Thousands of small-scale, uncoordinated units do not amount to a working (or manageable) industry.

No team of managers could have dealt with the total system in any effective manner. Mao's error was assuming that iron could be produced using the same peasant-based system (i.e. non-industrialised) that China had used to produce rice. There was no substantial iron industry created, and this would have been impossible even if that concept had been grafted onto the idea of small-scale production units. The switch to a small number of large-scale production units was a trend to *industrialise* iron manufacture. This case indicates that large-scale productive systems require an industrialised process. It does not prove that all productive units must be large-scale. It indicates the difficulties of managing where there is excessive proliferation of places in which production is being attempted.

Modern tourism is characterised by a number of mass destinations, which are to some degree the mid-points of highly industrialised tourist-processing systems. Modern tourism is also characterised by many small-scale destinations which, in some cases, are like peasant agriculture.

Hong Kong, Singapore and Australia as tourist destinations ➤

Hong Kong and Singapore are two of the world's prominent destinations, each recording more than five million tourist arrivals (in a technical sense) annually in recent years. Both places are widely regarded as well-managed tourist destinations. But is it reasonable for managers and policy makers in other countries to take Hong Kong or Singapore as a model for tourism administration? Arguably not.

The following analysis, related to the issue of proliferating variety, will reveal that in their roles as tourist destinations Hong Kong and Singapore have a natural advantage over most other countries, making them easier to manage. To that extent their success as destinations is not due to good management so much as good fortune. The good fortune was the small size of these places under independent government. If Hong Kong had been part of the People's Republic of China since 1949, just another city in that nation, and if Singapore had remained politically part of Malaysia, just another city in that nation, things might have been different.

Hong Kong and Singapore can be crossed in a car (plus a ferry for reaching offshore islands) in an hour or two. Therefore, wherever tourists are accommodated in either place, they can reach any other part on day trips; there is no need for tourists to move to a second accommodation base in order to comfortably cover the destination. Relating this point to concepts in Chapter 6, Hong Kong and Singapore each comprise just one tourist destination region (TDR), while most countries comprise dozens, hundreds or thousands. This makes Hong Kong and Singapore relatively easy to manage as TDRs in comparison to most countries. Consider just two of the practical implications.

First, in Hong Kong and Singapore, the governments, the national tourist organisations and other major tourism interests do not have to monitor activities in several TDRs within the country. Such activities might include the volumes of tourists visiting each one, the quantities of accommodation occupied in each one, and the levels of satisfaction derived by tourists in each one. In the case of either Hong Kong and Singapore, the whole country's performance as a tourist destination is reflected in just one TDR.

By contrast, in Australia a complex and expensive set of surveys is used to monitor the patterns and trends in 82 tourist regions designated for collecting data.

That degree of variety (82 regions) means that the tasks of monitoring and related managerial roles are quite complex, and tend to become more complex as tourism officials and planners demand more detailed information, an example of proliferating variety. In practice, nominating 82 official regions understates the true number of destination regions created by tourists. In Hong Kong and Singapore, on this issue there is no proliferating variety; as a result, managing is simpler.

A second implication relates to promotion. Tourism interests promoting Hong Kong or Singapore as destinations do not have to decide among several TDRs when planning the content of promotional messages for advertising, public relations or publicity. The question is superfluous, as there is only one TDR to promote and consequently no choice. Therefore, managerial attention can concentrate on deciding the best ways to promote that single TDR. This has intertwined advantages: economic, political, and managerial.

Consider this issue from a political perspective. In Hong Kong and Singapore, the national tourism offices and national airlines cannot be accused of favouring certain TDRs and neglecting others in promotional or operational strategies. By contrast, in New Zealand, in Australia and in dozens of other countries containing many TDRs, such accusations are recurring problems. Provincial interests around the country complain that their wonderful region has been overlooked in the national promotional campaign.

In practice, to be effective and efficient, the promotion of a largish country as a tourist destination requires that certain TDRs be singled out for special attention. This implies that other regions must be overlooked, or at least given no prominence. But what happens when national tourism promoters such as the Australian Tourist Commission, Qantas, Tourism New Zealand and Air New Zealand follow that rational and business-like strategy?

Around the country, many locals are devoted to their home region, convinced more by faith than by logic that it deserves inclusion in any national tourism promotion because it has 'unique' features that tourists would enjoy, and they exert pressure on national tourism promoters. They lobby directly and via the media and politicians.

At best, the consequence is that managers and directors of national tourism organisations and airlines have to spend time justifying promotional strategies in the face of prejudiced criticism. At worst, money is wasted promoting TDRs with insignificant appeal in the market. In Hong Kong and Singapore that problem is non-existent.

CONCLUSION

Proliferating variety is an underlying explanation of basic problems in managing. The ideal solution is for managers to reduce the variety in the systems being managed, and to resist the pressures from certain interest groups (e.g. bureaucrats, marketers and, especially, agitated tourism boosters representing many regions in a large country) to add variety. Managers should oppose unnecessary variety. The geographic aspect, used above to illustrate the theory, is just one way that proliferating variety affects the management of tourism.

Sustainability was noted in Chapter 10 and is explored in more detail here. The twin ideas, that tourism requires sustainable environments and that stakeholders in tourism industries should take special care to conserve environments, were controversial ideas before the 1980s, in Australia at least. Influential persons opposed these ideas when Edward St John, an environmental activist and a former minister in the Australian government, addressed the annual conference of the Australian National Travel Association (an interest group that later changed its name to Australian Tourism Industry Association and later again to Tourism Council Australia).

St John's (1974) address had a four-pronged argument. He said that natural environments are the principal resources useful in tourism, suggested that Australia's environments were being degraded by greedy exploitation and excessive pollution, pointed out that small groups of environmental activists were protesting in various ways, and remarked that tourism industry leaders were doing nothing about this issue, which was actually harming their interests.

St John's message was not favourably received by many of the persons at the conference. He was viewed as a radical troublemaker. Sixteen years later, however, the official policy of Australia's leading tourism industry association changed. A statement endorsed sustainable development for tourism and set out guidelines for development and operations. The basis of that policy, inferred from this quote from the policy document, is a restatement of what St John had said (ATIA 1990):

It is frequently the very unspoiled and unique nature of natural resources that attracts tourists. In most cases the attractions are irreplaceable. It seems self-evident that it is in the tourism industry's interests to ensure that such resources are managed in a manner which protects their intrinsic values. Regrettably, the logic of this self-interest has not always prevailed.

The discussion below begins with the origins of the idea of sustainable development of tourism (SDT) and then explains why it is now a popular idea. Next, it asks what is SDT or ST (sustainable tourism) really about? What is sustainable, and what is development? What are the managerial implications? Finally, a sting in the tail: the usual argument supporting SDT, as set out by St John and later adopted by environmentally mindful interests in tourism industries, will be revealed as deficient. This does not mean rejecting SDT; it points to a need for a different approach for fully effective strategies.

Origins of sustainable tourism policies

Increasingly over recent decades, experts who monitor particular environments (meteorologists, biologists, social researchers, zoologists, chemists and others) have been noticing problems and calling on all levels of governments, all sorts of industries and all kinds of people in their everyday lives to take action to reverse the causes of these problems.

Sustainability came to public attention, according to Hall (1995: 22), following the publication in 1980 of a World Conservation Strategy prepared via the United Nations. The most widely quoted definition of 'sustainable' comes from *Our Common Future*, a report prepared by Brundtland's committee for the World Commission on Environment and Development. The report defined sustainable activity as one which 'meets the goals of the present without comprising the ability of future generations to meet their own needs' (WCED 1987, cited in de Kadt 1992: 49).

Before 1987 the merit of sustainable development was ignored by all except committed environmentalists or greens; five years later (in 1992), de Kadt remarked that 'we have all become *greened* to a greater or lesser extent. In recent years environmental ecology and even sustainable development have moved progressively closer to centre of the stage of public concern and politics'.

Brundtland's definition and the policies in the WCED report have been widely endorsed, by governments, industry groups, academics and other persons interested in many fields, including tourism. In 1992 the United Nations Conference on Environment and Development (commonly known as the Earth Summit) held its first convention in Rio de Janeiro, attended by leaders and other representatives from 178 countries. Agreements at the Summit laid down principles for businesses and governments to follow.

Institutions representing tourism industries and academic researchers interested in links between tourism and environments took heed of these principles (Allcock et al. 1994; Smith & Eadington 1992; Bramwell & Lane 1993; Wahab & Pigram 1997; Wall 2000; R. Buckley 2002).

Are environments really in serious trouble?

Many environmental issues are debatable. For example, during the 1980s and 90s a hole in the ozone protecting the earth's biosphere grew larger, causing widespread alarm, and the cause was alleged to be environmentally damaging practices. However, by 2002 the hole had shrunk and seemed likely to close altogether; some scientists said it was merely a natural fluctuation, like swings in the earth's temperature over long periods.

An important book by Lomborg (2001) argued that many so-called 'problems' with our environments are not problems at all, and that certain things that are problematical (e.g. global warming, genetically modified food, malnutrition) are not doomsday problems, and can be managed.

Throughout human history, certain types of individuals have become easily alarmed at perceived threats and certain types have frightened others (especially the young and the credulous) by exaggerating the threats. This gives power to the alarmists who, in early days, frightened people with religious nonsense such as eternal hell for sinners. In the 1980s and 90s this type of character emerged in the form of environmental alarmists. These people led many to believe that the world's environments were on a slippery slope to doom and destruction. This has caused unnecessary gloom and depression. What has often been lacking in public debates, mass media reports and school lessons on environmental issues are three related things: a primary interest in truth, a skeptical attitude, and skills in scientific understanding.

Problems do exist in many environments, but many of these are manageable. Tourism and tourism industries are implicated, as later parts of this discussion will show.

Why SDT is a popular idea

Understanding why the idea of SDT and its common image, ecotourism, are now popular requires recognising how they affect a wide range of individuals. Overlapping categories can be identified.

Most numerous are individuals who have become concerned about environmental trends, learning about specific cases and the issue in general from their schooling, from the media and from personal observations. Certain tourism 'developments' are widely regarded as being environmentally damaging by this category. A recent example is a large resort constructed near Cardwell on the Queensland coast by Keith Williams. An environmental controversy led the Commonwealth government to place a stop-work order on the construction site in April 1995 and, while it was later lifted, environmentalists continued to protest on the grounds that the resort would cause major damage to fragile and rare environments.

Second, young people tend to be especially in favour of sustainable environments, in tourism and other fields. This is reflected in Brown's (1995) research, which found that students will pay more for accommodation with environmentally responsible practices than for accommodation with high standards of service.

Third, among workers whose livelihood depends directly on tourism the idea is popular because without it, they fear a future when demand for tourist services decreases and consequently their employment prospects suffer. If demand falls, the number of jobs decreases. Manley (1992) conveyed this idea in the title of his talk ('Protecting the Goose and Her Golden Egg') at a conference on ecotourism.

Fourth, besides seeming to protect their jobs, sustainable tourism offers tourism workers (including managers) an escape route from guilt. Many feel a degree of guilt about working in an industry widely accused of causing environmental problems. Countless publications have created that opinion, reiterated by the mass media and reflected in observations and conversations. An example is a letter in the Australian magazine *Corporate Review* (vol. 5, no. 4, 1994) alleging that 'the tourism industry is dirty and getting dirtier'.

Fifth, environmental activists ('greens') bring sharp insight and fierce voice to the issue. Committed environmentalists seem to be spiritually involved.

These categories reflect different explanations, in sequence: common sense, youthful perceptions, economic interests, intellectual reason, and spiritual belief.

The idea of SDT causes many people to feel good because it reconciles consumerism and environmentalism, contrary values existing side by side in many individuals' minds and sharply opposed in relation to tourism. Many (most?) people feel that going on holiday trips is very pleasurable and so, in effect, tourism is a highly valued form of consumption. However, tourism is a behaviour that many of these same people feel (and have been led to believe) is environmentally destructive.

Those contrary feelings are often reinforced. From the mass media and in casual conversations, we are encouraged to feel good about participating in tourism and simultaneously to feel guilty about participating. The phrase 'See Bali (or Byron Bay etc.) before it's destroyed by tourism' conveys this contradiction. By visiting a popular venue, consumers tend to feel they are one of its destroyers, one small increment in a degrading flow.

In that context, the idea of SDT is an opportunity to 'have your cake and eat it too'. SDT is popular because, by *seemingly* removing the conflict between environmentalism and consumerism, it reduces the feelings of guilt that consumers experience when participating in tourism. Also, it reduces any feelings of guilt that greenies experience when participating in tourism. An idea with strong emotional appeal across the spectrum from free-spending consumers to frugal greenies, also supported by scientists, children and young adults, is bound to be powerful and popular. In an era of mass tourism and mass threats to environments, SDT is an idea whose time has come.

If sustainable economics is an opportunity to have your cake and eat it too, it is analogous to Norman Lindsay's *Magic Pudding*, a children's story popular in Australia for 70 years about a pudding that remained the same size no matter how many slices were cut and eaten. In European culture this is the Gospel story about Jesus using five loaves and two fishes to feed 5000 people and having 12 full baskets when all had eaten. A variant is the goose that lays golden eggs. Those analogies, like others, cannot be extended very far, as magic puddings, miraculous loaves and golden geese are the stuff of fairy stories or sacred myths, with no relevance to everyday resource economics and management.

Do all indigenous societies possess ecological wisdom?

MacGregor (1993) claimed that the idea of sustainable development was not new, that what Brundtland advocated was analogous to what had been known and articulated in traditional cultures of indigenous peoples for countless generations. Knutson and Suzuki (1992) and other writers have advanced the same idea. The implication is that sustainability can be learned from indigenous cultures such as those of the Inuit in Canada, the Maori in New Zealand, and the Aborigines in Australia.

However, Ridley (1997) has shown that much of what MacGregor, Knutson and Suzuki and others have said on this theme is mythical, ignorant and misleading. In 'Ecology as religion', a chapter in his book, Ridley summarised research from around the world showing that indigenous peoples in traditional societies were, in effect, environmental vandals. The Maori for example, in the space of a few hundred years after arriving in New Zealand, ate all 12 species of moa (large birds) until they were extinct and then took up cannibalism (eating humans) to satisfy their desire for meat.

The spiritual basis of environmental sustainability attributed to many indigenous cultures in recent years has no basis in the distant past; it seems to have been invented in recent years, when environmental issues emerged. Indigenous cultures deserve respect, but that does not mean that everything attributed to them should be automatically accepted.

'Development' means different things to different people. Some view it as economic growth: more income, more jobs; some as modernisation: a social dimension where individuals in a developing society acquire new values. Some view it as distributive justice, giving poor people a more equitable share. An extension of this is development as socioeconomic transformation, away from capitalist modes of production.

The D in SDT cannot be merely economic growth, nor its social justice variations. Surely it should have a component of socioeconomic transformation, when tourists and tourism industries discover and apply new principles.

Managerial strategies for SDT

A range of managerial strategies relating to SDT can be identified. (The items below are not in order of importance.)

Environmentally acceptable practices ➤

Many businesses serving tourists are trying to minimise damage to environments in their immediate contexts. These strategies are often termed 'environmentally friendly', but 'acceptable' is more precise. Cases discussed by Harris and Leiper (1995) provide examples. Quicksilver Connection's strategies for moorings and pontoons, and for sullage disposal and selection of chemicals and cleaning agents, are illustrations of what this approach can involve. The Jemby Rinjah Lodge in the Blue Mountains West of Sydney is another model. Constructed from plantation timber, it uses self-composting toilets and solar power.

East's (1994) research found that a range of environmentally acceptable practices has become widespread in Australian hotels. An interesting finding in her survey is that larger hotels are more likely to have those practices than smaller hotels. At first glance, this evidence disputes the often-quoted environmental principle that 'small is beautiful'. East did not delve into this apparent contradiction of theory by practice. It is explored later.

Carrying capacity ➤

At particular places, keeping numbers (in a flow and/or stock) of tourists below a predetermined carrying capacity is one strategy for SDT. At Seal Bay on Kangaroo Island in South Australia, for example, in the mid-1990s the National Parks and Wildlife Service imposed an annual limit of 150 000 visitors, based on the estimate that more would impose unsustainable strains on the ecosystems for the sea lions (Harris & Leiper 1995).

A report by the Australian Department of Tourism titled *National Ecotourism Strategy* mentions several strategies for limiting visitor numbers (Allcock et al. 1994: 47), but rejects the simplest (raising prices until demand is sufficiently depressed) on equity grounds. The report seems to have overlooked a classic article titled 'The economics of wilderness' (Hardin 1969/1974), which analyses various methods for controlling visitor numbers and rejects all but one as flawed. Hardin's optimum method is not mentioned in the *Ecotourism Strategy*. It is based on a policy of merit, which at first glance seems quite inappropriate but is persuasively supported by argument. The strategy is to make visitors walk to sensitive wilderness areas and, if the numbers increase to the limit of carrying capacity, the walk is lengthened by moving the terminal for vehicles.

Rehabilitated or transformed precincts and structures ➤

Tourism development strategies might involve rehabilitating or transforming areas, structures and sites that are in poor condition. Examples were noted in Chapter 10.

Core strategy of the business ➤

Earth Sanctuaries Ltd is an unusual and special case of SDT strategies discussed by Harris and Leiper (1995), because the objective of the organisation from the start was to sustain particular ecosystems, providing a sustainable habitat for endangered Australian fauna. The strategies are feral-proof habitats, financed by selling distinctive eco-tourism experiences. Tourism is the means for achieving a higher goal.

Transformed business strategy ➤

The Penguin Reserve on Philip Island and Seal Bay on Kangaroo Island represent a differently evolved strategy from that of Earth Sanctuaries. In these cases (Harris & Leiper 1995), tourism-related enterprises began with tourism as the core business while the penguins and seals were environmental resources, used for tourism. In the 1980s, both radically transformed their priorities and so had to alter their strategies. Now the principal goals are to conserve ecosystems—the habitats of rare fauna—and tourism is used to serve that end.

Small is beautiful? ➤

Many people opposing certain activities linked to large industries because of environmental issues have proclaimed a solution in the belief that 'small is beautiful', that small-scale organisations are 'environmentally friendly'. The principle has benefits in certain contexts, but it can be environmentally disastrous. As noted earlier in this chapter, a small-is-beautiful policy caused drastic environmental problems when applied to iron manufacture in China and, as noted above, East's (1994) research found that large hotels in Australia are currently more in tune with environmentally acceptable practices than are small hotels. However, East's conclusion does not disprove the principle, as most 'large' hotels in Australia come within the 'small' range specified for organisations by the theorist who introduced the 'small-is-beautiful' principle (Schumacher 1974). A hotel with 400 employees is small in Schumacher's reckoning. More than 400 is large.

Any hotel with more than, say, 50 employees should have sufficient managerial personnel to work effectively on environmental issues. With more than 400, possible problems arise. Meanwhile, in hotels with only 10 or 20 employees, where there might be only one or two persons in managerial roles, no manager has time to do much about all the possibilities in environmental issues. These managers are usually too busy coping with a range of other matters.

In other words, very small can be too small for environmentally friendly practices and can be distinctly unfriendly. Very small operations tend to suffer diseconomies of scope, which limit the ability of their managers to deal with environmental issues. In managerial jargon, they suffer proliferating variety, a cause of managerial problems in any industry. Butler (1992) and Wight (1993) pointed out that mass tourism is not always environmentally problematical, and that small-scale tourism might cause problems.

Niche strategies? ➤

Associated with the 'small-is-beautiful' theory is another: that the best strategy is niche marketing. Some consultants, academics and policy advisers have advocated this as a general principle for sustainable tourism. Unfortunately, this one too is misused more often than not, probably because its advocates do not really understand niche strategy theory. Not all small-scale operators can or should adopt niche strategies. To be effective, a niche strategy requires significant protection from competition and from threats of competition, unusual conditions in industries in which small-scale firms abound.

The main aim of a niche strategy is to avoid having to compete. A genuine niche provides protection from competition and from threats of competition, so there is none. Thus, a sure sign that a commentator, consultant or academic is confused about niche strategies is when they suggest that niche strategies make business enterprises more competitive. Niche strategies, effectively practised, make an enterprise less competitive.

Moreover, no industry would survive if niche strategies were followed by all its component small-scale enterprises. The evolution of industries requires that managers in a proportion of small-scale enterprises ignore niches and, instead, challenge large organisations for their market shares.

One example of that issue is Budget Rent-a-Car (Blackwell & Stear 1989; King & Hyde 1989). If Budget had remained in a niche market, which was its original strategy, the Australian car rental industry could not have evolved as it did. When Bob Ansett wrested control of Budget from McIlree in the 1970s, he led the small-scale enterprise out of the niche McIlree had devised and challenged Avis and Hertz, the industry leaders. By 1981 Budget had become the industry leader, and the structure and character of the industry and its markets had been dramatically altered. The case indicates why a theory recommending niche strategies for an industry is a policy that would make the industry unsustainable.

Resource-based pricing ➤

MacGregor's (1993) list of SDT strategies includes a policy that all resources used in tourism are reflected in the prices tourists pay. Historically, tourism industries have not followed the user-pays policy. Instead, so-called 'free' resources such as natural environments have not been compensated for their use by tourists and tourism industries. This was (is) the mentality that nature is there to be exploited for economic gain. Seal Bay on Kangaroo Island is one of many cases where a user-pays policy has been adopted. The Great Barrier Reef Marine Park is another.

Regular environmental audits ➤

Audits can periodically assess SDT, at each business operation. Their scope includes evaluation of such items as recycling programs, impacts on carrying capacity, landscape aesthetics, local residents' lifestyles and values, and water quality. Stabler (1995) has reviewed methods of environmental auditing. The Great Barrier Reef Marine Park Authority is using this strategy, monitoring impacts on and near reefs used by tour operators.

Education, training and propaganda ➤

All reviews of SDT strategies include a recommendation for education and training. Tourists can be helped to learn about environmental issues, by their experiences at specific sites where particular issues are confronted, and by interpretation in static or live forms. Operating staff can be trained in various ways, for various purposes linked to SDT.

There can also be a propaganda strategy, not necessarily planned or even conscious but what Mintzberg (1991d) calls emergent strategy. With some environmental problems, there might be moral justification for manipulating opinions towards pro-conservation attitudes and pro-green activities.

Accredited promotion for SDT and eco-tourism ➤

MacGregor (1993) recommended that tourism businesses should reflect 'environmental sensitivity through *green* marketing and promoting the minimal environmental and cultural impacts' (1993: 788). Labels or brands informing tourists that a particular service, product or place conforms with principles of sustainability could be useful. A difficulty arises with the proliferation of such labels and brands, so that tourists do not know which, if any, are credible (Allcock et al. 1994; Buckley 2002).

Eco-tourism as a promotional gimmick ➤

As indicated above, some businesses and tourism promotional agencies use SDT under an eco-tourism label as a promotional gimmick, a ploy to attract consumers. Analysis set out above has shown why the ploy has powerful and widespread emotional appeal. In practice, the promoters might be doing little or nothing of substance in SDT and might be environmentally destructive. Geraghty's (1994) research found that the ploy was being widely used in Australia. McKercher's (1991) paper, titled 'The unrecognised threat to tourism: can tourism survive "Sustainability"?', also argued that much of what happens under the label of SDT or eco-tourism is environmentally damaging. Following McKercher's lead, Geraghty reviewed three cases.

Kingfisher Bay Resort is known as a leading exponent of environmentally friendly practices. Geraghty claimed that the resort had affected 'the environment of Fraser Island dramatically. It has rearranged the natural landscape and altered it to the stage where it is unrepairable. I think the promotional pamphlet for the Kingfisher Bay Resort is jumping on the bandwagon of ecotourism . . . It is not ecotourism at all . . . it is a nature-based resort' (Geraghty 1994: 21). Those criticisms might be accurate, but they miss an important point. Kingfisher Bay Resort has taken care to minimise certain factors which, in many nature resorts in other places around the world, are causing environmental harm. That is why Kingfisher Bay Resort has been a model for SDT. If in fact Kingfisher Bay Resort is keeping to its own standards, its impact on the island's ecosystems should be insignificant.

Geraghty was more critical of 'Eco-temptations', a Tasmanian promotion about four-wheel-drive tours and scenic flights, which 'are not environmentally-sensitive at all and do not fill any ecotourism criteria' (1994: 21).

His third case was a media-based tourism promotion titled 'Lismore was into eco-tourism before there was a word for it'. He described this as 'the most blatant abuse of the ecotourism term . . . [it is] just an advertisement for the Lismore/Nimbin region using the ecotourism phrase in its title solely for the purpose of attracting public attention' (1994: 22).

Research ➤

A major need for SDT is more research. Lines being followed include Moscardo's (1995) research on methods for assessing the ecological sustainability of tourist accommodation, and Sogar and Oostdyck's (1995) studies on sustainable tourism management in parks and forests. Jackson et al.'s (1995) interest in authenticity led to a suggested strategy for protecting fragile environments from mass tourism. Mathieson and Wall (1982) and Pigram (1992) indicated various relationships between tourism and environmental impacts, useful for strategies towards those aims. Less formal research observing real cases is another way of moving towards SDT, when cases showing some success become models to be copied.

Higher industrialisation: a useful state for SDT? ➤

Earlier in this chapter and elsewhere in this book, the point was made that some detrimental impacts of tourism occur beyond the scope of tourism industries. They occur because of activities by independent tourists. An underlying difficulty is that blaming 'the industry' or expecting 'the industry' to remedy the problems is futile. How can an industry be held responsible for Keith and Kylie setting off in their 4WD camper and littering every road and river bank from Killara to Kakadu with thousands of beer cans and cheeseburger containers?

Whatever might be regrettable in highly industrialised tourism, one of its advantages is that managers can be held responsible for a wide range of environmental matters and are generally able to do something. Under this scenario, the 4WD remains at home and the holiday-makers use public carriers, commercial accommodation and organised tours. Coach drivers and tour guides manage, by direct supervision, to reduce the undesirable environmental impacts stemming from Kylie's bad habits with beer cans and Keith's with cheeseburger packaging.

Defects in the conventional argument for SDT

Closely investigated, the conventional argument for sustainable tourism, as expressed by St John in 1974, can be revealed as defective. Sustainable tourism has been promoted by an unsustainable argument. The conventional argument assumes that tourists will tend not to visit destinations where the main attractive features have been ruined or where background environments have become polluted to a marked degree. There are three problems with that assumption.

First, empirical evidence contradicts it. If the assumption were valid, places where general environments had deteriorated drastically, or where the primary attractions had been totally destroyed, would decline in popularity as tourist destinations.

Thirty years ago Bangkok was commonly described by visitors as a city with degraded environments: noisy, smelly, with badly polluted air, overcrowded, appalling traffic congestion, and unpleasant to visit. Since the 1960s its environments have become much worse, by all accounts. Yet the city has seen increases in tourist arrivals, not merely in transit but for visits. Bangkok's history rebuts the argument that degraded environments destroy tourism.

After 1840, when discovered by Europeans, the pink and white terraces at Rotorua became New Zealand's most famous tourist attractions. Rock formations with steam pools, they were described as unique and remarkable, celebrated in writings and paintings. A flow of tourists came from overseas to see them, and nearby hotels, tour operators and transport firms flourished. Then, in 1886, the terraces and nearby hotels were totally destroyed by a huge volcanic eruption. Nothing was left. After a brief lull, tourism revived. New hotels were built. Now there are informative signs and paintings describing what the pink and white terraces looked like, and indicating the locations of ruined hotels. Rotorua remains one of New Zealand's major tourist destinations. Other features replaced the pink and white terraces as focal interests for tourists, but this does not alter the analysis. Rotorua's history undermines the argument that destroying key attractions in a region will destroy tourism there.

Second, there is a problem with the argument's underlying theory that tourism involves destinations attracting tourists. This is a superficial and misleading view of what happens (a point emphasised in Chapters 6 and 13). Notions about 'attractions' or 'pull factors' operating in any literal sense are illusions in tourism, with no scientific validity. Likewise, there is no scientific basis for claims such as 'each locality . . . has its special character [which] may well constitute its major attractiveness to tourists' (Oelrichs 1992: 14). That is never literally true, but is realistic in a few places for a few tourists. It should not be held up as a general principle about the big picture of tourism.

In general, as discussed earlier in this book, the causal factors of tourism are not in tourist destinations or their environmental qualities. Research has found that the major causes are push factors in places where people normally live. Push factors are motivations to travel away from home, motivations arising from environments at and near home, based on a range of human needs: a need for temporary escape from mundane routines, a need for self-evaluation, for regression, for esteem, social contacts and so on. Obviously other places are necessary to perform the roles of tourist destinations if those needs are to be satisfied via tourism, but environmental conditions there are not necessarily relevant.

The key factor is not the state of environments in destinations measured against some arbitrary model of environmental quality, but the *relative* states of environments in two locations at either end of each whole tourism system: the generating regions where tourists normally reside and the destinations they might visit. People residing in polluted cities will choose to travel for tourism in polluted destinations if they perceive a difference in the *relative* environments of those two places.

For example, many residents of Sydney live in badly polluted environments: their quality of life is affected by air pollution and virtually continuous aircraft noise. One of their popular holiday destinations is the coastal region 60 kilometres north. Over the past 30 years this region's environmental qualities have been badly damaged by pollutant sewage seeping into the lakes and rivers, so that what were formerly popular fishing and swimming areas are now virtually useless for those holiday recreations. Why has the region remained popular as a tourist destination for Sydneysiders? Part of the explanation is that it is quiet and peaceful, without noisy aircraft overhead every minute or two, and has clean air.

The third problem with the conventional argument is that it ignores time lags and new generations of tourists. Today's tourists are not all the same people from last year and last decade. Not all tourists assess changing environments in destinations based on personal experience of the trends. The tourists visiting Bangkok in 1995 are, with few exceptions, not those who were tourists in Bangkok years ago when the air was not so putrid as it is now, and no tourist in Rotorua during the past 50 years knew the place when tourists were visiting the pink and white terraces.

Also, new generations of tourists develop new forms of leisure behaviour, and so old forms that were popular become less common and might totally disappear. No tourists went swimming for pleasure before about 1780, and few (if any) tourists sunbathed for pleasure before about 1925 (Turner & Ash 1975). No tourists took photographs before 1839, when the habit began at Lake Como (Sontag 1979). Looking the other way on a time scale, few tourists these days visit the morgues or the sewers in Paris, two very popular attractions in the 19th century (MacCannell 1976). Relatively few tourists these days are totally fascinated by caves and grottoes, while 150 years ago those natural phenomena were sites for mass tourism. Reflecting on that trend in Capri, Norman Douglas questioned, in reference to the Blue Grotto, 'whether, if it were discovered today, it would attract the attention it once did. For it appeared on the crest of a wave of cavern and ruin worship that overswept Northern Europe' (Douglas (1911: 59).

Those patterns indicate that, while the fundamentals of tourism—recreational and creative leisure away from home—are constant, the forms of tourism evolve over generations, depending on social, cultural and other environments in generating regions and on perceptions of relative environments in and features of destination regions.

A better argument for SDT

The better argument in favour of SDT is not that it helps tourism, for that line merely reinforces erroneous theories about what causes tourism. The better argument in favour of SDT is that it conserves the biosphere.

Policies for environmental sustainability in other activities, such as manufacturing and mining, are not justified because they help manufacturing and mining, so attempts to justify SDT on the grounds that it helps tourism should seem suspicious. As shown above, the argument for a special case with tourism is spurious. SDT's best justification is that it conserves life, in all its essential diversity, conserving the complex and often fragile ecosystems of the biosphere. Benefits for tourism should be seen as a byproduct of that argument, not as its basis. Once that is recognised, tourism industry associations would endorse pro-environmental policies in general, not merely those which help certain forms of tourism.

Ideal SDT?

Tourism carries a handicap from its own history in relation to the possibility of making a complete change to sustainability. Historically, much tourism has been a form of imperialism, and the imperial attitude persists.

Tourists from rich, powerful societies continue to visit places where poorer, subject societies reside, and do not easily avoid an assumption that destinations should have something 'to offer the tourist'. That typical phrase has an imperial tone, implying that tourists are superior in some way and must, therefore, be offered something.

Chamberlin's (1983) book *Loot: The Plunder of Heritage* captures the origins and later forms of this attitude, beginning with 18th century aristocratic tourists from Western Europe plundering cultural artefacts of colonies or oppressed regions in those tourists' imperial systems, the empires of England, France etc. A famous case began in 1801–03 with Lord Elgin's removal of ancient marble sculptures from Athens. At great expense, he arranged for his loot to be taken home in several ships, and in 1816 sold the best pieces to the British Museum. In the 1980s, the Greek government began a campaign to have them returned.

Chamberlin and other writers claim that the same imperial attitude persists in those ordinary tourists today who feel that destinations have a duty to have something to offer the tourist. The same attitude is widely apparent in tourism industries. If so, progress towards perfect SDT is handicapped.

What are the alternatives? Perfect SDT is expressed in the famous motto of the Sierra Club: 'Take only photographs, leave only footprints'. It is ideal, but not comprehensive as it is impractical for most forms of tourism, which require facilities leaving more than footprints. The range of policies and strategies briefly described in the list above provides a more comprehensive approach.

WHO ACTUALLY MANAGES TOURISM?

Who manages tourism? The question might seem superfluous, as it does not appear to have been discussed by other writers. For instance, the journal *Tourism Management*, published several times annually for 27 years, so far as is known has never published articles pondering the question, even on the side of larger substantive topics.

The explanation for ignoring the question is simple. Conventional thinking assumes that tourism is entirely managed by persons employed in organisations that serve tourists:

travel agencies, tour operators, theme parks, airlines, hotels, national and regional tourism bodies. Conventional wisdom assumes that tourism is wholly industrialised, that every resource used by tourists comes from an industry or a collection of industries, managed by persons with routine managerial responsibilities. Once tourism is understood as a partly industrialised process and is viewed as a more complex picture, a different and much more realistic answer can emerge.

An educational diversion

Diverting the theme temporarily from tourism to education can clarify the issue. Who manages education? The quick answer is that education is managed by the teachers and administrators in what is often called the education industry, comprising kindergarten, primary and high schools, colleges and universities. But what if the question were rephrased and directed specifically at you: who has managed and now manages *your* education? Who plans, organises, coordinates and monitors the sequences of educational processes that you experience?

Before settling on an answer conclusively, reflect on the probability that your educational experiences are not merely what happens in classrooms and lecture theatres; they include educational experiences adding to your knowledge or understanding that occur when you are away from schools and universities. Would you agree that a lot of your education has come from normal everyday experiences that are not intended to be educational: conversations with acquaintances and family, observing the world around you, watching TV and films, listening to radio, reading newspapers, working, playing sport and playing games? In other words, would you agree that a large informal category of education exists outside any education industry? Now answer the question: who managed (and is managing) your education? Possibly your answer will be something like this:

> *My education was and is managed partly by teachers and administrators in the education industry, partly by myself and, in early years, by my parents. However, a large portion of my education is not managed in any real sense of the word—it is not planned, monitored, coordinated or controlled—it happens piecemeal.*

In a famous critique of modern education and conventional schools, Ivan Illich (1971) drew attention to a distinction between education and schooling that many people overlook. That distinction can be seen emerging from the answer in the previous paragraph. Education is the process of an individual acquiring knowledge and understanding from any source, while schooling is an institutionalised, teacher-related process with an obligatory curriculum. The two processes often go together, but they are not identical. Education overlaps schooling, and is a far wider process.

What has come to be called 'the education industry' or 'the education system' parades under a misleading title. It is more accurately called 'the schooling industry'. Teachers and administrators in schooling institutions (high schools, colleges, universities) are not involved in the total spectrum of an education system; they are limited to its schooling part, its institutionalised part. Education, like tourism, is a part-industrialised activity.

Back to tourism: who actually manages?

Who manages tourism? A precise answer comes from first recognising that tourism, like education, is a partly industrialised process. A portion of tourism transpires within the scope of tourism industries and that portion is managed by managers employed in those industries. What of the other part? To the extent that tourism is non-industrialised, it is managed by individual tourists and, to some degree, is not managed at all.

Individual tourists, no matter how clever and assiduous, cannot totally manage their own tourism. They might plan an itinerary, deciding where to go, the route and schedule, what to do, where to stay, how to get from place to place. But they normally cannot accomplish much regarding other elements of managing their trips, as they lack the knowledge of and authority over resources in places visited.

Tourism in its usual modern styles cannot be totally managed by managers employed in tourism industries, by managers in regional or national bureaucracies, by individual tourists, or by all those categories in combination. When any individual goes off on a trip, inevitably there will be future experiences that cannot be planned, or coordinated, or controlled for. On a mass scale this condition is merely multiplied, even while mass tourism seems stereotyped. Some remarks on the condition are made at the end of this chapter.

THE CONSEQUENCES OF PARTIAL INDUSTRIALISATION

In Chapters 7 and 11, arguments and evidence were set out to demonstrate a theory that tourism is partly industrialised. In the earlier sections of this chapter the relevance of varying levels of industrialisation was shown to be relevant to managerial issues of seasonality, feeback, proliferating variety, and sustainable tourism.

Broadly, the concept of partial industrialisation provides a more realistic understanding of what actually happens with tourism—especially in reference to managerial issues—than the simplistic notion that tourism is an industry with its implication of total industrialisation. The discussion below begins by noting a number of issues arising from the analysis and then identifies several consequences of partial industrialisation.

Two concepts of industry with different applications

The simple concept of tourism industry, based on economic impacts, sees it as very large and leads to claims that it is 'the world's largest industry'. The alternative, more complicated concept is based on managerial practices. It perceives multiple tourism industries and a large range of other resources supporting tourism.

The practical implications of these two concepts are, first, that each has its own applications and, second, that they should not be confused. For discussing broad economic impacts of tourism, the first is appropriate. For discussing policy, strategic and operational issues about how tourism is managed, and a range of other topics, the second concept is relevant.

The 'fragmented industry' myth

Many commentators, researchers and policy makers have tried to adapt the economic concept to managerial and policy issues. Then, discovering that most organisations supplying goods and services to tourists are managed in ways that ignore tourism issues, they fall back on the excuse that 'the tourism industry is fragmented'. Two cases in Chapter 12 (Wyndham Winery, and the Summit Restaurant before 1987) illustrate the basis of this conclusion; thousands of similar examples can be found. The excuse that 'the tourism industry is fragmented' is a misleading idea arising because the facts of business life do not match the theory. The excuse stems from confusion, and it spreads ignorance and frustration.

What happens is this. People wanting to boost tourism assume that all resources used by tourists belong to something called 'the industry' and that the managers of those resources should become active in that something to make it less fragmented. The under-lying assumption is that fragmented resources can be made cohesive (and thus more pro-ductive) by communicating with managers. Tourism boosters have tended to believe that once managers of any resources used by tourists are persuaded to believe that those resources are in the tourism industry, they will change their strategies and give more attention to tourism.

An example of this belief in New Zealand was a speech by Elspeth Kennedy, presi-dent of the South Island Promotion Association. According to a newspaper report, she was 'at a loss to understand why tourism marketing is left to tourism operators'. She suggested that all businesses offering goods or services used by tourists should 'get together' and help promotions aimed at tourists (reported in *The Dominion*, 20 September 1990). An expression of the belief in Australia was a comment by Ian Kennedy, vice-president of the Pacific Asia Travel Association, at a seminar at Ballina in July 1994. He described businesses that earn money from tourists without supporting tourism promotions as 'parasites'.

Countless other persons bound up in tourism promotion have made comments similar to these two. Despite the good intentions of the individuals, the assumptions on which their beliefs rest are flawed. The best interests of many businesses are served if their managers continue to treat tourists incidentally, not strategically. Arguing against that policy is futile. A more realistic approach, in tune with business practice, is to accept that tourism is partly industrialised, while allowing that some movements occur at the fringes, when enterprises such as the Summit Restaurant (in 1988) change strategies.

In economics theory, there is a valid concept known as a fragmented industry (Porter 1980). It is quite unlike the notion given that name by tourism boosters. Presumably the expression was picked up from economics and applied to tourism without close attention to its proper meaning.

Because tourism is partly industrialised, the numbers of real jobs created and sustained are fewer than the usual statistics imply, because the estimates are based on a false assumption of 100% industrialisation.

A report by the World Travel and Tourism Council (1993) was widely circulated in the mass media, and reiterated in magazines distributed to targeted readers around the world. Among countless claims that the tourism industry is the largest in the world, this one went out in the glossiest clothing. It asserted that this industry 'creates twice as many jobs as the average industry', according to the chief executive of American Express, Harvey Golub. A member of the WTTC, he wrote that research had shown that '204 million people, or 10% of the world's employees . . . are directly or indirectly employed in travel and tourism related work', and that by 2005, 'another 144 million new jobs' will be generated (Golub 1993: 8).

Those are misleading statistics. The true figures are very much smaller. Here is why. First, the data are based on technical definitions of tourist which, as explained in Chapter 2, encompass a wide scope of travellers and visitors, far wider that common sense would describe as 'tourists'. The second is a more substantial reason. When a report states that tourism employs a number of people, readers naturally infer that the data refer to a number of real and potentially identifiable jobs. And they infer that those jobs are in hotels, airlines, tour operators, theme parks, travel agencies and the like. Both of those inferences are illusions.

The data refer to a conglomeration of fractions of virtually every job in the workforce of the economy being discussed. Multiplier effects mean that even the grave-digger who buries a dead hotel employee is 'indirectly' paid by tourists' expenditure. A fraction of that job stems from 'the tourism industry'. And the shop assistant from whom the grave-digger bought his shovel is in the same category, one further round of spending away but still within Golub's scope—employed by the tourism industry.

Because tourism is partly industrialised, the numbers partly refer to fractions of jobs, fractions of virtually all jobs in the country, and partly to a number of whole jobs. Only the latter, the whole jobs, are tourism-related in the sense of dealing with tourism and requiring any tourism-related skills. When all those realities are teased out, the WTTC reports appear in a rather different light. A fuller explanation of this issue is set out elsewhere (Leiper 1999a).

The practical implication of the point in the previous section is that where the index of industrialisation is low, employment opportunities in tourism industries are much fewer than is stated in official statistics. For example, impact studies on domestic tourism in countries like Australia typically conclude that tourism is a very large industry supporting large-scale and growing employment. In truth, it involves large-scale consumption across a great many industries, most of which have no strategic links with tourists, so there are relatively few whole jobs working in tourism-related positions.

Many new jobs *have been* created in tourism industries, but not nearly so many as official statistics typically state. A consequence is that many people looking for employment become cynical about media stories of a boom in tourism jobs. A long-term consequence might be that the thousands of educational courses designed for students seeking careers in the tourism industry might be oversupplying the labour market.

Geographic dispersal

Part-industrialisation allows tourists' itineraries to be more widely dispersed than would be the case under total industrialisation. The explanation, and managerial implications, were set out in an earlier section of this chapter on the issue of proliferating variety.

Who manages tourism?

As discussed earlier in this chapter, part-industrialisation means that tourism is managed by employees in tourism industries to some degree and, in balance, by tourists. Because tourists have no authority over many of the resources that most will inevitably use during trips, they cannot manage everything. Consequently tourism is, inevitably, a partly managed process. Nobody has responsibility and authority for a portion of the resources used by tourists.

In those circumstances, beyond managed systems, environments of various sorts become problematical. Tourists become frustrated and complain that 'they should do something about it, if they want tourists here', implying that a tourism industry with its managers has responsibility.

Impediments to development

Partly industrialised tourism is handicapped in terms of its development, for the simple reason that the scale of the activity is not supported by an equivalent scale of industry. Partial industrialisation is an impediment to the work of tourism industry associations. These groups are activated by persons with interests in tourism who perceive, from economic impacts, that they represent a very large industry with much potential. They expect all the components of that 'industry' to join its associations and contribute to their groups' activities. However, most of those components are managed by persons who know that *their* own best interests are not linked to tourism, so they stay outside, or remain on the fringe. Wyndham Winery, described in Chapter 12, is a representative example of countless businesses in this condition. This is traditionally explained by saying that markets (in this instance, for tourism promotion) fail to perform in ways that economic theory suggests they should.

The true failure is simple economic theory. Such theory fails to deal with managed organisations, pretending they do not exist. Economic theory recognises as factors of production land, capital, labour and enterprise. In the 150 years since that theory was devised, important new factors of economic production have developed. They are organisations and management.

A reason for governmental and community involvement

Part-industrialisation is the main underlying (and largely unrecognised) reason why governments and community groups become directly involved in tourism. This differentiates tourism from wholly industrialised processes such as iron and steel manufacture, automobile manufacture and distribution, banking and insurance. O'Fallon's (1994) research, on governmental policy in tourism, included this line of analysis.

Because governments cannot subsidise an industry for no reason, and because the true reason is disguised, excuses have to be devised. A recent popular one is that tourism is 'a sunrise industry' and, like all new industries, needs support. In fact, Australia has had well-established tourism industries since at least 1882, when Thomas Cook Ltd opened an office in Melbourne. Australia's tourism industries are decades older than its electricity industries, its iron and steel industry and its car manufacturing industry.

The alternative concept, identifying industrial activity directed at tourism from the perspective of business management, sees multiple tourism industries. Some of them are fragmented industries, others are emerging, mature or in obsolence.

Targets for environmentalists

Impacts of tourism, good and bad, are caused partly by tourism industries and partly by independent tourism. Giving tourism industries all the credit and all the blame is irrational. To the extent that tourism is part-industrialised, 'the industry' is the wrong target. (This point was described in the discussion on sustainable development earlier in this chapter.)

Instability

Part-industrialisation is a cause of instability in tourist flows. Where there is a high degree of industrialisation, such as international tourism by residents of Japan, the numbers visiting each destination are relatively stable from one year to the next. On the other hand, where most tourists are independent, as in domestic tourism in Australia, the numbers going to each destination tend to vary more from year to year.

What causes the difference? The condition is similar to the seasonal fluctuations discussed earlier in this chapter. Managers in a tourism industry, as in any industry, take action to smooth out severe fluctuations, by synchromarketing and other strategies. Where there is capital invested, there are incentives to maintain income. At the other extreme, in independent tourism, managers play a relatively small role in influencing where tourists go. And there is little capital invested in tourism-specific plant (e.g. transport and accommodation) relative to tourist numbers.

Denying partial industrialisation: who gains?

Ten implications of tourism's partly industrialised condition have been identified and described briefly. These implications reflect several important issues that cause concern to many managers, planners, marketers, environmentalists and policy makers.

Denying or overlooking part-industrialisation is very beneficial for many tourism industry associations in one important respect. By pretending that tourism is an industry they can pose as representing the entire scope of resources used by tourists, and this can serve their own interests when seeking and gaining subsidies and other assistance from governments. Tourism industry associations tend to claim all the credit for the economic gains flowing into a country or region from tourism, even if most of the tourist visitors were largely independent of any tourism industry. Via this pretence, this denial strategy, tourism industry associations in many jurisdictions have been able to obtain substantial sums of assistance from governments, which they can use for their own interests. This might mean promoting the kinds of tourism that relies on tourism industries.

An example has been seen in Australia throughout recent years. A large flow of international inbound tourists (in the technical sense) comprised international students. Because of their large numbers, long-duration visits and large expenditures on fees as well as living expenses, in total they contributed greatly to the Australian economy. Indeed, they contributed more to the economy than did all tourists using hotels for accommodation (O'Dea 1997a, 1997b).

Meanwhile, various tourism industry organisations dependent on government subsidies do nothing substantial to promote the flow of international students (leaving the role to universities), while implicitly claiming credit for the economic impacts of students' spending as a sizable part of the total impact of 'tourists'.

CONCLUSION

Partial industrialisation helps explains many features of modern tourism. Ignoring it, by pretending that the process is wholly industrialised, leads to confusion and frustration when 'the tourism industry' does not perform in the way an industry is supposed to perform. The concept is relevant to business managers, policy makers, planners and bureaucratic administrators, consultants, researchers, educational administrators and environmentalists.

TOURISM MANAGEMENT: A REVIEW

A message running through this book is that tourism and its associated resources, industries, markets and environmental interactions can and should be viewed as highly complex phenomena. A theme is that complexities can be better understood by holistic and systemic approaches to the particular issue at hand. Another theme is that two fields of knowledge, relating to tourism and management, can be studied separately and can also be brought together, combined to gain understanding.

The pressing concerns of managers are quite properly with the aims, policies, strategies and operations of their organisations and, increasingly, with environmental issues. All those things are important, and the environment has become crucial to the future wellbeing of everyone, an issue with far greater importance and scope than might be inferred from considering its links with tourism. However important all those concerns are, the core of tourism management, which is the theme of this book, revolves around fostering appropriate experiences for tourists. Like most other human activities, tourism is managed; and, like some activities, it can be managed only so far, however knowledgeable the practitioners.

A limitation of that sort might seem problematical to persons with professional responsibilities for managing tourism, but it should not be a source of frustration. Fortunately, few managers in tourism industries have personalities like F.W. Taylor, creator of scientific management, who was unable to enjoy his own leisure and spoiled other persons' because he had to plan, measure and control everything in sight, including all kinds of recreation. At its core, tourism is a form of leisure behaviour, and therefore should never be too closely managed.

The leisure basis of modern tourism means that for many, if not most tourists, their trips are special periods for recreational and creative experiences. Neither form of human experience should be too closely managed, for then it loses spontaneity, loses some of its intrinsic value. One of the distinctive arts in tourism management is sensing that boundary, a skill not explored in this book. Ending on an admission of that sort is appropriate, for it recognises that no book on a subject as diverse as tourism management should ever be presumed to span all the themes implied by its title.

Discussion questions

1. Seasonal fluctuations are only one kind of time-related fluctuation occurring in tourism. What are the others?
2. Describe how seasonal fluctuations in tourism are caused by factors in TGRs and in TDRs.
3. Why would managers involved with very highly industrialised tourism want to reduce the severity of seasonal fluctuations?
4. How would managers involved with very highly industrialised tourism reduce the severity of seasonal fluctuations?
5. Describe why collecting information from feedback is relatively simple and economical in highly industrialised tourism but complicated and expensive under conditions of low-level industrialisation.
6. Explain the economic and managerial reasons why there would be fewer tourist destinations worldwide if the level of industrialisation in tourism systems were to rise.
7. Describe at least three reasons why SDT (sustainable development of tourism) has become a popular idea.
8. While the cultures of indigenous peoples deserve respect, according to writers such as Ridley we should not imagine that indigenous cultures contain wisdom for environmental sustainability. What research findings led Ridley to that conclusion?
9. List and discuss at least six managerial strategies that can contribute to SDT.
10. 'Small is beautiful' has become a slogan among environmental activists. According to the writer of the book with the title in which the slogan originated, how small is small, in terms of numbers of people working in a business organisation?

11. Explain why an industry would not develop and evolve if the managers of all its component business organisations adopted niche market strategies.

12. Is eco-tourism merely a promotional gimmick, in your opinion? What evidence do you have to either support or reject that possibility?

13. What are the defects in the conventional argument for SDT?

14. Who actually manages tourism under conditions of partial industrialisation?

15. List and describe at least six consequences of the partial industrialisation of tourism.

16. If you were a minister in the government of a country, discussing with other ministers and advisers how much financial subsidy should be given to promote tourism, how would the theory of partial industrialisation shape your thinking?

Recommended reading

Aguayo, R. 1990, *Dr Deming: The American Who Taught the Japanese About Quality*, New York: Simon & Schuster

Allcock, A., Jones, B., Lane, S. & Grant, J. 1994, *National Ecotourism Strategy*, Department of Tourism, Canberra: AGPS

Beeton, Sue 1998, *Ecotourism: A Practical Guide for Rural Communities,* Melbourne: Landlink Press

Bosselman, F. 1978, *In the Wake of the Tourist: Managing Special Places in Eight Countries,* Washington, DC: The Conservation Foundation

Buckley, Ralf 2001, Sustainable tourism management, *Annals of Tourism Research*, 28: 523–5

Buckley, Ralf 2002, Tourism ecolabels, *Annals of Tourism Research*, 29: 183–208

Butler, R. 1992, Alternative tourism: the thin edge of the wedge, pp 31–46 in Smith & Eadington (eds), op. cit.

Dredge, D. 1999, Destination, place, planning and design, *Annals of Tourism Research*, 26: 772–91

Garrod, Brian & Fyall, Alan 2000, Managing heritage tourism, *Annals of Tourism Research*, 27: 682–708

Hall, Colin Michael 2003, *Introduction to Tourism: Dimensions and Issues,* Sydney: Hospitality Press

Harris, Robert & Leiper, Neil 1995, *Sustainable Tourism in Australia: A Casebook Perspective,* Sydney: Butterworth Heinemann

Khan, M. 2003, Ecoserve: ecotourists' quality expectations, *Annals of Tourism Research*, 30: 109–24

Lomborg, Bjorn 2001, *The Skeptical Environmentalist: Measuring the Real State of the World,* Cambridge: Cambridge University Press

Moscardo, Gianna 1995, Developing a research agenda to assess the ecological sustainability of specialist tourist accommodation, pp 171–86 in Faulkner, Fagence, Davidson & Craig-Smith (eds), *Tourism Research and Education in Australia*, Proceedings of conference (Gold Coast, February 1994), Canberra: Bureau of Tourism Research

Mowforth, M. & Munt, I. 1998, *Tourism and Sustainability: New Tourism in the Third World,* London: Routledge

Smith, Valene & Eadington, William R. (eds) 1992, *Tourism Alternatives: Potentials and Problems in the Development of Tourism*, Philadephia: University of Pennsylvania Press

Swarbrooke, J. 1999, *Sustainable Tourism Management,* New York: CABI

Wahab, Salah & Pigram, John (eds) 1997, *Tourism Development and Growth: The Challenge of Sustainability,* London: Routledge

Wall, G. 2000, Sustainable development, pp 567–8 in *The Encyclopedia of Tourism,* J. Jafari (ed.), London: Routledge

Wight, P. 1993, Sustainable ecotourism: balancing economic, environmental and social goals within an ethical framework, *Journal of Tourism Studies*, 4(2): 54–66

World Commission on Environment and Development 1987, *Our Common Future,* New York: Oxford University Press

World Tourism Organisation 2000, *Sustainable Development of Tourism: A Compilation of Good Practices,* Madrid: WTO

BIBLIOGRAPHY

Ackoff, R. & Emery, F.E. 1972, *On Purposeful Systems*, London: Tavistock.

Aditjondro, George 1995, *Bali, Jakarta's Colony: Social & Ecological Impacts of Jakarta-Based Conglomerates on Bali's Tourism Industry*, Perth: Murdoch University, Asia Research Centre, Working Paper no. 58.

Adkin, Mark 1996, The Charge: The Real Reason why the Light Brigade was lost, London: Pimlico.

Adler, J. 1989, Origins of Sightseeing, *Annals of Tourism Research*, 16: 7–29.

Agarwal, Sheela 2002, Restructuring seaside tourism: the resort lifecyle, *Annals of Tourism Research*, 29: 25–55.

AGB McNair 1986, *Consumer Perceptions of Current Domestic Air Service Arrangements*, a report for the Independent Review of Economic Regulation of Domestic Aviation, Canberra: IRERDA.

Aguayo, Rafael 1990, *Dr Deming: The American Who Taught the Japanese about Quality*, New York: Simon & Schuster.

Ahituv, Niv & Neumann, Seev 1990, *Principles of Information Systems for Management*, (3rd edn), Dubuque: Wm C. Brown.

Airey, David & Nightingale, Michael 1981, Tourism Occupations, Career Profiles and Knowledge, *Annals of Tourism Research*, 8: 52–68.

Alexander, C. 1994, *The Way to Xanadu: Searches for the Source of Coleridge's Kubla Khan*, London: Phoenix.

Alexander, E. 1995, *How Organisations Act Together: Interorganisation Coordination in Theory & Practice*, Amsterdam: Gordon & Breach.

Allcock, Alison, Jones, Barbara, Lane, Susan & Grant, Jill 1994, *National Ecotourism Strategy*, Department of Tourism, Canberra: AGPS.

Andrews, K. 1991, The Concept of Corporate Strategy, pp 44–52 in Mintzberg & Quinn 1991, op. cit. (first pub. 1980).

Andronicus, Antonios 1979, Tourism in Cyprus, pp 237–64 in de Kadt 1979, op. cit.

Angyal, A. 1969, A logic of systems, pp 17–29 in Emery 1969, op. cit.

Ansett Holdings 1995, *Annual Report 1995*, Melbourne: Ansett.

——1996, *Annual Report 1996*, Melbourne: Ansett.

Ansett, Bob 1989, Case history: Budget Rent-A-Car, managing growth & maintaining corporate control, pp 153–64 in Blackwell & Stear, op. cit.

Ansoff, H. 1965, *Corporate Strategy: An Analytical Approach to Business Policy for Growth & Expansion*, New York: McGraw Hill.

Archer, B. 1982, The value of multipliers and their policy implications, *Tourism Management*, 3: 236–41.

Ardrey, R. 1967, *The Territorial Imperative: A Personal Inquiry into the Animal Origins of Property & Possessions*, London: Collins.

Argenti, John 1976, *Corporate Collapse: The Causes and Symptoms*, London: McGraw Hill.

——1984, *Predicting Corporate Failure: Notes for Businessmen*, London: Institute of Chartered Accountants.

Aristotle 1920, *Poetics* (trans. Ingram Bywater), Oxford: Clarenden Press (*c*. 330 BC).

Ashenden, D. & Milligan, S. 1994, Report takes aim at productivity in management education: special report, *The Weekend Australian*, 25–26 June, p. 41.

Australian Hotels Association 1988, *A History of the Australian Hotels Association in New South Wales 1873–1988*, Sydney: AHA.

Australian Tourism Industry Association 1990, *Environmental Guidelines for Tourism Developers*, Canberra: ATIA.

Axelrod, R. 1990, *The Evolution of Cooperation*, London: Penguin.

Bain, K. & Howells, P. 1988, *Understanding Markets: An Introduction to the Theory, Institutions and Practices of Markets*, London: Harvester-Wheatsheaf.

Baker, D. & Crompton, J. 2000, Quality, satisfaction and behaviour intention, *Annals of Tourism Research*, 27: 785–803.

Baker, G. & Funaro, B. 1955, *Motels*, New York: Reinhold.

Baker, Keith 1994, *Tourism Trends in New South Wales*, Sydney: Tourism NSW.

Ballantyne, J. 1994, The empowering of employees in Australian hotels and resorts (unpublished research report), Southern Cross University.

Balzar, J. 2002, Pirates of the Caribbean . . . and we're talking about USA executives, *Hong Kong Mail*, 25 May, p. 15.

Banks Group 1987, *Tourism Marketing Plan for Victoria: Three Year Strategy 1987–1990*, Sydney: The Banks Group.

Bar-On, Raymond 1993, Seasonality, pp 705–34 in Khan et al. 1993, op. cit.

Barr, T. 1990, *No Swank Here: The Development of the Whitsundays as a Tourist Destination to the early 1970s*, Townsville: James Cook University.

Bartholomeusz, S. 2001, Rundown and cashless, carrier was waiting to implode, *Sydney Morning Herald*, 15–16 September, p 76.

Barzun, J. 2001, *From Dawn to Decadence: 1500 to the Present, 500 Years of Western Cultural Life*, New York: HarperCollins.

Basho, M. 1966, *The Narrow Road to the Deep North and Other Travel Sketches* (c.1690, trans. Nobuyuki Yuasa), Harmondsworth: Penguin.

Bates, J. 1967, untitled paper presented to Tourism Seminar, Council of City of Blue Mountains, Katoomba, (ms at Tourism NSW, Sydney).

Baumol, W.J. & Blinder, A.S. 1988, *Economics Principles and Policies* (4th edn), New York: Harcourt Brace Jovanovich.

Baumol, W.J., Panzar, J.C. & Willig, R.D. 1982, *Contestable Markets and the Theory of Industry Structure*, New York: Harcourt Brace Jovanovich.

BCC (Boston Consulting Group) 1975, *Strategy Alternatives for the British Motorcycle Industry*, London: HMSO.

Beaumont, N. 1998, The meaning of ecotourism: is there now consensus for defining this 'natural' phenomenon? *Pacific Tourism Review*, 2: 239–50.

Beer, S. 1959, *Brain of the Firm*, Chichester: Wiley.

——1975, *Platform for Change*, Chichester: Wiley.

——1979, *Heart of the Enterprise*, Chichester: Wiley.

Beeton, Sue 1998, *Ecotourism: A Practical Guide for Rural Communities*, Melbourne: Landlink Press.

Bell, Clive 1928, *How to Make a Civilization*, in Larrabee & Meyerson (eds) op. cit., pp 31–8.

Bella, R., Marsden, R., Sullivan, W., Swidler, A. & Tipton, S. 1985, *Habits of the Heart: Individualism and Commitment in American Life*, Berkeley: University of California Press.

Benson, E.F. 1929, *Paying Guests*, London: Hogarth.

Berger, J. 1972, *Ways of Seeing*, London: BBC & Penguin.

Bertalanffy, L. 1972a, The history and status of general systems, pp 31–8 in *Trends in General systems theory*, G. Klir (ed.), New York: Wiley.

——1972b, General systems theory: a critical review, pp 29–49 in *Systems Behaviour*, J. Beishon & G. Peters (eds), London: Harper & Row.

Best, Michael 1990, *The New Competition: Institutions of Industrial Restructuring*, Cambridge: Polity Press.

Blackwell, James & Stear, Lloyd (eds) 1989, *Case Histories of Tourism and Hospitality*, Sydney: Australian-International Magazine Services.

Blainey, Geoffrey 1982, *Triumph of the Nomads: A History of Ancient Australia*, Melbourne: Macmillan.

——2002, *The Tyranny of Distance* (2nd edn), Melbourne: Text.

Blume, Mary 1992, *Cote d'Azure: Inventing the French Riviera*, New York: Thames & Hudson.

Bodewes, T. 1981, Development of tourism studies in Holland, *Annals of Tourism Research*, 8: 35–51.

414

Boer, A. 1992, The banking sector and small firm failure in the UK hotel and catering industry, *International Journal of Contemporary Hospitality Management*, 4(2): 13–16.

Boniface, B & Cooper, C. 1994, *The Geography of Travel and Tourism*, London: Butterworth–Heinemann.

Booker, John 1994, *Travellers' Money*, Stroud: Alan Sutton.

Boon, J. 1977, *The Anthropological Romance of Bali 1597–1972*, Cambridge: CUP.

Bosselman, Fred 1978, *In the Wake of the Tourist: Managing Special Places in Eight Countries*, Washington DC: The Conservation Foundation.

Boulding, K. 1987, The economy as an ecosystem: economics in the general system of the world, pp 3–18 in Karl A. Fox & Don G. Miles (eds), *Systems Economics: Concepts, Models and Multidisciplinary Perspectives*, Ames: Iowa State University Press.

Boyle, J. & Field, N. 2001, Ansett's relaunch suffers poor passenger interest, *Australian Financial Review*, 29–30 September, p 9.

Braithwaite, Dick (ed.) 2003, *Riding the Waves: Proceedings of Annual Conference, Council of Australian University Tourism & Hospitality Educators* (Coffs Harbour), Canberra: Bureau of Tourism Research.

Braithwaite, Dick, Greiner, Romy & Walker, Paul 1998, Success factors for tourism in regions of eastern Australia, pp 69–96 in Hall & O'Hanlon (eds), *Rural Tourism Management: Sustainable Options* (conference proceedings), Ayr: SAS.

Bramwell, B. & Lane, B. 1993, *Rural Tourism and Sustainable Rural Development* (conference proceedings), University College, Galway).

Braudel, F. 1982, *The Wheels of Commerce: Civilisation and Capitalism 15th–18th Centuries*, *Vol. 2*, trans. Sian Reynolds, London: Collins.

——1984, *The Perspective of the World: Civilisation & Capitalism 15th–18th Centuries*, *Vol. 3*, trans. Sian Reynolds, London: Collins.

Breth, R.M. 1977, *Mao's China: A Study of Socialist Economic Development*, Melbourne: Longman Cheshire.

Broinowski, Alison 1992, *The Yellow Lady: Australian Impressions of Asia*, Melbourne: Oxford University Press.

Brokensha, Peter & Guldberg, Hans 1992, *Cultural Tourism in Australia*, Canberra: AGPS.

Brown, Graham 1995, Attitudes towards hotel practices (unpublished research report), Southern Cross University: Centre for Tourism.

Brown, John 1986, (unpublished) Speech at the Annual Conference of the Australian Institute of Travel & Tourism, Canberra.

Brown, T. & Lefever, M. 1990, A 50 year renaissance: the hotel industry from 1939 to 1989, *Cornell Hotel & Restaurant Administration Quarterly*, May, pp 18–25.

Brymer, R. 1991, Employee empowerment: a guest-driven leadership strategy, *Cornell Hotel & Restaurant Administration Quarterly*, 32(1): 58–68.

Buck, Roy 1978, Towards a synthesis in tourism theory, *Annals of Tourism Research*, 5: 110–11.

Buckley, Geoff 2002, (unpublished) address to Graduands, Southern Cross University, Lismore.

Buckley, Ralf 2001, Sustainable tourism management, *Annals of Tourism Research*, 28: 523–5.

——2002, Tourism ecolabels, *Annals of Tourism Research*, 29: 183–208.

Buckminster-Fuller, Richard 1972, Designing a new industry, pp 153–220 in *The Buckminster Fuller Reader*, James Mellor (ed.), London: Penguin (first pub. 1946).

Bull, Adrian 1988, An evaluation of direct foreign investment in the Australian tourist industry, pp 103–13 in Faulkner & Fagence (eds), op. cit.

——1991, *The Economics of Travel and Tourism*, Melbourne: Longman.

Bureau of Tourism Research 1989, *Japanese Visitors in Australia*, Canberra: BTR.

——c. 1990, *Tourism Trends in New South Wales*, Canberra: BTR.

——2001, *National Visitor Survey, Annual Report*, Canberra: BTR.

Burkart A.J. 1981a, Tourism—a service industry? *Tourism Management*, 2: 2.

——1981b, How far is tourism a trade or industry?, *Tourism Management*, 2: 146.

Burkart, A.J. & Medlik, S. 1974, *Tourism: Past, Present, Future*, London: Heinemann.

——1981, ibid., 2nd edn.

Bushell, Robyn (ed.) 1997, *Tourism Research: Building a Better Industry: Proceedings of Annual Conference, Australian Universities' Tourism & Hospitality Educators* (Sydney), Canberra: Bureau of Tourism Research.

Butler, Richard 1980, The concept of a tourist area cycle of evolution, *Canadian Geographer*, 24(1): 5–12.

——1992, Alternative tourism: the thin edge of the wedge, pp 31–46 in Smith & Eadington (eds), op. cit.

——2000, Seasonality, pp 521–2 in *The Encyclopedia of Tourism*, J. Jafari, (ed.), op. cit.

Butterworth, G.V. & Smith, R. 1987, *Maori Tourism Task Force Report*, Wellington: Ministry of Maori Affairs.

Byers, G. 1988, The New Zealand Retail Travel Agency Industry and Travel Trade Distribution Systems (unpublished MBA research report), Massey University: Department of Management Systems.

Byron, Robert 1937, *The Road to Oxiana*, London: Macmillan.

Cameron, R. 1975, *The Golden Riviera*, London: Weidenfeld & Nicholson.

Carlsen, J. 1997, Economic evaluation of recreation and tourism in natural areas: a case study in New South Wales, *Tourism Economics*, 3: 227–39.

——(ed.) 2002, *Proceedings of Annual Conference, Australian Universities' Tourism & Hospitality Educators* (Fremantle), Canberra: Bureau of Tourism Research.

Carr, C. 1992, Planning priorities for empowered teams, *Journal of Business Strategy*, 13(5): 43–7.

Carroll, Stephen J. 1988, Managerial work in the future, pp 85–109 in *Futures of Organizations*, G. Hage (ed.), Lexington: Lexington Books.

Casson, L. 1974, *Travel in the Ancient World*. London: Allen & Unwin.

Cavafy, C.P. 1951, *Poems by CP Cavafy*, trans. John Mavrogordato, London: Chatto & Windus.

——1998, *C.P. Cavafy: Collected Poems*, trans. Edmund Keeley & Philip Sherrard, London: Chatto & Windus.

Central Planning Office 1985, *DP 9: Fiji's Ninth Development Plan*, Suva: CPO.

Chamberlin, E.R. 1983, *Loot! The Plunder of Heritage*, New York: Facts on File.

Chancellor, E. 2002, Dear Prudence, come back to stay, *Sydney Morning Herald*, 29 June, p 48.

Chandler, Alfred D. Jr 1962, *Structure and Strategy: Chapters in the History of the Industrial Enterprise*, Cambridge, MA: Harvard University Press.

——1977, *The Visible Hands: The Managerial Revolution in American Business*, Cambridge, MA: Harvard University Press.

Chatwin, B. 1987, *The Songlines*, London: Cape.

——1989, Nomad Invasions, pp 216–29 in *What Am I Doing Here?*, London: Cape.

——1996, The nomadic alternative (three essays), pp 75–108 in *Anatomy of Restlessness: Uncollected Writings of Bruce Chatwin*, London: Picador.

Chesney-Lind, M. & Lind, I.Y. 1986, Visitors as victims: crimes against tourists in Hawaii, *Annals of Tourism Research*, 13: 167–91.

Cheyne-Buchanan, Joanne 1992, Issues in marketing and promotion of farm tourism: a case study of the Manawatu region of New Zealand, *Australian Journal of Leisure & Recreation*, 2(3): 15–19.

Christaller, W. 1964, Some considerations of tourism location in Europe, *Papers, Regional Science Assoc*, pp 95–105.

Clark, N., Clift, S. & Page, S. 1993, *A Safe Place in the Sun? Health Precautions, Behaviours & Health Problems of British Tourists in Malta*, Canterbury (England): Christ Church College, Travel, Lifestyles & Health Working Paper #1.

Clarke, George 1975, Old and new towns as leisure experiences, in *Leisure: A New Perspective*, Canberra: AGPS.

Cohen, Eric 1978, The impacts of tourism on the physical environment, *Annals of Tourism Research*, 5: 215–37.

——1979, Rethinking the sociology of tourism, *Annals of Tourism Research*, 6: 18–35.

——2000, Souvenir, pp 547–8 in *The Encyclopedia of Tourism*, J. Jafari (ed.), op. cit.

Cohen, Stanley & Taylor, Laurie, 1978, *Escape Attempts: The Theory and Practice of Resistance to Everyday Life*, London: Penguin.

Collier, Alan 1989, *Principles of Tourism: A New Zealand Perspective*, Auckland: Longman Paul (1991, 2nd edn).

Collins, L. 2001, Shutdown may cost airlines $19.5bn, *Australian Financial Review*, 15 September, p 8.

Comptroller & Auditor General UK 2000, *The Millennium Dome*, London: National Audit Office.

Confucius 1997, *The Analects*, trans. Simon Leys, New York: Dutton.

Covey, Stephen R. 1989, *Seven Habits of Highly Effective People*, New York: Simon & Shuster.

Craig-Smith, Stephen & French, Christine 1990, Australian Hospitality and Tourism Education: Current Issues & Future Directions (Paper presented to the annual Hotel, Restaurant & Institutional Education Conference), Washington, DC.

Craik, J. 1988, The social impacts of tourism, pp 17–31 in Faulkner & Fagence (eds), op. cit.

Creedy, S. 2002, Payout hopes ride on grounded fleet, *Weekend Australian*, 7–8 Sept., p 6.

Creedy, S. & Bryden-Brown, S. 2002, Soft landings, hard landings, *Weekend Australian*, 7–8 Sept., p 19.

Creedy, S., Gilchrist, M. & Roberts, J. 2001, Ansett calls in receiver, *The Australian*, 13 September, p 1.

Crockett, S. & Wood, L. 1999, Brand Western Australia: a totally integrated approach to destination branding, *Journal of Vacation Marketing*, 5(3): 276–89.

Crompton, John 1979, Motivations for pleasure vacation, *Annals of Tourism Research*, 6: 408–24.

——1992, Structure of vacation destination choice sets, *Annals of Tourism Research*, 19: 420–34.

Crotts, J., Buhalis, D. & March, R. 2000, *Global Alliances in Tourism and Hospitality Management*, New York: Hayworth Press.

Cuervo, Raimondo 1967, *Tourism as a Medium for Human Communication*, Itaxapalapa, Mexican Government Department of Tourism.

Dalrymple, William 1989, *In Xanadu: A Quest*, London: Collins.

Dann, Graham 1977, Anomie, ego-enhancement and tourism, *Annals of Tourism Research*, 4: 184–94.

——1981, Tourist motivation, *Annals of Tourism Research*, 8: 187–219.

——1999, Writing out the tourist in space and time, *Annals of Tourism Research*, 26: 159–87.

——2000, Anomie, p 23 in *The Encyclopedia of Tourism*, J. Jafari (ed.), op. cit.

Dann, Graham & Cohen, Eric 1991, Sociology and Tourism, *Annals of Tourism Research*, 18: 154–69.

Dare, Byron, Welton, George & Coe, William 1988, *Concepts of Leisure in Western Civilisation: A Critical Review and Historical Analysis*, Dubuque, IA: Kendall Hunt.

Daruwalla, Pheroza & Weiler, Betty 1995, The training–attitudes nexus in the hospitality business, pp 391–98 in Faulkner et al., op. cit.

Darwin, Charles 1964, *On the Origin of Species*, Cambridge, MA: Harvard University Press (first pub. 1859).

David, Saul 1997, *Military Blunders: The How and Why of Military Failure*, London: Robinson.

Davidson, J. & Spearritt, P. 2000, *Holiday Business in Australia Since 1970*, Melbourne University Press.

Day, J., Skidmore, S. & Koller, T. 2002, Image selection in destination positioning, *Journal of Vacation Marketing*, 8(2): 177–86.

de Grazia, Sebastian 1962, *Of Time, Work and Leisure*, New York: Twentieth Century.

de Kadt, Emanuel 1979, *Tourism—Passport to Development?* Washington, DC: Oxford University Press, for UNESCO & World Bank.

——1992, Making the alternative sustainable: lessons from the development of tourism, pp 47–75 in Smith & Eadington (eds), op. cit.

Defoe, Daniel 1971, *A Tour Through the Whole Island of Great Britain*, London: Penguin (first pub. 1724).

Delouche, F. (ed.) 2001, *Illustrative History of Europe: A Unique Portrait of Europe's Common History*, London: Cassell.

Deming, W. Edwards 1986, *Out of the Crisis*, Cambridge, MA: MIT.

Department of the Treasury 1977, Submission to the House of Representatives' Select Committee on Tourism, *Reports of Hearings*, pp 1209–77, Canberra: House of Representatives.

Department of Tourism 1992, *Tourism—Australia's Passport to Growth: A National Tourism Strategy*, Canberra: Department of Tourism.

Doganis, R. 1987, *Flying Off Course: The Economics of International Airlines*, London: Allen & Unwin.

Douglas, Norman 1911, *Siren Land*, London: JM Dent.

——1915, *Old Calabria*, London: JM Dent.

Douglas, N. 1996, *They Came for Savages: A History of Tourism in Melanesia*, Lismore: Southern Cross University Press.

Douglas, N. & Douglas, N. 1991, Where the Tiki are wired for sound and the poi glow in the dark: a day at the Polynesian Cultural Centre, *Tok Blong SPPF*, May, pp 11–13.

Douglas, N., Douglas, N. & Derrett, R. (eds) 2001, *Special Interest Tourism*, Brisbane: Wiley.

Dowling, Ross 2000a, Developing ecotourism into the millennium, *International Journal of Tourism Research*, 2(30): 206–8.

——2000b, Global ecotourism and the new millennium, *World Leisure Journal*, 42(2): 11–19.

Doxey, G.V. 1975, A causation theory of visitor-resident irritants, pp 195–8 in *Proceedings of the Travel & Tourism Research Association's 6th Annual Conference*, San Diego.

Drake P.J. & Nieuwenhuysen, J.P. 1988, *Economic Growth for Australia: Agenda for Action*, Melbourne: CEDA.

Dredge, D. 1999, Destination, place, planning and design, *Annals of Tourism Research*, 26: 772–91.

Drucker, Peter F. 1955, *The Practice of Management*, Oxford: Heinemann.

——1968, *The Practice of Management*, London: Pan.

——1974, *Management: Tasks, Responsibilities, Practice*, New York: Harper & Row.

——1980, *Managing in Turbulent Times*, Oxford: Heinemann.

——1989, *Managing for Results: Economic Tasks and Risk Taking Decisions*, Oxford: Heinemann.

Dubrin, J. & Ireland, R. 1993, *Management and Organisation*, Cincinatti: Southwestern.

Dumazedier, J. 1967, *Towards a Society of Leisure*, London: Collier-Macmillan.

Dunford, Richard 1992, *Organisational Behaviour: An Organisational Analysis Perspective*, Sydney: Addison-Wesley.

Dunn, R. (ed.) 1989, *The Adventures of Ibn Battuta*, Berkeley: University of California Press.

Durschmied, Erik 1999, *The Hinge Factor: How Chance and Stupidity Have Changed History*, London: Coronet.

Dwyer, Larry & Forsyth, Peter 1995, Employment impacts of inbound tourism, pp 225–34 in Faulkner & Fagence (eds), op. cit.

East, Stephanie 1994, *Green Hotels* (unpublished research report), Lismore: Southern Cross University Centre for Tourism.

Easwaran, E. 1989, *The Compassionate Universe*, Pataluma, CA: Nilgiri Press.

Echtner, C. & Jamal, T. 1997, The disciplinary dilemma of tourism studies, *Annals of Tourism Research*, 24: 868–83.

Ehrenreich, Barbara 2000, *Nickel and Dimed: On (Not) Getting By in America*, New York: Owl Books.

Elias, Norbet & Dunning, Eric 1986, *The Quest for Excitement: Sport and Leisure in the Civilising Process*, Oxford: Basil Blackwell.

Emery, Fred (ed.) 1969, *Systems Thinking*, London: Penguin.

——1981, *Systems Thinking* (2nd edn), London: Penguin.

Emory, C.W. & Cooper, D.R. 1991, *Business Research Methods* (4th edn), Homewood: Irwin.

English, W., Josiam, B., Upchurch, S. & Willems, J. 1996, Restaurant attrition: a longitudinal analysis of restaurant failures, *International Journal of Contemporary Hospitality Management*, 8(2): 17–20.

Espejo, R. & Harnden, R. (eds) 1989, *The Viable Systems Model: Interpretations and Applications of Stafford Beer's VSM*, Chichester: Wiley.

Evans, S. & Drummond, M. 2001, Government's $3.5m loan helps Skywest fly again, *Australian Financial Review*, 22–23 September, 13.

Fagles, R. (ed.) 1996, *The Odyssey—Homer*, London: Viking.

Farrell, Brian 1982, *Hawaii: The Legend that Sells*, Honolulu: University of Hawaii Press.

Faulkner, B., & Fagence, M. (eds) 1988, *Frontiers in Australian Tourism* (conference proceedings), Canberra: Bureau of Tourism Research.

Faulkner, B., Fagence, M., Davidson, M. & Craig-Smith, S. (eds) 1995, *Tourism Research and Education in Australia*, Proceedings of conference (Gold Coast, February 1994), Canberra: Bureau of Tourism Research.

Faulkner, B., Tideswell, C. & Weaver, D. (eds) 1998, *Progress in Tourism and Hospitality Research* (conference proceedings, Gold Coast), Canberra: Bureau of Tourism Research.

Fayol, Henri 1987, *General and Industrial Management*, Belmont, CA: David S. Lake (first pub. 1916).

Feibleman, J. & Friend, J.W. 1945, The structure and function of organisations, *Philosophical Review*, 54: 19–44.

Ferrario, F. 1979, The evolution of tourist resources: an applied methodology, *Journal of Travel Research*, 17(3): 18–22, 17(4): 24–30.

Feynman, Richard 1999, Minority report to the Space Shuttle Challenger enquiry, pp 151–69 in *The Pleasure of Finding Things Out*, Richard P. Feynman (ed.), Cambridge, MA: Helix Books.

Finkelstein, S. & Hambrick, D. 1996, *Strategic Leadership: Top Executives and Their Effects on Organisations*, St Paul: West Publishing.

Firat, A. Faut, Dholakia, Nikhilesh & Bagozzi, Richard P. (eds) 1987, *Philosophical and Radical Thought in Marketing*, Lexington, KY: Lexington Books.

Firth, T. 2002, Business strategies and tourism: an investigation to identify factors which influence marginal firms to move into or remain on the fringes of tourism industries (unpublished PhD thesis), Southern Cross University.

Fisher A.G. 1935, *The Clash of Progress and Security*, London: Macmillan.

Fitzgerald, Shirley 1987, *Rising Damp: Sydney 1870–1890*, Melbourne: Oxford University Press.

——1992, *Sydney 1842–1992*, Sydney: Hale & Iremonger.

Flanagan, D. 1988, *Flanagan's Version: A Spectator's Guide to Science on the Eve of the Twentieth Century*, New York: Knopf.

Fletcher, J. 2000, Multiplier effect, in *The Encyclopedia of Tourism* pp 398–400, J. Jafari (ed.), London: Routledge.

Fletcher, T. 1977, The socio-economic impact of tourism, *World Travel*, 135: 24–7.

Fodness, D. & Murray, B. 1997, Tourist information search, *Annals of Tourism Research*, 24: 503–23.

Ford, H. 1916, speech reported in *The Chicago Tribune*, 16 May.

Forde, Kevin 1986, Investments put money where the mouth is, *Rydges*, July: 33–4.

Forster E.M. 1982, *Alexandria: A History and Guide*, London: Michael Haag (first pub. 1922).

Frater, J.M. 1983, Farm tourism in England: planning, funding, promotion and some lessons from Europe, *Tourism Management*, 4: 167–79.

Fredline, Elizabeth & Faulkner, Bill 2000, Host community reactions: a cluster analysis, *Annals of Tourism Research*, 27: 763–84.

Fucini, J. & Fucini, S. 1987, *Experience Inc: Men and Women Who Founded Famous Companies After the Age of 40*, New York: Free Press.

Funnell, Charles 1975, *By the Beautiful Sea: The Rise and High Times of That Great American Resort, Atlantic City*. New York: Knopf.

Galbraith, Jay 1983, Strategy and organisational planning, *Human Resource Management* (Spring/Summer), (also in Mintzberg & Quinn, *The Strategy Process*, 1991).

Gallarza, M., Saura, I. & Garcia, H. 2002, Destination image: towards a conceptual framework, *Annals of Tourism Research*, 29: 56–78.

George, Claude S. Jr 1972, *The History of Management Thought*, Englewood Cliffs, NJ: Prentice-Hall.

Geraghty, Grant 1994, Ecotourism and sustainable tourism: what is encompassed?, unpublished research report, Lismore: Southern Cross University Centre for Tourism.

Getz, Don 1986, Models in tourism planning, *Tourism Management*, 7: 21–32.

——1992, Tourism planning and the destination life cycle, *Annals of Tourism Research*, 19: 752–70.

——2000, Visiting friends and relatives, *Encyclopedia of Tourism*, J. Jafari (ed.), 621–2.

Gilbert, D.C. 1991, Conceptual issues in the meaning of tourism, pp 4–27 in *Progress in Tourism, Recreation and Hospitality Management*, C.P. Cooper (ed.), vol. 2.

Gilchrist, M. & Niesche, C. 2001, Huge losses stall Ansett rescue deal, *Weekend Australian*, 8–9 September, p 1.

Gnoth, J. 1997, Tourism motivation and expectation formation, *Annals of Tourism Research*, 24: 283–304.

Goeldner, Charles R. & Ritchie, J.R. Brent 2003, *Tourism: Principles, Practice, Philosophies*, 9th ed., Hoboken: John Wiley.

Goethe, J. 1970, *Italian Journey 1786–8*, Harmondsworth: Penguin.

Goffman, Erving 1964, *Stigma: Notes on the Management of Spoiled Identity*, London: Penguin.

Goldsmith, E. 1974, Pollution by tourism, *The Ecologist*, 4(2): 44–6.

Golub, H. 1993, Travel and tourism creates jobs, *Viewpoint* (World Travel & Tourism Council), 1 (1), pp 8–16.

Goodall, B. 1988, How tourists choose their holidays: an analytical framework, pp 1–17 in *Marketing in the Tourism Industry: The Promotion of Destination Regions*, B. Goodall & G. Ashworth (eds), London: Routledge.

Goodsir, D. & Doherty, L. 2001, Travel chaos for 47,000, *Sydney Morning Herald*, 15–16 September, p 1.

Goth, Paul 1994, *Living Downtown: The History of Residential Hotels in the US*, Los Angeles, CA: University of California Press.

Gottliebsen, R. 2002, Bad news bears, *Weekend Australian*, 29–30 June, pp 29, 32.

Graburn, Nelson 1978, Tourism—the sacred journey, pp 17–32 in Valene Smith, op. cit.

——2000a, Museums, in *The Encyclopedia of Tourism*, J. Jafari (ed.), pp 400–2, London: Routledge.

——2000b, Nostalgia, op. cit, pp 415–16.

Gray, H.P. 1970, *International Tourism—International Trade*, Lexington, KY: Lexington Books.

Greenwood, Davydd 1978, Culture by the pound: an anthropological perspective on tourism as cultural commoditisation, pp 129–38 in Valene Smith (ed.), op. cit.

Griggs, K. 2001, Kiwi flagship teeters as scrip hits record low, *Australian Financial Review*, 18 Sept., p 8.

Gronhaug, Knell & Dholakia, Nikhilesh 1987, Consumers, markets and supply systems, pp 3–14 in Firat et al., op. cit.

Grossman, P. 1987, *American Express: The Unofficial History of the People Who Built the Great Financial Empire*, New York: Crown.

Gunn, Clare 1972, *Vacationscape: Designing Tourist Regions*, Austin: University of Texas.

——1979, *Tourism Planning*, New York: Crane Russack.

——1988, *Vacationscape: Designing Tourist Regions* (2nd edn), New York: Van Nostrand Reinhold.

——1993, *Tourism Planning* (2nd edn), Washington, DC: Francis & Taylor.

——1994, *Tourism Planning* (3rd edn), Washington, DC: Taylor & Francis.

Haigh, Gideon 2003, *Bad Company: The Cult of the CEO*, Quarterly Essay, Issue 10, Melbourne.

Haines, M. & Davis, R. 1987, *Diversifying the Farm Business*, Oxford: BSP.

Hainsworth, D. 1981, *The Sydney Traders: Simeon Lord and his Contemporaries 1788–1821*, Melbourne University Press.

Halewood, C. & Hannam, K. 2001, Viking heritage tourism: authenticity and commodification, *Annals of Tourism Research*, 28: 565–80.

Hall, C.M. 1991, *Introduction to Tourism in Australia: Impacts, Planning and Development*, Melbourne: Longman Cheshire.

——1995, ibid. (2nd edn), Melbourne: Longman Cheshire.

——1997, Dissonant heritage: the management of the past, *Annals of Tourism Research*, 24: 496–8.

Hall, C.M., Johnson, G. Cambourne, B. Macionis, N. Mitchell, R. & Sharples L. 2000, Wine tourism: an introduction, in *Wine Tourism Around the World: Development, Management and Markets*, C.M. Hall & L. Sharples (eds), pp 1–23, Oxford: Butterworth Heinemann.

Hamilton-Smith, Elery 1987, Four kinds of tourism, *Annals of Tourism Research*, 14: 332–44.

Hanquin, Z.Q. & Lam, T. 1999, Mainland Chinese visitors' motivations to visit Hong Kong, *Tourism Management*, 20: 587–95.

Hanquin, Z., Wong, K. & Sik, L. 2001, An analysis of the development of tourism in Hong Kong, *Pacific Tourism Review*, 5: 15–21.

Hansard series, HR *House of Representatives Records*, Canberra; Government Printer.

Hardin, Garrett 1974, The economics of wilderness, *The Ecologist*, 4(1): 44–6 (first pub. in *Natural History*, June 1969).

Harley, R. 2001, Condition terminal for retailers, *Australian Financial Review*, 18 Sept., p 61.

Harris, Kerr, Forster & Co., Stanton, Robbins & Co 1965, *Australia's Travel and Tourist Industry*, Sydney: Australian National Travel Association.

Harris, Robert & Howard, Joy 1994, *The Australian Travel Agency*, Melbourne: Hospitality Press.

——1996, *Dictionary of Travel, Tourism and Hospitality Terms*, Melbourne: Hospitality Press.

Harris, Robert & Leiper, Neil 1995, *Sustainable Tourism in Australia: A Casebook Perspective*, Sydney: Butterworth Heinemann.

Harrison, Julia 1997, Museums and Touristic Expectations, *Annals of Tourism Research*, 24: 23–40.

Haukeland, Jan Vidar 1990, Non-travellers, the flip side of the coin, *Annals of Tourism Research*, 17: 172–84.

Hawke, Steve 1992, Diary—a personal note, *The Independent Monthly*, May, pp 2–3.

Hemingway, E. 1926, *The Sun Also Rises*, New York: Scribner.

——1985, *The Dangerous Summer*, London: Grafton.

Henderson, J. 2000, Strategic alliances and destination marketing: the Greater Mekong Subregion, *Pacific Tourism Review* 4: 149–160.

Henshall, B. (ed.) 1982, *Tourism and New Zealand, Strategic Analysis: Final Report*, University of Auckland: Department of Management Studies.

Henshall, B. & Roberts, R. 1985, Comparative assessment of tourist generating countries for New Zealand, *Annals of Tourism Research*, 12: 219–38.

Herodotus 1987, *The History*, trans. D. Green, University of Chicago Press.

Hewison, Robert 1987, *The Heritage Industry: Britain in a Climate of Decline*, New York: Methuen.

——1988, Great expectations: hyping heritage, *Tourism Management*, Sept., pp 239–40.

Hibbert, C. 1974, *The Grand Tour*, London: Spring Books.

——1979, Introduction, pp 7–14 in *Travels Through France and Italy*, Tobias Smollett (ed.), London: Folio.

Hilmer, Fred 1985, *When the Work Runs Out: The Future for Australians at Work*, Sydney: Harper & Row.

——1993, *National Competition Policy: Report by the Independent Committee of Inquiry*, Hilmer, F. (Chairman), Canberra: AGPS.

Hing, Nerilee & Dimmock, Kay 2000, From Bula to bust: events, reactions and recovery strategies for tourism surrounding Fiji's 2000 coup d'etat, *International Journal of Contemporary Hospitality Management, E Journal*, 1(1): 136–48.

Hitchcock, M., King, V.T. & Parnwell, M.J.G. (eds) 1993, *Tourism in South-East Asia*, London: Routledge.

Hobson, J.S.P. 2000, Tourist shopping in transit: the case of BAA Plc, *Journal of Vacation Marketing*, 6(2): 170–83.

——2002, Shopping and tourism, unpublished PhD thesis, Southern Cross University.

Hobson, J.S.P. & Christensen, M. 2001, Cultural and structural issues affecting Japanese shopping behaviour, *Asia Pacific Journal of Tourism Research*, 6: 37–45.

Hochschild, A. 1983, *The Managed Heart: Commercialisation of Human Feeling*, Berkeley: University of California Press.

Hockey, Joe 2002, *Delivering on the Promise: A Ten Year Growth Strategy for Tourism* (Keynote address, ATEC Symposium Adelaide), Canberra: Ministry for Small Business & Tourism.

Hofer, Charles 1991, Designing turnaround strategies, pp 793–9 in Mintzberg & Quinn, op. cit. (first pub. 1986).

Holmes, Scott 1995, Understanding business network brokers' manual, unpublished report for AusIndustry, Canberra: Department of Science, Technology & Industry.

Homer 1996, *The Odyssey*, trans. Robert Fagles, London: Viking.

Honey, M. 1999, *Ecotourism and Sustainable Development: Who Owns Paradise?* Washington: Island Press.

Hong, Evelyne 1985, *See the Third World While it Lasts: The Social and Environmental Impacts of Tourism, with Special Reference to Malaysia*, Georgetown: Consumers' Association of Penang.

Horne, Donald 1976, *Money Made Us*, Melbourne: Penguin.

——1984, *The Great Museum: The Re-Presentation of History*, London: Pluto.

Horwath & Horwath Services 1988, Market Study with Financial Projections for the Proposed Big Banana and Horticultural World, Coffs Harbour (Unpublished report for Total Project Control Pty Ltd), Brisbane: Horwath & Horwath.

Hovinen, G. 2002, Revisiting the destination lifecycle model, *Annals of Tourism Research*, 29: 209–30.

Howard, Claire 1914, *English Travellers of the Renaissance*, London: John Lane, The Bodley Head.

Howarth, S. 1982, *The Knights Templar*, London: Collins.

Hughes, Robert 1993, *Culture of Complaint: The Fraying of America*, New York: Oxford University Press.

Huizinga, J. 1950, *Homo Ludens*, Boston: Beacon.

Hultkrantz, L. 2002, Will there be a unified wireless marketplace for tourism?, *Current Issues in Tourism*, 5(2): 149–61.

Hunziker, W. 1951, *Social Tourism: Its Nature and Problems*, Geneva: Alliance Internationale de Tourisme.

Hwu, C.J. 1992, Woman Warrior, *Asia Travel Trade*, October, p. 52.

Illich, Ivan 1971, *De-Schooling Society*, London: Penguin.

Inglis, F. 2000, *The Delicious History of the Holiday*, London: Routledge.

IUOTO 1963, *The United Nations Conference on International Travel and Tourism* (proceedings), Geneva: International Union of Official Travel Organisations.

Jackson, M., White, G. & Schmierer, C. 1995, Development of an authenticity behavioural index in tourism, pp 342–56 in R. Shaw, op. cit.

Jafari, Jafar 1977, Editor's Page, *Annals of Tourism Research*, 5: 6–11.

——1987, Tourism models: socio-cultural aspects, *Tourism Management*, 8: 151–9.

——(ed.) 2000, *The Encyclopedia of Tourism*, London: Routledge.

——2002, Retracing and mapping tourism's landscape of knowledge, *ReVista: Harvard Review of Latin America*, Winter, pp 12–15.

Jafari, Jafar & Ritchie, J.R. Brent 1981, Towards a framework of tourism education: problems and prospects, *Annals of Tourism Research*, 8: 13–34.

James, David 1994, The dubious benefits of global competitiveness, *Business Review Weekly*, 30 May, pp 66–8.

Jansen-Verbeke, M. 1991, Leisure shopping: a magic concept for the tourism industry, *Tourism Management*, March, pp 9–14.

——2000, Shopping, *The Encyclopedia of Tourism*, J. Jafari, (ed.), p 532.

Jansen-Verbeke, M. & Rekom, J.V. 1996, Scanning museum visitors, *Annals of Tourism Research*, 23: 364–75.

Jaynes, Julian 1973, The problem of animate motion in the seventeenth century, pp 166–79 in *Historical conceptions in Psychology*, Mary Henle & Julian Jaynes (eds), New York: Springer.

——1982, *Origins of Consciousness in the Breakdown of the Bicameral Mind*, Boston: Houghton Mifflin.

Jefferson, Alan & Lickorish, Leonard 1988, *Marketing Tourism: A Practical Guide*, London: Longman.

Jevons, W. Stanley 1888, *Theory of Political Economy*, London: Macmillan.

Johnson, G. & Scholes, K. 1999, *Exploring Corporate Strategy*, London: Prentice Hall.

Jordan, N. 1981, Thinking about 'system' pp 15–39 in Emery, op. cit.

Kagan, J. 1998, *Three Seductive Ideas*, Cambridge: Harvard University Press.

Kaiser, C. & Helber, L. 1978, *Tourism Planning and Development*, Boston: CBI.

Kakuzo, O. 1956, *The Book of Tea*, Tokyo: Tuttle (first pub. 1906).

Kam, G. 2001a, *Suteja Neka and the Neka Art Museum*, Ubud: Yayasan Dharma Seni.

——2001b, *Insight Pocket Guide Bali* (3rd edn), Singapore: APA Publications.

Kaplan, Max 1975, *Leisure: Theory and Practice*, New York: Wiley.

Kaplan, Robert 1998, *An Empire Wilderness: Travels into America's Future*, New York: Vintage.

Karpin, David 1994a, Address to the Annual Conference of the Australian and New Zealand Academy of Management (Dec. 1993) in *Academy News*, 6(1) pp 2–4.

——1994b, *Report of the Taskforce on Leadership and Management Skills*, Canberra: Department of Industry.

Kaul, R. 1985, *Tourism—A Trilogy: Vol. One—The Phenomenon*, New Delhi: Sterling.

Kelly, John 1982, *Leisure Identities and Interactions*, London: Allen & Unwin.

Keynes, J.M. 1973, *A General Theory of Employment, Interest and Money*, London: Macmillan (first pub. 1936).

Khan, Maryam 2003, Ecoserve: ecotourists' quality expectations, *Annals of Tourism Research* 30: 109–24.

Khan, M., Olsen, M. & Var, T. (eds) 1993, *VNR's Encyclopedia of Hospitality and Tourism*, New York: Van Nostrand Reinhold.

Kim, S. & Littrell, M.A. 2001, Souvenir buying intentions, *Annals of Tourism Research*, 28: 638–57.

King, Brian 1991, Tour operators and the air-inclusive tour industry, *EIU Travel and Tourism Analyst*, 3: 66–87.

——1997, *Creating Island Resorts*, New York: Routledge.

King, Brian & Hyde, Geoff 1989, *Tourism Marketing in Australia*, Melbourne: Hospitality Press.

Knight, E. 1989, Bigger market share underpins Wyndham's profit, *Australian Financial Review*, 17 August.

Knutson, P. & Suzuki, D. 1992, *Wisdom of the Elders*, Toronto: Stoddart.

Kohler, A. 2001, Big government still haunts our skies, *Australian Financial Review*, 18 September, p 67.

——2002, Share-based remuneration: the root of all corporate evil, *Weekend Australian Financial Review*, 15–16 June, p 72.

Koke, Louise 1987, *Our Hotel in Bali*, Wellington: January Books.

Koloff, Mary Lynn, Moore, Ruth & Richardson, Rebecca 1989, The inbound tour operator sector of the Australian tourism industry, pp 226–80 in Blackwell & Stear, op. cit.

Kosters, Martinus 1988, Tourism and the environment (unpublished paper presented at a meeting of the editors of *Annals of Tourism Research*).

Kotler, Philip & Anderson, Alan R. 1987, *Strategic Marketing for Non-Profit Organizations*, Englewood Cliffs, NJ: Prentice-Hall.

Kotler, P., Chandler, P., Brown, L. & Adam, S. 1994, *Marketing* (3rd edn), Sydney: Prentice Hall.

Koutsoukis, J. 2001a, Government will duck all blame, *Australian Financial Review*, 15–16 September, 13.

——2001b, How Howard killed off Ansett's bid for survival, *Australian Financial Review*, 29–30 September, p 3.

Koutsoukis, J., Sandilands, B. & Walker, T. 2001, Bad faith, bad management: the Ansett disaster, *Australian Financial Review*, 21–22 September, pp 21–2.

Koza, M. & Lewin, A. 2000, Putting the S word back in alliances, pp 356–61 in *Mastering Strategy: The Complete MBA Companion*, T. Dickson (ed.), London: Pearson Education.

Kozak, M. 2000, Repeaters' behaviour at two distinct destinations, *Annals of Tourism Research*, 28: 784–807.

Krakuer, J. 1996, *Into the Wild*, New York: Anchor.

——1997, *Eiger Dreams: Voyages Among Men and Mountains*, New York: Anchor.

Krippendorf, Jost 1987, *The Holidaymakers: Understanding the Impacts of Leisure and Travel*, London: Heinemann.

Krugman, P. 2002, How to make a crooked squillion, *Sydney Morning Herald*, 29 June, p 1.

Lambert, R.S. 1950, *The Fortunate Traveller*, London: Melrose.

Lanchester, J. 1996, *The Debt to Pleasure*, London: Picador.

Lane, H. 1986, Marriages of necessity: airline–hotel liaisons, *Cornell Hotel & Restaurant Administration Quarterly*, May: 73–9.

Lang, T. 2000, The effect of the Internet on travel consumer purchasing behaviour and implications for travel agents, *Journal of Vacation Marketing*, 6: 368–85.

Larkin, J. 1994, The power of two, *Good Weekend*, *Sydney Morning Herald*, 18 June, pp 34–43.

Larrabee, Eric & Meyerson, Rolf (eds) 1958, *Mass Leisure*, Glencoe: The Free Press.

Law, R. & Leung, R. 2000, A study of airlines' reservation systems on the Internet, *Journal of Travel Research*, 39(2): 202–11.

Laws, Eric 1995, *Tourist Destination Management: Issues, Analysis and Policies*, London: Routledge.

Lecky, S. 2001, Plane stupid, *Sydney Morning Herald*, 22–3 September, p 34.

Lee, Laurie 1985, *As I Walked Out One Midsummer Morning*, London: Andre Deutch (first pub. 1969).

Leiper, Neil 1979, A framework of tourism, *Annals of Tourism Research*, 6: 390–407.

——1980a, An Interdisciplinary Study of Australian Tourism (unpublished thesis), Sydney: University of New South Wales.

——1980b, Developing Australia as a Tourist Destination (unpublished monograph, Sir Donald Anderson Award), Sydney: Australian Institute of Travel & Tourism.

——1980c, Grades in Hotels & Motels (unpublished working paper).

——1981a, Towards a cohesive curriculum in tourism: the case for a distinct discipline, *Annals of Tourism Research*, 8: 69–84.

——1981b, Tourist Precincts in the Hunter Region Plan (unpublished consultancy report), Sydney: NSW Dept of Tourism.

——1984, International travel by Australians 1946-1983: Travel propensities and travel frequencies, pp 67–83 in *Contemporary Issues in Australian Tourism*, Barry O'Rourke (ed.), University of Sydney: Dept of Geography.

——1985, *The Japanese Travel Market and its Potential for Australian Tourist Destionations*, Sydney: Qantas Airways.

——1989a, Tourism and gambling, *GeoJournal*, 19(3): 269–75.

——1989b, Main destination ratios: analysis of tourist flows, *Annals of Tourism Research*, 16: 530–41.

——1989c, Controlling in management systems, pp 103–18 in *Management: A Sourcebook*, M. Thompson (ed.), Palmerston North: The Dunmore Press.

——1990a, *Tourism Systems: An Interdisciplinary Perspective*, Massey University: Department of Management Systems, occasional paper #1.

——1990b, Partial industrialisation of tourism systems, *Annals of Tourism Research*, 17: 600–5.

——1998, Tourism in Cambodia: potential, problems, and illusions, *Pacific Tourism Review*, 1: 285–97.

——1999a, A conceptual analysis of tourism-supported employment which reduces the incidence of exaggerated, misleading statistics about jobs, *Tourism Management*, 20: 605–13.

——1999b, The Hajj: pilgrimage to Mecca, *Annals of Tourism Research*, 26: 474–6.

——2000, An emerging discipline, *Annals of Tourism Research*, 27: 805–8.

——2002, The formation of strategies to develop nature links and cultural corridors in ASEAN tourism, *ASEAN Journal of Hospitality & Tourism*, 1(1): 3–22.

Leiper, Neil & Hing, Nerilee 1998, Trends in Asia-Pacific tourism: optimism to uncertainty, *International Journal of Contemporary Hospitality Management*, 10: 245–51.

Leiper, Neil, Hing, Nerilee & Day, Michele 2001, What do tourists enjoy in Bali?, a paper presented at the CAUTHE Conference, Canberra.

Leiper, Neil & Stear, Lloyd 1978, Developing Australia as a tourist destination (paper for the House of Representatives' Select Committee on Tourism), Canberra: Select Committee, *Reports of Hearings*, 16 May 1978, pp 4788–849.

Leser, David 1997, See Bali and cry, *Good Weekend, Sydney Morning Herald*, 3 May, pp 16–25.

Levenstein, H. 1998, *Seductive Journey: American Tourists in France, From Jefferson to the Jazz Age*, Chicago: Univ. of Chicago Press.

Levitt, T. 1985, Marketing myopia, pp 3–19 in *Marketing Classics: A Selection of Influential Articles* (5th edn), B. Enis & K. Cox (eds), Newton: Allen & Bacon.

Lew, Alan 1987, A framework of tourist attraction research, *Annals of Tourism Research*, 14: 533–75.

Li, Yiping 2000, Geographical consciousness and tourism experience, *Annals of Tourism Research*, 27: 863–83.

Lickorish, L.J. & Kershaw, A.G. 1958, *The Travel Trade*, London: Practical Press.

Liddell, R. 1976, *Cavafy: A Biography*, New York: Schoken.

Limerick, David & Cunnington, Bert 1993, *Managing the New Organisation: A Blueprint for Networks and Strategic Alliances*, Sydney: Business & Professional Publishing.

Linder, S. 1970, *The Harried Leisure Class*, New York: Columbia University Press.

Links, J. G. 1973, *Venice for Pleasure*, London: Pallas.

Lippman, Walter 1922, *Public Opinion*, New York: Free Press.

Littlejohn, D. & Roper, A., 1991, Changes in international hotel strategies, in *Strategic Hotel Management*, R. Teare & A. Boer (eds) pp 20–9, London: Cassell.

Littlewood, I. 2000, *Sultry Climates: Travel and Sex Since the Grand Tour*, London: John Murray.

Lomborg, Bjorn 2001, *The Skeptical Environmentalist: Measuring the Real State of the World*, Cambridge, Cambridge University Press.

Long, S. 2001, Close ties? Absolutely, say unions, *Australian Financial Review*, 18 September, p 11.

Lound, M. & Battye, R. 1999, *International Visitors in Australia 1998*, Canberra: Bureau of Tourism Research.

Lovelock, C. & Wright, L. 1999, *Principles of Service Marketing and Management*, Englewood Cliffs, NJ: Prentice-Hall.

Lundberg, Donald 1985, *The Tourist Business* (5th edn), New York: Van Nostrand Reinhold.

Lundtorp, S. & Wanhill, S. 2001, The resort lifecycle theory: generating processes and estimation, *Annals of Tourism Research*, 28: 947–64.

Macartney-Snape, T. 1993, *Everest from Sea to Summit*, Sydney: Australian Geographical Society.

MacCannell, Dean 1976, *The Tourist: A New Theory of the Leisure Class*, New York: Schoken.

——1992, *Empty Meeting Grounds: The Tourist Papers*, New York: Routledge.

MacGregor, D. 1931, *The Evolution of Industry* (2nd edn), London: Thornton Butterworth (first pub. 1911).

MacGregor, James R. 1993, Sustainable Tourism Development, pp 781–9 in Khan et al., op. cit.

Mackay, Hugh 1977, *A Study of Tourists' Attitudes to the North Coast of New South Wales*, Sydney: NSW Department of Tourism.

Manley, B. 1992, Protecting the goose that laid the golden egg, pp 6–7 in proceedings of the conference, *Ecotourism Business in the Pacific* (Auckland) University of Auckland & East West Centre, Hawaii.

Manning, Frank 1979, Tourism and Bermuda's black clubs: a case of cultural revitalisation, pp 157–76 in de Kadt 1979, op. cit.

Mansfeld, Y. 1992, From motivation to actual travel, *Annals of Tourism Research*, 19: 399–419.

Marshall, Alfred 1920, *Principles of Economics* (8th edn), London: Macmillan (first pub. 1895).

Maslow, A. 1982, *Towards a Psychology of Being* (2nd edn), New York: Van Nostrand Reinhold (first pub. 1970).

Mathieson, A. & Wall, G. 1982, *Tourism: Economic, Social and Physical Impacts*, London: Longman,

Mavor, E. 1986, *The Grand Tour of William Beckford: Europe Before the Revolution Seen Through the Eyes of a Quizzical Young Man*, London: Penguin.

Mayo, Edward J., Jarvis, Lance P. & Lane, Paul M. 1989, The harried leisure class as consumers, pp 64–70 in *Quality of Life Studies in Marketing & Management* (conference papers), H. Meadows & M. Sirgy (eds), Blacksburg, VA: Virginia State Polytechnic & University.

Mayo, Elton 1945, *The Social Problems of an Industrial Civilization*, Boston: Division of Research, Harvard University.

——1987, Hawthorne and the Western Electric Company, in *The Great Writings on Management & Organizational Behaviour* (2nd edn), L. Boone & D. Bowen (eds), pp 77–91, New York: Random House.

McCabe, V., Poole, B., Weeks, P. & Leiper, N. 2000, *The Business and Management of Conventions*, Brisbane: Jacaranda-Wiley.

McCabe, V. & Weeks, P. 1999, Convention services management in Sydney's 4 & 5 star hotels, *Journal of Convention & Exhibition Management*, 1(4): 67–84.

McCrann, T. 2001a, Magnificent blunder, *Weekend Australian*, 15–6 September, p 38.

——2001b, Mark my words, Ansett Mark Two is a corporate camel, *Weekend Australian*, 29–30 September, p 36.

McDonnell, Ian 1994, Leisure Travel to Fiji and Indonesia from Australia 1982 to 1992: Some Factors Underlying Changes in Market Shares unpublished masters thesis, University of Technology, Sydney.

McGibbon, Jacqueline 2000, *The Business of Alpine Tourism in a Globalising World*, Rosenheim: Vetterling Druck.

McGibbon, Jacqueline & Leiper, Neil 2001, Perceptions of Business Failure in Australian Tourism Industries, paper presented at CAUTHE Conference, Canberra.

McGregor, James R. 1993, Sustainable tourism development, pp 781–9 in Khan et al., op. cit.

McGuiness, Padraic P. 1993, When chaos reigns, expect the unexpected, *The Australian*, 31 March.

McIntosh, Robert W. & Goeldner, Charles 1977, *Tourism: Principles, Philosophies* (2nd edn), New York: Wiley.

——1986, ibid., 5th edn.

——1992, ibid., 6th edn.

McKendrick, Neil 1959, Joseph Wedgewood: an eighteenth century entrepreneur in salesmanship and marketing techniques, *Economic History Review*, 12(3): 408–33.

McKercher, Bob 1991, The unrecognised threat to tourism: can tourism survive 'sustainability', in proceedings of *Ecotourism Conference*, Canberra: Bureau of Tourism Research.

McLaren, G. 1996, *Beyond Leichhardt: Bushcraft and the Exploration of Australia*, Fremantle: Fremantle Arts Centre Press.

Megalogenis, G. 2001, Access to air latest country status symbol, *Weekend Australian*, 22–23 September, p 14.

Memmler, R., Cohen, B. & Wood, D. 1996, *The Human Body in Health and Disease* (8th edn), Philadelphia: Lippincott.

Merkle, Judith A. 1980, *Management and Ideology: The Legacy of the International Scientific Management Movement*, Berkeley: University of California Press.

Middleton, V. 1998, *Sustainable Tourism*, Oxford: Butterworth.

Mill, Robert Christie & Morrison, A. 1985, *The Tourism System*, Englewood Cliffs, NJ: Prentice Hall.

Miller, Henry 1942, *The Colossus of Maroussi*, London: Secker & Warburg.

——1965 *The Air-Conditioned Nightmare*, London: Panther (first pub. 1943).

Mills, G. 2001, The need for intelligent airline regulation, *Australian Financial Review*, 22–23 September, p 5.

Milton, G. 1999, *Nathaniel's Nutmeg*, London: Hodder & Stoughton.

Mintz, Sidney 1985, *Sweetness and Power: A History of Sugar*, New York: Sefton Books/ Viking.

Mintzberg, H. 1987, The strategy concept 1: five Ps for strategy, *California Management Review*, 30(1): 11–25.

——1991a, 'The Manager's Job: Folklore and Fact', in *The Strategy Process* H. Mintzberg & J.B. Quinn (eds) pp 21–31, NJ: Prentice Hall.

——1991b, The structuring of organisations, in *The Strategy Process*, H. Mintzberg & J.B. Quinn, (eds), pp 331–49, NJ: Prentice-Hall.

——1991c, Generic strategies, pp 70–82 in *The Strategy Process*, H. Mintzberg & J.B. Quinn (eds) NJ: Printice Hall.

——1991d, Five Ps for strategy, pp 12–19 in H. Mintzberg & J.B. Quinn (eds) NJ: Prentice Hall.

Mintzberg, H. & Quinn, J. B. (eds) 1991, *The Strategy Process*, Englewood Cliffs, NJ: Prentice-Hall.

——1996, ibid. (3rd edn).

Mok, C. & Lam, T. 1997, A model for tourists' shopping propensity, *Pacific Tourism Review*, 1(1): 137–45.

Molloy, Janine & Davies, Jenny (eds) 1999, *Delighting the Senses: Proceedings of the Ninth Australian Tourism & Hospitality Education Conference* (Adelaide), Canberra: Bureau of Tourism Research.

Moore, K., Cushman, G. & Simmons, D. 1995, Behavioural conceptualization of tourism and leisure, *Annals of Tourism Research*, 22: 67–85.

Moorehead, A. 1982, *Darwin and the Beagle*, London: Hamish Hamilton.

Morgan, Gareth 1986, *Images of Organizations*, Beverley Hills, CA: Sage.

Morgan, G. 2002, Has the National Museum got it all wrong? A response to Keith Windshuttle, *Quadrant* 46, April, pp 23–9.

Morris, C. (ed.) 1995, *The Illustrated Journeys of Celia Fiennes 1685–1712*, Stroud: Alan Sutton.

Morris, Jan 1979, *Spain*, London: Faber.

Morrison, A. 1989, *Hospitality and Tourism Marketing*, Albany, NY: Dalmar.

Moscardo, Gianna 1995, Developing a research agenda to assess the ecological sustainability of specialist tourist accommodation, pp 171–86 in Faulkner et al., op. cit.

——1996, An activity based segmentation of visitors to Far North Queensland, pp 467–79 in *Tourism and Hospitality Research: Australian and International Perspectives* (proceedings of annual CAUTHE Conference, Coffs Harbour), G. Prosser (ed.), Canberra: Bureau of Tourism Research.

Moscardo, G. & Pearce, P. 1986, Historic theme parks: an Australian experience in authenticity, *Annals of Tourism Research*, 13: 467–79.

Mowforth, M. & Munt, I. 1998, *Tourism and Sustainability: New Tourism in the Third World*, London: Routledge.

Mules, Trevor (ed.) 2001, *Capitalising on Research: Proceedings of the Australian Tourism & Hospitality Education Conference*, Canberra: Bureau of Tourism Research.

Mumford, L. 1961, *Cities in History*, New York: Harcourt Brace.

Munsters, W. 2001, The Bonnefanten Museum—Maastricht, in Richards, op. cit., pp 93–110.

Murphy, Peter 1985, *Tourism: A Community Approach*, New York: Methuen.

——2000, *Proceedings of Annual Conference, Australian Universities' Tourism & Hospitality Educators* (Mt Buller), Canberra: Bureau of Tourism Research.

Needham, P. 1992, Ecotourism: going green, *Asia Travel Trade*, June, pp 16–17.

Neka, S. & Kam, G. 2000, *The Development of Painting in Bali: Selections from the Neka Art Museum* (2nd edn), Ubud: Yayasan Dharma Seni.

Nepal, Sanjay 2000, Tourism in protected areas: the Nepalese Himalaya, *Annals of Tourism Research*, 27: 661–81.

Neville, R. 1970, *Playpower*, London: Jonathon Cape.

Nolan, Sidney D. 1976, Tourists' use and evaluation of travel information sources, *Journal of Travel Research*, 14(3): 6–8.

Noronha, Raymond 1979a, *Social and Cultural Dimensions of Tourism*, Washington, DC: World Bank.

——1979b, Paradise reviewed: tourism in Bali, pp 177–204 in de Kadt, op. cit.

Nothomb, Amelie 1999, *Fear and Trembling* (trans. Adriana Hunter), New York: St Martin's Griffin.

O'Brien, J.A. 1990, *Management Information Systems: A Managerial End User Perspective*, Homewood, IL: Homewood Pub.

O'Dea, Daniel 1997a, *BTR Research Paper Number 3: Tourism's Direct Economic Contribution 1995–96*, Canberra: Bureau of Tourism Research.

——1997b, *BTR Research Paper Number 4: Tourism's Indirect Economic Effects 1995–96*, Canberra: Bureau of Tourism Research.

Oelrichs, Ian 1992, Endemic tourism: a profitable industry in a sustainable environment, pp 14–22 in proceedings of conference, *Ecotourism Business in the Pacific* (Auckland), University of Auckland & East West Centre, Hawaii.

O'Fallon, Carolyn E. 1994, The role of central government in tourism: a public choice perspective, PhD thesis, Lincoln University: Department of Parks, Recreation & Tourism.

Office of National Tourism 1996, *Projecting Success: Visitor Management Strategies for Sustainable Tourism Growth*, Canberra: ONT.

Oliva, Terence & Reidenbach, R. Erich 1987, Extensions of Bagozzi's holistic construal, pp 135–53 in Firat et al. (eds), op. cit.

Oppermann, Martin 1998, *Sex Tourism*, New York: Cognizant Press.

——1999, Sex tourism, *Annals of Tourism Research*, 26: 251–66.

Opperman, Martin & Chon, Kye-Sung 1997, Convention participation decision-making process, *Annals of Tourism Research*, 24: 178–91.

O'Riordan, B. & Oldfield, S. 2001, ASIC launches inquiry into Air NZ's directors, *Australian Financial Review*, 15–16 September, p 17.

Ornstein, Robert F. 1975, *The Psychology of Consciousness*, San Francisco: Freeman.

Orwell, George 1933, *Down and Out in Paris and London*, London: Gollancz.

——1970, Politics and the English Language, in *The Collected Essays, Journalism and Letters of George Orwell, Vol. Four—In Front of Your Nose*, S. Orwell & I. Angus (eds), pp 156–69, London: Penguin.

Ouchi, W. 1984, *The M Form Society: How American Teamwork Can Recapture the Competitive Edge*, Reading, MA: Addison-Wesley.

Overington, C. 2002, WorldCom, absolute fraud, *Sydney Morning Herald*, 29 June, pp 25, 28.

Page, Stephen 1995, *Urban Tourism*, London: Routledge.

Palmer, I & McGraw, P. 1990, Management Strategy towards Unions in the Australian Travel Industry, *Labour & Industry* 3: 389–403.

Pan, G.W. & Laws, E. 2001, Tourism marketing opportunities for Australia in China, *Journal of Vacation Marketing*, 8: 39–48.

Pandya, Anil 1987, Marketing as an exchange in an institutional framework, pp 77–93 in Firat et al., op. cit.

Pascal, Richard T. 1991, The Honda effect, pp 114–23 in Mintzberg & Quinn, op. cit. (first pub. 1984).

Peacock, R.W. 1984, *Small Business Mortality: Annotated Bibliography*, Adelaide: SA Institute of Technology, School of Accountancy.

Pearce, Douglas 1987, *Tourism Today: A Geographical Analysis*, London: Longman.

——1989 *Tourist Development* (2nd edn), London: Longman.

——1997, Competitive destination analysis in Southeast Asia, *Journal of Travel Research*, 35(4): 16–24.

——1999, Tourism in Paris: studies at the microscale, *Annals of Tourism Research*, 26: 77–97.

Pearce, J. & Robinson, R. 1989, *Management*, New York: McGraw Hill.

Pearce, Philip L. 1982, *The Social Psychology of Tourist Behaviour*, Oxford: Pergamon.

——1988, *The Ulysses Factor*, New York: Springer.

——1990, Farm tourism in New Zealand, *Annals of Tourism Research*, 17: 337–52.

——1991, Analysing tourist attractions, *Journal of Tourism Studies*, 2(1): 46–55.

——2000, Psychology, pp 471–3 in *The Encyclopedia of Tourism*, J. Jafari, (ed.), op. cit.

Pearce, Philip L. & Stringer, Peter F. 1991, Psychology and Tourism, *Annals of Tourism Research*, 18: 136–54.

Peat, Marwick, Mitchell & Co. 1977, *Holiday Accommodation in Australia*, Canberra: AGPS.

——1981, *Sydney's Tourism Accommodation and Needs*, Sydney: NSW Department of Tourism.

Penrose, Edith 1959, *The Theory of the Growth of the Firm*, Oxford: Basil Blackwell.

Perkins, Harvey C. & Cushman, Grant 1993, *Leisure, Recreation and Tourism*, Auckland: Longman Paul.

Perrow, C. 1986, *Complex Organisations* (3rd edn), New York: Random House.

Peters, F. 1994, *The Hajj: The Muslim Pilgrimage to Mecca*, Princeton, NJ: Princeton University Press.

Peters, T. & Waterman, R. 1991, *In Search of Excellence: Lessons from America's Best Run Companies*, New York: Harper & Row.

Petroski, Henry 1992a, History and Failure, *American Scientist*, Nov–Dec: pp 523–6.

——1992b, *The Evolution of Useful Things*, New York: Alfred Knopf.

——1994, *Design Paradigms: Case Histories of Error and Judgement in Engineering*, New York: Cambridge University Press.

Petty, S. & Towers, K. 2001, Traveland agencies face Monday deadline, *Australian Financial Review*, 15–16 September, p 12.

Picard, M. 1996, *Bali: Cultural Tourism and Touristic Culture*, trans. D. Darling, Singapore: Archipelago Press.

Pigram, J. 1983, *Outdoor Recreation and Resource Management*, Beckenham: Croom Helm.

——1992, Alternative tourism: tourism and sustainable resource management, pp 76–87 in Smith & Eadington (eds), op. cit.

Plog, Stanley 1974, Why destination areas rise and fall in popularity, *Cornell Hotel & Restaurant Administration Quarterly*, 15(November): 13–16.

Polo, M. 1958, *Marco Polo: The Travels*, trans. R. Latham, London: Penguin.

Popper, Karl 1959, *The Logic of Scientific Discovery*, London: Hutchinson.

Porter, M. 1980, *Competitive Strategy: Techniques for Analysing Industries and Competitors*, New York: The Free Press.

——1985, *Competitive Advantage: Creating and Sustaining Superior Performance*, New York: The Free Press.

——1990, *The Competitive Advantage of Nations*, London: Macmillan.

Porter, Roy 1999, *The Greatest Benefit to Mankind: A Medical History of Humanity*, London: Fontana.

Powers, Thomas F. 1992, The advent of the megachain: a case of the emperor's new clothes? *Hospitality Research Journal*, 15(3): 1–11.

Pretes, Michael 2003, Tourism and nationalism, *Annals of Tourism Research*, 30: 125–42.

PricewaterhouseCoopers 2001, Circular to Creditors (13 Sept. re Ansett Australia Ltd & subsidiaries), Melbourne: PC.

Prideaux, Bruce & Cooper, Malcolm 2002, Nature corridors: a strategy for regional tourism development in Indonesia, *ASEAN Journal on Tourism & Hospitality*, 1(1).

Prosser, G. 1995, Destination life cycles, pp 318–28 in R. Shaw, op. cit.

——(ed.) 1996, *Tourism and Hospitality Research: Australian and International Perspectives*, *Proceedings of CAUTHE Conference, Coffs Harbour*, Canberra: Bureau of Tourism Research.

Przeclawski, Krzysztof 1986, *Humanistic Foundations of Tourism*, Warsaw: Institute of Tourism.

Pudney, J. 1953, *The Thomas Cook Story*, London: Michael Joseph.

Purkayastha, D. 1981, *Note on the Motor Cycle Industry 1975*, Harvard Business School.

Putman, Robert, Leonardi, R. & Nanetti, R. 1992, *Making Democracy Work*, Princeton, NJ: Princeton University Press.

Qantas 1978, Qantas Airways Ltd: Submission to Select Committee on Tourism, in *Reports of Hearings* (House of Representatives), Canberra: Select Committees.

Quammen, D. 1996, *The Song of the Dodo: Island Biogeography in an Age of Extinctions*, London: Hutchinson.

Quine, W.V. 1981, What price bivalence?, *Journal of Philosophy*, 78: 90–5.

Quinn, R.E. 1988, *Beyond Rational Management: Mastering the Paradoxes and Competing Demands of High Performance*, San Francisco: Jossey Bass.

Quinn, Robert E., Faerman, S., Thompson, M. & McGrath, Michael R. 1990, *Becoming a Master Manager: A Competency Framework*, New York: Wiley.

——2003, ibid. (3rd edn).

Real, Michael 1977, *Mass-Mediated Culture*, Englewood Cliffs, NJ: Prentice-Hall.

Reich, R.B. 1987, Entrepreneurship reconsidered: the team as hero, *Harvard Business Review*, May–June: 77–83.

Reid, R. 1989, *Hospitality Marketing Management*, New York: Van Nostrand Reinhold.

Reuer, J. 2000, Collaborative strategy: the logic of alliances, pp 345–50 in *Mastering Strategy: The Complete MBA Companion*, T. Dickson (ed.), London: Pearson Education.

Richards, G. (ed.) 2001, *Cultural Attractions and European Tourism*, Oxford: CABI.

Richardson, G.B. 1972, The organisation of industry, *Economic Journal*, 82: 883–96.

Richardson, J.I. 1999, *A History of Australian Travel and Tourism*, Melbourne: Hospitality Press.

Ridley, M. 1997, *Origins of Virtue*, London: Penguin.

Riemer, Andrew 1993, *The Hapsburg Cafe*, Sydney: Angus & Robertson.

Ritchie, J.R. Brent 1992, New realities, new horizons: leisure, tourism and society in the third millenium, pp 13–26 in *The Annual Review of Travel, 1992 Edition*, New York: American Express.

Ritchie, J.R. Brent & Zinns, M. 1978, Culture as a determinant of the attractiveness of a tourist region, *Annals of Tourism Research*, 5: 252–67.

Rivais, R. 1993, Calais at the crossroads, *Guardian Weekly*, 30 May, p 13.

Robinson, E. 1931, *The Structure of Competitive Industry*, Cambridge: Cambridge University Press.

Rockel, I. 1986, *Taking the Waters: Early Spas in New Zealand*, Wellington: Government Printer.

Rodenburg, E. 1980, The effects of scale in economic development in Bali, *Annals of Tourism Research*, 7: 177–96.

Rumelt, R. 1991, The evaluation of business strategy, pp 52–9 in Mintzberg & Quinn, op. cit. (first pub. 1980).

Ryan, Chris 1991, *Recreational Tourism: A Social Science Perspective*, London: Routledge.

Ryan, Chris & Martin, A. 2001, Tourists and Strippers, *Annals of Tourism Research*, 28: 140–63.

Ryan, Chris & Mo, X. 2001, Chinese visitors to New Zealand: demographics and perceptions, *Journal of Vacation Marketing*, 8: 13–27.

Saarinen, Esa (ed.) 1982, *Conceptual Issues in Ecology*, Dordrecht: Reidel.

Sadleir, Michael 1983, *Blessington-d'Orsay—A Masquerade*, London: Folio.

Sakaran, Uma 1992, *Research Methods for Business* (2nd edn), New York: Wiley.

Sampson, A. 1975, *The Seven Sisters: The Great Oil Companies and the World They Made*, New York: Viking Press.

Sandilands, B. 2001a, Australia loses its points with Star Alliance, *Australian Financial Review*, 15–16 September, p 16.

——2001b, Ansett: flight of fools, *Australian Financial Review*, 15–16 Sept, p 24–5.

——2001c, Tourism hit as Qantas flies high, *Australian Financial Review*, 29–30 September, p 9.

Santayana, G. 1962, *The Life of Reason*, New York: Collins (first pub. 1906).

Saul, J.R. 1992, *Voltaire's Bastards: The Dictatorship of Reason in the West*, Toronto: Penguin.

——1995, *The Doubter's Dictionary*, Toronto: Penguin.

——1997, *The Unconscious Civilisation*, Toronto: Penguin.

——2001, *On Equilibrium*, Toronto: Penguin.

Schirmer, R. 1994, Overbooking: How is it Managed by Gold Coast Hotels?, unpublished report, Southern Cross University.

Schivelbusch, W. 1986, *The Railway Journey: The Industrialization of Time and Space in the 19th Century*, New York: Berg.

Schmidhauser, H. 1975, Travel propensity and travel frequency, pp 53–60 in *The Management of Tourism*, A.J. Burkart & S. Medlik (eds), London: Heinemann.

Schmidt, Catherine 1989, The guided tour, *Urban Life*, 7: 441–67.

Schoderbeck, P., Cosier, R.A. & Alpin, J.C. 1988, *Management*, Orlando, FL: Harcourt, Brace, Jovanovich.

Schon, D. 1983, *The Reflective Practitioner: How Professionals Think in Action*, New York: Basic Books.

Schumacher, F. 1974, *Small is Beautiful: A Study of Economics as if People Mattered*, London: Sphere.

Seaton, A. 1999, War and thanatourism: Waterloo 1815–1914, *Annals of Tourism Research*, 26: 130–58.

Select Committee on Tourism 1978, *Final Report of the House of Representatives' Select Committee on Tourism*, Canberra: AGPS.

Senge, P. 1990, *The Fifth Discipline: The Art and Practice of the Learning Organization*, New York: Doubleday.

Seth, Pran 1992, A living legend (interview with Oberoi), *Asia Travel Trade*, July, p. 41.

Sexton, E. & Crichton, S. 2001, Belly up, *Sydney Morning Herald*, 15–16 September.

Shaw, G. & Williams, A. 1997, *The Rise and Fall of British Coastal Resorts*, London: Mansell.

Shaw, Robin (ed.) 1995, *Proceedings of the National Tourism and Hospitality Conference*, Melbourne: Victoria University of Technology.

Shaw, S.D. 1994, ATT Probe—Hong Kong and Macau, *Asia Travel Trade*, 25(12): 18–30.

Sheehan, S. 2000, *Travelpack Bali and Lombok*, Singapore: AA Publishing.

Sheldon, P. 1997, *Tourism Information Technology*, Wallingford: CABI.

Simon, Herbert 1957, *Administrative Behaviour* (2nd edn), New York: Macmillan.

——1960, *A New Science of Management Decision*, New York: Harper & Row.

Singer, P. 1993, *How Are We to Behave? Ethics in an Age of Self Interest*, Melbourne: Text.

Skidelsky, R. 1994, *John Maynard Keynes—The Economist as Saviour 1920–1937*, London: Macmillan.

Smith, Adam 1952, *An Inquiry into the Nature and Causes of the Wealth of Nations*, Chicago: Benton (first pub. 1776).

Smith, A. 1982, *Management Systems: Analysis and Applications*, New York: CBS.

Smith, Stephen L.J. 1988, Defining tourism: a supply-side view, *Annals of Tourism Research*, 15: 179–90.

——1989, *Tourism Analysis: A Handbook*, London.

——1990a, A test of Plog's allocentric/psychocentric model: evidence from seven nations, *Journal of Travel Research*, 28(Spring): 40–3.

——1990b, Another look at the carpenter's tools: a reply to Plog, *Journal of Travel Research*, 28(Fall): 50–1.

——1991, The supply-side definition of tourism: reply to Leiper, *Annals of Tourism Research*, 18: 312–18.

——1999, How far is far enough? Operationalizing the concept of 'usual environment' in tourism definitions, *Tourism Analysis*, 4: 137–44.

——2000, Leisure, pp 354–6 in *The Encyclopedia of Tourism*, J. Jafari, (ed.), op. cit.

Smith, Valene (ed.) 1978, *Hosts and Guests: The Anthropology of Tourism*, Philadelphia: University of Pennsylvania Press.

——1989, ibid., 2nd edn.

Smith, Valene & Eadington, William R. (eds) 1992, *Tourism Alternatives: Potentials and Problems in the Development of Tourism*, Philadephia: University of Pennsylvania Press.

Smollett, Tobias 1979, *Travels through France and Italy*, London: Folio (first pub. 1766).

Snepenger, D., Houser, B. & Snepenger, M. 1990, Seasonality of demand, *Annals of Tourism Research*, 17: 628–30.

Sofield, T. & Li, S. 2000, Heritage, *The Encyclopedia of Tourism*, J. Jafari, (ed.), pp 275–7.

Sogar, D. Horace & Oostdyck, Willem 1995, Tourism management and the control of natural resources, pp 151–6 in Faulkner et al., op. cit.

Sontag, Susan 1979, *On Photography*, London: Penguin.

Solomon, R. 1992, *Ethics and Excellence: Cooperation and Integrity in Business*, New York: Oxford University Press.

Spigelman, J. 2002, Quality in an age of measurement, *Quadrant*, 46 Mar), 9–15.

St John, Edward 1974, Tourism and the environment, unpublished paper presented at the Annual Conference of the Australian National Travel Association, Sydney: ANTA.

Stabler, Mike 1995, An economic critique of tourism environmental auditing, pp 157–70 in Faulkner et al., op. cit.

Starbuck, W., Greve, A. & Hedberg, B. 1991, Responding to crises, pp 785–93 in Mintzberg & Quinn, op. cit. (first pub. 1978).

Stear, Lloyd 1981, Design of a curriculum for destination studies, *Annals of Tourism Research*, 8: 85–95.

——1984, Weekend social interaction in holiday and residential environments in New South Wales, pp 15–22 in *Contemporary Issues in Australian Tourism*, Barry O'Rourke (ed.), University of Sydney: Department of Geography.

——1995, Special interest tourism, *Annals of Tourism Research*, 22: 238–40.

——2002, The partial industrialisation of tourism, unpublished paper, University of Technology, Sydney.

——2003, A model of tourist attraction and of highly industrialised (international travel) tourism systems (publication pending University of Technology, Sydney).

Steinmeyer, M. 1994, Accor in Indonesia and Asia Pacific, *Asia Travel Trade*, April, p 46.

Stipanuk, D. 1996, The US lodging industry and the environment: an historical view, *Cornell Hotel and Restaurant Administration Quarterly*, 37(5): 39–50.

Strahan, N., Crosweller, A. & Crawford, B., 2001, Monopoly a concern: Fels, *Weekend Australian*, 15–16 September, p 4.

Stuart, T. 2000, Alliance networks: view from the hub, pp 361–7 in *Mastering Strategy: The Complete MBA Companion*, T. Dickson (ed.), London: Pearson.

Sugden, R. 1986, *The Economics of Rights, Cooperation and Welfare*, Oxford: Basil Blackwell.

Sumption Jonathon 1975, *Pilgrimage: An Image of Medieval Religion*, London: Faber & Faber.

Swarbrooke, J. 1999, *Sustainable Tourism Management*, New York: CABI.

Swinglehurst, Edmund 1974, *The Romantic Journey. The Story of Thomas Cook and Victorian Travel*, New York: Harper & Row.

Sykes, Trevor 1994, *The Bold Riders: Behind Australia's Corporate Collapses*, Sydney: Allen & Unwin.

——2001, Collapse shows limits of competition policy, *Australian Financial Review*, 15–16 September, p 19.

TAANSW 1993, *Tourist Attractions Association of New South Wales*, Sydney: TAANSW.

Taylor, D. 1974, *The Golden Age of British Hotels*, London: Northwood.

Taylor, F.W. 1972, *Scientific Management*, Westport, CT: Greenwood Press (first pub. 1911).

Thesiger, W. 1987, *The Life of My Choice*, London: Fontana.

Tideswell, C. 2001, The multi-destination travel behaviour of international visitors to Australia, unpublished PhD thesis, Griffith University.

Tisdell, Clem 1990, *The Nature of Sustainability and of Sustainable Development*, discussion paper # 48, University of Queensland: Dept of Economics.

Todd, M. & Crichton, S. 2001, Air New Zealand on course for a corporate crash, *Sydney Morning Herald*, 22–23 September, p 13.

Tolstoy, L. 1997, *A Calendar of Wisdom*, New York: Scribner (first pub. 1910).

Towner, J. 1985, The Grand Tour, a key phase in the history of tourism, *Annals of Tourism Research*, 12: 297–333.

——1996, *An Historical Geography of Recreation and Tourism in the Western World 1540–1940*, Chichester: Wiley.

Towner, J. & Wall, G. 1991, History and tourism, *Annals of Tourism Research*, 18: 71–84.

Townsend, R. 1970, *Up the Organization: How to Stop the Corporation from Stifling People and Strangling Profits*, London: Joseph.

Toynbee, Arnold 1935, *A Study in History, Vol. III*, Oxford: Oxford University Press.

Travis, D.J., Carleton, A.M. & Lauritsen, R.G. 2002, Contrails reduce daily temperature range, *Nature* 418: 601.

Tribe, J. 1997, The indiscipline of tourism, *Annals of Tourism Research*, 24: 638–57.

——2000, Indisciplined and unsubstantiated, *Annals of Tourism Research*, 27: 809–13.

Tufts, S. & Milne, S. 1999, Museums: a supply-side perspective, *Annals of Tourism Research*, 26: 613–31.

Turner, Luis & Ash, John 1975, *The Golden Hordes: International Tourism and the Pleasure Periphery*, London: Constable.

Turner, P. 2000, *Indonesia* (6th edn), Melbourne: Lonely Planet.

UNHCR 2002, UN High Commission for Refugees, http://www.unhcr.ch.

Urry, John 1990, *The Tourist Gaze*, London: Sage.

Veblen, Thorstein 1970, *The Theory of the Leisure Class*, London: Unwin (first pub. 1899).

——1904, *The Theory of Business Enterprise*, New York: Charles Scribner's Sons.

Venables, Cindy 1994, *A Comparison of Customer Complaints in the Fast Food Industry*, research report, Centre for Tourism, Southern Cross University.

Vickers, Adrian 1989, *Bali: A Paradise Created*, Melbourne: Penguin.

Waddell, H. 1927, *The Wandering Scholars*, London: Constable.

Wade, M. 2001, Watchdog concerned at lack of competition, *Sydney Morning Herald*, 15 September, p 32.

Waelchli, Fred 1989, The VSM and Ashby's law as illuminants of historical management thought, pp 51–76 in *The Viable System Model: Interpretations and Applications of Stafford Beer's VSM*, Raul Espejo & Roger Harnden (eds), Chichester: Wiley.

Wahab, Salah 1971, Introduction to tourism theory, *Travel Research Journal*, 1: 17–30.

——1974, *Elements of State Policy on Tourism, with Special Emphasis on Developing Countries*, Turin: Italigrafica.

——1975, *Wahab on Tourism Management*, London: Tourism International Press.

——(ed.) 1976, *Managerial Aspects of Tourism* (conference proceedings), Cairo: Ministry of Tourism.

Wahab, Salah & John Pigram (eds) 1997, *Tourism Development and Growth: The Challenge of Sustainability*, London: Routledge.

Wall, G. 2000, Sustainable development, in *The Encyclopedia of Tourism*, J. Jafari (ed.), pp 567–8.

Wall, S.J. & Wall, S.R. 1995, *The New Strategists: Creating Leaders at All Levels*, New York: The Free Press.

Waller, J. & Lea, S. 1999, Seeking the real Spain? Authenticity in motivation, *Annals of Tourism Research*, 26: 110–29.

Walmsley, D.J., Boskovic, R.M. & Pigram, John J. 1983, Tourism and crime, an Australian perspective, *Journal of Leisure Research*, 15: 133–55.

Walter, B. 2000, Looking for something more than a backyard blitz, *Sydney Morning Herald*, 13 Nov., p 28.

Walton, Isaac 1930, *The Compleat Angler*, London: Thames & Nelson (first pub. 1653).

Walton, J. 2000, The hospitality trades: a social history, in *In Search of Hospitality: Theoretical Perspectives and Debates*, C. Lashley & A. Morrison (eds), pp 56–76, Oxford: Butterworth-Heinemann.

Walton, Mary 1986, *The Deming Management Method*, New York: Putman.

Wang, N. 1999, Rethinking authenticity in tourists' experiences, *Annals of Tourism Research*, 26: 349–70.

——2000, Authenticity, pp 43–5 in *The Encyclopedia of Tourism*, J. Jafari, (ed.), op. cit.

Waterman, R., Peters, T. & Phillips, J. 1980, Structure is not organization, *Business Horizons*, 23(3): 14–26.

——1991, The 7-S framework, pp 309–14 in Mintzberg & Quinn, op. cit.

Watkins, L. 1989, *Billion Dollar Miracle: The Authentic Story of the Birth and Amazing Growth of the Tourism Industry in New Zealand*, Auckland: Travel Digest.

Weaver, David & Opperman, Martin 2000, *Tourism Management*, Brisbane: Wiley.

Weber, K. 2001, Outdoor adventure tourism: a review, *Annals of Tourism Research*, 28: 360–77.

Weiler, B. & Hall, C.M. (eds) 1992, *Special Interest Tourism*, London: Belhaven.

Westfield, M. 2001, Absolutely . . . going, going, gone, *Weekend Australian*, 15–6 September, pp 35–6.

Wheelwright, E. & MacFarlane, B. 1970, *The Chinese Road to Socialism*, London: Monthly Review Press.

Wiener, Norbert 1950, *The Human Use of Human Beings: Cybernetics and Society*, London: Eyre & Spottiswoode.

Wight, Pamela A. 1993, Sustainable ecotourism: balancing economic, environmental and social goals within an ethical framework, *Journal of Tourism Studies*, 4(2): 54–66.

Wild, Ronald 1979, Tourism in the Soviet Union, *Quadrant* April, pp 4–8.

Williams, A.M. & Shaw, G. (eds) 1988, *Tourism and Economic Development: Western European Experiences*, London: Belhaven.

Wilson, Colin 1975, *The Craft of the Novel*, Bath: Ashgrove Press.

Windshuttle, K. 2001, How not to run a museum, *Quadrant*, 45 (Sept), pp 11–19.

Winnifreth, T. & Jarrett, C. (eds) 1989, *The Philosophy of Leisure*, Basingstoke: Macmillan.

Witt, Christine A., Witt, Stephen F. & Wilson, Nick 1994, Forecasting international tourist flows, *Annals of Tourism Research*, 21: 612–28.

Wood, R. 1991, Hospitality's history: who wrote what and when, *Cornell Hotel & Restaurant Administration Quarterly*, August, pp 89–94.

World Commission on Environment and Development 1987, *Our Common Future*, New York: Oxford University Press.

434 World Tourism Organisation 1999, *Tourism Generating Markets: Overview and Country Profiles*, Madrid: WTO.

——no date (1990s), *Recommendations on Tourism Statistics*, Madrid: WTO.

——2000a, *Sustainable Development of Tourism: A Compilation of Good Practices*, Madrid: WTO.

——2000b, *Budgets of National Tourism Organisations*, Madrid: WTO.

——2002, Statistics, www.world-tourism.org

World Travel & Tourism Council 1993, *Travel and Tourism: A New Perspective*, London: WTTC.

Wykes, Alan 1973, *Abroad: A Miscellany of English Travel Writing 1700–1914*, London: MacDonald.

Yiannakis, A. & Gibson, H. 1992, Roles tourists play, *Annals of Tourism Research*, 19: 287–303.

Young, George 1973, *Tourism: Blessing or Blight?* London: Penguin.

Young, M. 1999, Cognitive maps of nature-based tourists, *Annals of Tourism Research*, 26: 817–39.